58th Annual Meeting of the Association for Computational Linguistics (ACL 2020)

Student Research Workshop

Online
5 – 10 July 2020

ISBN: 978-1-7138-1372-9

ACL 2020

The 58th Annual Meeting of the Association for Computational Linguistics

Proceedings of the Student Research Workshop

July 5 - July 10, 2020

Introduction

Welcome to the ACL 2020 Student Research Workshop!

The ACL 2020 Student Research Workshop (SRW) is a forum for student researchers in computational linguistics and natural language processing. The workshop provides a unique opportunity for student participants to present their work and receive valuable feedback from the international research community as well as from faculty mentors.

Following the tradition of the previous student research workshops, we have two tracks: research papers and thesis proposals. The research paper track is a venue for Ph.D. students, Masters students, and advanced undergraduates to describe completed work or work-in-progress along with preliminary results. The thesis proposal track is offered for advanced Masters and Ph.D. students who have decided on a thesis topic and are interested in feedback on their proposal and ideas about future directions for their work.

This year, the student research workshop has received considerable attention, reflecting the growth of the field. We received 137 submissions in total: 10 thesis proposals and 127 research papers. Among these, 12 research papers were non-archival. We accepted 49 papers, with an acceptance rate of 36%. After withdrawals and excluding non-archival papers, 43 papers appear in these proceedings, including six thesis proposals and 37 research papers. All the accepted papers will be presented virtually, as a part of the main conference, spread across three days (July 6th-8th).

Mentoring is at the heart of the SRW. In keeping with previous years, we had a pre-submission mentoring program before the submission deadline. A total of 57 papers participated in the pre-submission mentoring program. This program offered students the opportunity to receive comments from an experienced researcher to improve the writing style and presentation of their submissions. Additionally, authors of accepted SRW papers were matched with mentors to review their camera-ready drafts and conference presentations.

We are deeply grateful to our sponsors, including the National Science Foundation and the Don and Betty Walker Scholarship Fund. We also thank Grammarly for offering writing assistance to the authors of SRW papers. We thank our program committee members for their careful reviews of each paper and all of our mentors for donating their time to provide feedback to our student authors. Thank you to our faculty advisors, Omri Abend, Sujian Li, and Zhou Yu, for their essential advice and guidance, and to the ACL 2020 organizing committee for their support. Finally, thank you to our student participants!

Organizers:

Shruti Rijhwani - Carnegie Mellon University
Rotem Dror - Technion - Israel Institute of Technology
Jiangming Liu - The University of Edinburgh
Yizhong Wang - University of Washington

Faculty Advisors:

Omri Abend - Hebrew University of Jerusalem
Sujian Li - Peking University
Zhou Yu - University of California, Davis

Pre-submission Mentors:

Valerio Basile - University of Turin
Alexandra Birch - The University of Edinburgh
Yufeng Chen - Beijing Jiaotong University
David Chiang - University of Notre Dame
Eunsol Choi - Google AI
Lucia Donatelli - Saarland University
Greg Durrett - The University of Texas, Austin
Yansong Feng - Peking University
Lea Frermann - University of Melbourne
Yang Gao - Beijing Institute of Technology
Matt Gardner - Allen Institute for Artificial Intelligence
Gunhee Kim - Seoul National University
Pengfei Liu - Carnegie Mellon University
Vincent Ng - The University of Texas at Dallas
Dong Nguyen - Utrecht University
Yuval Pinter - Georgia Institute of Technology
Sai Krishna Rallabandi - Carnegie Mellon University
Melissa Roemmele - SDL
Sebastian Ruder - DeepMind
Rachel Rudinger - Allen Institute for Artificial Intelligence
Carolina Scarton - The University of Sheffield
Roy Schwartz - Allen Institute for Artificial Intelligence
Vered Shwartz - Allen Institute for Artificial Intelligence
Sameer Singh - University of California, Irvine
Sunayana Sitaram - Microsoft Research Lab India
David Smith - Northeastern University
Swabha Swayamdipta - Allen Institute for Artificial Intelligence
Alakananda Vempala - Bloomberg
Bonnie Webber - The University of Edinburgh
Arkaitz Zubiaga - Queen Mary University of London

Post-acceptance Mentors:

Sumeet Agarwal - Indian Institute of Technology Delhi
Reinald Kim Amplayo - University of Edinburgh
Jorge Balazs - University of Tokyo
Valerio Basile - University of Turin
Rishi Bommasani - Cornell University
Siddharth Dalmia - Carnegie Mellon University
Chris Develder - Ghent University
Denis Emelin - University of Edinburgh
Amir Feder - Technion - Israel Institute of Technology
Dayne Freitag - SRI International
Diana Galvan-Sosa - Tohoku University
Yang Gao - Beijing Institute of Technology
Tirthankar Ghosal - Indian Institute of Technology Patna
Dan Goldwasser - Purdue University
Nitish Gupta - University of Pennsylvania
Vivek Gupta - University of Utah
Junxian He - Carnegie Mellon University
saghar Hosseini - Microsoft Research
Dirk Hovy - Bocconi University
Ehsan Kamalloo - University of Alberta
Sudipta Kar - University of Houston
Alina Karakanta - University of Trento
Parisa Kordjamshidi - Michigan State University
Sachin Kumar - Carnegie Mellon University
Jonathan K. Kummerfeld - University of Michigan
Debanjan Mahata - Bloomberg
Emma Manning - Georgetown University
Amita Misra - IBM Research
Kenton Murray - Johns Hopkins University
Vincent Ng - University of Texas at Dallas
Vincent Nguyen - Australian National University
Natalie Parde - University of Illinois at Chicago
Jakob Prange - Georgetown University
Sebastian Ruder - DeepMind
sepideh sadeghi - Uber Technologies Inc.
Farig Sadeque - Boston Children's Hospital
Sebastian Schuster - Stanford University
Sunayana Sitaram - Microsoft Research India
Richard Sproat - Google, Japan
Gabriel Stanovsky - University of Washington
Rob Voigt - Northwestern University
Andy Way - Dublin City University
Bonnie Webber - University of Edinburgh
John Wieting - Carnegie Mellon University
Steven Wilson - University of Edinburgh
Michael Yoder - Carnegie Mellon University
Vicky Zayats - University of Washington
Shuyan Zhou - Carnegie Mellon University
Arkaitz Zubiaga - Queen Mary University of London

Program Committee:

Pranav A - Dayta AI
Oshin Agarwal - University of Pennsylvania
Sumeet Agarwal - Indian Institute of Technology Delhi
Piush Aggarwal - University of Duisburg-Essen
Manex Agirrezabal - University of Copenhagen
Afroz Ahamad - BITS Pilani Hyderabad Campus
Chris Alberti - Google
Rami Aly - University of Cambridge
Bharat Ram Ambati - Apple Inc.
Aida Amini - University of Washington
Reinald Kim Amplayo - University of Edinburgh
Maria Antoniak - Cornell University
Mattias Appelgren - University of Edinburgh
Zahra Azin - Istanbul Technical University
Vidhisha Balachandran - Carnegie Mellon University
Anusha Balakrishnan - Microsoft Semantic Machines
Jorge Balazs - University of Tokyo
Valerio Basile - University of Turin
Antonia Baumann - Trinity College Dublin
Rachel Bawden - University of Edinburgh
Eyal Ben-David - Technion - Israel Institute of Technology
Anjali Bhavan - Delhi Technological University
Tatiana Bladier - Heinrich Heine University of Düsseldorf
Eduardo Blanco - University of North Texas
Rishi Bommasani - Cornell University
Samuel R. Bowman - New York University
Rui Cai - University of Edinburgh
Ruket Cakici - NTENT Hispania
Ronald Cardenas - Charles University
Arlene Casey - University of Edinburgh
Lisa Andreevna Chalaguine - UCL
Khyathi Raghavi Chandu - Carnegie Mellon University
Jonathan P. Chang - Cornell University
Aditi Chaudhary - Carnegie Mellon University
Emily Chen - University of Illinois Urbana-Champaign
Liwei Chen - Peking University
Sihao Chen - University of Pennsylvania
Zhouhan Chen - New York University
Leshem Choshen - Hebrew University Jerusalem Israel
J. Alberto Conejero - Universitat Politècnica de València
Xiang Dai - University of Sydney
Siddharth Dalmia - Carnegie Mellon University
Samvit Dammalapati - Indian Institute of Technology Delhi
Alok Debnath - International Institute of Information Technology, Hyderabad
Luciano Del Corro - Goldman Sachs
Pieter Delobelle - KU Leuven
David Demeter - Northwestern University
Neşat Dereli - Boğaziçi University
Chris Develder - Ghent University
Flavio Di Palo - University of Illinois at Chicago

Radina Dobreva - University of Edinburgh
Lucia Donatelli - Saarland University
Rachel Dorn - Johns Hopkins University
Zi-Yi Dou - Carnegie Mellon University
Rafael Ehren - Heinrich-Heine-Universität Düsseldorf
Hicham El Boukkouri - LIMSI, CNRS, Université Paris-Saclay
Denis Emelin - University of Edinburgh
Carlos Escolano - Universitat Politècnica de Catalunya
Kurt Junshean Espinosa - University of the Manchester
Luis Espinosa Anke - Cardiff University
Tina Fang - University of Waterloo
Murhaf Fares - University of Oslo
Amir Feder - Technion - Israel Institute of Technology
Jared Fernandez - Northwestern University
Anjalie Field - Carnegie-Mellon University
Dayne Freitag - SRI International
Lea Frermann - Melbourne University
Daniel Fried - UC Berkeley
Yoshinari Fujinuma - University of Colorado
David Gaddy - University of California, Berkeley
Diana Galvan-Sosa - Tohoku University
Yang Gao - Beijing Institute of Technology
Marcos Garcia - Universidade da Corunha
Reza Ghaeini - Oregon State University
Tirthankar Ghosal - Indian Institute of Technology Patna
Arijit Ghosh Chowdhury - Manipal Institute of Technology
Seraphina Goldfarb-Tarrant - University of Washington
Dan Goldwasser - Purdue University
Vivek Gupta - University of Utah
Nitish Gupta - University of Pennsylvania
Abhinav Gupta - Mila
Sarah Gupta - University of Washington
Wen-Bin Han - National Tsing Hua University
Hardy Hardy - The University of Sheffield
Hiroaki Hayashi - Carnegie Mellon University
Junxian He - Carnegie Mellon University
Ji He - Citadel LLC
Jack Hessel - Cornell University
Barbora Hladka - Charles University
Ari Holtzman - University of Washington
saghar Hosseini - Microsoft Research
Dirk Hovy - Bocconi University
Phu Mon Htut - New York University
Junjie Hu - Carnegie Mellon University
Po-Yao Huang - Carnegie Mellon University
Glorianna Jagfeld - University of Lancaster
Labiba Jahan - Florida International University
Mimansa Jaiswal - University of Michigan
Mona Jalal - Boston University
Jyoti Jha - IIIT Hyderabad
Jad Kabbara - McGill University - MILA

Tomoyuki Kajiwara - Osaka University
Ehsan Kamalloo - University of Alberta
Zara Kancheva - IICT-BAS
Sudipta Kar - University of Houston
Alina Karakanta - Fondazione Bruno Kessler (FBK), University of Trento
Yohan Karunanayake - University of Moratuwa
Divyansh Kaushik - Carnegie Mellon University
Urvashi Khandelwal - Stanford University
Huda Khayrallah - Johns Hopkins University
Najoung Kim - Johns Hopkins University
Ekaterina Kochmar - University of Cambridge
Philipp Koehn - Johns Hopkins University
Taiwo Kolajo - Federal University Lokoja
Mamoru Komachi - Tokyo Metropolitan University
Xiang Kong - Carnegie Mellon University
Parisa Kordjamshidi - Michigan State University
Mandy Korpusik - Loyola Marymount University
Kalpesh Krishna - University of Massachusetts Amherst
Sachin Kumar - Carnegie Mellon University
Jonathan K. Kummerfeld - University of Michigan
Kemal Kurniawan - University of Melbourne
Yash Kumar Lal - Johns Hopkins University
Alexandra Lavrentovich - Amazon Alexa
Yiyuan Li - Carnegie Mellon University
Bowen Li - University of Edinburgh
Lei Li - Xidian University
Juncheng Li - Carnegie Mellon University
Junwei Liang - Carnegie Mellon University
Jasy Suet Yan Liew - Syracuse University
Kevin Lin - University of Washington
Zhengzhong Liu - Carnegie Mellon University
Jingzhou Liu - Carnegie Mellon University
Fei Liu - University of Central Florida
Pengfei Liu - Carnegie Mellon University
Fangyu Liu - University of Cambridge
Robert L Logan IV - University of California, Irvine
Di Lu - Dataminr
Kevin Lybarger - University of Washington
Chunchuan Lyu - The University of Edinburgh
Debanjan Mahata - Bloomberg
Shervin Malmasi - Harvard Medical School
Valentin Malykh - Huawei
Radhika Mamidi - IIIT Hyderabad
Emma Manning - Georgetown University
Pedro Henrique Martins - Instituto de Telecomunicações, Instituto Superior Técnico
Katherine McCurdy - University of Edinburgh
Shikib Mehri - Carnegie Mellon University
Omid Memarrast - University of Illinois at Chicago
Rui Meng - University of Pittsburgh
Antonio Valerio Miceli Barone - The University of Edinburgh
Tsvetomila Mihaylova - Instituto de Telecomunicações

Farjana Sultana Mim - Tohoku University
Koji Mineshima - Keio University
Gosse Minnema - University of Groningen
Amita Misra - IBM Research
Saif Mohammad - NRC
Seungwhan Moon - Facebook Conversational AI
Nora Muheim - University of Zürich
Kenton Murray - Johns Hopkins University
sachin nagargoje - Microsoft
Masaaki Nagata - NTT Corporation
Chirag Nagpal - Carnegie Mellon University
Aakanksha Naik - Carnegie Mellon University
Durgesh Nandini - University of Bamberg
Nikita Nangia - New York University
Nihal V. Nayak - Brown University
Denis Newman-Griffis - National Institutes of Health Clinical Center
Vincent Ng - University of Texas at Dallas
Dat Quoc Nguyen - VinAI Research
Vincent Nguyen - Australian National University, CSIRO Data61
Yasumasa Onoe - The University of Texas at Austin
Silviu Oprea - University of Edinburgh
Naoki Otani - Carnegie Mellon University
Endang Wahyu Pamungkas - University of Turin
Xiaoman Pan - University of Illinois at Urbana-Champaign
Alexander Panchenko - Skolkovo Institue of Science and Technology
Sheena Panthaplackel - The University of Texas at Austin
Natalie Parde - University of Illinois at Chicago
Archita Pathak - University at Buffalo (SUNY)
Tom Pelsmaeker - University of Edinburgh
Siyao Peng - Georgetown University
Jakob Prange - Georgetown University
Adithya Pratapa - Carnegie Mellon University
Longhua Qian - Soochow University
Yusu Qian - New York University
Ivaylo Radev - IICT-BAS
Sai Krishna Rallabandi - Carnegie Mellon University
Sree Harsha Ramesh - UMass Amherst
Vikas Raunak - CMU
Abhilasha Ravichander - Carnegie Mellon University
Kirk Roberts - University of Texas Health Science Center at Houston
Guy Rotman - Technion, IIT
Sebastian Ruder - DeepMind
Maria Ryskina - Carnegie Mellon University
sepideh sadeghi - Uber Technologies Inc.
Farig Sadeque - Boston Children's Hospital
Jin Sakuma - University of Tokyo
Younes Samih - Qatar Computing Research Institute
Ramon Sanabria - The University Of Edinburgh
Jainisha Sankhavara - DA-IICT
Enrico Santus - MIT
Ryohei Sasano - Nagoya University

Ramit Sawhney - Netaji Subhas Institute of Technology
Michael Sejr Schlichtkrull - University of Amsterdam
Sebastian Schuster - Stanford University
Roy Schwartz - The Allen Institute for AI
Indira Sen - GESIS
Hamed Shahbazi - Oregon State University
Gautam Kishore Shahi - University of Trento, Italy
Muhammad Abu Bakar Siddique - University of California, Riverside
Sonit Singh - Macquarie University
Kushagra Singh - Cure.fit
Sunayana Sitaram - Microsoft Research India
Sergey Smetanin - National Research University Higher School of Economics
Denis Smirnov - National Research University Higher School of Economics
Marco Antonio Sobrevilla Cabezudo - University of São Paulo
Katira Soleymanzadeh - Ege University
Thamar Solorio - UH
Sandeep Soni - Georgia Institute of Technology
Evangelia Spiliopoulou - Carnegie Mellon University
Daniel Spokoyny - CMU
Richard Sproat - Google, Japan
Tejas Srinivasan - Carnegie Mellon University
Marija Stanojevic - Temple University
Gabriel Stanovsky - University of Washington
Sanjay Subramanian - Allen Institute for Artificial Intelligence
Umut Sulubacak - University of Helsinki
Shabnam Tafreshi - The George Washington University
Tan Thongtan - Mahidol University
Taha Tobaili - The Open University
Elena Tutubalina - Kazan Federal University
Muaz Urwa - New york university
Sowmya Vajjala - National Research Council
Aline Villavicencio - University of Sheffield, UK
Rob Voigt - Northwestern University
Teodora Vukovic - University of Zurich
Ivan Vulić - University of Cambridge
Andy Way - ADAPT, Dublin City University
Bonnie Webber - University of Edinburgh
John Wieting - Carnegie Mellon University
Adina Williams - Facebook Inc.
Steven Wilson - University of Edinburgh
Shuly Wintner - University of Haifa
Yumo Xu - University of Edinburgh
Hitomi Yanaka - RIKEN AIP
Fan Yang - University of Houston
Rongtian Ye - Aalto University
Da Yin - Peking University
Michael Yoder - Carnegie Mellon University
Vicky Zayats - University of Washington
Omnia Zayed - PhD Student - National University of Ireland Galway
Meishan Zhang - Tianjin University, China
Haoran Zhang - University of Pittsburgh

Shiyue Zhang - The University of North Carolina at Chapel Hill
Yanpeng Zhao - The University of Edinburgh
Pei Zhou - University of Southern California
Chunting Zhou - Carnegie Mellon University
Zhong Zhou - Carnegie Mellon University
Shuyan Zhou - Carnegie Mellon University
Hao Zhu - Carnegie Mellon University
Arkaitz Zubiaga - Queen Mary University of London

Table of Contents

Adaptive Transformers for Learning Multimodal Representations

Prajjwal Bhargava
prajjwalgo@gmail.com

Abstract

The usage of transformers has grown from learning about language semantics to forming meaningful visiolinguistic representations. These architectures are often over-parametrized, requiring large amounts of computation. In this work, we extend adaptive approaches to learn more about model interpretability and computational efficiency. Specifically, we study attention spans, sparse, and structured dropout methods to help understand how their attention mechanism extends for vision and language tasks. We further show that these approaches can help us learn more about how the network perceives the complexity of input sequences, sparsity preferences for different modalities, and other related phenomena.

1 Introduction

Learning richer representations from visual and text data is a central task to solve multi-modal learning. Attention-based methods have proven to be very useful in learning long term dependencies and forming richer representations of the input sequences. Numerous approaches (Lu et al., 2019; Su et al., 2019; Li et al., 2019; Chen et al., 2019) have been proposed for learning visiolinguistic representations with transformers. Although these approaches have provided us with significant improvement on various benchmarks (language and visiolinguistic), the architectures used are over-parameterized require extensive training lasting for several weeks using multiple objectives to form a generalized representation of the task to be addressed, which is then followed by fine-tuning on a downstream task. This workflow has become a concerning problem. It results in deep learning methodologies being inaccessible and increased carbon footprints (Strubell et al., 2019). In this work, we specifically explore adaptive methods.

We refer to Adaptive mechanisms as those methods that change their behavior during training/run time and adapt stochastically to the environment based on data heuristics (parameters) learned by encountering samples from the same data distribution optimized by an objective function. Alternative approaches such as pruning, distillation (Hinton et al., 2015) and quantization are rigid to some extent and induce some form of permanent modifications to the model. Adaptive methods enforce the network to learn parameters such that their behavior changes as per the complexity of the input sequence as perceived by the neural network. The code to reproduce the results in this work is publicly available at this link[1].

Current self-attention approaches assume that the attention span of a head is invariant to the complexity of an input sequence. Attention heads can learn their optimal context size (Sukhbaatar et al., 2019), which results in a reduction of FLOPS. When an optimal attention span is learned, the amount of attention given to a particular input sequence by an attention head is determined by its context size. We show that the context size varies with the emergent complexity of the sequence, and spans can help us understand how much sensitive a layer is to an input sequence.

Training models with a quarter of a million parameters are not feasible and practical for most users. One effective way to facilitate neural network scaling is by making the weights of the network sparse. This configuration allows us to perform faster training of deeper networks with relatively less compute. To make attention distributions sparse, we use α entmax (Correia et al., 2019) to obtain probability distribution of weights. Normalized exponential functions like softmax cannot assign a zero attention weight. This property en-

[1] https://github.com/prajjwal1/adaptive_transformer

Proceedings of the 58th Annual Meeting of the Association for Computational Linguistics: Student Research Workshop, pages 1–7
July 5 - July 10, 2020. ©2020 Association for Computational Linguistics

forces the context vector to stay dense, resulting in non-relevant sequences to be considered even though the network has discarded them by putting a deficient weight. Adaptive sparsity can make an attention head to learn richer distributions by oscillating the behavior of distribution to stay between softmax and sparsemax. We show that this behavior can help us understand preferences for the density of attention weight distribution and how it varies amongst each head about different modality.

We also study a form of regularization method called Layerdrop (Fan et al., 2019) to understand its regularization impact for multi-modal features. If the network can learn to drop identical layers (*Data Driven* pruning), then it can be regarded as an adaptive depth mechanism. We specifically use the *Every other* pruning method where the user specifies the drop rate because it offers maximal gains as suggested compared to its counterpart pruning methods. This method has proven to be effective in reducing the number of parameters and pruning layers during inference.

The contribution of this work is as follows:

- The adaptive approaches have only been tested with linguistic features only. We extend these approaches to study how do they align to capture complex relationships between different modalities. We also study the effects of aligning these approaches to understand their compatibility through ablation analysis.

- We perform interpretability analysis to learn how these approaches can enhance our understanding of attention behavior and adaptive approaches.

- We provide experimental results on the recent adaptive approaches for the multi-modal input sequences.

2 Background

2.1 LXMERT

We use LXMERT (Tan and Bansal, 2019) as the baseline architecture. The adaptive approaches can be combined with any other self-attention mechanism based transformer. LXMERT uses self and cross attention layers to jointly attend to image and text inputs (input sequence). Specifically, it takes a word-level sentence and object-level image embeddings. The encoder consists of three main components: language (9 layers) and visual (5 layers) encoder (single-modality) to form textual and image representations and cross-modality encoder (5 layers) to jointly attend to both these representations. Cross attention is responsible for forming the mapping between ROI features and textual representations. Since the architecture used is identical, we refer the readers to (Tan and Bansal, 2019) for a detailed description of pre-training strategies. The network used has been pre-trained on four objectives: Masked Cross Modality LM, Masked Object Prediction, Cross Modality Matching, and Image Question Answering. Faster RCNN is used to extract ROI features from the input images.

2.2 Adaptive Attention Span

Unlike dynamic attention, which assumes that all attention heads require the same amount of span, learning an optimal attention span enables the gathering of information as per the context size determined by the attention head. A max upper bound span limit is enforced on each head, which helps reduce computation and memory requirements. As proposed in (Sukhbaatar et al., 2019), different heads emphasize on different context depending upon the task it is addressing. We explicitly show that these spans vary significantly based on the complexity of the task. We use the same masking function with minor modification:

$$m_z(x) = \min\left[\max\left[\frac{1}{R}(R + z - x), 0\right], 1\right] \tag{1}$$

Here, z acts as a model's parameter. We initialize it with kaiming normal (He et al., 2015) distribution. m_z is coupled with the attention weights. Hyperparameter R helps in controlling the softness of this attention distribution.

The attention head compute the similarities between current token t and past token r in the span $[t - S, t]$ as:

$$s_{tr} = x_t^T Q^T (K x_r + P_{t-r}) \tag{2}$$

where K, Q and P_{t-r} denote key, query vectors, and position embedding respectively. In the standard setting, attention weight distribution is obtained by applying softmax on the similarity vector.

$$A_{tr} = softmax(s_{tr}) \tag{3}$$

The attention weights from Equation 3 are then

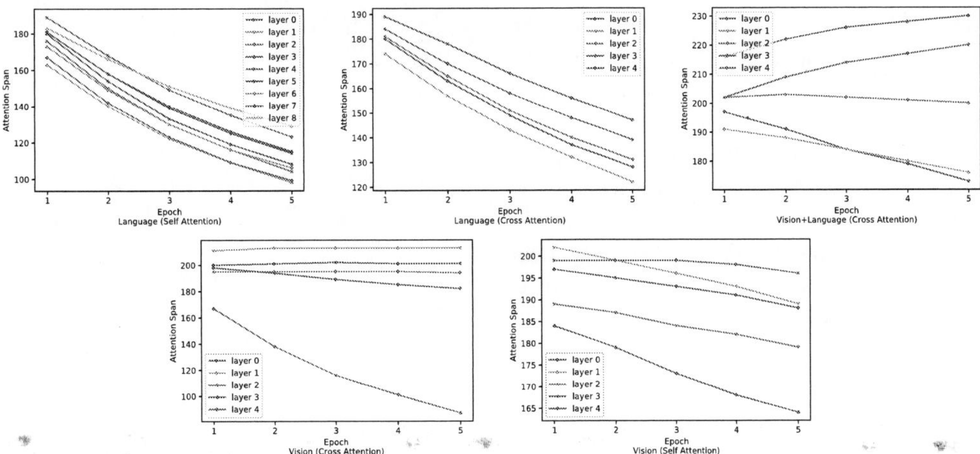

Figure 1: Variation of adaptive spans in different attention layers (single and cross-modality) as the training progresses. Accuracy on the local-validation set is reported per epoch. The maximum adaptive span limit was set to 1024

processed by the masking function as:

$$A_{tr} = \frac{m_z(t-r)exp(s_{tr})}{\sum\limits_{q=t-S}^{t-1} m_z(t-q)exp(s_{tr})} \tag{4}$$

The masking function is a non-increasing function that applies a transformation to the input values of attention scores to keep them in range of $[0, 1]$. The parameters of m_z are updated with model parameters to learn the optimal span.

2.3 Adaptive Sparse Attention

In order to make attention weights sparse, we use α entmax as proposed in (Correia et al., 2019). Specifically, softmax is replaced with α entmax to compute attention weights given attention scores in Equation 3.

$$\text{Att}(Q, K, V) = \pi \left(\frac{QK^{\top}}{\sqrt{d}} \right) V \tag{5}$$

$$\pi(Z)_{ij} = \alpha\text{-entmax} \ (z_i)_j \tag{6}$$

α plays a crucial role in determining the behavior of an attention head. If $\alpha > 1$, the weight distribution would move away from softmax's dense representation towards sparse mappings as its curvature changes. For $\alpha = 2$, we obtain complete sparse mappings. The value of alpha oscillates between 1 and 2. It is set as a network parameter, which is jointly optimized in the training process. Different values of α will govern the behavior of the attention head.

2.4 LayerDrop

Layerdrop (Fan et al., 2019) is a method to reduce the depth of the transformer in a controlled manner. This method drops the identical sub-layers in the transformer determined by a pruning strategy. We follow the *Every Other* strategy, which drops the layer as specified by a drop rate. It has been noted that this pruning strategy works well as compared to *Search on Valid* and *Data Driven* pruning strategies. Let N denote the total number of layers in the network. Setting $p = 1$ implies that we are dropping one layer out of all the layers assigned for a modality. The number of remaining layers becomes $N - p$. Although the network will consist of an equivalent amount of parameters as that of N layers, all the operations will be carried out equivalent to operations in $N - p$ layers. This strategy allows us to prune layers during inference time.

3   Experimental Setup

Visual Question Answering   To solve the VQA task, given an image and a question related to it, the network is supposed to predict the right answer from the given set of answer choices. We performed all the experimentation on the VQA 2.0 dataset (Antol et al., 2015). The dataset consists of three sets with a train set containing 83k images and 444k questions, a validation set containing 41k images and 214k questions, and a test set containing 81k images and 448k questions. In this case, the network is asked to predict an answer from 3129 answer choices for a particular question.

Implementation We use the pre-trained weights provided by (Tan and Bansal, 2019). We fine-tune LXMERT to form visiolinguistic representations based on image and text sequences with adaptive approaches mentioned above. This operation is followed by a classifier that receives the concatenated pooled features of image and text to predict the answer. Fine-tuning is performed on a single P100 GPU with 128 batch size. Optimization is performed with Lookahead (Zhang et al., 2019) with LAMB (You et al., 2019) as the inner optimizer. Learning rate schedule is regulated by Cyclical LR (Smith, 2017), with base and max learning rates set to $1e - 5$ and $1e - 4$.

4 Experimental Findings and Results

Adaptive span for understanding the complexity of the input sequence We demonstrate how learning spans can help in understanding the behavior of individual layers. Figure 1 shows how span varies amongst different attention layers. Studying spans can help us understand which layers are more sensitive to the input sequences encountered during the training process.

In the case of single modality encoder, spans for self-attention layers for vision and language decrease monotonically, indicating that the learning behavior is somewhat similar, although slopes tell us that the rate of learning is dissimilar. Similar behavior is seen in the cross-modality encoder for language.

Requiring a larger context size is indicative of the complexity of the sequences. When self-attention attends to both modalities, we observe that the intermediate layers responsible for forming complex representations increase their spans. This observation shows that a more significant span is necessary to attend both modalities jointly. Self-attention also requires a high span when attending to visual features in the cross-modality encoder. This observation shows that visual sequences are perceived as a more complex input to process than a language input in the cross-modality encoder.

Determining sparsity preferences for vision and language modality with α The value of α determines if the head is favoring sparse or dense attention weight distribution. For dealing with language modality, self-attention favors mostly sparse mapping of attention weights in intermediate layers. Similar behavior is observed inside cross-modality encoder as well. This observation shows that lan-

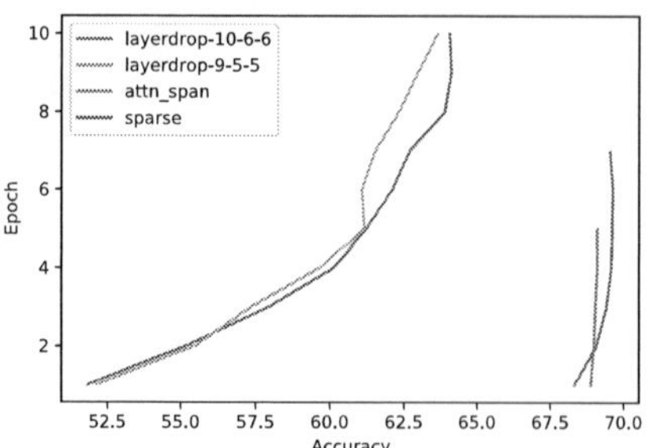

Figure 2: Regularization effect of layerdrop

guage modality benefits from sparse weights being assigned as attention distribution. The value of α is restricted below 1.5 for processing visual inputs. When vision modality is involved, heads that preferred sparse mapping initially are converging towards denser mapping, indicating that this representation of attention weights is preferred. We also observe that when both modalities are involved, the network prefers, even more, denser weight distribution. This observation shows that vision modality is given more preference (partly due to perceived complexity) over language inputs to process the sequence. Figure 3 shows variation of α values as training progresses.

Regularization effect of Layerdrop We consider two configurations of the model. The first one has 10 language, 6 vision, and 6 cross-modality layers with drop rate (p) set to 1 layer. In this case, the number of parameters is more, but the FLOPS is equivalent to the standard 9-5-5 baseline configuration. The later one has the 9-5-5 configuration with p set to 1. This rate causes a FLOP reduction of 17.54%. It is observed that layerdrop requires $\sim$3.5x more compute runtime for convergence during training. A possible explanation can be that additional training aids in forming a consolidated understanding of multi-modal representations. Even after ensuring the convergence of the model, a strong regularization effect (with a minimum value of p) prevents the network from achieving performance that is close enough with the mentioned adaptive methods with an equivalent number of parameters being used training. Figure 2 and Table 2 shows this noted observations.

Quantitative Analysis In this section, Table 1 compares the adaptive approaches with the baseline model and other state-of-the-art models, which rely upon standard softmax attention mechanism. We

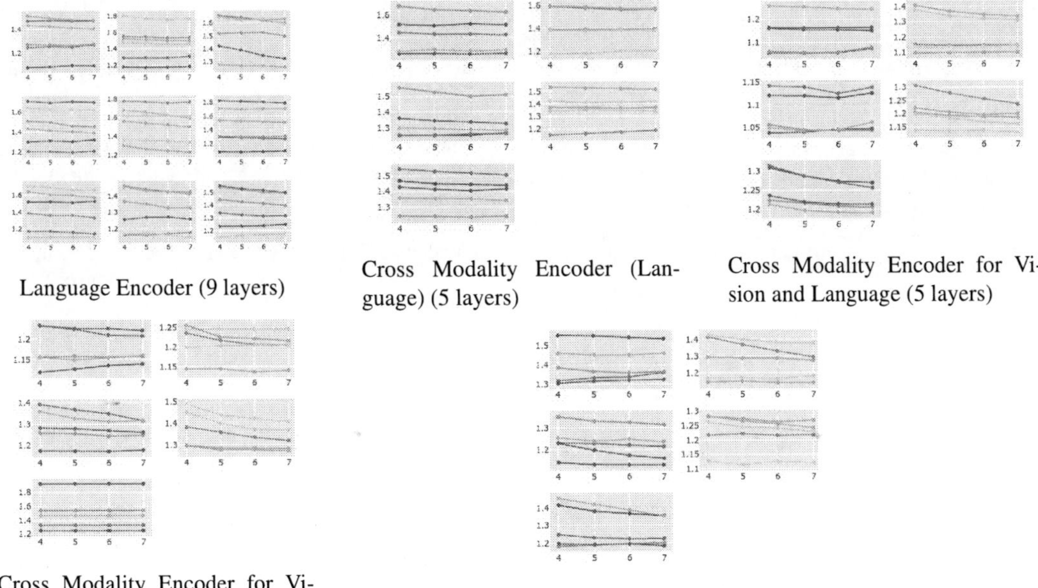

Language Encoder (9 layers)

Cross Modality Encoder (Language) (5 layers)

Cross Modality Encoder for Vision and Language (5 layers)

Cross Modality Encoder for Vision (5 layers)

Vision Encoder (5 layers)

Figure 3: Variation of Alpha in Entmax in first six attention heads during an intermediate training stage of 9-5-5 LXMERT model. X and Y axis denote epoch and alpha values, respectively. For simplicity, we only show alpha values for the first six attention heads (12). Color codes denote different attention heads.

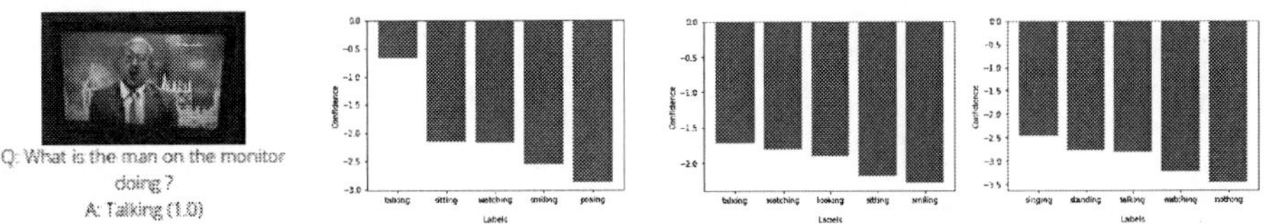

Figure 4: Top 5 confidence scores of an example input sequence **Left:** Adaptive Entmax **Center:** Adaptive Attention Span **Right:** 10-6-6 config with Layerdrop (p=1). Zoom in to see scores and labels.

notice that these approaches achieve near close performance as standard attention mechanisms by being computationally efficient. The results are reported without any hyperparameter tuning.

Qualitative Analysis In this section, we analyze the confidence scores on complex examples to better understand the network's predictions. We usually take the class with maximum confidence, but analyzing confidence scores of other classes can help us learn about what the network is learning about the similarity of different tasks in the image. Figure 4 shows confidence scores on an example input. We observe that entmax aids in forming a consolidated understanding of contrastive features. In most cases, the top 5 confidence scores include predictions present in the ground truth. Due to sparse mapping, the network makes strong, confident predictions about one label. When trained with an adaptive attention span, the network sometimes seems unsure about the correct label as ex-

pected from softmax behavior. It works well when a high probability is assigned to one label in the ground truth. We did not observe comparable performance from Layerdrop. In this example, the right answer is assigned a deficient score. The network does not seem to learn distinguishing features from similar classes properly.

5 Ablation Analysis

We normalize attention scores with entmax instead of softmax before applying the masking function to use both adaptive attention span and sparse attention weights mapping. It is evident from Table 2 that the adaptive span works better with the denser representation of attention weights to perform optimally. The effect of soft masking function is reduced when used with a sparse mapping function. We evaluate the layerdrop method with two configurations of the network 9-5-5 (language, vision, and cross-modality layers) and 10-6-6 with

Model	test-dev	test-std
BUTD (Anderson et al., 2018)	65.32	65.67
ViLBERT (Lu et al., 2019)	70.55	70.92
VLBERT (Su et al., 2019)	71.16	-
VisualBERT (Li et al., 2019)	70.80	71.00
UNITER (Chen et al., 2019)	72.27	72.46
LXMERT (Tan and Bansal, 2019)		
w/ softmax	72.42	72.54
w/ Adaptive Attetion Span	71.62	71.72
w/ Adaptive Sparse	71.73	71.97
w/ Layerdrop (10-6-6) (p=1)	66.4	66.72

Table 1: Comparison to the state-of-the-art methods with adaptive approaches on the VQA dataset.

Model	test-dev	test-std
LXMERT (Tan and Bansal, 2019)		
w/ Attention Span and Entmax	63.07	63.33
Default (10-6-6)	66.35	66.57
w/ Layerdrop (9-5-5) (p=1)	66.51	66.81

Table 2: Ablation study for Adaptive approaches

$p = 1$. From Table 2, we see that the shallower network performs better than the deeper-layered model. This observation shows that there is a specific threshold drop rate up until which layerdrop helps. It is plausible that this type of regularization is favorable in deeper networks.

6 Conclusion

While attention-based approaches are becoming universal, computationally efficient ways must be favored for broader adoption of provided pre-trained models on low resource hardware. Adaptive methods can significantly reduce the cost incurred to train such models and carbon footprints. In this work, we extend adaptive approaches to Visiolinguistic tasks to understand more about attention and adaptive mechanisms. While the empirical results are encouraging, important future work includes explorations of higher efficient adaptive and sparse mechanisms that can significantly cause FLOPS and parameter reduction with minimal loss in performance.

References

Peter Anderson, Xiaodong He, Chris Buehler, Damien Teney, Mark Johnson, Stephen Gould, and Lei Zhang. 2018. Bottom-up and top-down attention for image captioning and visual question answering. In *Proceedings of the IEEE conference on computer vision and pattern recognition*, pages 6077–6086.

Stanislaw Antol, Aishwarya Agrawal, Jiasen Lu, Margaret Mitchell, Dhruv Batra, C Lawrence Zitnick, and Devi Parikh. 2015. Vqa: Visual question answering. In *Proceedings of the IEEE international conference on computer vision*, pages 2425–2433.

Yen-Chun Chen, Linjie Li, Licheng Yu, Ahmed El Kholy, Faisal Ahmed, Zhe Gan, Yu Cheng, and Jingjing Liu. 2019. Uniter: Learning universal image-text representations. *arXiv preprint arXiv:1909.11740*.

Gonçalo M Correia, Vlad Niculae, and André FT Martins. 2019. Adaptively sparse transformers. *arXiv preprint arXiv:1909.00015*.

Angela Fan, Edouard Grave, and Armand Joulin. 2019. Reducing transformer depth on demand with structured dropout. *arXiv preprint arXiv:1909.11556*.

Kaiming He, Xiangyu Zhang, Shaoqing Ren, and Jian Sun. 2015. Delving deep into rectifiers: Surpassing human-level performance on imagenet classification. In *Proceedings of the IEEE international conference on computer vision*, pages 1026–1034.

Geoffrey Hinton, Oriol Vinyals, and Jeff Dean. 2015. Distilling the knowledge in a neural network. *arXiv preprint arXiv:1503.02531*.

Liunian Harold Li, Mark Yatskar, Da Yin, Cho-Jui Hsieh, and Kai-Wei Chang. 2019. Visualbert: A simple and performant baseline for vision and language. *arXiv preprint arXiv:1908.03557*.

Jiasen Lu, Dhruv Batra, Devi Parikh, and Stefan Lee. 2019. Vilbert: Pretraining task-agnostic visiolinguistic representations for vision-and-language tasks. In *Advances in Neural Information Processing Systems*, pages 13–23.

Leslie N Smith. 2017. Cyclical learning rates for training neural networks. In *2017 IEEE Winter Conference on Applications of Computer Vision (WACV)*, pages 464–472. IEEE.

Emma Strubell, Ananya Ganesh, and Andrew McCallum. 2019. Energy and policy considerations for deep learning in nlp. *arXiv preprint arXiv:1906.02243*.

Weijie Su, Xizhou Zhu, Yue Cao, Bin Li, Lewei Lu, Furu Wei, and Jifeng Dai. 2019. Vl-bert: Pretraining of generic visual-linguistic representations. *arXiv preprint arXiv:1908.08530*.

Sainbayar Sukhbaatar, Edouard Grave, Piotr Bojanowski, and Armand Joulin. 2019. Adaptive
attention span in transformers. *arXiv preprint
arXiv:1905.07799*.

Hao Tan and Mohit Bansal. 2019. Lxmert: Learning
cross-modality encoder representations from transformers. *arXiv preprint arXiv:1908.07490*.

Yang You, Jing Li, Sashank Reddi, Jonathan Hseu,
Sanjiv Kumar, Srinadh Bhojanapalli, Xiaodan Song,
James Demmel, and Cho-Jui Hsieh. 2019. Large
batch optimization for deep learning: Training bert
in 76 minutes. *arXiv preprint arXiv:1904.00962*,
1(5).

Michael Zhang, James Lucas, Jimmy Ba, and Geoffrey E Hinton. 2019. Lookahead optimizer: k steps
forward, 1 step back. In *Advances in Neural Information Processing Systems*, pages 9593–9604.

Story-level Text Style Transfer: A Proposal

Yusu Qian
Computer Science Department
Courant Institute of Mathematical Sciences
New York University
251 Mercer St 801, New York, NY 10012
`yq729@nyu.edu`

Abstract

Text style transfer aims to change the style of the input text to the target style while preserving the content to some extent. Previous works on this task are on the sentence level. We aim to work on story-level text style transfer to generate stories that preserve the plot of the input story while exhibiting a strong target style. The challenge in this task compared to previous work is that the structure of the input story, consisting of leading roles and their relations with each other, needs to be preserved, and that the generated story needs to be consistent after adding flavors. We plan to explore three methods including the BERT-based method, the Story Realization method, and the Graph-based method.

1 Introduction

Text style transfer has been extensively explored by the NLP community on the sentence level. In previous work, researchers defined style of a sentence as one or some of its attributes, including but not limited to sentiment (Xu et al., 2018; John et al., 2019; Liao et al., 2018), formality (Luo et al., 2019; Jain et al., 2018; Rao and Tetreault, 2018), factuality (Zhang et al., 2018), etc. The goal is to change the specified attribute or attributes in the input sentence to the target attribute or attributes. For example, changing a positive sentence to a negative sentence while keeping its key information. There are also works on transferring Shakespearean English to modern English and backward (Xu et al., 2012; Jhamtani et al., 2017).

In this paper, we propose methods to transfer text style on the story level. The task takes a story as input, and generates a story in the target style with the main plot of the input story preserved. In our work, we define *style* as the setting of the story which reveals time background and geographical information. For example, if a story starts with a boy receiving a package containing *parchments* and a *robe* delivered by an *owl*, a good guess is that this is a magic story most likely taken from or inspired by *Harry Potter*. If we want to change the above mentioned story into the *Alice in Wonderland* style, an ideal output maybe a story about a girl receiving a package containing an invitation to a tea party from a rabbit.

Compared with sentence-level text style transfer, our proposed work faces more challenges. It is impractical to collect parallel stories that have the same plot or structure but differ in settings. To deal with this, we break down the task into two parts. First, we explore methods to build a structural representation of the original story to preserve the main plot, including leading roles and their connections. Second, we generate a story given the retrieved information or graph and the target style.

2 Related Work

The work we propose is closely related to previous work on event extraction from text so that we have a structure representation of the input story, and text generation from events to produce the story in the target style.

Graph Extraction from Text Generating text on the story level from events ideally requires the events to be organized as a structural representation, otherwise the plot will not be consistent. While manually constructing graphs is expensive, there are multiple approaches to automatically construct graphs based on stories, including Named Entity Recognition (NER), Knowledge Graph, and other text graph generation methods. While NER has been studied for a while, the task of extracting named entities with semantic relations between nodes labelled has much room left to be explored. Most previous work on extracting entities together with relations either extract them separately and

Proceedings of the 58th Annual Meeting of the Association for Computational Linguistics: Student Research Workshop, pages 8–12
July 5 - July 10, 2020. ©2020 Association for Computational Linguistics

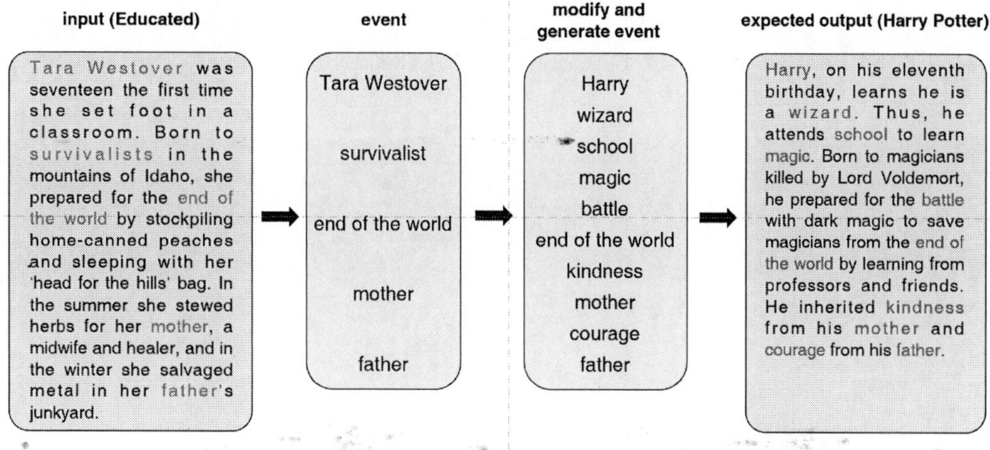

Figure 1: Illustration of how Story-realization Method works

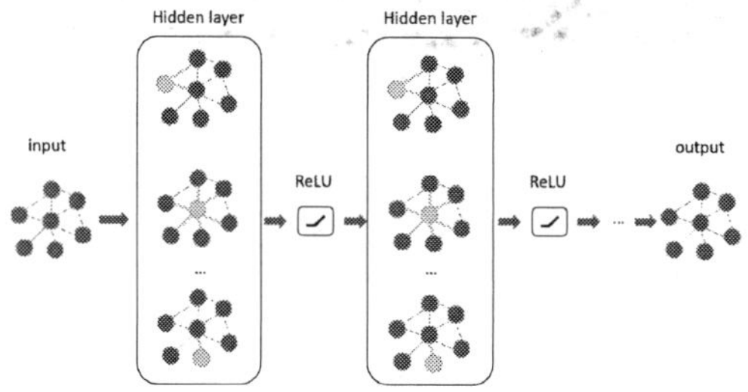

Figure 2: Structure of Graph Convolutional Network

predict the latter given the former (Chan and Roth, 2011; Zhou et al., 2005), or rely on feature engineering to extract them jointly (Ren et al., 2017).

Recently, Fu et al. (2019) employed relation-weighted graph convolutional networks (GCNs) (Kipf and Welling, 2016) to build an end-to-end relation extraction model, GraphRel, and reported SOTA results. Figure 2 illustrates how GCN works. GCN is a variant of convolutional neural networks (CNNs) that works on graphs. The representation of each node is updated based on its adjacent nodes.

Text Generation from Graph Due to the variety of graphs and information loss of long-distance dependencies, it is hard to generate coherent stories that span across multiple sentences from a graph. Koncel-Kedziorski et al. (2019) proposed a novel graph transformer to alleviate this problem by leveraging the relational structure of graphs without setting linearization or hierarchical constraints.

The usage of GCN for text generation from graphs is enjoying growing popularity among researchers. Marcheggiani and Perez-Beltrachini (2018) used GCNs to build an encoder which calculates the node representation of each node in a directed graph. After adding residual connections and dense connections between the GCN layers, they used an LSTM decoder. Guo et al. (2019) built Densely Connected Graph Convolutional Networks to address the issue of learning deeper GCNs, and achieved better results on graph-to-sequence learning and AMR-to-text generation than previous methods.

3 Proposed Methodology

Our goal is to adapt the original story to the target setting. A well-known example of such kind of adaptation is New York theatre production *Sleep No More*, which adapts the story of Macbeth deprived of its original time setting, and sets in a 1930s hotel called the McKittrick.

3.1 Data Set

The data sets ideal for our proposed work need to satisfy the following requirements. First, each corpus needs to have an abundant amount of text in the same *style*. Second, the *style* of each corpus should differ from each other significantly, to the extent that a snippet from a certain corpus tells enough for people to tell which corpus it is from.

We select paragraphs between 100 and 200 words from each corpus and use GraphRel to automatically build graphs from the text.

For each method described in the next section, we use different training data. For the BERT-based method, we use the story corpora as training data. For the Story-realization method, we use the selected paragraphs and corresponding extracted

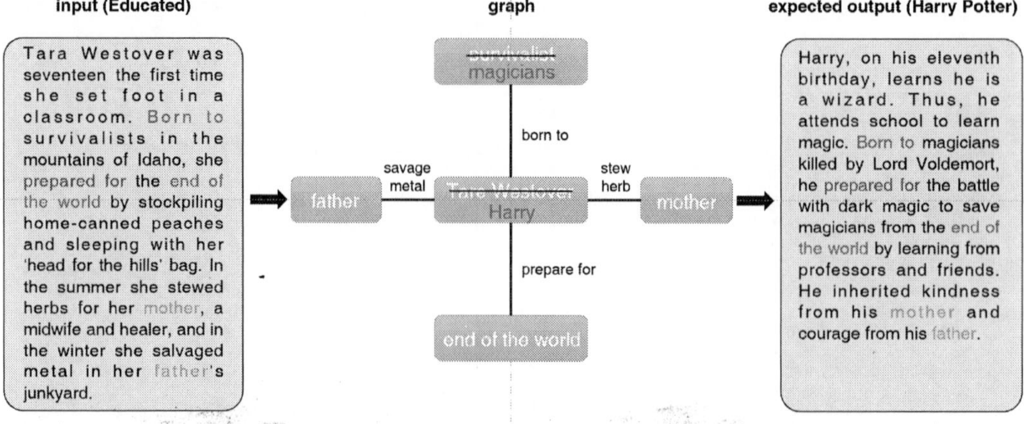

Figure 3: Illustration of how Graph-based Method works

named entities as training data. For the Graph-based method, we use the selected paragraphs and graphs built by GraphRel as training data.

To satisfy these requirements, we choose the *Harry Potter Series* and the *Game of the Throne Series* as our corpora. The former consists of 1,084,170 words and the latter consists of 1,736,054 words.

3.2 Models

We plan to experiment with the following three methods. The first two methods serve as baselines.

BERT-based Method This method will be based on Bidirectional Encoder Representations from Transformers (BERT) (Devlin et al., 2018). In this method, first we use the corpus in the target style to fine-tune BERT. Then we build a vocabulary for the target corpus, setting the threshold of minimum occurrence to 20. We examine each word in the input story to see if they are included in the vocabulary of the target corpus. If they are not, we use the fine-tuned BERT to mask and predict these words one by one. The BERT-based method serves as our baseline model as it modifies the input story sentence by sentence instead of as a whole.

In simpler cases where we only wish to change the era of the story and do not have any other requirements, we can add append a phrase indicating the era to the original sentences. For example, when we mask *video* in the sentence 'The boy spent a whole day playing video games.', BERT (large-cased version) correctly predicts the word to be *video*. If we add the phrase 'on the first day of the 18th century', the prediction becomes *card*, which matches the time setting.

Story Realization Method Ammanabrolu et al. (2019) proposed an ensemble-based model to generate sentences given plot events. This involves two steps. First, we need to extract events from the input story. This can be done through Named Entity Recognition (in this work we will use Allennlp NER) and finding VerbNet (Kipper-Schuler, 2005) classes of verbs and WordNet (Miller, 1995) Synsets for nouns recognized as events. The next step is to expand these events to a story. We plan to experiment with the ensemble model by Ammanabrolu et al. (2019) which is reported to combine the strength of the retrieve-and-edit method (Hashimoto et al., 2018), the template filling method, the sequence-to-sequence methods with finite state machine decoder, Monte Carlo beam decoding, and vanilla beam-decoding respectively. This method will conduct an event-to-event generation first to include more events before generating the output story. Figure 1 illustrates how this method works.

Here we need to note that sometimes extracted entities or relations are out-of-target-corpus-vocabulary words in the target style corpus. For example, *computer* is not in the corpus of *Harry Potter*. We need to replace these words with words that have the same part of speech and closest in the word embedding trained on the target corpus. Euclidean distance is used for distance calculation.

We expect that compared with the BERT-based method, the Story Realization method will perform better in terms of creativity while not as well in terms of content preservation.

Graph-based Method   In this method, a similar replacing scheme of out-of-target-corpus-vocabulary words as in the story realization method should be used on the input story. Then we plan to experiment with graph transformers and other graph-to-text generators trained on our data sets, compare their performance on our task, and examine the possibility to improve their performance by making modifications. Specifically, in the text-to-graph step we explore using Graph Neural Network. We plan to start with using GraphRel, the GCN-based SOTA entity and relation extraction model, to convert the input story to a graph.

Figure 3 illustrates how the Graph-based Method works. The input is an extract from the novel *Educated*. A graph containing key information is built upon the input story. Some modification is done to replace out-of-target-corpus-vocabulary words. We expect the output to preserve the structure of the input story while being creative and consistent. Towards this goal, we plan to experiment with different GCNs structures for text generation.

3.3 Evaluation

We plan to evaluate our generated stories using perplexity and human evaluation, with an emphasis on the latter considering the creative nature of this task.

The generated stories will be evaluated by linguists from these aspects: grammar and fluency; main plot preservation; strength of the target style; creativeness. Each aspect will be given a score between 1 and 5, with 1 representing total failure, 2 representing barely acceptable, 3 representing acceptable, 4 representing good, and 5 representing the most satisfying performance.

4   Summary

We propose to explore text style transfer on the story level. The challenge remains in preserving the main plot and generating consistent and meaningful text in the target style. We plan to focus mostly on studying the possible application of GCN in this task. We will perform extensive experiments and report results in future work.

5   Acknowledgment

We are grateful to He He, Junxian He, and Peng Xu for helpful advice and discussion, and reviewers for detailed feedback.

References

Prithviraj Ammanabrolu, Ethan Tien, Wesley Cheung, Zhaochen Luo, William L. White Ma, Lara J. Martin, and Mark O. Riedl. 2019. Story realization: Expanding plot events into sentences. *ArXiv*, abs/1909.03480.

Yee Seng Chan and Dan Roth. 2011. Exploiting syntactico-semantic structures for relation extraction. In *The 49th Annual Meeting of the Association for Computational Linguistics: Human Language Technologies, Proceedings of the Conference, 19-24 June, 2011, Portland, Oregon, USA*, pages 551–560. The Association for Computer Linguistics.

Jacob Devlin, Ming-Wei Chang, Kenton Lee, and Kristina Toutanova. 2018. BERT: pre-training of deep bidirectional transformers for language understanding. *CoRR*, abs/1810.04805.

Tsu-Jui Fu, Peng-Hsuan Li, and Wei-Yun Ma. 2019. GraphRel: Modeling text as relational graphs for joint entity and relation extraction. In *Proceedings of the 57th Annual Meeting of the Association for Computational Linguistics*, pages 1409–1418, Florence, Italy. Association for Computational Linguistics.

Zhijiang Guo, Yan Zhang, Zhiyang Teng, and Wei Lu. 2019. Densely connected graph convolutional networks for graph-to-sequence learning. *Transactions of the Association for Computational Linguistics*, 7:297–312.

Tatsunori B. Hashimoto, Kelvin Guu, Yonatan Oren, and Percy Liang. 2018. A retrieve-and-edit framework for predicting structured outputs. In *Proceedings of the 32nd International Conference on Neural Information Processing Systems*, NIPS'18, page 10073–10083, Red Hook, NY, USA. Curran Associates Inc.

Parag Jain, Abhijit Mishra, Amar Prakash Azad, and Karthik Sankaranarayanan. 2018. Unsupervised controllable text formalization. *CoRR*, abs/1809.04556.

Harsh Jhamtani, Varun Gangal, Eduard Hovy, and Eric Nyberg. 2017. Shakespearizing modern language using copy-enriched sequence-to-sequence models. *EMNLP 2017*, 6:10.

Vineet John, Lili Mou, Hareesh Bahuleyan, and Olga Vechtomova. 2019. Disentangled representation learning for non-parallel text style transfer. In *Proceedings of the 57th Annual Meeting of the Association for Computational Linguistics*, pages 424–434, Florence, Italy. Association for Computational Linguistics.

Thomas Kipf and Max Welling. 2016. Semi-supervised classification with graph convolutional networks. *ArXiv*, abs/1609.02907.

Karin Kipper-Schuler. 2005. *VerbNet: a broad-coverage, comprehensive verb lexicon*. Ph.D. thesis, Computer and Information Science Department, Universiy of Pennsylvania, Philadelphia, PA.

Rik Koncel-Kedziorski, Dhanush Bekal, Yi Luan, Mirella Lapata, and Hannaneh Hajishirzi. 2019. Text Generation from Knowledge Graphs with Graph Transformers. In *Proceedings of the 2019 Conference of the North American Chapter of the Association for Computational Linguistics: Human Language Technologies, Volume 1 (Long and Short Papers)*, pages 2284–2293, Minneapolis, Minnesota. Association for Computational Linguistics.

Yi Liao, Lidong Bing, Piji Li, Shuming Shi, Wai Lam, and Tong Zhang. 2018. QuaSE: Sequence editing under quantifiable guidance. In *Proceedings of the 2018 Conference on Empirical Methods in Natural Language Processing*, pages 3855–3864, Brussels, Belgium. Association for Computational Linguistics.

Fuli Luo, Peng Li, Jie Zhou, Pengcheng Yang, Baobao Chang, Xu Sun, and Zhifang Sui. 2019. A dual reinforcement learning framework for unsupervised text style transfer. In *IJCAI*.

Diego Marcheggiani and Laura Perez-Beltrachini. 2018. Deep graph convolutional encoders for structured data to text generation. In *Proceedings of the 11th International Conference on Natural Language Generation*, pages 1–9, Tilburg University, The Netherlands. Association for Computational Linguistics.

George A. Miller. 1995. Wordnet: A lexical database for english. *Commun. ACM*, 38(11):39–41.

Sudha Rao and Joel R. Tetreault. 2018. Dear sir or madam, may i introduce the gyafc dataset: Corpus, benchmarks and metrics for formality style transfer. In *NAACL-HLT*.

Xiang Ren, Zeqiu Wu, Wenqi He, Meng Qu, Clare R. Voss, Heng Ji, Tarek F. Abdelzaher, and Jiawei Han. 2017. Cotype. *Proceedings of the 26th International Conference on World Wide Web - WWW '17*.

Jingjing Xu, Xu Sun, Qi Zeng, Xiaodong Zhang, Xuancheng Ren, Houfeng Wang, and Wenjie Li. 2018. Unpaired sentiment-to-sentiment translation: A cycled reinforcement learning approach. In *Proceedings of the 56th Annual Meeting of the Association for Computational Linguistics (Volume 1: Long Papers)*, pages 979–988, Melbourne, Australia. Association for Computational Linguistics.

Wei Xu, Alan Ritter, Bill Dolan, Ralph Grishman, and Colin Cherry. 2012. Paraphrasing for style. In *Proceedings of COLING 2012*, pages 2899–2914, Mumbai, India. The COLING 2012 Organizing Committee.

Zhirui Zhang, Shuo Ren, Shujie Liu, Jianyong Wang, Peng Chen, Mu Li, Ming Zhou, and Enhong Chen. 2018. Style transfer as unsupervised machine translation.

GuoDong Zhou, Jian Su, Jie Zhang, and Min Zhang. 2005. Exploring various knowledge in relation extraction. In *Proceedings of the 43rd Annual Meeting of the Association for Computational Linguistics (ACL'05)*, pages 427–434, Ann Arbor, Michigan. Association for Computational Linguistics.

Unsupervised Paraphasia Classification in Aphasic Speech

Sharan Pai[‡†]**, Nikhil Sachdeva**[†]**, Prince Sachdeva**[†]**, Rajiv Ratn Shah**[†]
[‡] Department. of Mathematics
[†] Department of Computer Science
IIIT Delhi, India
{sharan16266, nikhil16061, prince17080, rajivratn}@iiitd.ac.in

Abstract

Aphasia is a speech and language disorder that results from brain damage, often characterized by word retrieval deficit (anomia) resulting in naming errors (paraphasia). Automatic paraphasia detection has many benefits for both treatment and diagnosis of Aphasia and its type. But supervised learning methods cant be utilized adequately as there is a lack of aphasic speech data. In this paper, we describe our novel unsupervised method, which can be implemented without the need for labeled paraphasia data. Our evaluations show that our method outperforms previous work based on supervised learning and transfer learning approaches for English. We demonstrate the utility of our method as an essential first step in developing augmentative and alternative communication (AAC) devices for patients suffering from aphasia in any language.

1 Introduction

Aphasia is a speech and language disorder commonly acquired by brain damage resulting from a stroke (Bhogal et al., 2003). Many people around the world suffer from Aphasia as there are at least 2 million patients in USA and 250,000 in Great Britain (National Aphasia Association, 2019).

Anomia, the difficulty in spoken word retrieval, is a common symptom in Aphasic speech (Laine and Martin, 2013). A majority of persons with aphasia (PWA) suffer from varying degrees of anomia (Nickels, 2002). Anomia further results in various types of Paraphasia (naming errors) which impedes the PWA's ability to carry out meaningful conversation leading to loneliness and social anxiety (Beeke et al., 2013).

There are three common types of paraphasia which occur in aphasic speech, namely *semantic, phonemic* and *neologistic* (Laine and Martin, 2013; Goodglass and Kaplan, 1972). In *semantic para-*

phasia, the PWA substitutes a semantically similar word *eg.* (substituting *elbow* with *knee*). In *phonemic paraphasia*, there are various sub types involving the type of phoneme substitution such as, substituting *bat* with *lat*, inserting or deleting a phoneme (*drake* as *dake*) or phoneme movements (*candle* with *cancle*). Lastly, in *neologistic paraphasia*, the target word is substituted with a nonword (*harmonica* with *parokada*). Detecting and classifying the type of paraphasia is useful to determine the type of aphasia and which treatment to prescribe (Nickels, 2002; Friedmann et al., 2013).

Aphasia TalkBank (MacWhinney, 2007), is a large scale multi-modal online database of aphasic speech data. It contains aphasic speech data for many languages such as English, French *etc* which is primarily used by clinical researchers to study aphasia (Forbes et al., 2012). While the amount of data is sufficient for clinical researchers, there is a lack of data to implement supervised learning methods. This is true not only for a well researched language like English, but also for low-resource [1] languages like Greek, Spanish *etc.*

To counter the lack of data and to extend the proposed method for low-resource languages too, we investigate an unsupervised approach. We first consider large and available speech corpuses such as LibriSpeech (Panayotov et al., 2015) to create speech embeddings of individual words similar to (Chung et al., 2016). We then perform soft clustering using HDBSCAN on these embeddings, and classify each word by using simple rules with a cutoff hyperparameter. The whole method is end-to-end unsupervised and can be applied to any language.

In our evaluations section, we demonstrate the efficacy of our method over a naive baseline and the transfer learning method used by (Le et al., 2017)

---

[1] we define low-resource *wrt* amount of available aphasic speech data

Proceedings of the 58th Annual Meeting of the Association for Computational Linguistics: Student Research Workshop, pages 13–19
July 5 - July 10, 2020. ©2020 Association for Computational Linguistics

for English. We hope that such an unsupervised method allows for development of AAC devices improving daily life of not only English-speaking PWA's but also PWA's in other languages.

2 Related Work

Recently, researchers have demonstrated the use of machine learning methods not only to diagnose the type of aphasia but also to rehabilitate and treat PWA's. Mainly focusing on obtaining a medical diagnosis, (Fraser et al., 2013) applied feature selection using a transcript and low-level acoustic features to classify between two sub-types of primary progressive aphasia. Likewise, (Peintner et al., 2008) used speech and language features to classify between three broad types of frontotemporal lobar degeneration, including progressive nonfluent aphasia. Further, given speech samples of PWA's, (Le et al., 2014; Le and Mower Provost, 2015; Le et al., 2016) proposed approaches for predicting the utterance-level pronunciation and prosody scores. (Abad et al., 2012, 2013) aimed to tackle the contextually similar problem through keyword spotting. It recognized target words from phrases spoken by the PWA but disregarded fine-grained word-level errors such as paraphasias.

Deep learning methods to detect paraphasia was first demonstrated in (Le et al., 2017). It worked around the notion of mispronunciation detection, adopting the methods of (Lee et al., 2013; Lee and Glass, 2013), which used Dynamic Time Warping (DTW) features to provide a quantitative comparison of word and phone-level pronunciations between native and non-native speakers. Similarly, (Le et al., 2017) has used DTW and other acoustic features like Phone Edit distance and Goodness of Pronunciation, to distinguish between target transcripts and paraphasias. Consequently, it has also used Automatic Speech Recognition (ASR) techniques to generate the target transcripts from the paraphasias automatically. In the end, all of these proposed methods require target transcripts for their core functioning.

To the best of our knowledge, no existing work provides an unsupervised approach to detecting and classifying paraphasia from aphasic speech. In this paper, we explore a realistic scenario where we have access only to the free form discussion with PWA's.

3 Method

Aphasic speech data can be collected in mainly two ways: as a free form discussion between a PWA and an interviewer or a PWA reading a set of provided scripts. While a PWA reading from scripts is conducive to supervised learning methods, it is rarely the case in real life. Hence, our goal is to perform paraphasia detection and classification in the wild *i.e.* without any target scripts. Another motivation for classification in the wild is the lack of labeled English aphasic speech data. Further, the available speech data has a class imbalance (phonemic and neologistic paraphasias account for 12.0 and 6.4 percent respectively). Low-resource languages such as Hindi, Greek *etc.* have a serious lack of aphasia speech data and almost non-existent labeled speech data. Using transfer-learning approaches similar to (Le et al., 2017), would not allow extending it to such low-resource languages. Hence, it was necessary to investigate unsupervised approaches for paraphasia classification. In this section, we outline our proposed unsupervised method which consists of first creating speech embeddings of non-aphasic speech data and then performing soft clustering to further classify the type of paraphasia detected.

3.1 Speech Embedding

In order to classify phonemic and neologistic paraphasia, capturing phoneme placement in a word is necessary.

Previous work, used features such as Goodness of Pronunciation and Phoneme Edit-Distance to do the same. Hence, we adopt speech embeddings which focus on phoneme pronunciation.

In particular, we use the Audio-Word2Vec embeddings outlined in (Chung et al., 2016) as they have demonstrated good performance in distinguishing utterances that have large (>3) phoneme sequence edit distance and grouping utterances with low phoneme sequence edit distance (0 to 2). These speech embeddings are created in an unsupervised fashion. Each word utterance is passed through a sequence-to-sequence encoder and reconstructed via a decoder. This process preserves the acoustic information in the embedding.

(Chung et al., 2016) further demonstrated that sequential phoneme structure is preserved in the vector space. This property can be exploited using density based clustering, the next step of our proposed method.

Classifying semantic paraphasia requires different approaches which cannot be encompassed in methods used to classify phonemic and neologistic paraphasia and hence is left as future work.

3.2 Probing Tasks

Unsupervised word embeddings can be improved further and geared specifically for aphasic speech, but in order to understand what these embeddings are capturing it is important to probe them. Taking inspiration from (Conneau et al., 2018), we create probing tasks specifically for paraphasia. Probing tasks are simple classification tasks for embeddings. We detail three probing tasks specifically for phonemic and neologistic paraphasia.

1. *Phoneme-Movement*: Phonemic paraphasia is often characterized with phoneme movement, usually involving a shift in the position of one or two phonemes. In this binary classification task, the embeddings are used to determine if a phoneme shift took place or not.

2. *Phoneme-Add/Delete*: The addition or deletion of a phoneme is seen in phonemic paraphasia. We use the generated embeddings to determine if the word utterance has a phoneme addition/deletion or is unchanged.

3. *In-Dictionary*: In this task, we check if the embeddings can classify if the word is in the language's dictionary or not. Neologistic paraphasia occurs when PWA's substitute target words with non-words.

These three probing tasks, while not exhaustive, can be used to determine how well the speech embeddings can perform for paraphasia detection.

3.3 Density based Clustering

As our method is unsupervised, we do not have access to whether each word utterance is a paraphasia (further what type) or not. To classify each utterance, we use techniques similar to anomaly detection.

Firstly, the embeddings generated for each word, represent only non-paraphasia words. This is because the dataset used to create these embeddings consists of only correct words utterances. We cluster these non-paraphasia embeddings into distinct clusters where the members of each cluster are embeddings of the same word. We use individual words as centroids rather than phoneme based centroids. This is because, phoneme based centroid choices such as monophones, senones *etc.* creates a surjective mapping from embeddings to centroids (*eg.* both words *cat* and *hat* contain the same phoneme *ae*, hence both words will be assigned to the same centroid), whereas word based centroids has a bijective mapping.

Secondly, we use HDBSCAN (McInnes et al., 2017) to perform density based clustering as it allows for cluster densities of varying size. The two most influential parameters namely, minimum cluster size and minimum samples are chosen so as to produce number of clusters equal to the vocabulary size of the dataset.

Lastly, we exploit the soft clustering property of HDBSCAN to detect paraphasias. We use simple rule based methods to perform classification. When a word utterance is correct *i.e* it is not a paraphasia, the top 1 cluster probability should be high, as the embedding should have a core distance of 0. Hence if the utterance satisfies top_1 probability $\geq \alpha$ then it is classified as a correct word. We use $\alpha = 0.75$ in our experiments.

Now, if a word utterance is phonemic paraphasia, HDBSCAN returns near similar cluster membership probabilities for 2 to 3 clusters (*eg.* *lat* will be clustered close to correct words *bat, late etc.*)

$$top_1 - top_2 \leq \beta \tag{1}$$

If a word utterance satisfies equation 1 then we can classify it as a phonemic paraphasia. We use $\beta = 0.2$ in our experiments.

For a neologistic paraphasia, the cluster membership probabilities are evenly low, as the word utterance is a non-word and was never seen by HDBSCAN while clustering. Hence, a utterance that satisfies

$$\sum^{k} top_i \leq \gamma$$

is classified as a neologistic paraphasia. In our experiments $k = 5$ and $\gamma = 0.5$

This clustering based method does not violate the unsupervised nature of the proposed goal. Our reasoning is validated by the empirical evaluations performed in further sections.

4 Evaluation

In order to validate the claims made in the previous section, we perform the following evaluations. For a fair comparison, we use the same test dataset used in (Le et al., 2017), and perform further analysis on our soft clustering approach. In this section, we detail the experimental setup used including the model structure and hyperparameters, the metrics and the baselines used to compare and finally expand on the results of our method.

4.1 Data

We use two speech datasets, one to create word utterance embeddings and perform HDBSCAN clustering and another to test our method.

As detailed in (Chung et al., 2016), we used the LibriSpeech corpus (Panayotov et al., 2015) to create audio-word2vec embeddings. We have used the *train-clean-100* subset to train the Seq2Seq autoencoder and a combination of *dev-clean* and *test-clean* subsets to perform density based soft clustering. MFCC's of 13 feature-coefficient were used as input to the models.

For our test dataset we used speech data from Aphasia TalkBank (MacWhinney, 2007), specifically, the *Scripts* section of the English section. *Scripts* contains recordings of PWA's reading a script, with each word utterance conveniently labeled as [*p:n] and [*n:k] for phonemic and neologistic paraphasia. (Le et al., 2017) uses the *Fridriksson* subset consisting of 12 PWA's reading 4 predefined scripts each, allowing (Le et al., 2017) to use supervised learning to classify paraphasia as they have access to the target word. We used this same subset, for our experiments to remain consistent.

4.2 Analysis

In this section we provide empirical evidence to substantiate our intuition while building our unsupervised method.

4.2.1 Probing Tasks

The three probing tasks are used to determine how well the unsupervised embeddings are performing on specific tasks. We examine three different types of embedding methods. First is the original setup (Chung et al., 2016) utilized, an Sequence-to-Sequence autoencoder with both the RNN Encoder and Decoder consisting of one hidden layer of 100 LSTM units was used. The networks were trained with SGD without momentum with a fixed learning rate of 0.3 and for 500 epochs. Secondly we improve upon the autoencoder architecture by using 2 instead of 1 hidden layer of 100 bidirectional LSTM units. (Chung et al., 2016) noticed that the embeddings favoured phonemes towards the end

of the word, this problem is alleviated by using bidirectional LSTM. The networks were trained with Adam with a learning rate of 0.01 and for 500 epochs.

Method	Ph-Move	Ph-Add/Del	In-Dict
Audio-word2vec	68%	**81%**	76%
Bi-LSTM	**73%**	77%	**83%**

Table 1: Performance of embedding generation methods on probing tasks reported as averaged accuracy values.

As seen in table 1, the bi-directional LSTM version of audio-word2vec performs better and hence going further we use this setup for creating word utterance embeddings.

4.2.2 Soft Clustering

We empirically demonstrate that the word embedding clusters behave similar to the format outlined in the Methods section. We use (McInnes et al., 2017) implementation of HDBSCAN in our experiments.

First we report the HDBSCAN cluster membership scores for correct, phonemic and neologistic paraphasias in Table 2. The paraphasia are transcribed in CHAT transcription format.

Word	Top 1	Top 2	Top 3
Correct Words			
weather	.882	.073	.032
hot	.821	.072	.053
rarely	.764	.213	.014
Phonemic Paraphasia			
u@u (to)	.537	.419	.065
duz@u (choose)	.501	.324	.171
fpł@u (spring)	.461	.253	.258
Neologistic Paraphasia			
ziz@u (easy)	.277	.102	.156
muz@u (use)	.196	.162	.153
zt@u (vast)	.234	.142	.077

Table 2: Top k cluster membership probability scores for correct, phonemic and neologistic paraphasia. Correct word for corresponding paraphasia is included in parenthesis

The cluster membership probabilities, align with the choice of cutoff rules used in the Methods section. Phonemic paraphasia is usually assigned a membership score split across two or three clusters.

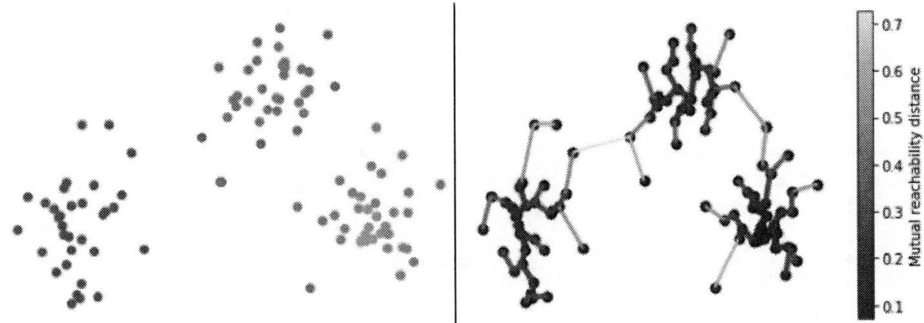

Figure 1: (a) TSNE projections of phonemic paraphasia (in red) with top 1,2 and 3 clusters. The darker the color the higher the cluster membership probability. (b) Minimum spanning tree based on mutual reachability scores

This is true because of the phoneme movement, addition or deletion property leaving rest of the word unaffected, causing confusion so as to which cluster the utterance belongs to. TSNE projection of a sample phonemic paraphasia with its top 1,2 and 3 clusters is displayed in Figure 1. The minimum spanning tree of the clusters also displays the confusion in allocating cluster membership to the phonemic error. Similarly neologistic paraphasia, has uniformly low cluster membership scores, as the utterance is never seen by HDBSCAN as it is a non-word.

A very small set of word utterances (≤ 20) satisfied the condition for both phonemic and neologistic paraphasia *eg.*(top 1,2 and 3 probabilities were .32 .11 and .09) These utterances were classified as phonemic due to the higher value of top 1 than the average neologistic paraphasia.

4.3 Results

As noted by (Le et al., 2017), it is necessary to classify if the word is correct in addition to phonemic or neologistic for future ASR and AAC system development. We report the averaged F1 score on three binary classification schemes, namely *C-pn* (correct vs. phonemic or neologistic), *C-p* (correct vs. phonemic) and *C-n* (correct vs. neologistic)

As baselines, we compare with a naive baseline which classifies all words as correct (the majority class) and the DBLSTM-RNN acoustic model by (Le et al., 2017). It is necessary to note that the DBLSTM-RNN was trained on supervised data using transfer learning methods.

Our method demonstrates results in table 3 which are comparable to the supervised learning method. It outperforms the other baselines for *C-pn* and *C-p*.

Method	C-pn	C-p	C-n
Majority Baseline	.442	.461	.484
(Le et al., 2017)	.704	.632	**.761**
Ours	**.761**	**.683**	.728

Table 3: Paraphasia detection and further classification reported as averaged F1 scores.

While, a tighter set of cutoff hyperparameters can be used to classify the paraphasias as the AAC devices and systems gets further personalized. Our choice of hyperparameters is purposely kept generalized so as to accommodate various PWA speakers. We also believe a better embedding method will allow for better scores even with our general cutoff hyperparameters, especially neologistic paraphasia as it will be further from any word cluster.

5 Conclusion

The work presented in this paper is heavily inspired by (Le et al., 2017), but differs and improves it in the following ways. We provide a completely unsupervised method which outperforms previous work in paraphasia classification and detection. While we maintain that our method can be used for all languages, irrespective of aphasic speech data, due to time constraints we could include only English in our evaluations. We lay the ground-work for paraphasia classification in low-resource languages allowing for development of ASR and AAC systems for not only English-speaking PWA's but also PWA's in developing nations. Our future work will target demonstrating the method on other languages. We also hope to address semantic paraphasia in future work and create, deploy AAC systems building on the method proposed in this paper.

Acknowledgement

Sharan Pai is partly supported by Mantle Labs and MIDAS Lab, IIIT Delhi. Nikhil and Prince Sachdeva are partly supported by MIDAS lab, IIIT Delhi. Rajiv Ratn Shah is partly supported by the Infosys Center for AI, IIIT Delhi and ECRA Grant (ECR/2018/002776) by SERB, Government of India. We would like to thank RAs Srimoyee Chaudhury and Sakshi Labhane for their help in earlier versions of the study.

References

Alberto Abad, Anna Pompili, Angela Costa, and Isabel Trancoso. 2012. Automatic word naming recognition for treatment and assessment of aphasia. *13th Annual Conference of the International Speech Communication Association 2012, INTERSPEECH 2012*, 2.

Alberto Abad, Anna Pompili, Angela Costa, Isabel Trancoso, Jos Fonseca, Gabriela Leal, Luisa Farrajota, and Isabel Martins. 2013. Automatic word naming recognition for an on-line aphasia treatment system. *Computer Speech Language*, 27:12351248.

Suzanne Beeke, Firle Beckley, Wendy Best, Fiona Johnson, Susan Edwards, and Jane Maxim. 2013. Extended turn construction and test question sequences in the conversations of three speakers with agrammatic aphasia. *Clinical linguistics & phonetics*, 27(10-11):784–804.

Sanjit K Bhogal, Robert W Teasell, Norine C Foley, and Mark R Speechley. 2003. Rehabilitation of aphasia: more is better. *Topics in Stroke Rehabilitation*, 10(2):66–76.

Yu-An Chung, Chao-Chung Wu, Chia-Hao Shen, Hung-Yi Lee, and Lin-Shan Lee. 2016. Audio word2vec: Unsupervised learning of audio segment representations using sequence-to-sequence autoencoder. *arXiv preprint arXiv:1603.00982*.

Alexis Conneau, Germán Kruszewski, Guillaume Lample, Loïc Barrault, and Marco Baroni. 2018. What you can cram into a single vector: Probing sentence embeddings for linguistic properties. *arXiv preprint arXiv:1805.01070*.

Margaret M Forbes, Davida Fromm, and Brian MacWhinney. 2012. Aphasiabank: A resource for clinicians. In *Seminars in speech and language*, volume 33, pages 217–222. Thieme Medical Publishers.

Kathleen Fraser, Frank Rudzicz, and Elizabeth Rochon. 2013. Using text and acoustic features to diagnose progressive aphasia and its subtypes.

Naama Friedmann, Michal Biran, and Dror Dotan. 2013. Lexical retrieval and its breakdown in aphasia and developmental language impairment. *The Cambridge handbook of biolinguistics*, pages 350–374.

Harold Goodglass and Edith Kaplan. 1972. *The assessment of aphasia and related disorders*. Lea & Febiger.

Matti Laine and Nadine Martin. 2013. *Anomia: Theoretical and clinical aspects*. Psychology Press.

Duc Le, Keli Licata, Elizabeth Mercado, Carol Persad, and Emily Mower Provost. 2014. Automatic analysis of speech quality for aphasia treatment. pages 4853–4857.

Duc Le, Keli Licata, Carol Persad, and Emily Mower Provost. 2016. Automatic assessment of speech intelligibility for individuals with aphasia. *IEEE/ACM Transactions on Audio, Speech, and Language Processing*, 24:1–1.

Duc Le, Keli Licata, and Emily Mower Provost. 2017. Automatic paraphasia detection from aphasic speech: A preliminary study. In *Interspeech*, pages 294–298.

Duc Le and Emily Mower Provost. 2015. Modeling pronunciation, rhythm, and intonation for automatic assessment of speech quality in aphasia rehabilitation.

Ann Lee and James R. Glass. 2013. Pronunciation assessment via a comparison-based system. In *SLaTE*.

Ann Lee, Yaodong Zhang, and James Glass. 2013. Mispronunciation detection via dynamic time warping on deep belief network-based posteriorgrams. pages 8227–8231.

Brian MacWhinney. 2007. The talkbank project. In *Creating and digitizing language corpora*, pages 163–180. Springer.

Leland McInnes, John Healy, and Steve Astels. 2017. hdbscan: Hierarchical density based clustering. *The Journal of Open Source Software*, 2(11):205.

National Aphasia Association. 2019. Aphasia statistics. [Online; accessed 30-January-2020].

Lyndsey Nickels. 2002. Therapy for naming disorders: Revisiting, revising, and reviewing. *Aphasiology*, 16(10-11):935–979.

Vassil Panayotov, Guoguo Chen, Daniel Povey, and Sanjeev Khudanpur. 2015. Librispeech: an asr corpus based on public domain audio books. In *2015 IEEE International Conference on Acoustics, Speech and Signal Processing (ICASSP)*, pages 5206–5210. IEEE.

Bart Peintner, William Jarrold, Dimitra Vergyri, Colleen Richey, Maria Luisa Gorno-Tempini, and

Jennifer Ogar. 2008. Learning diagnostic models using speech and language measures. *Conference proceedings : ... Annual International Conference of the IEEE Engineering in Medicine and Biology Society. IEEE Engineering in Medicine and Biology Society. Conference*, 2008:4648–51.

HGCN4MeSH: Hybrid Graph Convolution Network for MeSH Indexing

Miaomiao Yu   **Chenhui Li**   **Yujiu Yang** *

Tsinghua Shenzhen International Graduate School, Tsinghua University, China

`{yumm18,lch17}@mails.tsinghua.edu.cn`
`yang.yujiu@sz.tsinghua.edu.cn`

Abstract

Recently, deep learning has been used in *Medical Subject Headings* (MeSH) indexing to reduce the labor costs associated with manual annotation, including DeepMeSH, TextCNN, etc. However, these models fail to capture the complex correlations between MeSH terms. To this end, we use a Graph Convolution Network (GCN) to learn the relationship between these terms and present a novel Hybrid Graph Convolution Net for MeSH index (HGCN4MeSH). We utilize two bidirectional GRUs to learn the embedding representation of the abstract and the title of the MeSH index text respectively. We construct the adjacency matrix of MeSH terms, based on the co-occurence relationships in corpus, and use the matrix to learn representations using the GCN. On the basis of learning the joint representation, the prediction problem of the MeSH index keywords is an extreme multi-label classification problem after the attention layer operation. Experimental results on two datasets show that HGCN4MeSH is competitive with the state-of-the-art methods.

1 Introduction

MEDLINE[1] is an important database for publications of biomedical and life science containing more than 24 million journal citations. To facilitate information storage and retrieval, the National Library of Medicine (NLM) created *Medical Subject Headings* (MeSH)[2] to index articles in MEDLINE. MeSH is an annually-updated hierarchical glossary. There are 29368 concepts[3] of MeSH in 2019, covering various area from biomedicine to information technology. Currently, the articles in MEDLINE are indexed primarily by NLM human experts. It is estimated that it costs millions of dollars each year

---

Example1: [Animals, Blotting Western, Body, Weight, Heme, Oxygenase1, Male, Mice ,Mice Obese, Motor, Activity, Oxygen, Consumption, Protoporphyrins, Receptor Melanocortin Type 4, Thermogenesis, Weight]

Example2: [Animals, Blotting Western, Cell Hypoxia, Cell Line, Cell Survival, Cells Cultured, E2F1 Transcription Factor, Hepatocytes, Hypoxia-Inducible Factor 1 alpha Subunit, Membrane Proteins, Mice, Mice Inbred C57BL, Mitochondrial Proteins, RNA Small Interfering]

Example3: [Animals, Appetite Regulation, Energy Metabolism, Fats, Feedback Physiological, Glucose, Humans, Intestine Small, Signal Transduction]

Table 1: Examples of tags from article 26815432, 27391842, 26736497 in MEDLINE. It can be seen that when the tag 'Mice' appears, tag 'Animals' is likely to appear. However, when tag 'Animals' appears, the tag 'Mice' does not necessarily appear.

---

to index new articles (Mork et al., 2013). Therefore, it is necessary to build an efficient and accurate model for indexing documents — MeSH index.

Xun et al. (2019) demonstrated that the MeSH indexing problem can be cast as an extreme multi-label classification task. Each MeSH term can be regarded as a tag, with a total of 29368 tags, and each article has an average of 13 tags. Recently, there are some deep learning models applied to MeSH terms indexes successfully, such as AttentionMeSH (Jin et al., 2018), MeSHProbeNet (Xun et al., 2019), etc. However, these models do not considered the correlation and the co-occurrence relationship between MeSH terms. By ignoring the complexity between objects, these methods are inherently limited. Table 1 is a real example of article tags from the data.

In this paper, we propose a novel GCN (Kipf and Welling, 2016)-based MeSH term index model, HGCN4MeSH, which learns the co-occurrence representation of tags via a GCN-based mapping function. Specifically, we design a novel data-driven adjacency matrix to guide the information propagation between nodes. To solve the problem of too many tags in extreme multi-label classification

---

*The corresponding author.

[1] https://www.nlm.nih.gov/bsd/medline.html
[2] https://www.nlm.nih.gov/mesh/meshhome.html
[3] https://www.nlm.nih.gov/databases/download/mesh.html

Proceedings of the 58th Annual Meeting of the Association for Computational Linguistics: Student Research Workshop, pages 20–26
July 5 - July 10, 2020. ©2020 Association for Computational Linguistics

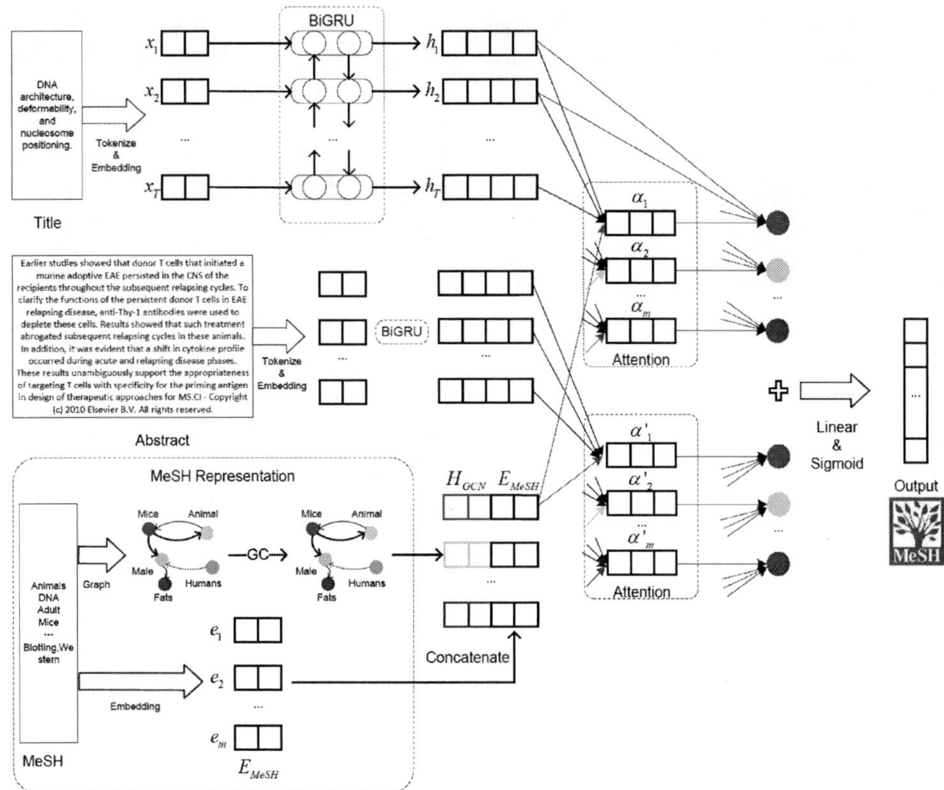

Figure 1: The proposed model framework. Balls of various sizes and colors represent different representations of MeSH terms, BiGRU is the bidirectional gated recurrent unit. First, A hybrid graph is constructed for MeSH terms, where each node represents a MeSH term. The abstract and title are input into GRU for feature extraction respectively and GCN updates the representation of MeSH terms by learning co-occurrences of MeSH terms during training. The final representation of MeSH terms consists of two parts, one is the representation generated by GCN, the other is the semantic representation of MeSH terms. Then we can calculate the attention weight between MeSH terms and title; abstract, output the final score via a linear layer and a sigmoid activation function.

cases, we propose a hybrid adjacency matrix, that is, constructing a bidirectional GCN between high-frequency tags and a unidirectional GCN between high-frequency and low-frequency tags to reduce the computation. The major contribution are:

- We propose a novel end-to-end extreme multi-label classification framework (Figure 1), which employs a GCN to learn tags representation.

- We utilize a partial block adjacency matrix to reduce calculation and noise for extreme multi-label classification. The experimental results show that our method is competitive with the state-of-the-art method.

2   Related Work

Aronson et al. (2004) introduced the Medical Text Index (MTI) to help experts find suitable MeSH terms for articles quickly and accurately. Peng et al. (2016) proposed DeepMeSH, which achieved the best results in the 2017 BioASQ challenge task A. BioASQ is a challenge funded by the European Union; the task A of BioASQ requires participants to use only the abstracts and titles to predict corresponding MeSH terms. DeepMeSH utilized TF-IDF (Jones, 1972) and document to vector (D2V) (Le and Mikolov, 2014) to represent each abstract and They used k-nearest-neighbor (KNN) (Altman, 1992) classifiers to generate candidate MeSH terms. AttentionMeSH (Jin et al., 2018) was also divided into two parts. The first part used KNN to generate candidate MeSH terms, and the second used bidirectional Recurrent Gated Unit (BiGRU) (Cho et al., 2014) architecture to capture context features. Xun et al. (2019) used the representation learned from the name of journal combine with the information from the abstract and a multi-view neural classifier to get results. Wang and Mercer (2019) provided a useable data set, including the title, abstract, paragraphs associated with the figures, and tables of each text, and used multi-channel TextCNN (Kim, 2014) to solve the problem.

MeSH terms were modelled independently in those methods, which ignored the relationships between MeSH terms. In this paper, we use a GCN to capture the more complex topological relationships.

3 HGCN4MeSH Model

3.1 Graph Convolutional Network and Correlation Matrix

We use Graph Convolutional Network (GCN) to model the relationship between MeSH terms. Kipf and Welling (2016) proposed GCN which induces embedding vectors of the nodes according to the properties of their neighbor nodes. Given a graph G = (V,E) where V and E denote the set of nodes and edges respectively. The GCN is a multi-layer neural network. With convolutional operations, the propagation of every layer can be written as

$$H^{l+1} = h(\tilde{A} \cdot H^l \cdot W^l).$$ (1)

Here, $H^l \in \mathbb{R}^{n \times d}$ and $H^{l+1} \in \mathbb{R}^{n \times d'}$ indicate the nodes representation of the lth and $(l+1)^{th}$ hidden layer respectively (where n is the number of nodes and d, d' are the dimensions of the node representations), $\tilde{A} \in \mathbb{R}^{n \times n}$ represents the normalized version of the correlation matrix $A \in \mathbb{R}^{n \times n}$, $h(\cdot)$ means a non-linear operation such as ReLU, $\cdot$ means the matrix product operation, $W^l \in \mathbb{R}^{d \times d'}$ is a layer-specific trainable transformation matrix.

GCN updates the node features by propagating the information between neighbor nodes, based on the corresponding correlation matrix. Hence, the crucial thing is how to build the adjacency matrix. In most applications, the adjacency matrix is predefined. However, there is no corresponding adjacency matrix already defined in the area of extreme multi-label text classification. Facing this problem, we propose the hybrid adjacency matrix construction method. We construct the adjacency matrix between tag frequencies and the co-occurrence relationships between tags.

In extreme multi-label text scenarios, the number of tags is often in the tens of thousands. If we consider the relationship between all the tags, the adjacency matrix would be huge and consume considerable memory and time during the computation. Considering that in the extreme multi-label classification task, the distribution of tags is long-tailed, which means that there are some tags appear rarely, hence $\tilde{A}$ is a sparse matrix.

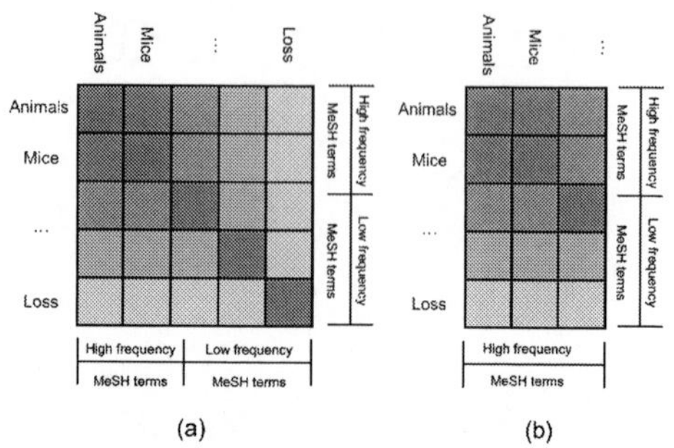

Figure 2: The construction of adjacency matrix. (a) the adjacency matrix of original GCN ($m \times m$) (b) the hybrid adjacency matrix of our model ($m \times n$)

Hence, we set a threshold frequency to divide tags into low-frequency and high-frequency groups. We find that the number of low-frequency tags co-occurring with high-frequency tags is larger than the number of low-frequency tags co-occurring with low-frequency tags through empirically. Thus, we build an adjacency matrix $\tilde{A} \in \mathbb{R}^{m \times n}$, where m is the number of the high-frequency tags and n denotes the total number of tags. It means that we utilize the information between high-frequency tags and low-frequency tags, so it is called hybrid adjacency matrix. Figure 2 shows the example of adjacency matrix. We use the empirical conditional probability to model the directed relationship between tags:

$$p(L_j|L_i) = \frac{M_{ij}}{N_i}$$ (2)

which means the occurrence probability of tag L_j when tag L_i appears, where N_i denotes the occurrences times of the tag L_i, and M_{ij} denotes the concurring times of tag L_i and tag L_j.

$$P_{ij} = p(L_j|L_i)$$ (3)

However, due to a large number of tags, these co-occurrencesmay be noisy estimate for some tags with low co-occurrence frequency, so we set a threshold τ as follows:

$$A_{ij} = \begin{cases} P_{ij} & P_{ij} > \tau \\ 0 & P_{ij} \leq \tau \end{cases}$$ (4)

3.2 Document Representation

The core challenging in MeSH idnexing is to learn representations for the title and abstract. After tokenizing the titles and abstracts, we derive the context-aware title representation via a bidirectional Gated Recurrent Unit (BiGRU) (Cho et al., 2014):

$$H_{title} = \text{BiGRU}(X_{title}) \in \mathbb{R}^{L \times 2d_h}$$
$$H_{abstract} = \text{BiGRU}(X_{abstract}) \in \mathbb{R}^{L' \times 2d_h} \quad (5)$$

where H_{title}, $H_{abstract}$ mean the hidden state of title, abstract respectively. $X_{title} \in \mathbb{R}^{L \times d_e}$, $X_{abstract} \in \mathbb{R}^{L' \times d_e}$ denote the feature of title, abstract respectively (d_e means the embedding dimension of word), L is the length of title, L' is the length of title, d_h is the hidden layer dimension. In this work, the title and the abstract share the same process.

3.3 MeSH Representation

First, we use the corresponding word embedding of all MeSH terms as the initial input (H_0) to GCN. In section 3.1, we introduced a novel adjacency matrix A, we can get the new representation of MeSH terms with co-occurrence information after multi-layers of GCN.

$$H_{GCN} = \sigma(\tilde{A} \cdot H^l \cdot W^l) \quad (6)$$

where $H^l \in \mathbb{R}^{m \times d_l}$ is the high-frequency MeSH terms representation of lth layer, $\tilde{A}$ is the normalized version of adjacency matrix and W^l is a layer-specific trainable transformation matrix. In other words, only the representations of high-frequency MeSH terms are propagated at each layer in GCN. After getting the representation of MeSH terms interrelation by GCN, we also use the embedding of MeSH terms to retain the semantic information.

$$H_{MeSH} = [H_{GCN} : e_{MeSH}] \quad (7)$$

where the symbol : means the concatenated operation; e_{MeSH} is the word embedding of MeSH terms.

Now we can utilize MeSH representations to select the most relevant text representation features for classification by attention mechanism (Bahdanau et al., 2014). We calculate the similarity between MeSH terms and text by dot products and use Softmax to normalize the word axis:

$$Sim = H_{title} \cdot H_{MeSH}$$
$$A_{attn} = softmax(Sim) \quad (8)$$

Ultimately, we can get the representation of MeSH terms by words representation:

$$H'_{MeSH} = A_{attn} H_{title} + A'_{attn} H_{abstract} \quad (9)$$

where A'_{attn} is the attention score between abstract and MeSH terms, and $H_{abstract}$ is the hidden state of abstract. Then we can gain the score of MeSH terms:

$$\hat{y} = \sigma(W H'_{MeSH} + b) \quad (10)$$

here, $\sigma(\cdot)$ is the sigmoid function, W is the trainable weight matrix and b is the bias. The binary cross-entropy loss function is applied in the model:

$$L_j = -(y_j log(\hat{y}_j) + (1 - y_j)log(1 - \hat{y}_j)) \quad (11)$$

where y_j is the ground truth, $\hat{y}_j \in [0, 1]$. The total loss is:

$$\mathcal{L} = \frac{1}{K} \sum_{j=1}^{K} L_j \quad (12)$$

Here, K is the total number of training data.

Finally, the MeSH multi-label classifier outputs the MeSH index that we want.

4 Experiments

4.1 Dataset

PMC Collection contains 257590 manually annotated biomedical articles and covers 22881 MeSH terms in total. Each documents contains 13.34 MeSH terms on average.

SETC2015 contains 14828 annotated articles created by Demner-Fushman and Mork (2015). Wang and Mercer (2019) used this dataset to create a new dataset, which covers 14365 MeSH terms and contains 13.15 MeSH terms per document.

4.2 Implementation Details

In the processing, non-English characters are removed. The embedding dimensions of title and abstract are both 200, GRU layer number is set to 2, and the hidden dimension is 200. In the part of GCN, we use a layer of GCN with both input and output dimensions of 200. LeakyReLU (Maas et al., 2013) with a negative slope of 0.2 is used as the non-linear activation function. For the division of word frequency, we choose the high-frequency MeSH terms with more than 1000 occurrences, the low-frequency MeSH terms with less than 1000 of the PMC Collection dataset. For SETC2015 dataset, the threshold is 500. We set τ in Eq.(4)

			$p@k$				$nDCG@k$	
	$p@1$	$p@3$	$p@5$	$p@10$	$p@15$	$nDCG@1$	$nDCG@3$	$nDCG@5$
PMC Collection								
multichannel TextCNN	0.8791	0.7214	0.6148	0.5179	0.4801	0.8791	0.7574	0.6752
HGCN4MeSH-1	0.9145	0.8250	0.7417	0.5773	0.4618	0.9145	0.8463	0.7832
HGCN4MeSH	**0.9267**	**0.8495**	**0.7707**	**0.6124**	**0.4953**	**0.9267**	**0.8677**	**0.8086**
SETC2015								
multichannel TextCNN	0.8051	0.6298	0.5206	0.4196	0.3959	0.8051	0.6698	0.5841
HGCN4MeSH-1	0.9054	0.7841	0.6921	0.5415	0.4450	0.9054	0.8124	0.7411
HGCN4MeSH	**0.9185**	**0.7930**	**0.7078**	**0.5581**	**0.4563**	**0.9185**	**0.8221**	**0.7555**

Table 2: Results for our Model in p@k and nDCG, HGCN4MeSH-1 is the model using the embedding of MeSH terms merely without GCN, HGCN4MeSH is the model with GCN

to be 0.1. Dropout (Srivastava et al., 2014) is 0.2, and learning rate 0.0005. Besides, we apply the Adam optimizer (Kingma and Ba, 2014) and early stopping strategies (Yao et al., 2007). The model is implemented with PyTorch (Paszke et al., 2017).

4.3 Evaluation Metrics

Due to the large space of the tags, only a few tags can match the text. Hence, the major metrics for performance evaluation are ranking-based methods.

Precision at k (p@k) and normalized discounted cumulative gain (nDCG) are ranking-based evaluation methods. In this paper, we also utilize these two authoritative metrics.

4.4 Experiments Results

Table 2 shows the rank-based matric result. Although there are some strong baselines of bioASQ challenge, the code is available to test on the two dataset. We compare with the state-of-art method, multichannel TextCNN (Wang and Mercer, 2019). For the proposed model, we report the results of the model with GCN or not. It is obvious that our model without GCN outperforms baseline, and the performance of the model with GCN is the best result, which may due to the fact that the model with GCN pays more attention to the co-occurrence relationships between the tags.

In addition, the score of the PMC Collection dataset increases by about 2-4 points after introducing GCN. However, the score of SETC2015 only increases by 1-2 points. The reason is that there are only 14000 samples of SETC2015. Thus the data-driven adjacency matrix is biased. Nevertheless, since the PMC Collection dataset contains about 250000 data, the adjacency matrix based on the dataset should be closer to the true co-occurrence relationship between the MeSH terms, and results to better performance.

Model			$p@k$		
l	f	$p@1$	$p@3$	$p@5$	$p@10$
1	0.5k	0.9116	0.8345	0.7597	0.6029
1	1k	**0.9267**	**0.8495**	**0.7707**	**0.6124**
1	1.5k	0.9185	0.8409	0.7518	0.6103
4	2k	0.9174	0.8359	0.7618	0.6046

Table 3: The result of MeSH terms on testing set for different frequency threshold. l is the GCN layer, f is the frequency threshold, f=1k means MeSH terms with less than 1000 occurrences is low-frequency tag, and those with more than 1000 occurrences are high-frequency tags.

Model			$p@k$		
l	f	$p@1$	$p@3$	$p@5$	$p@10$
1	1k	**0.9267**	**0.8495**	**0.7707**	**0.6124**
2	1k	0.9094	0.8323	0.7577	0.6008
3	1k	0.9170	0.8285	0.7494	0.5945

Table 4: The result of MeSH terms for different GCN layers. l=1 means the GCN layer is 1.

4.5 Ablation Studies

In the Table 3, we can observe effects of thresholds that define low-frequency MeSH terms and high-frequency MeSH terms. If the threshold is too high, it may cause fewer high-frequency MeSH terms, which causes the representation between different MeSH terms to be too smooth. However, when the frequency threshold is too low, there are many high-frequency words, and some co-occurrence of many words may become noise.

Table 4 shows that with the number of GCN layers increasing, the results decrease. As the number of GCN layers increasesthe information transmission between nodes may accumulate, resulting in excessive smoothness of the final representation.

Model	$p@1$	$p@3$	$p@5$	$p@10$
w/o atten	0.8897	0.7978	0.7235	0.5531
w/o GCN	0.9145	0.8250	0.7417	0.5773
w/o title	0.9094	0.8351	0.7589	0.5984
w/o abs	0.8763	0.7857	0.7050	0.5569
title&abs	0.9082	0.8361	0.7621	0.6058
ours	**0.9267**	**0.8495**	**0.7707**	**0.6124**

Table 5: The result of ablation studies. w/o: without; atten: attention; abs: abstract; ours:HGCN4MeSH; title&abs: title and abstract are concatenated as the input of GRU.

The results of the ablation experiment are shown in Table 5. Title contains a lot of useful information, the effect of extracting information from title and abstract separately is slightly better than directly concatenating both.

5   Conclusion

Modelling the relationship between MeSH terms is a key issue in MeSH indexing. This paper proposes a model for constructing specifying the relationship between MeSH terms based on GCN and a new end-to-end model for MeSH indexing.

In the field of biomedicine, the co-occurrence relationship of tags is very common and useful. We use the co-occurrence relationship between tags to design the adjacency matrix by the GCN using the data-driven method, which can also be extended to other extreme multi-label classification fields.

Acknowledgments

This work was supported in part by the National Key Research and Development Program of China (No. 2018YFB1601102), and Shenzhen special fund for the strategic development of emerging industries (No. JCYJ20170412170118573). In addition, we would like to thank Dr. Roy Schwartz; Dr. Rishi Bommasani and the anonymous reviewers for thoughtful feedback and constructive suggestions.

References

Naomi S Altman. 1992. An introduction to kernel and nearest-neighbor nonparametric regression. *The American Statistician*, 46(3):175–185.

Alan R Aronson, James G Mork, Clifford W Gay, Susanne M Humphrey, and Willie J Rogers. 2004. The nlm indexing initiative's medical text indexer. In *Medinfo*, pages 268–272.

Dzmitry Bahdanau, Kyunghyun Cho, and Yoshua Bengio. 2014. Neural machine translation by jointly learning to align and translate. *arXiv preprint arXiv:1409.0473*.

Kyunghyun Cho, Bart Van Merriënboer, Caglar Gulcehre, Dzmitry Bahdanau, Fethi Bougares, Holger Schwenk, and Yoshua Bengio. 2014. Learning phrase representations using rnn encoder-decoder for statistical machine translation. *arXiv preprint arXiv:1406.1078*.

Dina Demner-Fushman and James G Mork. 2015. Extracting characteristics of the study subjects from full-text articles. In *AMIA Annual Symposium Proceedings*, volume 2015, page 484. American Medical Informatics Association.

Qiao Jin, Bhuwan Dhingra, William Cohen, and Xinghua Lu. 2018. Attentionmesh: Simple, effective and interpretable automatic mesh indexer. In *Proceedings of the 6th BioASQ Workshop A challenge on large-scale biomedical semantic indexing and question answering*, pages 47–56.

Karen Sparck Jones. 1972. A statistical interpretation of term specificity and its application in retrieval. *Journal of documentation*.

Yoon Kim. 2014. Convolutional neural networks for sentence classification. *arXiv preprint arXiv:1408.5882*.

Diederik P Kingma and Jimmy Ba. 2014. Adam: A method for stochastic optimization. *arXiv preprint arXiv:1412.6980*.

Thomas N Kipf and Max Welling. 2016. Semi-supervised classification with graph convolutional networks. *arXiv preprint arXiv:1609.02907*.

Quoc Le and Tomas Mikolov. 2014. Distributed representations of sentences and documents. In *International conference on machine learning*, pages 1188–1196.

Andrew L Maas, Awni Y Hannun, and Andrew Y Ng. 2013. Rectifier nonlinearities improve neural network acoustic models. In *Proc. icml*, volume 30, page 3.

James G Mork, Antonio Jimeno-Yepes, and Alan R Aronson. 2013. The nlm medical text indexer system for indexing biomedical literature. In *BioASQ@ CLEF*.

Adam Paszke, Sam Gross, Soumith Chintala, Gregory Chanan, Edward Yang, Zachary DeVito, Zeming Lin, Alban Desmaison, Luca Antiga, and Adam Lerer. 2017. Automatic differentiation in pytorch.

Shengwen Peng, Ronghui You, Hongning Wang, Chengxiang Zhai, Hiroshi Mamitsuka, and Shanfeng Zhu. 2016. Deepmesh: deep semantic representation for improving large-scale mesh indexing. *Bioinformatics*, 32(12):i70–i79.

Nitish Srivastava, Geoffrey Hinton, Alex Krizhevsky, Ilya Sutskever, and Ruslan Salakhutdinov. 2014. Dropout: a simple way to prevent neural networks from overfitting. *The journal of machine learning research*, 15(1):1929–1958.

Xindi Wang and Robert E Mercer. 2019. Incorporating figure captions and descriptive text in mesh term indexing. In *Proceedings of the 18th BioNLP Workshop and Shared Task*, pages 165–175.

Guangxu Xun, Kishlay Jha, Ye Yuan, Yaqing Wang, and Aidong Zhang. 2019. Meshprobenet: a self-attentive probe net for mesh indexing. *Bioinformatics*.

Yuan Yao, Lorenzo Rosasco, and Andrea Caponnetto. 2007. On early stopping in gradient descent learning. *Constructive Approximation*, 26(2):289–315.

Grammatical Error Correction Using Pseudo Learner Corpus Considering Error Tendency of Learners

Yujin Takahashi, Satoru Katsumata[*] and **Mamoru Komachi**
Tokyo Metropolitan University
takahashi-yujin@ed.tmu.ac.jp, satoru.katsumata@retrieva.jp
komachi@tmu.ac.jp

Abstract

Recently, several studies have focused on improving the performance of grammatical error correction (GEC) tasks using pseudo data. However, a large amount of pseudo data are required to train an accurate GEC model. To address the limitations of language and computational resources, we assume that introducing pseudo errors into sentences similar to those written by the language learners is more efficient, rather than incorporating random pseudo errors into monolingual data. In this regard, we study the effect of pseudo data on GEC task performance using two approaches. First, we extract sentences that are similar to the learners' sentences from monolingual data. Second, we generate realistic pseudo errors by considering error types that learners often make. Based on our comparative results, we observe that $F_{0.5}$ scores for the Russian GEC task are significantly improved.

1 Introduction

Recently, several studies have proposed models to solve grammatical error correction (GEC) task as an application of writing support for language learners of various languages, such as English or Russian. A standard approach to improve GEC models is to incorporate pseudo errors into large monolingual datasets for pre-training. In particular, previous works achieved state-of-the-art performance by pre-training the model using pseudo data with a subsequent fine-tuning of the pre-trained model using a learner corpus (Zhao et al., 2019; Kiyono et al., 2019; Grundkiewicz et al., 2019; Náplava and Straka, 2019; Grundkiewicz and Junczys-Dowmunt, 2019).

Considering the aforementioned approach, several methods have been proposed for the generation of pseudo data for pre-training a GEC model.

In theory, it is possible to include all types of errors in a dataset via random error generation. However, considering the limitations of computational resources required to train a GEC model using large pseudo datasets, there is a need to generate pseudo datasets with only realistic errors.

Thus, in this study, we generate pseudo data to train GEC models considering the types of errors made by language learners and study the effect of this realistic pseudo training data. First, we extract sentences similar to the training data from monolingual datasets to generate pseudo data for pre-training. Second, we analyze the error tendency of learners and add pseudo errors considering the errors learners tend to make in English and Russian languages. Through experiments, we show that the proposed pseudo data generation method improves the $F_{0.5}$ scores of the GEC model.

In summary, the primary contributions of this study are as follows:

- We confirm that selecting training data similar to the learners' corpus instead of using randomly selected monolingual data improves the performance of the GEC model.

- We show the effect of realistic pseudo errors by considering the types of errors typically made by language learners for the Russian GEC task.

2 Related Works

Pseudo data have been generated for GEC tasks in several previous works. Zhao et al. (2019) generated pseudo data by adding randomly generated pseudo errors, in an error-free sentence. In particular, in this approach, randomly selected words were replaced or deleted from a large monolingual dataset. In addition, a random word was inserted into sentences, and words in a sentence

---

[*]Currently at Retrieva, Inc.

Proceedings of the 58th Annual Meeting of the Association for Computational Linguistics: Student Research Workshop, pages 27–32
July 5 - July 10, 2020. ©2020 Association for Computational Linguistics

En (CoNLL 2013)		Ru (RULEC-GEC dev)	
Error type	Ratio (%)	Error type	Ratio (%)
Art./Det.	19.9	Spelling	22.8
Collocation/Idiom	12.5	Insert	13.2
Noun number	11.4	Noun case	10.2
Preposition	8.98	Replace	9.99
Word form	6.56	Delete	9.58

Table 1: Comparison of error statistics between English and Russian learner corpora (Development Data).

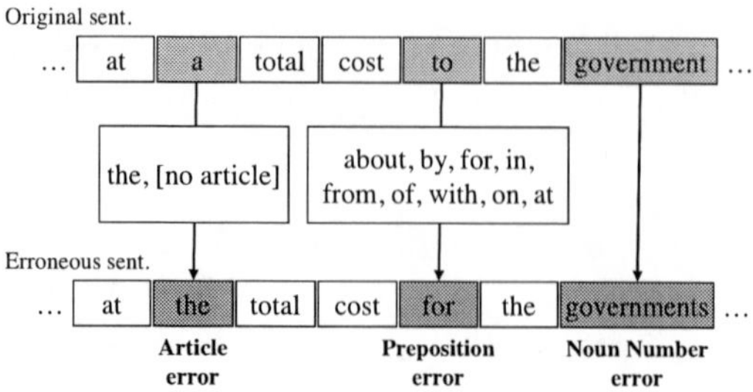

Figure 1: Example of pseudo error generation.

were swapped around. A similar approach was proposed by Kiyono et al. (2019), where an original word is masked or retained to generate pseudo data for pre-training. However, both of these methods generate errors that are not similar to the real errors made by language learners. The data in Table 1 indicates that English language learners tend to make errors related to article and word choice, while Russian language learners often make errors related to spelling, insertions, and noun inflections. In our study, we use these error tendencies to generate realistic errors to develop pre-training datasets for GEC tasks in those languages.

Furthermore, Grundkiewicz et al. (2019) generated realistic pseudo data by building a confusion set based on an unsupervised spellchecker to restrict word replacements made by learners in the resulting dataset. They used the conditional probability $P(cor|err)$ based on the spellchecker distribution; however, it is not the same as $P(err|cor)$, nor does it include error types other than spelling errors. Conversely, in our work, we approximate $P(err|cor)$ using a uniform distribution for the set of candidates for a correct word. This uniform distribution is developed using prior knowledge of error types instead of that obtained from a spellchecker. Thus, our generated pseudo data contains comparatively more realistic pseudo errors. Kasewa et al. (2018) determined the distribution of the pseudo error generation model $P(err|cor)$ from parallel data obtained using a grammatical error detection task.

Moreover, Grundkiewicz and Junczys-Dowmunt (2019) developed a confusion set that retained out-of-vocabulary words and preserved consistent letter casing. However, using this approach, unrealistic errors might be included in the pseudo data because it primarily considers the surface of words. Further, Náplava and Straka (2019) conducted a GEC experiment in multiple lan-

guages, such as English, Russian, German, and Czech, and proposed a pseudo error generation model for Czech, considering errors in diacritics. In the present study, we incorporate the most common error types in monolingual data based on language-specific prior knowledge to obtain development data.

3 Method for Pseudo Data Generation

First, we describe the method for pseudo data generation that considers learner error types. Subsequently, we use the generated pseudo data for pre-training a GEC model.

In this study, we combine the proposed method of pseudo data generation with previous methods. In particular, we incorporate the basic random approach (deletion, insertion, swapping) in our approach, as well as the more recent sophisticated approach proposed by Grundkiewicz et al. (2019) (character level perturb, confusion set based on an unsupervised spellchecker).

3.1 Data Selection

We assume that the sentences, where errors of the learners' error types are added, should be similar to that of the learners' sentences themselves. Thus, we used a data selection method (Moore and Lewis, 2010), where an N-gram language model (LM) is used to score input sentences. This method creates a generic LM N and targets LM I sets for the generic and target domains, respectively. Subsequently, the entropy H is calculated for the sentence s in monolingual data from these LM sets ($\text{LM}_{\text{model}} \in \{I, N\}$). Finally, the entropy difference (Equation 1) for the sentence is calculated. Data selection is then performed based on the similarity to the target domain in descending order of the assigned score.

$$\text{score}(s) = H(s; N) - H(s; I) \quad (1)$$

$$H(s; \text{LM}_{\text{model}}) = -\frac{1}{|s|} \log P_{\text{LM}_{\text{model}}}(s)$$

where $|s|$ indicates the sentence length, $P_{\text{LM}_{\text{model}}}(s)$ indicates the probability estimated by the LM_{model} for sentence s.

In this study, for each sentence in the monolingual data, the entropy difference is calculated between the LM trained on monolingual data and that trained on the data in the target domain. Subsequently, sentences are extracted according to the LM scores for pre-training data.

3.2 Error Types

Figure 1 shows an example of pseudo error generation according to the most common error types in learners' corpora. As an example of preposition errors, we limit the confusion set by defining the pseudo error generation model as $P(err|cor = \text{"to"})$ where $err \in$ {about, by, for, from, in, of, with, on, at}. The pseudo error is generated using a uniform distribution for the pseudo error generation model $P(err|cor)$.

English. As listed in Table 1, the common error types in English are those related to article/determiner, collocation/idiom, noun number, preposition, and word form. Thus, for English, we consider each error type as follows:

- For article/determiner errors, the set of replacement candidates is the entire vocabulary in the random baseline. However, we limit the set of replacement candidates to other articles and determiners only. This set contains an entry of "no article" as well (i.e., deletion).

- For noun number errors, the error can be generated by swapping the singular or plural form of a noun with the plural or singular form, respectively.

- For preposition errors, we define a candidate set as the top 10 most frequently used prepositions (Bryant and Briscoe, 2018). We only replace the preposition with one from the candidate sets.

- For word form errors, we define a candidate set for replacement using `word_forms` [1].

Lang.	Dataset	Corpus	Sent.
English	One Billion Corpus	mono	10M
	Lang-8 + NUCLE	para	134K
Russian	Russian News Crawl	mono	10M
	Lang-8 + RULEC-GEC	para	54K

Table 2: Data statistics.

We did not consider collocation and idiom errors in our study because defining a candidate set for those error types is challenging.

Russian. For the Russian language, we consider replacement and spelling errors as per the previously proposed methods (i.e., random and unsupervised spellchecker). For noun case errors, we define a candidate set for replacement using a dictionary. When the target word is a noun and is included in the dictionary, the candidates for replacement consist of the inflected patterns specified in the dictionary.

4 Experiments

4.1 Data

Table 2 lists the details of monolingual and parallel data used for training in our study. As training data, we used Lang-8 (Mizumoto et al., 2012) and NUS Corpus of Learner English (NUCLE) (Dahlmeier et al., 2013) for English, while we used Lang-8 and Russian Learner Corpus of Academic Writing-GEC (RULEC-GEC) (Rozovskaya and Roth, 2019) for Russian. As pre-training data (i.e., pseudo data), we used One Billion Corpus [2] for English and Russian News Crawl [3] for Russian.

4.2 Experimental Setting

We used the transformer model with copy-augmented architecture (Zhao et al., 2019) as the GEC model with almost the same hyperparameters. In particular, we set max-epoch = 3 for pre-training, and 15 for training. As an evaluation metric, we computed the precision, recall, and $F_{0.5}$ score for the CoNLL-2014 dataset and RULEC-GEC test set. Furthermore, we used the CoNLL-2013 (Ng et al., 2013) data and the RULEC-GEC dev data for development.

---

[1] `https://github.com/gutfeeling/word_forms`

[2] `https://www.statmt.org/lm-benchmark/`
[3] `http://www.statmt.org/wmt18/translation-task.html`

System	Pseudo data	CoNLL-2014 (En)			RULEC-GEC test (Ru)		
		Prec.	Rec.	$F_{0.5}$	Prec.	Rec.	$F_{0.5}$
Random errors w/o Data selection (baseline)	10M	67.5	34.1	56.5	22.7	3.6	11.1
Random errors w/ Data selection	2M	67.9	31.1	54.9	18.7	0.11	4.5
	4M	68.0	32.5	55.8	19.2	1.53	5.8
	6M	67.4	33.7	56.2	20.5	2.42	8.2
	8M	68.9	34.3	57.3	25.3	3.35	11.0
	10M	68.2	**34.9**	57.3	27.7	3.77	12.2
Error type w/o Data selection	10M	69.2	34.2	57.5	41.1	12.4	28.1
Error type w/ Data selection (proposed)	2M	67.5	31.3	54.8	32.8	2.5	9.7
	4M	68.8	33.1	56.6	37.2	6.7	19.5
	6M	**70.0**	33.5	57.5	44.2	11.9	28.6
	8M	68.5	34.6	57.2	**49.0**	15.0	33.7
	10M	69.1	34.5	**57.6**	48.6	**16.8**	**35.2**

Table 3: Results comparison of for each evaluated method. Best score in each column is indicated in bold.

As explained in Section 3.1, we trained the target LM to extract sentences from monolingual data using a part of the target side of the parallel data, where its domain matched the development data. We extracted the highest-scoring 10M sentences from the original monolingual datasets, One Billion Corpus, and Russian News Crawl, which have 30M and 80M sentences, respectively.

Furthermore, as discussed in Section 3.2, we generated pseudo data by incorporating pseudo errors into the monolingual corpus of each language. For noun case errors in Russian, we used a dictionary [4] containing noun inflections. We verified that the total number of pseudo errors in each experiment was similar to ensure a fair comparison. In our experiments, we compared the following three baselines to study the effects of pseudo errors and data selection in the monolingual corpus.

Random errors w/o Data selection In this approach, pseudo errors are added into randomly selected 10M monolingual data. The added errors include deleting, adding, and replacing randomly selected words, and shuffling the words in a sentence. This method corresponds to that of Zhao et al. (2019).

Random errors w/ Data selection First, we selected the top 10M sentences from the monolingual corpus using the LM scoring method described in Section 3.1. In our experiments, the amount of data is up to 10M sentences, increased by 2M sentences. In this approach, the process of adding pseudo errors is the same as in the Random

errors w/o Data selection approach.

Error type w/o Data selection In this approach, we introduced pseudo errors to randomly selected 10M monolingual data, as described in Section 3.2.

Error type w/ Data selection This method is our proposed approach, where we combine the data selection and error type approaches.

4.3 Result

Table 3 lists the results for each system.

Data selection. When comparing the results obtained using the Random errors, we can evaluate the effect of the data selection method. For English, the random methods, which incorporated the data selection approach, perform better than the random method without it ($56.5 \rightarrow 57.3$). In contrast, for Russian, similar improvements were noted for both approaches ($11.1 \rightarrow 12.2$).

Furthermore, when comparing the results obtained using the error type, we confirmed that the data selection approach significantly improved GEC performance for Russian data. However, for the English data, no significant improvements for GEC performance were observed. Moreover, for the Russian data, we found that both precision and recall improved when using the error type-based approach (Precision: $41.1 \rightarrow 48.6$, Recall: $12.4 \rightarrow 16.8$).

Error types. When comparing random and error type w/ data selection approaches, we observed the effect of pseudo data containing pseudo errors based on learners' error types in GEC performance. For the English data, the improvement is

---

[4] http://opencorpora.org/?page=downloads

System	Sentence
Source Sentence	We know each others' status, changements and so on through the social media.
Gold Sentence	We know each others' status, changes and so on through the social media.
Random w/ Data selection	We know each others' status, changements and so on through the social media.
Error type w/ Data selection	We know each others' status, changes and so on through the social media.
Source Sentence	Besides, we can make more friends by such interactions when our friends ...
Gold Sentence	Besides, we can make more friends through such interactions when our friends ...
Random w/ Data selection	Besides, we can make more friends through such interactions when our friends ...
Error type w/ Data selection	Besides, we can make more friends with such interactions when our friends ...
Source Sentence	В сочинение было много ошибок.
Gold Sentence	В сочинении было много ошибок. (En: There were many mistakes in the essay.)
Random w/ Data selection	В сочинение было много ошибок.
Error type w/ Data selection	В сочинении было много ошибок.

Table 4: Comparison of system outputs in English and Russian. Examples on the top indicate those word form errors that were successfully corrected, while those on the middle indicate preposition errors that were not successfully corrected. Those on the bottom indicate noun case errors that were successfully corrected in Russian.

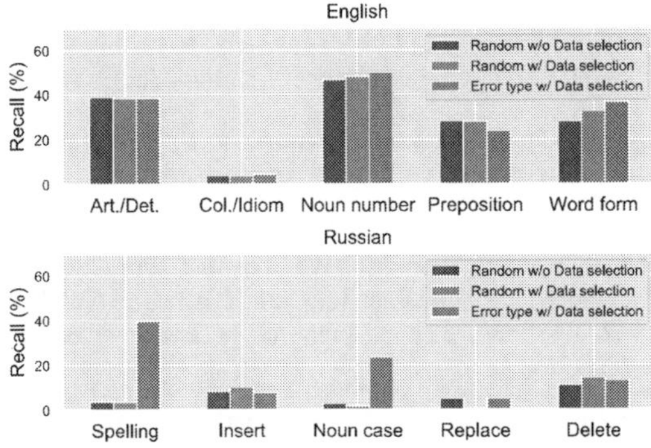

Figure 2: Comparison of recall for each error type. All systems were input with 10M pseudo data sentences.

not large. In contrast, for Russian data, the proposed method achieved the same level of accuracy using only one-third of the parallel corpus (8.23 → 9.68). Moreover, using the same amount of data, the score was almost tripled (12.2 → 35.2).

5 Analysis

Error type. Figure 2 shows the recall for each error type. We selected error types that most commonly appear in the development data.

For English data, the recall was comparable for all error types. Regarding error types other than preposition errors, an equal or improved recall was realized. In contrast, for preposition errors, the recall reduced significantly. It seems that this degradation in the recall can be attributed to the method used to add preposition errors in our study. In particular, we only considered replacement for preposition error generation, and not deletion or insertion. We believe this problem could be handled by generating preposition errors via insertion and deletion as well.

For Russian data, recall improved significantly for spelling and noun error cases. Note that these two error types are not considered explicitly during random error generation. In contrast, recalls for other error types are approximately comparable because the errors were generated using the same approach. Therefore, overall, we observed that the approach significantly improved by considering error types that could not be obtained using random error generation.

Example. Table 4 lists the output examples of two systems: Random errors w/ data selection and error type w/ data selection. Words in red indicate errors in the sentence, while those in blue indicate correct words.

At the top of Table 4, we present an instance of a word form error that was corrected using the proposed method. In particular, the random method outputted the input sentence as it stands. Conversely, the proposed method corrected the word form error by considering other word forms.

Furthermore, in the middle of Table 4, we present an output example wherein preposition errors were left uncorrected by the proposed method. In particular, the random method corrected the preposition error in an appropriately; however, our proposed method failed in performing the task. This difference in results is due to the limitations we posed on the dataset for the replacement to generate realistic pseudo errors. Thus, this example suggests that the recall degradation for preposition errors was caused by restricting the confusion set too strictly.

Finally, in the bottom of Table 4, we present an instance of a noun case error in Russian. The word "сочинение" is a neuter noun, and this case inflection of the word represents nominative or accusative case. When this word is used with the preposition "В", meaning English "in" in this example, it is necessary to change the case to prepositional case (сочинение → сочинении). From this example, our proposed method can correct noun case error, while the random method cannot correct them.

As an overall tendency of Russian noun case errors, the random method often outputted the input sentence as it is, according to our observation of the outputs, or it outputted a completely different word.

As a case of failure to correct, in our proposed method, we confirmed a tendency that the method changed case inflections to the wrong ones.

6 Conclusions

In this study, we studied the effect of pseudo data obtained using two approaches. In particular, we confirmed that combining data selection and realistic error injection approaches to obtain pseudo data improved the $F_{0.5}$ scores. Moreover, we analyzed the recall for each error type. Based on our experimental results, we observed that the recall for error types considered in our study improved or were comparable.

Acknowledgements

We would like to thank Yangyang Xi for granting permission to use text from Lang-8. We also thank Aizhan Imankulova and the anonymous reviewers for their insightful comments. This work was supported by JSPS KAKENHI, Grant Numbers JP19K12099 and JP19KK0286.

References

Christopher Bryant and Ted Briscoe. 2018. Language model based grammatical error correction without annotated training data. In *BEA*.

Daniel Dahlmeier, Hwee Tou Ng, and Siew Mei Wu. 2013. Building a large annotated corpus of learner English: The NUS corpus of learner English. In *BEA*.

Roman Grundkiewicz and Marcin Junczys-Dowmunt. 2019. Minimally-augmented grammatical error correction. In *W-NUT*.

Roman Grundkiewicz, Marcin Junczys-Dowmunt, and Kenneth Heafield. 2019. Neural grammatical error correction systems with unsupervised pre-training on synthetic data. In *BEA*.

Sudhanshu Kasewa, Pontus Stenetorp, and Sebastian Riedel. 2018. Wronging a right: Generating better errors to improve grammatical error detection. In *EMNLP*.

Shun Kiyono, Jun Suzuki, Masato Mita, Tomoya Mizumoto, and Kentaro Inui. 2019. An empirical study of incorporating pseudo data into grammatical error correction. In *EMNLP*.

Tomoya Mizumoto, Yuta Hayashibe, Mamoru Komachi, Masaaki Nagata, and Yuji Matsumoto. 2012. The effect of learner corpus size in grammatical error correction of ESL writings. In *COLING*.

Robert C. Moore and William Lewis. 2010. Intelligent selection of language model training data. In *ACL*.

Jakub Náplava and Milan Straka. 2019. Grammatical error correction in low-resource scenarios. In *W-NUT*.

Hwee Tou Ng, Siew Mei Wu, Yuanbin Wu, Christian Hadiwinoto, and Joel Tetreault. 2013. The CoNLL-2013 shared task on grammatical error correction. In *CoNLL*.

Alla Rozovskaya and Dan Roth. 2019. Grammar error correction in morphologically rich languages: The case of Russian. *TACL*.

Wei Zhao, Liang Wang, Kewei Shen, Ruoyu Jia, and Jingming Liu. 2019. Improving grammatical error correction via pre-training a copy-augmented architecture with unlabeled data. In *ACL*.

Research on Task Discovery for Transfer Learning in Deep Neural Networks

Arda Akdemir
University of Tokyo, Japan
`aakdemir@hgc.jp`

Abstract

Deep neural network based machine learning models are shown to perform poorly on unseen or out-of-domain examples by numerous recent studies. Transfer learning aims to avoid overfitting and to improve generalizability by leveraging the information obtained from multiple tasks. Yet, the benefits of transfer learning depend largely on task selection and finding the right method of sharing. In this thesis, we hypothesize that current deep neural network based transfer learning models do not achieve their fullest potential for various tasks and there are still many task combinations that will benefit from transfer learning that are not considered by the current models. To this end, we started our research by implementing a novel multi-task learner with relaxed annotated data requirements and obtained a performance improvement on two NLP tasks. We will further devise models to tackle tasks from multiple areas of machine learning, such as Bioinformatics and Computer Vision, in addition to NLP.

1 Introduction

Deep neural network based machine learning models have shown remarkable progress in the last decades across a wide range of tasks. The typical training regime uses a large amount of labeled data to get a general mapping of the elements in the input space to the label space, which is known as supervised learning. Yet, it is shown by numerous studies that these models suffer from overfitting and are sensitive to noise and examples that are not available in the training data (Jia and Liang, 2017; Belinkov et al., 2017). In addition, these models are usually trained from scratch for each new task where the weights of the models are initialized randomly. This approach does not follow the way humans learn new tasks, i.e. leveraging external world knowledge and information obtained from related tasks when learning a new task (Bruner, 1985; Hayes et al., 2002).

Transfer learning (TL) is a biologically motivated training paradigm that aims to mitigate the above mentioned real-world challenges of conventional supervised learning (Ruder, 2019). Signals in the training set of a source task are used as additional information for a given target task to enable better generalization. It is especially useful when the labeled data is limited for the target task and when the tasks are relatively similar (Collobert and Weston, 2008; Hashimoto et al., 2017; Ruder, 2019). Learning the structure among tasks is an essential first step to benefit most from transfer learning, and to this end Zamir et al. (2018) proposed a fully-computational framework to learn this structure in the Computer Vision domain. Straightforward application of transfer learning algorithms may lead to *catastrophic forgetting* where models forget the source task after being exposed to the target task. In addition, there is a lack of theoretical understanding of the task relationships, and as a result, tasks for transfer learning are usually determined with hindsight.

Multi-task learning (MTL) is a special case of transfer learning where multiple tasks are learned simultaneously. Caruana (1997) summarizes multi-task learning as leveraging information obtained from the training data of different tasks to improve generalization. It enables better generalization and lowers the annotated data requirements (Caruana, 1997; Maurer et al., 2016). Current multi-task learning systems typically use *hard-sharing*, where a low layer hidden representation is shared among all tasks to have an inductive bias (Collobert et al., 2011; Chu et al., 2015). It is recently shown that for dissimilar tasks *hard-sharing* may degrade the performance, which is also called *negative-transfer* (Yosinski et al., 2014). More sophisticated information sharing methodologies must be consid-

Proceedings of the 58th Annual Meeting of the Association for Computational Linguistics: Student Research Workshop, pages 33–41
July 5 - July 10, 2020. ©2020 Association for Computational Linguistics

ered in addition to finding useful task combinations, to make the most out of multi-task learning and to avoid *negative-transfer*.

The above findings and challenges motivate our research on transfer learning in deep neural networks. Specifically, we focus our research on investigating the task relations on the currently proposed models and on proposing new task combinations. Through our research, we plan to find answers to 'where to transfer from' (task selection), 'what to transfer' (datasets and data selection) and 'how to transfer' (pretraining and model architecture). Our main hypothesis is that, 1) neural network based transfer learning models improve over their single-task counterparts both in terms of generalizability and overall performance, 2) currently proposed transfer learning models do not achieve their fullest potential, and 3) there are many task combinations that will benefit from transfer learning. We will focus on the following research questions about transfer learning models throughout this thesis:

RQ1. How to optimize the model architecture and sharing methodology for a given task combination?

RQ2. What are some good auxiliary tasks to improve the perfomance of a target task?

RQ3. How to find useful pretraining schemes?

The first question aims to find the most useful architecture and the sharing methodology when the task combination is known/determined. Second is a higher-level research question to find useful task combinations and can be considered as the preliminary step for the first one. Finally, question three aims to find the right pretraining scheme to make the most ouf of transfer learning for a given set of target tasks. By combining these research questions, we aim to find the most useful multi-task learning setting for a given domain.

We started our research by analyzing the limitations of current supervised learning systems and showed the sensitivity of neural network based models to the changes in the domain (Akdemir et al., 2018). Next, we proposed a novel joint learning model that relaxes labeled data requirements for the Named Entity Recognition and Dependency Parsing tasks and showed improvements over the conventional methods. The results for the model are given in more detail in Section 4. We will further devise models to tackle tasks from multiple areas of machine learning, such as Bioinformatics and Computer Vision (CV) in addition to NLP. Specifically, we plan to focus on biomedical question answering and object detection tasks from Bioinformatics and CV areas, respectively. We motivate the choice of these two domains as follows: Transfer learning with ImageNet achieved a huge success, and almost all state-of-the-art models for downstream tasks in CV make use of transfer learning. The abundance of transfer learning based models makes CV a good test-domain for evaluating the contributions we will propose for different pretraining schemes for transfer learning. On the contrary, applications of transfer learning is scarce in Bioinformatics compared to CV and NLP. Hence, there should be various task combinations that can benefit from transfer learning in the Bioinformatics domain that were not investigated before. This motivated us to choose Bioinformatics as a target domain to find new task combinations.

The remainder of this paper is structured as follows. Section 2 gives a summary of the related work on transfer learning and multi-task learning. This is followed by the Research Plan, where we explain the methodology we will use regarding each research question. Finally, Section 4 describes the evaluation methods and datasets that will be used to assess the significance of our contributions regarding each research question.

2 Related Work

Our research is related to the works in the subtopics we summarize below.

2.1 Transfer Learning

We follow the taxonomy defined by Ruder (2019) to differentiate between transfer learning and multi-task learning. Specifically, transfer learning is an umbrella term for settings where information from a source task is leveraged to improve the performance of a target task. If the target and source are learned simultaneously, this methodology is defined as 'multi-task learning', whereas if we employ a sequential learning of each task, this is referred to as 'sequential transfer learning'. For instance, in the domain of reinforcement learning, Rusu et al. (2016) proposed 'progressive neural networks' which learn each task sequentially and fixes the parameters for the subsequent tasks. On the contrary, Hashimoto et al. (2017) proposed a joint many task model to simultaneously learn multiple NLP tasks.

In the area of Computer Vision, sequential transfer learning unlocked many potentials. Models pretrained on ImageNet are finetuned on the target task datasests (Krizhevsky et al., 2012) to achieve state-of-the-art results. Similarly, Peters et al. (2018) showed pretrained models improve performance across a wide range of NLP tasks. Radford et al. (2018) and Devlin et al. (2019) pretrained models over huge unlabeled datasets and these models are successfully applied to many downstream NLP tasks. However, Mou et al. (2016) showed that transferability depends largely on the semantic relatedness of the tasks. Finding related tasks is a key factor to achieve better transfer learning models, but a thorough understanding of how to find the most useful pretraining task is still missing (Ruder, 2019).

Another key factor to improve transferability is the selection of relevant data. Recently, Ruder and Plank (2017) proposed learning a similarity metric over the training sets by using Bayesian Optimization for transfer learning. Their work is limited to a domain adaptation setting where the source tasks are the same as the target task but the domains of the datasets are different. We propose extending their method to avoid *negative-transfer* in various multi-task settings.

2.2 Multi-task Learning

Ruder (2017) gives a comprehensive overview of multi-task learning models, where they define two main categories based on the information sharing methodology: *hard-sharing* and *soft-sharing*. In *Hard-sharing*, models contain a low-level layer which is shared among all task-specific layers, whereas in *soft-sharing* each model has its own weight set and regularization is applied to force these weights to be similar across all models. *Soft-sharing* based models are shown to benefit from multi-task learning when applied to related tasks. Yet, the benefits of this method are unclear for loosely related tasks.

Long and Wang (2015) attempted to learn the information flow between task-specific models. Ruder (2017) showed the effect of applying regularization to the network weights to generalize better. Using a more sophisticated approach to control the information flow and applying additional regularization terms on the network weights are promising ways to obtain improvements over the current models. Zhang et al. (2018) proposed learning the most suitable model for a given multi-task setting using

the previous results obtained for various (S, M) pairs where S is a set of tasks and M is the learning model. They find the best candidate covariance matrix which represents the task relations to estimate the relative error for a new multi-task setting and show the effectiveness of their approach. One drawback of these approaches is that they focus only on learning the task-relatedness between tasks and ignore the architectural variations. Meyerson and Miikkulainen (2019) showed that architectures can also be decomposed to allow sharing of various sub-modules for a set of tasks. Yet, more research is necessary to find out the best method of sharing and the best architecture for a given multi-task setting.

3   Research Plan

In this section, we restate the research questions and explain the approach we are planning to take.

RQ1: How to optimize the model architecture and sharing methodology for a given task combination?

Currently proposed multi-task learners mostly use hard sharing, where models share a common low-level layer, and task-specific sharing methods are not analyzed for many task combinations (Collobert et al., 2011; Søgaard and Goldberg, 2016; Hashimoto et al., 2017). Following Long and Wang (2015), we plan to use learnable parameters to control the information flow between each task-specific model. Learning joint label embeddings for disparate label classes (Augenstein et al., 2018) is another promising approach that goes beyond hard-sharing. Specifically, we will apply this method to leverage our previously proposed joint learner for Dependency Parsing and Named Entity Recognition. Part-of-speech tags strongly correlate with named entities and dependencies (Hashimoto et al., 2017; Akdemir and Güngör, 2019b). Thus, we argue that learning joint label embeddings of these tasks can help to further capture the relations between them.

RQ2: What are some good auxiliary tasks to improve the performance of a target task?

Regarding this research question, we will fix a target task and try to improve the performance by 1) incorporating a transfer learning framework and 2) applying a more sophisticated data selection mechanism. To better understand the task relations (where to transfer from), we will compare the performance on a fixed target task using several auxiliary tasks obtained through different task selection mechanisms. Lee et al. (2019) proposed pretraining the BERT model in the biomedical domain and apply the model to make predictions in several different downstream tasks in Bioinfomatics such as gene-disease relation extraction and biological named entity recognition. We argue that their approach can be combined with multi-task learning to further leverage the information available in the dataset of each task. Specifically, we claim that biological named entity recognition can be used as an auxiliary task to improve the performance of biological question answering systems. Our preliminary results are given in Section 4. The biological named entity dataset consists of several types of entities (genes, chemicals and disease mentions) and each type can be considered as a different task. We will use these set of tasks to compare the performance of the task selection mechanisms.

Deciding which data are useful (what to transfer), in addition to finding promising task combinations, is another key factor to increase transferability (Ruder and Plank, 2017). However, many of the current multi-task models use all the available data for all tasks (Long and Wang, 2015; Hashimoto et al., 2017; Lee et al., 2019). To this end, we will apply the previously proposed data selection mechanisms on our new task combinations to find the most useful and relevant examples from each dataset to improve the transferability and to avoid negative-transfer. Previous work on data selection successfully showed that using a Bayesian suite for deciding which data to use for multi-task learning brings significant improvements (Ruder and Plank, 2017). This motivated us to incorporate similar data selection mechanisms to further improve the performance of transfer learning models. We will compare several data selection mechanisms by fixing the model to be used and the task combination.

RQ3: How to find useful pretraining schemes?

The standard approach in sequential transfer learning is to pretrain a model using an objective that is relevant to and useful for the target task. In NLP, the prevailing method is to train a language model using the next sentence prediction and masked token prediction objectives over huge unlabeled datasets, e.g. the BERT model (Devlin et al., 2019). The pretrained models are usually fine-tuned on task-specific datasets, yet the characteristics of the downstream task are usually not considered during the pretraining process. Regarding this research question, our main goal is to find task-specific pretraining schemes and to compare the performance with fine tuned models that are not pretrained considering the downstream task (Lee et al., 2019).

Curriculum learning aims to find a good ordering of the training samples to go beyond random sampling (Bengio et al., 2009). The training samples are ordered according to their difficulties using prior knowledge. Recently, Jiang et al. (2015) proposed self paced curriculum learning which tries to learn this ordering dynamically during training to mitigate the drawbacks of defining static difficulties for training samples using external knowledge. Following this idea of changing the difficulty of the training samples (Bengio et al., 2009; Kumar et al., 2010; Jiang et al., 2015; Liang et al., 2016), we propose using 'adaptive masking' for pretraining language models. The standard approach for pretraining with masked language modeling involves predicting the distribution of a randomly masked word using its context (Devlin et al., 2019). Each masked word can be considered as an instance of a cloze test which is frequently used to assess the linguistic skills in humans. In a cloze test, students are expected to understand the context to fill in the masked word. Randomly selecting which words to mask causes the difficulty of each instance to change randomly as well. We propose adaptively changing the difficulty of the next training instance by observing the performance of the model. In this context, we define difficulty as the amount of contextual information necessary to select the most probable word, whereas Bengio et al. (2009) defined difficulty as the inverse of the frequency of each masked token regardless of their contexts. Table 1 illustrates why going beyond random masking is a promising method to improve the learning process. For the first example, the model (or the person tested) must predict 'school' from the context which includes the word 'students'. In the second example, the model must comprehend the overall negative meaning to predict 'low' instead of 'high'. [1] The idea can be extended easily to other domains of machine learning such as object detection where 'difficult words' are replaced with 'difficult objects'.

----

[1] The examples were taken from intermediate and advanced level cloze grammar tests from the englishlearner website: https://www.englishlearner.com/tests

Difficulty	Sentence
Intermediate	Two students from Cologne, Germany, ages 17 and 18, are accused <u>of</u> plotting an attack at their **school** on November 20.
Advanced	**Low** levels of **literacy** have a damaging impact <u>on</u> almost every aspect of adult life.

Table 1: Two example sentences for the masked language modeling task. The underlined tokens are the originally masked ones in the reference tests. Tokens that are more challenging to predict are shown in bold.

4 Evaluation

In order to evaluate the significance of our contributions, we will do evaluations for each research question separately. Below we give the evaluation methodology, together with example tasks and the related datasets that will be used for each research question.

4.1 RQ1.

We will compare our proposed methodology with the previously proposed multi-task learners and the state-of-the-art single-task learners in the same setting. We proposed a novel multi-task learning framework to improve the performance of the target task, Named Entity Recognition, using the information obtained from the auxiliary task, Dependency Parsing, for the Turkish language. Dependency Parsing is chosen as the auxiliary task following the previous work that showed the importance of dependencies for the Named Entity Recognition task, for morphologically rich languages, e.g the Turkish language (Güngör et al., 2018; Straka et al., 2019; Akdemir and Güngör, 2019a). The results in Table 2 show that our proposed model (Model 2) achieves an absolute 2.45% F-1 score overall improvement over the conventional joint learning model (Model 1). The conventional model requires a single dataset annotated with labels for both tasks, which is a delimiting constraint for less resourced languages. Instead, we proposed using separate datasets for each task (Akdemir and Güngör, 2019b) which allows the model to be trained on a larger dataset.

Next, we proposed a hierarchical multi-task learning framework (Akdemir et al., 2020) that builds on our previous work mentioned above. In this framework, each task-specific component is implemented following the state-of-the-art models and experiments are conducted using different sharing methodologies to find the most useful setting for this task combination. We followed Qi et al. (2018) and Lample et al. (2016) to implement a Highway Long Short Term Memory

	Model 1	Model 2
PER	84.50	86.48
LOC	81.97	86.36
ORG	78.34	78.63
Overall	82.11	**84.56**

Table 2: Results comparing the proposed model (Model 2) with the conventional joint learner (Model 1). All results are given in percentage (%) F-1.

(H-LSTM) based dependency parser and a BiL-STM Conditional Random Fields based named entity recognizer. In addition, we used BERT subword contextual embeddings as the common low-level layer shared by the task-specific components. This framework achieved absolute improvements of **18.86%** and **4.61%** F-1 over our previously proposed model for DEP and NER tasks respectively. In addition, the framework showed absolute improvements of **1.44%** and **0.13%** F-1 over the state-of-the-art models for the Turkish language for DEP and NER tasks respectively. The details about the implementation and the experiments conducted are given in (Akdemir et al., 2020).

We will further test the validity of our hypothesis on other less resourced morphologically rich languages such as the Czech Language (Demir and Özgür, 2014).

Dataset. To test our hierarchical multi-task learner on the Czech Language, we will use the 'Czech Named Entity Corpus 2.0' (Ševčíková et al., 2007) for the NER task and the PDT-UD treebank (Hajič et al., 2017) of the 'CoNLL 2018 Shared Task' (Zeman et al., 2018) for Dependency Parsing task. The NER dataset contains 8,993 sentences with 35,220 entities and uses a two-level named entity classification. For our purposes it is sufficient to use the first level classes (10 classes) as the named entity labels, referred as *supertypes*. PDT-UD contains 87,913 sentences obtained mainly from newswire.

4.2 RQ2.

To evaluate the significance of the contributions we make regarding **RQ2**, we will fix a target task and compare the performance using the newly proposed auxiliary task(s). As mentioned in Section 3, an example target task is biomedical question answering. We argue that detecting and categorizing diseases and biological entities is an important first step to answer biological questions. In addition, the effect of applying data selection will be evaluated by fixing a deep learning model for the object detection task. It was chosen because there are numerous models already proposed for multi-task object detection which allows us to clearly assess the significance of our contributions.

Dataset. We use the BC2GM (Smith et al., 2008), BC4CHEMD (Krallinger et al., 2017), and BC5CDR (Li et al., 2016) datasets for biological named entity recognition which contain gene entities, chemical entities and disease mentions respectively. To test our claim, we use the BioASQ dataset (Tsatsaronis et al., 2015) used during the biomedical question answering competition which contains yes-no, factoid and list type questions.

The preliminary results we obtained for Biological Question Answering task can be seen on Table 3. [2] We started with BERT (Devlin et al., 2019) embeddings and obtained improvements through 1) transfer learning on the biomedical abstracts from PubMed, 2) pretraining the question answering module on the Squad question answering dataset and 3) training a multi-task learning model for all question types. Step 3 is our contribution and has not been employed before, to the best of our knowledge. We aim to show further improvements by incorporating multi-task learning of biological named entities.

	BioAsq-6b - Factoid		
Model	LAcc	SAcc	MRR
BERT (baseline)	0.24	0.35	0.28
+TL on PubMed	0.32	0.50	0.39
+pretraining on Squad	0.39	0.58	0.47
+MTL of all questions	**0.42**	**0.61**	**0.49**

Table 3: Initial results on Biological Question Answering-6 factoid type questions.

For multi-task object detection from different domains, we will use the Office-Caltech (Gong et al., 2012) dataset, which is the standard benchmark for transfer learning in Computer Vision. The Office dataset contains images from three different domains; Amazon, Webcam and DSLR, containing 31 categories. Caltech dataset is the 10 overlapping categories from the Caltech-256 dataset (Griffin et al., 2007).

4.3 RQ3.

We will evaluate our newly proposed pretraining schemes both performance-wise and resource-wise. We choose the standard pretraining objective of BERT (Devlin et al., 2019) as the baseline and we will train the same model using our newly proposed 'adaptive masking'.

Dataset. We will use the unlabeled Wikipedia articles in English for pretraining the model using both pretraining tasks. Next, we will evaluate the performance of the system on the benchmark 'The Stanford Question Answering Dataset', SQuAD 2.0, which contains over 150,000 answerable and unanswerable questions. We choose question answering as the downstream task, as it was used as the downstream task to evaluate the performance of BERT (Devlin et al., 2019) .

5 Summary

Transfer learning is a promising area of research for deep neural network based machine learning models. It helps achieve better generalization and utilization of the training datasets. In this paper, we pointed out the current key challenges and unsolved problems: 1) Going beyond the conventional way of hard-sharing in multi-task learning and finding the most useful architecture for a given setting, 2) Finding good auxiliary tasks in a multi-task setting for a specific target task, and 3) Finding useful pretraining schemes. Our research aims to apply the current work on transfer learning to new tasks and also find novel methods to obtain better multi-task learning models.

References

Arda Akdemir and Tunga Güngör. 2019a. A Detailed Analysis and Improvement of Feature-Based Named Entity Recognition for Turkish. In *International Conference on Speech and Computer*, pages 9–19. Springer.

Arda Akdemir and Tunga Güngör. 2019b. Joint Learning of Named Entity Recognition and Dependency

---

[2]LAcc,SAcc and MRR are abbreviations for Lenient Accuracy, Strict Accuracy and Mean Reciprocal Rank, respectively.

Parsing using Separate Datasets. *Computación y Sistemas*, 23(3).

Arda Akdemir, Ali Hürriyetoğlu, Erdem Yörük, Burak Gürel, Çağri Yoltar, and Deniz Yüret. 2018. Towards generalizable place name recognition systems: analysis and enhancement of NER systems on English News from India. In *Proceedings of the 12th Workshop on Geographic Information Retrieval*, page 8. ACM.

Arda Akdemir, Tetsuo Shibuya, and Tunga Gungor. 2020. Hierarchical multi task learning with subword contextual embeddings for languages with rich morphology.

Isabelle Augenstein, Sebastian Ruder, and Anders Søgaard. 2018. Multi-task learning of pairwise sequence classification tasks over disparate label spaces. In *Proceedings of the 2018 Conference of the North American Chapter of the Association for Computational Linguistics: Human Language Technologies, Volume 1 (Long Papers)*, pages 1896–1906.

Yonatan Belinkov, Lluís Màrquez, Hassan Sajjad, Nadir Durrani, Fahim Dalvi, and James Glass. 2017. Evaluating layers of representation in neural machine translation on part-of-speech and semantic tagging tasks. In *Proceedings of the Eighth International Joint Conference on Natural Language Processing (Volume 1: Long Papers)*, pages 1–10.

Yoshua Bengio, Jérôme Louradour, Ronan Collobert, and Jason Weston. 2009. Curriculum learning. In *Proceedings of the 26th annual international conference on machine learning*, pages 41–48. ACM.

Jerome Bruner. 1985. Child's talk: Learning to use language. *Child Language Teaching and Therapy*, 1(1):111–114.

Rich Caruana. 1997. Multitask learning. *Machine learning*, 28(1):41–75.

Xiao Chu, Wanli Ouyang, Wei Yang, and Xiaogang Wang. 2015. Multi-task recurrent neural network for immediacy prediction. In *Proceedings of the IEEE international conference on computer vision*, pages 3352–3360.

Ronan Collobert and Jason Weston. 2008. A unified architecture for natural language processing: Deep neural networks with multitask learning. In *Proceedings of the 25th international conference on Machine learning*, pages 160–167. ACM.

Ronan Collobert, Jason Weston, Léon Bottou, Michael Karlen, Koray Kavukcuoglu, and Pavel Kuksa. 2011. Natural language processing (almost) from scratch. *Journal of machine learning research*, 12(Aug):2493–2537.

Hakan Demir and Arzucan Özgür. 2014. Improving named entity recognition for morphologically rich languages using word embeddings. In *2014 13th International Conference on Machine Learning and Applications*, pages 117–122. IEEE.

Jacob Devlin, Ming-Wei Chang, Kenton Lee, and Kristina Toutanova. 2019. BERT: Pre-training of Deep Bidirectional Transformers for Language Understanding. In *Proceedings of the 2019 Conference of the North American Chapter of the Association for Computational Linguistics: Human Language Technologies, Volume 1 (Long and Short Papers)*, pages 4171–4186.

Boqing Gong, Yuan Shi, Fei Sha, and Kristen Grauman. 2012. Geodesic flow kernel for unsupervised domain adaptation. In *2012 IEEE Conference on Computer Vision and Pattern Recognition*, pages 2066–2073. IEEE.

Gregory Griffin, Alex Holub, and Pietro Perona. 2007. Caltech-256 Object Category Dataset. *CalTech Report*.

Onur Güngör, Suzan Üsküdarli, and Tunga Güngör. 2018. Improving named entity recognition by jointly learning to disambiguate morphological tags. *arXiv preprint arXiv:1807.06683*.

Jan Hajič, Eva Hajičová, Marie Mikulová, and Jiří Mírovský. 2017. Prague dependency treebank. In *Handbook of Linguistic Annotation*, pages 555–594. Springer.

Kazuma Hashimoto, Caiming Xiong, Yoshimasa Tsuruoka, and Richard Socher. 2017. A Joint Many-Task Model: Growing a Neural Network for Multiple NLP Tasks. In *Proceedings of the 2017 Conference on Empirical Methods in Natural Language Processing*, pages 1923–1933.

Steven C Hayes, Dermot Barnes-Holmes, and Bryan Roche. 2002. Relational frame theory: A précis. In *Relational frame theory*, pages 141–154. Springer.

Robin Jia and Percy Liang. 2017. Adversarial examples for evaluating reading comprehension systems. In *Proceedings of the 2017 Conference on Empirical Methods in Natural Language Processing*, pages 2021–2031.

Lu Jiang, Deyu Meng, Qian Zhao, Shiguang Shan, and Alexander G Hauptmann. 2015. Self-paced curriculum learning. In *Twenty-Ninth AAAI Conference on Artificial Intelligence*.

Martin Krallinger, Obdulia Rabal, Saber A Akhondi, et al. 2017. Overview of the BioCreative VI chemical-protein interaction Track. In *Proceedings of the sixth BioCreative challenge evaluation workshop*, volume 1, pages 141–146.

Alex Krizhevsky, Ilya Sutskever, and Geoffrey E Hinton. 2012. Imagenet classification with deep convolutional neural networks. In *Advances in neural information processing systems*, pages 1097–1105.

M Pawan Kumar, Benjamin Packer, and Daphne Koller. 2010. Self-paced learning for latent variable models. In *Advances in Neural Information Processing Systems*, pages 1189–1197.

Guillaume Lample, Miguel Ballesteros, Sandeep Subramanian, Kazuya Kawakami, and Chris Dyer. 2016. Neural architectures for named entity recognition. In *Proceedings of the 2016 Conference of the North American Chapter of the Association for Computational Linguistics: Human Language Technologies*, pages 260–270.

Jinhyuk Lee, Wonjin Yoon, Sungdong Kim, Donghyeon Kim, Sunkyu Kim, Chan Ho So, and Jaewoo Kang. 2019. BioBERT: pre-trained biomedical language representation model for biomedical text mining. *arXiv preprint arXiv:1901.08746*.

Jiao Li, Yueping Sun, Robin J Johnson, Daniela Sciaky, Chih-Hsuan Wei, Robert Leaman, Allan Peter Davis, Carolyn J Mattingly, Thomas C Wiegers, and Zhiyong Lu. 2016. BioCreative V CDR task corpus: a resource for chemical disease relation extraction. *Database*, 2016.

Junwei Liang, Lu Jiang, Deyu Meng, and Alexander G Hauptmann. 2016. Learning to detect concepts from webly-labeled video data. In *IJCAI*, pages 1746–1752.

Mingsheng Long and Jianmin Wang. 2015. Learning multiple tasks with deep relationship networks. *arXiv preprint arXiv:1506.02117*, 2.

Andreas Maurer, Massimiliano Pontil, and Bernardino Romera-Paredes. 2016. The benefit of multitask representation learning. *The Journal of Machine Learning Research*, 17(1):2853–2884.

Elliot Meyerson and Risto Miikkulainen. 2019. Modular Universal Reparameterization: Deep Multi-task Learning Across Diverse Domains. In H. Wallach, H. Larochelle, A. Beygelzimer, F. d Alché-Buc, E. Fox, and R. Garnett, editors, *Advances in Neural Information Processing Systems 32*, pages 7901–7912. Curran Associates, Inc.

Lili Mou, Zhao Meng, Rui Yan, Ge Li, Yan Xu, Lu Zhang, and Zhi Jin. 2016. How Transferable are Neural Networks in NLP Applications? In *Proceedings of the 2016 Conference on Empirical Methods in Natural Language Processing*, pages 479–489.

Matthew E Peters, Mark Neumann, Mohit Iyyer, Matt Gardner, Christopher Clark, Kenton Lee, and Luke Zettlemoyer. 2018. Deep contextualized word representations. In *Proceedings of NAACL-HLT*, pages 2227–2237.

Peng Qi, Timothy Dozat, Yuhao Zhang, and Christopher D Manning. 2018. Universal dependency parsing from scratch. *Proceedings of the CoNLL 2018 Shared Task: Multilingual Parsing from Raw Text to Universal Dependencies*, pages 160–170.

Alec Radford, Karthik Narasimhan, Tim Salimans, and Ilya Sutskever. 2018. Improving Language Understanding by Generative Pre-Training.

Sebastian Ruder. 2017. An overview of multi-task learning in deep neural networks. *arXiv preprint arXiv:1706.05098*.

Sebastian Ruder. 2019. *Neural Transfer Learning for Natural Language Processing*. Ph.D. thesis, National University of Ireland, Galway.

Sebastian Ruder and Barbara Plank. 2017. Learning to select data for transfer learning with Bayesian Optimization. In *Proceedings of the 2017 Conference on Empirical Methods in Natural Language Processing*, pages 372–382.

Andrei A Rusu, Neil C Rabinowitz, Guillaume Desjardins, Hubert Soyer, James Kirkpatrick, Koray Kavukcuoglu, Razvan Pascanu, and Raia Hadsell. 2016. Progressive neural networks. *arXiv preprint arXiv:1606.04671*.

Magda Ševčíková, Zdeněk Žabokrtský, and Oldřich Krůza. 2007. Named entities in Czech: annotating data and developing NE tagger. In *International Conference on Text, Speech and Dialogue*, pages 188–195. Springer.

Larry Smith, Lorraine K Tanabe, Rie Johnson nee Ando, Cheng-Ju Kuo, I-Fang Chung, Chun-Nan Hsu, Yu-Shi Lin, Roman Klinger, Christoph M Friedrich, Kuzman Ganchev, et al. 2008. Overview of BioCreative II gene mention recognition. *Genome biology*, 9(2):S2.

Anders Søgaard and Yoav Goldberg. 2016. Deep multitask learning with low level tasks supervised at lower layers. In *Proceedings of the 54th Annual Meeting of the Association for Computational Linguistics (Volume 2: Short Papers)*, pages 231–235.

Milan Straka, Jana Straková, and Jan Hajič. 2019. Czech Text Processing with Contextual Embeddings: POS Tagging, Lemmatization, Parsing and NER. In *International Conference on Text, Speech, and Dialogue*, pages 137–150. Springer.

George Tsatsaronis, Georgios Balikas, Prodromos Malakasiotis, Ioannis Partalas, Matthias Zschunke, Michael R Alvers, Dirk Weissenborn, Anastasia Krithara, Sergios Petridis, Dimitris Polychronopoulos, et al. 2015. An overview of the BIOASQ large-scale biomedical semantic indexing and question answering competition. *BMC bioinformatics*, 16(1):138.

Jason Yosinski, Jeff Clune, Yoshua Bengio, and Hod Lipson. 2014. How transferable are features in deep neural networks? In *Advances in neural information processing systems*, pages 3320–3328.

Amir R Zamir, Alexander Sax, William Shen, Leonidas J Guibas, Jitendra Malik, and Silvio Savarese. 2018. Taskonomy: Disentangling task transfer learning. In *Proceedings of the IEEE Conference on Computer Vision and Pattern Recognition*, pages 3712–3722.

Daniel Zeman, Jan Hajič, Martin Popel, Martin Potthast, Milan Straka, Filip Ginter, Joakim Nivre, and Slav Petrov. 2018. Conll 2018 sharedtask: Multilingual parsing from raw text to universal dependencies. In *Proceedings of the CoNLL 2018 Shared Task: Multilingual parsing from raw text to universal dependencies*, pages 1–21.

Yu Zhang, Ying Wei, and Qiang Yang. 2018. Learning to multitask. In *Advances in Neural Information Processing Systems*, pages 5771–5782.

RPD: A Distance Function Between Word Embeddings

Xuhui Zhou,[1] **Zaixiang Zheng,**[2] **Shujian Huang,**[2]
[1]University of Washington
[2]National Key Laboratory for Novel Software Technology, Nanjing University
xuhuizh@uw.edu, zhengzx@smail.nju.edu.cn, huangsj@nju.edu.cn

Abstract

It is well-understood that different algorithms, training processes, and corpora produce different word embeddings. However, less is known about the relation between different embedding spaces, i.e. how far different sets of embeddings deviate from each other. In this paper, we propose a novel metric called Relative pairwise inner Product Distance (RPD) to quantify the distance between different sets of word embeddings. This metric has a unified scale for comparing different sets of word embeddings. Based on the properties of RPD, we study the relations of word embeddings of different algorithms systematically, and investigate the influence of different training processes and corpora. The results shed light on the poorly understood word embeddings and justify RPD as a measure of the distance of embedding spaces.

1 Introduction

Word embeddings are important in Natural language processing (NLP) which map words into a low-dimensional vector space. Many works have been proposed to generate word embeddings (Mnih and Kavukcuoglu, 2013; Mikolov et al., 2013; Pennington et al., 2014; Levy and Goldberg, 2014a; Bojanowski et al., 2017; Devlin et al., 2019).

With many different sets of word embeddings produced by different algorithms and corpora, it is interesting to investigate the relationships between these sets of word embeddings. Intrinsically, this would help us better understand word embeddings (Levy et al., 2015). Practically, knowing the relationship between different sets of word embeddings helps us build better word meta-embeddings (Yin and Schütze, 2016), reduce biases in word embeddings (Bolukbasi et al., 2016), pick better hyperparameters (Yin and Shen, 2018), and choose suitable algorithms in different scenarios (Kozlowski et al., 2019).

To study the relationship between different embedding spaces systematically, we propose RPD as a measure of the distance between different sets of embeddings. We derive statistical properties of RPD including its asymptotic upper bound and normality under the independence condition. We also provide a geometric interpretation of RPD. Furthermore, we show that RPD is strongly correlated with the performance of word embeddings measured by intrinsic metrics, such as comparing semantic similarity and evaluating analogies.

With the help of RPD, we study the relations among several popular embedding methods, including GloVe (Pennington et al., 2014), SGNS[1] (Mikolov et al., 2013), Singular Value Decomposition (SVD) factorization of PMI matrix, and SVD factorization of log count (LC) matrix. Results show that these methods are statistically correlated, which suggests that there is an unified theory behind these methods.

Additionally, we analyze the influence of training processes, i.e. hyperparameters (negative sampling), random initialization; and the influence of corpora towards word embeddings. Our findings include the fact that different training corpora result in significantly different GloVe embeddings, and that the main difference between embedding spaces comes from the algorithms although hyperparameters also have certain influence. Those findings not only provide some interesting insights of word embeddings but also fit nicely with our intuition, which further proves RPD as a suitable measure to quantify the relationship between different sets of word embeddings.

2 Background

Before introducing RPD, we review the theory behind some static word embedding methods, and

---

[1]Skip-gram with Negative Sampling

Proceedings of the 58th Annual Meeting of the Association for Computational Linguistics: Student Research Workshop, pages 42–50
July 5 - July 10, 2020. ©2020 Association for Computational Linguistics

discuss some previous works investigating the relationship between embedding spaces.

2.1 Word Embedding Models

We consider the following four word embedding models: SGNS, GloVe, SVD_{PMI}, SVD_{LC}. SGNS and GloVe are two widely used embedding methods, while SVD_{PMI} and SVD_{LC} are matrix factorization methods which are intrinsically related to SGNS and GloVe (Levy and Goldberg, 2014b; Levy et al., 2015; Yin and Shen, 2018).

The embedding of all the words forms an embedding matrix $E \in \mathbf{R}^{n \times d}$, where the d here is the dimension of each word vector and n is the size of the vocabulary.

SGNS maximizes a likelihood function for word and context pairs that occur in the dataset and minimizes it for randomly sampled unobserved pairs, i.e. negative samples (NS). We denote the method with k NS as $SGNS_k$.

GloVe factorizes the log-count matrix shifted by the entire vocabulary's bias term. The bias here are parameters learned stochastically with an objective weighted according to the frequency of words.

SVD_{PMI/LC} SVD factorizes a signal matrix $M = UDV^T$, which aims at reducing the dimensions of the cooccurrence matrix. The resulting embedding is $E = U_{:,1:d}D^{\frac{1}{2}}_{1:d,1:d}$, where d is the dimension of word embeddings. We denote the method as SVD_{PMI}, if the signal is the PMI matrix, and SVD_{LC} if the signal is the log count matrix.

Although the scope of this paper focuses on standard word embeddings that were learned at the word level, RPD could be adapted to analyze embeddings that were learned from word pieces, for example, fastText (Bojanowski et al., 2017) and contextualized embeddings (Peters et al., 2018; Devlin et al., 2019).

2.2 Relationship Between Embedding Spaces

Levy and Goldberg (2014b) provide a good analogy between SGNS and SVD_{PMI}. They suggest that SGNS is essentially factorizing the pointwise mutual information (PMI) matrix. However, their analogy is based on the assumption of no dimension constraint in SGNS, which is not possible in practice. Furthermore, their analogy is not suitable for analyzing methods besides SGNS and PMI models since their theoretical derivation relies on the specific objective of SGNS.

Yin and Shen (2018) provide a way to select the best dimension of word embeddings for specific tasks by exploring the relations of embedding spaces of different dimension. They introduce Pairwise Inner Product (PIP) loss (Yin and Shen, 2018), an unitary-invariant metric for measuring word embeddings' distance (Smith et al., 2017). The unitary-invariance of word embeddings states that two embedding vector spaces are equivalent if one can be obtained from another by multiplying a unitary matrix. However, PIP loss is not suitable for comparing numerically across embedding spaces since PIP loss has different energy for different embedding spaces.

3 Quantifying Distances between Embeddings

In this section, we describe the definition of RPD and its properties, which make RPD a suitable and effective method to quantify the distance between embedding spaces. Note that two embedding spaces do not necessarily have the same vocabulary for calculating the RPD.

3.1 RPD

For the following discussion, we always use the Frobenius norm as the norm of matrices.

Definition 1. (RPD) The RPD between embedding matrices E_1 and E_2 is defined as follows:

$$\mathrm{RPD}(E_1, E_2) = \frac{1}{2} \frac{\|\tilde{E}_1\tilde{E}_1^T - \tilde{E}_2\tilde{E}_2^T\|^2}{\|\tilde{E}_1\tilde{E}_1^T\|\|\tilde{E}_2\tilde{E}_2^T\|}.$$

where $\tilde{E}$ comes from dividing each entry of E by its standard deviation. For convenience, we let $\tilde{E} \equiv E$ for the following discussion.

The numerator of RPD respects the unitary-invariant property of word embeddings, which means that unitary transformation (i.e. rotation) preserves the relative geometry of an embedding space. The denominator is a normalization, which allows us to regard the whole embedding matrix as an integrated part (i.e. RPD does not correlate with the number of words of embedding spaces). This step makes comparisons across methods possible.

3.2 Statistical Properties of RPD

We assume the widely used isotropic assumption (Arora et al., 2016) that the ensemble of word vectors consists of i.i.d draws generated by $v = s\hat{v}$, where $\hat{v}$ is from the spherical Gaussian distribution, and s is a scalar random variable. In our case, we can assume each entry of embedding comes from a standard normal distribution E: $v_{ij} \sim \mathcal{N}(0,1)$.

Note that the assumption may not always work in practice, especially for other embeddings such as contextualized embeddings. However, under the isotropic conditions, the statistical properties derived are intuitively and empirically plausible. Besides, those properties serve to better interpret the value of RPD alone. Since RPD, in many cases, is used for comparison, we should be comfortable with the assumption.

Upper bound We estimate the asymptotic upper bound of RPD. By factorizing the numerator of RPD, we get (1).

$$\text{RPD}(E_1, E_2) = \frac{1}{2} \frac{\|E_1 E_1^T\|^2 + \|E_2 E_2^T\|^2}{\|E_1 E_1^T\|\|E_2 E_2^T\|} - \frac{\langle E_1 E_1^T, E_2 E_2^T \rangle}{\|E_1 E_1^T\|\|E_2 E_2^T\|} \quad (1)$$

Applying the Cauchy-Schwarz inequality to the last term of $(1)^2$, we have the following estimation.

$$2\text{RPD}(E_1, E_2) \leq \frac{\|E_1 E_1^T\|^2 + \|E_2 E_2^T\|^2}{\|E_1 E_1^T\|\|E_2 E_2^T\|}$$
$$= \frac{\|E_1 E_1^T\|}{\|E_2 E_2^T\|} + \frac{\|E_2 E_2^T\|}{\|E_1 E_1^T\|} \quad (2)$$

By the law of large numbers, we can prove that $\lim_{n \to \infty} \|EE^T\| = n\sqrt{d}$ (Appendix A). Then, we can tell from (2) that RPD is bounded by 1 when $n \to \infty$. In practice, the number of words n is large enough to let the maximum of RPD stay around 1, which means RPD is well-defined numerically.

Normality For $\text{RPD}(E_1, E_2)$, if E_1 is independent of E_2, we can prove that RPD distributes normally from both an empirical and a theoretical perspective. Theoretically, by applying the central limit theorem to the numerator and the law of large numbers to the denominator of RPD, we can get the normality of RPD under the condition $n \to \infty$, $\frac{d}{n} = c$, where c remains constant (Appendix B). Empirically, we can use Monte Carlo simulation to show the normality and estimate the mean and variance of RPD (Appendix C). With the help of RPD, we can perform hypothesis test (z-test) to evaluate the independence of two embedding spaces.

---

^{2}The inner product of matrix A and B is defined as $\langle A, B \rangle = trace(A^T B)$

3.3 Geometric Interpretation of RPD

From equation (1), we can tell that the first term goes to 1 when $n \to \infty$. So we only need to discuss the second term.

$$\frac{\langle E_1 E_1^T, E_2 E_2^T \rangle}{\|E_1 E_1^T\|\|E_2 E_2^T\|}$$

For the ith row in EE^T, we have vector $\hat{v}_i = (v_i v_1^T, v_i v_2^T, ..., v_i v_n^T)$, where v_i is the word i's vector in embedding E, n is the number of words. We can interpret $\hat{v}_i$ as another representation of word i projected onto the space spanned by $v_1, v_2, ..., v_n$. So for convenience, we denote $\hat{E} = EE^T$ with its ith row as $\hat{v}_i$.

We can prove that $\lim_{n \to \infty} \text{RPD}(E_1, E_2) = 1 - \frac{1}{n} \sum_{i=1}^{n} \cos(\theta_i)$. The $\theta_i \in (0, \frac{\pi}{2})$ is the angle between $\hat{v}_i^{(1)}$ (i^{th} row vector of $\hat{E}_1$) and $\hat{v}_i^{(2)}$ (i^{th} row vector of $\hat{E}_2$) (Appendix D). Therefore, we can understand the value of RPD from the perspective of cosine similarity between vectors.

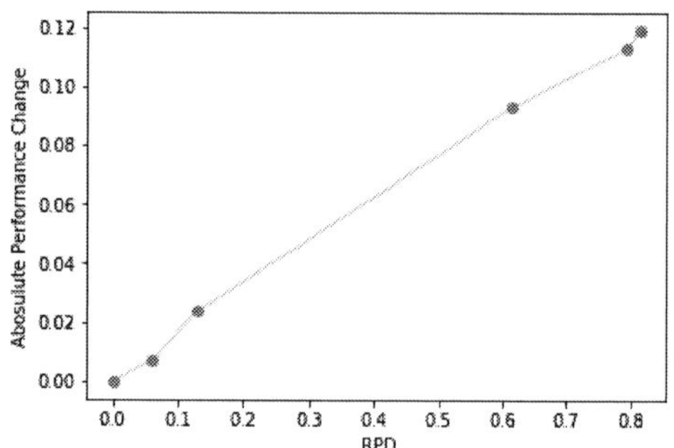

Figure 1: The plot shows the difference in performance as a function of RPD score. The x-axis for each point represents the RPD between word embeddings produced by SGNS (with NS 15, 5, 1), GloVe, SVD$_{\text{PMI}}$, SVD$_{\text{LC}}$ and word embeddings produced by SGNS$_{25}$. The y-axis for each point represents the sum of absolute variation in the performance (word similarity and word analogy).

3.4 RPD and Performance

As Yin and Shen (2018) discussed, usability of word embeddings, such as using them to solve analogy and relatedness tasks, is important to practitioners. Through applying different sets of word embeddings to word similarity and word analogy tasks (Mikolov et al., 2013), we study the relationship between RPD and word embeddings' performance. Specifically, we set the word embeddings produced by SGNS with 25 NS as a starting point and use

44

other word embeddings, for example, GloVe as an end point. Then we get a two dimensional point with x as their RPD, y as their absolute performance change in word similarity[3] and analogy[4] tasks.

By putting those points in Figure 1, we can tell in a certain range of RPD, the larger RPD between the two sets of word embedding means the bigger gap in their absolute performance. Intuitively, RPD is strongly related to cosine similarity, which is the measure of word similarity. RPD also shares the same property of PIP loss, where a small RPD leads to a small difference in relatedness and analogy tasks. We obtain similar results when the starting point is a different embedding space.

Note that this section serves to demonstrate the performance (at least in word similarity and analogy tasks) variation of different embedding spaces is correlated with their RPD. While we are aware of the relevance of other downstream tasks, we do not explore further since our focus lies in investigating the intrinsic geometry relation of embedding spaces.

4 Experiment

The following experiments serve to apply RPD to explore some questions of interest and further demonstrate that RPD is suitable for investigating the relations between embedding spaces. We leave applying RPD to help improve specific NLP tasks to future research. For example, RPD could be used for combining different embeddings together, which could help us produce better meta-embeddings (Kiela et al., 2018).

4.1 Setup

If not explicitly stated, the experiments are performed on Text8 corpus (Mahoney, 2011), a standard benchmark corpus used for various natural language tasks (Yin and Shen, 2018). For all methods we experiment, we train 300 dimension embeddings, with window size of 10, and normalize the embedding matrices with their standard deviation[5]. The default NS for SGNS is 15.

---

[3]Our word similarity task can be found here: `https://aclweb.org/aclwiki/WordSimilarity-353_Test_Collection_(State_of_the_art)`

[4]Our word analogy task can be found here: `https://aclweb.org/aclwiki/Google_analogy_test_set_(State_of_the_art)`

[5]The code can be found on Bitbucket: `https://bitbucket.org/omerlevy/hyperwords`

Methods	GloVe	SVD$_{\text{PMI}}$	SVD$_{\text{LC}}$
SGNS$_{25}$	0.792	0.609	0.847
SGNS$_{15}$	0.773	0.594	0.837
SGNS$_5$	0.725	0.550	0.805
SGNS$_1$	0.719	0.511	0.799

Table 1: RPDs of SGNS vs other methods

4.2 Different Algorithms Produce Different Embeddings

Dependence of SGNS and SVD$_{\text{PMI}}$

As discussed in the introduction, the relationship between embeddings trained with SGNS and SVD$_{\text{PMI}}$ remains controversial (Arora et al., 2016; Mimno and Thompson, 2017). We use the results we obtain in Section 3.2 to test their dependence. For example, if one believes that E_1 trained with SGNS and E_2 trained with SVD$_{\text{PMI}}$ have no relationship, then the null hypothesis H_0 would be: E_1 and E_2 are independent.

Under H_0, RPD(E_1, E_2) asymptotically follows $\mathcal{N}(\mu, \sigma^2)$. Then the test statistic z is calculated as follows.

$$z = \frac{\text{RPD}(E_1, E_2) - \mu}{\sigma}$$

In our case, we estimate $\mu = 0.953$ and $\sigma = 0.001$ with Monte Carlo simulation with randomly initialized embeddings. Take RPD$(E_{\text{SGNS}_1}, E_{\text{SVD}_{\text{PMI}}}) = 0.511$ from Table 1 as an example, the statistic $z = 442$, which means the p-value $\ll 0.01$. Thus, we can confidently reject H_0. Notice that we can test any two sets of word embeddings with this method. It is not hard to see that no pair of word embeddings in Table 1 are independent, which suggests that there exists an unified theory behind these methods.

SGNS is Closest to SVD$_{\text{PMI}}$

With the help of RPD, it is also interesting to investigate distances between embeddings produced by different methods. Here, we calculate the RPDs among SGNS (with negative sampling 25, 15, 5, 1), GloVe, SVD$_{\text{PMI}}$, SVD$_{\text{LC}}$.

Table 1 shows the RPDs between SGNS with different negative sampling numbers and other methods. From the table, we can tell that SGNS stays close to SVD$_{\text{PMI}}$, which confirms Levy and Goldberg (2014b)'s theory.

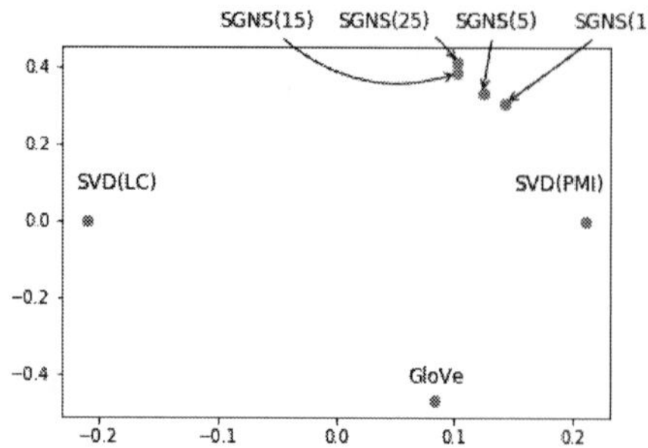

Figure 2: Plot of different methods. We create the plot by fixing the position of SVD_{LC} and SVD_{PMI}. We then derive the position of other word embeddings according to their RPD with existing points on the plot.

	SGNS	GloVe
Text8-WMT14	0.168	0.686
Text8-TED	0.119	0.758
WMT14-TED	0.175	0.716

Table 2: RPDs between same method trained from different corpora

Hyper-parameters Have Influence on Embeddings

From Table 1, an interesting phenomenon is that SGNS becomes closer to other methods with the decrease of negative samples, which suggests that negative sampling is one of the factors driving SGNS away from matrix factorization methods.

With RPDs between different sets of word embeddings, we plot the embeddings in 2D by treating each embedding space as a single point. We first fix point SVD_{PMI} and SVD_{LC}, then we draw other points according to their RPDs with the other methods. Figure 2 helps us see how negative sampling affects the embedding intuitively. Increasing the number of negative samples pulls SGNS away from SVD_{PMI}. Combining Table 1 and Figure 2, we can tell that although the hyper-parameters can influence the embeddings to some extent, the main difference comes from the algorithms.

4.3 Different Initializations Barely Influence Embeddings

Random initializations produce different embeddings with the same algorithms and hyperparameters. While those embeddings usually get similar performance on the downstream tasks, people are still concerned about their effects. We investigate the influence of random initializations for GloVe and SGNS.

We train the embedding in the same setting multiple times and get the average RPDs for each method. For SGNS, the average RPDs of random initialization is 0.027. For GloVe, the value is 0.059.

We can tell that different random initializations produce essentially the same embeddings. Neither SGNS or GloVe has a significant RPD in different initializations, which suggests random initialization has little influence over word embeddings' performance (Section 3.4). However, SGNS seems to be more stable in this setting.

4.4 Different Corpora Produce Different Embeddings

It is well known that different corpora produce different word embeddings. However, it is hard for us to tell how different they are and whether the difference influences downstream applications (Antoniak and Mimno, 2018). Knowing this would help researchers choose the algorithms in specific scenarios, for example, evolving semantic discovery (Yao et al., 2018; Kozlowski et al., 2019). They focus on the semantic evolution of words, but corpora are different in different time scales. Their methods use word embeddings to study semantic shift, which might be influenced by the word embeddings being trained on different corpora, thus getting unreliable results. In this case, it would be important to chose an algorithm less prone to influences by differences in corpora.

We train word embeddings using each of text8 (Wikipedia domain, 25097 unique words), WMT14 news crawl[6] (Newswire domain, 24359 unique words), TED speech[7] (Speech domain, 7389 unique words). We compute RPD on the intersections of their vocabulary

From Table 2, we can tell that SGNS is consistently more stable than GloVe in different domains. We suggest that this is because GloVe trains the embedding with co-occurrence matrix, which gets influenced more by the corpus.

5 Discussion

While our work investigates some interesting problems about word embeddings, there are many other

---

[6] http://www.statmt.org/wmt14/
[7] https://workshop2016.iwslt.org/

problems about embeddings that can be demonstrated with the help of RPD. We discuss some of them as follows.

5.1 RPD and Crosslingual Word Embeddings

Artetxe et al. (2018) provide a framework to obtain bilingual embeddings, whose the core step of the framework is an orthogonal transformation and other existing methods can be seen as its variations. The framework proposes to train monolingual embeddings separately and then map them into a shared-embedding space with linear transformation.

While linear transformation is no guarantee for the alignment of two embedding spaces from different languages, RPD could potentially serve as a way to indicate how different language pairs benefit from mapping them with an orthogonal transformation. Since RPD is unitary-invariant, we can calculate RPD between embedding spaces from different language pairs. The smaller RPD is, the better the framework could align this two language embedding spaces.

5.2 RPD and Post-Processing Word Embeddings

Post-processing word embeddings can be useful in many ways. For example, Vulić et al. (2018) retrofit word embeddings with external linguistic resources, such as WordNet to obtain better embeddings; Rothe and Schütze (2016) decompose embedding space to get better performance at specialized domains; and Mu and Viswanath (2018) obtain stronger embeddings by eliminating the common mean vector and a few top dominating directions.

RPD could serve as a metric to evaluate how the embedding space changes intrinsically after post-processing.

5.3 RPD and Contextualized Word Embeddings

Contextualized embeddings are popular NLP techniques which significantly improve a wide range of NLP tasks (Bowman et al., 2015; Rajpurkar et al., 2018). To understand why contextualized embeddings are beneficial to those NLP tasks, many works investigate the the nature of syntactic (Liu et al., 2019), semantic (Liu et al., 2019), and commonsense knowledge (Zhou et al., 2019) contained in such representations.

However, we still know little about the vector space of contextualized embeddings and their rela-
tionship with traditional word embeddings, which is important to further apply contextualized embeddings in various scenarios (Lin and Smith, 2019). RPD can potentially serve to help us better understand contextualized embeddings in future research.

6 Conclusion

In this paper, we propose RPD, a metric to quantify the distance between embedding spaces (i.e different sets of word embeddings). With the help of RPD and its properties, we verify some intuitions and answer some questions. Justifying RPD theoretically and empirically, we believe RPD can offer us a new perspective to understand and compare word embeddings.

Acknowledgments

I would like to thank Dr. Zi Yin, Dr. Vered Shwartz, Maarten Sap, and Jorge Balazs for their feedback that greatly improved the paper.

References

Maria Antoniak and David Mimno. 2018. Evaluating the stability of embedding-based word similarities. *Transactions of the Association for Computational Linguistics*, 6:107–119.

Sanjeev Arora, Yuanzhi Li, Yingyu Liang, Tengyu Ma, and Andrej Risteski. 2016. A latent variable model approach to pmi-based word embeddings. *Transactions of the Association for Computational Linguistics*, 4:385–399.

Mikel Artetxe, Gorka Labaka, and Eneko Agirre. 2018. Generalizing and improving bilingual word embedding mappings with a multi-step framework of linear transformations.

Piotr Bojanowski, Edouard Grave, Armand Joulin, and Tomas Mikolov. 2017. Enriching word vectors with subword information. *Transactions of the Association for Computational Linguistics*, 5:135–146.

Tolga Bolukbasi, Kai-Wei Chang, James Y Zou, Venkatesh Saligrama, and Adam T Kalai. 2016. Man is to computer programmer as woman is to homemaker? debiasing word embeddings. In D. D. Lee, M. Sugiyama, U. V. Luxburg, I. Guyon, and R. Garnett, editors, *Advances in Neural Information Processing Systems 29*, pages 4349–4357. Curran Associates, Inc.

Samuel R. Bowman, Gabor Angeli, Christopher Potts, and Christopher D. Manning. 2015. A large annotated corpus for learning natural language inference. In *Proceedings of the 2015 Conference on Empirical Methods in Natural Language Processing*, pages

632–642, Lisbon, Portugal. Association for Computational Linguistics.

Jacob Devlin, Ming-Wei Chang, Kenton Lee, and Kristina Toutanova. 2019. BERT: Pre-training of deep bidirectional transformers for language understanding. In *Proceedings of the 2019 Conference of the North American Chapter of the Association for Computational Linguistics: Human Language Technologies, Volume 1 (Long and Short Papers)*, pages 4171–4186, Minneapolis, Minnesota. Association for Computational Linguistics.

Douwe Kiela, Changhan Wang, and Kyunghyun Cho. 2018. Dynamic meta-embeddings for improved sentence representations. In *Proceedings of the 2018 Conference on Empirical Methods in Natural Language Processing*, pages 1466–1477, Brussels, Belgium. Association for Computational Linguistics.

Austin C. Kozlowski, Matt Taddy, and James A. Evans. 2019. The geometry of culture: Analyzing the meanings of class through word embeddings. *American Sociological Review*, 84(5):905–949.

Omer Levy and Yoav Goldberg. 2014a. Dependency-based word embeddings. In *Proceedings of the 52nd Annual Meeting of the Association for Computational Linguistics (Volume 2: Short Papers)*, pages 302–308, Baltimore, Maryland. Association for Computational Linguistics.

Omer Levy and Yoav Goldberg. 2014b. Neural word embedding as implicit matrix factorization. In *Proceedings of the 27th International Conference on Neural Information Processing Systems - Volume 2*, NIPS'14, pages 2177–2185, Cambridge, MA, USA. MIT Press.

Omer Levy, Yoav Goldberg, and Ido Dagan. 2015. Improving distributional similarity with lessons learned from word embeddings. *Transactions of the Association for Computational Linguistics*, 3:211–225.

Lucy H. Lin and Noah A. Smith. 2019. Situating sentence embedders with nearest neighbor overlap. *ArXiv*, abs/1909.10724.

Nelson F. Liu, Matt Gardner, Yonatan Belinkov, Matthew E. Peters, and Noah A. Smith. 2019. Linguistic knowledge and transferability of contextual representations. In *Proceedings of the 2019 Conference of the North American Chapter of the Association for Computational Linguistics: Human Language Technologies, Volume 1 (Long and Short Papers)*, pages 1073–1094, Minneapolis, Minnesota. Association for Computational Linguistics.

Matt Mahoney. 2011. Large text comparison benchmark, 2011.

Tomas Mikolov, Kai Chen, Greg S. Corrado, and Jeffrey Dean. 2013. Efficient estimation of word representations in vector space.

David Mimno and Laure Thompson. 2017. The strange geometry of skip-gram with negative sampling. In *Proceedings of the 2017 Conference on Empirical Methods in Natural Language Processing*, pages 2873–2878.

Andriy Mnih and Koray Kavukcuoglu. 2013. Learning word embeddings efficiently with noise-contrastive estimation. In C. J. C. Burges, L. Bottou, M. Welling, Z. Ghahramani, and K. Q. Weinberger, editors, *Advances in Neural Information Processing Systems 26*, pages 2265–2273. Curran Associates, Inc.

Jiaqi Mu and Pramod Viswanath. 2018. All-but-the-top: Simple and effective postprocessing for word representations. In *International Conference on Learning Representations*.

Jeffrey Pennington, Richard Socher, and Christopher Manning. 2014. Glove: Global vectors for word representation. In *Proceedings of the 2014 Conference on Empirical Methods in Natural Language Processing (EMNLP)*, pages 1532–1543, Doha, Qatar. Association for Computational Linguistics.

Matthew Peters, Mark Neumann, Mohit Iyyer, Matt Gardner, Christopher Clark, Kenton Lee, and Luke Zettlemoyer. 2018. Deep contextualized word representations. In *Proceedings of the 2018 Conference of the North American Chapter of the Association for Computational Linguistics: Human Language Technologies, Volume 1 (Long Papers)*, pages 2227–2237, New Orleans, Louisiana. Association for Computational Linguistics.

Pranav Rajpurkar, Robin Jia, and Percy Liang. 2018. Know what you don't know: Unanswerable questions for SQuAD. In *Proceedings of the 56th Annual Meeting of the Association for Computational Linguistics (Volume 2: Short Papers)*, pages 784–789, Melbourne, Australia. Association for Computational Linguistics.

Sascha Rothe and Hinrich Schütze. 2016. Word embedding calculus in meaningful ultradense subspaces. In *Proceedings of the 54th Annual Meeting of the Association for Computational Linguistics (Volume 2: Short Papers)*, pages 512–517, Berlin, Germany. Association for Computational Linguistics.

Samuel L. Smith, David H. P. Turban, Steven Hamblin, and Nils Y. Hammerla. 2017. Offline bilingual word vectors, orthogonal transformations and the inverted softmax. *CoRR*, abs/1702.03859.

Ivan Vulić, Goran Glavaš, Nikola Mrkšić, and Anna Korhonen. 2018. Post-specialisation: Retrofitting vectors of words unseen in lexical resources. In *Proceedings of the 2018 Conference of the North American Chapter of the Association for Computational Linguistics: Human Language Technologies, Volume 1 (Long Papers)*, pages 516–527, New Orleans, Louisiana. Association for Computational Linguistics.

Zijun Yao, Yifan Sun, Weicong Ding, Nikhil Rao, and Hui Xiong. 2018. Dynamic word embeddings for evolving semantic discovery. In *Proceedings of the Eleventh ACM International Conference on Web Search and Data Mining*, WSDM 18, page 673681, New York, NY, USA. Association for Computing Machinery.

Wenpeng Yin and Hinrich Schütze. 2016. Learning word meta-embeddings. In *Proceedings of the 54th Annual Meeting of the Association for Computational Linguistics (Volume 1: Long Papers)*, pages 1351–1360, Berlin, Germany. Association for Computational Linguistics.

Zi Yin and Yuanyuan Shen. 2018. On the dimensionality of word embedding. In S. Bengio, H. Wallach, H. Larochelle, K. Grauman, N. Cesa-Bianchi, and R. Garnett, editors, *Advances in Neural Information Processing Systems 31*, pages 887–898. Curran Associates, Inc.

Xuhui Zhou, Yue Zhang, Leyang Cui, and Dandan Huang. 2019. Evaluating commonsense in pretrained language models.

A   Appendix A. Limitation of $||EE^T||$

As discuss before, in our case, we can assume i.i.d. $v_{ij} \sim \mathcal{N}(0,1)$, where v_{ij} is the jth entry in the ith word vector v_i of E.

$$
\begin{aligned}
||EE^T|| &= n\sqrt{\frac{\sum_{i,j}^{n}(v_i v_j^T)^2}{n^2}} \\
&= n\sqrt{\frac{\sum_{i \neq j}^{n}(v_i v_j^T)^2}{n^2} + \frac{\sum_{i=j}^{n}(v_i v_j^T)^2}{n^2}}
\end{aligned}
\tag{3}
$$

By the assumption, we know that $v_i v_j^T$ identically distributes for any $i \neq j, 1 \geq i \leq n, 1 \geq j \leq n$. By applying the law of large numbers, the term $\frac{\sum_{i \neq j}^{n}(v_i v_j^T)^2}{n^2}$ goes to $E((v_i v_j^T)^2)$ as n goes to ∞. The term $\frac{\sum_{i=j}^{n}(v_i v_j^T)^2}{n^2}$ goes to zero as n goes to ∞. Then, we know that $||EE^T|| \rightarrow n\sqrt{E((v_i v_j^T)^2)}, n \rightarrow \infty$.

We only need to calculate $E((v_i v_j^T)^2)$.

$$
E((v_i v_j^T)^2) = Var(v_i v_j^T) + (E(v_i v_j^T))^2 \tag{4}
$$

Simple calculation shows that $Var(v_i v_j^T) = d$, $E(v_i v_j^T) = 0$. Then $E((v_i v_j^T)^2) = d$, d is the dimension of word embedding here. Thus, $||EE^T|| \rightarrow n\sqrt{d}, n \rightarrow \infty$.

B   Appendix B. Normality of RPD

Let's review the form of RPD.

$$
\text{RPD}(E_1, E_2) = \frac{1}{2} \frac{||E_1 E_1^T - E_2 E_2^T||^2}{||E_1 E_1^T||||E_2 E_2^T||} \tag{5}
$$

As we discuss in A, $\frac{||E_1 E_1^T||||E_2 E_2^T||}{n^2} \rightarrow d$, as $n \rightarrow \infty$. We only have to prove $\frac{||E_1 E_1^T - E_2 E_2^T||^2}{n^2}$ distributes normally. The key is how to apply the central limit theorem (CLT).

We denote as follows.

$$
\begin{aligned}
H_n &= \frac{||E_1 E_1^T - E_2 E_2^T||^2}{n^2} \\
&= \frac{||E_1 E_1^T||^2 + ||E_2 E_2^T||^2 - 2\langle E_1 E_1^T, E_2 E_2^T \rangle}{n^2}
\end{aligned}
\tag{6}
$$

Notice that the term $\langle E_1 E_1^T, E_2 E_2^T \rangle$ does not contribute to the variance if we analyze the second moment of the numerator. So it is equivalent to prove $T_n = \frac{||E_1 E_1^T||^2 + ||E_2 E_2^T||^2}{n^2}$ distributes normally.

We project the T_n to
$$
S_n = \sum_{i,j}^{n} E(T_n | v_{ij}) - (n-1)E(T_n)
$$

Simple calculation would show that $\frac{Var(T_n)}{Var(S_n)} \rightarrow 1, n \rightarrow \infty, \frac{n}{d} = c$. Then by the Hajek projection theorem, we get T_n has the same distribution as S_n. It is not hard to see that each random variable $E(T_n | v_{ij})$ in S_n is independent of others. This allows us to apply CLT to S_n and get $S_n \sim \mathcal{N}(\mu, \sigma^2)$. Thus, $H_n \sim \mathcal{N}(\mu, \sigma^2)$.

C   Appendix C. Monte Carlo Simulation

Here is how we perform Monte Carlo simulation. We independently produce two matrix $E_1, E_2 \in \mathbf{R}^{n \times d}$ with each entry i.i.d as $\mathcal{N}(0,1)$. Then we calculate $\text{RPD}(E_1, E_2)$ and get the first RPD value. Repeat the process for 5000 times, we get a vector of RPDs. Drawing the histogram of this vector yields a normal distribution and we can estimate the mean and variance of the distribution by calculating the mean and variance of the vector of RPDs.

D   Appendix D. Geometry Interpretation of RPD

Now we consider a general case, where $\hat{E}_1$ and $\hat{E}_2$ are embeddings with n words.

$$
\begin{bmatrix} v_1^{(1)} \\ v_2^{(1)} \\ \vdots \\ v_n^{(1)} \end{bmatrix}, \begin{bmatrix} v_1^{(2)} \\ v_2^{(2)} \\ \vdots \\ v_n^{(2)} \end{bmatrix}
$$

Then

$$
\begin{aligned}
\frac{\langle \hat{E}_1, \hat{E}_2 \rangle}{||\hat{E}_1||||\hat{E}_2||} &= \frac{\sum_{i=1}^{n} v_i^{(1)T} v_i^{(2)}}{||\hat{E}_1||||\hat{E}_2||} \\
&= \sum_{i=1}^{n} \frac{v_i^{(1)T} v_i^{(2)}}{||v_i^1||||v_i^{(2)}||} \frac{||v_i^1||||v_i^{(2)}||}{||\hat{E}_1||||\hat{E}_2||}
\end{aligned}
\tag{7}
$$

We denote $\frac{||v_i^1||||v_i^{(2)}||}{||\hat{E}_1||||\hat{E}_2||}$ as w_i, $\frac{v_i^{(1)T} v_i^{(2)}}{||v_i^1||||v_i^{(2)}||}$ as $\cos(\theta_i)$

It is not hard to see that the $w_i \approx \frac{1}{n}$, when n is large enough. Then we get $\text{RPD}(E_1, E_2) \approx 1 - \frac{\sum_{i=1}^{n} \cos(\theta_i)}{n}$. Considering the isotropic assumption again, another observation is that the $\cos(\theta_i)$ distributes normally.

Reflection-based Word Attribute Transfer

Yoichi Ishibashi, Katsuhito Sudoh, Koichiro Yoshino, Satoshi Nakamura

Nara Institute of Science and Technology

{ishibashi.yoichi.ir3, sudoh, koichiro, s-nakamura}@is.naist.jp

Abstract

Word embeddings, which often represent such analogic relations as $\overrightarrow{king} - \overrightarrow{man} + \overrightarrow{woman} \approx \overrightarrow{queen}$, can be used to change a word's attribute, including its gender. For transferring *king* into *queen* in this analogy-based manner, we subtract a difference vector $\overrightarrow{man} - \overrightarrow{woman}$ based on the knowledge that *king* is male. However, developing such knowledge is very costly for words and attributes. In this work, we propose a novel method for word attribute transfer based on reflection mappings without such an analogy operation. Experimental results show that our proposed method can transfer the word attributes of the given words without changing the words that do not have the target attributes.

1 Introduction

Word-embedding methods handle word semantics in natural language processing (Mikolov et al., 2013a,b; Pennington et al., 2014; Vilnis and McCallum, 2015; Bojanowski et al., 2017). Such word-embedding models as skip-gram with negative sampling (SGNS; Mikolov et al., 2013b) or GloVe (Pennington et al., 2014) capture such analogic relations as $\overrightarrow{king} - \overrightarrow{man} + \overrightarrow{woman} \approx \overrightarrow{queen}$. Previous work (Levy and Goldberg, 2014b; Arora et al., 2016; Gittens et al., 2017; Ethayarajh et al., 2019; Allen and Hospedales, 2019) offers theoretical explanation based on Pointwise Mutual Information (PMI; Church and Hanks, 1990) for maintaining analogic relations in word vectors.

These relations can be used to transfer a certain attribute of a word, such as changing *king* into *queen* by transferring its gender. This transfer can be applied to perform data augmentation; for example, rewriting *He is a boy* to *She is a girl*. It can be used to generate negative examples for natural language inference, for example. We tackle a novel

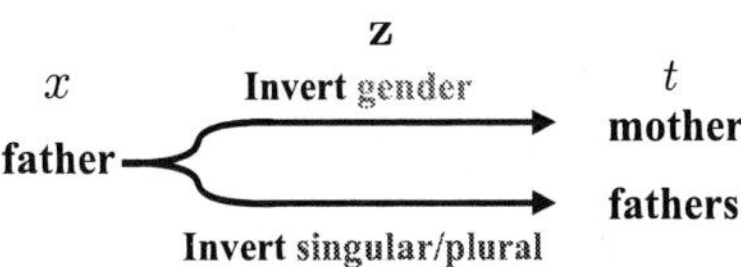

Figure 1: Examples of word attribute transfer

task that transfers any word associated with certain attributes: *word attribute transfer.*

A naive way for word attribute transfer is to use a difference vector based on analogic relations, such as adding $\overrightarrow{woman} - \overrightarrow{man}$ to $\overrightarrow{king}$ to obtain $\overrightarrow{queen}$. This requires explicit knowledge whether an input word is male or female; we have to add a difference vector to a male word and subtract it from a female word for the gender transfer. We also have to avoid changing words without gender attributes, such as *is* and *a* in the example above, since they are non-attribute words. Developing such knowledge is very costly for words and attributes in practice. In this work, we propose a novel framework for a word attribute transfer based on *reflection* that does not require explicit knowledge of the given words in its prediction.

The contribution of this work is two-fold: (1) We propose a word attribute transfer method that obtains a vector with an inverted binary attribute without explicit knowledge. (2) The proposed method demonstrates more accurate word attribute transfer for words that have target attributes than other baselines without changing the words that do not have the target attributes.

2 Word Attribute Transfer Task

In this task, we focus on modeling the binary attributes (e.g. male and female[1]). Let x denote a word and let $\mathbf{v}_x$ denote its vector representation. We assume that $\mathbf{v}_x$ is learned in advance

---

[1]Gender-specific words are sometimes considered socially problematic. Here we use this as an example from the man-woman relation.

Proceedings of the 58th Annual Meeting of the Association for Computational Linguistics: Student Research Workshop, pages 51–58
July 5 - July 10, 2020. ©2020 Association for Computational Linguistics

with an embedding model, such as skip-gram. In this task, we have two inputs, word x and vector $\mathbf{z}$, which represent a certain target attribute, and output word t with the inverted attribute of x for $\mathbf{z}$. In this paper, $\mathbf{z}$ is a 300-dimensional vector embedded from a target attribute ID using an embedding function of a deep learning framework. For example, given a set of attributes $\mathcal{Z} = \{\text{gender}, \text{antonym}\}$, we assign different random vectors $\mathbf{z}_{\text{gender}}$ for gender and $\mathbf{z}_{\text{antonym}}$ for antonym, respectively. Let $\mathcal{A}$ denote a set of triplets $(x, t, \mathbf{z})$, e.g., $(man, woman, \mathbf{z}_{\text{gender}}) \in \mathcal{A}$, and $\mathcal{N}$ denote a set of words without attribute $\mathbf{z}$, e.g., $(person, \mathbf{z}_{\text{gender}}) \in \mathcal{N}$. This task transfers input word vector $\mathbf{v}_x$ to target word vector $\mathbf{v}_t$ by transfer function $f_{\mathbf{z}}$ that inverts attribute $\mathbf{z}$ of $\mathbf{v}_x$:

$$\mathbf{v}_t \approx \mathbf{v}_y = f_{\mathbf{z}}(\mathbf{v}_x). \quad (1)$$

The following property must be satisfied: (1) attribute words $\{x | (x, t, \mathbf{z}) \in \mathcal{A}\}$ are transferred to their counterparts and (2) non-attribute words $\{x | (x, \mathbf{z}) \in \mathcal{N}\}$ are not changed (transferred back into themselves). For instance with $\mathbf{z}_{\text{gender}}$, given input word *man*, gender attribute transfer $f_{\mathbf{z}_{\text{gender}}}(\mathbf{v}_{man})$ should result in a vector close to $\mathbf{v}_{woman}$. Given another input word *person* as x, the results should be $\mathbf{v}_{person}$.

3 Analogy-based Word Attribute Transfer

Analogy is a general idea that can be used for word attribute transfer. PMI-based word embedding, such as SGNS and GloVe, captures analogic relations, including Eq. 2 (Mikolov et al., 2013c; Levy and Goldberg, 2014a; Linzen, 2016). By rearranging Eq. 2, Eq. 3 is obtained:

$$\mathbf{v}_{queen} \approx \mathbf{v}_{king} - \mathbf{v}_{man} + \mathbf{v}_{woman}, \quad (2)$$
$$\approx \mathbf{v}_{king} - (\mathbf{v}_{man} - \mathbf{v}_{woman}). \quad (3)$$

The analogy-based transfer function is

$$f_{\mathbf{z}}(\mathbf{v}_x) = \begin{cases} \mathbf{v}_x - \mathbf{d} & \text{if } x \in \mathcal{M}, \\ \mathbf{v}_x + \mathbf{d} & \text{if } x \in \mathcal{F}, \end{cases} \quad (4)$$

where $\mathcal{M}$ is a set of words with a target attribute (e.g., male) and $\mathcal{F}$ is a set of words with an inverse attribute (e.g., female). $\mathbf{d}$ is a difference vector, such as $\mathbf{v}_{man} - \mathbf{v}_{woman}$. Eq. 4 indicates that the operation changes depending on whether input word x belongs to $\mathcal{M}$ or $\mathcal{F}$. However, to transfer

the word attribute by analogy, we need such explicit knowledge as attribute value ($\mathcal{M}$, $\mathcal{F}$ or others) that is contained by the input word.

4 Reflection-based Word Attribute Transfer

4.1 Ideal Transfer without Knowledge

What is ideal transfer function $f_{\mathbf{z}}$ for a word attribute transfer? The following are the ideal natures of such a transfer function:

$$\forall (m, w, \mathbf{z}) \in \mathcal{A}, \qquad \mathbf{v}_m = f_{\mathbf{z}}(\mathbf{v}_w), \quad (5)$$
$$\forall (m, w, \mathbf{z}) \in \mathcal{A}, \qquad \mathbf{v}_w = f_{\mathbf{z}}(\mathbf{v}_m), \quad (6)$$
$$\forall (u, \mathbf{z}) \in \mathcal{N}, \qquad \mathbf{v}_u = f_{\mathbf{z}}(\mathbf{v}_u). \quad (7)$$

This function $f_{\mathbf{z}}$ enables a word to be transferred without explicit knowledge because operation $f_{\mathbf{z}}$ does not change depending on whether input word belongs to $\mathcal{M}$ or $\mathcal{F}$. By combining Eqs. 5, 6 and 7, we obtain the following formulas:

$$\forall (m, w, \mathbf{z}) \in \mathcal{A}, \qquad \mathbf{v}_m = f_{\mathbf{z}}(f_{\mathbf{z}}(\mathbf{v}_m)), \quad (8)$$
$$\forall (m, w, \mathbf{z}) \in \mathcal{A}, \qquad \mathbf{v}_w = f_{\mathbf{z}}(f_{\mathbf{z}}(\mathbf{v}_w)), \quad (9)$$
$$\forall (u, \mathbf{z}) \in \mathcal{N}, \qquad \mathbf{v}_u = f_{\mathbf{z}}(f_{\mathbf{z}}(\mathbf{v}_u)). \quad (10)$$

Hence, the ideal transfer function is a mapping that becomes an identity mapping when we apply it twice for any $\mathbf{v}$. Such a mapping is called *involution* in geometry. For example, $f: \mathbf{v} \mapsto -\mathbf{v}$ is one example of an involution.

4.2 Reflection

Reflection $\text{Ref}_{\mathbf{a},\mathbf{c}}$ is an ideal function because this mapping is an involution:

$$\forall \mathbf{v} \in \mathbb{R}^n, \qquad \mathbf{v} = \text{Ref}_{\mathbf{a},\mathbf{c}}(\text{Ref}_{\mathbf{a},\mathbf{c}}(\mathbf{v})). \quad (11)$$

Reflection reverses the location between two vectors in a Euclidean space through an hyperplane called a *mirror*. Reflection is different from inverse mapping. When m and w are paired words, reflection can transfer $\mathbf{v}_m$ and $\mathbf{v}_w$ each other with identical reflection mapping as in Eqs. 5 and 6, but an inverse mapping cannot. Given vector $\mathbf{v}$ in Euclidean space $\mathbb{R}^n$, the formula for the reflection in the mirror is given:

$$\text{Ref}_{\mathbf{a},\mathbf{c}}(\mathbf{v}) = \mathbf{v} - 2\frac{(\mathbf{v} - \mathbf{c}) \cdot \mathbf{a}}{\mathbf{a} \cdot \mathbf{a}}\mathbf{a}, \quad (12)$$

where $\mathbf{a} \in \mathbb{R}^n$ is a vector orthogonal to the mirror and $\mathbf{c} \in \mathbb{R}^n$ is a point through which the mirror passes. $\mathbf{a}$ and $\mathbf{c}$ are parameters that determine the mirror.

4.3 Proposed method: Reflection-based Word Attribute Transfer

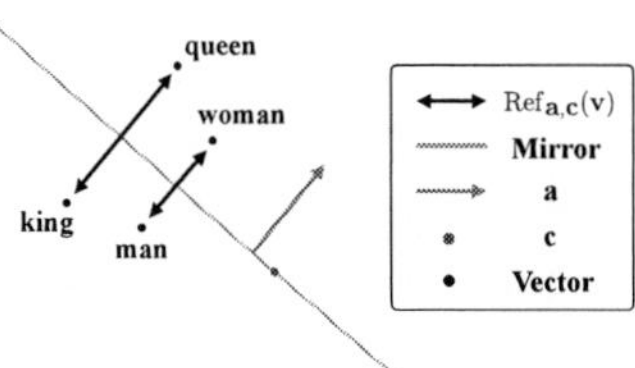

Figure 2: Reflection-based word attribute transfer with a single mirror

We apply reflection to the word attribute transfer. We learn a mirror (hyperplane) in a pre-trained embedding space using training word pairs with binary attribute $\mathbf{z}$ (Fig. 2). Since the mirror is uniquely determined by two parameter vectors, $\mathbf{a}$ and $\mathbf{c}$, we estimate $\mathbf{a}$ and $\mathbf{c}$ from target attribute $\mathbf{z}$ using fully connected multi-layer perceptrons:

$$\mathbf{a} = \mathrm{MLP}_{\theta_1}(\mathbf{z}), \qquad (13)$$

$$\mathbf{c} = \mathrm{MLP}_{\theta_2}(\mathbf{z}), \qquad (14)$$

where θ is a set of trainable parameters of MLP_θ. Here, θ_1 and θ_2 are optimized for each attribute dataset. Transferred vector $\mathbf{v}_y$ is obtained by inverting attribute $\mathbf{z}$ of $\mathbf{v}_x$ by reflection:

$$\mathbf{v}_y = \mathrm{Ref}_{\mathbf{a},\mathbf{c}}(\mathbf{v}_x). \qquad (15)$$

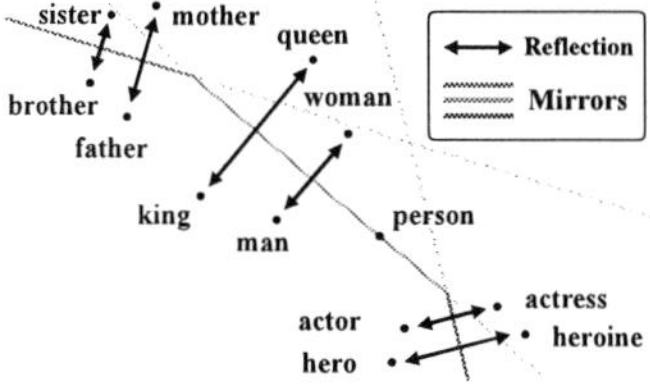

Figure 3: Reflection with parameterized mirrors

Reflection with a mirror by Eqs. 13 and 14 assumes a single mirror that only depends on $\mathbf{z}$. Previous discussion assumed pairs that share a stable pair, such as *king* and *queen*. However, since gendered words often do not come in pairs, gender is not stable enough to be modeled by a single mirror. For example, although *actress* is exclusively feminine, *actor* is clearly neutral in many cases. Thus, *actor* is not obviously a masculine counterpart like *king*. In fact, bias exists in gender words in the embedding space (Zhao et al., 2018; Kaneko and Bollegala, 2019). This phenomenon can occur not only with gender attributes but also with other attributes. The single mirror assumption forces the

mirror to be a hyperplane that goes through the midpoints for all the word vector pairs. However, the vector pair *actor-actress* shown on the right in Fig. 3 cannot be transferred well since the single mirror (the green line) does not satisfy this constraint due to the bias of the embedding space. To solve this problem, we propose *parameterized mirrors*, based on the idea of using different mirrors for different words. We define mirror parameters $\mathbf{a}$ and $\mathbf{c}$ using word vector $\mathbf{v}_x$ to be transferred in addition to attribute vector $\mathbf{z}$:

$$\mathbf{a} = \mathrm{MLP}_{\theta_1}([\mathbf{z}; \mathbf{v}_x]), \qquad (16)$$

$$\mathbf{c} = \mathrm{MLP}_{\theta_2}([\mathbf{z}; \mathbf{v}_x]), \qquad (17)$$

where $[\cdot; \cdot]$ indicates the vector concatenation in the column. The *parameterized mirrors* are expected to work more flexibly on different words than a single mirror because *parameterized mirrors* dynamically determine similar mirrors for similar words. For instance, as shown in Fig. 3, suppose we learned the mirror (the blue line) that transfers $\mathbf{v}_{hero}$ to $\mathbf{v}_{heroine}$ in advance. If input word vector $\mathbf{v}_{actor}$ resembles $\mathbf{v}_{hero}$, a mirror that resembles the one for $\mathbf{v}_{hero}$ should be derived and used for the transfer.

On the other hand, the reflection works as an identity mapping for a vector on the mirror (e.g., $\mathbf{v}_{person}$ in Fig 3). That is, the proposed method assumes that non-attribute word vectors are located on the mirror. Since we used a 300-dimensional embedded space in the experiment, we assume that the non-attribute word vector exists in a 299-dimensional subspace.

Here, it should be noted that Eq. 11 may not hold for parameterized mirrors. In reflection with a single mirror, it is true that $\mathbf{v} = \mathrm{Ref}_{\mathbf{a},\mathbf{c}}(\mathrm{Ref}_{\mathbf{a},\mathbf{c}}(\mathbf{v}))$. However, with the $\mathbf{v}$-parameterized reflection $\mathrm{Ref}_{\mathbf{a_v},\mathbf{c_v}}(\mathbf{v})$, this is not guaranteed. Because mirror parameters $\mathbf{a_v}$ and $\mathbf{c_v}$ depend on an input word vector as Eqs. 16 and 17. Thus, we exclude this constraint and employ the constraints given by Eqs. 5-7 for our loss function.

The following property must be satisfied in word attribute transfer: (1) words with attribute $\mathbf{z}$ are transferred and (2) words without it are not transferred. Thus, loss $L(\theta_1, \theta_2)$ is defined:

$$L(\theta_1, \theta_2) = \frac{1}{|\mathcal{A}|} \sum_{(x,t,\mathbf{z}) \in \mathcal{A}} (\mathbf{v}_y - \mathbf{v}_t)^2 \qquad (18)$$

$$+ \frac{1}{|\mathcal{N}|} \sum_{(x,\mathbf{z}) \in \mathcal{N}} (\mathbf{v}_y - \mathbf{v}_x)^2, \qquad (19)$$

where Eq. 18 is a term that draws target word vector $\mathbf{v}_{t_i}$ closer to corresponding transferred vector $\mathbf{v}_{y_i}$ and Eq. 19 is a term that prevents words without a target attribute from being moved by transfer function. $\mathbf{v}_y$ is the output of a reflection (Eq. 15).

5   Experiment

We evaluated the performance of the word attribute transfer using data with four different attributes. We used 300-dimensional word2vec and GloVe as the pre-trained word embedding. We used four different datasets of word pairs with four binary attributes: Male-Female, Singular-Plural, Capital-Country, and Antonym (Table 1). These word pairs were collected from analogy test sets (Mikolov et al., 2013a; Gladkova et al., 2016) and the Internet. Noun antonyms were taken from the literature (Nguyen et al., 2017). For non-attribute dataset $\mathcal{N}$, we sampled words from the vocabulary of word embedding. We sampled from 4 to 50 words for training and 1000 for the test ($|\mathcal{N}_{\text{test}}| = 1000$).

Table 1: Statistics of binary attribute word pair datasets (in number of word pairs)

Dataset $\mathcal{A}$	Train	Val	Test	Total
Male-Female (MF)	29	12	12	53
Singular-Plural (SP)	90	25	25	140
Capital-Country (CC)	59	25	25	109
Antonym (AN)	1354	290	290	1934

5.1   Evaluation Metrics

We measured the accuracy and stability performances of the word attribute transfer. The accuracy measures how many input words in $\mathcal{A}_{\text{test}}$ were transferred correctly to the corresponding target words. The stability score measures how many words in $\mathcal{N}_{\text{test}}$ were not mapped to other words. For example, in the Male-Female transfer, given *man*, the transfer is regarded as correct if *woman* is the closest word to the transferred vector; otherwise it is incorrect. Given *person*, the transfer is regarded as correct if *person* is the closest word to the transferred vector; otherwise it is incorrect. The accuracy and stability scores are calculated by the following formula:

$$\delta(\mathbf{v}_y, t) = \begin{cases} 1 & \text{if } \arg\max_{k \in \mathcal{V}}(\cos(\mathbf{v}_y, \mathbf{v}_k)) = t \\ 0 & \text{otherwise,} \end{cases} \quad (20)$$

$$\text{Accuracy} = \frac{1}{|\mathcal{A}_{\text{test}}|} \sum_{(x,t,\mathbf{Z}) \in \mathcal{A}_{\text{test}}} \delta(\mathbf{v}_y, t), \quad (21)$$

$$\text{Stability} = \frac{1}{|\mathcal{N}_{\text{test}}|} \sum_{(x,\mathbf{Z}) \in \mathcal{N}_{\text{test}}} \delta(\mathbf{v}_y, x), \quad (22)$$

where $\mathcal{V}$ is the vocabulary of the word embedding model and $\cos(\mathbf{v}_y, \mathbf{v}_k)$ is the cosine similarity measure, defined as: $\cos(\mathbf{v}_y, \mathbf{v}_k) = \frac{\mathbf{v}_y \cdot \mathbf{v}_k}{\|\mathbf{v}_y\| \|\mathbf{v}_k\|}$.

5.2   Methods and Configurations

In our experiment, we compared our proposed method with the following baseline methods[2]:

REF Reflection-based word attribute transfer with a single mirror. We used a fully connected 2-layer MLP with 300 hidden units and ReLU (Glorot et al., 2011) to estimate $\mathbf{a}$ and $\mathbf{c}$.

REF+PM Reflection-based word attribute transfer with *parameterized mirrors*. We used the same architecture of MLP as the REF.

MLP Fully connected MLP with 300 hidden units and ReLU: $\mathbf{v}_y = \text{MLP}([\mathbf{v}_x; \mathbf{z}])$. The highest accuracy models in SGNS are a 2-layer MLP for Capital-Country and 3-layer MLP for the other datasets. The highest accuracy models in GloVe are a 2-layer MLP for Singular-Plural and 3-layer MLP for the other datasets.

DIFF Analogy-based word attribute transfer with a difference vector: $\mathbf{d} = \mathbf{v}_m - \mathbf{v}_w$, where m and w are in the training data of $\mathcal{A}$. We chose $\mathbf{d}$ that achieved the best accuracy in the validation data of $\mathcal{A}$. We determined whether to add or subtract $\mathbf{d}$ to $\mathbf{v}_x$ based on the explicit knowledge (Eq. 4). DIFF$^+$ and DIFF$^-$ transfer with a difference vector regardless of the explicit knowledge. $^+$ and $^-$ add or subtract the difference vector to any input word vector.

MEANDIFF Analogy-based word attribute transfer with a mean difference vector $\bar{\mathbf{d}}$: $\bar{\mathbf{d}} = \frac{1}{|\mathcal{A}_{\text{train}}|} \sum_{(m_i, w_i, \mathbf{Z}) \in \mathcal{A}_{\text{train}}} (\mathbf{v}_{m_i} - \mathbf{v}_{w_i})$. We determined whether to add or subtract $\bar{\mathbf{d}}$ to $\mathbf{v}_x$ based on the explicit knowledge (Eq. 4).

For proposed methods, we used the Adam optimizer (Kingma and Ba, 2015) with $\alpha = 10^{-4}$ for Male-Female, Singular-Plural and Capital-Country,

---

[2]Our code and datasets are available at: `https://github.com/ahclab/reflection`

and $\alpha = 15^{-3}$ for Antonym (the other hyperparameters were the same as the original one (Kingma and Ba, 2015)). We did not use such regularization methods as dropout (Srivastava et al., 2014) or batch normalization (Ioffe and Szegedy, 2015) because they did not show any improvement in our pilot test. We implemented REF, REF+PM and MLP with Chainer (Tokui et al., 2019), which is one of the best deep learning frameworks.

5.3 Evaluation in Accuracy and Stability

Table 2 shows the accuracy and stability results. Different pre-trained word embeddings GloVe or word2vec gave similar results. REF+PM achieved the best accuracy among the methods that did not use explicit attribute knowledge. For example, the accuracy of REF+PM was 76% in Capital-Country, but the accuracy of DIFF$^+$ was 26%. For stability, reflection-based transfers achieved outstanding stability scores that exceeded 99%. The results show that our proposed method transfers an input word if it has a target attribute and does not transfer an input word with better score than the baselines otherwise, even though the proposed method does not use attribute knowledge of the input words. MLP worked poorly both in accuracy and stability. On the antonym dataset, although the transfer accuracy by the proposed method was a bit lower than that by MLP, the proposed methods stability was 100% and that of MLP was extremely poor: about 1%.

We investigated the relation between the training data size of the non-attribute words, and the stability of the learning-based methods by conducting an additional experiment that varied $|\mathcal{N}_{\mathrm{train}}|$. The stability scores by MLP did not improve (Table 3). On the other hand, REF+PM achieved high stability scores with $|\mathcal{N}_{\mathrm{train}}| = 0$ and maintained the accuracy. We hypothesized that the high stability came from the distance between the word and its mirror. If non-attribute words are distributed on the mirror, they will not be transferred. We investigated the distance between input word vector $\mathbf{v}_x$ and its mirror (Fig. 4). The result shows that non-attribute words are close to the mirror, and attribute words are distributed away from it. In Male-Female and Singular-Plural, the distance is not significantly farther than Antonym and Capital-Country. If the distance between paired words is very small, the distance between the word and its mirror is also small. Fig. 5 shows the distribution of the distance between input $\mathbf{v}_x$ and target word vector $\mathbf{v}_t$.

The distance of Male-Female and Singular-Plural is much smaller than Capital-Country and Antonym.

5.4 Visualization of Parameterized Mirrors

Figure 6 shows the t-SNE results of mirror parameter $\mathbf{a}$ obtained for the test words. Paired mirror, $(\mathbf{a}_x, \mathbf{a}_t)$, is connected by a line segment. Fig. 6 suggests that the mirror parameters of the paired words are similar to each other and that those with the attribute form a cluster; words with the same attribute have similar mirror parameters $\mathbf{a}$.

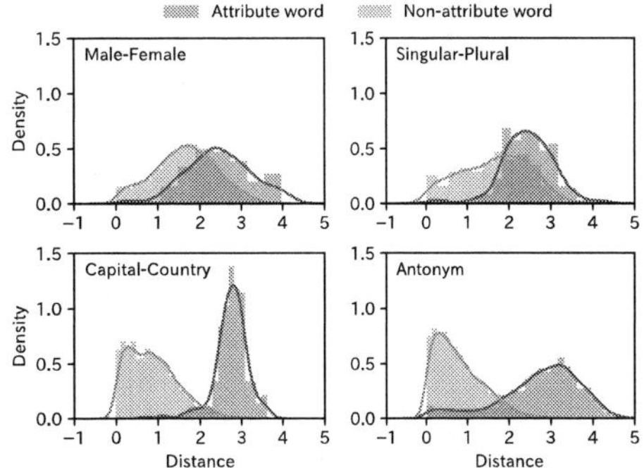

Figure 4: Distribution of distance between input word vector and its mirror $\frac{|(\mathbf{v}_x - \mathbf{c}) \cdot \mathbf{a}|}{\|\mathbf{a}\|}$ learned by REF+PM. Non-attribute words are close to the mirror, and attribute words are distributed away from it.

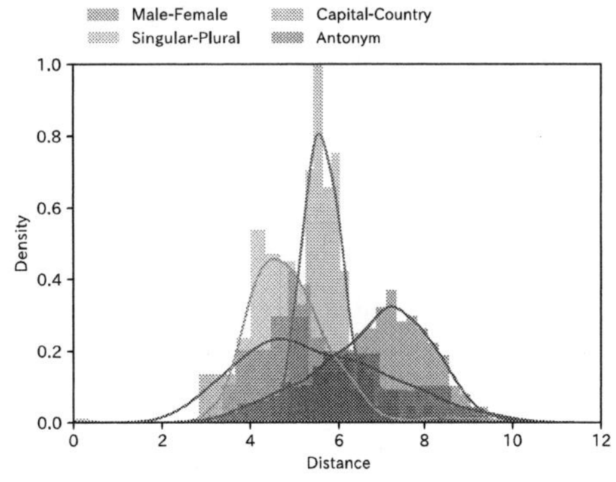

Figure 5: Distribution of distance between input word vector $\mathbf{v}_x$ and target word vector $\mathbf{v}_t$

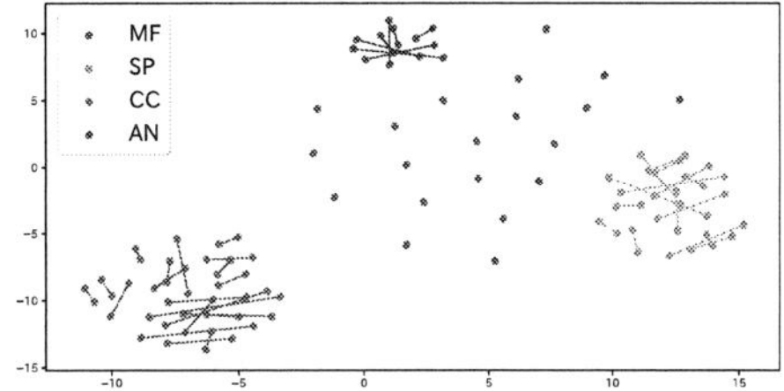

Figure 6: Two-dimensional t-SNE projection of $\mathbf{a}$

Table 2: Results in accuracy and stability scores: MF, SP, CC, and AN are datasets.

Method	Knowledge	word2vec								GloVe							
		Accuracy (%)				Stability (%)				Accuracy (%)				Stability (%)			
		MF	SP	CC	AN	MF	SP	CC	AN	MF	SP	CC	AN	MF	SP	CC	AN
REF		20.8	0.0	36.0	0.0	99.8	**100.0**	**99.8**	**100.0**	12.5	2.0	26.0	0.0	**100.0**	**100.0**	**100.0**	**100.0**
REF+PM		**41.7**	**22.0**	**58.0**	28.8	**99.9**	99.4	99.4	**100.0**	**45.8**	**50.0**	**76.0**	33.5	99.7	99.1	99.2	**100.0**
MLP		8.3	4.0	12.0	**35.9**	2.2	0.0	2.7	1.9	4.2	10.0	18.0	**36.7**	5.1	7.0	5.2	1.2
DIFF $^+$		25.0	2.0	32.0	-	72.1	77.9	53.9	-	25.0	2.0	26.0	-	99.3	94.2	99.3	-
DIFF $^-$		25.0	2.0	30.0	-	49.6	78.2	56.3	-	25.0	2.0	24.0	-	**100.0**	99.9	99.5	-
MEANDIFF $^+$		4.2	0.0	22.0	-	98.6	99.4	87.6	-	0.0	0.0	22.0	-	**100.0**	**100.0**	**100.0**	-
MEANDIFF $^-$		8.3	0.0	14.0	-	97.2	99.3	92.4	-	0.0	0.0	0.0	-	**100.0**	**100.0**	**100.0**	-
DIFF	✓	62.5	4.0	64.0	-	-	-	-	-	50.0	4.0	44.0	-	-	-	-	-
MEANDIFF	✓	12.5	0.0	36.0	-	-	-	-	-	0.0	0.0	0.0	-	-	-	-	-

Table 3: Relation among size of $|\mathcal{N}_{\text{train}}|$ and stability of learning-based methods

		Accuracy (%)				Stability (%)			
		$|\mathcal{N}_{\text{train}}|$				$|\mathcal{N}_{\text{train}}|$			
		0	4	10	50	0	4	10	50
MF	REF	12.5	12.5	12.5	12.5	**100.0**	**100.0**	**100.0**	**100.0**
	REF+PM	**45.8**	**41.7**	**37.5**	**41.7**	99.7	99.9	99.9	99.9
	MLP	0.0	4.2	0.0	4.2	0.0	0.4	1.0	5.0
SP	REF	0.0	0.0	2.0	0.0	**100.0**	**100.0**	**100.0**	**100.0**
	REF+PM	**48.0**	**40.0**	**50.0**	**46.0**	53.3	99.1	99.1	99.8
	MLP	4.0	6.0	6.0	10.0	0.0	0.5	1.7	7.0
CC	REF	24.0	26.0	24.0	20.0	**100.0**	**100.0**	**100.0**	**100.0**
	REF+PM	**76.0**	**72.0**	**74.0**	**74.0**	99.2	**100.0**	99.9	99.9
	MLP	16.0	10.0	14.0	18.0	0.0	0.4	1.0	5.2
AN	REF	0.0	0.0	0.0	0.0	**100.0**	**100.0**	**100.0**	**100.0**
	REF+PM	26.9	26.7	33.5	25.7	**100.0**	**100.0**	**100.0**	**100.0**
	MLP	**29.5**	**29.7**	**36.7**	**36.6**	0.1	0.5	1.2	4.6

5.5 Transfer Example

Table 4 shows the gender transfer results for a tiny example sentence. Here the attribute transfer was applied to every word in the sentence. MLP made many wrong transfers. Analogy-based transfers can transfer only in one direction. REF+PM can transfer only attribute words. Table 5 shows that words with different target attributes were transferred by each reflection-based transfer.

Table 4: Comparison of gender transfers. Each method transfers words in a sentence one by one.

X	the woman got married when you were a boy.
REF	the **woman** got married when you were a **boy**.
REF+PM	the **man** got married when you were a **girl**.
DIFF $^+$	the **man** got married when you were a **boy**.
DIFF $^-$	she **woman** got married she you were a **girl**.
MLP	By_Katie_Klingsporn **girlfriend** Valerie_Glodowski fiancee Doughty_Evening_Chronicle ma'am Bob_Grossweiner_& a **mother**.

Table 5: Transfer of different attributes with REF+PM

X	the rich actor wants to visit the beautiful city in tokyo.
+ MF	the rich **actress** wants to visit the beautiful city in tokyo.
+ SP	the rich **actresses** wants to visit the beautiful **cities** in tokyo.
+ CC	the rich actresses wants to visit the beautiful cities in **japan**.
+ AN	the **poor** actresses wants to visit the beautiful cities in japan.

6 Related Work

The theory of analogic relations in word embeddings has been widely discussed (Levy and Goldberg, 2014b; Arora et al., 2016; Gittens et al., 2017; Ethayarajh et al., 2019; Allen and Hospedales, 2019; Linzen, 2016). In our work, we focus on the analogic relations in a word embedding space and propose a novel framework to obtain a word vector with inverted attributes. The style transfer task (Niu et al., 2018; Prabhumoye et al., 2018; Logeswaran et al., 2018; Jain et al., 2019; Dai et al., 2019; Lample et al., 2019) resembles ours. In style transfer, the text style of the input sentences is changed. For instance, Jain et al. (2019) transferred from formal to informal sentences. These style transfer tasks use sentence pairs; our word attribute transfer task uses word pairs. Style transfer changes sentence styles, but our task changes the word attributes. Soricut and Och (2015) studied morphological transformation based on character information. Our work aims for more general attribute transfer, such as gender transfer and antonym, and is not limited to morphological transformation.

7 Conclusion

This research aims to transfer word binary attributes (e.g., gender) for applications such as data augmentation of a sentence. We can transfer the word attribute with analogy of word vectors, but it requires explicit knowledge whether the input word has the attribute or not (e.g., *man* $\in$ gender, *woman* $\in$ gender, *person* $\notin$ gender). The proposed method transfers binary word attributes using reflection-based mappings and keeps non-attribute words unchanged, without attribute knowledge in inference time. The experimental results showed that the proposed method outperforms analogy-based and MLP baselines in transfer accuracy for attribute words and stability for non-attribute words.

References

Carl Allen and Timothy M. Hospedales. 2019. Analogies Explained: Towards Understanding Word Embeddings. In *Proceedings of the 36th International Conference on Machine Learning, ICML 2019, 9-15 June 2019, Long Beach, California, USA*, pages 223–231.

Sanjeev Arora, Yuanzhi Li, Yingyu Liang, Tengyu Ma, and Andrej Risteski. 2016. A Latent Variable Model Approach to PMI-based Word Embeddings. *Transactions of the Association for Computational Linguistics*, 4:385–399.

Piotr Bojanowski, Edouard Grave, Armand Joulin, and Tomas Mikolov. 2017. Enriching Word Vectors with Subword Information. *Transactions of the Association for Computational Linguistics*, 5:135–146.

Kenneth Ward Church and Patrick Hanks. 1990. Word Association Norms, Mutual Information, and Lexicography. *Computational Linguistics*, 16(1):22–29.

Ning Dai, Jianze Liang, Xipeng Qiu, and Xuanjing Huang. 2019. Style Transformer: Unpaired Text Style Transfer without Disentangled Latent Representation. In *Proceedings of the 57th Conference of the Association for Computational Linguistics, ACL 2019, Florence, Italy, July 28- August 2, 2019, Volume 1: Long Papers*, pages 5997–6007.

Kawin Ethayarajh, David Duvenaud, and Graeme Hirst. 2019. Towards Understanding Linear Word Analogies. In *Proceedings of the 57th Conference of the Association for Computational Linguistics, ACL 2019, Florence, Italy, July 28- August 2, 2019, Volume 1: Long Papers*, pages 3253–3262.

Alex Gittens, Dimitris Achlioptas, and Michael W. Mahoney. 2017. Skip-Gram - Zipf + Uniform = Vector Additivity. In *Proceedings of the 55th Annual Meeting of the Association for Computational Linguistics, ACL 2017, Vancouver, Canada, July 30 - August 4, Volume 1: Long Papers*, pages 69–76.

Anna Gladkova, Aleksandr Drozd, and Satoshi Matsuoka. 2016. Analogy-based detection of morphological and semantic relations with word embeddings: what works and what doesn't. In *Proceedings of the Student Research Workshop, SRW@HLT-NAACL 2016, The 2016 Conference of the North American Chapter of the Association for Computational Linguistics: Human Language Technologies, San Diego California, USA, June 12-17, 2016*, pages 8–15.

Xavier Glorot, Antoine Bordes, and Yoshua Bengio. 2011. Deep Sparse Rectifier Neural Networks. In *Proceedings of the Fourteenth International Conference on Artificial Intelligence and Statistics, AISTATS 2011, Fort Lauderdale, USA, April 11-13, 2011*, pages 315–323.

Sergey Ioffe and Christian Szegedy. 2015. Batch Normalization: Accelerating Deep Network Training by Reducing Internal Covariate Shift. In *Proceedings of the 32nd International Conference on Machine Learning, ICML 2015, Lille, France, 6-11 July 2015*, pages 448–456.

Parag Jain, Abhijit Mishra, Amar Prakash Azad, and Karthik Sankaranarayanan. 2019. Unsupervised Controllable Text Formalization. In *The Thirty-Third AAAI Conference on Artificial Intelligence, AAAI 2019, The Thirty-First Innovative Applications of Artificial Intelligence Conference, IAAI 2019, The Ninth AAAI Symposium on Educational Advances in Artificial Intelligence, EAAI 2019, Honolulu, Hawaii, USA, January 27 - February 1, 2019.*, pages 6554–6561.

Masahiro Kaneko and Danushka Bollegala. 2019. Gender-preserving Debiasing for Pre-trained Word Embeddings. In *Proceedings of the 57th Conference of the Association for Computational Linguistics, ACL 2019, Florence, Italy, July 28- August 2, 2019, Volume 1: Long Papers*, pages 1641–1650.

Diederik P. Kingma and Jimmy Ba. 2015. Adam: A Method for Stochastic Optimization. In *3rd International Conference on Learning Representations, ICLR 2015, San Diego, CA, USA, May 7-9, 2015, Conference Track Proceedings*.

Guillaume Lample, Sandeep Subramanian, Eric Michael Smith, Ludovic Denoyer, Marc'Aurelio Ranzato, and Y-Lan Boureau. 2019. Multiple-Attribute Text Rewriting. In *7th International Conference on Learning Representations, ICLR 2019, New Orleans, LA, USA, May 6-9, 2019*.

Omer Levy and Yoav Goldberg. 2014a. Linguistic Regularities in Sparse and Explicit Word Representations. In *Proceedings of the Eighteenth Conference on Computational Natural Language Learning, CoNLL 2014, Baltimore, Maryland, USA, June 26-27, 2014*, pages 171–180.

Omer Levy and Yoav Goldberg. 2014b. Neural Word Embedding as Implicit Matrix Factorization. In *Advances in Neural Information Processing Systems 27: Annual Conference on Neural Information Processing Systems 2014, December 8-13 2014, Montreal, Quebec, Canada*, pages 2177–2185.

Tal Linzen. 2016. Issues in evaluating semantic spaces using word analogies. In *Proceedings of the 1st Workshop on Evaluating Vector-Space Representations for NLP, RepEval@ACL 2016, Berlin, Germany, August 2016*, pages 13–18.

Lajanugen Logeswaran, Honglak Lee, and Samy Bengio. 2018. Content preserving text generation with attribute controls. In *Advances in Neural Information Processing Systems 31: Annual Conference on Neural Information Processing Systems 2018, NeurIPS 2018, 3-8 December 2018, Montréal, Canada.*, pages 5108–5118.

Tomas Mikolov, Kai Chen, Greg Corrado, and Jeffrey Dean. 2013a. Efficient Estimation of Word Representations in Vector Space. In *1st International Conference on Learning Representations, ICLR 2013, Scottsdale, Arizona, USA, May 2-4, 2013, Workshop Track Proceedings*.

Tomas Mikolov, Ilya Sutskever, Kai Chen, Gregory S. Corrado, and Jeffrey Dean. 2013b. Distributed Representations of Words and Phrases and their Compositionality. In *Advances in Neural Information Processing Systems 26: 27th Annual Conference on Neural Information Processing Systems 2013. Proceedings of a meeting held December 5-8, 2013, Lake Tahoe, Nevada, United States.*, pages 3111–3119.

Tomas Mikolov, Wen-tau Yih, and Geoffrey Zweig. 2013c. Linguistic Regularities in Continuous Space Word Representations. In *Human Language Technologies: Conference of the North American Chapter of the Association of Computational Linguistics, Proceedings, June 9-14, 2013, Westin Peachtree Plaza Hotel, Atlanta, Georgia, USA*, pages 746–751.

Kim Anh Nguyen, Sabine Schulte im Walde, and Ngoc Thang Vu. 2017. Distinguishing Antonyms and Synonyms in a Pattern-based Neural Network. In *Proceedings of the 15th Conference of the European Chapter of the Association for Computational Linguistics, EACL 2017, Valencia, Spain, April 3-7, 2017, Volume 1: Long Papers*, pages 76–85.

Xing Niu, Sudha Rao, and Marine Carpuat. 2018. Multi-Task Neural Models for Translating Between Styles Within and Across Languages. In *Proceedings of the 27th International Conference on Computational Linguistics, COLING 2018, Santa Fe, New Mexico, USA, August 20-26, 2018*, pages 1008–1021.

Jeffrey Pennington, Richard Socher, and Christopher D. Manning. 2014. Glove: Global Vectors for Word Representation. In *Proceedings of the 2014 Conference on Empirical Methods in Natural Language Processing, EMNLP 2014, October 25-29, 2014, Doha, Qatar, A meeting of SIGDAT, a Special Interest Group of the ACL*, pages 1532–1543.

Shrimai Prabhumoye, Yulia Tsvetkov, Ruslan Salakhutdinov, and Alan W. Black. 2018. Style Transfer Through Back-Translation. In *Proceedings of the 56th Annual Meeting of the Association for Computational Linguistics, ACL 2018, Melbourne, Australia, July 15-20, 2018, Volume 1: Long Papers*, pages 866–876.

Radu Soricut and Franz Josef Och. 2015. Unsupervised Morphology Induction Using Word Embeddings. In *NAACL HLT 2015, The 2015 Conference of the North American Chapter of the Association for Computational Linguistics: Human Language Technologies, Denver, Colorado, USA, May 31 - June 5, 2015*, pages 1627–1637.

Nitish Srivastava, Geoffrey E. Hinton, Alex Krizhevsky, Ilya Sutskever, and Ruslan Salakhutdinov. 2014. Dropout: a simple way to prevent neural networks from overfitting. *J. Mach. Learn. Res.*, 15(1):1929–1958.

Seiya Tokui, Ryosuke Okuta, Takuya Akiba, Yusuke Niitani, Toru Ogawa, Shunta Saito, Shuji Suzuki, Kota Uenishi, Brian Vogel, and Hiroyuki Yamazaki Vincent. 2019. Chainer: A Deep Learning Framework for Accelerating the Research Cycle. In *Proceedings of the 25th ACM SIGKDD International Conference on Knowledge Discovery & Data Mining, KDD 2019, Anchorage, AK, USA, August 4-8, 2019*, pages 2002–2011.

Luke Vilnis and Andrew McCallum. 2015. Word Representations via Gaussian Embedding. In *3rd International Conference on Learning Representations, ICLR 2015, San Diego, CA, USA, May 7-9, 2015, Conference Track Proceedings*.

Jieyu Zhao, Yichao Zhou, Zeyu Li, Wei Wang, and Kai-Wei Chang. 2018. Learning Gender-Neutral Word Embeddings. In *Proceedings of the 2018 Conference on Empirical Methods in Natural Language Processing, Brussels, Belgium, October 31 - November 4, 2018*, pages 4847–4853.

Topic Balancing with Additive Regularization of Topic Models

Veselova Eugeniia
Moscow Institute
of Physics and Technology
Moscow, Russia
veselova.er@phystech.edu

Vorontsov Konstantin
Moscow Institute
of Physics and Technology
Moscow, Russia
vokov@forecsys.ru

Abstract

This article proposes a new approach for building topic models on unbalanced collections in topic modelling, based on the existing methods and our experiments with such methods. Real-world data collections contain topics in various proportions, and often documents of the relatively small theme become distributed all over the larger topics instead of being grouped into one topic. To address this issue, we design a new regularizer for Θ and Φ matrices in probabilistic Latent Semantic Analysis (pLSA) model. We make sure this regularizer increases the quality of topic models, trained on unbalanced collections. Besides, we conceptually support this regularizer by our experiments.

1 Introduction

Topic modelling is a widespread approach to unsupervised text analysis and clustering. Given the number of latent variables — topics — topic models extract hidden word$\times$topic and topic$\times$document probability distributions from text corpora. Topic models have proven to be relevant in a wide range of contexts and uni- and multilingual tasks (Uys et al., 2008; De Smet and Moens, 2009; Boyd-Graber et al., 2017).

Two fundamental topic models are probabilistic Latent Semantic Analysis — pLSA (Hofmann, 1999) and Latent Dirichlet Allocation — LDA (Blei et al., 2003). Various extensions of pLSA and LDA models have emerged over the past years, e.g. Additive Regularization of Topic Models (ARTM) (Vorontsov and Potapenko, 2015) modification of pLSA, where required solution properties are induced by the additional regularizer part in the model. Through regularizers one can take into consideration various problem-specific features of data, and this is a reason why we apply ARTM-framework in our work.

Despite almost 30 years of model development history, lots of problems and issues were raised in the topic modelling field. Problem of the "order effect" in LDA (Agrawal et al., 2018), for example. It consists in converging to the different topics set while during training on the unstructured data. Even with the structured data solution in the pLSA or LDA model is non-unique and unstable. Such unstability may be reduced by tuning the model with regularizers, as in the ARTM model. Inserting Φ and Θ prior distribution into the model, according to the (Wallach et al., 2009), promotes convergence to the better and stable solution along with regularization. However, many problems with models itself and with quality metrics remain unsolved.

In this article, we point out the topic balancing problem. At this moment problem of training topic models on the unbalanced collections is not studied thoroughly and is far from the comprehensive solution. We examine previously suggested approach to the topic balancing and propose a balancing procedure, based on the a priori ratio between topic capacities.

2 Problem statement

2.1 Topic modelling introduction

Let D denote the text corpora, W denote the set of words in the corpora, or the corpora vocabulary, and T denote the set of the topics. Every document $d \in D$ is presented as a token sequence $(w_1, w_2, \ldots, w_{n_d})$ of length n_d from the vocabulary of size n. In the models, based on the "bag-of-words" hypothesis, the more compact way to represent a document is to consider the document as a vocabulary multiset, where each token $w \in d$ occurs n_{dw} times in the document.

Topic model describes conditional probabilities $p(w|d)$ of the appearance of the tokens w in the documents d through the probabilities of the to-

Proceedings of the 58th Annual Meeting of the Association for Computational Linguistics: Student Research Workshop, pages 59–65
July 5 - July 10, 2020. ©2020 Association for Computational Linguistics

kens in the topics $\varphi_{wt} = p(w|t)$ and topics in the documents $\theta_{td} = p(t|d)$. To build a probabilistic generative model, we consider further hypotheses fulfilled:

- conditional independence hypothesis: each topic generates tokens regardless of the document;

$$p(w|d, t) = p(w|t)$$

- "bag-of-words" hypothesis: words order in the document does not affect desired distributions;

- a finite set of topics T exist in the corpora, and each token occurrence in each document refers to some latent topic from T.

According to the law of total probability and the assumption of conditional independence

$$p(w|d) = \sum_{t \in T} \varphi_{wt} \theta_{td}$$

This probabilistic model describes how the collection D is generated from the known distributions $p(w|t)$ and $p(t|d)$. Learning a topic model is an inverse problem: obtaining tokens–topics and topics–documents distributions $p(w|t)$ and $p(t|d)$ given a corpora D. This problem is equivalent to finding a stochastic matrix decomposition of counter matrix as a product $F \approx \Phi\Theta$, where matrix Φ represents *tokens probabilities for the topics* and Θ represents *topic probabilities for the documents*:

$$F = (\hat{p}(w|d))_{W \times D}, \ \hat{p}(w|d) = \frac{n_{wd}}{n_d}$$

$$\Phi = (\varphi_{wt})_{W \times T}, \ \varphi_{wt} = p(w|t)$$

$$\Theta = (\theta_{td})_{T \times D}, \ \theta_{td} = p(t|d)$$

In pLSA the topic model is learned by log-likelihood maximization through EM-algorithm

$$L(\Phi, \Theta) = \sum_{d \in D, w \in d} n_{dw} \log \sum_{t \in T} \varphi_{wt} \theta_{td} \to \max_{\Phi, \Theta} \tag{1}$$

Further details can be found in the Appendix A.

Since the matrix product $\Phi\Theta$ is defined up to a linear transformation, solution of the problem is not unique and, therefore, is unstable. Additional objectives called *regularizers*, depending on the Θ and Φ matrices, can be included in the log-likelihood along with their non-negative *regularization coefficients* τ to reduce the solution domain.

Likelihood maximization problem (1) with r regularizers then takes the following form:

$$L(\Phi, \Theta) + \sum_{i=1}^{r} \tau_i R_i(\Phi, \Theta) \to \max_{\Phi, \Theta} \tag{2}$$

Solution of the problem therefore transforms to

$$p_{\hat{t}dw} = \frac{\varphi_{w\hat{t}} \theta_{\hat{t}d}}{\sum\limits_{t \in T} \varphi_{wt} \theta_{td}}$$

$$\varphi_{wt} = \underset{w \in W}{\text{norm}} \left(n_{wt} + \varphi_{wt} \frac{\partial R}{\partial \varphi_{wt}} \right)$$

$$\theta_{wt} = \underset{t \in T}{\text{norm}} \left(n_{td} + \theta_{td} \frac{\partial R}{\partial \theta_{td}} \right)$$

where

$$n_{wt} = \sum_{d \in D} n_{dw} p_{tdw}, \ n_{td} = \sum_{w \in d} n_{dw} p_{tdw}$$

Regularization approach and theorem proofs can be found in (Vorontsov and Potapenko, 2015)

2.2 Topic balancing problem statement

Let $n_t = \sum\limits_{d \in D} p(t|d) n_d$ denote the *topic capacity* of the topic t. Let $k = \frac{n_{t_{max}}}{n_{t_{min}}}$ denote the *imbalance degree* of the model; with $p(t) = \frac{n_t}{n}$ denoting the *topic probability* and $N(\hat{t}) = |\{d \in D | \underset{t}{\text{argmax}} \ \theta_{td} = \hat{t}\}|$, we can denote *documents imbalance degree* $k = \frac{N_{t_{max}}}{N_{t_{min}}}$ too. Probabilistic topic models, based on the matrix factorization, tend to spread documents by topics uniformly and extract topics with the equal capacity. In order to maximize log-likelihood, model should engage all inner parameters for data description. Reducing the topics number, meaning reducing the number of available parameters, is unprofitable for the model in terms of EM-algorithm optimization, therefore strong proportion reduction of the particular topic is unprofitable too. Experiments show that in the pLSA and LDA models imbalance degree rarely exceeds 3-4.

Similar problem arises in the multiclass classification with imbalanced data, where classifying model prefers predicting the label of the most common class for every object to reduce the number of errors in classification. The standard approach to imbalanced data problem is a class weighting. It can help to provide some bias towards the minority classes while training the model, and thus help in improving performance of the model while classifying various classes. Documents imbalance leads to overweight of the vocabulary of predominant topics in the collection. This effect exaggerates "word burstiness" in the model (Doyle and Elkan, 2009; Lei et al., 2011) in terms of documents: if a collection has disproportion of topics, a document is likely to belong to the widely represented topic.

Let us call the model *imbalanced* if it can extract and maintain topics with the imbalance degree k up to 10. In this article, we examine different ways of balancing topics in topic models and building imbalanced models.

3 Topic balancing hypotheses

3.1 Iterative renormalization of parameter in the Dirichlet distribution

While formulating the probabilistic generative model in terms of LDA, topic distributions over words and document distributions over topics are generated from prior Dirichlet distributions. A learning algorithm for LDA can also be considered as an EM-like algorithm with modified M-step (Asuncion et al., 2009). The most simple and frequently used modification is the following:

$$\varphi_{wt} \propto n_{wt} + \beta_w, \; \theta_{td} \propto n_{td} + \alpha_t$$

Thus probabilities of words in topics and probabilities of topics in documents are estimated with apriori shift. This LDA modification is covered by the ARTM framework through the LDA regularizer

$$R(\Phi, \Theta) = \sum_t \sum_w (\beta_w - 1) \log \varphi_{wt} +$$
$$+ \sum_d \sum_t (\alpha_t - 1) \log \theta_{td}$$

and parameters of Dirichlet distributions can be manually adjusted.

We put forward a hypothesis that increasing Dirichlet parameters in proportion to the topic capacities similar to the classes weighing in unbalanced classification can countervail tendency of the EM-algorithm to decrease the capacity of the big topics and increase the capacity of the small topics.

For the modelling experiment we chose synthetic collection which consists of the two themes — business and music — with 1000 and 150 documents respectively. Two pairs of models were built to compare modelling results and evaluate balancing opportunity. First models were trained with two topics with and without renormalization, second — with six topics. In the second pair, the separation of topics was evident through each topic size and top-tokens: five topics had top-tokens from a big theme (with ~ 200 documents in each topic), the last one topic had top-tokens from a small theme. However, better topics were obtained with balanced Dirichlet parameters. In the first pair of models we implied that through the process of rebalancing Dirichlet parameters we could obtain two topics with ~ 150 and ~ 1000 documents each and different top-tokens. This hypothesis was not fully confirmed in the experiment: without the parameter renormalization EM-algorithm had converged to the topics with almost similar topic capacities, with parameter renormalization model maintained documents imbalance degree equal 2 instead of 7. Results of the experiment can be seen in Figure 1.

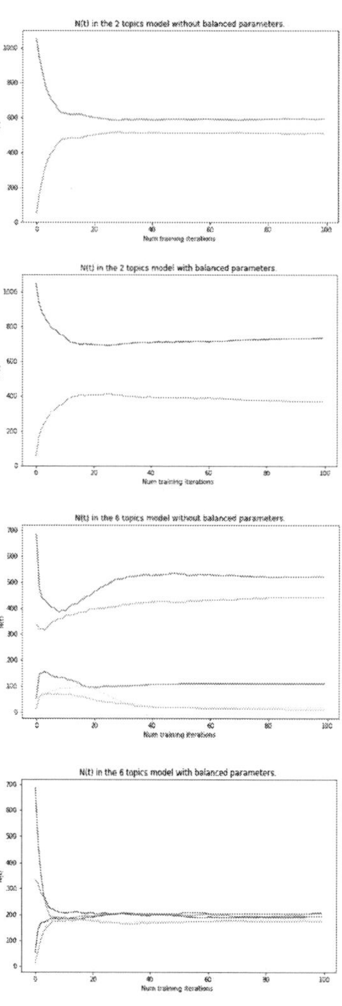

Figure 1: Results of LDA renormalization.

3.2 Rebalancing $p(t|d, w)$

Referring a weighting classes approach in the unbalanced classification task, we considered possibility to rebalance $p(t|d, w)$ (4). We proposed dividing n_{tdw} by n_t. However, the same experiment as with LDA model gave no positive results, and later, in the subsection, we are going to prove this hypothesis failure.

We show that dividing $p(t|d, w)$ by any value Z_t, which depends on t only, does not change Φ, but only leads to minor the topics redistribution in documents. Proof can be found in the Appendix B. We prove that during renormalization in the EM-algorithm, M-step formulas for Φ does not change, because normalizing multiplier Z_t is reduced. Therefore, pLSA renormalization does not influence the topics.

3.3 Φ initialization

According to the (Wallach et al., 2009), Φ and Θ prior distribution, inserted into the model, could promote stability of the solution. We followed this assumption and conducted an experiment, in which Φ matrix was initialized not randomly, as in the unmodified topic models, but with the previously calculated probabilities according to the foregone distribution of documents by topics. We suppose that the "real" Φ initialization along with the Θ, calculated from Φ, are the optimal factorization of the counter matrix F in terms of log-likelihood. Therefore, the overall topic balance and relative change of Φ matrix value must not be small enough ($\sim 1 - 3\%$).

For this experiment chose four synthetic collections with two themes about business and music: first collection consisted of 1000 and 10 documents per theme respectively, second consisted of 1000 and 100 documents, third consisted of 1000 and 300 documents, and fourth consisted of 1000 and 600 documents respectively.

The experiment was split into two levels: at the first level, we trained models without a priori Φ initialization, at the second level, beforehand calculated Φ matrix was used as an initial tokens–topics distribution for each model. All zero a priori probabilities in the calculated Φ matrix were replaced with the minimal possible probability value $\propto 10^{-5}$. Zero probabilities emerge when a word does not occur in any document of the foregone topic; hence we are not artificially limiting topic vocabularies by preserving zeroes. We were training

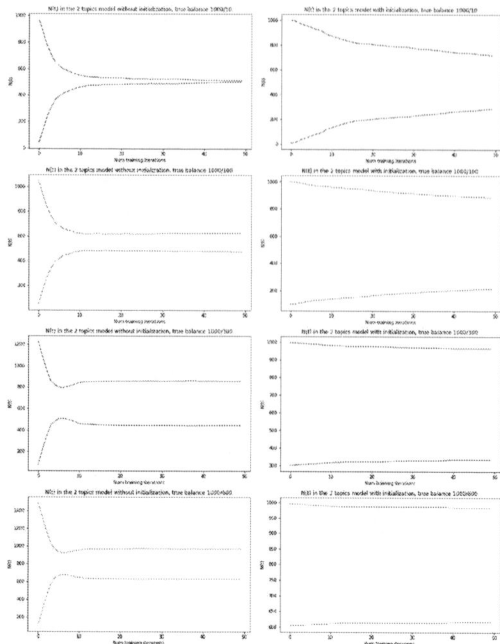

Figure 2: Results of a priori Φ initialization in pLSA model.

and comparing pairs of basic model with two topics and model with the initialization of the Φ matrix with two topics for each collection, eight models in sum. Regardless of the data collection, after first 10 training iterations, uninitialized models converged to the balanced solutions with almost equal $N(t)$, though initial initialization supported documents imbalance degree up to 6. This result is represented in Figure 2 through the topic's N(t). The left column represents the model without initialization, the right column represents the model with initialization with true topic's balance [10:1000, 100:1000, 300:1000, 600:1000] respectively.

4 Topic prior regularizer

4.1 Description of the regularizer

According to our experiments and modelling experience, log-likelihood functional optimization does not preserve topic balance in models and does not converge to the optimal solution from the user's point of view. We want an optimal solution to allow topics with relatively small topic capacities or topics with relatively small $p(t|d)$ for the most of corpora documents. Optimality in such terms can be achieved in a solution, where some topic variables, or degrees of freedom, are not fully utilized. Current functional during the optimization via EM-algorithm tends to redistribute $p(t|d)$ in the most efficient way, without degenerate distributions. Thus topic capacities obtain similar values during the training process.

We formed the hypothesis from our experiments, that additional shift in tokens–topics Φ may influence the EM-algorithm as a restriction of the degrees of freedom, supporting topics imbalance. By setting relative collection balance in Φ in advance, we can control possible collection balance after the training process. During the optimization, all φ_{wt} are specified according to the tokens distribution in documents. We implemented this hypothesis in a new ARTM regularizer $R_{TopicPrior}$ called *TopicPriorRegularizer* with the parameter β to describe a priori topic balance in the collection.

$$R_{TopicPrior}(\Phi, \Theta) = \sum_{t} \sum_{w} \beta_t \log \phi_{wt}$$

To better understand the $R_{TopicPrior}$ influence on the EM-algorithm, we calculated the $R_{TopicPrior}$ partial derivative:

$$\frac{\partial R}{\partial \Phi_{wt}} = \frac{\beta_t}{\varphi_{wt}}$$

and modified log-likelihood in case of one additional regularizer with regularization coefficient τ, determining regularizing strength:

$$\varphi_{wt} \propto n_{wt} + \tau \beta_t$$

In most of the cases, we lack knowledge about topic capacities in the researched data collection, therefore we cannot set precise β value. We generalize our regularization approach and propose $R_{TopicPriorSampled}$ regularizer, where β parameter is being sampled from the Dirichlet distribution with the parameter $\gamma \in \mathbb{R}^1$. γ is responsible for the estimated data sparsity, thus $\gamma = 1$ stands for the random topic capacities in a model, $\gamma \ll 1$ stands for the equal topic capacities, $\gamma \gg 1$ stands for the significantly uneven topic capacities.

$$\beta \sim \text{Dir}(\gamma), \ \gamma \in \mathbb{R}^1$$

4.2 Modelling experiments

For the first modelling experiment we chose synthetic collection with the two themes — business and music — with 1000 and 100 documents respectively. We build two models with two topics in

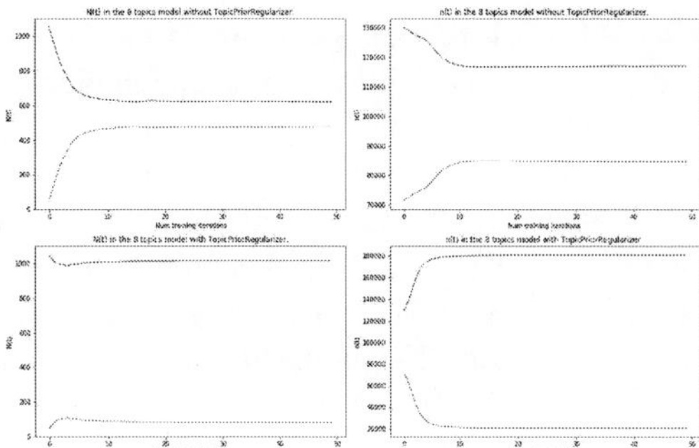

Figure 3: Results of unregularized and regularized pLSA model training with 2 topics.

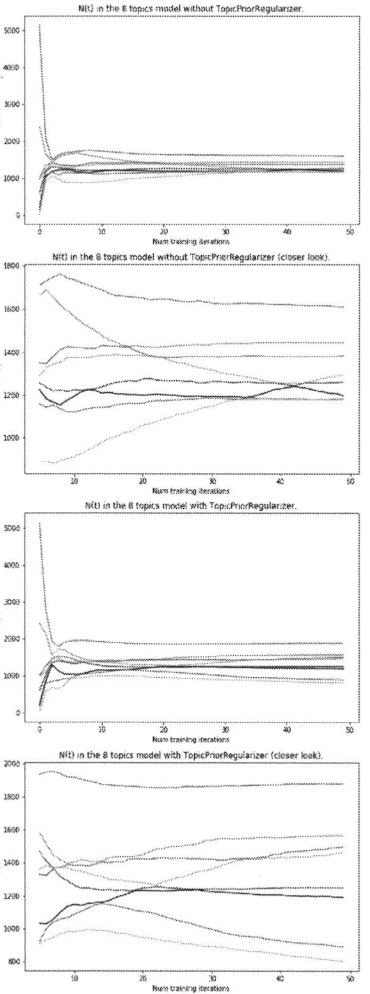

Figure 4: Results (N(t)) of unregularized and regularized pLSA model training with 8 topics.

each and train them for 15 epochs, however, the second model is trained with the $R_{TopicPrior}$, where $\beta = [0.1, 0.9]$. After training we evaluate both models by their perplexity, top-tokens and $n(t)$ for every topic in the model. The second model had extracted a small theme as a distinct topic, while the first unregularized model has two similar topics. Training results are presented in Figure 3: the first row represents model without regularizer, the second row represents regularized model; the left column represents N(t) of the topics, the right column represents n(t) of the topics.

For the second modelling experiment we choose collection with the eight themes, balanced with the following documents proportion: $doc\_prop =$ $[3000, 2000, 1500, 1000, 1000, 1000, 700, 350]$. Two models were trained on this collection: unregularized and regularized model, where regularizer was initialized with $\beta = \frac{doc\_prop}{sum(doc\_prop)}$. Figure Figure 4 and Figure 5 show better topics composition in the second model, compared to the first model results.

5   Discussion and conclusion

Learning an unbalanced topic model from unbalanced text collection is a non-trivial task for all of the existing modelling methods. In this paper we discussed the problem of training topic models with unbalanced text collections. No previous research provides a thorough analysis of this problem or an efficient training procedure for unbalanced models. After reviewing the problem, we proposed an approach to building topic models, able to maintain relatively high imbalance degree. We described our approach in terms of pLSA regularization and brought theoretical justification for the $R_{TopicPrior}$ regularizer.

References

Amritanshu Agrawal, Wei Fu, and Tim Menzies. 2018. What is wrong with topic modeling? And how to fix it using search-based software engineering. *Information and Software Technology*, 98:74–88.

Arthur Asuncion, Max Welling, Padhraic Smyth, and Yee Whye Teh. 2009. On smoothing and inference for topic models. In *Proceedings of the twenty-fifth conference on uncertainty in artificial intelligence*, pages 27–34. AUAI Press.

David M Blei, Andrew Y Ng, and Michael I Jordan. 2003. Latent Dirichlet allocation. *Journal of machine Learning research*, 3(Jan):993–1022.

Jordan Boyd-Graber, Yuening Hu, David Mimno, et al. 2017. Applications of topic models. *Foundations and Trends® in Information Retrieval*, 11(2-3):143–296.

Wim De Smet and Marie-Francine Moens. 2009. Cross-language linking of news stories on the web using interlingual topic modelling. In *Proceedings of the 2nd ACM workshop on Social web search and mining*, pages 57–64. ACM.

Gabriel Doyle and Charles Elkan. 2009. Accounting for burstiness in topic models. In *Proceedings of the 26th Annual International Conference on Machine Learning*, pages 281–288.

Thomas Hofmann. 1999. Probabilistic latent semantic analysis. In *Proceedings of the Fifteenth conference on Uncertainty in artificial intelligence*, pages 289–296. Morgan Kaufmann Publishers Inc.

Shaoze Lei, JianWen Zhang, Shifeng Weng, and Changshui Zhang. 2011. Topic model with constrained word burstiness intensities. In *The 2011 International Joint Conference on Neural Networks*, pages 68–74. IEEE.

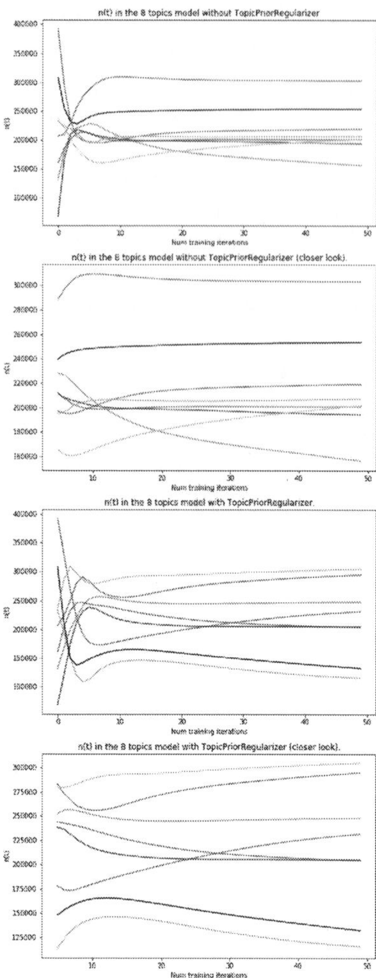

Figure 5: Results (n(t)) of unregularized and regularized pLSA model training with 8 topics.

JW Uys, ND Du Preez, and EW Uys. 2008. Leveraging unstructured information using topic modelling. In *PICMET'08-2008 Portland International Conference on Management of Engineering & Technology*, pages 955–961. IEEE.

Konstantin Vorontsov and Anna Potapenko. 2015. Additive regularization of topic models. *Machine Learning*, 101(1-3):303–323.

Hanna M Wallach, David M Mimno, and Andrew McCallum. 2009. Rethinking LDA: Why priors matter. In *Advances in neural information processing systems*, pages 1973–1981.

A pLSA and ARTM model optimization problem

In pLSA the topic model is learned by log-likelihood maximization through EM-algorithm

$$L(\Phi, \Theta) = \sum_{d \in D, w \in d} n_{dw} \log \sum_{t \in T} \varphi_{wt} \theta_{td} \to \max_{\Phi, \Theta}$$

$$(3)$$

with linear constraints of non-negativity and normalization:

$$\sum_{w \in W} \varphi_{wt} = 1, \ \varphi_{wt} \geq 1; \quad \sum_{t \in T} \theta_{td} = 1, \ \theta_{td} \geq 1$$

Solution of the pLSA problem satisfies the following system of equations with auxiliary variables p_{tdw}:

$$p_{\hat{t}dw} = \frac{\varphi_{w\hat{t}} \theta_{\hat{t}d}}{\sum_{t \in T} \varphi_{wt} \theta_{td}}$$

$$\varphi_{wt} = \operatorname*{norm}_{w \in W} (n_{wt}), \ n_{wt} = \sum_{d \in D} n_{dw} p_{tdw} \quad (4)$$

$$\theta_{wt} = \operatorname*{norm}_{t \in T} (n_{td}), \ n_{td} = \sum_{w \in d} n_{dw} p_{tdw}$$

Process of the calculation auxiliary variables p_{tdw} is an E-step, while model parameters elaboration by the calculated p_{tdw} is an M-step in the EM-algorithm.

B Proof of rebalancing failure

We considered possibility to rebalance $p(t|d, w)$ in accordance with weighting classes approach. We proposed dividing n_{tdw} by n_t.

We show that dividing $p(t|d, w)$ by any value Z_t, which depends on t only, doesn't change Φ, but only leads to minor the topics redistribution in documents. We put $R = 0$ in (2) for the sake of simplicity.

Investigating M-step of the EM-algorithm, we write down log-likelihood with renormalizing factor $\frac{1}{Z_t}$:

$$\frac{1}{Z_t} \sum_{d \in D} \sum_{w \in d} \sum_{t \in T} n_{dw} \varphi_{wt} \theta_{td} \to \max_{\Phi, \Theta}$$

and then separate variables Φ and Θ:

$$\sum_{w \in W} \sum_{t \in T} \frac{n_{wt}}{Z_t} \log \varphi_{wt} +$$

$$+ \sum_{d \in D} \sum_{t \in T} \frac{n_{td}}{Z_t} \log \theta_{td} \to \max_{\Phi, \Theta}$$

To solve this linear programming task, we apply Karush–Kuhn–Takker conditions. We write Lagrangian:

$$\mathcal{L}(\Phi, \Theta) = \sum_{w \in W} \sum_{t \in T} \frac{n_{wt}}{Z_t} \log \varphi_{wt} -$$

$$- \sum_{t \in T} \lambda_t \left(\sum_w \varphi_{wt} - 1 \right) +$$

$$+ \sum_{d \in D} \sum_{t \in T} \frac{n_{td}}{Z_t} \log \theta_{td} -$$

$$- \sum_{d \in D} \mu_d \left(\sum_{t \in T} \theta_{td} - 1 \right)$$

and equate its derivations to zero:

$$\frac{\partial \mathcal{L}}{\partial \varphi_{wt}} = \frac{n_{wt}}{Z_t \varphi_{wt}} - \lambda_t = 0$$

$$\lambda_t \varphi_{wt} = \frac{n_{wt}}{Z_t} \quad \Rightarrow \quad \lambda_t = \frac{n_t}{Z_t}$$

$$\varphi_{wt} = \operatorname*{norm}_{w \in W} (n_{wt})$$

and

$$\frac{\partial \mathcal{L}}{\partial \theta_{td}} = \frac{n_{td}}{Z_t \theta_{td}} - \mu_d = 0$$

$$\mu_d \theta_{td} = \frac{n_{td}}{Z_t} \quad \Rightarrow \quad \mu_d = \sum_{t \in T} \frac{n_{td}}{Z_t}$$

$$\theta_{td} = \operatorname*{norm}_{t \in T} \left(\frac{n_{td}}{Z_t} \right)$$

M-step formulas for Φ does not change, because normalizing multiplier Z_t is reduced. Therefore, pLSA renormalization has no influence on the topics.

Combining Subword Representations into
Word-level Representations in the Transformer Architecture

Noe Casas   **Marta R. Costa-jussà**   **José A. R. Fonollosa**
Universitat Politècnica de Catalunya
{noe.casas,marta.ruiz,jose.fonollosa}@upc.edu

Abstract

In Neural Machine Translation, using word-level tokens leads to degradation in translation quality. The dominant approaches use subword-level tokens, but this increases the length of the sequences and makes it difficult to profit from word-level information such as POS tags or semantic dependencies.

We propose a modification to the Transformer model to combine subword-level representations into word-level ones in the first layers of the encoder, reducing the effective length of the sequences in the following layers and providing a natural point to incorporate extra word-level information.

Our experiments show that this approach maintains the translation quality with respect to the normal Transformer model when no extra word-level information is injected and that it is superior to the currently dominant method for incorporating word-level source language information to models based on subword-level vocabularies.

1 Introduction

Currently dominant Neural Machine Translation (NMT) architectures receive as input sequences of discrete tokens taken from fixed-size source and target token vocabularies defined a priori. Before being fed to the network, the input text is tokenized and the positions of those tokens within the vocabulary table are the actual network inputs. The granularity of the tokens in those vocabularies can range from character-level, to subword-level, to word-level.

Character-level token granularity, while allowing maximum representation ability with minimal vocabulary size for alphabet-based scripts, also delegates word formation modeling to the network and makes token sequences to be much longer than with word-based tokens.

Using word-level tokens leads to very large vocabulary sizes, especially for morphologically rich languages, where the number of surface forms per lemma is high. Large token vocabularies are impractical for the current neural architectures and hardware. It is frequent to constrain the vocabulary size to a few tens of thousand tokens, which is hardly enough to fit the number of symbols in a complete word-based vocabulary. Compositional word structures like numbers pose further problems with such a granularity level, as well as proper nouns. When word-based vocabularies are used, the vocabulary is built with the most frequent surface forms in the training data, which normally leads to degradation of translation quality.

Subword-level token granularity offers a compromise between representational power and vocabulary size, especially statistically extracted subword vocabulary strategies like Byte Pair Encoding (BPE) (Sennrich et al., 2016b).

Models with word-level token vocabularies can incorporate word-level information as extra input to the model by combining it one-to-one with the token representations. Some examples of word-level information are Part of Speech (POS) tags, syntactic dependency relationships or lemmas. In order to make use of word-level information in models with subword-level token vocabularies, a usual approach is to assign the word information to all its subwords (Sennrich and Haddow, 2016). This approach, despite improving the translation quality, introduces an information assignment mismatch.

We propose to modify the Transformer architecture (Vaswani et al., 2017) to combine the learned subword representations into word representations in the encoder block. This allows to naturally incorporate any extra word-level information directly at the level of word-level representations.

This work is structured as follows: the relevant related work is described in section 2; the proposed

Proceedings of the 58th Annual Meeting of the Association for Computational Linguistics: Student Research Workshop, pages 66–71
July 5 - July 10, 2020. ©2020 Association for Computational Linguistics

approach is described in section 3, while the experimental setup is presented in section 4 and the results are described and discussed in section 5. Finally, the conclusions are drawn in section 6.

2 Related Work

The main difficulty in profiting from word-level information in subword-based NMT architectures is the word-subword token level mismatch.

Several lines of research have studied how to combine subword-level representations into word-level information in a task-agnostic way. While the approaches by Bojanowski et al. (2017), Zhao et al. (2018) and Li et al. (2018) aim at computing pre-trained word representations, other proposals integrate the computation of the word representation in the overall NMT model, either combining information from character level, like those by Luong and Manning (2016) Costa-jussà and Fonollosa (2016), from n-gram level, like the one by Ataman and Federico (2018), or from multiple granularities like the work by Chen et al. (2018). Some other approaches like those by Wang et al. (2019) and Gu et al. (2018b) try to extend this idea to obtain multilingual *conceptual* representations from character-level representations.

Nevertheless, in all those approaches, the decoder only has access to the aggregated word-level information and not to the original subword-level information. This, while mitigating the unknown word problem, cannot handle the scenario where copying from source to target is necessary, like with unseen proper names or with compositional structures like numbers. To the best of our knowledge, this type of neural architectures that condense subword/character-level information into word-level representations have not been used for integrating extra word-level information as an additional input to the model in a translation task.

On the other hand, word level information has been injected to subword-based NMT models: Sennrich and Haddow (2016) copy the word-level linguistic information (e.g. lemma, POS tag) to each of the subwords in a word. Such information is used in an embedding and is concatenated with the subword token embedding. In this method, the subwords are also injected information about whether they are the leading subword in a word or they appear in the middle of a sequence of subwords or they are the last subword.

3 Subword to Word Transformer

In the standard Transformer architecture from Vaswani et al. (2017), the encoder applies a series of self-attention layers to the input token embeddings. The output of the encoder is then used at every layer of the decoder as key and value of the multi-head attention. In these operations, the token representations in the sequences in the source batch are masked according to the original sequence lengths in tokens.

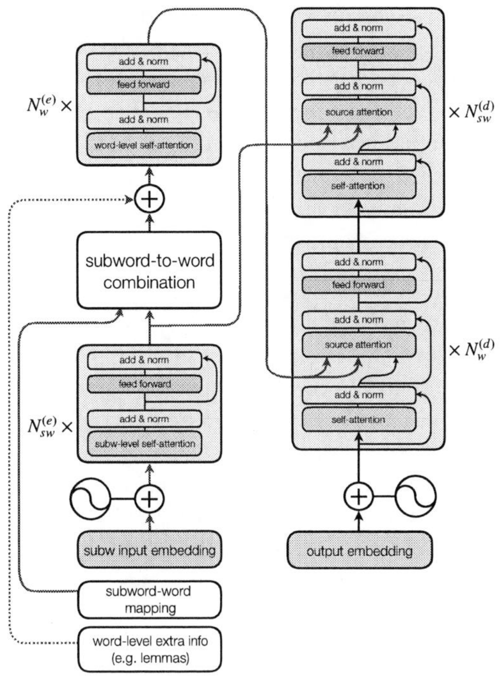

Figure 1: Subword to Word Transformer model.

We propose to divide the encoder into two blocks of self-attention layers. The first block receives the embedded subword-level token representations and processes them through $N_{sw}^{(e)}$ layers of self-attention like those from the nominal Transformer. The subword-level representations obtained as result of the first block are then combined into word level representations. A second block of $N_w^{(e)}$ self-attention layers processes these word-level representations. The output of the second encoder block is then fed to the first $N_w^{(d)}$ layers of the decoder, while the following $N_{sw}^{(d)}$ decoder layers are fed with the output of the first block of the encoder. The appropriate padding masks are used in the decoder depending on whether the encoder output used is subword or word-level. This architecture is shown in Figure 1.

In our first tests we directly used the encoder word representations as keys and values to every decoder layer (instead of using the encoder subword representations in the last layers of the decoder). This, however, led to poor results. We understand that such a configuration made it impossible for the network to properly handle token copying from source to target, which is usually needed in cases of proper nouns or compositional structures like numbers. Other possible causes for this degradation could be some mismatch on the encoder side e.g. positional embeddings being subword-based but encoder embeddings being word-level. To test this hypothesis, we added positional encodings after the point where subword representations are combined into word-level representations. This led to no improvement, indicating that the inability to copy was certainly the cause of the degradation.

The specific approach chosen to combine subword representations into word representations is a layer of Gated Recurrent Units (GRU) (Cho et al., 2014), which receives as input the output of the first encoder block. We take the output of the GRU at the positions of the last subword tokens in each word, providing the appropriate padding positions to handle the minibatch sequences. This way, the lengths of the sequences in the batch are now the number of word tokens in each sentence.

Other subword-to-word combination approaches tested during the early stages of this work included using Long-Short Term Memories (LSTM) (Hochreiter and Schmidhuber, 1997) and simply adding all subwords within each word.

The proposed approach provides a natural point to incorporate word-level information: after the subword-level representations have been combined into word-level ones. This way, as shown in Figure 1, the extra word-level information is embedded into a vector space and added to the word-level representations of the source sentence, after the word-to-subword combination.

Note that, while applying this approach to the encoder part is straightforward, applying it to the decoder presents a key challenge: at inference time, the target side tokens are generated one by one, which implies that it is not possible to combine all of the subword tokens of a word until they have all been generated.

4 Experimental Setup

We understand that there are two desirable properties for the proposed word-subword combination model: to be able to retain the translation quality obtained with the analogous subword-based model and to be able to better profit from word-level information than other approaches.

In order to verify that the translation quality is retained, we performed experiments on the IWSLT14 English-German data, both in English→German and German→English translation directions, with a BPE shared subword vocabulary with 10K merge operations. We studied the resulting translation quality with different hyperparameter sets in order to understand their effect on the model.

In order to study the effectiveness of the proposed model with other approaches to incorporate word-level information into a subword-based model, we used the WMT16 English-Romanian data with the back-translated synthetic data from (Sennrich et al., 2016a), using a shared subword vocabulary of 40k merge operations.

We used the proposal by (Sennrich and Haddow, 2016) as baseline, and compared it to a vanilla Transformer baseline and to our proposed method.

For all experiments, we used the `fairseq` library (Ott et al., 2019), either with its built-in models for the baselines or with custom model implementations for the approach by Sennrich and Haddow (2016) and for our own proposed architecture.

For the IWSLT14 de-en and en-de baselines we used the Transformer architecture (Vaswani et al., 2017) with the hyperparameters proposed by the `fairseq` authors[1], namely 6 layers in encoder and decoder, 4 attention heads, embedding size of 512 and 1024 for the feedforward expansion size, together with dropout of 0.3 and a total batch size of 4000 tokens, using label smoothing of 0.1. For the WMT16 en-ro baseline we used the base configuration of the Transformer model offered in `fairseq`, that is, 6 layers in encoder and decoder, 8 attention heads, embedding size of 512 and 2048 for the feedforward expansion size, together with dropout of 0.1 and total batch size of 32000 tokens, without label smoothing (following the baseline used by Gu et al. (2018a)).

All reported BLEU scores are computed with the model weights averaged over the last 10 checkpoints after training until convergence.

---

[1] `https://github.com/pytorch/fairseq/tree/master/examples/translation`

5   Results

We studied the effect of different hyperparameter values over translation quality. We measured the results obtained on the IWSLT14 de-en data by using different types of subword combination strategies, as well as combining subwords at different layer levels, chosen arbitrarily. Table 1 shows how the subword combination strategy that obtains best results is to use GRU units that receive the subwords as input and return the outputs at the positions of the final subword in each word. The difference with the other alternatives is minimal, though. The rest of the hyperparameters are the same as the IWSLT14 baseline, with a total batch size of 12000 and the subword merging layers being $N_{sw}^{(e)} = 3$ and $N_{sw}^{(d)} = 3$.

Combination	BLEU
Addition	33.93
GRU	34.02
LSTM	33.92

Table 1:   BLEU scores on IWSLT14 German-English for different subword combination strategies.

Regarding the influence over the translation quality of the level at which subword representations are merged, Table 2 shows that the best results are obtained when merging subwords after the fifth encoder layer, and using again the subword representations in the decoder after the third layer. The rest of hyperparameters are the same as the IWSLT14 baseline, with a total batch size of 12000 and GRU as subword combination strategy.

$N_{sw}^{(e)}$	$N_{sw}^{(d)}$	BLEU
3	5	33.53
3	3	34.02
5	3	34.46

Table 2:   BLEU scores on the IWSLT14 German-English test set for different values of $N_{sw}^{(e)}$ and $N_{sw}^{(d)}$, using GRU as subword combination strategy.

Once determined that using GRU as subword combination and setting $N_{sw}^{(e)} = 5$ and $N_{sw}^{(d)} = 3$ is the hyperparameter configuration that gives the best results, we checked whether the proposed architecture maintains the translation quality with respect to a vanilla Transformer baseline. As shown in Table 3, the BLEU scores are practically the same for both architectures and both German→English

while for English→German there is a small decrease. As commented in section 4, the baseline uses a batch size of 4000 while our approach uses 12000. Note that for the baseline architecture, larger batch sizes actually decrease the resulting translation quality.

	en-de	de-en
Base Transformer	28.75	34.44
Word-subword model	28.29	34.46

Table 3:   BLEU scores on the IWSLT14 German-English data, using no extra word-level information.

Finally, in order to assess our proposed approach at incorporating extra word-level information, we compared it against the approach by Sennrich and Haddow (2016) (with the Transformer as base architecture), which copies the word level information to each of the subwords in the word; in our implementation, the subword embedding and the linguistic information are combined by adding them together, which is analogous to the original alternative that concatenates them. For the vanilla Transformer and the approach by Sennrich and Haddow (2016) we used a total batch size of 32000 while for the word-subword model (our proposal), we used a total batch size of 40000, GRU as subword combination strategy and $N_{sw}^{(e)} = 5$ and $N_{sw}^{(d)} = 3$.

	en-ro
Base Transformer	27.02
Word-level info copied to subwords	27.29
Word-subword model + word-level info	27.82

Table 4:   BLEU scores measured on the WMT16 English-Romanian data, with lemmas as linguistic info.

The word-level linguistic information used was only the lemma (using a vocabulary of 40k lemmas), which is the feature that should provide the largest improvement according to Sennrich and Haddow (2016). We used Stanford CoreNLP (Manning et al., 2014) to annotate the corpus with the English lemmas. The obtained results are shown in Table 4, where our proposed approach obtains the best BLEU score compared to the base Transformer model (Vaswani et al., 2017) without any word-level information, and to copying the word-level info to subwords (Sennrich and Haddow, 2016).

6 Conclusion

In this work, we proposed a modification to the Transformer architecture to merge the subword representations from the first layers of the encoder into word-level representations. Merging word-level representations inside the model allows it to use the subword-level representations in the final decoder layers so that it can handle compositional structures and other situations where copying from source is needed. This approach provided an appropriate point to incorporate linguistic word-level information and it is superior at doing so compared with the reference approach by Sennrich and Haddow (2016).

Future extensions to this work may include applying it to character-level instead of subword representations, and using it for morphologically richer languages, especially low-resourced agglutinative ones, where our approach, together with the incorporation of linguistic information, may provide larger improvements in translation quality. Further extensions may include studying the behavior of more powerful subword combination strategies (e.g. convolutions, self-attention) and the application of subword merging to the target side.

Acknowledgements

This work is partially supported by Lucy Software / United Language Group (ULG) and the Catalan Agency for Management of University and Research Grants (AGAUR) through an Industrial PhD Grant. This work is also supported in part by the the Spanish Ministerio de Economía y Competitividad, the European Regional Development Fund through the postdoctoral senior grant Ramón y Cajal and by the Agencia Estatal de Investigación through the project EUR2019-103819.

References

Duygu Ataman and Marcello Federico. 2018. Compositional representation of morphologically-rich input for neural machine translation. In *Proceedings of the 56th Annual Meeting of the Association for Computational Linguistics (Volume 2: Short Papers)*, pages 305–311, Melbourne, Australia. Association for Computational Linguistics.

Piotr Bojanowski, Edouard Grave, Armand Joulin, and Tomas Mikolov. 2017. Enriching word vectors with subword information. *Transactions of the Association for Computational Linguistics*, 5:135–146.

Huadong Chen, Shujian Huang, David Chiang, Xinyu Dai, and Jiajun Chen. 2018. Combining character and word information in neural machine translation using a multi-level attention. In *Proceedings of the 2018 Conference of the North American Chapter of the Association for Computational Linguistics: Human Language Technologies, Volume 1 (Long Papers)*, pages 1284–1293, New Orleans, Louisiana. Association for Computational Linguistics.

Kyunghyun Cho, Bart van Merrienboer, Caglar Gulcehre, Dzmitry Bahdanau, Fethi Bougares, Holger Schwenk, and Yoshua Bengio. 2014. Learning phrase representations using RNN encoder–decoder for statistical machine translation. In *Proceedings of the 2014 Conference on Empirical Methods in Natural Language Processing (EMNLP)*, pages 1724–1734, Doha, Qatar. Association for Computational Linguistics.

Marta R. Costa-jussà and José A. R. Fonollosa. 2016. Character-based neural machine translation. In *Proceedings of the 54th Annual Meeting of the Association for Computational Linguistics (Volume 2: Short Papers)*, pages 357–361, Berlin, Germany. Association for Computational Linguistics.

Jiatao Gu, James Bradbury, Caiming Xiong, Victor O.K. Li, and Richard Socher. 2018a. Non-autoregressive neural machine translation. In *International Conference on Learning Representations*.

Jiatao Gu, Hany Hassan, Jacob Devlin, and Victor O.K. Li. 2018b. Universal neural machine translation for extremely low resource languages. In *Proceedings of the 2018 Conference of the North American Chapter of the Association for Computational Linguistics: Human Language Technologies, Volume 1 (Long Papers)*, pages 344–354, New Orleans, Louisiana. Association for Computational Linguistics.

Sepp Hochreiter and Jürgen Schmidhuber. 1997. Long short-term memory. *Neural Computation*, 9(8):1735–1780.

Bofang Li, Aleksandr Drozd, Tao Liu, and Xiaoyong Du. 2018. Subword-level composition functions for learning word embeddings. In *Proceedings of the Second Workshop on Subword/Character Level Models*, pages 38–48, New Orleans. Association for Computational Linguistics.

Minh-Thang Luong and Christopher D. Manning. 2016. Achieving open vocabulary neural machine translation with hybrid word-character models. In *Proceedings of the 54th Annual Meeting of the Association for Computational Linguistics (Volume 1: Long Papers)*, pages 1054–1063, Berlin, Germany. Association for Computational Linguistics.

Christopher D. Manning, Mihai Surdeanu, John Bauer, Jenny Finkel, Steven J. Bethard, and David McClosky. 2014. The Stanford CoreNLP natural language processing toolkit. In *Association for Computational Linguistics (ACL) System Demonstrations*, pages 55–60.

Myle Ott, Sergey Edunov, Alexei Baevski, Angela Fan, Sam Gross, Nathan Ng, David Grangier, and Michael Auli. 2019. fairseq: A fast, extensible toolkit for sequence modeling. In *Proceedings of NAACL-HLT 2019: Demonstrations*.

Rico Sennrich and Barry Haddow. 2016. Linguistic input features improve neural machine translation. In *Proceedings of the First Conference on Machine Translation*, pages 83–91, Berlin, Germany. Association for Computational Linguistics.

Rico Sennrich, Barry Haddow, and Alexandra Birch. 2016a. Edinburgh neural machine translation systems for WMT 16. In *Proceedings of the First Conference on Machine Translation*, pages 371–376, Berlin, Germany. Association for Computational Linguistics.

Rico Sennrich, Barry Haddow, and Alexandra Birch. 2016b. Neural machine translation of rare words with subword units. In *Proceedings of the 54th Annual Meeting of the Association for Computational Linguistics, ACL 2016, August 7-12, 2016, Berlin, Germany, Volume 1: Long Papers*.

Ashish Vaswani, Noam Shazeer, Niki Parmar, Jakob Uszkoreit, Llion Jones, Aidan N Gomez, Łukasz Kaiser, and Illia Polosukhin. 2017. Attention is all you need. In I. Guyon, U. V. Luxburg, S. Bengio, H. Wallach, R. Fergus, S. Vishwanathan, and R. Garnett, editors, *Advances in Neural Information Processing Systems 30*, pages 6000–6010. Curran Associates, Inc.

Xinyi Wang, Hieu Pham, Philip Arthur, and Graham Neubig. 2019. Multilingual neural machine translation with soft decoupled encoding. In *International Conference on Learning Representations*.

Jinman Zhao, Sidharth Mudgal, and Yingyu Liang. 2018. Generalizing word embeddings using bag of subwords. In *Proceedings of the 2018 Conference on Empirical Methods in Natural Language Processing*, pages 601–606, Brussels, Belgium. Association for Computational Linguistics.

Zero-shot North Korean to English Neural Machine Translation by Character Tokenization and Phoneme Decomposition

Hwichan Kim **Tosho Hirasawa** **Mamoru Komachi**

Tokyo Metropolitan University

6-6 Asahigaoka, Hino, Tokyo 191-0065, Japan

{kim-hwichan, hirasawa-tosho}@ed.tmu.ac.jp, komachi@tmu.ac.jp

Abstract

The primary limitation of North Korean to English translation is the lack of a parallel corpus; therefore, high translation accuracy cannot be achieved. To address this problem, we propose a zero-shot approach using South Korean data, which are remarkably similar to North Korean data. We train a neural machine translation model after tokenizing a South Korean text at the character level and decomposing characters into phonemes. We demonstrate that our method can effectively learn North Korean to English translation and improve the BLEU scores by +1.01 points in comparison with the baseline.

1 Introduction

Neural machine translation (NMT) has been adapted to many languages; however, machine translation of the North Korean language[1] has seldom been performed. One of the reasons is the lack of large-scale bilingual data for training North Korean neural models. It is known that large-scale bilingual data are required to improve the translation accuracy of an NMT model. For example, one of the previous works suggests that an NMT system is less accurate than a phrase-based statistical machine translation system if there are no more than 100 million words in the bilingual training data (Koehn and Knowles, 2017).

There are three approaches to solve low language resource bottleneck. First, Wang et al. (2006) proposed a method to train a translation model using a pivot language as an intermediate language. This approach translates from the source language to the pivot language and from the pivot language to the target language. However, there is no good pivot language between North Korean and English. Second, Johnson et al. (2017) proposed a many-to-many translation model, where multiple languages are translated into other languages using a single shared encoder and decoder. They demonstrated that this model can translate a language pair that is unseen in training data. However, North Korean does not have any bilingual data between any languages. Third, Marujo et al. (2011) proposed a rule-based method to convert similar languages into a target language, such as Brazilian Portuguese to European Portuguese, and extended the target language resources. North Korean is a language remarkably similar to South Korean, but conversion from South Korean to North Korean needs to be determined considering the context, which makes rule-based conversion difficult.

Therefore, in this study, we propose a method to tokenize South Korean input sentences at the character level and decompose them into phonemes to mitigate the grammatical differences between South Korean and North Korean, and demonstrate that the translation model from North Korean to English can be effectively learned using bilingual South Korean-English data. The main contributions of this study are as follows.

- Because there is no evaluation dataset between North Korean and English, we create a North Korean-English evaluation dataset by manually translating the South Korean-English bilingual evaluation dataset into a North Korean one.

- We demonstrate that the North Korean-English translation model can be trained effectively on bilingual South Korean-English data by character-level tokenization and phoneme-level decomposition.

---

[1]Korean is a language mainly used in the Korean peninsula; however, there are some grammatical differences between the Republic of Korea and the Democratic People's Republic of Korea. In this study, we refer to the Korean language used in the Republic of Korea as "South Korean," and the Korean language used in the Democratic People's Republic of Korea as "North Korean."

Proceedings of the 58th Annual Meeting of the Association for Computational Linguistics: Student Research Workshop, pages 72–78

July 5 - July 10, 2020. ©2020 Association for Computational Linguistics

Grammar differences	SK	NK	EN	Percentage
Word segmentation	많은 것	많은것	many things	86.9
Initial sound rule	농구	롱구	basketball	19.6
	이행	리행	fulfillment	
		이행	move	
Compound word	바닷가	바다가	beach	0.3

Table 1: Grammatical differences between South Korean (SK) and North Korean (NK), and the percentage of sentences with grammatical differences in South Korean evaluation data.

2   Related Work

The pivot language approach increases the translation error between the source language and the target language, because the translation model of each language is independently trained. Cheng et al. (2017) addressed this problem by allowing interaction during the translation model training. Moreover, Chen et al. (2017) proposed a method to train a source-to-target model using a pretrained teacher model as its guide.

Marujo et al. (2011) proposed a rule-based method to convert similar languages into a target language to extend the language resources of the target side. Wang et al. (2016) presented a method to extract the conversion rules between similar languages.

Firat et al. (2016) proposed a many-to-many translation model with several encoders and decoders. However, the accuracy of a many-to-many translation model with a single shared encoder and decoder was found to be higher (Johnson et al., 2017).

Finally, the translation accuracy was improved by preprocessing of the bilingual data. Zhang and Komachi (2018) demonstrated that higher translation accuracy can be obtained by decomposing Kanji into ideographic characters and strokes in Japanese-Chinese NMT. Stratos (2017) proposed a speech-parsing model for South Korean with character-level tokenization and decomposition into phonemes, demonstrating an improvement in the speech-parsing accuracy.

3   South-North Differences in the Korean Language

3.1   Grammatical differences

The two Korean languages have grammatical differences, including differences in word segmentation (WS), initial sound rule (ISR), and compound words. Table 1 presents examples of grammatical differences between South Korean and North Korean words or phrases that have the same meaning. We only consider the differences in the WS and ISR in our study, as differences in compound words in the evaluation data rarely appear.

Word segmentation.   South Korean and North Korean differ in the way to tokenize words containing formal and proper nouns and in quantitative expressions. For example, words are separated in both South Korean and North Korean when particles appear; however, they are not separated in North Korean if the next word after a particle is a formal noun. In Table 1, the word meaning "many things" is written as "많은 것" in South Korean and is separated because "은" is a particle. However, since "것" is a formal noun, it is written consecutively in North Korean as "많은것." To convert WS from South Korean grammar to North Korean grammar, it is necessary to consider the context.

Initial sound rule.   In South Korean, a consonant "ㄹ" changes into "ㅇ" or "ㄴ" when it is combined with "ㅑ, ㅕ, ㅛ, ㅜ, ㅠ, ㅣ, ㅖ," or other vowels, whereas it does not change in North Korean. For example, the word that means "basketball" in Table 1 is represented as "농구" in South Korean because of the ISR, but is represented as "롱구" in North Korean. Additionally, some South Korean words become polysemous owing to the ISR. In Table 1, the words that mean "fulfillment" and "move" both become "이행" in South Korean, but remain "리행" and "이행" in North Korean, respectively. It is difficult to mitigate the difference in the ISR without considering the context.

3.2   Creating North Korean Evaluation Data

We created the North Korean to English translation evaluation dataset by having a North Korean native speaker manually convert the evaluation dataset in the News Korean-English parallel corpus[2] into

---

[2]https://github.com/jungyeul/korean-parallel-corpora

Hyperparameter	Value
Embedding size	512
Hidden layer size	1,024
Enc./Dec. depth	1
Enc./Dec. recurrence transition depth	2
Tie decoder embeddings	yes
Layer normalization	yes
Hidden/Embedding dropout	0.5
Source/Target Word dropout	0.3
Label smoothing	0.2
Optimizer	adam
Learning rate	0.0005
Batch size (tokens)	1,000
Early stopping patience	10
Validation interval	8,000

Table 2: Hyperparameters.

		Words		
	Sent.	EN	SK	NK
train	93,975	2,297,744	1,567,469	-
dev	1,000	25,804	18,126	15,613
test	2,000	53,904	36,641	31,645
WS	1,733	48,720	33,574	28,578
ISR	350	10,766	7,283	6,184

Table 3: Statistics of News Korean-English parallel corpus and North Korean-English evaluation data.

North Korean grammar. This North Korean-English evaluation dataset will be published at the same address 2. Table 1 presents the percentage of sentences with grammatical differences between North Korean and South Korean evaluation data. From this table, we can see that the WS and ISR are the main grammatical differences between South Korean and North Korean.

4 Korean Neural Machine Translation using Character Tokenization and Phoneme Decomposition

We propose a method to tokenize input sentences into characters or decompose them into phonemes. Using this method, it is possible to reduce the influence of grammatical differences between South Korean and North Korean to train a machine translation model in North Korean using bilingual South Korean data. In the following South Korean or North Korean sentences, we indicate the word boundary as □ for better understanding.

Character model. In character level tokenization, we split each word into characters. For example, the word that means "many things" in Table 1 is written as "많은□것" in South Korean and "많은것" in North Korean, but when we tokenize it at the character level, it becomes "많□은□것," and there is no difference between the two languages. Therefore, character level tokenization can overcome the difference in WS to some extent.

Word (phoneme BPE) model. In word level (phoneme BPE) tokenization, we decompose the characters in a word into phonemes (vowels and consonants). As a result, we can reduce the effect of ISR. For example, the word "basketball" is written as "농구" in South Korean and "롱구" in North Korean; therefore, only one out of two tokens are common at the character level. When they are decomposed into phonemes, the former is "ㄴ ㅗ ㅇ ㄱ ㅜ" in South Korean, and the latter is "ㄹ ㅗ ㅇ ㄱ ㅜ" in North Korean, resulting in four out of five tokens being common. In this way, decomposition into phonemes can reduce the effect of ISR.

In addition, we retain the word or phrase boundary in the input sentence in this model. For example, when decomposing the sentence "롱구는□운동" into phonemes, it is decomposed as "ㄹ ㅗ ㅇ ㄱ ㅜ ㄴ ㅡ ㄴ □ ㅇ ㅜ ㄴ ㄷ ㅗ ㅇ." By applying byte-pair encoding (BPE, Sennrich et al., 2016) to the sentence that has been decomposed into phonemes, it is possible to segment the sentence at the phoneme level while considering word or phrase boundaries.

Character (phoneme BPE) model. In character (phoneme BPE) tokenization, we tokenize a sentence at the character level and decompose it into phonemes. Tokenization at the character level and decomposition into phonemes can mitigate the differences in WS and ISR, and it is possible to combine both. For example, when the sentence "롱구는□운동" is tokenized at the character level and decomposed into phonemes, it becomes "ㄹ ㅗ ㅇ □ ㄱ ㅜ □ ㄴ ㅡ ㄴ □ ㅇ ㅜ ㄴ □ ㄷ ㅗ ㅇ." By applying BPE to this sentence, it is possible to segment the sentence at the phoneme level while considering character boundaries.

| | South Korean | | | | North Korean | | | |
Model	dev	test	WS	ISR	dev	test	WS	ISR
S&Z (2019)	-	10.37	-	-	-	-	-	-
word	6.96	7.40	7.61	8.22	5.54±.22	5.32±.03	5.34±.03	5.53±.05
word (charBPE)	9.09	9.38	9.59	10.01	8.54±.32	9.02±.22	9.18±.21	9.28±.30
char	10.26	9.89	10.17	10.49	10.15±.07	9.84±.20	10.12±.22	10.32±.31
word (phonBPE)	9.38	9.67	9.71	10.67	8.87±.11	9.10±.06	9.21±.06	9.62±.37
char (phonBPE)	**10.28**	**10.05**	**10.30**	**10.69**	**10.20±.16**	**10.03±.21**	**10.29±.19**	**10.60±.16**

Table 4: Evaluation of each model in South Korean / North Korean to English translation. These are BLEU scores of evaluation data set and WS and ISR subsets. These BLEU scores are the average of three models. The char (phonBPE) model achieved the highest scores in dev, test and two subsets.

		Types	Tokens
	word	213,552	1,567,469
	word (charBPE)	32,083	2,057,155
SK	char	15,372	4,231,099
	word (phonBPE)	29,442	2,091,575
	char (phonBPE)	1,736	4,316,529
EN	word	53,222	2,297,744
	word (charBPE)	16,024	2,494,763

Table 5: Data statistics after each preprocessing.

5 Experiment

5.1 Settings

We train a BiDeep recurrent neural network using Nematus[3] for implementation. We adjust the hyperparameters as in Sennrich and Zhang (2019) (Table 2). We use a News Korean-English parallel corpus for training the model and convert it into North Korean grammar (3.2) for evaluating the model. We perform tokenization and truecasing using Moses scripts for all the input sentence pairs. We delete sentences with more than 200 words from the training data. Table 3 presents the training, development, and test data statistics. In the evaluation, we perform detruecasing and detokenization for the translation outputs using Moses script and evaluate the bilingual evaluation understudy (BLEU) score using sacreBLEU (Post, 2018). We select the model using South Korean and North Korean development data.

In this study, in addition to the word level data of South Korean and North Korean as input languages, we use the four preprocessing methods, which are described in the following paragraphs and presented in Table 5.

Word (character BPE) model. According to Sennrich and Zhang (2019), we apply character level BPE to each of the South Korean, North Korean, and English sides that had been split with words. We set the merge operation to 30k and the frequency threshold to 10. For the following South Korean and North Korean preprocessing steps, the English side used only the word (character BPE) model. In addition to our re-implementation of Sennrich and Zhang (2019), we cite the BLEU score reported in their paper.

Character model. We perform character level tokenization. As for English and Hanja included in the South Korean and North Korean data, we treat them as words without further tokenization. In addition, we limit the token types to a maximum frequency of 1,700.

Word (phoneme BPE) model. We decompose the words into phonemes and apply BPE. We set the merge operation to 30k and the frequency threshold to 10. We use hgtk (Hangul toolkit)[4] for the decomposition into phonemes.

Character (phoneme BPE) model. We perform the character level tokenization, decomposition into phonemes, and application of BPE. We set the merge operation to 1k.

5.2 Results

Table 4 presents the BLEU scores for the evaluation data. In the cases of both the South Korean and North Korean languages, the char (phonBPE) models achieved the highest scores in the dev data. The test data reveals an improvement of +0.67 points for South Korean and +1.01 points for North Korean in comparison with the word (charBPE) model, respectively.

[3]https://github.com/EdinburghNLP/nematus

[4]https://github.com/bluedisk/hangul-toolkit

Reference	A division of General Motors is getting some **financial help** from the **Federal** Reserve:
Source	GM의 자회사가 **연방**준비제도로부터 **재정적 지원**을 받게 되었습니다.
word (charBPE)	GM's job company is getting **financial assistance** from the **Federal** Reserve.
char	GM's automaker has been receiving **financial assistance** from the **Federal** Reserve.
word (phonBPE)	GM's company has received **financial assistance** from the **Federal** Reserve.
char (phonBPE)	GM's company has been receiving **financial assistance** from the **Federal** Reserve.
Source	GM의 자회사가 **련방**준비제도로부터 **재정적지원**을 받게 되었습니다.
word (charBPE)	GM's own company is getting money from a scusty system.
char	GM's automaker has been receiving **financial assistance** from the **Federal** Reserve.
word (phonBPE)	GM's ZGM company gets **financial assistance** from the getaway.
char (phonBPE)	GM has received **financial assistance** from the **Federal** Reserve.

Table 6: Translation examples that differ in the WS and ISR (upper: South Korean, lower: North Korean). The word that means "financial help" is written as "재정적 지원" in South Korean, and in North Korean, it is written consecutively as "재정적지원." Additionally, in South Korean, the word that means "federal" becomes "연방" because of the head ISR but remains "련방" in North Korean.

Reference	It added that it was **consulting** with the Ministry of Unification on the plan.
Source	해양수산부는 이 방안에 대해 통일부와 **논의 중**이라고 덧붙였다.
char	The Ministry ⋯ said it is **discussing** the plan.
char (phonBPE)	The Ministry ⋯ said it was **discussing** the plan.
Source	해양수산부는 이 방안에 대해 통일부와 **론의중**이라고 덧붙였다.
char	The Ministry ⋯ said the plan is under way with the Unification Ministry.
char (phonBPE)	The Ministry ⋯ said the plan would be **discussed** with the Unification Ministry.

Table 7: The word that means "consulting" becomes "논의 중" in South Korean owing to the ISR, but remains "론의중" in North Korean.

Model	Fluency	Adequacy
word (charBPE)	2.71	1.91
char	**2.82**	1.91
word (phonBPE)	2.67	1.90
char (phonBPE)	**2.82**	**1.93**

Table 8: Human evaluation of each model for North Korean to English translation. These scores are the average of the those assigned by three evaluators. In human evaluation, also, the char (phonBPE) model achieved the highest scores.

6 Discussion

We extract two subsets that have differences in the WS or ISR in the test data to test the hypothesis that each preprocessing step can absorb the grammatical differences. Table 3 presents the WS and ISR subset data statistics.

Word segmentation. Table 4 presents the results of a test with a subset of WS. The char (phonBPE) model exhibits the highest BLEU score in the North Korean test. In addition, the BLEU difference between South Korean and North Korean is 0.01 point, indicating that the difference in WS is well-absorbed.

Initial sound rule. Table 4 presents the results of a test with a subset of the ISR. Even for a subset of the ISR, the char (phonBPE) model exhibits the highest BLEU score in the North Korean test, and the BLEU difference between South Korean and North Korean is 0.09 point, indicating that the difference in ISR is well-absorbed.

Output of each model. Table 6 presents the outputs of each model. The words that include grammatical differences, such as "재정적지원" and "련방," are not well-translated in the word-based models. However, the character-based models can translate them correctly. Character-level tokenization can mitigate both grammatical differences as shown in the example of Table 6; however, character-level tokenization cannot solve all the grammatical differences. For example, Table 7 presents an example, wherein the word "론의중" is affected by the ISR, and only the char (phonBPE) model can translate it in North Korean translation. Therefore, tokenization at the character level and decomposition into phonemes are necessary to reduce the differences of the WS and ISR.

Human evaluation We randomly extracted 50 lines from each model output in the North Korean to English test. Three evaluators evaluated the fluency and adequacy on a scale of 1–5. Table 8 presents the results of the human evaluation. The char (phonBPE) model exhibits the highest scores in both metrics, with an improvement of +0.11 points in the fluency evaluation and +0.02 points in the adequacy evaluation in comparison with the word (charBPE) model. Additionally, the human evaluation results indicate that character tokenization and phoneme decomposition can improve the accuracy of the North Korean to English translation.

7   Conclusions and Future Work

In this study, to solve the language resource bottleneck in North Korean translation, we proposed a method to tokenize input sentences in South Korean and North Korean at the character level and decompose them into phonemes. This method is simple and mitigates the grammatical differences between South Korean and North Korean; moreover, the method demonstrates improvement in translation accuracy for North Korean to English translation.

However, the differences that exist between South Korean and North Korean are not only grammatical ones. There are some words that have the same pronunciation and notation but different meanings. For example, the meaning of "낙지" is "squid" in South Korean, but "octopus" in North Korean. Therefore, the differences in word meanings are a major challenge. In the future, we intend to use the English translation data of North Korean news articles to create an evaluation dataset that considers differences in words, and attempt to develop a translation method using a language model with context, such as BERT (Devlin et al., 2019).

Acknowledgement

We would like to thank Rico Sennrich for his help with the hyperparameters and preprocess setting, and thank John Wieting and anonymous reviewers for their help. We would also like to thank Ayami Higuchi, Kinnam Lee, and Susil Kim for their help with the human evaluation. This work was supported by JSPS KAKENHI Grant Numbers JP19K12099 and JP19KK0286.

References

Yun Chen, Yang Liu, Yong Cheng, and Victor O.K. Li. 2017. A teacher-student framework for zero-resource neural machine translation. In *Proceedings of the 55th Annual Meeting of the Association for Computational Linguistics (Volume 1: Long Papers)*, pages 1925–1935, Vancouver, Canada. Association for Computational Linguistics.

Yong Cheng, Qian Yang, Yang Liu, Maosong Sun, and Wei Xu. 2017. Joint training for pivot-based neural machine translation. In *Proceedings of the Twenty-Sixth International Joint Conference on Artificial Intelligence, IJCAI-17*, pages 3974–3980, Melbourne, Australia. International Joint Conferences on Artificial Intelligence Organization.

Jacob Devlin, Ming-Wei Chang, Kenton Lee, and Kristina Toutanova. 2019. BERT: Pre-training of deep bidirectional transformers for language understanding. In *Proceedings of the 2019 Conference of the North American Chapter of the Association for Computational Linguistics: Human Language Technologies, Volume 1 (Long and Short Papers)*, pages 4171–4186, Minneapolis, Minnesota. Association for Computational Linguistics.

Orhan Firat, Baskaran Sankaran, Yaser Al-onaizan, Fatos T. Yarman Vural, and Kyunghyun Cho. 2016. Zero-resource translation with multi-lingual neural machine translation. In *Proceedings of the 2016 Conference on Empirical Methods in Natural Language Processing*, pages 268–277, Austin, Texas. Association for Computational Linguistics.

Melvin Johnson, Mike Schuster, Quoc V. Le, Maxim Krikun, Yonghui Wu, Zhifeng Chen, Nikhil Thorat, Fernanda Viégas, Martin Wattenberg, Greg Corrado, Macduff Hughes, and Jeffrey Dean. 2017. Google's multilingual neural machine translation system: Enabling zero-shot translation. *Transactions of the Association for Computational Linguistics*, 5:339–351.

Philipp Koehn and Rebecca Knowles. 2017. Six challenges for neural machine translation. In *Proceedings of the First Workshop on Neural Machine Translation*, pages 28–39, Vancouver. Association for Computational Linguistics.

Luis Marujo, Nuno Grazina, Tiago Luis, Wang Ling, Luisa Coheur, and Isabel Trancoso. 2011. BP2EP - Adaptation of Brazilian Portuguese texts to European Portuguese. In *In Proceedings of the 15th International Conference of the European Association for Machine Translation (EAMT)*, pages 129–136, Leuven, Belgium. European Association for Machine Translation.

Matt Post. 2018. A call for clarity in reporting BLEU scores. In *Proceedings of the Third Conference on Machine Translation: Research Papers*, pages 186–191, Belgium, Brussels. Association for Computational Linguistics.

Rico Sennrich, Barry Haddow, and Alexandra Birch. 2016. Neural machine translation of rare words with subword units. In *Proceedings of the 54th Annual Meeting of the Association for Computational Linguistics (Volume 1: Long Papers)*, pages 1715–1725, Berlin, Germany. Association for Computational Linguistics.

Rico Sennrich and Biao Zhang. 2019. Revisiting low-resource neural machine translation: A case study. In *Proceedings of the 57th Annual Meeting of the Association for Computational Linguistics*, pages 211–221, Florence, Italy. Association for Computational Linguistics.

Karl Stratos. 2017. A sub-character architecture for Korean language processing. In *Proceedings of the 2017 Conference on Empirical Methods in Natural Language Processing*, pages 721–726, Copenhagen, Denmark. Association for Computational Linguistics.

Haifeng Wang, Hua Wu, and Zhanyi Liu. 2006. Word alignment for languages with scarce resources using bilingual corpora of other language pairs. In *Proceedings of the COLING/ACL 2006 Main Conference Poster Sessions*, pages 874–881, Sydney, Australia. Association for Computational Linguistics.

Pidong Wang, Preslav Nakov, and Hwee Tou Ng. 2016. Source language adaptation approaches for resource-poor machine translation. *Computational Linguistics*, 42(2):277–306.

Longtu Zhang and Mamoru Komachi. 2018. Neural machine translation of logographic language using sub-character level information. In *Proceedings of the Third Conference on Machine Translation: Research Papers*, pages 17–25, Belgium, Brussels. Association for Computational Linguistics.

Media Bias, the Social Sciences, and NLP: Automating Frame Analyses to Identify Bias by Word Choice and Labeling

Felix Hamborg

Dept. of Computer and Information Science
University of Konstanz, Germany
`felix.hamborg@uni-konstanz.de`

Abstract

Media bias can strongly impact the public perception of topics reported in the news. A difficult to detect, yet powerful form of slanted news coverage is called bias by word choice and labeling (WCL). WCL bias can occur, for example, when journalists refer to the same semantic concept by using different terms that frame the concept differently and consequently may lead to different assessments by readers, such as the terms "freedom fighters" and "terrorists," or "gun rights" and "gun control." In this research project, I aim to devise methods that identify instances of WCL bias and estimate the frames they induce, e.g., not only is "terrorists" of negative polarity but also ascribes to aggression and fear. To achieve this, I plan to research methods using natural language processing and deep learning while employing models and using analysis concepts from the social sciences, where researchers have studied media bias for decades. The first results indicate the effectiveness of this interdisciplinary research approach. My vision is to devise a system that helps news readers to become aware of the differences in media coverage caused by bias.

1 Introduction

Media bias describes differences in the content or presentation of news (Hamborg et al., 2018). It is a ubiquitous phenomenon in news coverage that can have severely negative effects on individuals and society, e.g., when slanted news coverage influences voters and, in turn, also election outcomes (Alsem et al., 2008; DellaVigna and Kaplan, 2007). Potential issues of biased coverage, whether through the selection of topics or how they are covered, are compounded by the fact that in many countries only a few corporations control large parts of the media landscape–in the US, for example, six corporations control 90% of the media (Business Insider, 2014).

Even subtle changes in the words used in a news text can strongly impact readers' opinions (Papacharissi and de Fatima Oliveira, 2008; Price et al., 2005; Rugg, 1941; Schuldt et al., 2011). When referring to a semantic concept, such as a politician or other named entities (NEs), authors can label the concept, e.g., "illegal aliens," and choose from various words to refer to it, e.g., "immigrants" or "aliens." Instances of bias by word choice and labeling (WCL) frame the referred concept differently (Entman, 1993, 2007), whereby a broad spectrum of effects occurs. For example, the frame may change the polarity of the concept, i.e., positively or negatively, or the frame may emphasize specific parts of an issue, such as the economic or cultural effects of immigration (Entman, 1993).

In the social sciences, research over the past decades has resulted in comprehensive models to describe media bias as well as effective methods for the analysis of media bias, such as content analysis (McCarthy et al., 2008) and frame analysis (Entman, 1993). Because researchers need to conduct these analyses mostly manually, the analyses do not scale with the vast amount of news that is published nowadays (Hamborg et al., 2019a). In turn, such studies are always conducted for topics in the past and do not deliver insights for the current day (McCarthy et al., 2008; Oliver and Maney, 2000); this would, however, be of primary interest to people reading the news. Revealing media bias to news consumers would also help to mitigate bias effects and, for example, support them in making more informed choices (Baumer et al., 2017).

In contrast, in computational linguistics and computer science, fewer approaches systematically analyze media bias (Hamborg et al., 2019a). The models used to analyze media bias tend to be simpler (Hamborg et al., 2018; Park et al., 2009) compared to previously mentioned models. Many approaches analyze media bias from the perspective

Proceedings of the 58th Annual Meeting of the Association for Computational Linguistics: Student Research Workshop, pages 79–87
July 5 - July 10, 2020. ©2020 Association for Computational Linguistics

of news consumers while neglecting both the established approaches and the comprehensive models that have already been developed in the social sciences (Evans et al., 2004; Mehler et al., 2006; Munson et al., 2013, 2009; Oelke et al., 2012; Park et al., 2009; Smith et al., 2014). Correspondingly, their results are often inconclusive or superficial, despite the approaches being technically superior.

2 Research Question, Tasks, and Contributions

To address the issues described in Section 1, I define the following research question for my Ph.D. research: *How can an automated approach identify instances of bias by word choice and labeling in a set of English news articles reporting on the same event?* To address this research question, I derive the following research tasks:

T1. Identify the strengths and weaknesses of manual and of automated methods used to identify media bias.

T2. Research NLP techniques and required datasets to address these weaknesses. To do so, use established bias models and (semi-) automate currently manual analysis methods.

T3. Implement a prototype of a media bias identification system that employs the developed methods to demonstrate the applicability of the approach in real-world news article collections. The target group of the prototype are non-expert people.

T4. Evaluate the effectiveness of the bias identification methods with a test corpus and evaluate the effectiveness of using the prototype in a user study.

Combining the expertise of the social sciences and computational linguistics appears beneficial for research on media bias. Thus, the main contribution of my Ph.D. research will be an approach that combines models and methods from multiple disciplines. On the one hand, it will leverage established models from the social sciences to describe media bias and will follow currently manual methods to analyze media bias. On the other hand, it will take advantage of scalable methods for text analysis developed and used in computational linguistics. I need to employ and extend the state-of-the-art in two closely related NLP fields (cf. Section 4): (1) cross-document coreference resolution (CDCR) as

well as (2) target-dependent sentiment classification (TSC) including "sentiment shift" and identification of framing effects and causes (see Section 4.2). I plan to embed both techniques into an approach that is inspired by the procedure of manually conducted, inductive frame analyses (cf. Section 3.1).

For the first technical contribution, a sieve-based CDCR approach was already devised that addresses characteristics of coreferences as they often occur in bias by WCL. The examples in the Abstract show that even phrases that are usually considered contrary may be coreferential in a set of articles reporting on a specific event. For the second technical contribution, i.e., to estimate how a semantic concept may be perceived by people when reading a news article, I primarily plan to devise and test neural models that I will design specifically for the task. I also plan to implement a prototype that includes visualizations to reveal the identified instances of bias by WCL to users of the system.

In the remainder of this document, I will give a brief overview of manual techniques for the analysis of bias by WCL and exemplary results from the social sciences as well as related, automated approaches (Section 3). Section 3 concludes with the current research gap, which motivates my Ph.D. research. Section 4 describes the tasks that I have already conducted as well as current and future tasks to complete my Ph.D. research. Section 5 describes a preliminary evaluation, which I already completed, as well as remaining tasks.

3 Related Work

The following summarizes an interdisciplinary literature review that I conducted as part of my Ph.D. research (T1) (Hamborg et al., 2019a).

3.1 Manual Approaches

In the social sciences, the news production process is an established model that defines nine forms of media bias and describes where these forms originate from (Baker et al., 1994; Hamborg et al., 2019a, 2018; Park et al., 2009). For example, journalists select events, sources, and from these sources the information they want to publish in a news article. While these initial selections are necessary due to the multitude of real-world events, they may also introduce bias to the resulting story. While writing an article, authors can affect readers' perception of a topic through word choice (cf. Section 1, Baker et al., 1994; Gentzkow and Shapiro, 2006; Oelke et al., 2012). Lastly, for example, the placement and size of an article on a website determine how much attention the article will receive.

Researchers in the social sciences primarily conduct frame analyses or, more generally, content analyses to identify instances of bias by WCL (McCarthy et al., 2008; Oliver and Maney, 2000). In content analysis, researchers first define one or more analysis questions or hypotheses. Then, they gather the relevant news data, and coders systematically read the texts, annotating parts of the texts that indicate instances of bias relevant to the analysis question, e.g., phrases that change readers' perception of a specific person or topic. In inductive content analysis, coders read and annotate the texts without prior knowledge other than the analysis question. In deductive content analysis, coders must adhere to a set of coding rules defined in a codebook, which is usually created using the findings from an earlier inductive content analysis. After the coding, researchers quantify the annotated instances to lastly accept or reject their hypotheses.

Content analyses conducted for WCL bias are typically either topic-oriented or person-oriented. Annotations range from basic forms, e.g., targeted sentiment (Niven, 2002), to fine-grained "perception" categories, causes thereof, or other features, e.g., Papacharissi and de Fatima Oliveira (2008) investigated WCL in the coverage of different news outlets on topics related to terrorism. One high-level finding was that the New York Times used more dramatic tones than the Washington Post, e.g., news articles dehumanized terrorists by not ascribing any motive to terrorist attacks or use of metaphors, such as "David and Goliath." Both the Financial Times and the Guardian focused their articles on factual reporting.

3.2 (Semi-)Automated Approaches

Many automated approaches treat media bias vaguely and view it only as "differences of [news] coverage" (Park et al., 2011b), "diverse opinions" (Munson and Resnick, 2010), "different perspectives" (Hamborg et al., 2018), or "topic diversity" (Munson et al., 2009), resulting in inconclusive or superficial findings (Hamborg et al., 2019a). Only a few approaches use comprehensive bias models or focus on a specific form of media bias (cf. Section 3.1). Likewise, few approaches aim to specifically identify instances of WCL bias. For

example, Lim et al. (2018); Spinde et al. (2020b) propose to investigate words with a low document frequency in a set of news articles reporting on the same event, to find potentially biasing words that are characteristic for a single article. NewsCube 2.0 employs crowdsourcing to estimate the bias of articles reporting on a topic. The system allows users to annotate WCL in news articles collaboratively (Park et al., 2011a).

The most related, fully automated field of methods is TSC, which aims to find the connotation of a phrase regarding a given target. On news texts, however, to-date TSC methods perform poorly for at least three reasons. First, news texts have rather subtle connotations due to the expected journalistic objectivity (Gauthier, 1993; Hamborg et al., 2018). Second, to my knowledge, no news-tailored TSC approaches, dictionaries, nor annotated datasets exist; generic approaches tend to perform poorly on news texts (Balahur et al., 2010; Kaya et al., 2012; Oelke et al., 2012). Third, the one-dimensional polarity scale used by all mature TSC methods may fall short of representing complex news frames (cf. Section 1). To avoid the difficulties of highly context-dependent connotations in news texts, researchers have proposed to perform TSC only on quotes (Balahur et al., 2010) or on the readers' comments (Park et al., 2011b), which more likely contain explicit connotations. Researchers also suggested to investigate emotions induced by headlines, but they achieved mixed results (Strapparava and Mihalcea, 2007).

3.3 Research Gap

To my knowledge, there are currently no automated approaches that identify or compare instances of WCL bias, despite reliable analysis concepts used in the social sciences and automated text analysis methods in related fields, such as CDCR and TSC.

To address the difficulties due to the expected objectivity of news texts and other previously mentioned factors, I plan to follow two main ideas: first, the use of knowledge and models from sciences that have long studied media bias. Second, I expect the recent advent of word embeddings and deep learning, including neural language models, such as BERT (Devlin et al., 2018), to be strongly beneficial to the outcome of this project. The advancements in these fields have led to a performance leap in many NLP disciplines, including coreference resolution and TSC, where, e.g., in the latter macro F1 gained from $F1_m = 63.3$ (Kiritchenko et al., 2014) to $F1_m = 75.8$ on the Twitter set (Zeng et al., 2019).

4 Methodology

Research task T2 will be the main contribution of my Ph.D. research; hence, this section focuses on completed and future tasks related to T2. Technically, addressing the research question represents two main challenges. First, resolving coreferences of semantic concepts across a set of news articles. In bias by WCL, journalists often use coreferences in a broader, sometimes even contradictory, sense than the state-of-the-art in coreference resolution and CDCR is capable of (Balahur et al., 2010; Baumer et al., 2017; Hamborg et al., 2019b). Second, classifying how actors and other semantic concepts are framed due to their mentions and their mentions' contexts, for which I will use TSC.

I plan to integrate the two tasks into the analysis shown in Figure 1 (RT3). Given a set of news articles reporting on the same event, the analysis will find subsets of articles and in-text phrases that similarly frame the concepts involved in the event. Lastly, the system will visualize the results to news consumers. Because RT3 is not directly related to NLP, it is described only briefly in Section 4.3.

4.1 Broad Cross-doc. Coreference Resolution

After the system has completed state-of-the-art preprocessing (Manning et al., 2014), the second phase in the analysis is broad CDCR, which aims to resolve coreferences as they occur in WCL bias (Hamborg et al., 2019b). The first task within this phase is *candidate extraction*. Relevant phrases containing bias by WCL commonly are noun phrases (NPs), e.g., NEs such as politicians, or verb phrases (VPs), i.e., describing an action, such as "cross the border" or "invade the country." The approach currently focuses only on NPs and extracts mentions from two sources. First, mentions from coreference chains identified by coreference resolution, and second, NPs identified by parsing.

The second task, *candidate merging*, addresses the main difficulty of broad CDCR. Journalists often use divergent terms to refer to the same semantic concept (Hamborg et al., 2019a), sometimes even terms that typically have opposing meanings, such as "intervene" vs. "invade," "coalition forces" vs. "invading forces." Such coreferences are highly context-dependent and may only be valid in a sin-

gle news article or across related articles (Hamborg et al., 2019b,c). Related state-of-the-art techniques for coreference resolution capably resolve generally valid synonyms, nominal and pronominal coreferences, such as "Donald Trump," "US president," and "he." However, they cannot reliably resolve the previously mentioned, broader examples of coreferences, which often occur in bias by WCL (Hamborg et al., 2019a).

The candidate merging task uses a series of sieves, where each analyzes specific characteristics of two candidates to determine whether they should be merged (see Figure 1). For example, the first sieve merges candidates if they have similar core meanings, specifically, if the head of each candidate's representative phrase is identical (Hamborg et al., 2019b). For a given coreference chain, the representative phrase is defined as the mention that best represents the chain's meaning (Manning et al., 2014). This way, the first sieve merges cases such as "Donald Trump" and "President Trump." The second sieve merges candidates if most of their mentions are semantically similar. The sieve currently uses non-contextualized word embeddings, specifically word2vec (Mikolov et al., 2013), to vectorize each mention. Then, it calculates the unweighted mean of all vectorized mentions of a candidate. Lastly, the sieve will merge two candidates if their mean vectors are similar by cosine similarity. Analogously, the remaining sieves address specific characteristics, e.g., using word embeddings (Le and Mikolov, 2014) and clustering methods, such as affinity propagation (Frey and Dueck, 2007). More information on the approach is described by Hamborg et al. (2019b).

Future research directions for the CDCR task most importantly include extending the capabilities of the approach and improving its performance. For the former, we want to investigate how coreferential mentions of activities (VPs) can be resolved. To improve the CDCR performance, we plan to devise a method that uses a language model to resolve coreferential mentions. For example, BERT increased the performance on single-document coreference resolution from F1=73.0 to F1=77.1. Using SpanBERT, a pre-training method focused on spans rather than tokens, the performance is increased to F1=79.6 (Joshi et al., 2019). We expect that using a language model can yield similar improvements for CDCR.

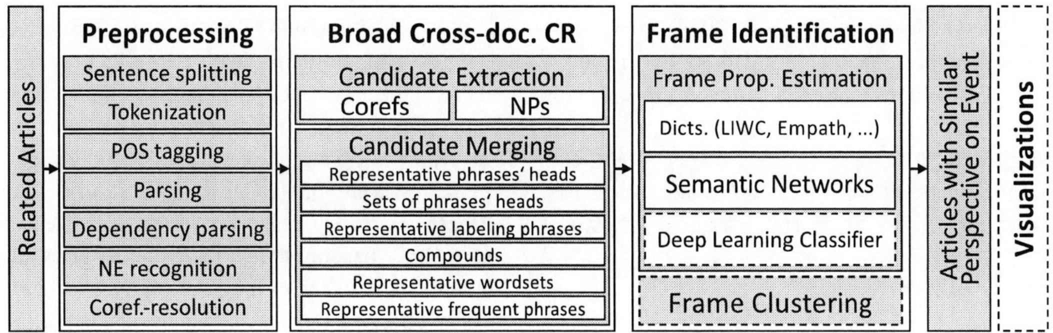

Figure 1: Shown is the plan for the three-phase analysis pipeline as it preprocesses news articles reporting on the same event, resolves coreferential mentions of semantic concepts across documents, and groups articles framing these concepts similarly. Source: (Hamborg et al., 2019b)

4.2 Frame Identification

Approaches aiming to estimate how semantic concepts are perceived, e.g., in the closely related field of TSC by classifying the concepts' polarity, or, more broadly, approaches to identify bias, traditionally employ manually created dictionaries or manually engineered features for machine learning (ML). Such approaches can achieve high performances in various domains, e.g., Recasens et al. (2013) propose an approach that capably identifies single bias-words in Wikipedia articles by using dictionaries and further, non-complex features.

In news texts, however, such approaches fall short. Since neutral language is expected (cf. Section 3), token-based and ML methods fail to catch the "meaning between the lines" (Hamborg et al., 2019a,b; Balahur et al., 2010; Godbole et al., 2007). Yet, recent NLP advancements, most importantly language models, have proven to be very effective in the news domain as in various other domains and tasks (see Section 3.3).

I plan to devise a neural model that will, in part, be inspired by state-of-the-art TSC approaches such as LCF-BERT (Zeng et al., 2019) and domain-adapted SPC-BERT (Rietzler et al., 2019), with three main differences. First, the model will need to consider characteristics specific to news articles. For example, in news articles, sentiment may more strongly depend on global context compared to TSC prime domains, e.g., because the latter are typically shorter texts (Adhikari et al., 2019).

Second, besides "absolute" sentiment polarity, the model needs to consider the "sentiment shift" induced by the context of a target mention. For example, while TSC traditionally focuses on the event's or text's sentiment regarding a target (cf.

"text-level" as defined by Balahur et al. (2010)), bias by WCL is concerned explicitly with the language, e.g., words, used in the sentence. So, given a target mention, I am interested in whether the mention or its context sway the perception more positively or negatively, also in relation to the sentiment at event- or text-level (Balahur et al., 2010).

Third, for an identified non-neutral polarity, the approach should be able to find in-text causes and potential effects thereof. Causes include the use of emotional words, loaded language, or aggressive repetition of specific facts. Effects include particularly how the target is framed (cf. "frame properties" as defined by Hamborg et al. (2019b) or "frames types" by Card et al. (2015)). Resolving the dependencies of a target and its context is an issue that is subject of current TSC research (Zeng et al., 2019; Rietzler et al., 2019), which I expect to be important in the proposed project as well.

4.3 System and Visualization

A system will integrate the previously described analysis workflow and will visualize the results to non-expert users (RT3). I devised visualizations that are similar to UIs of popular news aggregators, such as Google News, and bias-aware aggregators, such as AllSides. In contrast to these, the system will be able to identify in-text instances of bias (Hamborg et al., 2017, 2020; Spinde et al., 2020a). Hence, the system will not only give a bias-aware overview of current topics but also will have a visualization for single articles, which will highlight identified instances of WCL bias.

For research and evaluation of the previously described system and its analysis methods, I currently use the datasets AllSides (Chen et al., 2018), NewsWCL50 (Hamborg et al., 2019c), and PO-

LUSA (Gebhard and Hamborg, 2020), which have high diversity concerning outlets' political slant.

I plan to publish the code of the system and methods. Due to the system's modularity, researchers can extend it to support further forms of bias, e.g., commission and omission of information or picture selection (Torres, 2018; Hamborg et al., 2019a).

5   Evaluation

I conducted preliminary evaluations of the two main methods described in Section 4 (RT4). To measure the CDCR performance on broad coreferences as they occur in WCL bias (Section 4.1), I created a test dataset named NewsWCL50. The dataset was created by manually annotating coreferential mentions of persons, actions, and also vaguely defined, abstract concepts across 50 news articles (Hamborg et al., 2019b). The evaluation seems to confirm the research direction for this task. The approach currently achieves $F1 = 45.7$, or 84.4 if evaluated only on technically feasible annotations, compared to 29.8, or 42.1, respectively, achieved by the best baseline. Technically feasible refers to only comparing to annotations that the approach theoretically should be able to resolve, e.g., currently only NPs while excluding VPs.

A future evaluation will include a comparison to state-of-the-art CDCR methods (Barhom et al., 2019; Intel AI Lab, 2018). For improved soundness, we plan to create a second dataset similar to the NewsWCL50 dataset but with more coders and more articles. To do so, we will crowdsource the annotations of concept mentions on MTurk and use an improved codebook. The improvements will address issues of NewsWCL50's codebook, e.g., by making annotation types less ambiguous (Hamborg et al., 2019b). Further, we plan to use two additional datasets: ECB+ (Cybulska and Vossen, 2014) and NIdent (Recasens et al., 2012). Both datasets are commonly used to evaluate CDCR approaches and contain cross-document coreferences.

To evaluate the second task, frame identification, I plan to create a comprehensive training and test set for the TSC method described in Section 4.2. I already created a preliminary dataset of 3000 sentences, each including a target mention and a sentiment label agreed on by three coders. The dataset was created analogously to established TSC datasets (Dong et al., 2014; Pontiki et al., 2014; Nakov et al., 2016; Rosenthal et al., 2017).

Preliminary results seem to indicate that TSC on the news domain is in part more difficult than on TSC prime domains, such as product reviews, where authors often express their opinion explicitly. State-of-the-art TSC achieves average recall $AvgRec = 70.0$ on news articles, whereas performances on common TSC test datasets range from $AvgRec = 75.6$ (Twitter dataset) to 82.2 (Restaurant). Other baselines, e.g., using dictionaries and semantic networks, such as ConceptNet, perform very poorly ($F1 < 15.0$), which seems to confirm that token-based approaches fail to catch the subtlety common to WCL bias.

Finally, we plan to evaluate the system's effectiveness regarding visualization of the identified biases to non-expert users. An already conducted pre-study confirmed the study design (Spinde et al., 2020a). I will revisit this task once the classification methods described in Section 4 can be used within the study.

6   Conclusion and Implications

In summary, both everyday news consumers, as well as researchers in the social sciences, could benefit strongly from the automated identification of bias by word choice and labeling (WCL) in news articles. Devising suitable methods to resolve broad coreferences across news articles reporting on the same event and estimating the frames of the found instances of WCL bias are at the heart of this research project. One primary result of the project will be the first automated approach capable of identifying instances of bias by WCL in a set of news articles reporting on the same event or topic.

My vision is that at a later point in time, such methods might be integrated into popular news aggregators, such as Google News, helping news readers to explore and understand media bias through their daily news consumption. Also, I think that these methods could be integrated into the analysis workflow of content analyses and frame analyses, helping to automate further these currently mostly manual and thus time-consuming analysis concepts prevalent in the social sciences.

Acknowledgments

This research is supported by the Heidelberger Akademie der Wissenschaften (Heidelberg Academy of Sciences). I thank the Carl Zeiss Foundation for the scholarship that supports my Ph.D. research. Also, I thank the anonymous reviewers and Sudipta Kar for their valuable comments.

References

Ashutosh Adhikari, Achyudh Ram, Raphael Tang, and Jimmy Lin. 2019. DocBERT: BERT for Document Classification.

Karel Jan Alsem, Steven Brakman, Lex Hoogduin, and Gerard Kuper. 2008. The impact of newspapers on consumer confidence: Does spin bias exist? *Applied Economics*, 40(5):531–539.

Brent H Baker, Tim Graham, and Steve Kaminsky. 1994. *How to identify, expose & correct liberal media bias*. Media Research Center, Alexandria, VA.

Alexandra Balahur, Ralf Steinberger, Mijail Kabadjov, Vanni Zavarella, Erik Van Der Goot, Matina Halkia, Bruno Pouliquen, and Jenya Belyaeva. 2010. Sentiment analysis in the news. In *Proceedings of the Seventh International Conference on Language Resources and Evaluation ({LREC}'10)*, Valletta, Malta. European Language Resources Association (ELRA).

Shany Barhom, Vered Shwartz, Alon Eirew, Michael Bugert, Nils Reimers, and Ido Dagan. 2019. Revisiting Joint Modeling of Cross-document Entity and Event Coreference Resolution. In *Proceedings of the 57th Annual Meeting of the Association for Computational Linguistics*, pages 4179–4189, Stroudsburg, PA, USA. Association for Computational Linguistics.

Eric P.S. Baumer, Francesca Polletta, Nicole Pierski, and Geri K. Gay. 2017. A Simple Intervention to Reduce Framing Effects in Perceptions of Global Climate Change. *Environmental Communication*.

Business Insider. 2014. These 6 Corporations Control 90% Of The Media In America.

Dallas Card, Amber E. Boydstun, Justin H. Gross, Philip Resnik, and Noah A. Smith. 2015. The Media Frames Corpus: Annotations of Frames Across Issues. In *Proceedings of the 53rd Annual Meeting of the Association for Computational Linguistics and the 7th International Joint Conference on Natural Language Processing (Volume 2: Short Papers)*, pages 438–444, Stroudsburg, PA, USA. Association for Computational Linguistics.

Wei-Fan Chen, Henning Wachsmuth, Khalid Al-Khatib, and Benno Stein. 2018. Learning to Flip the Bias of News Headlines. In *Proceedings of the 11th International Conference on Natural Language Generation*, pages 79–88, Stroudsburg, PA, USA. Association for Computational Linguistics.

Agata Cybulska and Piek Vossen. 2014. Using a sledgehammer to crack a nut? Lexical diversity and event coreference resolution. In *Proceedings of the Ninth International Conference on Language Resources and Evaluation (LREC'14)*, pages 4545–4552, Reykjavik, Iceland. European Language Resources Association (ELRA).

Stefano DellaVigna and Ethan Kaplan. 2007. The Fox News effect: Media bias and voting. *The Quarterly Journal of Economics*, 122(3):1187–1234.

Jacob Devlin, Ming-Wei Chang, Kenton Lee, and Kristina Toutanova. 2018. BERT: Pre-training of Deep Bidirectional Transformers for Language Understanding. *arXiv preprint arXiv: 1810.04805*.

Li Dong, Furu Wei, Chuanqi Tan, Duyu Tang, Ming Zhou, and Ke Xu. 2014. Adaptive Recursive Neural Network for target-dependent Twitter sentiment classification. In *52nd Annual Meeting of the Association for Computational Linguistics, ACL 2014*, pages 49–54, Baltimore, MD, USA.

Robert M Entman. 1993. Framing: Toward Clarification of a Fractured Paradigm. *Journal of Communication*, 43(4):51–58.

Robert M Entman. 2007. Framing Bias: Media in the Distribution of Power. *Journal of Communication*, 57(1):163–173.

David Kirk Evans, Judith L. Klavans, and Kathleen R. McKeown. 2004. Columbia Newsblaster. In *Demonstration Papers at HLT-NAACL 2004 on XX - HLT-NAACL '04*, pages 1–4, Morristown, NJ, USA. Association for Computational Linguistics.

Brendan J. Frey and Delbert Dueck. 2007. Clustering by Passing Messages Between Data Points. *Science*, 315(5814):972–976.

Gilles Gauthier. 1993. In Defence of a Supposedly Outdated Notion: The Range of Application of Journalistic Objectivity. *Canadian Journal of Communication*, 18(4):497.

Lukas Gebhard and Felix Hamborg. 2020. The PO-LUSA Dataset: 0.9M Political News Articles Balanced by Time and Outlet Popularity. In *Proceedings of the ACM/IEEE Joint Conference on Digital Libraries (JCDL)*, pages 1–2, Wuhan, CN.

Matthew Gentzkow and Jesse M. Shapiro. 2006. Media Bias and Reputation. *Journal of Political Economy*, 114(2):280–316.

Namrata Godbole, Manja Srinivasaiah, and Steven Skiena. 2007. Large-Scale Sentiment Analysis for News and Blogs. In *Proceedings of the International Conference on Weblogs and Social Media (ICWSM)*, volume 7, pages 219–222, Boulder, CO, USA.

Felix Hamborg, Karsten Donnay, and Bela Gipp. 2019a. Automated identification of media bias in news articles: an interdisciplinary literature review. *International Journal on Digital Libraries*, 20(4):391–415.

Felix Hamborg, Norman Meuschke, Akiko Aizawa, and Bela Gipp. 2017. Identification and Analysis of Media Bias in News Articles. In *Proceedings of the 15th International Symposium of Information*

Science, pages 224–236, Berlin, DE. Verlag Werner Hülsbusch.

Felix Hamborg, Norman Meuschke, and Bela Gipp. 2018. Bias-aware news analysis using matrix-based news aggregation. *International Journal on Digital Libraries*.

Felix Hamborg, Anastasia Zhukova, and Bela Gipp. 2019b. Automated Identification of Media Bias by Word Choice and Labeling in News Articles. In *2019 ACM/IEEE Joint Conference on Digital Libraries (JCDL)*, pages 196–205, Urbana-Champaign, IL, USA. IEEE.

Felix Hamborg, Anastasia Zhukova, and Bela Gipp. 2019c. Illegal Aliens or Undocumented Immigrants? Towards the Automated Identification of Bias by Word Choice and Labeling. In *Proceedings of the iConference 2019*, pages 179–187. Springer, Cham, Washington, DC, USA.

Felix Hamborg, Anastasia Zhukova, and Bela Gipp. 2020. Newsalyze: Enabling News Consumers to Understand Media Bias. In *Proceedings of the ACM/IEEE Joint Conference on Digital Libraries (JCDL)*, pages 1–2, Wuhan, CN.

Intel AI Lab. 2018. NLP Architect.

Mandar Joshi, Danqi Chen, Yinhan Liu, Daniel S. Weld, Luke Zettlemoyer, and Omer Levy. 2019. SpanBERT: Improving Pre-training by Representing and Predicting Spans.

Mesut Kaya, Guven Fidan, and Ismail H Toroslu. 2012. Sentiment Analysis of Turkish Political News. In *2012 IEEE/WIC/ACM International Conferences on Web Intelligence and Intelligent Agent Technology*, pages 174–180. IEEE Computer Society, IEEE.

Svetlana Kiritchenko, Xiaodan Zhu, Colin Cherry, and Saif Mohammad. 2014. NRC-Canada-2014: Detecting Aspects and Sentiment in Customer Reviews. In *Proceedings of the 8th International Workshop on Semantic Evaluation (SemEval 2014)*, pages 437–442, Dublin, Ireland. Association for Computational Linguistics.

Quoc V. Le and Tomas Mikolov. 2014. Distributed Representations of Sentences and Documents. *International Conference on Machine Learning - ICML 2014*, 32.

Sora Lim, Adam Jatowt, and Masatoshi Yoshikawa. 2018. Towards Bias Inducing Word Detection by Linguistic Cue Analysis in News Articles.

Christopher Manning, Mihai Surdeanu, John Bauer, Jenny Finkel, Steven Bethard, and David McClosky. 2014. The Stanford CoreNLP Natural Language Processing Toolkit. In *Proceedings of 52nd Annual Meeting of the Association for Computational Linguistics: System Demonstrations*, pages 55–60, Stroudsburg, PA, USA. Association for Computational Linguistics.

John McCarthy, Larissa Titarenko, Clark McPhail, Patrick Rafail, and Boguslaw Augustyn. 2008. Assessing stability in the patterns of selection bias in newspaper coverage of protest during the transition from communism in Belarus. *Mobilization: An International Quarterly*, 13(2):127–146.

Andrew Mehler, Yunfan Bao, X. Li, Y. Wang, and Steven Skiena. 2006. Spatial Analysis of News Sources. *IEEE Transactions on Visualization and Computer Graphics*, 12(5):765–772.

Tomas Mikolov, Greg Corrado, Kai Chen, and Jeffrey Dean. 2013. Efficient Estimation of Word Representations in Vector Space. *Proceedings of the International Conference on Learning Representations (ICLR 2013)*.

Sean A. Munson, Stephanie Y. Lee, and Paul Resnick. 2013. Encouraging reading of diverse political viewpoints with a browser widget. In *Proceedings of the 7th International Conference on Weblogs and Social Media, ICWSM 2013*.

Sean A Munson and Paul Resnick. 2010. Presenting diverse political opinions. In *Proceedings of the 28th international conference on Human factors in computing systems - CHI '10*, pages 1457–1466, New York, New York, USA. ACM, ACM Press.

Sean A Munson, Daniel Xiaodan Zhou, and Paul Resnick. 2009. Sidelines: An Algorithm for Increasing Diversity in News and Opinion Aggregators. In *ICWSM*.

Preslav Nakov, Alan Ritter, Sara Rosenthal, Fabrizio Sebastiani, and Veselin Stoyanov. 2016. SemEval-2016 Task 4: Sentiment Analysis in Twitter. In *Proceedings of the 10th International Workshop on Semantic Evaluation (SemEval-2016)*, pages 1–18, San Diego, CA, USA. Association for Computational Linguistics.

David Niven. 2002. *Tilt?: The search for media bias.* Praeger.

Daniela Oelke, Benno Geißelmann, and Daniel A Keim. 2012. Visual Analysis of Explicit Opinion and News Bias in German Soccer Articles. In *EuroVis Workshop on Visual Analytics*, Vienna, Austria.

Pamela E. Oliver and Gregory M. Maney. 2000. Political Processes and Local Newspaper Coverage of Protest Events: From Selection Bias to Triadic Interactions. *American Journal of Sociology*, 106(2):463–505.

Zizi Papacharissi and Maria de Fatima Oliveira. 2008. News Frames Terrorism: A Comparative Analysis of Frames Employed in Terrorism Coverage in U.S. and U.K. Newspapers. *The International Journal of Press/Politics*, 13(1):52–74.

Souneil Park, Seungwoo Kang, Sangyoung Chung, and Junehwa Song. 2009. NewsCube. In *Proceedings of the 27th international conference on Human factors in computing systems - CHI 09*, page 443, New York, New York, USA. ACM Press.

Souneil Park, Minsam Ko, Jungwoo Kim, H Choi, and Junehwa Song. 2011a. NewsCube 2.0: An Exploratory Design of a Social News Website for Media Bias Mitigation. In *Workshop on Social Recommender Systems*.

Souneil Park, Minsam Ko, Jungwoo Kim, Ying Liu, and Junehwa Song. 2011b. The politics of comments. In *Proceedings of the ACM 2011 conference on Computer supported cooperative work - CSCW '11*, pages 113–122, New York, New York, USA. ACM, ACM Press.

Maria Pontiki, Dimitris Galanis, John Pavlopoulos, Harris Papageorgiou, Ion Androutsopoulos, and Suresh Manandhar. 2014. SemEval-2014 Task 4: Aspect Based Sentiment Analysis. In *Proceedings of the 8th International Workshop on Semantic Evaluation (SemEval 2014)*, pages 27–35, Dublin, Ireland.

Vincent Price, Lilach Nir, and Joseph N. Cappella. 2005. Framing public discussion of gay civil unions.

Marta Recasens, Cristian Danescu-Niculescu-Mizil, and Dan Jurafsky. 2013. Linguistic Models for Analyzing and Detecting Biased Language. In *Proceedings of the 51st Annual Meeting on Association for Computational Linguistics*, pages 1650–1659, Sofia, BG. Association for Computational Linguistics.

Marta Recasens, M. Antonia Marti, and Constantin Orasan. 2012. Annotating Near-Identity from Coreference Disagreements. In *Proceedings of the Eighth International Conference on Language Resources and Evaluation (LREC'12)*, pages 165–172, Istanbul, Turkey. European Language Resources Association (ELRA).

Alexander Rietzler, Sebastian Stabinger, Paul Opitz, and Stefan Engl. 2019. Adapt or Get Left Behind: Domain Adaptation through BERT Language Model Finetuning for Aspect-Target Sentiment Classification. *arXiv preprint arXiv:1908.11860*.

Sara Rosenthal, Noura Farra, and Preslav Nakov. 2017. SemEval-2017 Task 4: Sentiment Analysis in Twitter. In *Proceedings of the 11th International Workshop on Semantic Evaluation (SemEval-2017)*, pages 502–518, Vancouver, Canada. Association for Computational Linguistics.

Donald Rugg. 1941. Experiments in Wording Questions: II. *Public Opinion Quarterly*.

Jonathon P. Schuldt, Sara H. Konrath, and Norbert Schwarz. 2011. Global warming or climate change? Whether the planet is warming depends on question wording. *Public Opinion Quarterly*.

Alison Smith, Timothy Hawes, and Meredith Myers. 2014. Hiérarchie: Interactive Visualization for Hierarchical Topic Models. *Proceedings of the Workshop on Interactive Language Learning, Visualization, and Interfaces*, pages 71–78.

Timo Spinde, Felix Hamborg, Angelica Becerra, Karsten Donnay, and Bela Gipp. 2020a. Enabling News Consumers to View and Understand Biased News Coverage: A Study on the Perception and Visualization of Media Bias. In *Proceedings of the ACM/IEEE Joint Conference on Digital Libraries (JCDL)*, pages 1–4, Wuhan, CN.

Timo Spinde, Felix Hamborg, and Bela Gipp. 2020b. An Integrated Approach to Detect Media Bias in German News Articles. In *Proceedings of the ACM/IEEE Joint Conference on Digital Libraries (JCDL)*, pages 1–2, Wuhan, CN.

Carlo Strapparava and Rada Mihalcea. 2007. Semeval-2007 task 14: Affective text. In *Proceedings of the 4th International Workshop on Semantic Evaluations*, pages 70–74, Prague, Czech Republic. Association for Computational Linguistics.

Michelle Torres. 2018. Give me the full picture: Using computer vision to understand visual frames and political communication.

Biqing Zeng, Heng Yang, Ruyang Xu, Wu Zhou, and Xuli Han. 2019. LCF: A Local Context Focus Mechanism for Aspect-Based Sentiment Classification. *Applied Sciences*, 9(16):1–22.

SCAR: Sentence Compression using Autoencoders for Reconstruction

Chanakya Malireddy
IIIT Hyderabad
`chanakya.malireddy`
`@research.iiit.ac.in`

Tirth Maniar
IIIT Hyderabad
`tirth.maniar`
`@students.iiit.ac.in`

Manish Shrivastava
IIIT Hyderabad
`m.shrivastava`
`@iiit.ac.in`

Abstract

Sentence compression is the task of shortening a sentence while retaining its meaning. Most methods proposed for this task rely on labeled or paired corpora (containing pairs of verbose and compressed sentences), which is often expensive to collect. To overcome this limitation, we present a novel unsupervised deep learning framework (SCAR) for deletion-based sentence compression. SCAR is primarily composed of two encoder-decoder pairs: a compressor and a reconstructor. The compressor masks the input, and the reconstructor tries to regenerate it. The model is entirely trained on unlabeled data and does not require additional inputs such as explicit syntactic information or optimal compression length. SCAR's merit lies in the novel Linkage Loss function, which correlates the compressor and its effect on reconstruction, guiding it to drop inferable tokens. SCAR achieves higher ROUGE scores on benchmark datasets than the existing state-of-the-art methods and baselines. We also conduct a user study to demonstrate the application of our model as a text highlighting system. Using our model to underscore salient information facilitates speed-reading and reduces the time required to skim a document.

1 Introduction

Our fast-paced lifestyle precludes us from reading verbose and lengthy documents. How about a system that highlights the salient content for us (as shown in Fig.1)? We model this problem as the well-known sentence compression task. Sentence compression aims to generate a shorter representation of the input that captures its gist and preserves its intent. Compression algorithms are broadly classified as abstractive and extractive. Extractive compression or deletion-based algorithms only select relevant words from the input, whereas abstractive compression algorithms also allow paraphrasing.

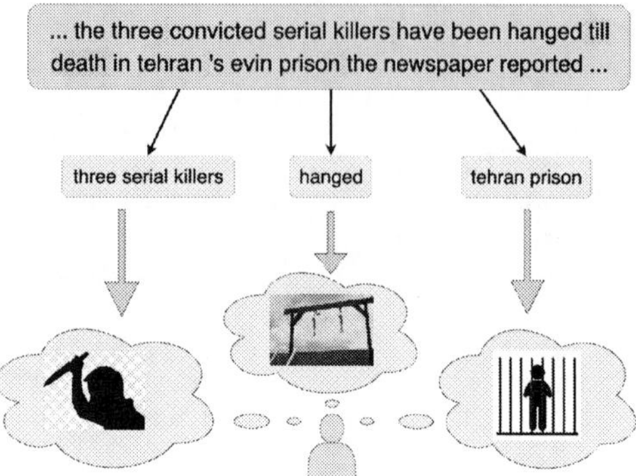

Figure 1: An example of a system that highlights the salient content, allowing the user to skim through the document quickly.

In the past, compression approaches have revolved around statistical methods (Knight and Marcu, 2000) and syntactic rules (McDonald, 2006). Current state-of-the-art methods model the problem as a sequence-to-sequence learning task (Filippova et al., 2015). Although these methods perform well, they require massive parallel training datasets that are difficult to collect (Filippova and Altun, 2013). Recently, unsupervised approaches have been explored to overcome this limitation. Fevry and Phang (2018) model compression as a denoising task but barely reach the baselines. Baziotis et al. (2019) propose SEQ^3, an autoencoder which uses a Gumbel-softmax to represent the distribution over summaries. But a qualitative analysis of their outputs shows that SEQ^3 mimics the lead baseline.

In this work, we present an unsupervised deep learning framework (SCAR) for deletion-based sentence compression. SCAR is composed of a compressor and a reconstructor. For each word in the input, the compressor determines whether or not to include it in the compression. A length loss restricts the compression length. The reconstruc-

Proceedings of the 58th Annual Meeting of the Association for Computational Linguistics: Student Research Workshop, pages 88–94
July 5 - July 10, 2020. ©2020 Association for Computational Linguistics

tor tries to regenerate the input using the words retained by the compressor. A reconstruction loss motivates the compressor to include words that aid in reconstruction. However, without an additional loss to govern word masking, the network fails to converge. We introduce a novel linkage loss that ties together the compressor and the reconstructor. It penalizes the network if a) it decides to drop a word but is unable to reconstruct it or b) it decides to include a word which it could reconstruct easily.

2 Related Work

Early compression algorithms were formulated using strong linguistic priors and language heuristics (Jing, 2000; Knight and Marcu, 2002; Dorr et al., 2003; Cohn and Lapata, 2008). McDonald (2006) use syntactical evidence to condition the output of the model. Berg-Kirkpatrick et al. (2011) prune dependency edges to remove constituents for compression.

Deep learning-based approaches have gained popularity owing to their success in core NLP tasks such as machine translation (Bahdanau et al., 2014). Filippova et al. (2015) propose an RNN based encoder-decoder network for deletion based compression. Although this approach achieves superior performance over metric-based approaches, a large amount of paired sentences are needed to train the network.

The first attempt to reduce the dependence on paired corpora for deletion based deep learning compression models was made by Miao and Blunsom (2016). They train separate compressor and reconstruction models, to allow for both supervised and unsupervised training. The compressor consists of a discrete variational autoencoder. The model is trained end-to-end using the REINFORCE algorithm. However, the reported results still use a sizeable amount of labeled data.

Recent approaches have sought completely unsupervised solutions. Fevry and Phang (2018) use a denoising autoencoder (DAE) for sentence compression. The input sentence is shuffled and extended to add noise. DAE tries to reconstruct the original denoised sentence from the noisy input. An additional signal is needed to specify the output length. At test time, the sentence is fed to the model without any noise. In an attempt to denoise the input, the network generates a compressed output. However, the model often fails to capture the information present in the input and is barely able

to reach the baselines.

SEQ^3 (Baziotis et al., 2019) proposes an autoencoder using a Gumbel-softmax to represent the distribution over summaries. A compressor generates a summary, and a reconstructor tries to reconstruct the input using the summary. A pre-trained language model acts as a prior, to incentivize the compressor to produce human-readable summaries. An additional topic loss is required to ensure that the summary contains relevant words, making the model non-generic and fine-tuned to the domain. A qualitative analysis of the outputs shows that SEQ^3 merely mimics the lead baseline and generates compressions by blindly copying a prefix of the input.

3 SCAR

SCAR is composed of two encoder-decoder pairs: compressor **C** and reconstructor **R**, as shown in Fig. 2. Given an input sentence $\mathbf{s} = w_1, w_2 ..., w_k$ containing k words, **C** generates an indicator vector $\mathbf{I_v} = I_{v1}, I_{v2}, ..., I_{vk}$ which indicates the presence/absence of each word in the summary. The summary is represented as $\mathbf{s'} = \mathbf{s} \odot \mathbf{I_v}$, where $\odot$ represents element-wise multiplication. Therefore, words corresponding to $\mathbf{I_{vi}} \approx 0$ are effectively skipped. The network tries to reconstruct the input sentence from $\mathbf{s'}$.

Formally, the network tries to find an I_v^* such that the probability $p(\mathbf{s}|\mathbf{s} \odot \mathbf{I_v})$ is maximized and $\sum_{t=1}^{k} I_{vt}$ is minimized, jointly. The probability $p(\mathbf{s}|\mathbf{s} \odot \mathbf{I_v})$ can be decomposed further as shown in Eq.(1)

$$I_v^* = \arg\max_{I_v} \prod_{t=1}^{k} p(w_t|(w_1 \times I_{v1}),$$
$$..., (w_{k-1} \times I_{vk-1})) \quad (1)$$

For every word in the sentence, we learn a 300-dimensional embedding initialized with GloVe (Pennington et al., 2014). These embeddings are sequentially fed as input to the **Sentence Encoder** (E_s), composed of a bi-LSTM. The input is fed forwards and backward. The hidden states are a concatenation of the forward and backward states. The sentence representation is obtained from the final hidden state of E_s $(i.e., h_{e1})$. The **Indicator Extraction Module (IEM)**, a bi-LSTM decoder, is initialized using h_{e1}. The output of this decoder at each time step is passed through a network of two fully connected layers to generate

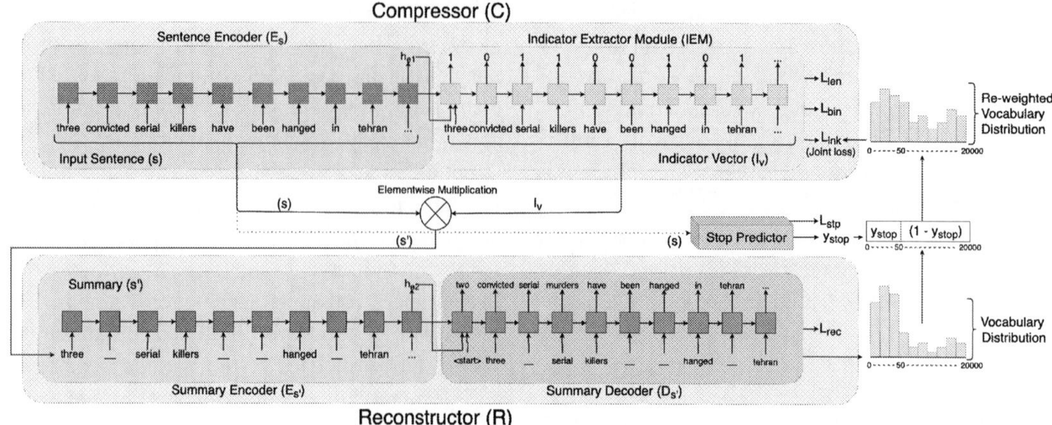

Figure 2: The figure shows the proposed SCAR architecture (details are described in Section 3)

a single indicator value. We intend this value to be close to either one or zero, denoting the presence/absence of each word from the summary.

The masked sentence, $\mathbf{s}' = \mathbf{s} \odot \mathbf{I}_v$, is encoded using the **Summary Encoder** ($E_{s'}$), composed of a bi-LSTM. The **Summary Decoder** ($D_{s'}$), also a bi-LSTM, is initialized using the final hidden state of $E_{s'}(h_{e2})$. This decoder aims to regenerate the input sentence $\mathbf{s}$ from $\mathbf{s}'$. This motivates IEM to generate $\mathbf{I}_v$ such that $\mathbf{s}$ can be easily reconstructed. The output at each time step in $D_{s'}$ is fed to a dense layer, W_s, which computes a distribution over the vocabulary from the decoder's hidden states.

3.1 Loss functions

Compression Length loss (L_{len}) is used to constrain the summary length. It is calculated from the output of IEM as shown in Eq. (2). $Len(\mathbf{s}')$ is the sum of elements of $\mathbf{I}_v$. We set $r = 0.4$ in our experiments.

$$L_{len} = \left(\frac{Len(\mathbf{s}')}{Len(\mathbf{s})} - r \right)^2 \qquad (2)$$

Sentence Reconstruction loss (L_{rec}) is applied to ensure $\mathbf{s}'$ contains enough information to reconstruct $\mathbf{s}$. It is calculated from the output of $D_{s'}$ as shown in Eq. (3).

$$L_{rec} = - \sum_{i=1}^{Len(s)} log P(w_i | w'_{<i}, h_{e2}) \qquad (3)$$

To help ease reconstruction, L_{rec} steers the network to keep larger summaries, whereas L_{len} forces it to it cut down. This makes it hard for the model to converge optimally. We introduce a novel **Linkage loss** (L_{lnk}), which correlates the indicator vector and its effect on reconstruction. It penalizes the network if a) it decides to mask a word but is unable to reconstruct it or b) it decides to include a word which it could reconstruct easily. It is applied to the outputs of IEM and $D_{s'}$, as shown in Eq. (4).

Ref:	the olympic village for the winter games in turin was officially opened on tuesday
Summ:	___ olympic village ___ ___ winter _____ __ turin ___ _________ opened __ _______
Recon:	the olympic village of the winter olympics a turin was officially opened here wednesday

Figure 3: Linkage loss guides the model to drop words that can be inferred during reconstruction (light green) and retain words that are harder to infer (dark green).

$$L_{lnk} = \sum_{i=1}^{Len(s)} \left(\mathbf{I}_{vi} e^{(1-\chi_i)} + (1-\mathbf{I}_{vi}) e^{\chi_i} - 1 \right) \qquad (4)$$

The variable $\chi_i \in [0, 1]$, in Eq. (5), is the normalized value of a word's logit in a sentence. It denotes the relative difficulty of decoding word w_i, given $w'_{<i}$ and h_{e2}. L_{lnk} is minimized when either a) $\chi_i = 0$ and $\mathbf{I}_{vi} = 0$ (signifying that w_i is easy to decode and should be dropped) or b) $\chi_i = 1$ and $\mathbf{I}_{vi} = 1$ (signifying that hard-to-decode words should be retained). The effect of L_{lnk} can be seen in Fig. 3. The model retains words with a higher χ_i (dark green), whereas words with a lower χ_i (light green) can be inferred during reconstruction and

90

therefore dropped.

$$\chi_i = \frac{|logP(w_i|w'_{<i}, h_{e2})|}{\max_{1 \leq j \leq Len(s)}|logP(w_j|w_{<j}, h_{e2})|} \quad (5)$$

Binarization loss (L_{bin}) is applied to the output of IEM, as shown in Eq. (6), to push the values of $\mathbf{I_v}$ close to 0 and 1 (since setting them to these hard values directly introduces non-differentiability). In our experiments, b is set to 5 and a is such that L_{bin} is always non-negative. At test time, only the words with $I_{vi} > 0.5$ are included in the compression.

$$L_{bin} = \frac{1}{Len(s)} \sum_{i=1}^{Len(s)} (a - b(I_{vi} - 0.5)^2) \quad (6)$$

3.2 Re-weighting Vocabulary Distribution

Due to the nature of Zipf's law (Zipf, 1949), most of the probability mass in the vocabulary distribution output by the Summary Decoder is retained by *stopwords*. As a result, χ_i corresponding to *stopwords* is much lower compared to *content words*. This causes the network to blindly drop *stopwords* and retain most *content words*. In this case, many content words that may be inferable are not dropped. To remedy this, we introduce **Stop Predictor** (D_{stop}), which assigns a score to the next word based on whether it is a *stopword* or not. When the network believes that the next word is not a *stopword*, it re-distributes the probability mass from *stopwords* proportionally among *content words* and vice-versa.

The word embeddings' of **s** are sequentially fed as input to D_{stop}, a bi-LSTM decoder. The output of D_{stop} at each time step is passed through a network of two fully connected layers to generate a single score, $y_{stop,i} \in [0,1]$. In order to train D_{stop} we apply L_{stp} (mean-square-error loss with the ground truth) as shown in Eq.(7). The ground truth is obtained from the *stopword-list*, defined as the collection of 50 most frequent words (0.25% of the vocabulary size) found in the dataset.

We re-weight the vocabulary distribution using $y_{stop,i}$, similar to p_{gen} in (See et al., 2017), as shown in Eq. (8). $\mathbb{I}_s$ is a vocabulary sized vector with the 50 elements of *stopword-list* set to 1 and the rest to 0.

$$L_{stp} = \frac{1}{Len(s)} \sum_{i=1}^{Len(s)} (y_{stop,i} - y_{stop,i}^{gt})^2 \quad (7)$$

$$P'(w_i|w'_{<i}, h_{e2}) = softmax(\mathbb{I}_s \cdot y_{stop,i} \cdot P(w_i)$$
$$+ (1 - \mathbb{I}_s) \cdot (1 - y_{stop,i}) \cdot P(w_i)) \quad (8)$$

This re-weighted distribution is plugged into Eq.(5) and used to calculate L_{lnk}.

The final loss function (L) is a linear combination of the above losses. Since this is an unsupervised approach, currently, the weights are experimentally determined. Initial weights for each loss were selected to normalize the output range of all loss functions. We performed a grid search in the neighborhood of these initial weight values to determine optimal weights that maximized the ROUGE scores on the validation set. The weights have been set to 8 (L_{len}), 1 (L_{rec}), 5 (L_{lnk}), 100 (L_{bin}) and 10 (L_{stp}) in our experiments.

3.3 Training

In our experiments, we used the annotated Gigaword corpus (Rush et al., 2015). The model is trained only on the reference section. We only considered sentences where the length was between 15 and 40 words (3.5M samples). A small portion of the training set (200k samples) was held out for validation. The batch size is set to 128. Vocabulary is restricted to 20000 most frequent words from the dataset. All bi-LSTM cells are of size 600 and weights are initialized normally $\mathcal{N}(\mu = 0, \sigma = 0.1)$. The output from IEM and D_{stop} is passed through a hidden layer (150 units) and an output layer with ReLU and sigmoid activations, respectively. We use Adam optimizer (Kingma and Ba) (lr=0.001, β_1=0.9 and β_2=0.999). Gradients larger than 1.0 are clipped. The model is trained for 5 epochs using early stopping by monitoring the performance on the validation set.[1]

4 Experiments

Since the test set of the Gigaword corpus is small (1.9k samples) and does not capture the true behavior of the models, we report our results on the significantly larger validation set (189k samples). Note that SCAR does not make use of the validation set during training, and it can be treated as a test set. We also test (without retraining) SCAR on DUC-2003 and DUC-2004 shared tasks (Over et al., 2007), containing 624/500 news articles each, paired with 4 reference summaries capped at 75

---

[1] https://github.com/m-chanakya/scar

	Gigaword			DUC-2003			DUC-2004		
	R-1	**R-2**	**R-L**	**R-1**	**R-2**	**R-L**	**R-1**	**R-2**	**R-L**
Baselines									
All-Text	28.07	10.02	24.49	-	-	-	-	-	-
Prefix	26.28	9.54	24.73	20.82	6.14	18.44	22.18	6.30	19.33
Lead50	**30.22**	**10.99**	**27.40**	**20.92**	**6.22**	**18.59**	**22.26**	**6.33**	**19.38**
Unsupervised									
SEQ^3	30.23	10.24	27.26	20.89	6.07	18.54	22.12	6.17	19.29
DAE	26.84	7.35	23.15	18.45	3.94	15.79	20.06	4.73	17.03
SCAR	**29.80**	**7.52**	**26.10**	**21.71**	**4.73**	**18.81**	**22.92**	**5.52**	**19.85**
Supervised									
Seq2Seq	33.72	14.18	30.65	26.12	9.67	23.37	27.31	10.43	24.18
Ablation									
w/o L_{lnk}	27.24	5.16	23.87	20.31	3.41	17.60	19.94	3.25	17.07
w/o D_{stop}	28.86	7.02	25.29	21.46	4.66	18.62	21.94	4.70	19.10
$r = 0.3$	27.80	5.07	24.39	20.25	3.16	17.46	20.28	3.09	17.53
$r = 0.2$	25.36	3.36	22.38	18.97	2.31	16.23	18.43	2.20	15.90

Table 1: Average ROUGE scores on Gigaword and DUC datasets.

bytes. We report average ROUGE (1,2,L) F1 scores (Lin, 2004) obtained by all the models in Table 1.

We compare our model with three standard baselines - **Prefix** (first 8 words for Gigaword/first 75 bytes for DUC), **Lead50** (50% tokens) and **All-Text** (entire input). To compare with supervised approaches, we train a baseline **Seq2Seq** model, similar to (Fevry and Phang, 2018). Finally, we compare our model with the recent unsupervised approaches, **DAE** (Fevry and Phang, 2018) [2], and SEQ^3 (Baziotis et al., 2019) [3].

4.1 Pitfalls of SEQ^3

Lead50 achieves the highest ROUGE scores, but it does not make for a viable compression method as it blindly drops the latter half of the sentence. The scores obtained by SEQ^3 are strikingly similar to Lead50. The authors of SEQ^3 note that "the model tends to copy the first words of the input sentence in the compressed text". We observed that SEQ^3 introduces very little abstractiveness (only 0.001% of the words are different from the input) and copies the first half of the sentence.

To corroborate our findings, we introduce the notion of *summary coverage*. It is a measure of how well each position of the input is represented in the compression. We divide the input sentence into equal-sized segments and measure how often

[2] https://github.com/zphang/usc_dae
[3] https://github.com/cbaziotis/seq3.git

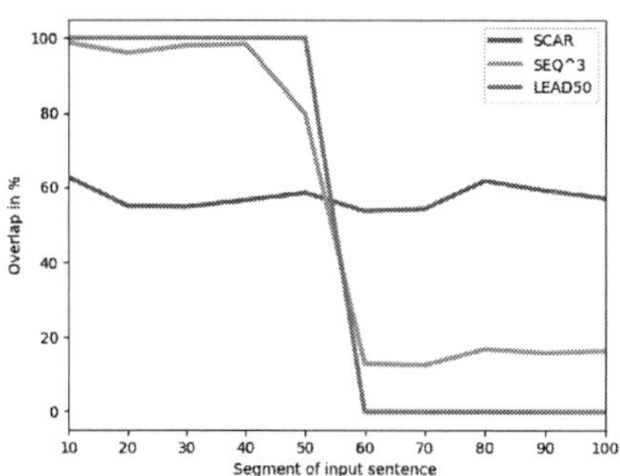

Figure 4: We divide the input sentence into equal-sized segments and measure how often each segment (x-axis) is included in the compression (y-axis).

each segment is included in the compression. We plot the summary coverage for Lead50, SEQ^3, and SCAR, as shown in Fig.4. A visualization is shown in Fig.5. Lead50 and SEQ^3 only cover the first half (initial segments) of the input, leading to incomplete/incorrect compressions. SCAR has more uniform coverage and represents all segments of the input well, leading to more informative compressions.

4.2 Quantitative evaluation

Given the pitfalls of SEQ^3, SCAR achieves state-of-the-art performance in unsupervised sentence compression on Gigaword and DUC datasets. SCAR's R-2 scores on both benchmark sets are low because it tends to drop the inferable portion

LEAD50:	malaysia 's government on monday announced an immediate ##-million dollar plan to expand roads , build underground bypasses and overhead bridges to ease kuala lumpur 's traffic jams .
SEQ³:	malaysia 's government on monday announced an immediate ##-million dollar plan to expand roads , build underground bypasses and overhead bridges to ease kuala lumpur 's traffic jams .
SCAR	malaysia 's government on monday announced an immediate ##-million dollar plan to expand roads , build underground bypasses and overhead bridges to ease kuala lumpur 's traffic jams .
Headline:	malaysia announces ##-million dollar plan to ease kuala lumpur traffic woes

Figure 5: Visualization of summary coverage by overlaying the compressions onto the reference.

Ref (SCAR Highlight)	president bill clinton this week unveils a budget proposal offering nearly ### billion dollars in tax relief over the next six years and calling for the elimination of the federal deficit by #### .
SEQ³	president bill clinton this week unveils a budget proposal offering nearly ### billion dollars in tax relief deficit (Wrong content retained)
DAE	president bill clinton unveils the federal budget deficit this week by offering nearly ### billion dollars (Wrong content retained)
SCAR	bill this budget proposal nearly billion tax relief next six calling elimination federal deficit
Headline	clinton calls for elimination of the federal deficit by ####

Figure 6: An example of the reference (with SCAR highlight), compressions, and headline.

	Correct	Unsure	Time
Reference	93.4%	6.6%	2m 31s
SCAR (Highlight)	93.4%	6.6%	**1m 54s**
Compressions			
SEQ^3	53.3%	46.67%	**2m 13s**
DAE	26.67%	73.34%	2m 29s
SCAR	**66.67%**	33.33%	2m 42s

Table 2: Average correctness and time scores.

of a bi-gram. Without Linkage loss (L_{lnk}), SCAR loses its ability to drop inferable portions of the input. Without D_{stop}, a mechanism to re-distribute probability mass from stop words, SCAR tends only to drop stopwords. Lower values of r, cause the model to generate smaller compressions. As expected, all of the above factors cause a dip in performance.

4.3 Qualitative evaluation

ROUGE only measures the content overlap and does not account for coherence. We conduct a Qualitative study to address the known issues with ROUGE (Schluter, 2017) and evaluate SCAR's effectiveness as a speed reading system.

Human evaluators are asked to match the reference/compression that they are shown with the correct headline from a set of 5 options. 3 incorrect options are generated by selecting Gigaword headlines that share tokens with the reference. The fifth option is "unsure." Fifteen English speaking participants were divided into 5 sets. They were shown the reference (1), the reference with SCAR highlighting (2), compressions generated by SCAR (3), SEQ^3 (4), and DAE (5), respectively. Each user was asked to match 10 samples.

An example is shown in Fig.6. Compressions generated by DAE fail to preserve the meaning and intent of the reference. SEQ^3 habitually retains the first half of the input, and the evaluators fail to match the headline if it corresponds to the latter half. Due to collocation, SCAR tends to drop the inferable portion of a bi-gram. For example, "Bill" is retained, and "Clinton" is dropped. The average correctness and time scores are reported in Table 2. Compared to other compressions, SCAR has the highest score in terms of correctness. Using SCAR to highlight, reduces reading time by 25%.

5 Conclusion and Future Work

SCAR addresses a significant limitation of the unavailability of labeled data for sentence compression. It outperforms the existing state-of-the-art unsupervised models. Since SCAR learns to drop inferable components of the input and therefore reduces noise, it can be used as a preprocessing step for machine translation and other information retrieval tasks.

References

Dzmitry Bahdanau, Kyunghyun Cho, and Yoshua Bengio. 2014. Neural machine translation by jointly learning to align and translate. *arXiv preprint arXiv:1409.0473*.

Christos Baziotis, Ion Androutsopoulos, Ioannis Konstas, and Alexandros Potamianos. 2019. Seq^3: Differentiable sequence-to-sequence-to-sequence autoencoder for unsupervised abstractive sentence compression. *arXiv preprint arXiv:1904.03651*.

Taylor Berg-Kirkpatrick, Dan Gillick, and Dan Klein. 2011. Jointly learning to extract and compress. In *Proceedings of the 49th Annual Meeting of the Association for Computational Linguistics: Human Language Technologies-Volume 1*, pages 481–490. Association for Computational Linguistics.

Trevor Cohn and Mirella Lapata. 2008. Sentence compression beyond word deletion. In *Proceedings of the 22nd International Conference on Computational Linguistics-Volume 1*, pages 137–144. Association for Computational Linguistics.

Bonnie Dorr, David Zajic, and Richard Schwartz. 2003. Hedge trimmer: A parse-and-trim approach to headline generation. In *Proceedings of the HLT-NAACL 03 on Text summarization workshop-Volume 5*, pages 1–8. Association for Computational Linguistics.

Thibault Fevry and Jason Phang. 2018. Unsupervised sentence compression using denoising autoencoders. In *Proceedings of the 22nd Conference on Computational Natural Language Learning*, pages 413–422, Brussels, Belgium. Association for Computational Linguistics.

Katja Filippova, Enrique Alfonseca, Carlos A Colmenares, Lukasz Kaiser, and Oriol Vinyals. 2015. Sentence compression by deletion with lstms. In *Proceedings of the 2015 Conference on Empirical Methods in Natural Language Processing*, pages 360–368.

Katja Filippova and Yasemin Altun. 2013. Overcoming the lack of parallel data in sentence compression. In *Proceedings of the 2013 Conference on Empirical Methods in Natural Language Processing*, pages 1481–1491.

Hongyan Jing. 2000. Sentence reduction for automatic text summarization. In *Proceedings of the sixth conference on Applied natural language processing*, pages 310–315. Association for Computational Linguistics.

Diederik P Kingma and Jimmy Ba. Adam: A method for stochastic optimization. In *Proceedings of the 3rd International Conference on Learning Representations (ICLR), arXiv preprint arXiv*, volume 1412.

Kevin Knight and Daniel Marcu. 2000. Statistics-based summarization – step one: Sentence compression. In *In Proceedings of AAAI*.

Kevin Knight and Daniel Marcu. 2002. Summarization beyond sentence extraction: A probabilistic approach to sentence compression. *Artificial Intelligence*, 139(1):91–107.

Chin-Yew Lin. 2004. ROUGE: A package for automatic evaluation of summaries. In *Text Summarization Branches Out*, pages 74–81, Barcelona, Spain. Association for Computational Linguistics.

Ryan McDonald. 2006. Discriminative sentence compression with soft syntactic evidence. In *11th Conference of the European Chapter of the Association for Computational Linguistics*.

Yishu Miao and Phil Blunsom. 2016. Language as a latent variable: Discrete generative models for sentence compression. In *Proceedings of the 2016 Conference on Empirical Methods in Natural Language Processing*, pages 319–328, Austin, Texas. Association for Computational Linguistics.

Paul Over, Hoa Dang, and Donna Harman. 2007. Duc in context. *Information Processing & Management*, 43(6):1506–1520.

Jeffrey Pennington, Richard Socher, and Christopher Manning. 2014. Glove: Global vectors for word representation. In *Proceedings of the 2014 conference on empirical methods in natural language processing (EMNLP)*, pages 1532–1543.

Alexander M. Rush, Sumit Chopra, and Jason Weston. 2015. A neural attention model for abstractive sentence summarization. In *Proceedings of the 2015 Conference on Empirical Methods in Natural Language Processing*, pages 379–389, Lisbon, Portugal. Association for Computational Linguistics.

Natalie Schluter. 2017. The limits of automatic summarisation according to rouge. In *Proceedings of the 15th Conference of the European Chapter of the Association for Computational Linguistics: Volume 2, Short Papers*, pages 41–45.

Abigail See, Peter Liu, and Christoper Manning. 2017. Get to the point: Summarization with pointer-generator networks. pages 1073–1083.

George K. Zipf. 1949. *Human Behaviour and the Principle of Least Effort*. Addison-Wesley.

Feature Difference Makes Sense:
A Medical Image Captioning Model Exploiting Feature Difference and Tag Information

Hyeryun Park[1], Kyungmo Kim[1], Jooyoung Yoon[1], Seongkeun Park[2], Jinwook Choi[2,3]

[1]Interdisciplinary Program for Bioengineering, Graduate School, Seoul National University
[2]Department of Biomedical Engineering, College of Medicine, Seoul National University
[3]Institute of Medical and Biological Engineering, MRC, Seoul National University
{helena.park, medinfoman, joo0yoon, ilj, jinchoi}@snu.ac.kr

Abstract

Medical image captioning can reduce the workload of physicians and save time and expense by automatically generating reports. However, current datasets are small and limited, creating additional challenges for researchers. In this study, we propose a feature difference and tag information combined long short-term memory (LSTM) model for chest x-ray report generation. A feature vector extracted from the image conveys visual information, but its ability to describe the image is limited. Other image captioning studies exhibited improved performance by exploiting feature differences, so the proposed model also utilizes them. First, we propose a difference and tag (DiTag) model containing the difference between the patient and normal images. Then, we propose a multi-difference and tag (mDiTag) model that also contains information about low-level differences, such as contrast, texture, and localized area. Evaluation of the proposed models demonstrates that the mDiTag model provides more information to generate captions and outperforms all other models.

1 Introduction

Image captioning is a research area that generates text describing natural images, representing a convergence of computer vision and natural language processing. There are several existing methods for image captioning. One way involves filling up templates with detected objects or properties (Li et al., 2011; Yang et al., 2011), but this has limitations about diversity. Especially, sentences describing abnormal findings in medical images are relatively diverse and rare. Another involves retrieving the captions of images that are similar to the query image and selecting relevant phrases from those captions to generate new captions (Gupta et al., 2012; Kuznetsova et al., 2014). However, this method does not generalize well when applied to unfamiliar images.

To overcome the weaknesses of current methods, we adopted the encoder-decoder architecture with an attention mechanism. The encoder encodes an image into a feature vector, and the decoder decodes the feature vector into text. The encoder-decoder is one of the neural networks successfully used in other recent image captioning studies (Vinyals et al., 2015; Xu et al., 2015; Karpathy and Fei-Fei, 2015; You et al., 2016; Zhou et al., 2017; Anderson et al., 2018).

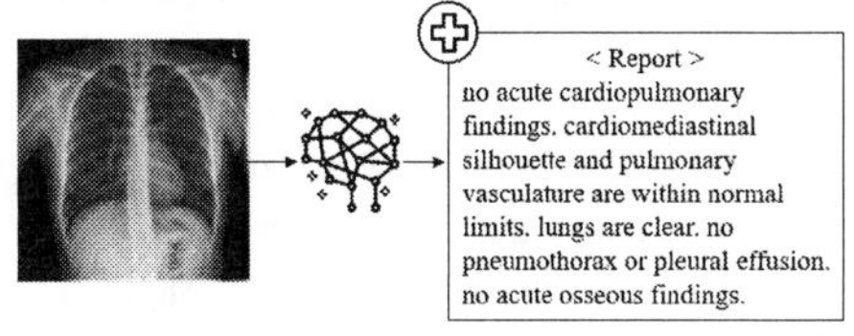

Figure 1: An example of a medical image captioning system that generates a report given a chest x-ray image.

Medical image captioning is the field of generating medical reports that describe medical images, as shown in Figure 1. The first challenge in medical image captioning is the lack of quality in training sets. Researchers have difficulty accessing chest x-ray datasets, which slows the development of related technologies. There are publicly available datasets that have images and reports: IU X-RAY, PEIR GROSS, and ICLEF-CAPTION (Kougia et al., 2019). Using only these datasets, state-of-the-art caption generation models do not generate medical reports correctly. Recently, MIMIC-CXR (Johnson et al., 2019), the largest dataset with images, reports, and labels, is released. The second challenge is that there are too many normal descriptions in the dataset, which creates a skewed dataset that poses problems for

Proceedings of the 58th Annual Meeting of the Association for Computational Linguistics: Student Research Workshop, pages 95–102
July 5 - July 10, 2020. ©2020 Association for Computational Linguistics

supervised learning. Besides, some types of significant abnormal findings appear too rarely in the dataset to appropriately train the model.

In this study, we propose a model that can identify and focus on abnormal findings more specifically and precisely, similar to the way that physicians would typically read, interpret, and write chest x-ray reports. Since physicians look for the differences between the normal group and the disease group, we also focus on image feature differences. Therefore, the proposed model sets the criteria based on a normal x-ray image and creates a feature difference vector that explains the difference between a normal x-ray image and a patient's x-ray image. This feature difference vector is a subtraction of visual feature vectors extracted from the two images. To improve the model, we also exploit tag information obtained from the medical report. Tags provide important information about the images and also convey meaningful semantics to the decoder. Several previous studies (Jhamtani and Berg-Kirkpatrick, 2018; Tan et al., 2019; Forbes et al., 2019) show methods that leverage feature vectors of images to account for differences between two images.

Next, since physicians obtain information not only from the overall image but also from the localized lesion areas, we consider that each convolutional level would also convey meaningful details such as contrast, texture, and localized area. Therefore, another proposed model fully exploits information contained in each layer. Previous studies (Darlow et al., 2018; Bau et al., 2017; Zhou et al., 2018) analyze and interpret convolutional neural networks (CNNs) utilizing feature vectors extracted from lower convolutional layers.

The following section describes the organization of the dataset, and section 3 introduces the baseline and our proposed models. Section 4 provides the experimental settings and results with analysis, and draws some conclusions in Section 5.

2   Dataset

This study uses IU X-RAY, which consists of a series of image-text-tag triplets. This dataset is anonymous and is from the Open Access Biomedical Image Search Engine (OpenI) [1] (Demner-Fushman et al., 2016).

The 7,470 chest x-ray images have two views: posteroanterior (PA) and lateral. The baseline model uses all images, but the proposed model uses only 3,821 images, which are PA views. The report corresponding to each image has four sections: comparison, indication, findings, and impression. The output of the model is a concatenation of the findings and the impression section (Jing et al., 2018). The findings section describes observations in each area of the body, and the most crucial impression section explains the problem and then provides a diagnosis. The output excludes the comparison and indication sections, which contain patient information and symptoms.

One or more tags are automatically extracted from each report using the Medical Text Indexer (MTI) [2] program (Jing et al., 2018). MTI produces index recommendations based on Medical Subject Heading (MeSH) [3] terms. There are a total of 210 unique tags, with an average of 2 tags per image. Without the normal tag, there is an average of 25 images per tag. Class imbalance arises because 1,502 images contain normal tag, so we randomly sample 75 images for a better balance between tags. The tags still have a class imbalance because the scope is too broad, making the term rare.

The prepared datasets are 3,821 image-text-tag triplets, all PA view images. After adjusting the number of images with the normal tag, we use random selection to get 1,911, 238, and 245 triplets for the training, validation, and test sets.

3   Models

3.1   Baseline Model

Among the recent models, the basis is the Jing (2018) model [4]. Our baseline model is similar to this model, which includes a CNN-RNN (encoder-decoder) with an attention mechanism. The Jing (2018) model's encoder part utilizes VGG-19 (Simonyan and Zisserman, 2014) for the visual feature extractor, multi-label classification (MLC) for tag classification, and decoder part uses Hierarchical LSTM (Hochreiter and Schmidhuber,

---

[1] https://openi.nlm.nih.gov/
[2] https://ii.nlm.nih.gov/MTI/
[3] https://www.nlm.nih.gov/mesh/meshhome.html

[4] Reference code available at
https://github.com/ZexinYan/Medical-Report-Generation

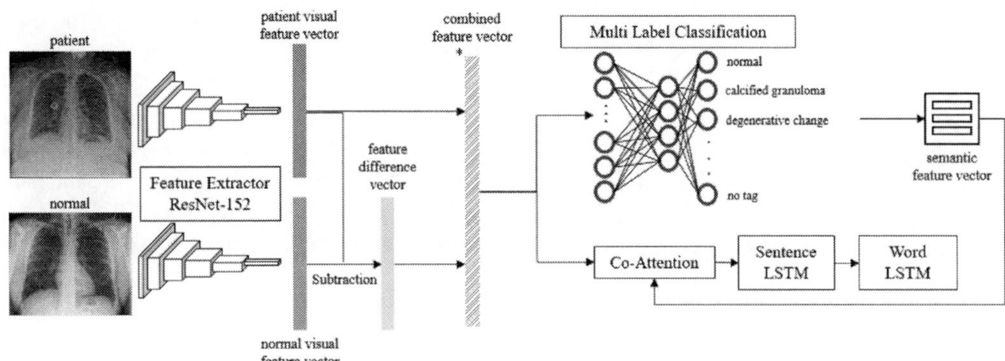

Figure 2: Two difference and tag (DiTag) model structures. The DiTag model uses only feature difference vector and sends it to MLC and co-attention. The combined DiTag (cDiTag) model uses a combined feature vector (*), which is a concatenation of patient visual feature vector and feature difference vector.

1997) with a co-attention mechanism. The only difference between the Jing (2018) model and our baseline model is that we use ResNet-152 (He et al., 2016) instead of VGG-19 to extract the visual feature vector. MLC uses the visual feature vector to predict one or more tags and generates semantic feature vectors that are word embedding of the predicted tags. To obtain an embedding vector of each tag, we train an embedding layer from the training data. Hierarchical LSTM combines sentence LSTM with co-attention and word LSTM. Sentence LSTM creates a topic vector and a stop vector by independently attending to the visual feature vector and semantic feature vector using co-attention. The word LSTM concatenates the topic vector and previous word embedding for a new embedding as input to generate words. The way to get a word embedding vector is the same as the tag, but the embedding matrix is different.

The overall loss is the sum of tag loss, stop loss, and word loss. First, tag loss L_{tag} is a cross-entropy loss between predicted tag distributions by MLC and the normalized real tag distributions. Second, stop loss L_{stop} is a cross-entropy loss between predicted stop distributions by Sentence LSTM and ground truth distributions. The stop loss is binary cross-entropy, and the class is stop or continue. Third, word loss L_{word} is a cross-entropy loss between predicted word distribution by Word LSTM and real word distribution. λ_{tag}, λ_{stop}, λ_{word} scale all the losses. The report consists of S sentences, with each sentence having W_s words. Total loss for the baseline model is:

$$L_{base} = \lambda_{tag}L_{tag} + \lambda_{stop}\sum_{s=1}^{S} L^s{}_{stop} + \lambda_{word}\sum_{s=1}^{S}\sum_{w=1}^{W_s} L^{s,w}{}_{word} \quad (1)$$

3.2 Difference and Tag Model

The weakness of our baseline model is that it mainly generates general content (such as "the heart is normal in size" and "the lungs are clear") and does not correctly describe the aspects of the patient image associated with the disease. The model does not adequately capture the differences between the images because the chest x-ray images are similar. Also, when clinicians diagnose patients, they look for the differences between the patient group and the normal group.

Therefore, the first goal of this study was to provide the model with more information about these differences. Our difference and tag (DiTag) model creates a feature difference vector that contains the differences between the patient image and the normal image. The feature difference vector is the result of subtracting the visual feature vector of the normal image from the visual feature vector of the patient image extracted through ResNet-152. The visual feature vector is a global average pooling of feature map produced by the last convolution layer.

We experimented with this feature difference vector using two model structures, as shown in Figure 2. The first structure, the DiTag model, passes the feature difference vector directly to the MLC and the co-attention and does not use the combined feature vector. Co-attention allows the model to attend to the feature difference vector $\{d_n\}_{n=1}^{N}$ and the semantic feature vector $\{t_m\}_{m=1}^{M}$ independently to create a context vector, which is then passed to the sentence LSTM to generate topic vector and stop vector, as shown in Figure 3. The co-attention is only associated with the sentence LSTM, not the word LSTM. The co-attention

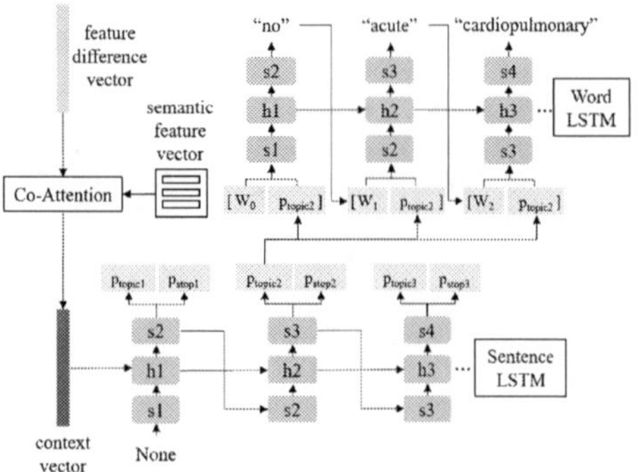

Figure 3: An example of generating a second sentence. For each sentence LSTM step, the co-attention creates a context vector, and the sentence LSTM outputs a topic vector and a stop vector. The word LSTM generates words based on the topic vector and embedding of the previous word.

computes attention score α independently to create a feature difference context vector d^s and a semantic context vector t^s at time step s:

$$d^s = \sum_{n=1}^{N} \alpha_{d,n} d_n \,, \ t^s = \sum_{m=1}^{M} \alpha_{t,m} t_m \quad (2)$$

Concatenate these context vectors, then use a fully connected layer W to obtain the final context vector c^S at time step s:

$$c^s = W[d^s; t^s] \quad (3)$$

A topic vector contains context information by combining the current hidden state of the sentence LSTM and the context vector of the current step. A stop vector decides to stop or continue generating the topic vector and words by combining the previous and current hidden state of sentence LSTM to calculate the probability of stopping. Figure 3 also shows how the word LSTM works.

The second structure is the combined DiTag (cDiTag) model, which sends the combined feature vector that represents the concatenation of the feature difference vector and the patient visual feature vector to the MLC and the co-attention. Co-attention is the same as DiTag model, except that it attends to the combined feature vector rather than the feature difference vector. The overall loss of both structures is the same as the baseline model.

3.3   Multi-Difference and Tag Model

Physicians provide diagnoses using information obtained not only from the overall image but also from localized lesion areas. Therefore, the second goal of this study was to offer lower-level differences to the model, such as the contrast,

texture, and localized area. The DiTag model extracts the visual feature vector from the last convolutional layer of ResNet-152, while the mDiTag model further extracts additional visual feature vectors from three lower convolutional layers. Using four visual features from the patient images and four from the normal images, we experimented with the three model structures to compare the effects of model components, as shown in Figure 4.

The mDiTag(-) model subtracts the normal visual feature vector from the patient visual feature vector obtained in each layer to generate four feature difference vectors and then sends all four vectors to the co-attention. The model excludes the MLC, and co-attention attends to the four feature difference vectors and creates a context vector and sends it to the LSTM. Total loss for the mDiTag(-) model is:

$$L_{DiTag} = \lambda_{stop} \sum_{s=1}^{S} L^s_{stop} + \lambda_{word} \sum_{s=1}^{S} \sum_{w=1}^{W} L^{s,w}_{word} \quad (4)$$

The mDiTag(+) model obtains new visual feature vectors by sending the visual feature vectors of each layer into four different MLCs, one for each layer. The co-attention is identical to that of the mDiTag(-) model. The total loss is the sum of the four tag losses, each occurring in four layers, stop loss and word loss. The model is backpropagated based on the previous four tag losses and then backpropagated based on the overall loss.

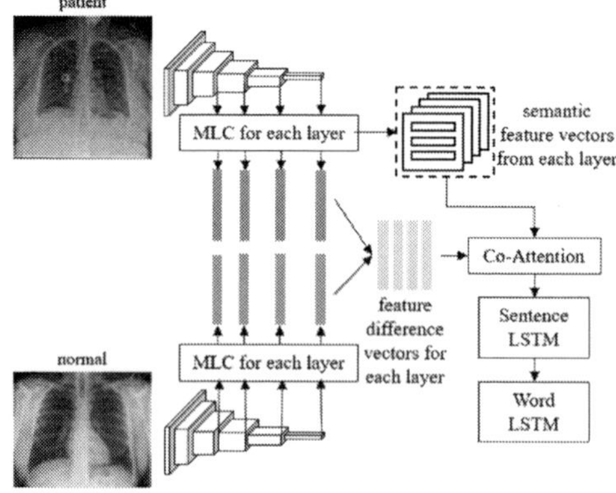

Figure 4: Three mDiTag model structures. The mDiTag(-) model excludes MLC and semantic feature vectors. The mDiTag(+) model excludes only the semantic feature vectors. The whole structure is mDiTag(s) model.

Model	BLEU-1	BLEU-2	BLEU-3	BLEU-4	ROUGE-L	CIDEr
Baseline model	0.2738	0.1585	0.1045	0.0682	0.2099	0.1226
DiTag model	0.3015	0.1795	0.1204	0.0811	0.2438	0.1939
cDiTag model	0.2501	0.1413	0.0913	0.0597	0.2177	0.0903
mDiTag(-) model	**0.3293**	**0.1985**	**0.1354**	**0.0945**	**0.2731**	**0.1944**
mDiTag(+) model	0.3227	0.1919	0.1271	0.0852	0.2575	0.1829
mDiTag(s) model	0.2086	0.1225	0.0795	0.0566	0.1719	0.1252

Table 1: Metric Evaluation for all models. The DiTag model utilizes feature difference vector, the cDiTag model uses combined feature vector, and the mDiTag models use multiple feature difference vectors. The mDiTag(-) model excludes MLC and semantic feature vectors, the mDiTag(+) model excludes semantic feature vectors, and the mDiTag(s) model uses all. The best model for all metric scores is the mDiTag(-) model.

The mDiTag(s) model is similar to the mDiTag(+) model, but MLC obtains a new visual feature vector and a semantic feature vector. The model sends four feature difference vectors and four semantic feature vectors to the decoder. Co-attention attends to the four feature difference vectors and four semantic feature vectors to create a context vector, and then sends it to the LSTM. The loss function and backpropagation method of this model is the same as that of the mDiTag(+) model. There are four tag losses in each intermediate convolutional layer of mDiTag(+) and mDiTag(s) model. Total loss for these models is:

$$L_{mDiTag} = \lambda_{tag\_1} L_{tag\_1} + \lambda_{tag\_2} L_{tag\_2} + \\ \lambda_{tag\_3} L_{tag\_3} + \lambda_{tag\_4} L_{tag\_4} + \\ \lambda_{stop} \sum_{s=1}^{S} L^{s}_{stop} + \\ \lambda_{word} \sum_{s=1}^{S} \sum_{w=1}^{W} L^{s,w}_{word}$$

$$(5)$$

4 Experimental Settings and Results

4.1 Experimental Settings

All model experiments use the same parameters and hyperparameters. For MLC, the number of classes corresponding is 210, the number of classes to predict is 10, and the generated semantic feature vector dimension is 512. In the decoder, the Sentence LSTM is 1 layer, the Word LSTM is 1 layer, the hidden vector dimension is 512, the maximum number of sentences generated is 6, and the maximum number of words created is 30. The learning rate starts from $1e-4$ and is optimized by Adam optimizer. Total epoch is 1,000 but tested with a model of minimum loss. It took four days to train with a 1080Ti GPU with 11G Memory.

4.2 Metric Evaluation

Table 1 provides information on the performance of the models evaluated for the test dataset. We use BLEU score (Papineni et al., 2002), ROUGE-L

(Lin, 2004), and CIDEr (Vedantam et al., 2015) for the metrics. The DiTag model has higher metric scores than the baseline model, and for cDiTag model, only the ROUGE-L score increases. Since the DiTag model structure is more suitable, mDiTag model structures also only utilizes the feature difference vector.

Next, based on all metric scores, the best model is the mDiTag(-) model. When the model includes MLC, the metric score reduces. Since there are two tags per image on average, when predicting 10 tags, there are wrong tag information. Also, the

Model	generation result
Baseline Model	no acute cardiopulmonary abnormality the heart is normal in size the heart and lungs have in the interval
mDiTag(-) Model	<num> no acute cardiopulmonary abnormality <num> chronic changes consistent with emphysema the heart is normal in size the lungs are clear no pleural effusion or pneumothorax is seen
mDiTag(+) Model	no acute cardiopulmonary abnormality the heart is normal in size the lungs are clear there is no focal air space opacity to suggest a pneumonia
Ground Truth Report	left base atelectasis lungs otherwise clear there is minimal opacity in the left lung base representing atelectasis the lungs are otherwise clear heart size is normal no <unk>
Image	

Table 2: The first example of the models' outputs with corresponding ground truth report, and image.

significant class imbalance makes MLC challenging to train. Further, when the model uses the semantic feature vector, metric scores reduce. The semantic feature vector is word embedding of the top 10 tags predicted by MLC. However, the semantic feature vector provides incorrect information because of the wrong tags among the 10 predicted tags.

4.3 Analysis of Model Output

Table 2 and Table 3 show examples of the models' output. To make the model outputs easier to see, we eliminate the repeated sentences in the table. The mDiTag(-) model generates more detailed reports than the other models. There are some abnormal findings in the images and ground truth reports in Table 2 and Table 3. The baseline model only explains about the normal findings, while the mDiTag(-) model produces some disease-related sentences, but is not accurate. The outputs show that exploiting multiple feature differences allows the model to generate a relatively diverse explanation of the patient's disease. However, the output still produces general description and does not present enough information about specific features of the disease. As expected, there are incorrect disease descriptions because the tag prediction is not accurate. In addition, as there are too many types of abnormal findings, the terms become too rare to train the model adequately. The components of the text generation part should be modified to resolve the issue of the repeated sentence. Another limitation of this paper is the lack of human evaluation.

5 Conclusion

We propose models that exploit feature differences and tag information. As expected, the model that uses low-level convolutional features from the CNN model can convey low-level details, such as contrast, texture, and localized area. Some of our models outperform the conventional image captioning models in terms of BLEU score, ROUGE-L, and CIDEr. The mDiTag(-) model performs best according to every metric. Based on these experiments, we can conclude that the feature differences between images and semantic tags are crucial elements necessary for training. In the future, we will strengthen tags that contain semantic information to extract keywords for more accurate information, such as disease information, location, and size. Furthermore, improving the accuracy of multiple tag prediction is crucial to deliver semantic facts accurately. We are also considering obtaining more images from hospitals to reduce the proportion of abnormal images in the datasets.

Acknowledgments

The authors would like to thank the three anonymous reviewers and mentor Steven Wilson for their valuable feedback on this work. This research was supported by a grant of the Korea Health Technology R&D Project through the Korea Health Industry Development Institute (KHIDI), funded by the Ministry of Health & Welfare, Republic of Korea (grant number : HI18C0316).

Model	generation result
Baseline Model	no acute cardiopulmonary abnormality the heart is normal in size the lungs are clear
mDiTag(-) Model	<num> no acute cardiopulmonary abnormality <num> left midlung subsegmental atelectasis versus scar the heart is normal in size the mediastinum is unremarkable no pleural effusion or pneumothorax no acute bony abnormality
mDiTag(+) Model	no acute cardiopulmonary abnormality the heart is normal in size the lungs are clear no focal airspace consolidation or pleural <unk>
Ground Truth Report	low lung volumes no acute cardiopulmonary findings the cardiomediastinal silhouette is stable lung volumes remain low there is no pleural line to suggest pneumothorax or costophrenic blunting to suggest large pleural effusion bony structures are within normal <unk>
Image	

Table 3. The second example of the models' outputs with corresponding ground truth report, and image.

References

Peter Anderson, Xiaodong He, Chris Buehler, Damien Teney, Mark Johnson, Stephen Gould, and Lei Zhang. 2018. Bottom-Up and Top-Down Attention for Image Captioning and Visual Question Answering. In *2018 IEEE/CVF Conference on Computer Vision and Pattern Recognition*. IEEE, pages 6077-6086. https://doi.org/10.1109/CVPR.2018.00636.

David Bau, Bolei Zhou, Aditya Khosla, Aude Oliva, and Antonio Torralba. 2017. Network Dissection: Quantifying Interpretability of Deep Visual Representations. In *Proceedings of the IEEE Conference on Computer Vision and Pattern Recognition (CVPR)*. IEEE, pages 3319-3327. http://doi.org/10.1109/CVPR.2017.354.

Luke Nicholas Darlow, and Amos Storkey. 2018. What Information Does a ResNet Compress? In *Proceedings of the International Conference on Learning Representations*.

Dina Demner-Fushman, Marc D. Kohli, Marc B. Rosenman, Sonya E. Shooshan, Laritza Rodriguez, Sameer Antani, George R. Thoma, and Clement J. McDonald. 2016. Preparing a collection of radiology examinations for distribution and retrieval. *Journal of the American Medical Informatics Association*, 23(2):304–310. https://doi.org/10.1093/jamia/ocv080.

Maxwell Forbes, Christine Kaeser-Chen, Piyush Sharma, and Serge Belongie. 2019. Neural Naturalist: Generating Fine-Grained Image Comparisons. In *Proceedings of the 2019 Conference on Empirical Methods in Natural Language Processing and the 9th International Joint Conference on Natural Language Processing (EMNLP-IJCNLP)*. Association for Computational Linguistics, pages 708-717. http://doi.org/10.18653/v1/D19-1065.

Ankush Gupta, Yashaswi Verma, and C. V. Jawahar. 2012. Choosing linguistics over vision to describe images. In *Proceedings of the Twenty-Sixth AAAI Conference on Artificial Intelligence*. Association for the Advancement of Artificial Intelligence, pages 606-612.

Kaiming He, Xiangyu Zhang, Shaoqing Ren, and Jian Sun. 2016. Deep Residual Learning for Image Recognition. In *Proceedings of the IEEE Conference on Computer Vision and Pattern Recognition*. IEEE, pages 770-778. https://doi.org/10.1109/CVPR.2016.90.

Sepp Hochreiter, and Jürgen Schmidhuber. 1997. Long Short-Term Memory. *Neural Computation*, 9(8):1735–1780. https://doi.org/10.1162/neco.1997.9.8.1735.

Harsh Jhamtani, and Taylor Berg-Kirkpatrick. 2018. Learning to Describe Differences Between Pairs of Similar Images. In *Proceedings of the 2018 Conference on Empirical Methods in Natural Language Processing*. Association for Computational Linguistics, pages 4024-4034. https://doi.org/10.18653/v1/D18-1436.

Xu Jia, Efstratios Gavves, Basura Fernando, and Tinne Tuytelaars. 2015. Guiding the Long-Short Term Memory Model for Image Caption Generation. In *Proceedings of the IEEE International Conference on Computer Vision*. IEEE, pages 2407-2415. https://doi.org/10.1109/ICCV.2015.277.

Baoyu Jing, Pengtao Xie, and Eric Xing. 2018. On the Automatic Generation of Medical Imaging Reports. In *Proceedings of the 56th Annual Meeting of the Association for Computational Linguistics (Volume 1: Long Papers)*. Association for Computational Linguistics, pages 2577–2586. http://doi.org/10.18653/v1/P18-1240.

Alistair E. W. Johnson, Tom J. Pollard, Seth Berkowitz, Nathaniel R. Greenbaum, Matthew P. Lungren, Chih-ying Deng, Roger G. Mark, and Steven Horng. 2019. MIMIC-CXR: A Large Publicly Available Database of Labeled Chest Radiographs. https://arxiv.org/abs/1901.07042.

Andrej Karpathy, and Li Fei-Fei. 2015. Deep Visual-Semantic Alignments for Generating Image Descriptions. In *Proceedings of the IEEE Conference on Computer Vision and Pattern Recognition. IEEE*, pages 3128-3137. https://doi.org/10.1109/CVPR.2015.7298932.

Vasiliki Kougia, John Pavlopoulos, and Ion Androutsopoulos. 2019. A Survey on Biomedical Image Captioning. In *Proceedings of the Second Workshop on Shortcomings in Vision and Language*. Association for Computational Linguistics, pages 26–36. http://doi.org/10.18653/v1/W19-1803.

Polina Kuznetsova, Vicente Ordonez, Tamara L. Berg and Yejin Choi. 2014. TreeTalk: Composition and Compression of Trees for Image Descriptions. *Transactions of the Association for Computational Linguistics*, 2:351-362. https://doi.org/10.1162/tacl_a_00188.

Siming Li, Girish Kulkarni, Tamara L. Berg, Alexander C. Berg, and Yejin Choi. 2011. Composing Simple Image Descriptions using Web-scale N-grams. In *Proceedings of the Fifteenth Conference on Computational Natural Language Learning*. Association for Computational Linguistics, pages 220-228. https://www.aclweb.org/anthology/W11-0326.

Chin-Yew Lin. 2004. ROUGE: A Package for Automatic Evaluation of Summaries. In *Text Summarization Branches Out*. Association for

Computational Linguistics, pages 74–81. https://www.aclweb.org/anthology/W04-1013.

Kishore Papineni, Salim Roukos, Todd Ward, and Wei-Jing Zhu. 2002. BLEU: a Method for Automatic Evaluation of Machine Translation. In *Proceedings of the 40th Annual Meeting of the Association for Computational Linguistics*. Association for Computational Linguistics, pages 311–318. https://doi.org/10.3115/1073083.1073135.

Karen Simonyan and Andrew Zisserman. 2014. Very Deep Convolutional Networks for Large-scale Image Recognition. In *Computing Research Repository*. http://arxiv.org/abs/1409.1556.

Hao Tan, Franck Dernoncourt, Zhe Lin, Trung Bui, and Mohit Bansal. 2019. Expressing Visual Relationships via Language. In *Proceedings of the 57th Annual Meeting of the Association for Computational Linguistics*. Association for Computational Linguistics, pages 1873-1883. http://doi.org/10.18653/v1/P19-1182.

Ramakrishna Vedantam, C. Lawrence Zitnick, and Devi Parikh. 2015. CIDEr: Consensus-based image description evaluation. In Proceedings of the IEEE Conference on Computer Vision and Pattern Recognition. IEEE, pages 4566-4575. https://doi.org/10.1109/CVPR.2015.7299087.

Oriol Vinyals, Alexander Toshev, Samy Bengio, and Dumitru Erhan. 2015. Show and Tell: A neural image caption generator. In *Proceedings of the IEEE Conference on Computer Vision and Pattern Recognition*. IEEE, pages 3156-3164. https://doi.org/10.1109/CVPR.2015.7298935.

Kelvin Xu, Jimmy Lei Ba, Ryan Kiros, Kyunghyun Cho, Aaron Courville, Ruslan Salakhudinov, Richard S. Zemel, and Yoshua Bengio. 2015. Show, Attend and Tell: Neural Image Caption Generation with Visual Attention. In *Proceedings of the 32nd International Conference on Machine Learning (Volume 37)*. PMLR, pages 2048-2057.

Yezhou Yang, Ching Lik Teo, Hal Daumé III, and Yiannis Aloimonos. 2011. Corpus-Guided Sentence Generation of Natural Images. In *Proceedings of the 2011 Conference on Empirical Methods in Natural Language Processing*. Association for Computational Linguistics, pages 444–454.

Quanzeng You, Hailin Jin, Zhaowen Wang, Chen Fang, and Jiebo Luo. 2016. Image Captioning with Semantic Attention. In *Proceedings of the IEEE Conference on Computer Vision and Pattern Recognition. IEEE*, pages 4651-4659. https://doi.org/10.1109/CVPR.2016.503.

Bolei Zhou, David Bau, Aude Oliva, and Antonio Torralba. 2018. Interpreting Deep Visual Representations via Network Dissection. In *IEEE Transactions on Pattern Analysis and Machine Intelligence*. IEEE, 41(9):2131-2145. http://doi.org/10.1109/TPAMI.2018.2858759.

Luowei Zhou, Chenliang Xu, Parker Koch, and Jason J. Corso. 2017. Watch What You Just Said: Image Captioning with Text-Conditional Attention. In *Proceedings of the on Thematic Workshops of ACM Multimedia 2017*. Association for Computing Machinery, pages 305-313. https://doi.org/10.1145/3126686.3126717.

Multi-Task Neural Model for Agglutinative Language Translation

Yirong Pan[1,2,3], **Xiao Li**[1,2,3], **Yating Yang**[1,2,3], and **Rui Dong**[1,2,3]
[1] Xinjiang Technical Institute of Physics & Chemistry, Chinese Academy of Sciences, China
[2] University of Chinese Academy of Sciences, China
[3] Xinjiang Laboratory of Minority Speech and Language Information Processing, China
panyirong15@mails.ucas.ac.cn
{xiaoli, yangyt, dongrui}@ms.xjb.ac.cn

Abstract

Neural machine translation (NMT) has achieved impressive performance recently by using large-scale parallel corpora. However, it struggles in the low-resource and morphologically-rich scenarios of agglutinative language translation task. Inspired by the finding that monolingual data can greatly improve the NMT performance, we propose a multi-task neural model that jointly learns to perform bi-directional translation and agglutinative language stemming. Our approach employs the shared encoder and decoder to train a single model without changing the standard NMT architecture but instead adding a token before each source-side sentence to specify the desired target outputs of the two different tasks. Experimental results on Turkish-English and Uyghur-Chinese show that our proposed approach can significantly improve the translation performance on agglutinative languages by using a small amount of monolingual data.

1 Introduction

Neural machine translation (NMT) has achieved impressive performance on many high-resource machine translation tasks (Bahdanau et al., 2015; Luong et al., 2015a; Vaswani et al., 2017). The standard NMT model uses the encoder to map the source sentence to a continuous representation vector, and then it feeds the resulting vector to the decoder to produce the target sentence.

However, the NMT model still suffers from the low-resource and morphologically-rich scenarios of agglutinative language translation tasks, such as Turkish-English and Uyghur-Chinese. Both Turkish and Uyghur are agglutinative languages with complex morphology. The morpheme structure of the word can be denoted as: *prefix1 + ... + prefixN + stem + suffix1 + ... + suffixN*

(Ablimit et al., 2010). Since the suffixes have many inflected and morphological variants, the vocabulary size of an agglutinative language is considerable even in small-scale training data. Moreover, many words have different morphemes and meanings in different context, which leads to inaccurate translation results.

Recently, researchers show their great interest in utilizing monolingual data to further improve the NMT model performance (Cheng et al., 2016; Ramachandran et al., 2017; Currey et al., 2017). Sennrich et al. (2016) pair the target-side monolingual data with automatic back-translation as additional training data to train the NMT model. Zhang and Zong (2016) use the source-side monolingual data and employ the multi-task learning framework for translation and source sentence reordering. Domhan and Hieber (2017) modify the decoder to enable multi-task learning for translation and language modeling. However, the above works mainly focus on boosting the translation fluency, and lack the consideration of morphological and linguistic knowledge.

Stemming is a morphological analysis method, which is widely used for information retrieval tasks (Kishida, 2005). By removing the suffixes in the word, stemming allows the variants of the same word to share representations and reduces data sparseness. We consider that stemming can lead to better generalization on agglutinative languages, which helps NMT to capture the in-depth semantic information. Thus we use stemming as an auxiliary task for agglutinative language translation.

In this paper, we investigate a method to exploit the monolingual data of the agglutinative language to enhance the representation ability of the encoder. This is achieved by training a multi-task neural model to jointly perform bi-directional translation and agglutinative language stemming, which utilizes the shared encoder and decoder. We treat stemming as a sequence generation task.

Proceedings of the 58th Annual Meeting of the Association for Computational Linguistics: Student Research Workshop, pages 103–110
July 5 - July 10, 2020. ©2020 Association for Computational Linguistics

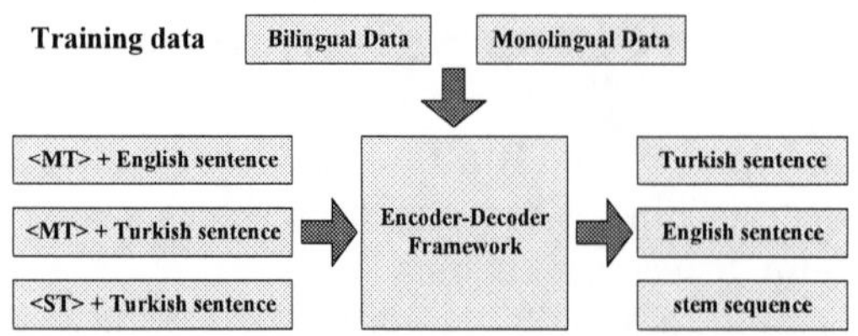

Figure 1: The architecture of the multi-task neural model that jointly learns to perform bi-directional translation between Turkish and English, and stemming for Turkish sentence.

2 Related Work

Multi-task learning (MTL) aims to improve the generalization performance of a main task by using the other related tasks, which has been successfully applied to various research fields ranging from language (Liu et al., 2015; Luong et al., 2015a), vision (Yim et al., 2015; Misra et al., 2016), and speech (Chen and Mak, 2015; Kim et al., 2016). Many natural language processing (NLP) tasks have been chosen as auxiliary task to deal with the increasingly complex tasks. Luong et al. (2015b) employ a small amount of data of syntactic parsing and image caption for English-German translation. Hashimoto et al. (2017) present a joint MTL model to handle the tasks of part-of-speech (POS) tagging, dependency parsing, semantic relatedness, and textual entailment for English. Kiperwasser and Ballesteros (2018) utilize the POS tagging and dependency parsing for English-German machine translation. To the best of our knowledge, we are the first to incorporate stemming task into MTL framework to further improve the translation performance on agglutinative languages.

Recently, several works have combined the MTL method with sequence-to-sequence NMT model for machine translation tasks. Dong et al. (2015) follow a ***one-to-many*** setting that utilizes a shared encoder for all the source languages with respective attention mechanisms and multiple decoders for the different target languages. Luong et al. (2015b) follow a ***many-to-many*** setting that uses multiple encoders and decoders with two separate unsupervised objective functions. Zoph and Knight (2016) follow a ***many-to-one*** setting that employs multiple encoders for all the source languages and one decoder for the desired target language. Johnson et al. (2017) propose a more simple method in ***one-to-one*** setting, which trains a single NMT model with the shared encoder and decoder in order to enable multilingual translation.

The method requires no changes to the standard NMT architecture but instead requires adding a token at the beginning of each source sentence to specify the desired target sentence. Inspired by their work, we employ the standard NMT model with one encoder and one decoder for parameter sharing and model generalization. In addition, we build a joint vocabulary on the concatenation of the source-side and target-side words.

Several works on morphologically-rich NMT have focused on using morphological analysis to pre-process the training data (Luong et al., 2016; Huck et al., 2017; Tawfik et al., 2019). Gulcehre et al. (2015) segment each Turkish sentence into a sequence of morpheme units and remove any non-surface morphemes for Turkish-English translation. Ataman et al. (2017) propose a vocabulary reduction method that considers the morphological properties of the agglutinative language, which is based on the unsupervised morphology learning. This work takes inspiration from our previously proposed segmentation method (Pan et al., 2020) that segments the word into a sequence of sub-word units with morpheme structure, which can effectively reduce language complexity.

3 Multi-Task Neural Model

3.1 Overview

We propose a multi-task neural model for machine translation from and into a low-resource and morphologically-rich agglutinative language. We train the model to jointly learn to perform both the bi-directional translation task and the stemming task on an agglutinative language by using the standard NMT framework. Moreover, we add an artificial token before each source sentence to specify the desired target outputs for different tasks. The architecture of the proposed model is shown in Figure 1. We take the Turkish-English translation task as example. The "**<MT>**" token denotes the bilingual translation task and the "**<ST>**" token denotes the stemming task on Turkish sentence.

3.2 Neural Machine Translation (NMT)

Our proposed multi-task neural model on using the source-side monolingual data for agglutinative language translation task can be applied in any NMT structures with encoder-decoder framework. In this work, we follow the NMT model proposed by Vaswani et al. (2017), which is implemented as Transformer. We will briefly summarize it here.

Task	Data	# Sent	# Src	# Trg
Tr-En	train	355,251	6,356,767	8,021,161
	valid	2,455	37,153	52,125
	test	4,962	69,006	96,291
Uy-Ch	train	333,097	6,026,953	5,748,298
	valid	700	17,821	17,085
	test	1,000	20,580	18,179

Table 1: The statistics of the training, validation, and test datasets on Turkish-English and Uyghur-Chinese machine translation tasks. The "**# Src**" denotes the number of the source tokens, and the "**# Trg**" denotes the numbers of the target tokens.

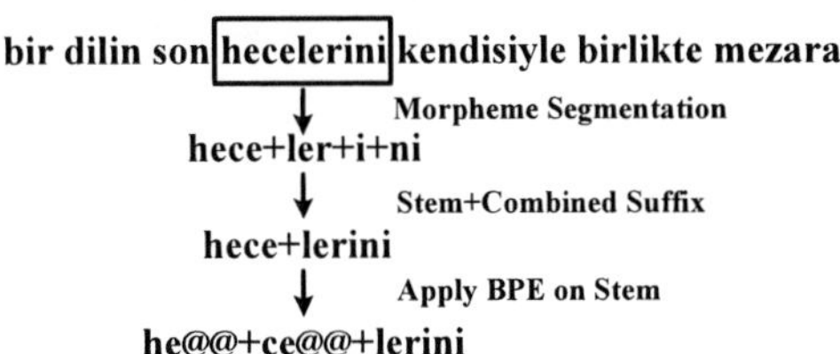

Figure 2: The example of morphological segmentation method for the word in Turkish.

Firstly, the Transformer model maps the source sequence $x = (x_1, ..., x_m)$ and the target sentence $y = (y_1, ..., y_n)$ into a word embedding matrix, respectively. Secondly, in order to make use of the word order in the sequence, the above word embedding matrices sum with their positional encoding matrices to generate the source-side and target-side positional embedding matrices. The encoder is composed of a stack of N identical layers. Each layer has two sub-layers consisting of the multi-head self-attention and the fully connected feed-forward network, which maps the source-side positional embedding matrix into a representation vector.

The decoder is also composed of a stack of N identical layers. Each layer has three sub-layers: the multi-head self-attention, the multi-head attention, and the fully connected feed-forward network. The multi-head attention attends to the outputs of the encoder and decoder to generate a context vector. The feed-forward network followed by a linear layer maps the context vector into a vector with the original space dimension. Finally, the *softmax* function is applied on the vector to predict the target word sequence.

4 Experiment

4.1 Dataset

The statistics of the training, validation, and test datasets on Turkish-English and Uyghur-Chinese machine translation tasks are shown in Table 1.

For the Turkish-English machine translation, following (Sennrich et al., 2015a), we use the WIT corpus (Cettolo et al., 2012) and the SETimes corpus (Tyers and Alperen, 2010) as the training dataset, merge the dev2010 and tst2010 as the validation dataset, and use tst2011, tst2012, tst2013, tst2014 from the IWSLT as the test datasets. We also use the talks data from the IWSLT evaluation campaign[1] in 2018 and the news data from News Crawl corpora[2] in 2017 as external monolingual data for the stemming task on Turkish sentences.

For the Uyghur-Chinese machine translation, we use the news data from the China Workshop on Machine Translation in 2017 (CWMT2017) as the training dataset and validation dataset, use the news data from CWMT2015 as the test dataset. Each Uyghur sentence has four Chinese reference sentences. Moreover, we use the news data from the Tianshan website[3] as external monolingual data for the stemming task on Uyghur sentences.

4.2 Data Preprocessing

We normalize and tokenize the experimental data. We utilize the jieba toolkit[4] to segment the Chinese sentences, we utilize the Zemberek toolkit[5] with morphological disambiguation (Sak et al., 2007) and the morphological analysis tool (Tursun et al., 2016) to annotate the morpheme structure of the words in Turkish and Uyghur, respectively.

We use our previously proposed morphological segmentation method (Pan et al., 2020), which segments the word into smaller subword units with morpheme structure. Since Turkish and Uyghur only have a few prefixes, we combine the prefixes with stem into the stem unit. As shown in Figure 2, the morpheme structure of the Turkish word "*hecelerini*" (syllables) is: *hece + lerini*. Then the byte pair encoding (BPE) technique (Sennrich et al., 2015b) is applied on the stem unit "*hece*" to segment it into "*he@@*" and "*ce@@*". Thus the Turkish word is segmented into a sequence of subword units: *he@@ + ce@@ + lerini*.

---

[1] https://wit3.fbk.eu/archive/2018-01/additional_TED_xml/
[2] http://data.statmt.org/wmt18/translation-task/
[3] http://uy.ts.cn/
[4] https://github.com/fxsjy/jieba
[5] https://github.com/ahmetaa/zemberek-nlp

Task	Training Sentence Samples
En-Tr Translation	<MT> We go through initiation rit@@ es.
	Başla@@ ma ritüel@@ lerini yaş@@ ıyoruz.
Tr-En Translation	<MT> Başla@@ ma ritüel@@ lerini yaş@@ ıyoruz.
	We go through initiation rit@@ es.
Turkish Stemming	<ST> Başla@@ ma ritüel@@ lerini yaş@@ ıyoruz.
	Başla@@ ritüel@@ yaş@@

Table 2: The training sentence samples for multi-task neural model on Turkish-English machine translation task. We add "<MT>" and "<ST>" before each source sentence to specify the desired target outputs for different tasks.

Lang	Method	# Merge	Vocab	Avg.Len
Tr	Morph	15K	36,468	28
Tr	BPE	36K	36,040	22
En	BPE	32K	31,306	25
Uy	Morph	10K	38,164	28
Uy	BPE	38K	38,292	21
Ch	BPE	32K	40,835	19

Table 3: The detailed statistics of using different word segmentation methods on Turkish, English, Uyghur, and Chinese.

In this paper, we utilize the above morphological segmentation method for our experiments by applying BPE on the stem units with 15K merge operations for the Turkish words and 10K merge operations for the Uyghur words. The standard NMT model trained on this experimental data is denoted as "**baseline NMT model**". Moreover, we employ BPE to segment the words in English and Chinese by learning separate vocabulary with 32K merge operations. Table 2 shows the training sentence samples for multi-task neural model on Turkish-English machine translation task.

In addition, to certify the effectiveness of the morphological segmentation method, we employ the pure BPE to segment the words in Turkish and Uyghur by learning a separate vocabulary with 36K and 38K merge operations, respectively. The standard NMT model trained on this experimental data is denoted as "**general NMT model**". Table 3 shows the detailed statistics of using different word segmentation methods on Turkish, English, Uyghur, and Chinese. The "**Vocab**" token denotes the vocabulary size after data preprocessing. The "**Avg.Len**" token denotes the average sentence length.

4.3 Training and Evaluation Details

We employ the Transformer model implemented in the *Sockeye* toolkit (Hieber et al., 2017). The number of layer in both the encoder and decoder is set to $N=6$, the number of head is set to 8, and the number of hidden unit in the feed-forward network is set to 1024. We use an embedding size of both the source and target words of 512 dimension, and use a batch size of 128 sentences. The maximum sentence length is set to 100 tokens with 0.1 label smoothing. We apply layer normalization and add dropout to the embedding and transformer layers with 0.1 probability. Moreover, we use the Adam optimizer (Kingma and Ba, 2015) with an initial learning rate of 0.0002, and save the checkpoint every 1500 updates.

Model training process stops after 8 checkpoints without improvements on the validation perplexity. Following Niu et al. (2018a), we select the 4 best checkpoint based on the validation perplexity values and combine them in a linear ensemble for decoding. Decoding is performed by using beam search with a beam size of 5. We evaluate the machine translation performance by using the case-sensitive BLEU score (Papineni et al., 2002) with standard tokenization.

4.4 Neural Translation Models

In this paper, we select 4 neural translation models for comparison. More details about the models are shown below:

General NMT Model: The standard NMT model trained on the experimental data segmented by BPE.

Baseline NMT Model: The standard NMT model trained on the experimental data segmented by morphological segmentation. The following models also use this word segmentation method.

Bi-Directional NMT Model: Following Niu et al. (2018b), we train a single NMT model to perform bi-directional machine translation. We concatenate the bilingual parallel sentences in both directions. Since the source and target sentences come from the same language pairs, we share the source and target vocabulary, and tie their word embedding during model training.

Multi-Task Neural Model: We simply use the monolingual data of the agglutinative language from the bilingual parallel sentences. We use a joint vocabulary, tie the word embedding as well as the output layer's weight matrix.

Task	Model	tst11	tst12	tst13	tst14
Tr-En	general	25.92	26.55	27.34	**26.35**
	baseline	**26.48**	**27.02**	**27.91**	26.33
En-Tr	general	13.73	14.68	13.84	14.65
	baseline	**14.85**	**15.93**	**15.45**	**15.93**

Table 4: The BLEU scores of the general NMT model and baseline NMT model on the machine translation task between Turkish and English.

Task	Model	tst11	tst12	tst13	tst14
Tr-En	baseline	26.48	27.02	27.91	26.33
	bi-directional	26.21	27.17	28.68	26.90
	multi-task	**26.82**	**27.96**	**29.16**	**27.98**
En-Tr	baseline	14.85	15.93	15.45	15.93
	bi-directional	15.08	16.20	16.25	**16.56**
	multi-task	**15.65**	**17.10**	**16.35**	16.41

Table 5: The BLEU scores of the baseline NMT model, bi-directional NMT model, and multi-task neural model on the machine translation task between Turkish and English.

5 Results and Discussion

Table 4 shows the BLEU scores of the general NMT model and baseline NMT model on machine translation task. We can observe that the baseline NMT model is comparable to the general NMT model, and it achieves the highest BLEU scores on almost all the test datasets in both directions, which indicates that the NMT baseline based on our proposed segmentation method is competitive.

5.1 Using Original Monolingual Data

Table 5 shows the BLEU scores of the baseline NMT model, bi-directional NMT model, and multi-task neural model on the machine translation task between Turkish and English. The table shows that the multi-task neural model outperforms both the baseline NMT model and bi-directional NMT model, and it achieves the highest BLEU scores on almost all the test datasets in both directions, which suggests that the multi-task neural model is capable of improving the bi-directional translation quality on agglutinative languages. The main reason is that compared with the bi-directional NMT model, our proposed multi-task neural model additionally employs the stemming task for the agglutinative language, which is effective for the NMT model to learn both the source-side semantic information and the target-side language modeling.

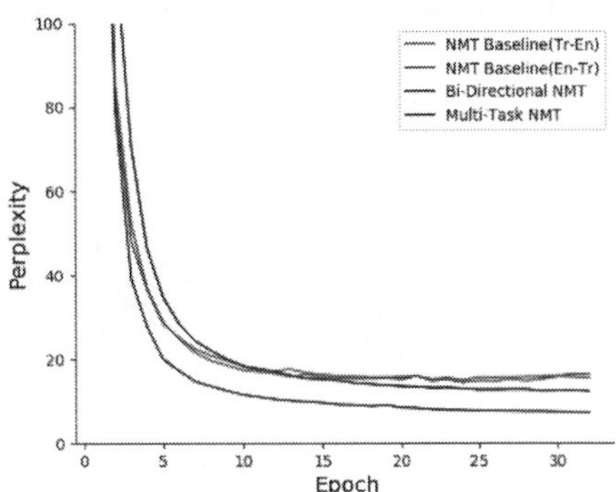

Figure 3: The function of epochs (x-axis) and perplexity (y-axis) values on the validation dataset in different neural translation models for the translation task.

Translation Examples	
source	üniversite hayatı taklit ediyordu.
reference	College was imitating life.
baseline	It was emulating a university life.
bi-directional	The university was emulating its lives.
multi-task	The university was imitating life.

Table 6: A translation example for the different NMT models on Turkish-English.

The function of epochs and perplexity values on the validation dataset in different neural translation models are shown in Figure 3. We can see that the perplexity values are consistently lower on the multi-task neural model, and it converges rapidly.

Table 6 shows a translation example for the different models on Turkish-English. We can see that the translation result of the multi-task neural model is more accurate. The Turkish word "**taklit**" means "imitate" in English, both the baseline NMT and bi-directional NMT translate it into a synonym "emulate". However, they are not able to express the meaning of the sentence correctly. The main reason is that the auxiliary task of stemming forces the proposed model to focus more strongly on the core meaning of each word (or stem), therefore helping the model make the correct lexical choices and capture the in-depth semantic information.

5.2 Using External Monolingual Data

Moreover, we evaluate the multi-task neural model on using external monolingual data for Turkish stemming task. We employ the parallel sentences and the monolingual data in a 1-1 ratio, and shuffle them randomly before each training epoch. More details about the data are shown below:

Task	Data	tst11	tst12	tst13	tst14
Tr-En	original	**26.82**	27.96	29.16	27.98
	talks	26.55	27.94	29.13	**28.02**
	news	26.47	**28.18**	28.89	27.40
	mixed	26.60	27.93	**29.58**	27.32
En-Tr	original	15.65	17.10	16.35	16.41
	talks	15.57	16.97	16.22	**16.91**
	news	15.67	17.19	16.26	16.69
	mixed	**15.96**	**17.35**	**16.55**	16.89

Table 7: The BLEU scores of the multi-task neural model on using external monolingual data of talks data, news data, and mixed data.

Task	Model	BLEU
Uy-Ch	general NMT model	35.12
	baseline NMT model	35.46
	multi-task neural model with external monolingual data	**36.47**
Ch-Uy	general NMT model	21.00
	baseline NMT model	21.57
	multi-task neural model with external monolingual data	**23.02**

Table 8: The BLEU scores of the general NMT model, baseline NMT model, and the multi-task neural model with external monolingual data on Uyghur-Chinese and Chinese-Uyghur machine translation tasks.

Original Data: The monolingual data comes from the original bilingual parallel sentences.
Talks Data: The monolingual data contains talks.
News Data: The monolingual data contains news.
Talks and News Mixed Data: The monolingual data contains talks and news in a 3:4 ratio as the same with the original bilingual parallel sentences.

Table 7 shows the BLEU scores of the proposed multi-task neural model on using different external monolingual data. We can see that there is no obvious difference on Turkish-English translation performance by using different monolingual data, whether the data is in-domain or out-of-domain to the test dataset. However, for the English-Turkish machine translation task, which can be seen as agglutinative language generation task, using the mixed data of talks and news achieves further improvements of the BLEU scores on almost all the test datasets. The main reason is that the proposed multi-task neural model incorporates many morphological and linguistic information of Turkish rather than that of English, which mainly pays attention to the source-side representation ability on agglutinative languages rather than the target-side language modeling.

We also evaluate the translation performance of the general NMT model, baseline NMT model, and multi-task neural model with external news data on the machine translation task between Uyghur and Chinese. The experimental results are shown in Table 8. The results indicate that the multi-task neural model achieves the highest BLEU scores on the test dataset by utilizing external monolingual data for the stemming task on Uyghur sentences.

6 Conclusions

In this paper, we propose a multi-task neural model for translation task from and into a low-resource and morphologically-rich agglutinative language. The model jointly learns to perform bi-directional translation and agglutinative language stemming by utilizing the shared encoder and decoder under standard NMT framework. Extensive experimental results show that the proposed model is beneficial for the agglutinative language machine translation, and only a small amount of the agglutinative data can improve the translation performance in both directions. Moreover, the proposed approach with external monolingual data is more useful for translating into the agglutinative language, which achieves an improvement of +1.42 BLEU points for translation from English into Turkish and +1.45 BLEU points from Chinese into Uyghur.

In future work, we plan to utilize other word segmentation methods for model training. We also plan to combine the proposed multi-task neural model with back-translation method to enhance the ability of the NMT model on target-side language modeling.

Acknowledgements

We are very grateful to the mentor of this paper for her meaningful feedback. Thanks three anonymous reviewers for their insightful comments and practical suggestions. This work is supported by the High-Level Talents Introduction Project of Xinjiang under Grant No.Y839031201, the National Natural Science Foundation of China under Grant No.U1703133, the National Natural Science Foundation of Xinjiang under Grant No.2019BL-0006, the Open Project of Xinjiang Key Laboratory under Grant No.2018D04018, and the Youth Innovation Promotion Association of the Chinese Academy of Sciences under Grant No.2017472.

References

Mijit Ablimit, Graham Neubig, Masato Mimura, Shinsuke Mori, Tatsuya Kawahara, and Askar Hamdulla. 2010. Uyghur morpheme-based language models and ASR. In *IEEE International Conference on Signal Processing*.

Duygu Ataman, Matteo Negri, Marco Turchi, and Marcello Federico. 2017. Linguistically motivated vocabulary reduction for neural machine translation from Turkish to English. *Journal of the Prague Bulletin of Mathematical Linguistics*, 108:331-342.

Dzmitry Bahdanau, Kyunghyun Cho, and Yoshua Bengio. 2014. Neural machine translation by jointly learning to align and translate. *arXiv preprint arXiv:1409.0473*.

Mauro Cettolo, Christian Girardi and Marcello Federico. 2012. WIT3: Web inventory of transcribed and translated talks. In *Proceedings of the 16th Conference of the European Association for Machine Translation*.

Dongpeng Chen and Brian Kan-Wing Mak. 2015. Multitask learning of deep neural networks for low-resource speech recognition. In *IEEE/ACM Transactions on Audio, Speech, and Language Processing*.

Yong Cheng, Wei Xu, Zhongjun He, Wei He, Hua Wu, Maosong Sun, and Yang Liu. 2016. Semi-Supervised learning for neural machine translation. In *Proceedings of the 54th Annual Meeting of ACL*.

Kyunghyun Cho, Bart Van Merrienboer, Caglar Gulcehre, Dzmitry Bahdanau, Fethi Bougares, Holger Schwenk, and Yoshua Bengio. 2014. Learning phrase representations using RNN encoder-decoder for statistical machine translation. *arXiv preprint arXiv:1406.1078*.

Anna Currey, Antonio Valerio Miceli Barone, and Kenneth Heafield. 2017. Copied monolingual data improves low-resource neural machine translation. In *Proceedings of the Second Conference on Machine Translation*.

Tobias Domhan and Felix Hieber. 2017. Using target-side monolingual data for neural machine translation through multi-task learning. In *Proceedings of EMNLP*.

Daxiang Dong, Hua Wu, Wei He, Dianhai Yu, and Haifeng Wang. 2015. Multi-task learning for multiple language translation. In *Proceedings of ACL*.

Caglar Gulcehre, Orhan Firat, Kelvin Xu, Kyunghyun Cho, et al. 2015. On using monolingual corpora in neural machine translation. *arXiv preprint arXiv:1503.03535v2*.

Kazuma Hashimoto, Caiming Xiong, Yoshimasa Tsuruoka, and Richard Socher. 2017. A joint many-task model: Growing a neural network for multiple NLP tasks. In *Proceedings of EMNLP*.

Felix Hieber, Tobias Domhan, Michael Denkowski, David Vilar, Artem Sokolov, Ann Clifton, and Matt Post. 2017. Sockeye: A toolkit for neural machine translation. *arXiv preprint arXiv:1712.05690*.

Matthias Huck, Simon Riess, and Alexander Fraser. 2017. Target-side word segmentation strategies for neural machine translation. In *Proceedings of the Second Conference on Machine Translation*.

Sébastien Jean, Kyunghyun Cho, Roland Memisevic, and Yoshua Bengio. 2015. On using very large target vocabulary for neural machine translation. In *Proceedings of ACL*.

Melvin Johnson, Mike Schuster, Quoc V. Le, Maxim Krikun, Yonghui Wu, Zhifeng Chen, Nikhil Thorat, Fernanda Viégas, Martin Wattenberg, Greg Corrado, Macduff Hughes, and Jeffrey Dean. 2017. Google's multilingual neural machine translation system: Enabling zero-shot translation. In *Proceedings of ACL*.

Suyoun Kim, Takaaki Hori, and Shinji Watanabe. 2016. Joint CTC-Attention based end-to-end speech recognition using multi-task learning. *arXiv preprint arXiv:1609.06773*.

Diederik Kingma and Jimmy Ba. 2015. Adam: A method for stochastic optimization. In *Proceedings of ICLR*.

Eliyahu Kiperwasser, Miguel Ballesteros. 2018. Scheduled multi-task learning: From syntax to translation. In *Transactions of the Association for Computational Linguistics*.

Kazuaki Kishida. 2005. Technical issues of cross-language information retrieval: A review. *Journal of the Information Processing and Management*, 41(3):433-455. https://doi.org/10.1016/j.ipm.2004.06.007.

Xiaodong Liu, Jianfeng Gao, Xiaodong He, Li Deng, Kevin Duh, and Ye-Yi Wang. 2015. Representation learning using multi-task deep neural networks for semantic classification and information retrieval. In *Proceedings of NAACL*.

Minh-Thang Luong, Hieu Pham, and Christopher D Manning. 2015a. Effective approaches to Attention-based neural machine translation. In *Proceedings of EMNLP*.

Minh-Thang Luong, Quoc V Le, Ilya Sutskever, Oriol Vinyals, and Lukasz Kaiser. 2015b. Multi-task sequence to sequence learning. *arXiv preprint arXiv:1511.06114*.

Minh-Thang Luong, Christopher D. Manning. 2016. Achieving open vocabulary neural machine translation with hybrid word-character models. In *Proceedings of ACL*.

Ishan Misra, Abhinav Shrivastava, Abhinav Gupta, and Martial Hebert. 2016. Cross-Stitch networks for multi-task learning. In *Proceedings of CVPR*.

Xing Niu, Sudha Rao, and Marine Carpuat. 2018a. Multi-task neural models for translating between styles within and across languages. In *Proceedings of COLING*.

Xing Niu, Michael Denkowski, and Marine Carpuat. 2018b. Bi-Directional neural machine translation with synthetic parallel data. *arXiv preprint arXiv: 1805.11213*.

Prajit Ramachandran, Peter Liu, and Quoc Le. 2017. Unsupervised pretraining for sequence to sequence learning. In *Proceedings of the 2017 Conference on EMNLP*.

Yirong Pan, Xiao Li, Yating Yang, and Rui Dong. 2020. Morphological word segmentation on agglutinative languages for neural machine translation. *arXiv preprint arXiv: 2001.01589*.

Kishore Papineni, Salim Roukos, Todd Ward, and WeiJing Zhu. 2002. BLEU: A method for automatic evaluation of machine translation. In *Proceedings of ACL*.

Ha¸Sim Sak, Tunga Güngör, and Murat Saraçlar. 2007. Morphological disambiguation of Turkish text with perceptron algorithm. In *International Conference on Intelligent Text Processing and Computational Linguistics*.

Rico Sennrich, Barry Haddow, and Alexandra Birch. 2015a. Improving neural machine translation models with monolingual data. *arXiv preprint arXiv:1511.06709*.

Rico Sennrich, Barry Haddow, and Alexandra Birch. Neural machine translation of rare words with subword units. 2015b. *arXiv preprint arXiv: 1508.07909*.

Rico Sennrich, Barry Haddow, and Alexandra Birch. 2016. Controlling politeness in neural machine translation via side constraints. In *Proceedings of NAACL*.

Ilya Sutskever, Oriol Vinyals, and Quoc VV Le. 2014. Sequence to sequence learning with neural networks. In *Proceedings of NIPS*.

Ahmed Tawfik, Mahitab Emam, Khaled Essam, Robert Nabil, and Hany Hassan. 2019. Morphology-aware word-segmentation in dialectal Arabic adaptation of neural machine translation. In *Proceedings of the Fourth Arabic Natural Language Processing Workshop*.

Eziz Tursun, Debasis Ganguly, Turghun Osman, Yating Yang, Ghalip Abdukerim, Junlin Zhou, and Qun Liu. 2016. A semi-supervised tag-transition-based Markovian model for Uyghur morphology analysis. In *ACM Transactions on Asian and Low-Resource Language Information Processing*.

Francis M. Tyers and Murat Alperen. 2010. South-East European Times: A parallel corpus of the Balkan languages, In *Proceedings of the LREC Workshop on Exploitation of Multilingual Resources and Tools for Central and (South-) Eastern European Languages*.

Ashish Vaswani, Noam Shazeer, Niki Parmar, Jakob Uszkoreit, Llion Jones, Aidan N Gomez, Ł ukasz Kaiser, and Illia Polosukhin. 2017. Attention is all you need. In *Advances in Neural Information Processing Systems*.

Junho Yim, Heechul Jung, ByungIn Yoo, Changkyu Choi, Dusik Park, and Junmo Kim. 2015. Rotating your face using multi-task deep neural network. In *Proceedings of CVPR*.

Jiajun Zhang and Chengqing Zong. 2016. Exploiting source-side monolingual data in neural machine translation. In *Proceedings of EMNLP*.

Barret Zoph and Kevin Knight. 2016. Multi-source neural translation. In *Proceedings of NAACL*.

Considering Likelihood in NLP Classification Explanations with Occlusion and Language Modeling

David Harbecke and **Christoph Alt**

German Research Center for Artificial Intelligence (DFKI), Berlin, Germany

`{firstname}.{lastname}@dfki.de`

Abstract

Recently, state-of-the-art NLP models gained an increasing syntactic and semantic understanding of language, and explanation methods are crucial to understand their decisions. Occlusion is a well established method that provides explanations on discrete language data, e.g. by removing a language unit from an input and measuring the impact on a model's decision. We argue that current occlusion-based methods often produce invalid or syntactically incorrect language data, neglecting the improved abilities of recent NLP models. Furthermore, gradient-based explanation methods disregard the discrete distribution of data in NLP. Thus, we propose **OLM**: a novel explanation method that combines **o**cclusion and language **m**odels to sample valid and syntactically correct replacements with high likelihood, given the context of the original input. We lay out a theoretical foundation that alleviates these weaknesses of other explanation methods in NLP and provide results that underline the importance of considering data likelihood in occlusion-based explanation.[1]

1 Introduction

Explanation methods are a useful tool to analyze and understand the decisions made by complex non-linear models, e.g. neural networks. For example, they can attribute *relevance* scores to input features (e.g. word or sub-word units in NLP). Nevertheless, explanation methods can be misleading (Adebayo et al., 2018) and they need to be analyzed for their well-foundedness.

Gradient-based methods provide explanations by analyzing local infinitesimal changes to determine the shape of a network's function. The implicit assumption is that the local shape of a function is

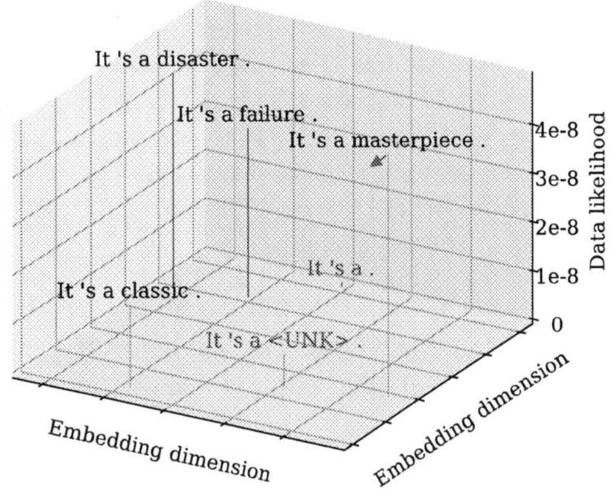

Figure 1: Schematic display of data likelihood in NLP. There are discrete inputs, i.e. combination of tokens, with a data likelihood greater than zero. All other inputs in the embedding space have likelihood zero because they have no corresponding tokens. Occlusion methods (green) create unlikely input. Gradient-based explanation methods (red arrow) consider infinitesimal changes to the input and thus data with no likelihood.

indicative or useful to calculate the relevance of an input feature for a model's prediction. In computer vision, for example, infinitesimal changes to an input image still produce another valid image and the change in prediction is a valid tool to analyze what led to it (e.g., Zintgraf et al., 2017). The same applies to methods that analyze the function's gradient at multiple points, such as *Integrated Gradients* (Sundararajan et al., 2017).

In NLP, however, the input consists of natural language, which is discrete, i.e., the data that has positive likelihood is a discrete distribution (see Figure 1). This means that local neighborhoods need not be indicative of the model's prediction behaviour and a model's prediction function at points with zero likelihood need not be relevant to the model's decision. Thus, we argue that black-box

---

[1] Our experiments are available at `https://github.com/DFKI-NLP/OLM`

111

Proceedings of the 58th Annual Meeting of the Association for Computational Linguistics: Student Research Workshop, pages 111–117

July 5 - July 10, 2020. ©2020 Association for Computational Linguistics

Method	Relevances						Max. value
OLM (ours)	forced	, familiar	and	thoroughly	condescending	.	0.76
OLM-S (ours)	forced	, familiar	and	thoroughly	condescending	.	0.47
Delete	forced	, familiar	and	thoroughly	condescending	.	1
UNK	forced	, familiar	and	thoroughly	condescending	.	0.35
Sensitivity Analysis	forced	, familiar	and	thoroughly	condescending	.	0.025
Gradient*Input	forced	, familiar	and	thoroughly	condescending	.	0.00011
Integrated Gradients	forced	, familiar	and	thoroughly	condescending	.	0.68

Table 1: Relevance scores of different gradient- and occlusion-based explanation methods for a sentence from the SST-2 dataset, correctly classified as negative sentiment by *RoBERTa*. Red indicates an input token, with a contribution to the true label (negative sentiment), blue indicates a detraction from the true label. Coloring are normalized for each method for visibility, the maximum value of each method is indicated in the last column. The relevances of the first four and last method can be interpreted as prediction difference if that token is missing (see *Sensitivity-1* in 2.1). The first token "forced" only has high relevance for our methods, the most commonly resampled tokens can be found in Table 2. Punctuation marks have less relevance than words for our method compared to gradient methods.

models in NLP should be analyzed only at inputs of non-zero likelihood and explanation methods should not rely on gradients.

Occlusion is a well suited method due to its ability to produce explanations on data with discrete likelihood. For example, by replacing or deleting a language unit in the original input and measuring the impact on the model's prediction. However, the likelihood of the replacement data is usually low. Consider, for example, a sentiment classification task and assume a model that assigns syntactically incorrect inputs a negative sentiment. It correctly predicts *"It 's a masterpiece ."* as positive, but assigns negative sentiment to syntactically incorrect inputs produced by occlusion, e.g. *"It 's a ."* or *"It 's a <UNK> ."*, which have low data likelihood (see Figure 1). This may result in a large prediction difference for many tokens in a positive sentiment example and no prediction difference for many tokens in a negative sentiment example (see Table 1), independent of whether they carry any sentiment information and thus may be relevant to the model. This example shows that the relevance attributed by current occlusion-based methods may depend solely on the model's syntactic understanding instead of the input feature's information regarding the task.

We argue that current NLP state-of-the-art models have increasing syntactic (Hewitt and Manning, 2019) and hierarchical (Liu et al., 2019a) understanding. Therefore, methods that explain these

models should consider syntactically correct replacement that is likely given the unit's context, e.g. in Figure 1 *"classic"* or *"failure"* as replacements for *"masterpiece"* in *"It 's a masterpiece ."* Our experiments show that presenting these models with perturbed ungrammatical input changes the explanations.

1.1 Contributions

- We present **OLM**, a novel black-box relevance explanation method which considers syntactic understanding. It is suitable for any model that performs an NLP classification task and we analyze which axioms for explanation methods it fulfills.
- We introduce the **class zero-sum axiom** for explanation methods.
- We experimentally compare the relevances produced by our method to those of other black-box and gradient-based explanation approaches.

2 Methods

In this section, we introduce our novel explanation method that combines occlusion with language modeling. Instead of deleting or replacing a linguistic unit in the input with an unlikely replacement, *OLM* substitutes it with one generated by a language model. This produces a contextualized distribution of valid and syntactically likely reference inputs and allows a more faithful analysis of models with increasing syntactic capabilities. This is followed by an axiomatic analysis of *OLM*'s properties. Finally, we introduce **OLM-S**, an extension that measures sensitivity of a model at a feature's position.

For our approach we employ the difference of probabilities formula from Robnik-Šikonja and Kononenko (2008). Let x_i be an attribute of input x and $x_{\backslash i}$ the incomplete input without this attribute. Then the relevance r given the prediction function f and class c is

$$r_{f,c}(x_i) = f_c(x) - f_c(x_{\backslash i}). \tag{1}$$

Note that $f_c(x_{\backslash i})$ is not accurately defined and needs to be approximated, as $x_{\backslash i}$ is an incomplete input. For vision, Zintgraf et al. (2017) approximate $f_c(x_{\backslash i})$ by using the input data distribution p_{data} to sample $\hat{x}_i$ independently of x or use a Gaussian distribution for $\hat{x}_i$ conditioned on surrounding pixels. We argue sampling should be conditioned on the whole input and depend on the probability of the data distribution. We argue that in NLP a language model p_{LM} generates input that is as natural as possible for the model and thus approximate

$$f_c(x_{\backslash i}) \approx \sum_{\hat{x}_i} p_{LM}(\hat{x}_i|x_{\backslash i}) f_c(x_{\backslash i}, \hat{x}_i). \tag{2}$$

In general, x_i should be units of interest such as phrases, words or subword tokens. Thus, *OLM*'s relevance for a language unit is the difference in prediction between the original input and inputs with the unit resampled by conditioning on information in its context. The relevance of every language unit is in the interval $[-1, 1]$, with the sign indicating contradiction or support, and can be interpreted as the value of information added by the unit for the model.

2.1 Axiomatic Analysis

Sundararajan et al. (2017) introduced axiomatic development and analysis of explanation methods. We follow their argument that an explanation method should be derived theoretically, not experimentally, as we want to analyze a model, not our understanding of it. First, we introduce a new axiom. Then we discuss which existing axioms our method fulfills.[2]

Class Zero-Sum Axiom. We introduce an axiom that follows from the intuition that for a normalized DNN every input feature contributes as

---

[2]Proofs for the following analysis can be found in Appendix A.

token	freq.	pred.	token	freq.	pred.
familiar	9	1	old	2	1
warm	4	7e-4	perfect	2	3.9e-4
ancient	3	0.074	quiet	2	1
cold	3	1	real	2	6.5e-3
beautiful	2	1.4e-4	sweet	2	1.9e-4
bold	2	0.63	wonderful	2	3.1e-4
low	2	1	yes	2	1
nice	2	8.3e-4	young	2	0.99

Table 2: Most frequently resampled words for "forced" in "*forced* , familiar and thoroughly condescending ." from Table 1. The last column indicates the prediction of the negative sentiment neuron, which is the true label. We sample 100 times per token, the prediction is rounded to two significant digits. Many resampled words (pred. < 0.5) lead to a positive sentiment classification. The high variance of the model prediction for replacements of this token is not captured by another method.

much to a specific class as it detracts from all other classes. Let f be a prediction function where the output is normalized over all classes C. Every input feature contributes as much to the classification of a specific class as it detracts from other classes. A relevance method that gives a feature positive relevance for every class is not helpful in understanding the model. An explanation method satisfies *Class Zero-Sum* if the summed relevance of each input feature x_i over all classes is zero.

$$\sum_{c \in C} r_{f,c}(x_i) = 0 \tag{3}$$

This axiom can be seen as an alternative to the **Completeness** axiom given by Bach et al. (2015). *Completeness* states that the sum of the relevances of an input is equal to its prediction. They can not be fulfilled simultaneously. Gosiewska and Biecek (2019) show that a linear distribution of relevance as with *Completeness* is not necessarily desirable for non-linear models. They argue that explanations that force the sum of relevances to be equal to the prediction do not capture the interaction of features faithfully. *OLM* fulfills *Class Zero-Sum*, as do other occlusion methods and gradient methods. Other axioms *OLM* fulfills are:

Implementation Invariance. Two neural networks that represent the same function, i.e. give the same output for each possible input, should receive the same relevances for every input (Sundararajan et al., 2017).

Linearity. A network, which is a linear combination of other networks, should have explanations which are the same linear combination of the original networks explanations (Sundararajan et al., 2017).

Sensitivity-1. The relevance of an input variable should be the difference of prediction when the input variable is occluded (Ancona et al., 2018).

2.2 OLM-S

From our approach we can also deduce a method that describes the sensitivity of the classification at the position of an input feature. To this end, we compute the standard deviation of the language model predictions.

$$s_{f,c}(x_i) = \sqrt{\sum_{\hat{x}_i} p_{LM}(\hat{x}_i|x_{\setminus i}) \left(f_c(x_{\setminus i}, \hat{x}_i) - \mu\right)^2},$$
(4)

where μ is the mean value from equation 2. We call this *OLM-S(ensitivity)*. Note that this measure is independent of x_i and only describes the sensitivity of the feature's position. This means that it measures a model's sensitivity at a given language unit's position given the context. *OLM* and *OLM-S* are thus using mean and standard deviation, respectively, of the prediction when resampling a token.

3 Experiments

In our experiments, we aim to answer the following question: Do relevances produced by our method differ from those that either ignore the discrete structure of language data or produce syntactically incorrect input, and if so, how?

We first train a state-of-the-art NLP model (*RoBERTa*, Liu et al., 2019b) on three sentence classification tasks (Section 3.2). We then compare the explanations produced by *OLM* and *OLM-S* to five occlusion and gradient-based methods (Section 3.1). To this end, we calculate the relevances of words over a whole input regarding the true label. We calculate the Pearson correlation coefficients of these relevances for every sentence and average this over the whole development set of each task. In our experiments we use *BERT base* (Devlin et al., 2019) for *OLM* resampling.

3.1 Baseline Methods

We compare *OLM* with occlusion (Robnik-Šikonja and Kononenko, 2008; Zintgraf et al., 2017) in two variants. One method of occlusion is **deletion** of the word. The other method is replacing the word with the <UNK> token for unknown words.

These methods can produce ungrammatical input, as we argue in Section 1.

Furthermore, we compare with the following gradient-based methods. **Sensitivity Analysis** (Simonyan et al., 2013) is the absolute value of the gradient. **Gradient*Input** (Shrikumar et al., 2016) is simple component-wise multiplication of an input with its gradient. **Integrated Gradients** (Sundararajan et al., 2017) integrate the gradients from a reference input to the current input. As these gradient-based methods provide relevance for every word vector value, we sum up all vector values belonging to a word. Gradient-based methods do not consider likelihood in NLP (see Section 1) and are thus also merely a comparison and not a gold standard.

3.2 Tasks

We select a representative set of NLP sentence classification tasks that focus on different aspects of context and linguistic properties:

MNLI (matched) The Multi-Genre Natural Language Inference Corpus (Williams et al., 2018) contains 400k pairs of premise and hypothesis sentences and the task is to predict whether the premise entails the hypothesis. We re-use the *RoBERTa large* model fine-tuned on MNLI (Liu et al., 2019b), with a dev set accuracy of 90.2.

SST-2 The Stanford Sentiment Treebank (Socher et al., 2013) contains 70k sentences labeled with positive or negative sentiment. We fine-tune the pre-trained *RoBERTa base* to the classification task and achieve an accuracy of 94.5 on the dev set.

CoLA The Corpus of Linguistic Acceptability (Warstadt et al., 2018) contains 10k sentences labeled as grammatical or ungrammatical, e.g. 'They can sing.' (acceptable) vs. 'many evidence was provided.' (unacceptable). Similar to SST-2, we fine-tune *RoBERTa base* to the task and achieve a Matthew's corr. of 61.3 on the dev set.

3.3 Results

Table 3 shows the correlation of our two proposed occlusion methods (*OLM* and *OLM-S*) with other explanation methods on three NLP tasks. For *OLM-S* we only report correlation to *Sensitivity* because both inform about the magnitude of possible change. They both provide non-negative values and therefore are not necessarily comparable to the other methods. We find that across all tasks *OLM* correlates the most with the two occlusion-based

	MNLI		SST-2		CoLA	
	OLM	OLM-S	OLM	OLM-S	OLM	OLM-S
Delete	0.60	-	0.52	-	0.25	-
UNK	0.58	-	0.47	-	0.21	-
Sensitivity Analysis	0.27	0.35	0.30	0.37	0.20	0.29
Gradient*Input	-0.03	-	0.02	-	0.02	-
Integrated Gradients	0.28	-	0.35	-	0.15	-

Table 3: Correlation between explanation methods on MNLI, SST-2, and CoLA development sets. OLM correlates with every method except for Gradient*Input. The correlation is highest with the other Occlusion methods for MNLI and SST-2 but not close to 1. For all methods, the correlation is lowest on CoLA.

methods (*Unk* and *Delete*) but the overall correlation is low, with a maximum of 0.6 on MNLI. Also the level differs greatly between tasks, ranging from 0.21 and 0.25 (*Unk*, *Delete*) on CoLA to 0.58 and 0.6 on MNLI. As this is an average of correlations, this shows that resampling creates distinctive explanations that can not be approximated by other occlusion methods. An example input from SST-2 can be found in Table 1, which clearly highlights the difference in explanations. Table 2 shows the corresponding tokens resampled by *OLM*, using *BERT base* as the language model. For gradient-based methods the correlation with *OLM* is even lower, ranging from -0.03 for *Gradient*Input* on MNLI to 0.35 for *Integrated Gradients* on SST-2. For *OLM-S* we observe a correlation between 0.29 (CoLA) and 0.35 (MNLI), which is still low. *Gradient*Input* shows almost no correlation to *OLM* across tasks. The overall low correlation of gradient-based methods with *OLM* and *OLM-S* suggests that ignoring the discrete structure of language data might be problematic in NLP.

4   Related Work

There exist many other popular black-box explanation methods for DNNs. *SHAP* (Lundberg and Lee, 2017) is a framework that uses Shapley Values which are a game-theoretic black-box approach to determining relevance by occluding subsets of all features. They do not necessarily consider the likelihood of data. The occlusion *SHAP* employs may be combined with *OLM* but the approximation error of the language model could increase with more features occluded. *LIME* (Ribeiro et al., 2016) explains by learning a local explainable model. *LIME* tries to be locally faithful to a model, which is, as we argue, not as important as likely data for explanations in NLP.

There are also explanation methods for DNNs which give layer-specific rules to retrieve relevance. *LRP* (Bach et al., 2015) propagates relevance from the output to the input such that *Completeness* is satisfied for every layer. *DeepLIFT* (Shrikumar et al., 2017) compares the activations of an input with activations reference inputs. In contrast to *OLM*, these layer-specific explanation methods have been shown not to satisfy *Implementation Invariance* (Sundararajan et al., 2017).

Most state-of-the-art models in NLP are transformers which use attention. There is a discussion on whether attention weights (Bahdanau et al., 2015; Vaswani et al., 2017) should be considered as explanation method in Jain and Wallace (2019) and Wiegreffe and Pinter (2019). They are not based on an axiomatic attribution of relevances. It is unclear whether they satisfy any axiom. An advantage to analyzing attention weights is that attention weights naturally show what the model does. Thus, even if they do not always provide a faithful explanation, their analysis might be helpful for a specific input.

5   Conclusion

We argue that current black-box and gradient-based explanation methods do not yet consider the likelihood of data and present *OLM*, a novel explanation method, which uses a language model to resample occluded words. It is especially suited for word-level relevance of sentence classification with state-of-the-art NLP models. We also introduce the *Class Zero-Sum Axiom* for explanation methods, compare it with an existing axiom. Furthermore, we show other axioms that *OLM* satisfies. We argue that with this more solid theoretical foundation *OLM* can be regarded as an improvement over existing NLP classification explanation methods. In our experiments, we compare our methods to other occlusion and gradient explanation methods. We do not consider these experiments to be exhaustive. Unfortunately, there is no general evaluation for explanation methods.

We show that our method adds value by showing distinctive results and better founded theory. A practical difficulty of *OLM* is the approximation with a language model. First, a language model can create syntactically correct data, that does not make sense for the task. Second, even state-of-the-art language models do not always produce syntactically correct data. However, we argue that using a language model is a suitable way for finding reference inputs.

In the future, we want to extend this method to language features other than words. NLP tasks with longer input are probably not very sensitive to single word occlusion, which could be measured with *OLM-S*.

Acknowledgments

We would like to thank Leonhard Hennig, Robert Schwarzenberg, Dirk Hovy and the anonymous reviewers for their feedback on the paper. This work was partially supported by the German Federal Ministry of Education and Research as part of the projects BBDC2 (01IS18025E) and XAINES.

References

Julius Adebayo, Justin Gilmer, Michael Muelly, Ian Goodfellow, Moritz Hardt, and Been Kim. 2018. Sanity checks for saliency maps. In *Advances in Neural Information Processing Systems*, pages 9525–9536.

Marco Ancona, Enea Ceolini, Cengiz Öztireli, and Markus Gross. 2018. Towards better understanding of gradient-based attribution methods for deep neural networks. *International Conference on Learning Representations*.

Sebastian Bach, Alexander Binder, Grégoire Montavon, Frederick Klauschen, Klaus-Robert Müller, and Wojciech Samek. 2015. On pixel-wise explanations for non-linear classifier decisions by layer-wise relevance propagation. *PloS one*, 10(7):e0130140.

Dzmitry Bahdanau, Kyunghyun Cho, and Yoshua Bengio. 2015. Neural machine translation by jointly learning to align and translate. *International Conference on Learning Representations*.

Jacob Devlin, Ming-Wei Chang, Kenton Lee, and Kristina Toutanova. 2019. BERT: Pre-training of deep bidirectional transformers for language understanding. In *Proceedings of the 2019 Conference of the North American Chapter of the Association for Computational Linguistics: Human Language Technologies, Volume 1 (Long and Short Papers)*, pages 4171–4186. Association for Computational Linguistics.

Alicja Gosiewska and Przemyslaw Biecek. 2019. Do not trust additive explanations. *CoRR*, arXiv:1903.11420.

John Hewitt and Christopher D. Manning. 2019. A structural probe for finding syntax in word representations. In *Proceedings of the 2019 Conference of the North American Chapter of the Association for Computational Linguistics: Human Language Technologies, Volume 1 (Long and Short Papers)*, pages 4129–4138.

Sarthak Jain and Byron C. Wallace. 2019. Attention is not Explanation. In *Proceedings of the 2019 Conference of the North American Chapter of the Association for Computational Linguistics: Human Language Technologies, Volume 1 (Long and Short Papers)*, pages 3543–3556.

Nelson F. Liu, Matt Gardner, Yonatan Belinkov, Matthew E. Peters, and Noah A. Smith. 2019a. Linguistic knowledge and transferability of contextual representations. In *Proceedings of the 2019 Conference of the North American Chapter of the Association for Computational Linguistics: Human Language Technologies, Volume 1 (Long and Short Papers)*, pages 1073–1094.

Yinhan Liu, Myle Ott, Naman Goyal, Jingfei Du, Mandar Joshi, Danqi Chen, Omer Levy, Mike Lewis, Luke Zettlemoyer, and Veselin Stoyanov. 2019b. Roberta: A robustly optimized BERT pretraining approach. *CoRR*, arXiv:1907.11692.

Scott M. Lundberg and Su-In Lee. 2017. A unified approach to interpreting model predictions. In I. Guyon, U. V. Luxburg, S. Bengio, H. Wallach, R. Fergus, S. Vishwanathan, and R. Garnett, editors, *Advances in Neural Information Processing Systems 30*, pages 4765–4774. Curran Associates, Inc.

Marco Tulio Ribeiro, Sameer Singh, and Carlos Guestrin. 2016. Why should i trust you?: Explaining the predictions of any classifier. In *Proceedings of the 22nd ACM SIGKDD international conference on knowledge discovery and data mining*, pages 1135–1144. ACM.

Marko Robnik-Šikonja and Igor Kononenko. 2008. Explaining classifications for individual instances. *IEEE Transactions on Knowledge and Data Engineering*, 20(5):589–600.

Avanti Shrikumar, Peyton Greenside, and Anshul Kundaje. 2017. Learning important features through propagating activation differences. In *International Conference on Machine Learning*, pages 3145–3153.

Avanti Shrikumar, Peyton Greenside, Anna Shcherbina, and Anshul Kundaje. 2016. Not just a black box: Learning important features through propagating activation differences. *CoRR*, arXiv:1605.01713.

Karen Simonyan, Andrea Vedaldi, and Andrew Zisserman. 2013. Deep inside convolutional networks: Visualising image classification models and saliency maps. *CoRR*, arXiv:1312.6034.

Richard Socher, Alex Perelygin, Jean Wu, Jason Chuang, Christopher D. Manning, Andrew Ng, and Christopher Potts. 2013. Recursive deep models for semantic compositionality over a sentiment treebank. In *Proceedings of EMNLP*, pages 1631–1642.

Mukund Sundararajan, Ankur Taly, and Qiqi Yan. 2017. Axiomatic Attribution for Deep Networks. In *International Conference on Machine Learning*, pages 3319–3328.

Ashish Vaswani, Noam Shazeer, Niki Parmar, Jakob Uszkoreit, Llion Jones, Aidan N. Gomez, Lukasz Kaiser, and Illia Polosukhin. 2017. Attention is all you need. In *Advances in Neural Information Processing Systems*, pages 5998–6008.

Alex Warstadt, Amanpreet Singh, and Samuel R. Bowman. 2018. Neural network acceptability judgments. *CoRR*, arXiv:1805.12471.

Sarah Wiegreffe and Yuval Pinter. 2019. Attention is not not explanation. In *Proceedings of the 2019 Conference on Empirical Methods in Natural Language Processing and the 9th International Joint Conference on Natural Language Processing (EMNLP-IJCNLP)*, pages 11–20.

Adina Williams, Nikita Nangia, and Samuel Bowman. 2018. A broad-coverage challenge corpus for sentence understanding through inference. In *Proceedings of the 2018 Conference of the North American Chapter of the Association for Computational Linguistics: Human Language Technologies, Volume 1 (Long Papers)*, pages 1112–1122.

Luisa M. Zintgraf, Taco S. Cohen, Tameem Adel, and Max Welling. 2017. Visualizing deep neural network decisions: Prediction difference analysis. *International Conference on Learning Representations*.

A   Proof Appendix

Let f be a neural network that predicts a probability distribution over classes C, i.e. $\sum_{c \in C} f_c(x) = 1$. Let $x = (x_1, ..., x_n)$ be a input split into n input features.

1. **Class Zero-Sum** and **Completeness** rule each other out. Assume $r_{f,c}$ fulfills both, then we have

$$\sum_{i=1}^{n} \sum_{c \in C} r_{f,c}(x_i) = 0 \qquad (5)$$

from **Class Zero-Sum** and

$$\sum_{c \in C} \sum_{i=1}^{n} r_{f,c}(x_i) = 1 \qquad (6)$$

from *Completeness*. Contradiction.

2. **OLM** satisfies **Class Zero-Sum**. Let $r_{f,c}$ now be the *OLM* relevance method from equations (1) and (2) in the paper.

$$
\begin{aligned}
&\sum_{c \in C} r_{f,c}(x_i) \\
&= \sum_{c \in C} \left(f_c(x) - \sum_{\hat{x}_i} p_{LM}(\hat{x}_i | x_{\setminus i}) f_c(x_{\setminus i}, \hat{x}_i) \right) \\
&= \sum_{c \in C} f_c(x) - \sum_{\hat{x}_i} p_{LM}(\hat{x}_i | x_{\setminus i}) \sum_{c \in C} f_c(x_{\setminus i}, \hat{x}_i) \\
&= 1 - \sum_{\hat{x}_i} p_{LM}(\hat{x}_i | x_{\setminus i}) = 0.
\end{aligned}
\qquad (7)
$$

3. **OLM** satisfies **Implementation Invariance**. *OLM* is a black box method and only evaluates the function of the neural network. Thus, it has to satisfy *Implementation Invariance*.

4. **OLM** satisfies **Sensitivity-1**. *OLM* is defined as an Occlusion method, so it necessarily gives the difference of prediction when an input variable is occluded.

5. **OLM** satisfies **Linearity**. Let $f = \sum_{j=1}^{n} \alpha_j g^j$ be a linear combination of models. Then we have

$$
\begin{aligned}
r_{f,c}(x_i) &= f_c(x) - \sum_{\hat{x}_i} p_{LM}(\hat{x}_i | x_{\setminus i}) f_c(x_{\setminus i}, \hat{x}_i) \\
&= \sum_{j=1}^{n} \alpha_j g_c^j(x) - \\
&\quad \sum_{\hat{x}_i} p_{LM}(\hat{x}_i | x_{\setminus i}) \sum_{j=1}^{n} \alpha_j g_c^j(x_{\setminus i}, \hat{x}_i) \\
&= \sum_{j=1}^{n} \alpha_j r_{g^j,c}(x_i).
\end{aligned}
\qquad (8)
$$

Non-Topical Coherence in Social Talk:
A Call for Dialogue Model Enrichment

Alex Lưu
Brandeis University
`alexluu@brandeis.edu`

Sophia A. Malamud
Brandeis University
`smalamud@brandeis.edu`

Abstract

Current models of dialogue mainly focus on utterances within a topically coherent discourse segment, rather than new-topic utterances (NTUs), which begin a new topic not correlating with the content of prior discourse. As a result, these models may sufficiently account for discourse context of task-oriented but not social conversations. We conduct a pilot annotation study of NTUs as a first step towards a model capable of rationalizing conversational coherence in social talk. We start with the naturally occurring social dialogues in the Disco-SPICE corpus, annotated with discourse relations in the Penn Discourse Treebank (PDTB) and Cognitive approach to Coherence Relations (CCR) frameworks. We first annotate content-based coherence relations that are not available in Disco-SPICE, and then heuristically identify NTUs, which lack a coherence relation to prior discourse. Based on the interaction between NTUs and their discourse context, we construct a classification for NTUs that actually convey certain non-topical coherence in social talk. This classification introduces new sequence-based social intents that traditional taxonomies of speech acts do not capture. The new findings advocates the development of a Bayesian game-theoretic model for social talk.[1]

1 Introduction and Background

Social talk or casual conversation, one of the most popular instances of spontaneous discourse, is commonly defined as the speech event type in which "all participants have the same role: to be "equals;" no purposes are pre-established; and the range of possible topics is open-ended, although conventionally constrained" (Scha et al., 1986). Even though we do not establish any purposes in terms of information exchange or practical tasks, we do share certain social goal from the back of our mind when deciding to engage in a casual conversation. This work rests upon the assumption that casual conversations can be modeled as ***goal-directed rational interactions***, similar to task-oriented conversations, and therefore both of these types demonstrate Grice's Cooperative Principle, i.e. conversational moves are constrained by "a common purpose or set of purposes, or at least a mutually accepted direction" which "may be fixed from the start" or "evolve during the exchange", "may be fairly definite" or "so indefinite as to leave very considerable latitude to the participant" (Grice, 1975). A similar assumption is made in Grosz and Sidner (1986)'s discourse structure framework as it affirms the primary role of speakers' intentions in "explaining discourse structure, defining discourse coherence, and providing a coherent conceptualization of the term "discourse" itself." We adopt the following terminology from Grosz and Sidner (1986):

- utterances – basic discourse units.
- discourse segments – functional sequences of naturally aggregated utterances (not necessarily consecutive), each corresponding to a discourse segment purpose (DSP) – an extension of Gricean utterance-level intentions.

To account for conversational coherence, current models[2] of dialogue mainly focus on utterances within a topically coherent discourse segment, rather than **new-topic utterances** (NTUs), which begin a new topic not linguistically[3] correlating with the content of prior discourse. For example, the excerpt shown in Table 1 has two NTUs, utterances 119 and 123.

In terms of theoretical models, Asher and Las-

---

[1]The live version of this publication is located at https://osf.io/nvtkq/.

[2]Here we only consider the dialogue models that involve symbolic representation of discourse context (in comparison with, for example, end-to-end trained neural dialogue models).

[3]"Linguistically" means "via linguistic calculation at the meaning levels such as semantic or pragmatic."

Proceedings of the 58th Annual Meeting of the Association for Computational Linguistics: Student Research Workshop, pages 118–133
July 5 - July 10, 2020. ©2020 Association for Computational Linguistics

Utt.	Simplified transcript
104-B	*And what 's the story with them*
105-B	*Are they still separated*
106-A	*Yes still separated*
107-A	*And Mummy was going she can't have children*
108-A	*Why Mummy it 's not her fault she can't have children*
109-A	*If he love her they could adopt*
110-A	*If he really wanted children of his own they [unclear speech]*
111-B	*I know*
112-B	*Sure he 's what forty odd five*
113-B	*Isn't he*
114-A	*Aye*
115-B	*Fucking hell*
116-B	*If he really wanted children he could 've had them long ago*
117-A	*That 's what I say*
118-B	*So uhm*
119-A	*Uh uh hold on*
120-A	*[unclear speech]*
121-A	*Think my mobile 's about to go*
122-A	*Ah it 's only John*
123-A	*Alright so how was your day*
124-B	*Not bad*

Table 1: An except, with indexed utterances, from dialogue P1A-095 in the SPICE-Ireland corpus (Kallen and Kirk, 2012) between two interlocutors A and B.

carides (2003)'s Segmented Discourse Representation Theory attributes conversational coherence to the existence of rhetorical relations between utterances, while Ginzburg (2012) and (Roberts, 1996/2012) propose that a conversational move is coherent if it is relevant to the Question Under Discussion. Computational models such as Belief-Desire-Intention (Allen, 1995, chapter 17) and Information State Update (Larsson and Traum, 2000) assume coherence to be a natural property of dialogues within a specific task domain. These models, both theoretical and computational, may adequately account for discourse dynamics of task-oriented conversations, where adjacent utterances tend to share a lot of linguistic material and speakers' intents are drawn from a narrow set of task-related goals. However, without any enrichment, they are not capable of handling the complexity of conversational coherence in social talk in which both speaker goals and utterances are less con-strained. Specifically, all of these models treat NTUs as incoherent conversational moves.

This work, therefore, seeks to identify the constraints on new topics in casual conversations as a first step towards a model which is capable of rationalizing NTUs and accounting for conversational coherence in social talk. The main contributions of this paper are as follows. We introduce NTUs as a novel research object that is capable of advancing our understanding of the *interactive* and *rational* aspects of social talk. We propose an annotation strategy for exploring NTUs in naturally occurring dialogues. A pilot annotation study of NTUs in a significant amount of spoken conversation text led us to amend the available taxonomies of speech acts with new **sequence-based social intents** that shed light on non-topical coherence in social talk. These new findings feed into a framework for the ***Bayesian game-theoretic models*** that are capable of predicting the emergence of the newly identified intents and accounting for conversational coherence in social talk.

2 Methodology Overview

Before studying the interaction between NTUs and their discourse context, we need to locate them in instances of social talk. Riou (2015) handles a similar task by annotating every turn-constructional unit (TCU) in casual conversations with two topic-related variables:

- topic transition vs. topic continuity.
- stepwise vs. disjunctive transition (Jefferson, 1984) if the TCU is annotated as a transition.

The TCUs triggering disjunctive transitions are intentionally equivalent to NTUs and the corresponding transitions can also be called **disjunctive topic changes**[4] (DTCs), i.e. conversational moves whose linguistic representation is an NTU. To perform the annotation task in Riou (2015), the annotators completely rely on their own intuition rather than guidelines.[5] This negatively affects annotation reliability, especially for topic transition cases, which are much less frequent in the studied data.

---

[4]Sharing Jefferson's characterization of troubles-telling exit devices in that the new topic "does not emerge from [prior talk], is not topically coherent with it, but constitutes a break from it" (Jefferson, 1984), and comparable to TOPIC-SHIFT (Carlson and Marcu, 2001) in RST Discourse Treebank.

[5]This is because the author aims to investigate the linguistic design of topic transitions and therefore cannot give the annotators the linguistic description of these transitions. Otherwise, she would face the risk of circularity in her study.

To improve the reliability and rigor of NTU detection, we approach the task reversely: we first annotate content-based coherence relations between utterances and then identify NTUs as those utterances that bear no coherence relation to the content of prior discourse. This approach shares certain features with the integration of new utterances in free dialogues presented in Reichman (1978): if a new utterance is not covered by the current conversational topic, the hearer can expand the current topic to cover it, or connect its topic with the current topic using a semantic relation from a predefined set. This similarity reflects the following view of discourse coherence: "[a discourse is] coherent just in case (a) every proposition (and question and request) that's introduced in the discourse is rhetorically connected to another bit of information in the discourse, resulting in a 'single' connected structure for the whole discourse; and (b) all anaphoric expressions can be resolved"; and therefore, "[a] discourse is incoherent whenever there's a proposition introduced in the discourse which doesn't seem to be connected to any of the other bits of the discourse in any meaningful way." (Asher and Lascarides, 2003, p. 4).

The main difference between Reichman (1978)'s model of topic shift and our work is that the former allows the total shift relation, the succeeding topic of which is totally new, only when all of the preceding topics have been exhausted and closed, while we do not impose any constraints on the nature of DTCs. We assume that interlocutors are coherent in naturally occurring conversations (wherein incoherent moves need convincing evidence). Analyzing the coherence of a conversation, we put ourselves in conversational participants' shoes and rely on our communicative competence to identify all possible DSPs that account for the relevance of each conversational move. We are interested in the cases where an identified DSP cannot be assigned to a pre-existing coherence relation. We hypothesize that the pre-existing coherence relations account for topical coherence (i.e. talk-about), but not non-topical coherence such as interactional coherence (i.e. talk-that-does) (Clift, 2016, p.92).

3 Annotating Coherence Relations

We start with the casual telephone dialogues in the Disco-SPICE corpus[6] (Rehbein et al., 2016),

based on the SPICE-Ireland corpus[7] (Kallen and Kirk, 2012), in which discourse relations – triples consisting of a discourse-level predicate and its two arguments – are annotated with the CCR (Sanders et al., 1992) and the early version of the PDTB 3.0 (Webber et al., 2016) schemes. We ignore the CCR annotations in favour of the PDTB 3.0-based annotation because the latter covers more discourse relations in the corpus, including:

- explicit discourse relations between any two discourse segments (whose predicate is an explicit discourse connective such as *"because"* or *"however"*).
- implicit/AltLex relations between utterances given by the same speaker (whose predicate is not represented by an explicit discourse connective but can be inferred or alternatively lexicalized by some non-connective expression, respectively).[8]
- entity-based coherence relations (EntRel) between adjacent utterances given by the same speaker (whose predicate is an abstract placeholder linking two arguments that mention the same entity).

In the excerpt shown in Table 1, utterances 104 and 105 are two arguments of an implicit relation that can be realized by a connective *"in particular"*, while 121 and 122 are the arguments of an entity-based relation that is signaled by the pronoun *"it"*.

We enrich Disco-SPICE with SPICE-Ireland's original pragmatic annotation, consisting of Searlean speech acts (Searle, 1976), prosody, and quotatives among others. This information is helpful in identifying, for example, the quote content, or speech act *query*, i.e. asking for information, even in declarative clauses.

We use the latest version of the PDTB 3.0 taxonomy of discourse relations (Webber et al., 2019), and annotate the instances which are not covered in the Disco-SPICE corpus, such as:

- implicit/AltLex discourse relations between utterances given by different speakers.
- entity-based coherence relations between adjacent utterances given by different speakers.
- entity-based coherence relations between non-adjacent utterances.

---

annotated in a significant amount of spoken conversation text.

[7]This corpus can be obtained upon request to its directors.

[8]Here we make an assumption that the same annotation strategy is applied to both implicit and AltLex discourse relations, since AltLex relations must first be identified as implicit ones (Webber et al., 2016).

---

[6]This corpus is unique as it is publicly accessible, and highly relevant to our work in that the discourse relations are

Specifically, if a relation is not entity-based, it will be labeled with a sense in the PDTB 3.0 sense hierarchy. Annotators are encouraged to choose the most fine-grained labels. For example, *expansion.equivalence* is preferred over *expansion* for an *expansion.equivalence* relation, although both are acceptable. In total, there are 53 sense labels available for explicit/implicit/AltLex discourse relations.

We also enrich our repertory of content-based coherence relations with additional semantic relations from ISO 24617-8 and ISO 24617-2, which take care of the interactive nature of dialogue:

- functional dependence relations characterizing the semantic dependence between two dialogue acts due to their communicative functions (cf. adjacency pairs in Conversation Analysis)[9], named after the first pair part:
  - information-seeking: *propositionalQ, checkQ, setQ, choiceQ*.
  - directive: *request, instruct, suggest*.
  - commissive: *promise, offer*.
  - social obligation management: *apology, thanking, greeting, goodbye*.
- *feedback* dependence relations connecting a stretch of discourse and a response utterance that provides or elicits information about the success in processing that stretch.
- additional entity-based coherence relations relating to other communicative functions such as *topic closing* (as a discourse structuring function) and *completion* (as a partner communication management function).

In Table 1, utterances 105 and 106 are two arguments of a *propositionalQ* functional dependence relation, while 109 and 111 are the arguments of a *feedback* relation.

It is worth noting that the argument order of annotated coherence relations is chronological, i.e. the second argument always appears after the first argument in the conversational flow.

We aim at annotating coherence relations that cover as many utterances as possible (rather than exhaustively annotating every relation), adding notes to the ones that are not very clear and therefore can be considered non-existent in the next step – NTU identification. In case of multiple relations available to the same pair of arguments, annotating just one relation is sufficient. Table 2 shows the key

---

10 dialogues - 2,719 utterances	
Inherited from Disco-SPICE:	
1,273 coherence relations (158 entity-based)	
Newly annotated:	
1,870 coherence relations	
implicit discourse relations	10
entity-based discourse relations	1,490
functional dependence relations	324
• information seeking	291
• directive	4
• commissive	1
• social obligation management	28
feedback dependence relations	487

Table 2: Statistics of coherence relation annotation.

statistics of the annotation in this work, performed solely by the student author (see further details of the annotation in Appendix A).

As seen in Table 2, the ratio of the coherence relations inherited from Disco-SPICE to the newly annotated ones is $1,273/1,870 \approx 2/3$, which means that using Disco-SPICE saves us a considerable portion of annotation workload. While this efficiency is optimal for a pilot study, it does not provide the full picture of our proposed annotation task. We plan to use this study's annotation guidelines to conduct a full-blown annotation project on the data set[10] composed by Riou (2015), aiming at (1) performing in-depth empirical studies such as detailed analyses of the distribution of annotated relations and annotation disagreements, and (2) enriching the linguistic resources for studying dialogue coherence. In addition, the results of this study can serve as an assessment of the reliability of Riou (2015)'s annotation methodology.

4 Identifying NTU Candidates

Based on both inherited and newly annotated relations described in Section 3, excluding those relations noted as "not very clear", which account for less than *3%* of the newly annotated relations, we heuristically identified *72* candidates for NTUs, each of which is:

- not the first utterance of a dialogue,
- the first utterance token of the first argument of some coherence relation,

---

[9]Examples of adjacency pairs are *greeting - greeting, question - answer, request - grant/refuse*, etc.

[10]This data set includes 15-min extracts of 8 conversations from the Santa Barbara Corpus of Spoken American English (Du Bois et al., 2000). The advantage of this data set over Disco-SPICE is that its audio files are publicly accessible, which is invaluable for our annotation.

- not part of 2nd argument of another relation,
- not in the dialogue span of another relation.

5 Identifying NTUs and Patterns of DTCs

An NTU candidate identified in Section 4 is valid only if there is no a content-based coherence relation with respect to prior discourse, which can be missed or annotated as "not very clear" in Section 3. To separate genuine NTUs from other NTU candidates, we carry out a more detailed inspection. Specifically, the following pieces of information are further annotated for each NTU candidate:

- the immediately preceding topic.
- the current topic, its focused entity[11], and its information status, i.e. given-new w.r.t. discourse/hearer (Prince, 1992; Birner, 2006).
- the interlocutors involved in content, if any, and their roles (speaker/hearer).
- the links between the current topic and:
  - the pre-dialogue common ground.
  - the utterance situation (time and space).
  - the content of prior discourse.

We were able to single out *38* true cases of NTUs, roughly *50%* of NTU candidates, which contain discourse-new topics and new focused entities. Based on the annotated information about the interaction between the NTUs and their discourse context, we identified the following patterns of DTCs (see detailed examples in Appendix B):

- Grosz and Sidner (1986)'s true interruption.
- forgotten topic (when the speaker cannot articulate the topic she intents to talk about).
- the first topic after greeting.
- goodbye-initialized topic (when saying goodbye opens a new discussion thread).
- interlocutor-decentric move (from a topic focusing on one of the interlocutors).
- interlocutor-centric move:
  - interlocutor-centric return (from a topic not focusing on the interlocutors).
  - interlocutor-centric switching (from a topic focusing on one interlocutor to a topic focusing on the other).
  - urgent interlocutor-centric topic in extra-linguistic utterance situation (when the speaker suddenly prioritizes an urgent topic related to one of the interlocutors).

- speaker-centric distraction (an off-track topic focusing on the speaker).
  - speaker-centric wrap-up (when the attempt to wrap up the conversation opens a new discussion thread).
  - hearer-centric related topic (from a topic not focusing on interlocutors).
- cushioning topic (from interlocutor-decentric to interlocutor-centric) - topic immediately relevant to an interlocutor's life.

The presence of cushioning topics implies that the speaker may plan, at least, "two steps ahead", including:

- the interpretation the hearer may have, and
- the potential of topic extension based on that interpretation.

In addition, the patterns of goodbye-initialized topic and speaker-centric wrap-up can elicit better insight into the findings in Gilmartin et al. (2018) about the extended leave-taking sequences.

6 Classifying NTUs

The patterns of DTCs identified in Section 5 (except for Grosz and Sidner (1986)'s true interruption and the forgotten topic, covering *7* identified instances of NTUs) show that non-topical coherence, sustained or built by DTCs, is created via sequential adjustment of the distances between the active conversational topic and each interlocutor. This adjustment seems to be constrained by the relational work between the interlocutors, i.e. the social aspect of the conversations, rather than the content-based relevance.

Based on the interlocutors' intents, a simple version of the classification of NTUs in social dialogues, covering 31 identified instances of NTUs, can be proposed as below:

- socially initialized topic (the first topic after greeting) - *2* instances.
- topic merely motivated by changing social focus (urgent interlocutor-centric topic in extra-linguistic utterance situation, speaker-centric distraction) - *3* instances.
- topic merely motivated by changing the degree of relevance of social domains (interlocutor-decentric move, cushioning topic, interlocutor-centric return) - *9* instances.
- topic motivated by changing both social focus and the degree of relevance of social domains (generally embodied in the other patterns of

---

[11]Inspired by the ideas of focus of attention and local coherence in Grosz et al. (1995).

DTCs) - *17* instances.

This classification introduces new sequence-based social intents[12] that traditional taxonomies of speech acts do not capture as the social intents proposed in these taxonomies, if any, do not demonstrate the sequential dynamics of the relational work between the interlocutors (e.g. ISO 24617-2's social obligation management functions, Klüwer (2011)'s dialogue acts for social talk, or van der Zwaan et al. (2012)'s social support categories).

These newly found intents, characterizing non-topical coherence in social talk, convincingly demonstrate social talk as a sophisticated form of goal-directed rational interactions rather than a random walk through loosely connected topics. This shows real promise and new perspectives for research in dialogue modeling. We hypothesize that a workable dialogue model for social talk needs to explicitly handle all of the key aspects of goal-directed rational interactions.

7 Toward a Game-theoretic Model

To formally capture the interactive and rational aspects of social conditioned language use in conversation, recent work such as Iterated Best Response (Franke, 2009), Rational Speech Act (Frank and Goodman, 2012), and Social Meaning Game (Burnett, 2019) pairs Lewis (1969/2002)'s signaling games with the Bayesian approach to speaker/listener reasoning. In essence, these models formalize Gricean inference by predicting:

Speaker behavior: the probability $P_s(o|h, C_s)$ that the speaker uses the observed linguistic value o to convey hidden meaning h in the speaker's context model C_s is a function of $U_s(o, h, C_s)$, the utility of o in C_s given the speaker's desire to communicate h.

- $P_s(o|h, C_s) \propto exp(\alpha \times U_s(o, h, C_s))$
  (where α is a normalizing constant)

Listener behavior: the probability $P_l(h|o, C_l)$ that the listener interprets the meaning of o as h in the listener's context model C_l depends on the prior probability $P(h)$ of the speaker having h in mind (e.g. based on certain sociocultural convention) and on the probability $P_s(o|h, C_l)$ that the speaker uses o to convey h in C_l, estimated by the listener.

- $P_l(h|o, C_l) \propto P(h) \times P_s(o|h, C_l)$

Based on this framework, we can develop a minimally workable model that accounts for the emer-gence of sequence-based social intents in marked linguistic environments where NTUs occur (cf. Acton and Burnett (2019) for social meaning):

- Hidden: the speaker's social intents.
- Observed: Topics chosen / topic transitions.
- Cost: content-based complexity of the topic transitions (e.g. from the perspective of cognitive processing).
- Utility: subtraction of the cost from the coherence measure (which reflects both types of coherence: topical and non-topical).

However, this model design is not robust enough to predict the emergence of the newly classified sequence-based social intents due to the simplicity of the utility function. Specifically, the forthright division of labor between the cost and coherence measure does not capture the real interactions between the components of these metric concepts, such as multiple sociolinguistic dimensions of the discourse context. We will address this challenge in our further work.

8 Conclusion and Future Work

In this paper, we present a pilot annotation study[13] as a first step towards a dialogue model which is capable of rationalizing NTUs and conversational coherence in social talk. Analyzing the interaction between the identified NTUs and their discourse context, we discover a set of patterns of DTCs, represented by the NTUs. Based on these patterns, we propose a simple classification of NTUs in social talk, yet introducing new sequence-based social intents that traditional taxonomies of speech acts do not capture. These intents not only adequately account for non-topical coherence in social talk but also convincingly demonstrate social talk as a sophisticated form of goal-directed rational interactions. We hypothesize that the Bayesian game-theoretic framework, which explicitly models the interactive and rational aspects of social interaction, is a sensible architecture for handling social talk.

Next, we aim to develop an actionable Bayesian game-theoretic model for social talk, focusing on decomposing its utility function. Particularly, we seek to learn from social interaction work such as Stevanovic and Koski (2018) for designing the ***goal-directedness*** aspect of the model.

---

[12]These intents should be taken with the caveat concerning the cross-cultural generalization about their validity.

[13]The annotation results can be accessible upon the evidence of the possession of SPICE-Ireland corpus.

Acknowledgments

We would like to thank Marine Riou for fully sharing her annotation methodology and data of topic transitions in conversation so that we can gain important insights into her work. We are extremely grateful to Maarten van Gompel, the main author of the FoLiA annotation format and FLAT annotation tool, who provided key technical solutions and support to our annotation project. We owe a debt of gratitude to the organizers and attendees of the inaugural Natural Language, Dialog and Speech (NDS) Symposium, who gave us a unique opportunity to present our work, receive constructive feedback, and experience genuine interest from the audience. We would like to thank the 2020 ACL SRW Pre-submission Mentorship Program for providing valuable suggestions to improve the readability, overall presentation, and technical level of our paper to put it on a par with other accepted submissions. Our deepest gratitude goes to the anonymous reviewers and post-acceptance mentor, Vicky Zayats, whose detailed comments helped us further develop our paper into a fine piece of work that we are very happy with. Last but not least, we are very grateful to all of the readers and look forward to having thought-provoking discussions with you at https://osf.io/nvtkq/, where the live version of our paper is located.

References

Eric K. Acton and Heather Burnett. 2019. Markedness, rationality, and social meaning. Poster session presented at LSA 2019 Annual Meeting, New York, NY.

James Allen. 1995. *Natural Language Understanding.* Pearson.

Nicholas Asher and Alex Lascarides. 2003. *Logics of Conversation.* Cambridge University Press.

Betty J. Birner. 2006. Inferential relations and non-canonical word order. *Drawing the boundaries of meaning: Neo-Gricean studies in pragmatics and semantics in honor of Laurence R. Horn*, pages 31–51.

Heather Burnett. 2019. Signalling games, sociolinguistic variation and the construction of style. *Linguistics and Philosophy.*

Lynn Carlson and Daniel Marcu. 2001. Discourse tagging reference manual. *ISI Technical Report ISI-TR-545*, 54:56.

Rebecca Clift. 2016. *Conversation Analysis.* Cambridge University Press.

John W Du Bois, Wallace L Chafe, Charles Meyer, Sandra A Thompson, and Nii Martey. 2000. Santa barbara corpus of spoken american english. *CD-ROM. Philadelphia: Linguistic Data Consortium.*

Michael C. Frank and Noah D. Goodman. 2012. Predicting pragmatic reasoning in language games. *Science*, 336(6084):998–998.

Michael Franke. 2009. *Signal to act: Game theory in pragmatics.* Ph.D. thesis, Universiteit van Amsterdam.

Emer Gilmartin, Christian Saam, Brendan Spillane, Maria O'Reilly, Ketong Su, Arturo Calvo Devesa, Loredana Cerrato, Killian Levacher, Nick Campbell, and Vincent Wade. 2018. The ADELE corpus of dyadic social text conversations: Dialog act annotation with ISO 24617-2. In *Proceedings of the 11th International Conference on Language Resources and Evaluation (LREC 2018)*, pages 4016–4022, Miyazaki, Japan.

Jonathan Ginzburg. 2012. *The Interactive Stance: Meaning for Conversation.* Oxford University Press.

Maarten van Gompel, Ko van der Sloot, Martin Reynaert, and Antal van den Bosch. 2017. *FoLiA in Practice: The Infrastructure of a Linguistic Annotation Format*, pages 71–82. Ubiquity Press.

H Paul Grice. 1975. Logic and conversation. *Syntax and Semantics*, 3:41–58.

Barbara J Grosz and Candace L Sidner. 1986. Attention, intentions, and the structure of discourse. *Computational linguistics*, 12(3):175–204.

Barbara J Grosz, Scott Weinstein, and Aravind K Joshi. 1995. Centering: A framework for modeling the local coherence of discourse. *Computational linguistics*, 21(2):203–225.

ISO 24617-2. 2012. Language resource management – semantic annotation framework (SemAF) – part 2: Dialogue acts. Technical report, International Organization for Standardization.

ISO 24617-8. 2016. Language resource management – semantic annotation framework (SemAF) – part 8: Semantic relations in discourse, core annotation schema (DR-core). Technical report, International Organization for Standardization.

Gail Jefferson. 1984. On stepwise transition from talk about a trouble to inappropriately next-positioned matters. *Structures of social action: Studies in conversation analysis*, pages 191–222.

Jeffrey L Kallen and John Monfries Kirk. 2012. *SPICE-Ireland: A User's Guide; Documentation to Accompany the SPICE-Ireland Corpus: Systems of Pragmatic Annotation in ICE-Ireland.* Cló Ollscoil na Banríona.

Tina Klüwer. 2011. "I like your shirt" - Dialogue acts for enabling social talk in conversational agents. In *Proceedings of the 11th International Workshop on Intelligent Virtual Agents (IVA 2011)*, pages 14–27, Reykjavik, Iceland. Springer.

Staffan Larsson and David R Traum. 2000. Information state and dialogue management in the TRINDI dialogue move engine toolkit. *Natural language engineering*, 6(3-4):323–340.

David Lewis. 1969/2002. *Convention: A philosophical study*. John Wiley & Sons.

Ellen F Prince. 1992. The ZPG letter: Subjects, definiteness, and information-status. *Discourse description: Diverse analyses of a fund raising text*, pages 295–325.

Ines Rehbein, Merel Scholman, and Vera Demberg. 2016. Annotating discourse relations in spoken language: A comparison of the PDTB and CCR frameworks. In *Proceedings of the 10th International Conference on Language Resources and Evaluation (LREC 2016)*, pages 1039–1046, Portorož, Slovenia. European Language Resources Association (ELRA).

Rachel Reichman. 1978. Conversational coherency. *Cognitive science*, 2(4):283–327.

Marine Riou. 2015. *The grammar of topic transition in American English conversation. Topic transition design and management in typical and atypical conversations (schizophrenia)*. Ph.D. thesis, Université Sorbonne Paris Cité.

Craige Roberts. 1996/2012. Information structure: Towards an integrated formal theory of pragmatics. *Semantics and Pragmatics*, 5:6–1.

Ted JM Sanders, Wilbert PM Spooren, and Leo GM Noordman. 1992. Toward a taxonomy of coherence relations. *Discourse processes*, 15(1):1–35.

Remko JH Scha, Bertram C Bruce, and Livia Polanyi. 1986. Discourse understanding. *Center for the Study of Reading Technical Report; no. 391*.

John R. Searle. 1976. A classification of illocutionary acts. *Language in Society*, 5(1):1–23.

Melisa Stevanovic and Sonja E Koski. 2018. Intersubjectivity and the domains of social interaction: Proposal of a cross-sectional approach. *Psychology of Language and Communication*, 22(1):39–70.

Bonnie Webber, Rashmi Prasad, Alan Lee, and Aravind Joshi. 2016. A discourse-annotated corpus of conjoined VPs. In *Proceedings of the 10th Linguistic Annotation Workshop held in conjunction with ACL 2016 (LAW-X 2016)*, pages 22–31, Berlin, Germany. Association for Computational Linguistics.

Bonnie Webber, Rashmi Prasad, Alan Lee, and Aravind Joshi. 2019. The Penn Discourse Treebank 3.0 annotation manual. Technical report, University of Edinburgh.

JM van der Zwaan, V Dignum, and CM Jonker. 2012. A BDI dialogue agent for social support: Specification and evaluation method. In *AAMAS 2012: Proceedings of the 11th International Conference on Autonomous Agents and Multiagent Systems, Workshop on Emotional and Empathic Agents, Valencia, Spain; authors' version*. International Foundation for Autonomous Agents and Multiagent Systems (IFAAMAS).

A Coherence relation annotation in practice

As the input data of this annotation task includes different useful information layers, namely the PDTB 3.0 discourse relations of Disco-SPICE and pragmatic annotation of SPICE-Ireland, the FoLiA format is selected for data representation because this rich XML-based annotation format accommodates multiple linguistic annotation types with arbitrary tagsets and is accompanied by FLAT, a modern web-based annotation tool whose user-interface can show different linguistic annotation layers at the same time (van Gompel et al., 2017). Specifically, each dialogue is a sequence of utterances, as shown in Figure 1, each of which includes:

- the 'speaker' token (highlighted in green), combining the dialogue ID and the speaker ID, whose "Description" field contains SPICE-Ireland pragmatic annotations (see Figure 3 for an example of an utterance annotated as a directive, i.e. <dir>, and a complete intonational unit, i.e. ended with %, whose final token *them* is spoken in a rising tone, i.e. 2),

- the tokenized content, which may consist of:

  - explicit discourse connectives or AltLex expressions, i.e. non-connective expressions which lexicalize the corresponding discourse relations, (highlighted in various colors).

  - implicit discourse connective tokens (in gray).

  - real *[None]* tokens (in black), equivalent to empty event tokens in the original Disco-SPICE *.xml* file.

  - hidden *[None]* tokens (in gray), placeholders of EntRel discourse relations.

Figure 2 shows that when a token is hovered over, it is highlighted in black while its text turns yellow, and its annotation layers are displayed in a pop-up box.

Figure 3 shows that when a token is clicked, it is highlighted in yellow, and its annotation layers become editable in the **Annotation Editor**.

The annotation of one coherence relation is treated as the annotation of one 'connective' entity and two 'argument' chunks. Each 'connective' entity has its co-index with its 'argument' chunks in its "Description" field. Figure 4 shows that the 'connective' entity *in_particular* has its co-index *72* with its 'argument' chunks, namely *ARG1-72* and *ARG2-72*. This is an example of an implicit relation inherited from Disco-SPICE.

Figures 5, 6 and 7 show several newly annotated relations, namely *propositionalQ*, *EntRel*, and *feedback* respectively. Notice that the 'argument' chunks only need associating with the 'speaker' tokens of the utterances containing the actual chunks. To annotate a 'connective' entity that does not connect to any real text token, we create a hidden token *[None]* right before the 'speaker' token of the '2nd argument' chunk in the corresponding relation.

B Examples of DTCs

Table 3 displays the DTCs, corresponding to the NTUs of the excerpt shown in Table 1. ICP and OCP stand for initiating conversational participant and other conversational participant(s) respectively (Grosz and Sidner, 1986).

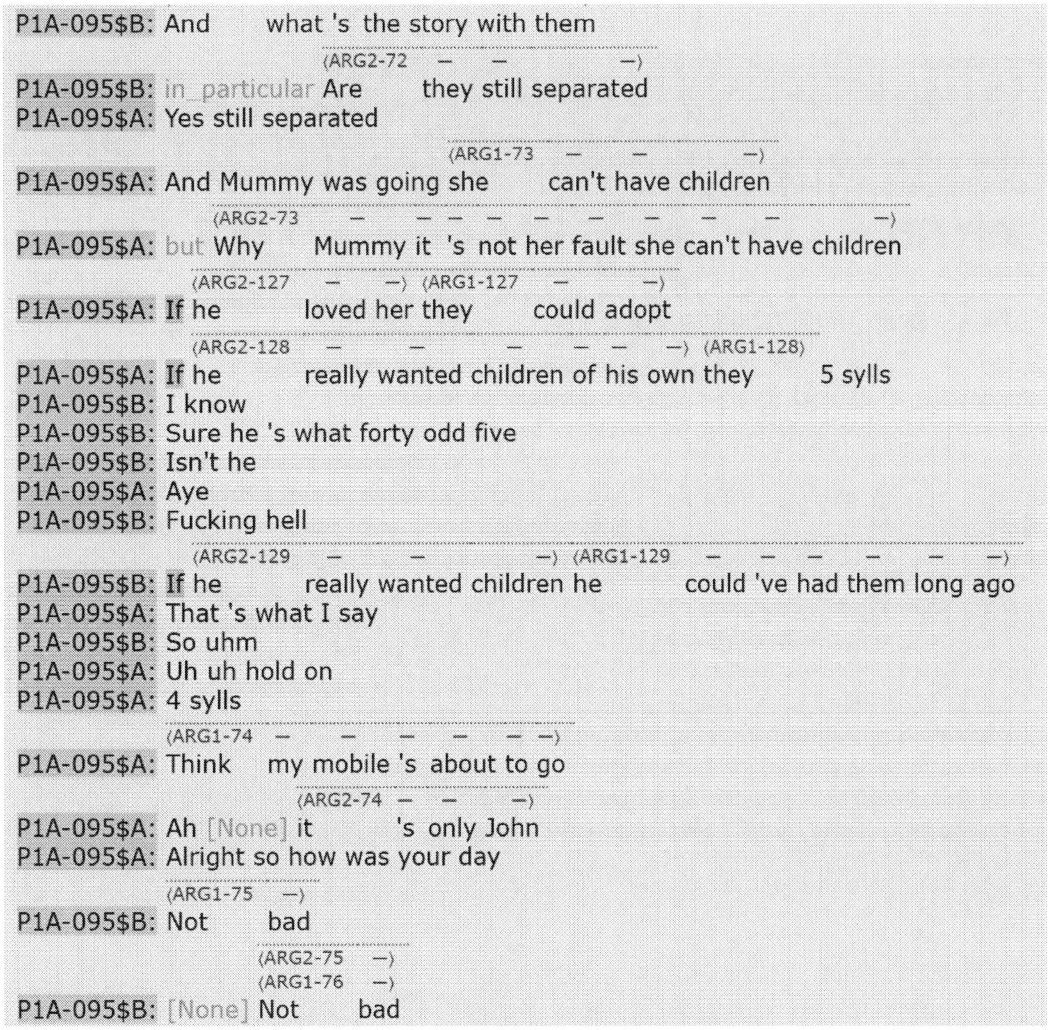

P1A-095$B: And   what 's the story with them
                    (ARG2-72   —   —   —)
P1A-095$B: in_particular Are   they still separated
P1A-095$A: Yes still separated
                                  (ARG1-73   —   —   —)
P1A-095$A: And Mummy was going she   can't have children
              (ARG2-73   —   — — — — — — —   —)
P1A-095$A: but Why   Mummy it 's not her fault she can't have children
              (ARG2-127   —   —) (ARG1-127   —   —)
P1A-095$A: If he   loved her they   could adopt
              (ARG2-128   —   —   —   — —   —) (ARG1-128)
P1A-095$A: If he   really wanted children of his own they   5 sylls
P1A-095$B: I know
P1A-095$B: Sure he 's what forty odd five
P1A-095$B: Isn't he
P1A-095$A: Aye
P1A-095$B: Fucking hell
              (ARG2-129   —   —   —) (ARG1-129   —   —   —   —   —   —)
P1A-095$B: If he   really wanted children he   could 've had them long ago
P1A-095$A: That 's what I say
P1A-095$B: So uhm
P1A-095$A: Uh uh hold on
P1A-095$A: 4 sylls
              (ARG1-74 —   —   —   — —)
P1A-095$A: Think   my mobile 's about to go
                    (ARG2-74 —   —   —)
P1A-095$A: Ah [None] it   's only John
P1A-095$A: Alright so how was your day
              (ARG1-75   —)
P1A-095$B: Not   bad
                        (ARG2-75   —)
                        (ARG1-76   —)
P1A-095$B: [None] Not   bad

Figure 1: FLAT-based representation of the excerpt shown in Table 1.

Utt.	Preceding topic	Current topic	Involved CPs	Topic change type
119	Jamie's husband having another woman	Reaction to an event in the utterance situation - Discourse New	ICP (A) as the speaker	Grosz and Sidner's true interruption
123	An event happening in ICP's place	New focused entity: OCP's day - Discourse New	OCP (B) as the hearer	Hearer-centric related topic

Table 3: Examples of DTC patterns in the excerpt shown in Table 1.

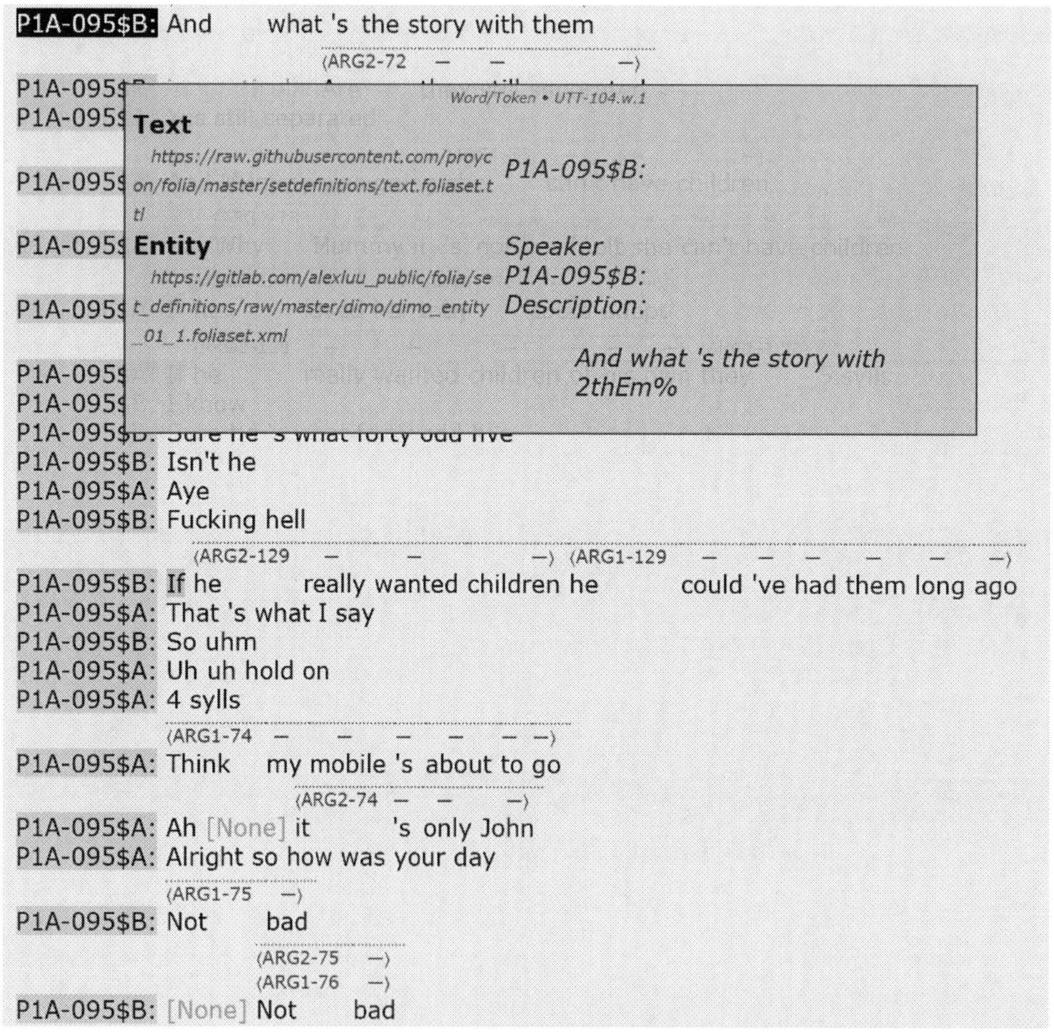

Figure 2: Quick access to the annotation of a token in FLAT.

128

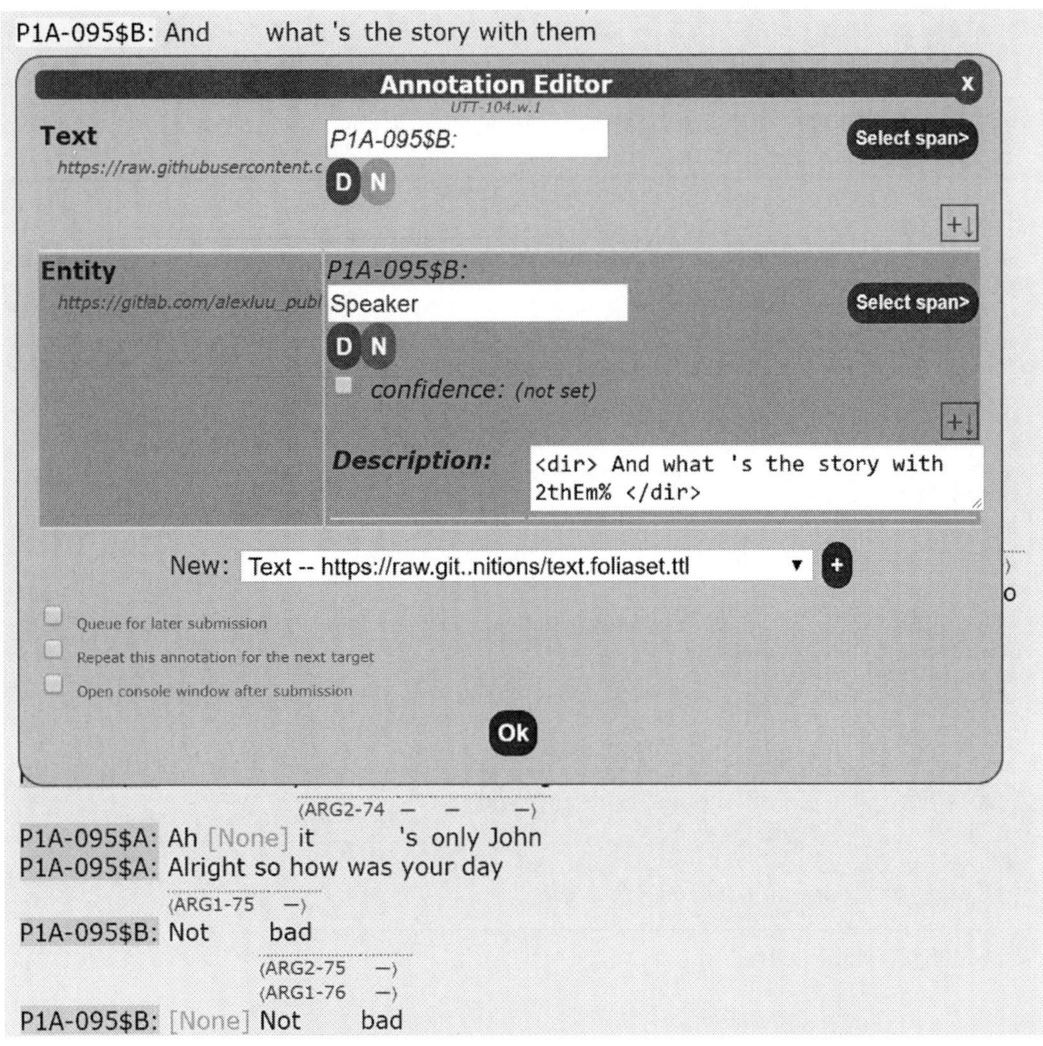

Figure 3: **Annotation Editor** for a token in FLAT.

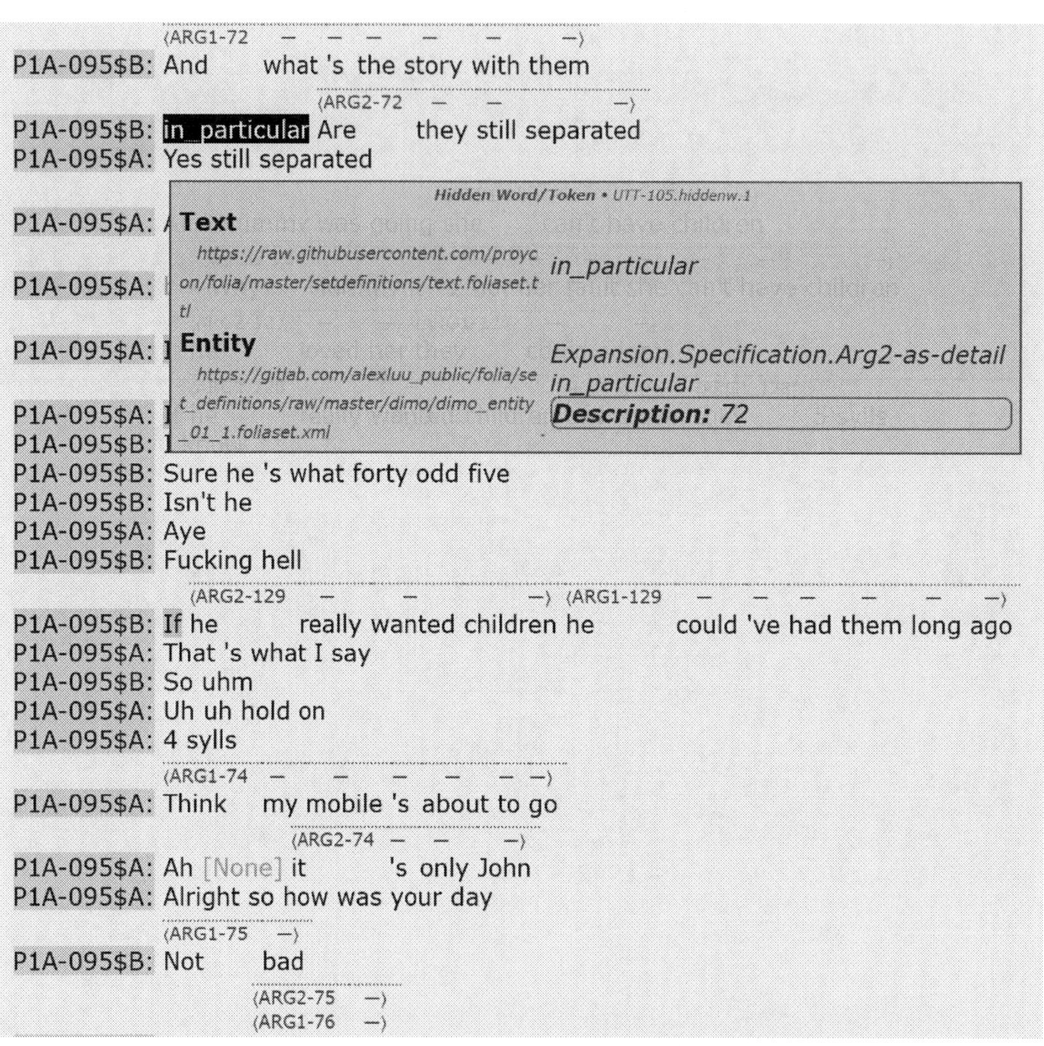

Figure 4: FLAT-based representation of a coherence relation inherited from Disco-SPICE.

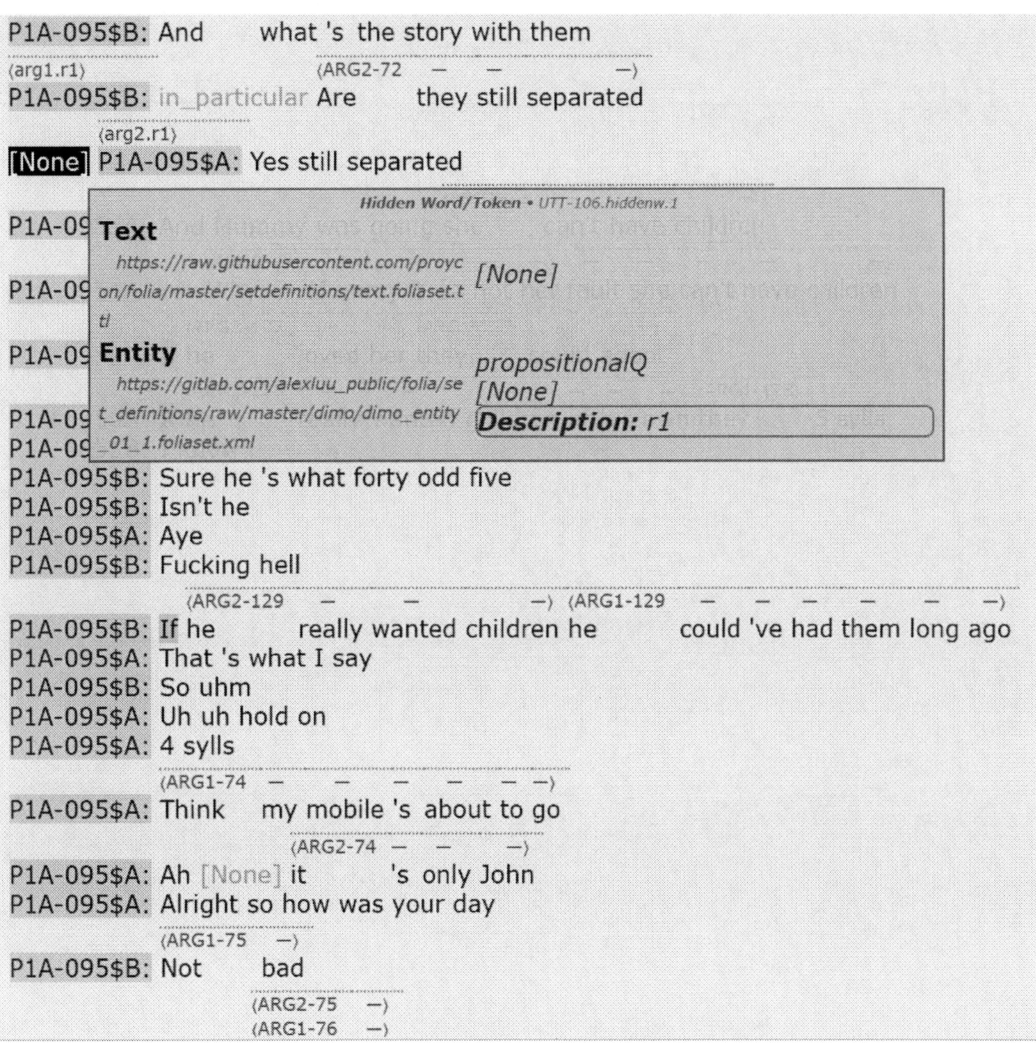

Figure 5: FLAT-based representation of a *propositionalQ* relation.

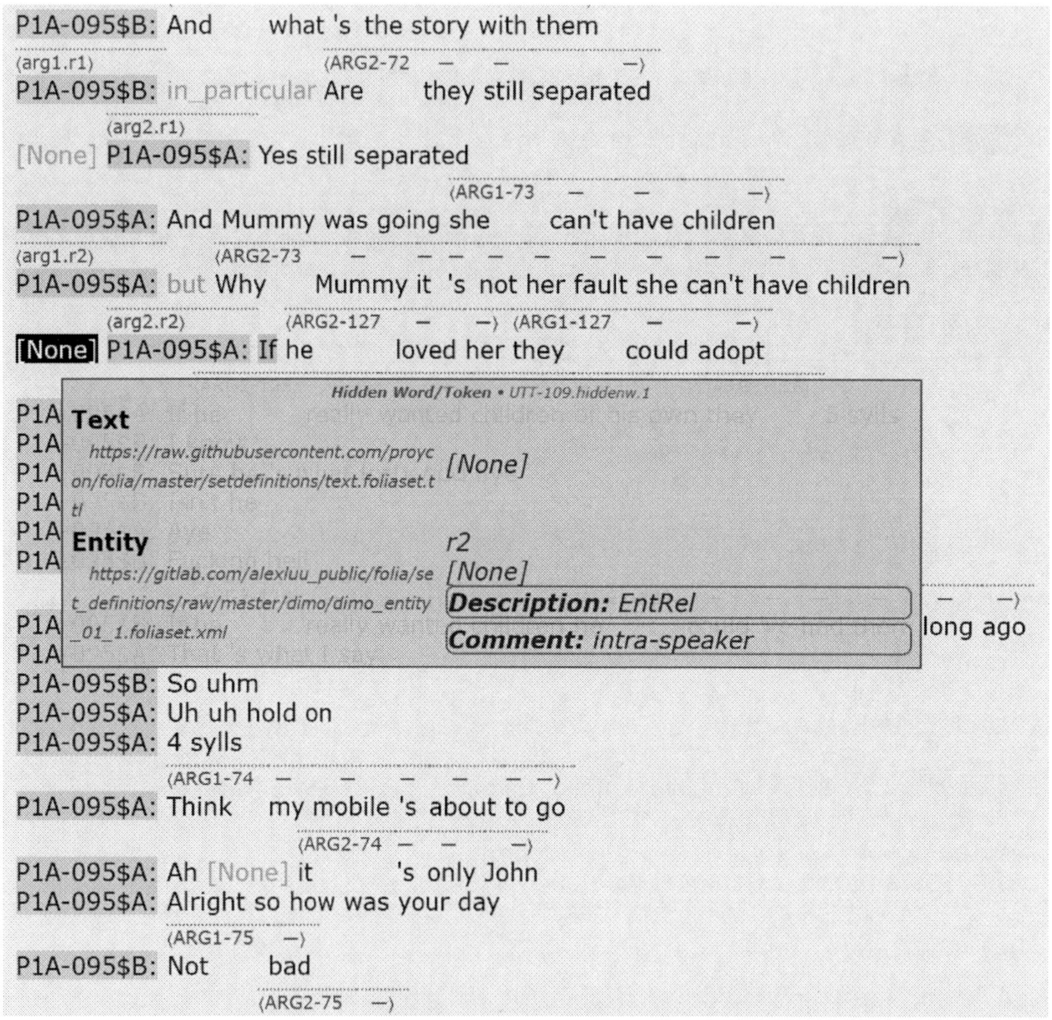

Figure 6: FLAT-based representation of an *EntRel* relation.

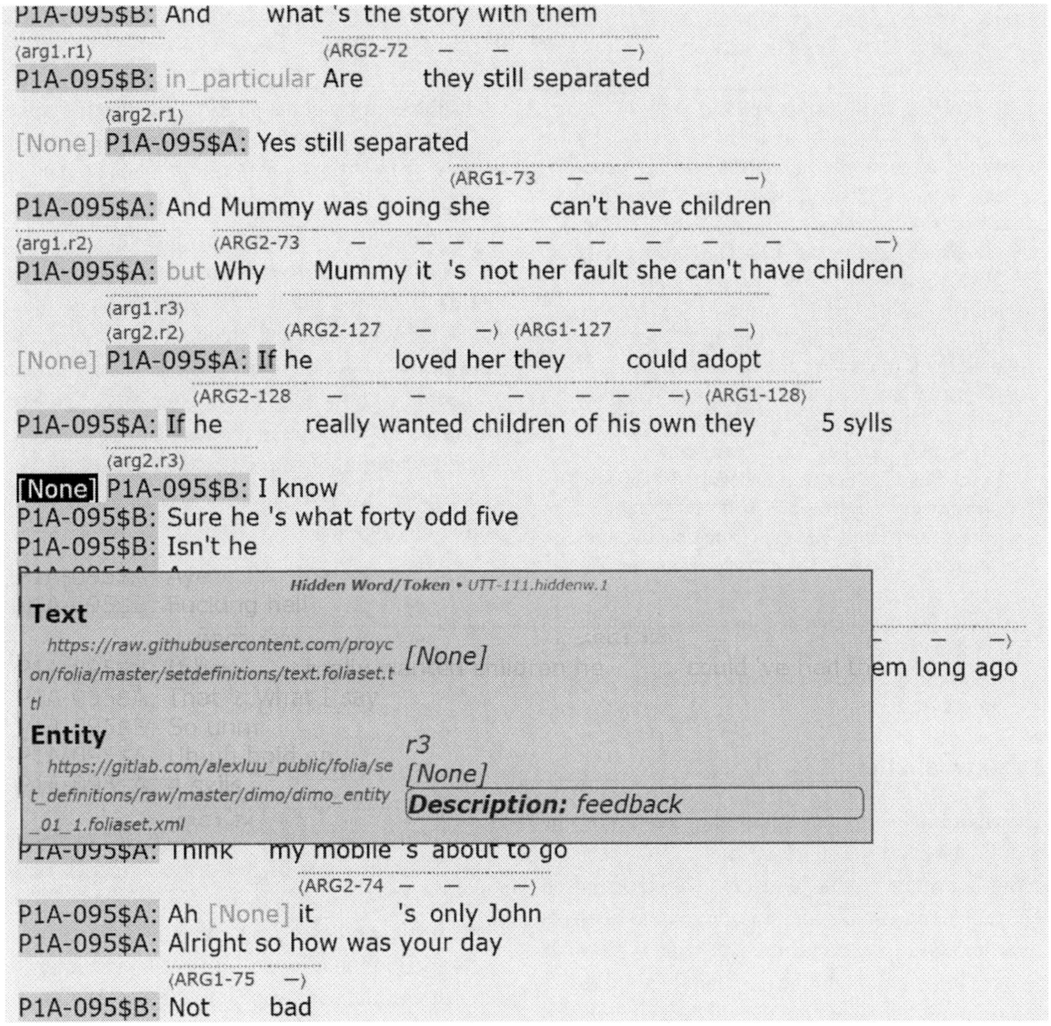

Figure 7: FLAT-based representation of a *feedback* relation.

Why is *penguin* more similar to *polar bear* than to *sea gull*?
Analyzing conceptual knowledge in distributional models

Pia Sommerauer
Computational Lexicology and Terminology Lab
Vrije Universiteit Amsterdam
De Boelelaan 1105 Amsterdam, The Netherlands
`pia.sommerauer@vu.nl`

Abstract

What do powerful models of word meaning created from distributional data (e.g. Word2vec (Mikolov et al., 2013) BERT (Devlin et al., 2019) and ELMO (Peters et al., 2018)) represent? What causes words to be similar in the semantic space? What type of information is lacking? This thesis proposal presents a framework for investigating the information encoded in distributional semantic models. Several analysis methods have been suggested, but they have been shown to be limited and are not well understood. This approach pairs observations made on actual corpora with insights obtained from data manipulation experiments. The expected outcome is a better understanding of (1) the semantic information we can infer purely based on linguistic co-occurrence patterns and (2) the potential of distributional semantic models to pick up linguistic evidence.

1   Introduction

Distributional semantic representations capture semantic similarity and relatedness and, perhaps more importantly, enable machine learning-based Natural Language Processing models to abstract over lexical representations. But what type of semantic information do they contain? Could distributional models show that the concepts *lemon* and *moon* share shape and color, but differ with respect to almost everything else? Understanding what semantic knowledge is represented in embeddings can not only help us improve those representations but also shed light on questions about lexical representation raised in cognitive linguistics (e.g. the suitability of embeddings for models of metaphor interpretation (Utsumi, 2011)). Understanding the way components of meaning are represented could eventually enable us to use data-derived, distributional representations for lexical reasoning.

While exiting model analysis methods (Hupkes et al., 2018; Belinkov and Glass, 2019; Saphra and Lopez, 2018) have yielded initial insights, they are still limited when applied to distributional word representations. Gaining insights into semantic representations derived from massive amounts of textual data thus entails answering two core questions: (1) What information about concepts can we find in the linguistic data and how does it relate to people's knowledge about concepts? (2) What linguistic information in the data can be picked up by a distributional semantic model and how is it represented? Answering these questions entails the following four steps:

1. Formulate linguistic hypotheses about what kind of knowledge about concepts we expect to be reflected by linguistic corpora based on theoretical and experimental research.
2. Build a corpus of human judgments reflecting human knowledge about concepts suitable to test the hypotheses.
3. Investigate the potential of distributional models and model analysis methods by simulating different types of linguistic evidence of semantic properties in text corpora.
4. Test hypotheses about what is represented in distributional models and data and interpret the results with respect to the potential of distributional models and analysis methods.

The core questions of this research proposal and their interaction are illustrated in Figure 1. The remainder of this paper is structured as follows: After discussing related work in Section 2, I present linguistic hypotheses in Section 3. The corpus of human judgments of property-concept pairs for testing these hypotheses is presented in Section 4. Section 5 outlines model analysis methods and simulation experiments, followed by a conclusion and reflection on possible outcomes in Section 6.

Proceedings of the 58th Annual Meeting of the Association for Computational Linguistics: Student Research Workshop, pages 134–142
July 5 - July 10, 2020. ©2020 Association for Computational Linguistics

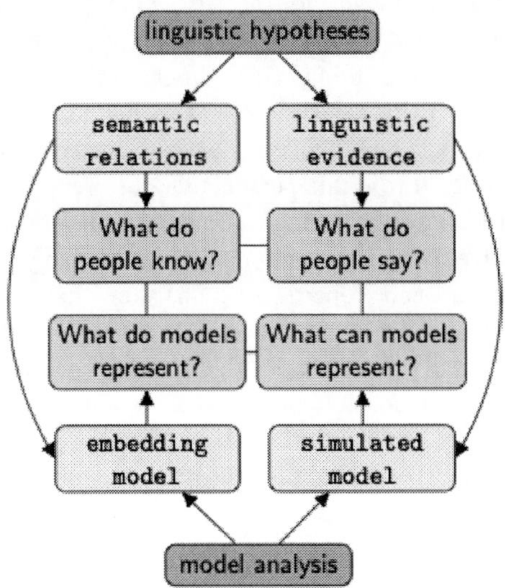

Figure 1: Framework for investigating conceptual knowledge in distributional models from two perspectives: (1) linguistic hypotheses about semantic knowledge and textual evidence and (2) the potential of model analysis methods and models. The questions are approached through model analysis methods on real and simulated data.

2   Related work

Several studies investigate the relation between semantic features recorded in feature norm datasets (McRae et al., 2005; Devereux et al., 2014; Vinson and Vigliocco, 2008; Vigliocco et al., 2004) and embedding vectors (Fagarasan et al., 2015; Tsvetkov et al., 2015, 2016; Herbelot and Vecchi, 2015; Herbelot, 2013; Riordan and Jones, 2011; Glenberg and Robertson, 2000; Derby et al., 2018; Forbes et al., 2019; Rubinstein et al., 2015). These studies indicate that (at least partial) mappings between distributional and conceptual spaces are possible and that conceptual knowledge can complement distributional representations. Erk (2016) shows that distributional similarity can indicate property-overlap. Gupta et al. (2015) show that attributes of the type of knowledge recorded in knowledge bases can, to some extent, be learned from word embeddings. Herbelot (2013) hypothesizes that Gricean maxims determine what is mentioned in text, based on limited datasets. These studies provide partial evidence for conceptual knowledge in distributional data, but they do not provide a systematic account of the underlying factors at play.

A major reason for this gap is the difficulty of interpreting representations resulting from machine learning models. Diagnostic classification has proven successful in the analysis of such representations (Hupkes et al., 2018; Belinkov and Glass, 2019) and word embedding representations (Yaghoobzadeh and Schütze, 2016; Sommerauer and Fokkens, 2018; Yaghoobzadeh et al., 2019). However, the results of these experiments provide limited insights.

Unverified negative examples. For instance, in the CSLB norms (Devereux et al., 2014), **has_legs** is listed for several birds, but not for *owl*, *duck*, and *eagle*. This introduces noise to already rather small datasets used to investigate property knowledge in distributional data (Derby et al., 2018). Yaghoobzadeh et al. (2019) apply diagnostic classification to investigate semantic classes using a large, automatically generated dataset derived from Wikipedia, which is likely to contain noise. Sommerauer and Fokkens (2018) and Herbelot and Vecchi (2015) have provided small sets of verified examples to combat this issue.

Distribution of examples. A classifier is likely to be able to separate words which are located in entirely different areas of the semantic space, but this does not mean it has recognized a specific property. For instance, the ability to separate red fruits (e.g. *strawberry*) from furniture (e.g. *table*) does not indicate that the property **red** was recognized. Sommerauer and Fokkens (2018) provide a small, qualitative analysis with respect to example distribution, but to the best of my knowledge, this has not been investigated systematically. Rubinstein et al. (2015) show that taxonomic properties yield higher performance in diagnostic classification experiments than (mostly physical) attributes. A possible explanation for this could be that taxonomic properties (e.g. **is_animal** are much easier to detect because of many correlating properties resulting in high general similarity in the semantic space.

Interpretation of performance. Saphra and Lopez (2018) point out that diagnostic classifiers can achieve high performance purely based in noise in the data instead of meaningful signals (Zhang and Bowman, 2018; Wieting and Kiela, 2018). To the best of my knowledge, this has not been taken into account yet in studies on embeddings.

The research proposed here is the first attempt to combine a systematic analysis in terms of linguistic hypotheses with with a methodological investigation addressing these limitations.

3 Linguistic hypotheses

This sections presents hypotheses about (a) *what* aspects of conceptual information people mention in texts (Section 3.1) and (b) *how* they mention it (Section 3.2).

3.1 Semantic relations

I define semantic relations representative of four major factors: impliedness, typicality, affordedness and variability. The factors are based on theoretical and empirical accounts in cognitive and computational linguistics (Grice, 1975; Gibson, 1954; Glenberg, 1997; Dale and Reiter, 1995; Sommerauer et al., 2019). The relations are used to label a corpus of property-concept pairs. To test the hypotheses by means of model analysis methods, it is necessary to have reliable information about negative examples of properties. I distinguish several negative relations (e.g. it can be impossible or unusual that a property applies to instances of a concept) to facilitate the annotation task.

Impliedness. Most conceptual knowledge can be seen as highly implied. Mentioning it would constitute a violation of the Gricean maxim of quantity. This is likely to be particularly relevant for properties which are inherited from lexical categories. For instance, the knowledge that a dog is an animate being with a heartbeat is unlikely to be mentioned explicitly. This tendency could be connected to claims about lexical retrieval (Collins and Quillian, 1970). Whether this is indeed the case is a question for further research.

Typicality. Corpus research has shown that people tend to express property-concept relations explicitly for cases in which a concept is a particularly good example of a property (Veale and Hao, 2007; Veale, 2011, 2013). For instance, colors tend to be described in terms of things which illustrate them particularly well (e.g. *as white as snow, as red as blood, as black as ebony wood*[1]). In contrast, properties which are typical of a concept (and evoked in many participants in elicitation tasks such as the CSLB norms (Devereux et al., 2014)) are most likely strongly implied conceptual knowledge and not mentioned explicitly (e.g. **green** - *broccoli*).

Affordedness. According to research in cognitive linguistics, a central component of semantic knowledge consists of the actions which are available to a person in a particular situation (called

afforded actions) (Gibson, 1954; Glenberg, 1997; Glenberg and Robertson, 2000). For instance, you can do several things with a rock, such as throw or drop it (Fulda et al., 2017). Many texts refer to events, which consist of actions involving participants. From this perspective, it is very likely that activities in which instances of concepts are involved are also mentioned in natural language. Glenberg and Robertson (2000) show that distributional models give good indications of activities usually associated with concepts, but cannot distinguish possible but unusual from impossible activities. Fulda et al. (2017) show that embedding models are helpful in affordance extraction. It can thus be expected that frequently performed actions are mentioned in text and can give indications about other properties (e.g. round objects such as bowling balls tend to roll). Possible but unusual activities are unlikely to be mentioned consistently.

Variability. Instances of concepts can vary with respect to a particular property. For instance, bell peppers can be red, green or yellow. Since neither of the colors is implied by the concept, information about it is more likely to be mentioned. In some cases, the property can even indicate an important distinction between different sub-concepts (e.g. brown, black and grey can distinguish different types of bears). In such cases, important and potentially distinguishing information is expressed via the property.

Negative relations. Several relations with no or only a loose association between property and concept can be distinguished. Linguistic corpora are unlikely to contain consistent evidence of such cases. The main reason for defining different types of negative relations is to facilitate the annotation task. Furthermore, they can be informative for further analysis. The relations include: properties which apply to concepts in rare cases, properties which can apply in unusual (such as fictional) cases and impossible combinations. We also include properties which can apply in creative, figurative expressions.

3.2 Linguistic evidence

Linguistic evidence of a semantic property can appear in different forms:

Direct. A property is expressed by its corresponding lexical form. For instance, a direct expression of the semantic property **red** is the adjective *red* and its morphological variants (if they exist),

---

[1] `https://www.pitt.edu/~dash/grimm053.html` (last accessed 2020-02-18)

for instance *reddish*.

Indirect. Semantic properties can be expressed indirectly in terms of a logical consequence or behavior that is tied to a property. For instance, things which have the semantic property **round** usually roll. Words such as *roll* and their morphological variants act as indirect evidence.

Property-preserving. Words can express properties which partially overlap with the semantic property in question. For instance, the semantic property **swim** can be expressed by *float* or *glide* in some contexts. Those expressions can also express other semantic properties and are thus not exclusively tied to the target property.

Related. Semantic properties can be related to other properties of concepts. For instance, the semantic property **swim** is closely related to different kinds of water, such as *sea*, *river* or *pond* and possibly also *beach* or *sand*. These expressions are related to a wide variety of properties and most certainly not exclusively tied to instances of concepts which swim.

Correlation. Properties which are not expressed can correlate strongly with an entire category of concepts. For instance, all birds **lay eggs**. While this is something *chickens* usually do/are used for, the activity is less prominent for *canaries* and thus unlikely to be mentioned in texts. However, it is likely that something like **belonging to the category of birds** is apparent from linguistic context, as indicated by Hearst patterns (Hearst, 1992) and research about predicting hyponymy relations from embeddings (Fu et al., 2014). Thus, the close connection between category and property may result in a form of linguistic evidence indicating a category which is very closely tied to a semantic property.

Property-category. Expressions of properties belonging to the same category (e.g. *red*, *yellow* and *green* express colors) in the context of a concept can indicate an entire property-category. This is likely to be the case if instances of a concept can have one of a variety of properties that belong to the same category (e.g. color) and the properties occur with similar frequencies (e.g. white, red, blue (etc.) t-shirts).

Table 1 shows the specific semantic relations with respect to the (sub-)set of instances of a concept they apply to and the type of corpus evidence we expect to find for property-concept pair.

4 Dataset design and crowd annotation

The dataset for this thesis should contain concept-property pairs annotated with the fine-grained semantic relations introduced in Section 3.1. The dataset should contain (1) enough positive and negative examples of a property to allow for diagnostic experiments and (2) positive and negative examples which cannot easily be separated based on general similarity in the semantic space (Sommerauer and Fokkens, 2018; Sommerauer et al., 2019).

To address these aspects, the property-concept pairs were collected following the strategy outlined in Sommerauer et al. (2019). Firstly, properties which are expected to apply to concepts across different semantic categories were selected (e.g. colors). Secondly, existing resources (the CSLB feature norms (Devereux et al., 2014) (an extended and improved version of the norms collected by (McRae et al., 2005)), but also WordNet (Miller, 1995; Fellbaum, 2010), ConceptNet (Speer and Havasi, 2012) and stereotype data (Veale, 2013) were used to collect positive and negative example candidates for these properties. Where possible, candidates were selected from diverse semantic categories. The candidates were extended by using a large-scale distributional model (GoogleNews Word2vec model[2]).

The candidate pairs are labeled with semantic relations in a crowd task. Crowd workers are presented with natural language statements about a specific pair illustrating a semantic relation and asked to indicate whether they agree or disagree.[3] Test runs indicate that workers can complete around 70 questions in about 10 minutes.[4]

Each property-concept pair should have at least one relation which is perceived as appropriate by most participants (and is thus labeled with 'agree').[5] However, it has been shown that ambiguity is inherent to many semantic annotation tasks (Dumitrache et al., 2018), leading to disagreements. Disagreement in this task is likely to arise

---

[2]Downloaded from `https://code.google.com/archive/p/word2vec/`

[3]An example of such a statement illustrating `typical_of_concept` would be: *"Fly" is one for the first things which come to mind when I hear "stork' because flying is one of the typical movements of (a/an) stork'*. The full set of statements can be found at `https://github.com/cltl/SPT_annotation`

[4]The task was set up using the Lingoturk framework (Pusse et al., 2016) and is being distributed via the platform Prolific `https://www.prolific.co/`.

[5]More than one relation can apply (e.g. both typicality relations).

set of instances	factor	relation	evidence
most - all	impliedness	`implied`	correlation
	typicality	`typical_of_concept`	sparse - none
		`typical_of_property`	direct, property-preserving, related
	affordedness	`affording_activity`	indirect, property-preserving, related
		`afforded_usual`	direct, property-preserving, related
		`afforded_unusual`	sparse to none
some	variability	`variability_limited`	direct, property-category
		`variability_open`	property-category
few-none	negative cases	`rare`	sparse - none
		`unusual`	sparse - none
		`impossible`	sparse - none
		`creative`	sparse - none

Table 1: Summary of linguistic hypotheses about semantic relations and types of evidence.

from two factors: (1) ambiguity in the interpretation of the concept, property, relation or combination and (2) different levels of knowledge about the world. Disagreement caused by interpretation differences is particularly relevant for this dataset, as this is can indicate polysemy, which has been shown to have an impact on embedding representations (Del Tredici and Bel, 2015; Yaghoobzadeh et al., 2019, e.g.). It is, however, still an open question how exactly it relates to the representation of semantic properties. Table 2 shows the answers collected for a clear pair, an ambiguous pair and an ambiguous pair additionally perceived as difficult.

relation	p1	p2	p3
`typical_of_property`	10	3	3
`typical_of_concept`	10	5	5
`affording_activity`	10	4	5
`implied_category`	8	6	4
`variability_limited`	7	7	3
`variability_open`	2	3	7
`rare`	1	2	5
`unusual`	0	4	4
`impossible`	0	3	0
`creative`	0	4	3

Table 2: Number of annotators (out of 10) who selected 'agree' for a semantic relation shown for three pairs of varying difficulties: sweet-honey (p1) (clear), made of wood - beam (p2) (ambiguous) and hot-chutney (p3) (not well known according to a worker).

Inter-annotator agreement alone cannot be used to evaluate the quality of the dataset. Disagreement is not only an expected, but a desired and meaningful outcome. Instead, I consider the quality of the annotations from multiple perspectives: (1) As a basis for comparison, I apply IAA metrics to the entire dataset and portions of the dataset which I expect to trigger high or low agreement. These portions have been selected in advance. (2) I consider the quality of the workers in terms of whether they contradict themselves in their answers (e.g. label a single pair as typical *and* impossible). A low number of contradictions can be seen as an indication of a clear task. Workers with high contradiction rates can be excluded, which should increase the IAA on the remaining annotations.(3) I analyze the data with the crowd-truth framework (Dumitrache et al., 2018), which provides a fine-grained analysis of workers, annotation units and labels. (4) A subset of pairs is being annotated by trained experts. These annotations serve as a gold standard and can provide more insights into disagreements and worker behavior. They can help to reveal additional, possibly unexpected factors causing disagreement.

5   Method

Various analysis methods have been suggested to interpret latent representations resulting from machine learning (particularly deep learning) models. While they have yielded important insights, they still struggle with a number of limitations (Belinkov and Glass, 2019; Saphra and Lopez, 2018). I plan to approach these limitations by pairing analysis methods (described in Section 5.1) with data simulation experiments (described in Section 5.2). This combination is expected to yield insights into (1) the analysis methods and their potential and (2) the representation of linguistic evidence in a text corpus in distributional models.

5.1 Analyzing latent representations

I plan to use diagnostic classification (Hupkes et al., 2018; Belinkov and Glass, 2019) and SVCCA (Singular Vector Canonical Correlation Analysis) (Raghu et al., 2017). SVCCA has been suggested to address some of the limitations of diagnostic classification (Saphra and Lopez, 2018).

Both methods require a specific distribution of positive and negative examples. Distributional models place generally similar concepts in similar areas in the embedding space because they occur in similar contexts. This means that positive examples which are similar to one another, but dissimilar from the negative examples will be easily recognizable (e.g. **fly**: *seagull* vs *table*). Distinguishing them, however, does not mean that evidence of the particular property was discovered. If however, a diverse group of positive examples can be distinguished from negative examples similar to the positive ones (e.g. **fly**: *seagull* vs *penguin*), we conclude that the property has actually been identified with higher confidence. While this type of dataset control cannot eliminate all possible correlations, it is a first step towards more solid evidence.

5.2 Simulation experiments

The following questions should be answered before we can draw conclusions from the analysis of embedding models trained on natural language corpora:

1. How much evidence in the context of a concept is necessary to have an impact on the representation in an embedding model?
2. How do embedding models represent different kinds of evidence? Can they abstract over morphological variants or synonyms of a word?
3. What is the performance of a model analysis methods if there is very clear evidence of a property? What is the difference between embeddings with clear evidence and embeddings without clear evidence?

I approach these questions by introducing artificial evidence to text corpora and training distributional models on these corpora. In the case of distributional models and linguistic evidence, it is challenging to design small and controlled experiments, as the models rely on a substantial amount of data. Building an entirely artificial corpus (as for instance done by Yaghoobzadeh and Schütze (2016)) would entail the risk of losing information

responsible for the general structure of a semantic space. Therefore, I will simulate textual evidence of a property by introducing artificial 'evidence words' to the contexts of a random set of words in an otherwise unchanged corpus. Embeddings resulting from this manipulated corpus can then be used to test how much evidence is sufficient for information to be recognized by analysis methods. I expect this approach to show how the performance of diagnostic methods relates to the presence or absence of textual evidence. These insights are crucial form the interpretation of analysis methods applied to a natural corpus.

6 Conclusion

This proposal presents a framework for investigating the semantic content of distributional word representations from two perspectives: Firstly, I propose to test linguistic hypotheses about what aspects of conceptual knowledge are represented in natural language. Secondly, I propose to interpret the results against the background of a methodological investigation of model analysis methods and the potential of distributional models.

The linguistic hypotheses to be tested may be falsified. While this would be a negative result, it is still a relevant insight and can be used as a basis for new predictions. Furthermore, it can be expected that the methodological insights gained in the simulation experiments can inform other approaches investigating non-transparent embedding representations and yield important insights about the behavior of distributional models.

I expect that the corpus and insights gathered in this project can be complementary to resources capturing common-sense knowledge explicitly, such as Conceptnet (Speer et al., 2017) and common sense challenges (e.g. (Talmor et al., 2019)).

Acknowledgments

I would like to thank my supervisors Piek Vossen and Antske Fokkens for their support, feedback and guidance in developing this proposal. I would also like to thank Vivek Gupta for his helpful comments and the anonymous reviewers for their feedback. This research is funded by the PhD in the Humanities Grant provided by the Netherlands Organization of Scientific Research (Nederlandse Organisatie voor Wetenschappelijk Onderzoek, NWO) PGW.17.041.

References

Yonatan Belinkov and James Glass. 2019. Analysis methods in neural language processing: A survey. *Transactions of the Association for Computational Linguistics*, 7:49–72.

Allan M Collins and M Ross Quillian. 1970. Facilitating retrieval from semantic memory: The effect of repeating part of an inference. *Acta Psychologica*, 33:304–314.

Robert Dale and Ehud Reiter. 1995. Computational interpretations of the gricean maxims in the generation of referring expressions. *Cognitive science*, 19(2):233–263.

Marco Del Tredici and Núria Bel. 2015. A word-embedding-based sense index for regular polysemy representation. In *Proceedings of the 1st Workshop on Vector Space Modeling for Natural Language Processing*, pages 70–78.

Steven Derby, Paul Miller, Brian Murphy, and Barry Devereux. 2018. Representation of word meaning in the intermediate projection layer of a neural language model. In *Proceedings of the 2018 EMNLP Workshop BlackboxNLP: Analyzing and Interpreting Neural Networks for NLP*, pages 362–364.

Barry J. Devereux, Lorraine K. Tyler, Jeroen Geertzen, and Billi Randall. 2014. The centre for speech, language and the brain (cslb) concept property norms. *Behavior research methods*, 46(4):1119–1127.

Jacob Devlin, Ming-Wei Chang, Kenton Lee, and Kristina Toutanova. 2019. Bert: Pre-training of deep bidirectional transformers for language understanding. In *Proceedings of the 2019 Conference of the North American Chapter of the Association for Computational Linguistics: Human Language Technologies, Volume 1 (Long and Short Papers)*, pages 4171–4186.

Anca Dumitrache, Lora Aroyo, and Chris Welty. 2018. Capturing ambiguity in crowdsourcing frame disambiguation. In *Sixth AAAI Conference on Human Computation and Crowdsourcing*.

Katrin Erk. 2016. What do you know about an alligator when you know the company it keeps? *Semantics and Pragmatics*, 9:17–1.

Luana Fagarasan, Eva Maria Vecchi, and Stephen Clark. 2015. From distributional semantics to feature norms: grounding semantic models in human perceptual data. In *Proceedings of the 11th International Conference on Computational Semantics*, pages 52–57.

Christiane Fellbaum. 2010. Wordnet. In *Theory and applications of ontology: computer applications*, pages 231–243. Springer.

Maxwell Forbes, Ari Holtzman, and Yejin Choi. 2019. Do neural language representations learn physical commonsense? *arXiv preprint arXiv:1908.02899*.

Ruiji Fu, Jiang Guo, Bing Qin, Wanxiang Che, Haifeng Wang, and Ting Liu. 2014. Learning semantic hierarchies via word embeddings. In *Proceedings of the 52nd Annual Meeting of the Association for Computational Linguistics (Volume 1: Long Papers)*, pages 1199–1209.

Nancy Fulda, Daniel Ricks, Ben Murdoch, and David Wingate. 2017. What can you do with a rock? affordance extraction viaword embeddings. In *Proceedings of the 26th International Joint Conference on Artificial Intelligence*, pages 1039–1045.

James J Gibson. 1954. The visual perception of objective motion and subjective movement. *Psychological Review*, 61(5):304.

Arthur M Glenberg. 1997. What memory is for. *Behavioral and brain sciences*, 20(1):1–19.

Arthur M Glenberg and David A Robertson. 2000. Symbol grounding and meaning: A comparison of high-dimensional and embodied theories of meaning. *Journal of memory and language*, 43(3):379–401.

HP Grice. 1975. Logic and conversation. *Foundations of Cognitive Psychology*, page 719.

Abhijeet Gupta, Gemma Boleda, Marco Baroni, and Sebastian Padó. 2015. Distributional vectors encode referential attributes. In *Proceedings of the 2015 Conference on Empirical Methods in Natural Language Processing*, pages 12–21.

Marti A Hearst. 1992. Automatic acquisition of hyponyms from large text corpora. In *Proceedings of the 14th conference on Computational linguistics-Volume 2*, pages 539–545. Association for Computational Linguistics.

Aurélie Herbelot. 2013. What is in a text, what isn't, and what this has to do with lexical semantics. In *Proceedings of the 10th International Conference on Computational Semantics (IWCS 2013)–Short Papers*, pages 321–327.

Aurélie Herbelot and Eva Maria Vecchi. 2015. Building a shared world: Mapping distributional to model-theoretic semantic spaces. In *Proceedings of the 2015 Conference on Empirical Methods in Natural Language Processing*, pages 22–32.

Dieuwke Hupkes, Sara Veldhoen, and Willem Zuidema. 2018. Visualisation and'diagnostic classifiers' reveal how recurrent and recursive neural networks process hierarchical structure. *Journal of Artificial Intelligence Research*, 61:907–926.

Ken McRae, George S Cree, Mark S Seidenberg, and Chris McNorgan. 2005. Semantic feature production norms for a large set of living and nonliving things. *Behavior research methods*, 37(4):547–559.

Tomas Mikolov, Wen-tau Yih, and Geoffrey Zweig. 2013. Linguistic regularities in continuous space word representations. In *HLT-NAACL*, volume 13, pages 746–751.

George A Miller. 1995. Wordnet: a lexical database for english. *Communications of the ACM*, 38(11):39–41.

Matthew E Peters, Mark Neumann, Mohit Iyyer, Matt Gardner, Christopher Clark, Kenton Lee, and Luke Zettlemoyer. 2018. Deep contextualized word representations. In *Proceedings of NAACL-HLT*, pages 2227–2237.

Florian Pusse, Asad Sayeed, and Vera Demberg. 2016. Lingoturk: managing crowdsourced tasks for psycholinguistics. In *Proceedings of the 2016 Conference of the North American Chapter of the Association for Computational Linguistics: Demonstrations*, pages 57–61.

Maithra Raghu, Justin Gilmer, Jason Yosinski, and Jascha Sohl-Dickstein. 2017. Svcca: Singular vector canonical correlation analysis for deep learning dynamics and interpretability. In *Advances in Neural Information Processing Systems*, pages 6076–6085.

Brian Riordan and Michael N Jones. 2011. Redundancy in perceptual and linguistic experience: Comparing feature-based and distributional models of semantic representation. *Topics in Cognitive Science*, 3(2):303–345.

Dana Rubinstein, Effi Levi, Roy Schwartz, and Ari Rappoport. 2015. How well do distributional models capture different types of semantic knowledge? In *Proceedings of the 53rd Annual Meeting of the Association for Computational Linguistics and the 7th International Joint Conference on Natural Language Processing (Volume 2: Short Papers)*, pages 726–730.

Naomi Saphra and Adam Lopez. 2018. Understanding learning dynamics of language models with svcca. *Proceedings of NAACL-HLT*.

Pia Sommerauer and Antske Fokkens. 2018. Firearms and tigers are dangerous, kitchen knives and zebras are not: Testing whether word embeddings can tell. In *Proceedings of the 2018 EMNLP Workshop BlackboxNLP: Analyzing and Interpreting Neural Networks for NLP*, pages 276–286.

Pia Sommerauer, Antske Fokkens, and Piek Vossen. 2019. Towards interpretable, data-derived distributional semantic representations for reasoning: A dataset of properties and concepts. In *Wordnet Conference*, page 85.

Robert Speer and Catherine Havasi. 2012. Representing general relational knowledge in conceptnet 5. In *LREC*, pages 3679–3686.

Robyn Speer, Joshua Chin, and Catherine Havasi. 2017. Conceptnet 5.5: An open multilingual graph of general knowledge. In *Thirty-First AAAI Conference on Artificial Intelligence*.

Alon Talmor, Jonathan Herzig, Nicholas Lourie, and Jonathan Berant. 2019. Commonsenseqa: A question answering challenge targeting commonsense knowledge. In *Proceedings of NAACL-HLT*, pages 4149–4158.

Yulia Tsvetkov, Manaal Faruqui, and Chris Dyer. 2016. Correlation-based intrinsic evaluation of word vector representations. In *Proceedings of the 1st Workshop on Evaluating Vector-Space Representations for NLP*, pages 111–115.

Yulia Tsvetkov, Manaal Faruqui, Wang Ling, Guillaume Lample, and Chris Dyer. 2015. Evaluation of word vector representations by subspace alignment. In *Proceedings of EMNLP*.

Akira Utsumi. 2011. Computational exploration of metaphor comprehension processes using a semantic space model. *Cognitive science*, 35(2):251–296.

Tony Veale. 2011. Creative language retrieval: A robust hybrid of information retrieval and linguistic creativity. In *Proceedings of the 49th Annual Meeting of the Association for Computational Linguistics: Human Language Technologies-Volume 1*, pages 278–287. Association for Computational Linguistics.

Tony Veale. 2013. The agile cliché: using flexible stereotypes as building blocks in the construction of an affective lexicon. In *New Trends of Research in Ontologies and Lexical Resources*, pages 257–275. Springer.

Tony Veale and Yanfen Hao. 2007. Learning to understand figurative language: from similes to metaphors to irony. In *Proceedings of the Annual Meeting of the Cognitive Science Society*, volume 29.

Gabriella Vigliocco, David P Vinson, William Lewis, and Merrill F Garrett. 2004. Representing the meanings of object and action words: The featural and unitary semantic space hypothesis. *Cognitive psychology*, 48(4):422–488.

David P. Vinson and Gabriella Vigliocco. 2008. Semantic feature production norms for a large set of objects and events. *Behavior Research Methods*, 40(1):183–190.

John Wieting and Douwe Kiela. 2018. No training required: Exploring random encoders for sentence classification.

Yadollah Yaghoobzadeh, Katharina Kann, Timothy J Hazen, Eneko Agirre, and Hinrich Schütze. 2019. Probing for semantic classes: Diagnosing the meaning content of word embeddings. In *Proceedings of the 57th Annual Meeting of the Association for Computational Linguistics*, pages 5740–5753.

Yadollah Yaghoobzadeh and Hinrich Schütze. 2016. Intrinsic subspace evaluation of word embedding representations. In *Proceedings of the 54th Annual Meeting of the Association for Computational Linguistics (Volume 1: Long Papers)*, volume 1, pages 236–246.

Kelly W Zhang and Samuel R Bowman. 2018. Language modeling teaches you more syntax than translation does: Lessons learned through auxiliary task analysis. *EMNLP 2018*, page 359.

A Simple and Effective Dependency parser for Telugu

Sneha Nallani, Manish Shrivastava, Dipti Misra Sharma
Kohli Center on Intelligent Systems (KCIS),
International Institute of Information Technology, Hyderabad
Telangana, India
`sneha.nallani@research.iiit.ac.in`
`{m.shrivastava, dipti}@iiit.ac.in`

Abstract

We present a simple and effective dependency parser for Telugu, a morphologically rich, free word order language. We propose to replace the rich linguistic feature templates used in the past approaches with a minimal feature function using contextual vector representations. We train a BERT model on the Telugu Wikipedia data and use vector representations from this model to train the parser. Each sentence token is associated with a vector representing the token in the context of that sentence and the feature vectors are constructed by concatenating two token representations from the stack and one from the buffer. We put the feature representations through a feed forward network and train with a greedy transition based approach. The resulting parser has a very simple architecture with minimal feature engineering and achieves state-of-the-art results for Telugu.

1 Introduction

Dependency parsing is extremely useful for many downstream tasks. However, robust dependency parsers are not available for several Indian languages. One reason is the unavailability of annotated treebanks. Another reason is that most of the existing dependency parsers for Indian languages use hand-crafted features using linguistic information like part-of-speech and morphology (Kosaraju et al., 2010; Bharati et al., 2008; Jain et al., 2012) which are very expensive to annotate. Telugu is a low resource language and there hasn't been much recent work done on parsing. Most of the previous work on Telugu dependency parsing has been focused on rule based systems or data-driven transition based systems. This paper focuses on improving feature representations for a low resource, agglutinative language like Telugu using the latest developments in the field of NLP such as contextual vector representations.

Contextual word representations (Howard and Ruder, 2018; Peters et al., 2018; Devlin et al., 2019) are derived from a language model and each word can be uniquely represented based on its context. One such model is BERT (Devlin et al., 2019). BERT vectors are deep bidirectional representations pre-trained by jointly conditioning on both left and right context of a word and have been shown to perform better on variety of NLP tasks.

In this paper, we use BERT representations for parsing Telugu. We replace the rich hand-crafted linguistic features with a minimal feature function using a small number of contextual word representations. We show that for a morphologically rich, agglutinative language like Telugu, just three word features with good quality vector representations can effectively capture the information required for parsing. We put the feature representations through a feed forward network and train using a greedy transition based parser (Nivre, 2004, 2008).

Past work on Telugu dependency parsing has only been focused on predicting inter-chunk dependency relations (Kosaraju et al., 2010; Kesidi et al., 2011; Kanneganti et al., 2016, 2017; Tandon and Sharma, 2017). In this paper, we also report parser accuracies on intra-chunk annotated Telugu treebank for the first time.

2 Related Work

Extensive work has been done on dependency parsing in the last decade, especially due to the CoNLL shared tasks on dependency parsing. Creation of Universal Dependencies (Nivre et al., 2016) led to an increased focus on common approaches to parsing several different languages. There were new transition based approaches making use of more robust input representations (Chen and Manning, 2014; Kiperwasser and Goldberg, 2016) and improved network architectures (Ma et al., 2018).

Proceedings of the 58th Annual Meeting of the Association for Computational Linguistics: Student Research Workshop, pages 143–149
July 5 - July 10, 2020. ©2020 Association for Computational Linguistics

Graph based approaches to dependency parsing have also become more common over the last few years (Kiperwasser and Goldberg, 2016; Dozat and Manning, 2017, inter alia).

However, there hasn't been much recent work on parsing Indian languages and much less on Telugu. Most of the previous work on Telugu dependency parsing has been focused on rule based systems (Kesidi et al., 2011) or data-driven transition based systems (Kanneganti et al., 2016) using Malt parser (Nivre et al., 2006). The Malt parser uses a classifier to predict the transition operations taking a feature template as input. The feature templates used in Telugu parsers commonly consist of several hand-crafted features like words, their part-of-speech tags, gender, number and other morphological features (Kosaraju et al., 2010; Kanneganti et al., 2016). There has been some work done on representing these linguistic features using dense vector representations in a neural network based parser (Tandon and Sharma, 2017).

Recent developments in the field of NLP led to the arrival of contextual word vectors (Howard and Ruder, 2018; Peters et al., 2018; Devlin et al., 2019) and their extensive use in downstream NLP tasks, from POS tagging (Peters et al., 2018) to more complex tasks like Question Answering and Natural Language Inference tasks (Devlin et al., 2019). Contextual vectors have also been applied to dependency parsing systems. The top-ranked system in CoNLL-2018 shared task on Dependency Parsing(Che et al., 2018) used ELMo representations along with conventional word vectors in a graph based parser. Kulmizev et al. (2019); Kondratyuk and Straka (2019) use contextual vector representations for multilingual dependency parsing.

In this paper, we train a BERT-baseline model (Devlin et al., 2019) on Telugu Wikipedia data and use these vector representations to improve Telugu dependency parsing.

3   Telugu Dependency Treebank

We use the Telugu treebank made available for ICON 2010 tools contest. We extend this treebank by another 900 sentences from the HCU Telugu treebank. The size of the combined treebank is around 2400 sentences. The treebank is annotated using Computational Paninian grammar (Bharati et al., 1995; Begum et al., 2008) proposed for Indian languages. The treebank is annotated at inter-chunk level (Bharati et al., 2009) in SSF (Bharati

et al., 2007) format. Only chunk heads in a sentence are annotated with dependency labels.

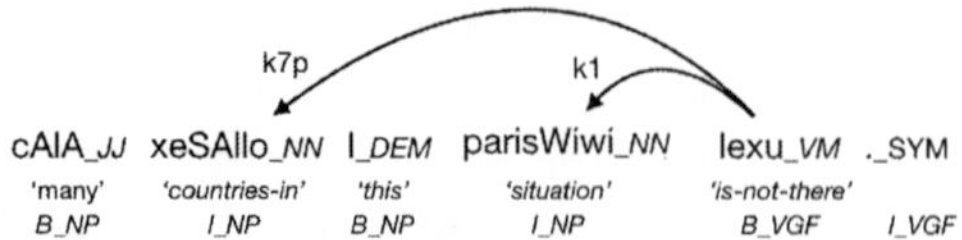

Figure 1: Inter-chunk dependency tree. B_* denotes the beginning of a new chunk.

We automatically annotate the intra-chunk dependencies (Bhat, 2017) using a Shift-Reduce parser based on Context Free Grammar rules within a chunk, written for Telugu[1]. Annotating the intra-chunk dependencies provides a complete parse tree for each sentence.

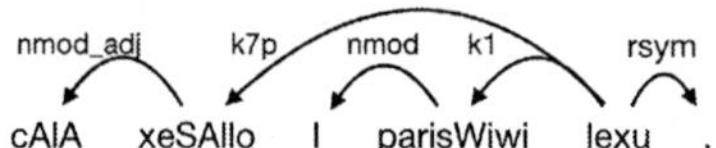

Figure 2: Intra-chunk dependency tree

The treebank is converted from SSF to CoNLL-X format (Buchholz and Marsi, 2006)[2].

4   Our Approach

We propose to replace the rich hand-crafted feature templates used in Malt parser systems with a minimally defined feature set which uses automatically learned word representations from BERT. We do not make use of any additional pipeline features like POS or morphological information assuming this information is captured within the vectors. We train a BERT baseline model (Devlin et al., 2019) on the Telugu wikipedia data, which comprises 71289 articles. We use the ILMT tokenizer included in the Telugu shallow parser [3] to segment the data into sentences. The sentence segmented data consists of approximately 2.6M sentences. We convert all of the data from UTF to WX[4] notation for faster processing. We use byte-pair encoding (Sennrich et al., 2016) to tokenize the data and generate a vocabulary file. We pass this vocabulary

---

[1] https://github.com/ltrc/
Shift-Reduce-Chunk-Expander
[2] https://github.com/ltrc/
SSF-to-CONLL-Convertor
[3] https://ltrc.iiit.ac.in/showfile.php?
filename=downloads/shallow_parser.php
[4] https://en.wikipedia.org/wiki/WX_
notation

file to BERT [5] for pre-training. After pre-training, we extract contextual token representations for all the sentences in the treebank from the pre-trained BERT model. In case a single word is split into multiple tokens, we treat these tokens as continuous bag of words and add the representations of all the tokens in a word to obtain the word representation. We find that this approach works better than considering only the first word-piece vector (Kulmizev et al., 2019; Kondratyuk and Straka, 2019). We use these word representations as input features to the parser. Our feature function is a concatenation of a small number of BERT vectors and we integrate it into a transition based parser. The specific details are mentioned in Section 4.2

4.1 Transition based Dependency Parsing

Transition based parsers process a sentence sequentially and treat parsing as a sequence of actions that produce a parse tree. They predict a sequence of transition operations starting from an initial configuration to a terminal configuration, and construct a dependency parse tree in the process. A configuration consists of a stack, an input buffer of words, and a set of relations representing a dependency tree. They make use of a classifier to predict the next transition operation based on a set of features derived from the current configuration. A couple of widely used transition systems are Arc-standard (Nivre, 2004) and Arc-eager (Nivre, 2008). We make use of the Arc-standard transition system in our parser and briefly describe it here.

4.1.1 Arc-standard Transition System

In the arc-standard system, a configuration consists of a stack, a buffer, and a set of dependency arcs. The initial configuration for a sentence $s = w_1, ..., w_n$ consists of stack = $[ROOT]$, buffer = $[w_1, ..., w_n]$ and dependencies = $[]$. In the terminal configuration, buffer = $[]$ and stack = $[ROOT]$, and the parse tree is given by dependencies. The root node of the parse tree is attached as the child of $ROOT$.

The arc-standard system defines three types of transitions that operate on the top two elements of the stack and first element of the buffer:

- LEFT-ARC: Adds a head-dependent relation between the word at the top of stack and the

word below it and removes the lower word from the stack.

- RIGHT-ARC: Adds a head-dependent relation between the second word on the stack and the top word and removes the top word from the stack.

- SHIFT: Moves the word from the front of the buffer onto the stack.

In the labeled version of parsing, there are a total of $2\ell + 1$ transitions, where ℓ is the number of different dependency labels. There is a left-arc and a right-arc transition corresponding to each label. The label *left-arc_vmod* adds a head-dependent relation between the top two words of the stack (s_0, s_1) with label *vmod*, dependencies=$[(s_0, s_1, vmod),...]$

4.2 Feature Function

We use a minimally defined feature set consisting solely of word representations obtained from BERT. We do not incorporate any part-of-speech or morphological information separately. The intuition is that such information is already captured within the BERT representations. Our feature set consists of word representations of the top two elements of the stack (s_0, s_1) and the first element of the buffer (b_0). We compute a feature vector,

$$F = v_{s_0} \circ v_{s_1} \circ v_{b_0}$$

by concatenating ($\circ$) the vector representations of all the words in the feature set, where v_i is the vector representation of the word i,

4.3 Classifier

We use a fully connected Feed Forward Network with one hidden layer with ReLU activation to score all the possible parser transitions. The next transition is predicted based on the features extracted from the current configuration. We compute the scores of all transitions,

$$transition\_scores(f) = W^2 \cdot relu(W^1 \cdot f + b^1) + b^2$$

where f is the feature vector obtained from the current configuration. A softmax layer is applied over the transition scores to get the probability distribution. We pick a valid transition with the highest probability. We use a dropout layer with probability 0.2 for regularization.

---

[5] https://github.com/google-research/bert

Intra-chunk	UAS	LS	LAS
Max	95.43	83.05	81.81
Min	85.04	67.09	64.17
Average	90.92	71.95	70.49

Table 1: Parser 10-fold cross-validation results on intra-chunk annotated treebank.

Inter-chunk	UAS	LS	LAS
Max	94.50	78.90	77.20
Min	78.16	56.14	52.14
Average	90.37	67.57	65.74

Table 2: Parser 10-fold cross-validation results on inter-chunk annotated treebank.

5 Experiments and Results

The Telugu dependency treebank is quite small in size consisting of only 2400 sentences. We also observe that the sentence length and quality of annotation in the treebank is not uniform and has a high amount of variation. We therefore evaluate our parser on the treebank using ten-fold cross-validation. We report the cross-validation accuracies on both inter-chunk (Table 2) and intra-chunk (Table 1) annotated treebanks. Parser accuracies on intra-chunk annotated Telugu treebank are reported for the first time in this paper. The overall parser accuracies improve on the intra-chunk annotated treebank.

We compare these results with a baseline using only word2vec word representations and subsequently adding Part-of-speech (POS) and suffix representations described in (Tandon and Sharma, 2017). We also try to reproduce Tandon and Sharma (2017) experiments on both inter-chunk and intra-chunk annotated treebanks. Tandon and Sharma (2017) report their best results for Telugu on the inter-chunk annotated treebank using word, POS and suffix representations. Their results are reported on a test set and since their exact dataset is not available, we report average 10-fold cross validation accuracies. The reproduced results are listed in Table 3. As can be seen from the table the average cross-validation accuracies are lower. The discrepancy between rows 3 and 4 is because of a larger feature set and a different optimizer. Tandon and Sharma (2017) use 13 features from the parse configuration instead of our three features which introduce unnecessary noise, when the average sentence length is as small as five. We also find that Adam optimizer performs better than the Adagard optimizer used in their setup.

Implementation details: The parser comprises of simple feed forward neural network with one hidden layer consisting of 1024 hidden units and a relu activation function and a dropout layer with dropout probability of 0.2. We use xavier uniform initialization (Glorot and Bengio, 2010) to initialize the network parameters and Adam optimizer (Diederik P. Kingma, 2015) with default momentum and learning rates provided by PyTorch. We use BERT baseline model for pre-training and each BERT token representation is of dimension 768.

Arc-standard vs Arc-eager: We experiment with both Arc-standard (Nivre, 2004) and Arc-Eager (Nivre, 2008) transition systems and find that Arc-standard works better in our case (Table 4). We use Arc-standard transition system in all further experiments.

Feature Function: We experiment with different feature sets and find that using just three features, the top two elements of the stack and the top-most element of the buffer result in the highest accuracies. Extending the feature set to include more elements from the stack or buffer causes the accuracies to fall. Parser accuracies using different feature sets are reported in Table 5.

Peters et al. (2018) and Che et al. (2018) suggest that concatenating conventional word vectors with contextual word vectors could result in a boost in accuracies. We try out the same by concatenating *word2vec* vectors with BERT vectors and observe some improvement in label scores. The results are mentioned in Table 6.

BERT layers: We also experiment with vector representations from different layers of BERT. The results are mentioned in Table 7. We find that the 4_{th} layer from the top of our BERT baseline model results in the highest accuracy for the parser. This finding is consistent with the work of Tenney et al. (2019) which suggests that dependencies are better captured between layers 6 and 9. We use the vector representations from 4_{th} layer from the top in all our experiments.

BPE vs Inverse-BPE: Byte-pair encoding (Sennrich et al., 2016) segments words from left to right. In Telugu, most grammatical information

System	Annotation	Method	UAS	LS	LAS
Baseline	Intra-chunk	MLP with word	84.56	65.87	63.39
Baseline + POS	Intra-chunk	MLP with word, POS	88.90	68.99	67.46
Baseline + POS + suffix	Intra-chunk	MLP with word, POS, suffix	89.93	71.97	70.38
Tandon et al, 2017 re-impl	Intra-chunk	MLP with word, POS, suffix	88.67	67.27	65.29
This work	Intra-chunk	MLP using BERT	90.92	71.95	70.49
Tandon et al, 2017	Inter-chunk	MLP with word, POS, suffix	$94.11^{\dagger}$	$74.32^{\dagger}$	$73.14^{\dagger}$
Tandon et al, 2017 re-impl	Inter-chunk	MLP with word, POS, suffix	88.13	61.48	59.54
This work	Inter-chunk	MLP using BERT	90.37	67.57	65.74

Table 3: Parsing results on Telugu treebank. The results with † are reported test-set accuracies and the rest are 10-fold cross-validation accuracies.

Transition System	UAS	LS	LAS
Arc-Standard	90.92	71.95	70.49
Arc-Eager	89.91	71.15	69.52

Table 4: Cross-validation results for arc-standard and arc-eager transition systems using features (s_0, s_1, b_0).

Feature set	UAS	LS	LAS
(s_0, s_1, b_0)	90.92	71.95	70.49
$(s_0, s_1, b_0, lc_1s_0, rc_1s_0)$	90.85	71.57	70.08
$(s_0, s_1, s_2, b_0, lc_1s_0, rc_1s_0)$	90.91	71.50	70.13
$(s_0, s_1, s_2, b_0, lc_1s_0, rc_1s_0, lc_1s_1, rc_1s_1)$	90.76	71.25	69.86

Table 5: Parser cross-validation results using different feature sets. (lc_1, rc_1) refer to the left-most and right-most children.

Vector representation	UAS	LS	LAS
$BERTvector$	90.92	71.95	70.49
$BERTvector \circ wordvector$	90.89	72.11	70.60

Table 6: Parser cross-validation results with and without concatenating word vectors with BERT vectors for the feature set (s_0, s_1, b_0)

BERT Layers	UAS	LS	LAS
Layer -1	90.21	71.22	69.59
Layer -2	90.58	71.63	69.99
Layer -3	90.19	71.20	69.65
Layer -4	**90.92**	**71.95**	**70.49**
Layer -5	90.31	71.52	69.99
Layer -6	90.22	71.70	70.20

Table 7: Parser cross-validation results using representations from different layers of BERT. Layer $-n$ represents the n_{th} layer from the top.

Tokenization	UAS	LS	LAS
BPE	90.92	71.95	70.49
Inverse-BPE	91.06	71.71	70.22

Table 8: Parser cross-validation results on BERT models trained with BPE and Inverse-BPE.

is encoded in the suffixes. Intuitively, segmenting the words from right to left (inverse-BPE) could lead to linguistically better word segments. We test out this assumption (Table 8). We use 60k merge operations in both cases. Inverse-BPE leads to slightly better unlabeled attachment scores but causes a slight drop in label scores.

6   Error Analysis

In this section we look at some of the most common errors made by this parser and try to understand why those errors might be occurring. We evaluate the parser on a test-set of 240 sentences. The most frequently occurring errors are $k1(agent/subject)$ and $k2(object/patient)$ mismatch, $k1$ is labeled as $k2$ and vice versa. $k1$ and $k2$ are the most frequently occurring labels after $ROOT$. 78% sentences in the test-set contain $k1$ dependency and 50% sentences contain $k2$ dependency. $k1$ is labeled as $k2$ 15% of the time and $k2$ is labeled as $k1$ 18% of the time. These errors are usually seen when the words occur without case-markers. In these cases, $k1$ and $k2$ can be distinguished by looking at the verb agreement. Fixing these two errors would greatly improve the parser.

Other frequently occurring errors are confusion between $k2$ and $k4(recipient)$ since they sometimes take the same case-markers, $nmod$ and $nmod\_adj$, $vmod$ and adv, $sent\_adv$ labels. The label $vmod$ is ambiguous in general and can be easily confused with adverbs.

7 Conclusion and Future Work

We present a simple yet effective dependency parser for Telugu using contextual word representations. We demonstrate that even with vectors trained on a small corpus of 2.6M sentences, we can reduce the need for explicit linguistic features in deep learning based models. We show based on the results of the parser that BERT vectors effectively capture much of the linguistic information required for parsing. We also show that with good vector representations, a small feature set is more effective for a morphologically rich, agglutinative language like Telugu.

Future work could include finding a way to incorporate other linguistic features like case-markers, gender, number, person, tense, aspect and verb agreement information into the parser.

References

Rafiya Begum, Samar Husain, Arun Dhwaj, Dipti Misra Sharma, Lakshmi Bai, and Rajeev Sangal. 2008. Dependency annotation scheme for indian languages. In *Proceedings of the Third International Joint Conference on Natural Language Processing: Volume-II*.

Akshar Bharati, Vineet Chaitanya, Rajeev Sangal, and KV Ramakrishnamacharyulu. 1995. *Natural language processing: a Paninian perspective*. Prentice-Hall of India New Delhi.

Akshar Bharati, Samar Husain, Bharat Ambati, Sambhav Jain, Dipti Sharma, and Rajeev Sangal. 2008. Two semantic features make all the difference in parsing accuracy. *Proceedings of ICON*, 8.

Akshar Bharati, Rajeev Sangal, and Dipti M Sharma. 2007. Ssf: Shakti standard format guide. *Language Technologies Research Centre, International Institute of Information Technology, Hyderabad, India*, pages 1–25.

Akshara Bharati, Dipti Misra Sharma, Samar Husain, Lakshmi Bai, Rafiya Begam, and Rajeev Sangal. 2009. Anncorra: Treebanks for indian languages, guidelines for annotating hindi treebank. *IIIT Hyderabad*.

Riyaz Ahmad Bhat. 2017. *Exploiting linguistic knowledge to address representation and sparsity issues in dependency parsing of indian languages*. Phd thesis, IIIT Hyderabad.

Sabine Buchholz and Erwin Marsi. 2006. CoNLL-x shared task on multilingual dependency parsing. In *Proceedings of the Tenth Conference on Computational Natural Language Learning (CoNLL-X)*, pages 149–164, New York City. Association for Computational Linguistics.

Wanxiang Che, Yijia Liu, Yuxuan Wang, Bo Zheng, and Ting Liu. 2018. Towards better ud parsing: Deep contextualized word embeddings, ensemble, and treebank concatenation. In *Proceedings of the CoNLL 2018 Shared Task: Multilingual Parsing from Raw Text to Universal Dependencies*.

Danqi Chen and Christopher Manning. 2014. A fast and accurate dependency parser using neural networks. In *Proceedings of the 2014 Conference on Empirical Methods in Natural Language Processing (EMNLP)*, pages 740–750, Doha, Qatar. Association for Computational Linguistics.

Jacob Devlin, Ming-Wei Chang, Kenton Lee, and Kristina Toutanova. 2019. BERT: Pre-training of deep bidirectional transformers for language understanding. In *Proceedings of the 2019 Conference of the North American Chapter of the Association for Computational Linguistics: Human Language Technologies, Volume 1 (Long and Short Papers)*, pages 4171–4186, Minneapolis, Minnesota. Association for Computational Linguistics.

Jimmy Ba Diederik P. Kingma. 2015. Adam: A method for stochastic optimization. In *Proceedings of the 3rd International Conference for Learning Representations*.

Timothy Dozat and Christopher D. Manning. 2017. Deep biaffine attention for neural dependency parsing. In *Proceedings of the 5th International Conference on Learning Representations*.

Xavier Glorot and Yoshua Bengio. 2010. Understanding the difficulty of training deep feedforward neural networks. In *Proceedings of the thirteenth international conference on artificial intelligence and statistics*, pages 249–256.

Jeremy Howard and Sebastian Ruder. 2018. Universal language model fine-tuning for text classification. In *Proceedings of the 56th Annual Meeting of the Association for Computational Linguistics (Volume 1:*

Long Papers), pages 328–339, Melbourne, Australia. Association for Computational Linguistics.

Naman Jain, Karan Singla, Aniruddha Tammewar, and Sambhav Jain. 2012. Two-stage approach for Hindi dependency parsing using MaltParser. In *Proceedings of the Workshop on Machine Translation and Parsing in Indian Languages*, pages 163–170, Mumbai, India. The COLING 2012 Organizing Committee.

Silpa Kanneganti, Himani Chaudhry, and Dipti Misra Sharma. 2016. Comparative error analysis of parser outputs on telugu dependency treebank. In *International Conference on Intelligent Text Processing and Computational Linguistics*, pages 397–408. Springer.

Silpa Kanneganti, Vandan Mujadia, and Dipti M Sharma. 2017. Classifier ensemble approach to dependency parsing. In *International Conference on Computational Linguistics and Intelligent Text Processing*, pages 158–169. Springer.

Sruthilaya Reddy Kesidi, Prudhvi Kosaraju, Meher Vijay, and Samar Husain. 2011. A constraint based hybrid dependency parser for telugu. *International Journal of Computational Linguistics and Applications*, 2(1-2):53–72.

Eliyahu Kiperwasser and Yoav Goldberg. 2016. Simple and accurate dependency parsing using bidirectional LSTM feature representations. *Transactions of the Association for Computational Linguistics*, 4:313–327.

Dan Kondratyuk and Milan Straka. 2019. 75 languages, 1 model: Parsing universal dependencies universally. In *Proceedings of the 2019 Conference on Empirical Methods in Natural Language Processing and the 9th International Joint Conference on Natural Language Processing (EMNLP-IJCNLP)*, pages 2779–2795, Hong Kong, China. Association for Computational Linguistics.

Prudhvi Kosaraju, Sruthilaya Reddy Kesidi, Vinay Bhargav Reddy Ainavolu, and Puneeth Kukkadapu. 2010. Experiments on indian language dependency parsing. *Proceedings of the ICON10 NLP Tools Contest: Indian Language Dependency Parsing*, pages 40–45.

Artur Kulmizev, Miryam de Lhoneux, Johannes Gontrum, Elena Fano, and Joakim Nivre. 2019. Deep contextualized word embeddings in transition-based and graph-based dependency parsing - a tale of two parsers revisited. In *Proceedings of the 2019 Conference on Empirical Methods in Natural Language Processing and the 9th International Joint Conference on Natural Language Processing (EMNLP-IJCNLP)*, pages 2755–2768, Hong Kong, China. Association for Computational Linguistics.

Xuezhe Ma, Zecong Hu, Jingzhou Liu, Nanyun Peng, Graham Neubig, and Eduard Hovy. 2018. Stack-pointer networks for dependency parsing. In *Proceedings of the 56th Annual Meeting of the Association for Computational Linguistics (Volume 1: Long Papers)*, pages 1403–1414, Melbourne, Australia. Association for Computational Linguistics.

Joakim Nivre. 2004. Incrementality in deterministic dependency parsing. In *Proceedings of the Workshop on Incremental Parsing: Bringing Engineering and Cognition Together*, pages 50–57, Barcelona, Spain. Association for Computational Linguistics.

Joakim Nivre. 2008. Algorithms for deterministic incremental dependency parsing. *Computational Linguistics*, 34(4):513–553.

Joakim Nivre, Johan Hall, and Jens Nilsson. 2006. MaltParser: A data-driven parser-generator for dependency parsing. In *Proceedings of the Fifth International Conference on Language Resources and Evaluation (LREC'06)*, Genoa, Italy. European Language Resources Association (ELRA).

Joakim Nivre, Marie-Catherine de Marneffe, Filip Ginter, Yoav Goldberg, Jan Hajič, Christopher D. Manning, Ryan McDonald, Slav Petrov, Sampo Pyysalo, Natalia Silveira, Reut Tsarfaty, and Daniel Zeman. 2016. Universal dependencies v1: A multilingual treebank collection. In *Proceedings of the Tenth International Conference on Language Resources and Evaluation (LREC 2016)*, pages 1659–1666, Portorož, Slovenia. European Language Resources Association (ELRA).

Matthew Peters, Mark Neumann, Mohit Iyyer, Matt Gardner, Christopher Clark, Kenton Lee, and Luke Zettlemoyer. 2018. Deep contextualized word representations. In *Proceedings of the 2018 Conference of the North American Chapter of the Association for Computational Linguistics: Human Language Technologies, Volume 1 (Long Papers)*, pages 2227–2237, New Orleans, Louisiana. Association for Computational Linguistics.

Rico Sennrich, Barry Haddow, and Alexandra Birch. 2016. Neural machine translation of rare words with subword units. In *Proceedings of the 54th Annual Meeting of the Association for Computational Linguistics (Volume 1: Long Papers)*, pages 1715–1725, Berlin, Germany. Association for Computational Linguistics.

Juhi Tandon and Dipti Misra Sharma. 2017. Unity in diversity: A unified parsing strategy for major indian languages. In *Proceedings of the Fourth International Conference on Dependency Linguistics (Depling 2017), September 18-20, 2017, Università di Pisa, Italy*, 139, pages 255–265. Linköping University Electronic Press.

Ian Tenney, Dipanjan Das, and Ellie Pavlick. 2019. BERT rediscovers the classical NLP pipeline. In *Proceedings of the 57th Annual Meeting of the Association for Computational Linguistics*, pages 4593–4601, Florence, Italy. Association for Computational Linguistics.

Pointwise Paraphrase Appraisal is Potentially Problematic

Hannah Chen, Yangfeng Ji, David Evans
Department of Computer Science
University of Virginia
Charlottesville, VA 22904
{yc4dx, yangfeng, evans}@virginia.edu

Abstract

The prevailing approach for training and evaluating paraphrase identification models is constructed as a binary classification problem: the model is given a pair of sentences, and is judged by how accurately it classifies pairs as either paraphrases or non-paraphrases. This pointwise-based evaluation method does not match well the objective of most real world applications, so the goal of our work is to understand how models which perform well under pointwise evaluation may fail in practice and find better methods for evaluating paraphrase identification models. As a first step towards that goal, we show that although the standard way of fine-tuning BERT for paraphrase identification by pairing two sentences as one sequence results in a model with state-of-the-art performance, that model may perform poorly on simple tasks like identifying pairs with two identical sentences. Moreover, we show that these models may even predict a pair of randomly-selected sentences with higher paraphrase score than a pair of identical ones.

1 Introduction

Paraphrase identification is a well-studied sentence pair modeling task that refers to the problem of determining whether two sentences are semantically equivalent. Detecting paraphrases can be very useful for many NLP applications such as machine translation (MT), question answering (QA), and information retrieval (IR). In a QA system, we would like to find the most probable question paraphrases from a database of question answer pairs for a given input question (Rinaldi et al., 2003; Dong et al., 2017). In a MT model, we would like to obtain the best translation by comparing the target sentence to a list of translated sentences. Even though pretrained language models have reached state-of-the-art performance on paraphrase identification tasks, the current problem setup is insufficient to produce models with consistent and robust performance on unseen samples and real world problems.

The typical current problem setup for paraphrase identification is different from intended uses in real world applications. They often involve finding best paraphrases from a group of documents given a particular query, rather than just determining whether two sentences are paraphrases of each other. Besides, getting the order and identifying the most relevant documents is usually more important than getting the binary decision of a pair of sentences (Zuccon et al., 2012). However, to make the task simpler, current methods and existing datasets such as Quora Question Pairs (QQP) (Iyer et al., 2017) and Microsoft Research Paraphrase Corpus (MRPC) (Lan et al., 2017) are all framed as a binary classification problem at the sentence pair level.

Contributions As a first step to improve the way paraphrase identification is evaluated for ranking tasks, we analyze some of the anomalies found in the current pointwise task setting. We first demonstrate the standard way of fine-tuning BERT for pointwise paraphrase evaluation makes the model sometimes fails on simple problems including recognizing two identical sentences and reversing the order of two sentences in a pair (Section 3). We find that it performs worse than a bag-of-words model due to its asymmetrical model architecture. Lastly, we show that the model may fail to capture the correct relative order of two sentence pairs using the pointwise approach, sometimes even predicting a pair of random sentences with a higher paraphrase score than a pair of identical ones (Section 4).

2 Background

This section provides background on the paraphrase identification task, evaluation methods, and the datasets and models we use in our experiments.

150

Proceedings of the 58th Annual Meeting of the Association for Computational Linguistics: Student Research Workshop, pages 150–155
July 5 - July 10, 2020. ©2020 Association for Computational Linguistics

2.1 Paraphrase Identification

We consider the general definition of paraphrase as sentences having the same meaning. In addition, paraphrase requires a symmetric relation. Paraphrase identification originates from the real-world applications such as machine translation (Dolan et al., 2004; Quirk et al., 2004) and document summarization (Barzilay and McKeown, 2001), where an essential task is to evaluate the semantic relatedness of translated sentences or generated texts.

2.2 Evaluation Methods

The current problem setting for paraphrase identification is similar to the pointwise method for learning-to-rank problems in information retrieval (Li, 2011). There are three types of approaches to solve learning-to-rank: pointwise, pairwise, and listwise (Liu, 2009). The *pointwise* approach learns to predict a binary relevance judgement for a single document given a specific query. It retrieves the most relevant document by computing the relevance score between each candidate document and the query and returning the document with the maximum score. The *pairwise* approach learns to predict the relative order of a pair of documents, (d_1, d_2), for a given query q. This is closer to the nature of ranking than the pointwise approach. However, both the pointwise and pairwise approaches neglect the fact that some documents are related to the same query. The *listwise* approach directly optimizes the model on the permutations of a list of documents $D = \{d_1, d_2, ..., d_n\}$ (Cao et al., 2007), and hence it most closely matches the objective of ranking.

2.3 Datasets

For our experiments, we use four datasets designed for evaluating paraphrase identification models.

Quora Question Pairs (QQP) consists of 400k question pairs from Quora (Iyer et al., 2017). The goal is to reduce the number of duplicate questions on the platform. Each question pair is either labeled as duplicate or non-duplicate. Recently, it has been shown to have selection bias, where models can simply rely on the frequency of the sentences or the intersection of the neighbor sentences to make predictions (Zhang et al., 2019a).

Paraphrase Adversaries from Word Scrambling (PAWS) contains two datasets constructed from Wikipedia and QQP (Zhang et al., 2019b). To

Dataset	BERT		BOW	
	Acc	F1	Acc	F1
QQP	90.10	86.7	64.75	51.56
QQP+PAWS$_{QQP}$	90.69	87.48	64.13	51.28
MRPC	83.65	87.97	68.12	79.45
Twitter URL	89.98	76.75	84.32	50.44

Table 1: Model accuracy and F1 scores trained on different datasets. Both metrics are scaled by 100. QQP + PAWS$_{QQP}$ indicates models are trained and evaluated on both datasets.

compare with the original QQP dataset, we only tested PAWS$_{QQP}$. The sentence pairs are created by swapping words that have the same part-of-speech or named entity tags to construct higher lexical overlap sentences. The training set contains 11,988 sentence pairs, and the testing set contains 667.

Microsoft Research Paraphrase Corpus (MRPC) contains 5801 sentence pairs extracted from online news articles (Dolan and Brockett, 2005). The sentence pairs are created with very similar syntactic features and high *n*-gram overlap causing the model to make skewed decisions based on these shallow features (Das and Smith, 2009).

Twitter URL Paraphrase Corpus is extracted from tweets posted by 22 English news accounts on Twitter (Lan et al., 2017). Relevant tweets are paired up based on the same embedded URLs, and each pair is then labeled by 6 human annotators. After discarding sentence pairs with neutral decisions (3 out of 6 annotators labeled it as paraphrase), the dataset consists of 42k sentence pairs for training and 9k pairs for testing.

2.4 Models

We fine-tuned the BERT$_{BASE}$ model on different paraphrase datasets with the default configuration (Devlin et al., 2018). We also implemented early stopping during the training process. For baseline comparison, we trained a bag-of-words (BOW) model with unigram and bigram encodings. The model makes predictions based on the consine similarity between the encodings of the two sentences. A consine similarity value above 0.5 is considered a paraphrase. The performance of both models for each task is shown in Table 1.

We include the results for testing QQP model on its adversarial set, PAWS$_{QQP}$, in Table 2, and it shows BERT performing as poorly as BOW of this

Models	QQP → PAWS$_{QQP}$	
	Acc	F1
BERT	32.94	42.68
BOW	28.21	44.01

Table 2: Model accuracy and F1 score tested in the adversarial setting, where models are trained on QQP and evaluated on PAWS$_{QQP}$ development set.

dataset. We also report the results of models that trained and tested on a concatenated set of QQP and PAWS$_{QQP}$ in Table 1.

3 Asymmetry

For semantic matching tasks, the BERT paraphrase identification model considers two sentences (s_1, s_2) as a single sequence by concatenating them with a separator token. However, due to this asymmetrical approach, the sequence representations before the final classification layer would be entirely different if we permute the order of the two input sentences. We explore two implications of this method for identifying paraphrases: sensitivity to input order (Section 3.1) and possibility of considering identical sentences non-paraphrases (Section 3.2).

3.1 Sensitivity to Sentence Order

In the original datasets, each sentence pair is only concatenated in one way as (s_1, s_2) and a label y will be predicted by the model. We constructed new sentence pairs in the reverse order as (s_2, s_1), and tested the model on these sentence pairs and got their predicted labels y'. To find out how much it would affect the prediction results, we computed the ratio of sentence pairs that are predicted with a different label $(y \neq y')$. The results for BERT and BOW models are shown in the second and third column of Table 3.

In normal setting (model is trained and evaluated on the the same dataset), there are more than 3% of sentence pairs that are predicted with an opposite label by BERT. The ratio decreases on PAWS$_{QQP}$, but it increases when the model includes adversarial examples in the training data. The percentages are even higher on MRPC and Twitter corpus. BOW, trivially, has zero disagreement since the order does not effect the bag-of-words model.

We reproduced the same experiment in section 3.1 on the RoBERTa$_{BASE}$ model (Liu et al., 2019), and found that the model also has inherent

asymmetry issue as BERT. The ratio of sentence pairs from the QQP development set with opposite labels is around 4.7% (But it performs well on identifying identical sentences with an error rate less than 1%). We further tried fine-tuning BERT on the augmented QQP dataset that includes sentence pairs in both original and reverse order. Although the ratio of sentence pairs with opposite predicted labels decreases about half, the asymmetrical issue is not completely eliminated. These results suggest that these pre-trained language model do not really understand the symmetric relation within paraphrases. One possible reason is combining two sentences as a single input encourages the model to learn paraphrase as an asymmetric relation.

Datasets	Reverse Order		Identical	
	BERT	BOW	BERT	BOW
QQP→QQP	3.70	0.0	2.40	0.0
QQP→PAWS$_{QQP}$	2.66	0.0	7.36	0.0
QQP+PAWS$_{QQP}$	4.0	0.0	0.54	0.0
MRPC	8.46	0.0	0.0	0.0
Twitter URL	7.08	0.0	0.0	0.0

Table 3: The percentage (%) of sentence pairs with asymmetrical prediction results. Reverse Order: sentence pairs predicted with different labels when reversing the order of the sentences. Identical: identical pairs that are predicted as non-paraphrases. (Please see Section 2.3 for actual data sizes.)

3.2 Inability to Recognize Identical Sentences

We would like to know if the asymmetrical structure also affect BERT's ability to identify identical sentences as paraphrases. We collected distinct sentences for each dataset and constructed a new set of sentence pairs by pairing each one with itself. Each pair is labeled as paraphrase. We calculated the ratio of pairs that are predicted as non-paraphrase by the model. As shown in Table 3, BERT trained on QQP recognizes 2.4% of identical pairs as non-paraphrases and the ratio increases about 5% when tested on PAWS$_{QQP}$. BOW trivially achieves perfect accuracy on pairs of identical sentences, since they have exactly the same bags of words.

The models trained on MRPC and Twitter corpus do recognize all the identical pairs as paraphrases. This may be the fact that many sentences appear in Twitter corpus multiple times pairing with different sentence each time. Thus, the model may better capture the difference between a variety of sentences. As for MRPC, many sentence pairs look

	QQP $\rightarrow$ QQP	QQP $\rightarrow$ PAWS$_{\text{QQP}}$	QQP + PAWS$_{\text{QQP}}$	MRPC	Twitter URL
Paraphrase $>$ Identical	30.51	41.88	21.27	4.18	1.76
Avg Score Difference	5.09	3.07	2.58	0.12	0.60
Non-paraphrase $>$ Identical	0.97	43.21	0.41	0.0	0.03
Avg Score Difference	6.28	2.53	3.01	0.0	1.52

Table 4: Percentage of paraphrase and non-paraphrase pairs with higher paraphrase score (%) than a pair of identical sentences given the same query sentence. Avg Score Differences: average score difference between paraphrase/non-paraphrase and identical pairs. (Only pairs with higher scores than the identical ones are included.)

quite alike, and hence the model can better identify small differences between sentences even though most sentences only appear once. Since PAWS$_{\text{QQP}}$ contains higher lexical overlap sentence pairs, the model trained on both QQP and PAWS$_{\text{QQP}}$ decreases the error rate to less than 1%.

We also fine-tuned a BERT model on the augmented QQP training set with identical sentence pairs, and it can correctly identify every identical pairs as paraphrases. This suggests that the amount of lexical overlap in the dataset would affect the model's ability to identify identical sentences.

4 Problems with Pointwise Evaluation

For a given query sentence, we assume that a well-generalized paraphrase identification model should output a higher paraphrase score to the query sentence itself than a randomly-selected sentence. However, models trained with pointwise evaluation cannot learn the relative order based on the degree of semantic equivalence. We test this by considering how often models recognize a random sentence as more similar than the query sentence itself, and looking at the distribution of paraphrase scores across a dataset.

4.1 Random Sentences

We augmented the original datasets with sentence pairs concatenated in opposite order, as in Section 3.1, and labeled them same as their original pairs. We then compared each sentence pair, (s, s'), to a pair of identical sentences, (s, s), given the same query sentence s. We fine-tuned BERT on each dataset to learn a paraphrase score function f, and computed the fraction of tests where a randomly-selected pair gets a higher paraphrase score than an identical pair, $f(s, s') > f(s, s)$. Table 4 shows the results, revealing a similar pattern as in Section 3.2. The model trained on QQP considers more than 30% of randomly-selected paraphrase sentence pairs to be more similar than the

identical pairs, but the ratio decreases to 21% when adding the adversarial set into training. For MRPC and Twitter URL corpus, less than 5% of paraphrase pairs are considered to be more similar than the identical pairs.

For a randomly-selected sentence pair, (s, s'), and a pair of identical sentences, (s, s), given the same query s sentence, we computed the score difference as $f(s, s') - f(s, s)$. The distributions of the score differences are shown in Figure 1a. We filtered out the pairs that have lower paraphrase score than the identical pairs, and report the average score difference in Table 4. In Figure 1a, the model trained on QQP has the largest score difference between paraphrase and identical pairs. After augmenting the training set with PAWS$_{\text{QQP}}$, the right tail of the distribution for paraphrase pairs diminishes. This indicates that the model considers fewer non-identical sentences as more similar to the query sentence than itself.

4.2 Paraphrase Score Distribution

To better understand how the scores are distributed, we plot the histograms of paraphrase score for random, paraphrase, non-paraphrase, and identical sentence pairs in Figure 1b. In the normal setting, there are two peaks in the distributions of randomly-selected pairs since they include both paraphrase and non-paraphrase pairs. On the other hand, the sentence pairs from PAWS$_{\text{QQP}}$ all seem very similar to the model. The distributions clearly show the model cannot distinguish them. Compared with the distribution for the Twitter corpus, the distribution of paraphrase pairs from QQP is more spread out, and it has slightly larger gap between the distribution of paraphrase and identical pairs.

5 Discussion

Defining Paraphrases. Our experiments assume that the "best" paraphrase for a given sentence s

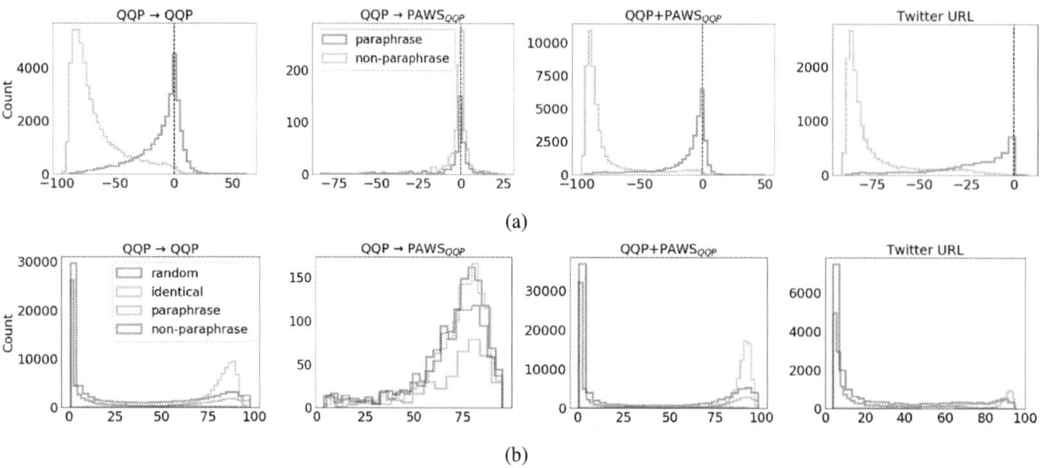

Figure 1: Histograms of (a) the score difference between randomly-selected and identical pairs and (b) paraphrase score for sentence pairs. Randomly-selected pairs contain the sentence pairs their original and reverse order. (We do not include the plot for MRPC since most paraphrase pairs from the dataset look alike, and it is hard to distinguish the distributions from the graph.)

is s itself. This assumes an equivalent in meaning definition of paraphrase, but other definitions may be appropriate. Bhagat and Hovy (2013) defined paraphrases as "sentences that convey the same meaning using different wording". By this definition, identical sentences are not paraphrases. Of course, we do not need a complex model to identify identical sentences when a simple equality test will do. However, when considering paraphrase detection as a test for how well language models can understand meaning, it would be counterproductive to consider identical sentences non-paraphrases, and require a trivial modification to consider them perfect paraphrases. Thus, we would expect a model to be able to identify sentence pairs with the same meaning as paraphrases regardless of whether they are the same in their surface forms.

Our experiments also assume that the paraphrase relationship should be symmetrical. This is consistent with the notion that the paraphrase identification task is meant to identify sentences with similar meaning, but not consistent with the purpose of many uses of paraphrase identification (e.g., in some real world question retrieval tasks, finding questions that contain the query, or that have the opposite meaning, would still be useful). This suggests the importance of a clear notion of what a paraphrase is, in both constructing test datasets and in determining how a given application can use a paraphrase detection model.

Selection Bias in the Pointwise Setting. Previ-

ous studies have addressed the problem of selection bias when constructing the task as a pointwise learning problem (Wang et al., 2016; Zadrozny, 2004). Datasets tend to have inconsistent frequency of sentences causing the model biased towards the dominating sentences. For instance, we found that some sentences from the Twitter corpus are repeated almost a hundred times as the first input sentence. This is part of the reason that the model gets more asymmetrical prediction results for sentences in reverse order (Table 3).

6 Conclusion

Although the state-of-art paraphrase identification models can achieve impressive performance under the pointwise evaluation method, they cannot handle real-world problems and unseen data well and even have worse results than a BOW model on simple tasks. We show that the asymmetry in BERT can produce inconsistent prediction results when reversing the order of the two sentences. We examined the relation of semantic equivalence learned by models trained with pointwise approach, and found that they may consider a random sentence as more similar to the query sentence itself. This suggests future work to reconsider how to match the training and evaluation to the actual objective of downstream applications, and thus create more reliable evaluation metrics and benchmarks.

References

Regina Barzilay and Kathleen McKeown. 2001. Extracting paraphrases from a parallel corpus. In *Proceedings of the 39th annual meeting of the Association for Computational Linguistics*, pages 50–57.

Rahul Bhagat and Eduard Hovy. 2013. What is a paraphrase? *Computational Linguistics*, 39(3):463–472.

Zhe Cao, Tao Qin, Tie-Yan Liu, Ming-Feng Tsai, and Hang Li. 2007. Learning to rank: From pairwise approach to listwise approach. In *Proceedings of the 24th International Conference on Machine Learning*, ICML 07, page 129136, New York, NY, USA. Association for Computing Machinery.

Dipanjan Das and Noah Smith. 2009. Paraphrase identification as probabilistic quasi-synchronous recognition. In *Proceedings of the Joint Conference of the 47th Annual Meeting of the ACL and the 4th International Joint Conference on Natural Language Processing of the AFNLP*, pages 468–476. Association for Computational Linguistics.

Jacob Devlin, Ming-Wei Chang, Kenton Lee, and Kristina Toutanova. 2018. BERT: pre-training of deep bidirectional transformers for language understanding. *CoRR*, abs/1810.04805.

Bill Dolan and Chris Brockett. 2005. Automatically constructing a corpus of sentential paraphrases. In *Third International Workshop on Paraphrasing (IWP2005)*. Asia Federation of Natural Language Processing.

Bill Dolan, Chris Quirk, and Chris Brockett. 2004. Unsupervised construction of large paraphrase corpora: Exploiting massively parallel news sources. In *Proceedings of the 20th International Conference on Computational Linguistics*, COLING 04, page 350es, USA. Association for Computational Linguistics.

Li Dong, Jonathan Mallinson, Siva Reddy, and Mirella Lapata. 2017. Learning to paraphrase for question answering. In *Proceedings of the 2017 Conference on Empirical Methods in Natural Language Processing*, pages 875–886, Copenhagen, Denmark. Association for Computational Linguistics.

Shankar Iyer, Nikhil Dandekar, and Kornl Csernai. 2017. First quora dataset release: Question pairs. https://www.quora.com/q/quoradata/First-Quora-Dataset-Release-Question-Pairs.

Wuwei Lan, Siyu Qiu, Hua He, and Wei Xu. 2017. A continuously growing dataset of sentential paraphrases. *CoRR*, abs/1708.00391.

Hang Li. 2011. A short introduction to learning to rank. *IEICE Transactions*, 94-D:1854–1862.

Tie-Yan Liu. 2009. Learning to rank for information retrieval. *Found. Trends Inf. Retr.*, 3(3):225331.

Yinhan Liu, Myle Ott, Naman Goyal, Jingfei Du, Mandar Joshi, Danqi Chen, Omer Levy, Mike Lewis, Luke Zettlemoyer, and Veselin Stoyanov. 2019. Roberta: A robustly optimized BERT pretraining approach. *CoRR*, abs/1907.11692.

Chris Quirk, Chris Brockett, and William B Dolan. 2004. Monolingual machine translation for paraphrase generation. In *Proceedings of the 2004 conference on empirical methods in natural language processing*, pages 142–149.

Fabio Rinaldi, James Dowdall, Kaarel Kaljurand, Michael Hess, and Diego Mollá. 2003. Exploiting paraphrases in a question answering system. In *Proceedings of the Second International Workshop on Paraphrasing - Volume 16*, PARAPHRASE 03, page 2532, USA. Association for Computational Linguistics.

Xuanhui Wang, Michael Bendersky, Donald Metzler, and Marc Najork. 2016. Learning to rank with selection bias in personal search. In *Proceedings of the 39th International ACM SIGIR Conference on Research and Development in Information Retrieval*, SIGIR 16, page 115124, New York, NY, USA. Association for Computing Machinery.

Bianca Zadrozny. 2004. Learning and evaluating classifiers under sample selection bias. In *Proceedings of the Twenty-First International Conference on Machine Learning*, ICML 04, page 114, New York, NY, USA. Association for Computing Machinery.

Guanhua Zhang, Bing Bai, Jian Liang, Kun Bai, Shiyu Chang, Mo Yu, Conghui Zhu, and Tiejun Zhao. 2019a. Selection bias explorations and debias methods for natural language sentence matching datasets. *CoRR*, abs/1905.06221.

Yuan Zhang, Jason Baldridge, and Luheng He. 2019b. PAWS: paraphrase adversaries from word scrambling. *CoRR*, abs/1904.01130.

Guido Zuccon, Leif Azzopardi, Dell Zhang, and Jun Wang. 2012. Top-k retrieval using facility location analysis. In *Proceedings of the 34th European Conference on Advances in Information Retrieval*, ECIR12, page 305316, Berlin, Heidelberg. Springer-Verlag.

Paper #21 spanning pages 156–161 was removed from the proceedings.

Efficient Neural Machine Translation for Low-Resource Languages via Exploiting Related Languages

Vikrant Goyal, Sourav Kumar, Dipti Misra Sharma
Language Technologies Research Center (LTRC)
IIIT Hyderabad, India
{vikrant.goyal, sourav.kumar}@research.iiit.ac.in, dipti@iiit.ac.in

Abstract

A large percentage of the world's population speaks a language of the Indian subcontinent, comprising languages from both Indo-Aryan (e.g. Hindi, Punjabi, Gujarati, etc.) and Dravidian (e.g. Tamil, Telugu, Malayalam, etc.) families. A universal characteristic of Indian languages is their complex morphology, which, when combined with the general lack of sufficient quantities of high-quality parallel data, can make developing machine translation (MT) systems for these languages difficult. Neural Machine Translation (NMT) is a rapidly advancing MT paradigm and has shown promising results for many language pairs, especially in large training data scenarios. Since the condition of large parallel corpora is not met for Indian-English language pairs, we present our efforts towards building efficient NMT systems between Indian languages (specifically Indo-Aryan languages) and English via efficiently exploiting parallel data from the related languages. We propose a technique called Unified Transliteration and Subword Segmentation to leverage language similarity while exploiting parallel data from related language pairs. We also propose a Multilingual Transfer Learning technique to leverage parallel data from multiple related languages to assist translation for low-resource language pair of interest. Our experiments demonstrate an overall average improvement of 5 BLEU points over the standard Transformer-based NMT baselines.

1 Introduction

In recent years, Neural Machine Translation (Luong et al., 2015; Bahdanau et al., 2014; Johnson et al., 2017; Wu et al., 2017; Vaswani et al., 2017) (NMT) has become the most prominent approach to Machine Translation (MT) due to its simplicity, generality and effectiveness. In NMT, a single neural network often consisting of an encoder and a decoder is used to directly maximize the conditional probabilities of target sentences given the source sentences in an end-to-end paradigm. NMT models have been shown to surpass the performance of previously dominant statistical machine translation (SMT) (Koehn, 2009) on many well-established translation tasks.

However, in order to reach high accuracies, NMT systems tend to require very large parallel training corpora (Koehn and Knowles, 2017). As a matter of fact, such corpora are not yet available for many language pairs. Indian languages are not an exception to this; however they are extremely diverse, belonging to different language families, employing various scripts and spanning a multitude of dialects. The majority of Indian languages are morphologically rich and depict unique characteristics, which are significantly different from languages such as English.

Since NMT models learn poorly from small corpora, building effective NMT systems for low-resource languages (e.g. Indian languages) becomes a primary challenge. The bulk of research on low-resource NMT has focused on exploiting monolingual data, or parallel data involving other language pairs. Some of the most well-known methods to improve NMT models with monolingual data range from backtranslation (Sennrich et al., 2016), dual learning (He et al., 2016) to Unsupervised MT (Artetxe et al., 2017; Lample et al., 2017, 2018). Similarly, parallel data from other languages can be exploited to either pretrain the network or jointly learn the representations (Zoph et al., 2016; Firat et al., 2017; Johnson et al., 2017; Kocmi and Bojar, 2018).

Currently, Transfer Learning (TL) is being widely used for low-resource language translation because it is one of the vital directions for addressing the data sparsity problem in low-resource NMT (Zoph et al., 2016; Nguyen and Chiang, 2017; Pass-

Proceedings of the 58th Annual Meeting of the Association for Computational Linguistics: Student Research Workshop, pages 162–168
July 5 - July 10, 2020. ©2020 Association for Computational Linguistics

ban et al., 2017; Kocmi and Bojar, 2018). However, most of the existing approaches that take advantage of transfer learning have a major limitation: they do not exploit multiple languages together and in an efficient manner. The idea presented by Zoph et al. (2016) may have the shortcoming of exploiting only one high-resource model (parent) at a time to optimize the low-resource model (child). Actually, the use of highly related multiple language pairs might help to increase the translation quality of the child model. The original Transfer Learning method (Zoph et al., 2016) also makes no assumption about the relatedness of the parent and child languages. Multilingual NMT (Firat et al., 2017; Johnson et al., 2017) approaches which also use parallel data from different languages to improve the translation quality of NMT models does not exploit language relatedness either.

In this paper, we present our efforts towards building efficient NMT systems between Indian languages (specifically Indo-Aryan languages) and English by exploiting parallel data from related languages. We aim to deal with the problem of how to make full use of these corpora of highly related languages, to increase the translation quality of low-resource languages. To this end, we introduce two simple and yet effective approaches:

- Multilingual Transfer Learning: to enable the low-resource languages (child model) to exploit parallel data from multiple related languages which may or may not be high-resourced, and

- Unified Transliteration and Subword Segmentation: to exploit the language similarity between the related language pairs.

Experiments show that our approaches are effective and significantly outperform the state-of-the-art Transformer (Johnson et al., 2017) baseline. Our proposed approach of Multilingual Transfer Learning also significantly outperforms simple Transfer Learning (Zoph et al., 2016) approach, where NMT models are also built using Unified Transliteration and Subword Segmentation approach.

2 Methodology

The core idea of our method is to extend the Multilingual Learning (Johnson et al., 2017) and Transfer Learning (Zoph et al., 2016) approaches to effectively exploit parallel data from multiple related languages. In Section 2.2, we explain our Unified Transliteration and Subword Segmentation technique to exploit language relatedness among the parallel data of related languages. Sections 2.3 and 2.4 describe our modified Multilingual Learning and Transfer Learning techniques for NMT. In Section 2.5, we describe our Multilingual Transfer Learning approach.

2.1 Language Relatedness

In this work, we experiment on Indo-Aryan languages specifically Hindi, Punjabi, Gujarati, Marathi and Bengali. Being from one language family, these languages are closely related to each other and share many features. These languages are morphologically rich and depict unique characteristics, which are significantly different from languages such as English. Some of these characteristics are the relatively free word-order with a tendency towards the Subject-Object-Verb (SOV) construction, a high degree of inflection, usage of reduplication and conjunct verbs. These languages share many common words which have the same root and meaning. They use different Indic scripts derived from the ancient Brahmi script, but correspondences can be established between equivalent characters across scripts.

2.2 Unified Transliteration and Subword Segmentation

Unlike the original Transfer Learning (Zoph et al., 2016) and the Multilingual Neural MT (Johnson et al., 2017) methods which do not exploit any language relatedness, the basic idea of this approach is to exploit the relationship between the related language lexicons while using parallel data from related languages to assist with translation of low-resource languages. To do so, we find a representation of the data that ensures a sufficient overlap between the vocabularies of the related languages.

Since the languages involved in the models have different orthographies, the data processing should help to map them into a common orthography but here we take a minimalist approach; we transliterate all the Indian languages (Hindi, Gujarati, Bengali, Marathi and Punjabi) into a common Devanagari script to share the same surface form. This unified transliteration is a string homomorphism, replacing characters in all the languages mentioned above with Hindi characters (script conversion to Devanagari) or consonant clusters independent of context.

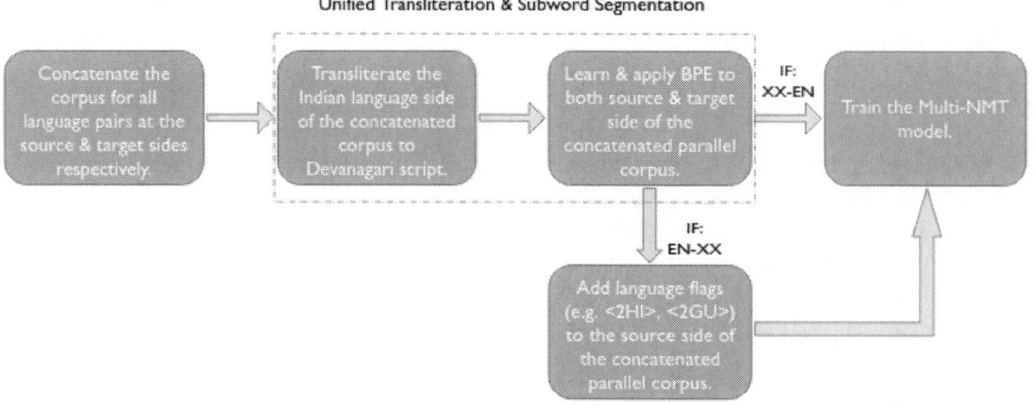

Figure 1: Our pipeline for building Multilingual NMT models for Indian languages.

Now, to increase the overlap between the vocabularies of the languages used in a model, which are already transliterated into a common script and consequently share the same surface form, we use Byte Pair Encoding (BPE) (Sennrich et al., 2015) to break words into subwords. For the BPE merge rules to not only find the common subwords between two related languages but also ensure consistency between source and target segmentation among each language pair, we learn the rules from the union of source and target data of all the language pairs involved in the model construction. The rules are then used to segment the corpora. It is important to note that this results in a single vocabulary, used for both the source and target languages in all the language pairs.

2.3 Multilingual Learning for NMT

The objective of Multilingual Learning for NMT is to construct a single model for translating to and from multiple languages. Early work in multilingual NMT utilizes a separate encoder, decoder and an attention mechanism to support the translation of either one-to-many or many-to-one language directions. Firat et al. (2017) introduced a many-to-many system, which still relied upon separate encoder-decoder setup with a shared attention mechanism. In a simplified manner and yet delivering better performance, Johnson et al. (2017) introduced a "language flag"-based approach that shares the attention mechanism and a single encoder-decoder network to enable multilingual models. A language flag or token is prepended to the input sequence to indicate which direction to translate in.

The decoder learns to generate the target given this input.

However, the Multilingual NMT approaches do not consider the relatedness of the languages or how many shared words there are among the different source and target languages. Mainly, they aim at exploiting many different source and target languages rather than focusing on similarities between many languages that are used in the training and the languages that is used in testing. Accordingly, we modify the Multilingual NMT approach (Johnson et al., 2017) with Unified Transliteration and Subword segmentation technique to exploit the language relatedness. We experiment with this modified approach in our work on efficient NMT for Indian languages.

2.4 Transfer Learning for NMT

Zoph et al. (2016) proposed how Transfer Learning between two NMT models can improve a low-resource NMT task. In their approach, a language pair with a relatively large amount of parallel data is first utilized to train a parent model in a phase known as "pretraining". Then the encoder-decoder parameters are transferred to initialize a child model for a low-resource language pair of interest. After initializing, the model enters the "fine-tuning" stage, where the child model is fine-tuned on the low-resource language pair. This enables the inductive transfer of knowledge from the parent model to the child model. This approach does not make any assumption between the relatedness of the parent and child language pair. However, in our work we use a relatively high-resource lan-

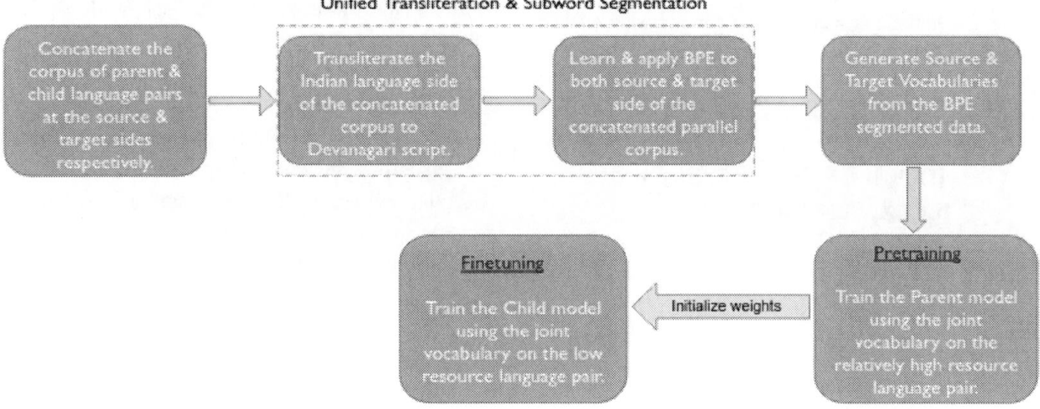

Figure 2: Our pipeline for building Transfer Learning models for Indian languages.

guage pair as our parent model which has similar syntactic and morphological properties as the child language pair. We further exploit the language relatedness of parent and child language pairs via our Unified Transliteration and Subword Segmentation technique. We experiment with this modified Transfer Learning technique and demonstrate huge BLEU improvements over the Transformer NMT baseline for low-resource Indian languages.

2.5 Multilingual Transfer Learning for NMT

In the normal Transfer Learning (Zoph et al., 2016) approach for NMT, the parent model is trained on a single high-resource language pair which may or may not be related to the child language pair of interest. Passban et al. (2017) presented a double transfer learning technique which first trains a parent model on a single high-resource language pair, then initializes the next parent model on the same single high-resource language pair but with different domain and corpus size, and finally fine-tunes it on the child task. To the best of our knowledge, previous Transfer Learning approaches do not exploit parallel data from multiple languages. However, learning from multiple languages can result in better knowledge transfer.

Therefore, in this work, we propose a new Transfer Learning approach called as Multilingual Transfer Learning to enable the low-resource languages to efficiently learn from multiple related languages which may or may not be high-resourced. In this approach, the parent model is a Multilingual NMT model of related languages and also the child language pair. This Multilingual parent NMT model

also uses the Unified Transliteration and Subword Segmentation technique to exploit language relatedness more efficiently as discussed in Section 2.2. After pretraining the parent model, the child model is initialyzed with parent model parameters and is then fine-tuned on the low-resource language pair of interest.

The proposed approach may deliver better results than Multilingual NMT and Transfer Learning because adding more languages into one model may result in better knowledge transfer (i.e multilingual NMT) but it can also result in ambiguities between languages at the inference time. Accordingly, a multilingual NMT model fine-tuned on the language pair of interest can potentially remove all the inconsistencies at the inference time.

3 Experimental Settings

3.1 Dataset

In our experiments, we use the IIT-Bombay (Kunchukuttan et al., 2017) parallel data for Hindi-English. The training corpus consists of data from mixed domains. We use the multilingual ILCI (Indian Language Corpora Initiative) corpus (Jha, 2010), which contains roughly 50,000 parallel sentences for each of the Indian languages (Gujarati, Punjabi, Marathi, Bengali) and also for English. The ILCI data is from tourism and health domains. For every XX-EN language pair (where XX is Gujarati, Marathi, Bengali or Punjabi), the English side of the data is same because of the multilingual nature of the corpus. We check and clean the ILCI corpus manually as it contains a lot of misalignments and mistranslations.

Table 1: Statistics of our cleaned and processed parallel data, where XX is Gujarati, Marathi, Bengali or Punjabi

Dataset	Sentences
IITB HI-EN Train	1,528,631
ILCI XX-EN Train	46,490
ILCI XX-EN Test	2,000
ILCI XX-EN Dev	500

3.2 Data Processing

We use the Moses (Koehn et al., 2007) toolkit[1] for tokenization and cleaning the English side of the data. All the Indian language data is first normalized with the Indic NLP library[2] followed by tokenization with the same library. As our preprocessing step, we remove all sentences of length greater than 80 words from our training corpus and lowercase the English side of the data. In all cases, we use BPE segmentation with 16k merge operations as described in Section 2.2.

3.3 Training Details

For all of our experiments, we use the OpenNMT-py (Klein et al., 2018) toolkit[3]. We use the Transformer model with 6 layers in both the encoder and decoder, each with 512 hidden units. The word embedding size is set to 512 with 8 heads. The training is done in batches of maximum 4096 tokens at a time with dropout set to 0.3. We use the Adam (Kingma and Ba, 2014) optimizer to optimize model parameters. We validate the model every 5,000 steps via BLEU (Papineni et al., 2002) and perplexity on the development set. We train all our NMT models for 150k steps except for fine-tuning which is done for 10k steps. After translation at the test time, we rejoin the translated BPE segments and convert the translated sentences back to their original language scripts. Finally, we evaluate the accuracy of our translation models using BLEU.

4 Results

We report the results of Multilingual Learning, Transfer Learning and Multilingual Transfer Learning for Gujarati-English, Bengali-English, Marathi-

English and Punjabi-English language pairs for both translation directions (XX-EN and EN-XX). Table 2 shows our main results for the Indian language to English (XX-EN) translation direction. Multilingual models for XX-EN language direction do not show any improvements. The reason for this might be the multiparallel nature of the ILCI data where each English sentence on the target side appears 4 times in the model, thereby creating ambiguities in the model. The transfer learning model built using Unified Transliteration and Subword Segmentation that was trained on the IITB HI-EN data and then fine-tuned on XX-EN data (see model no. 8 in Table 2) resulted in an average improvement of 5 BLEU points.

Table 3 shows our main results for the English to Indian language (EN-XX) translation direction. In this case, the multilingual model using all ILCI data shows significant improvements over the baseline, unlike in the XX-EN translation direction. The reason for this is that in the EN-XX direction, language flags are used on the source side which guides the decoder to which language the model translate in, whereas the same is not possible for the XX-EN direction as verified by our preliminary experiments. The other two multilingual models containing the IITB EN-HI data show performance degradation, potentially due to the mismatch between the size of the IITB EN-HI (1.5M sentences) and ILCI data (47k sentences). The transfer learning model that was trained on IITB EN-HI data and then fine-tuned on EN-XX data (see model no. 8 in Table 3) also resulted in an average improvement of 5 BLEU points.

In both translation directions, the multilingual models do not prove to be effective. Fine-tuning the multilingual models (multilingual transfer learning) on XX-EN or EN-XX data removes some ambiguities in the model and shows significant improvements compared to their simple multilingual model counterparts. The best performance (almost 5-6 BLEU improvements over the baseline) is achieved by fine-tuning the multilingual model (trained on IITB HI-EN or EN-HI data and all the ILCI data) on EN-XX or XX-EN outperforming all the NMT, Multilingual NMT and Transfer Learning baselines thus demonstrating the effectiveness of our technique.

[1] https://github.com/moses-smt/mosesdecoder
[2] https://anoopkunchukuttan.github.io/indic_nlp_library/
[3] https://github.com/OpenNMT/OpenNMT-py/

Table 2: BLEU scores of the contrastive experiments for Indian Language to English translation (XX to EN).

Model No.	Model Description	Gujarati	Bengali	Marathi	Punjabi
1	Baseline	28.37	22.40	25.29	30.51
2	Multilingual Model of all ILCI data	25.14	21.47	23.56	25.43
3	Multilingual Model of IITB HI-EN data & all ILCI data	28.62	22.71	26.90	29.46
4	Multilingual Model of IITB HI-EN data & ILCI data of XX-EN	29.18	23.93	27.15	30.54
5	Fine-tuning model no. 2 on XX-EN	26.83	22.72	25.36	27.12
6	Fine-tuning model no. 3 on XX-EN	**33.78 (+5.41)**	**27.55 (+5.15)**	**31.79 (+6.5)**	**34.70 (+4.19)**
7	Fine-tuning model no. 4 on XX-EN	33.72	27.40	31.80	34.68
8	Fine-tuning model pretrained on IITB HI-EN data on XX-EN	33.13	27.06	31.27	34.54

Table 3: BLEU scores of the contrastive experiments for English to Indian Language translation (EN to XX).

Model No.	Model Description	Gujarati	Bengali	Marathi	Punjabi
1	Baseline	20.67	16.59	15.13	25.20
2	Multilingual Model of all ILCI data	24.61	19.81	17.92	28.02
3	Multilingual Model of IITB EN-HI data & all ILCI data	20.63	16.51	15.05	21.76
4	Multilingual Model of IITB EN-HI data & ILCI data of EN-XX	14.30	6.38	8.88	14.54
5	Fine-tuning model no. 2 on EN-XX	24.75	20.25	18.75	28.16
6	Fine-tuning model no. 3 on EN-XX	**26.22 (+5.55)**	**21.62 (+5.03)**	**19.90 (+4.77)**	**30.27 (+5.07)**
7	Fine-tuning model no. 4 on EN-XX	25.52	20.45	19.77	29.53
8	Fine-tuning model pretrained on IITB EN-HI data on EN-XX	25.35	21.77	19.58	29.54

5 Conclusion & Future Work

In this paper, we explore effective methods to exploit parallel data from multiple related languages to improve the translation between Indian languages and English. Our results show that Multilingual Learning for translation between Indian Languages and English is not very effective given the set of data we have. However, the performance of multilingual models can easily be enhanced by fine-tuning them on the low-resource language pairs of interest. Our experiments show that using a Multilingual NMT model as a parent model (consisting of multiple language pairs with related languages either on the source side or on the target side) and fine-tuning it on the low-resource language pair of interest yields an overall average improvement of 5 BLEU points over a standard Transformer-based NMT baseline. Our proposed Multilingual Transfer Learning approach also outperforms the simple Transfer Learning approach by a significant amount. In future, we would like to work on effective techniques to exploit monolingual data and parallel data from other languages together to improve the translation of low-resource languages.

Acknowledgements

We would like to thank Prof. Andy Way for his valuable and detailed comments in improving the paper.

References

Mikel Artetxe, Gorka Labaka, Eneko Agirre, and Kyunghyun Cho. 2017. Unsupervised neural machine translation. *arXiv preprint arXiv:1710.11041*.

Dzmitry Bahdanau, Kyunghyun Cho, and Yoshua Bengio. 2014. Neural machine translation by jointly learning to align and translate. *arXiv preprint arXiv:1409.0473*.

Orhan Firat, Kyunghyun Cho, Baskaran Sankaran, Fatos T Yarman Vural, and Yoshua Bengio. 2017. Multi-way, multilingual neural machine translation. *Computer Speech and Language*, 45(C):236–252.

Di He, Yingce Xia, Tao Qin, Liwei Wang, Nenghai Yu, Tie-Yan Liu, and Wei-Ying Ma. 2016. Dual learning for machine translation. In *Advances in Neural Information Processing Systems*, pages 820–828.

Girish Nath Jha. 2010. The tdil program and the indian langauge corpora intitiative (ilci). In *LREC*.

Melvin Johnson, Mike Schuster, Quoc V Le, Maxim Krikun, Yonghui Wu, Zhifeng Chen, Nikhil Thorat, Fernanda Viégas, Martin Wattenberg, Greg Corrado, et al. 2017. Google's multilingual neural machine translation system: Enabling zero-shot translation. *Transactions of the Association for Computational Linguistics*, 5:339–351.

Diederik P Kingma and Jimmy Ba. 2014. Adam: A method for stochastic optimization. *arXiv preprint arXiv:1412.6980*.

Guillaume Klein, Yoon Kim, Yuntian Deng, Vincent Nguyen, Jean Senellart, and Alexander M Rush. 2018. Opennmt: Neural machine translation toolkit. *arXiv preprint arXiv:1805.11462*.

Tom Kocmi and Ondřej Bojar. 2018. Trivial transfer learning for low-resource neural machine translation. *arXiv preprint arXiv:1809.00357*.

Philipp Koehn. 2009. *Statistical machine translation*. Cambridge University Press.

Philipp Koehn, Hieu Hoang, Alexandra Birch, Chris Callison-Burch, Marcello Federico, Nicola Bertoldi, Brooke Cowan, Wade Shen, Christine Moran, Richard Zens, et al. 2007. Moses: Open source toolkit for statistical machine translation. In *Proceedings of the 45th annual meeting of the association for computational linguistics companion volume proceedings of the demo and poster sessions*, pages 177–180.

Philipp Koehn and Rebecca Knowles. 2017. Six challenges for neural machine translation. In *Proceedings of the First Workshop on Neural Machine Translation*, pages 28–39.

Anoop Kunchukuttan, Pratik Mehta, and Pushpak Bhattacharyya. 2017. The iit bombay english-hindi parallel corpus. *arXiv preprint arXiv:1710.02855*.

Guillaume Lample, Alexis Conneau, Ludovic Denoyer, and Marc'Aurelio Ranzato. 2017. Unsupervised machine translation using monolingual corpora only. *arXiv preprint arXiv:1711.00043*.

Guillaume Lample, Myle Ott, Alexis Conneau, Ludovic Denoyer, and Marc'Aurelio Ranzato. 2018. Phrase-based & neural unsupervised machine translation. *arXiv preprint arXiv:1804.07755*.

Minh-Thang Luong, Hieu Pham, and Christopher D Manning. 2015. Effective approaches to attention-based neural machine translation. *arXiv preprint arXiv:1508.04025*.

Toan Q Nguyen and David Chiang. 2017. Transfer learning across low-resource, related languages for neural machine translation. In *Proceedings of the Eighth International Joint Conference on Natural Language Processing (Volume 2: Short Papers)*, pages 296–301.

Kishore Papineni, Salim Roukos, Todd Ward, and Wei-Jing Zhu. 2002. Bleu: a method for automatic evaluation of machine translation. In *Proceedings of the 40th annual meeting on association for computational linguistics*, pages 311–318. Association for Computational Linguistics.

Peyman Passban, Qun Liu, and Andy Way. 2017. Translating low-resource languages by vocabulary adaptation from close counterparts. *ACM Transactions on Asian and Low-Resource Language Information Processing (TALLIP)*, 16(4):1–14.

Rico Sennrich, Barry Haddow, and Alexandra Birch. 2015. Neural machine translation of rare words with subword units. *arXiv preprint arXiv:1508.07909*.

Rico Sennrich, Barry Haddow, and Alexandra Birch. 2016. Improving neural machine translation models with monolingual data. In *Proceedings of the 54th Annual Meeting of the Association for Computational Linguistics (Volume 1: Long Papers)*, pages 86–96.

Ashish Vaswani, Noam Shazeer, Niki Parmar, Jakob Uszkoreit, Llion Jones, Aidan N Gomez, Łukasz Kaiser, and Illia Polosukhin. 2017. Attention is all you need. In *Advances in Neural Information Processing Systems*, pages 5998–6008.

Lijun Wu, Yingce Xia, Li Zhao, Fei Tian, Tao Qin, Jianhuang Lai, and Tie-Yan Liu. 2017. Adversarial neural machine translation. *arXiv preprint arXiv:1704.06933*.

Barret Zoph, Deniz Yuret, Jonathan May, and Kevin Knight. 2016. Transfer learning for low-resource neural machine translation. In *Proceedings of the 2016 Conference on Empirical Methods in Natural Language Processing*, pages 1568–1575.

Exploring Interpretability in Event Extraction: Multitask Learning of a Neural Event Classifier and an Explanation Decoder

[†]**Zheng Tang**, [‡]**Gustave Hahn-Powell**, [†]**Mihai Surdeanu**
[†]Department of Computer Science
[‡]Department of Linguistics
University of Arizona, Tucson, Arizona, USA
`{zhengtang, hahnpowell, msurdeanu}@email.arizona.edu`

Abstract

We propose an interpretable approach for event extraction that mitigates the tension between generalization and interpretability by jointly training for the two goals. Our approach uses an encoder-decoder architecture, which jointly trains a classifier for event extraction, and a rule decoder that generates syntactico-semantic rules that explain the decisions of the event classifier. We evaluate the proposed approach on three biomedical events and show that the decoder generates interpretable rules that serve as accurate explanations for the event classifier's decisions, and, importantly, that the joint training generally improves the performance of the event classifier. Lastly, we show that our approach can be used for semi-supervised learning, and that its performance improves when trained on automatically-labeled data generated by a rule-based system.

1 Introduction

Interpretability is a key requirement for machine learning (ML) in many domains, e.g., legal, medical, finance. In the words of (Ribeiro et al., 2016), "if users do not trust the model or a prediction, they will not use it." However, there is a tension between generalization and interpretability in deep learning, as interpretable models are often generated by "distilling" a model with good generalization, e.g., a deep learning one that relies on distributed representations, into models that are more interpretable but lose some generalization, e.g., linear models or decision trees (Craven and Shavlik, 1996; Ribeiro et al., 2016; Frosst and Hinton, 2017). Here, we argue that both generalization and interpretability are equally important. For example, in the medical space, a patient will likely reject a treatment recommended by an algorithm without an explanation. Closer to natural language processing (NLP), a statistical information extraction method that converts free text in a specific domain to structured knowledge should also provide human-understandable explanations of its extractions. This allows the subject matter expert to quality check such output without a deep knowledge of the underlying machinery, which is a necessity in successful inter-disciplinary NLP collaborations.

In this work, we propose an interpretable approach for event extraction (EE) that mitigates the tension between generalization and interpretability through multitask learning (MTL). Our approach uses an attention-based encoder to encode the input text and given entities of interest (e.g., proteins in the biomedical domain), and a decoder that jointly trains two tasks. The first task is event classification, which identifies which event applies for a given entity (e.g., phosphorylation). The second task decodes a rule in the Odin language (Valenzuela-Escárcega et al., 2018; Valenzuela-Escárcega et al., 2016), which explains the prediction of the classifier in a format that can be read and understood by human end users. An example of such a rule is shown in Figure 1. Importantly, both tasks share the same encoder, and are trained using a joint objective function.

Supporting earlier findings, we observe that joint training leads to performance improvements both within and across tasks. In our unique pairing of tasks, however, we are able to shed light on an opaque process by generating rules that provide an interpretable distillation of an event classifier's decisions.

The major contributions of this paper are:

(1) A simple neural architecture for EE that jointly learns to extract events and explain its decisions. While here we investigate event extraction, we believe this approach is applicable to many other information extraction tasks.

(2) We extend a subset of the BioNLP 2013 GENIA

Proceedings of the 58th Annual Meeting of the Association for Computational Linguistics: Student Research Workshop, pages 169–175
July 5 - July 10, 2020. ©2020 Association for Computational Linguistics

```
label:   Phosphorylation
pattern: |
  trigger =
    [lemma=/phosphorylation/ & !word=/(?i)^(de|auto)/]
  theme:Protein =
    prep_of appos? /nn|conj_(and|or)|cc/{,2}
```

Label(s) to assign to a match.
Lexical constraints on the event's predicate.
`argName:ArgType`, where `ArgType` indicates the semantic category expected for this argument.

Figure 1: An example of an event extraction rule in the Odin language that extracts phosphorylation events driven by a nominal trigger ("phosphorylation"). The event's sole argument or `theme` (the phosphorylated protein) is identified through both semantic constraints (its type must be `Protein`), and syntactic ones (it must be attached to the trigger through a certain syntactic dependency pattern: a `prep_of` followed by an optional (`?`) appositive (`appos`), followed by up to two (`{,2}`) other dependencies, e.g., nn). This rule would extract a `Phosphorylation(PKC)` event from the text "…which includes the phosphorylation of PKC by…".

event extraction (Kim et al., 2013) dataset with a set of rules designed to extract and explain three of the GENIA biomedical events: protein *phosphorylation*, *localization*, and *gene expression*. The result is a parallel dataset that aligns some of the GENIA event labels with rules that extract them. We release this dataset[1] for reproducibility.

(3) We train and evaluate our approach on this dataset and demonstrate that: (a) our approach achieves reasonable event classification performance, despite the fact that it uses no syntactic or part-of-speech information; (b) it decodes explanations with high accuracy, e.g., with a BLEU overlap score between the generated rules and hand-written rules of up to 93%, and (c) most importantly, we show that MTL improves performance over the individual event classification task. To our knowledge, this is the first work that demonstrates that interpretability improves classification performance.

(4) Our approach can be easily extended to a semi-supervised setting, where we use the rules associated with the events of interest to extract additional training data with "silver" labels, i.e., where we use the rule predictions as training labels for the classifier. We show that despite the inherent noise in this process, the performance of our approach improves considerably in this semi-supervised setting.

[1]https://github.com/clulab/releases/tree/master/aclsrw2020-edin/

2   Related Work

Interpretability in machine learning is an area of active research involving a multitude of approaches. In this work, we focus on *post-hoc* interpretations that explain a model's output (Lipton, 2016).

A common theme of prior research in interpretable machine learning is producing a definite decision process (e.g., a decision tree) that preserves generalization. (Craven and Shavlik, 1996) explored converting a trained network to a decision tree. Similarly, (Frosst and Hinton, 2017) trained soft binary decision trees using the predictions of a neural model. These decision trees are trained with mini-batch gradient descent using as labels a trained network's results. In the same vein, (Che et al., 2016) proposed a mimic learning framework, which trains gradient boosting trees to mimic the soft predictions of the original neural network. One unaddressed challenge with this direction, however, is that a decision tree's interpretability tends to decay as the tree increases in size.

Rather than converting a statistical model into an interpretable model such as a decision tree, other efforts have focused on *jointly* learning a statistical model with explanations for the model's output. Our work falls in this camp as well. (Hendricks et al., 2016) proposed a system for image classification that generates a natural language (NL) explanation to accompany each decision. Similarly, (Blunsom et al., 2018) learned NL explanations for the natural language inference (NLI) task, and (Ye et al., 2018) applied this idea to crime case prediction. Inspired by such approaches, here we learn to generate declarative information extraction rules that serve to explain the predictions of an event classifier.

3   Approach

Our approach jointly addresses classification and interpretability through an encoder-decoder architecture, where the decoder uses MTL for event extraction (Task 1) and rule generation (Task 2). In this paper, we apply this architecture to the extraction of unary events in the biomedical domain. The two tasks are framed as follows:

Task 1 (T1): Given a sentence and an entity in focus, it must identify which event applies to the entity, and what is its trigger, i.e., the verbal or nominal predicates that drives the lexicalization of the event (e.g., "phosphorylation").

Task 2 (T2): Decode a rule in the Odin language that explains the prediction of the event classifier. That is, the rule should identify the lexical constraints on the event trigger, e.g., its lemma, the semantic type expected of the argument, e.g., that is must be a `Protein`, and the syntactic pattern that connects the event trigger with the argument (Figure 1 shows a complete example for such a rule).

Consider this text as a walkthrough example: *which includes the phosphorylation of* **PKC** *by . . . ,* where the text in bold indicates the entity that is provided in the input in this task. This follows the settings of the standard event extraction task of BioNLP 2013 (Kim et al., 2013). For Task 1, we train a series of binary event classifiers (one for each event type), which predict the position of the event's lexical predicate (i.e., trigger) that modifies each given entity (*phosphorylation* here). Drawing upon the state information from Task 1, we prime our decoder in Task 2 using a contextualized representation of the predicted event trigger to generate an information extraction rule in the Odin language that captures the same event (i.e., entity-predicate structure) identified in Task 1 (see Figure 1). We detail these two tasks next.

3.1 Task 1: Event Classifier

We train a binary event classifier for each event type, which must identify if the corresponding event type applies to the entity under consideration, and, if so, which token in the input sentence is the event's trigger.

The classifier uses an encoder with entity attention to encode its input. For each sentence with words $w_1, \ldots, w_n$ and a given entity z, we associate each word i with a representation x_i that concatenates three embeddings: $x_i = e(w_i) \circ e(p_i) \circ char(w_i)$, where $e(w_i)$ is the word embedding of token i, p_i is the word's relative position to the *entity* under consideration, and $char(w_i)$ is the output of a bidirectional character-level LSTM (charLSTM) applied over w_i. $e(w_i)$ is initialized with the pretrained embeddings of (Hahn-Powell et al., 2016) using the word2vec Skip-gram model (Mikolov et al., 2013) trained on the full text of over 1 million biomedical papers taken from the PubMed Central Open Access Subset.[2] while $e(p_i)$ and $char(w_i)$ are initialized randomly.

The sequence of x_is serves as input to a sentence-level bidirectional LSTM (biLSTM), whose hidden states h_is serve as input to the attention layer below.

The entity-attention layer computes a sequence of context vectors (the matrix C in the equations below), which weighs the biLSTM's hidden states by their importance to the entity z. Our attention mechanism is inspired by the transformer network (Vaswani et al., 2017). Similarly, we compute the attention function on a set of keys and values that are packed together into matrices K and V. The difference is that our approach is entity-focused in its query, so we only compute the attention on a single query vector q. Further, unlike the conventional encoder in a transformer network, we don't produce a single vector, but a sequence of vectors (the matrix C).

$$q = W_q h_z \tag{1}$$

$$K = W_k H^E \tag{2}$$

$$V = W_v H^E \tag{3}$$

$$s = qK \tag{4}$$

$$a = \mathrm{softmax}(s) \tag{5}$$

$$C = V \odot a \tag{6}$$

where W_q, W_k, W_v are learned matrices of dimension 200×200, H^E contains the biLSTM's hidden states, and h_z is the hidden state of the entity z from H^E. We concatenate each context vector (C_i) with the entity vector (H_i^E) and feed the concatenated vector to two feedforward layers with a softmax function, and use its output to predict if there is a trigger in this position. We calculate the classifier's loss using the binary log loss function.

3.2 Task 2: Rule Decoder

Inspired by neural machine translation (Luong et al., 2015), we use another LSTM with attention as the decoder. To center rule decoding around the trigger, which must be generated first, we first feed the trigger vector from the encoder's context as the initial state in the decoder. Then, in each timestep t, we generate the attention context vector C_t^D by using the current hidden state of the decoder, h_t^D:

$$s_t(j) = C_j^E W^A h_t^D \tag{7}$$

---

[2] `https://www.ncbi.nlm.nih.gov/pmc/tools/openftlist/`

$$a_t = \text{softmax}(s_t) \tag{8}$$

$$C_t^D = \sum_j a_t(j) h_j^E \tag{9}$$

where W^A is a learned matrix of dimensions 100×200, and C^E are the context vectors from the previous entity-focused attention layer. Note that the learned matrix W^A here is distinct from the matrices learned in the previous entity-attention layer. We feed this C_t^D vector to a single feed forward layer that is coupled with a softmax function. We predict the next word from a vocabulary extracted from the existing Odin rules used in our experiments (see next section for details). During training, we calculate the decoder's loss using the multiclass cross-entropy loss function.

Note that the losses corresponding to these two tasks are jointly optimized. Formally, the loss function is defined as:

$$\text{loss} = \text{loss}_c + \text{loss}_d \tag{10}$$

$$\text{loss}_c = \sum_i -(t_i^c \log(y_i) + (1 - t_i^c) \log(1 - y_i)) \tag{11}$$

$$loss_d = \sum_i - \log(p_i) \tag{12}$$

where $loss_c$ is the cross-entropy loss of the event classifier, which relies on: t^c, the target label (i.e., 1 for positive examples, 0 for negative), and y, the likelihood predicted by the model. $loss_d$ is the cross-entropy loss of the rule decoder, where i iterates over the tokens in the rule, and p_i is the decoder's probability of the correct token at position i.

4 Experiments

4.1 Dataset

We train and evaluate on three events from the BioNLP 2013 GENIA Events extraction shared task (Kim et al., 2013): Phosphorylation (P), Localization (L), and Gene Expression (GE). To facilitate comparison with previous work, we use the standard training, development, and test partitions from the original dataset. To generate data for the rule decoder, we extend this dataset with rules from the rule-based system of (Valenzuela-Escárcega et al., 2018), which reported high-precision results for Phosphorylation (92%). We manually added new rules using existing syntactic templates that cover

common syntactic forms of subject-verb-object patterns to cover more events. Further, because the system of Valenzuela-Escárcega et al. (2018) did not cover L and GE events, we extended it with rules for these two events. All in all, we used: 32, 20, and 21 rules for P, L, and GE, respectively. Most of these rules rely on syntactic structures denoted in terms of dependency paths to extract event arguments (see Figure 1 for an example of such a rule). From these rules, we obtained a token-level vocabulary for the rule decoder. This poses an additional challenge on our decoder, which must now decode from raw text both the semantics necessary for these events, and the syntactic patterns needed to match event arguments. Further, note that these rules do not have perfect recall, i.e., there are events in the data that are not covered by rules. In other words, the two tasks in our MTL framework are not perfectly aligned: there are data points which are part of the training examples of T1, but not of T2 (for those training examples, the loss of decoder is set to be 0).

In addition to using these rules for explainability, we used the rule-based system to generate additional "silver" training data for these three events, by using its extractions from a collection of PubMed publications. From these papers, we extracted an additional 6592, 6321, and 2056 positive training examples for P, L, and GE, respectively. To avoid biasing the classifier to the positive classes, we also generated 3467, 3532, and 2876 negative training examples for P, L, and GE by extracting entities assign to extract evented to other event types in the BioNLP data.

4.2 Evaluation Metrics

We used precision, recall, and F1 scores to measure the performance of the event extractor (classifier), and used the BLEU score to measure the quality of generated rules, i.e., how close they are to the corresponding gold rules that extracted the same output. Note that the BLEU score provides an incomplete evaluation of rule quality. The more complete solution would be to evaluate these rules by executing them over free text and verifying the quality of the extracted output. However, this is not a trivial process, as some of the decoded rules break the Odin syntax, and are only executable after a manual cleanup process. We leave this evaluation for future work.

	Phosphorylation (P)			Localization (L)			Gene Expression (GE)		
	Precision	Recall	F1	Precision	Recall	F1	Precision	Recall	F1
Rule baseline	92.68	48.12	63.35	66.13	44.44	53.16	51.08	69.79	58.98
T1	87.78	49.38	63.20	100.00	4.04	7.77	89.32	64.30	74.77
T1 + Silver	62.75	82.50	71.28	54.55	34.34	42.15	68.43	74.31	71.25
T1 + Silver + T2	84.38	68.75	75.77	76.60	39.39	52.03	69.92	71.24	70.58
BioNLP best	83.95	85.62	84.78	86.21	53.54	66.05	91.29	82.55	86.70
BioNLP median	79.83	81.57	80.64	88.55	40.91	55.89	82.58	78.11	80.09

Table 1: Results for the three events in the BioNLP 2013 test partition. T1 and T2 indicate the two tasks in our MTL approach, i.e., the event classifier and the rule decoder, respectively. Silver indicates that that configuration used the silver data created by the rule-based system (see §4.1). BioNLP best and median indicate the best/median results during the 2013 shared task. We do not include T1 + T2 results because in this configuration we observed that there is not sufficient data to train the decoder.

4.3 Baseline

We compared our proposed methods with the rule-based baseline proposed by (Valenzuela-Escárcega et al., 2018). They used their rule-based system to extract Phosphorylation events in BioNLP 2013 Genia Events (GE) task data using 42 manually written rules (which we extended for our experiments – see Section 4.1). On the development partition, they reported a precision of 92.9%, a recall of 56.0%, and an F1 score of 69.9%. We also evaluated their system on the formal test partition and obtained a precision of 84.2%, a recall of 43.8%, and an F1 score of 57.6%. As mentioned in Section 4.1, we adjusted the grammar in this system to cover gene expression and localization events. The complete results for this system are listed in Table 1 as "Rule baseline."

4.4 Results and Discussion

Tables 1 analyzes the performance of our approach for the three events, compared against the rule-based system described in §4.1. These results highlight several important observations:

(1) T1 by itself performs generally worse than the rule baseline and the median BioNLP result. This is caused by: (a) the small size of this dataset, e.g., there are only 117 training examples for P; and (b) the fact that our approach uses no part-of-speech (POS) or syntactic information, which have been shown to be important for this BioNLP task (Kim et al., 2013). However, adding the silver data improves T1 performance considerably, e.g., 35 F1 points for Localization. This demonstrates that our approach provides a simple but effective platform for semi-supervised learning.

(2) Most importantly, jointly training for classification and explainability helps the classification task (T1) itself. As shown in the tables, combining T1

	BLEU	Exact Matches	Non-exact, Explainable Matches
P	93.80	86.11	2/15
L	83.78	84.33	1/9
GE	78.99	76.45	10/43

Table 2: Evaluation of decoded rules, on the BioNLP development partition. BLEU measures the overlap with hand-written rules. Exact Matches shows the percentage of decoded rules that exactly match hand-written ones. Explainable Matches shows the number of decoded rules that do not match exactly hand-written ones, but were considered good explanations by human experts.

and T2 generally improves F1 scores considerably, e.g., 4 F1 points for Phosphorylation and 10 for Localization. To our knowledge, this is the first NLP work to demonstrate that aiming for interpretability also helps the main task addressed. All in all, we approach the median performance in the shared task, a respectable result considering that our approach uses only raw text as input, whereas all participants in this shared task used some form of syntactic representation. Importantly, our approach outperforms considerably the rule-based method of (Valenzuela-Escárcega et al., 2018), which served as the starting point of this work (see Section 4.3).

(3) The only negative results in our experiments are the GE results in the test partition, where T1 outperforms both T1 + Silver and T1 + Silver + T2. We hypothesize that this is caused by the larger training data for this event, e.g., there are 6 times more training samples for GE than P, which allows the T1 classifier to learn by itself, without the scaffolding offered by MTL, and the additional (noisy) data in the silver dataset. This suggests that our approach is best suited for EE scenarios with minimal training data, an important subset of information extraction tasks.

But are the decoded rules actually interpretable? To answer this, we compared in Table 2 the decoded rules against the hand-written rules that matched in the BioNLP development partition.

Hand-written Rule	Decoded Rule
trigger = [lemma = /phosphorylate/ & ! word = /(?i)^(de|auto)/ & tag = /^(V|JJ)/ & ! mention = ModificationTrigger]	trigger = [lemma = /phosphorylate/ & ! word = /(?i)^(de|auto)/ & tag = /^(V|JJ)/ & ! = ModificationTrigger]
theme : BioChemicalEntity = > nsubjpass prep_of ? /conj_(and|or|nor)|nn|cc/ { , 2 }	theme : BioChemicalEntity = > nsubjpass prep_of ? /conj_(and|or|nor)|nn|cc/ { , 2 }
trigger = [lemma = /detect|localiz|locat|releas|secret|translocat/ & ! word = /(?i)^de/]	trigger = [lemma = /detect|localiz|locat|releas|secret|translocat/ & ! word = /(?i)^de/ & ! outgoing = /prep_(by|of)/]
theme : BioChemicalEntity = prep_of ? appos ? /conj_(and|or|nor)|cc|nn/ { , 2 }	theme : BioChemicalEntity = < /conj_(and|or|nor)/ ? /conj_(and|or|nor)|cc|nn|prep_of/ { , 2 }
trigger = [lemma = / phosphorylation / & ! word = / (? i) ^ (de | auto) / & ! outgoing = / prep_ (by | of) /]	trigger = [lemma = / phosphorylate / & ! word = / (? i) ^ (de | auto) / & tag = / ^ (V | JJ) / & ! mention = ModificationTrigger]
theme : BioChemicalEntity = < / conj_ (and | or | nor) / ? / conj_ (and | or | nor) | cc | nn | prep_of / { 2 } site : Site ? = nn | < dobj ? / prep_ (at | on) / num ?	cause : BioChemicalEntity ? = < xcomp ? (nsubj | agent | < vmod) / appos | nn | conj_ (and | or | nor) | cc / { 2 }
	theme : BioChemicalEntity = (dobj | xcomp) / conj_ (and | or | nor) | dep | cc | nn | prep_of / { 2 } (> > [word = by]) { 2 } site : Site ? = dobj ? / prep_ (at | on) | nn | conj_ (and | or | nor) | cc / { 2 }

Table 3: Examples of mistakes in the decoded rules. The first column shows hand-written rules, while the second shows the rules decoded by our approach from sentences where the corresponding hand-written rules matched. We highlight in the hand-written rules the tokens that were missed during decoding (false negatives) in green, and in the decoded rules we highlight the spurious tokens (false positives) in red. The first row lists a partial mistake, which does not affect the interpretability of the decoded rule, since it only misses one token that can be inferred by the human experts from context. The second row lists a partial mistake, which impacts the semantics of the rule. For example, the decoder missed that the path between the trigger and the `theme` argument starts with an optional `prop_of` and `appos`. This rule was marked as partially correct because some simple syntactic patterns, e.g., `nn`, can still be correctly matched by the decoded rule. The last row lists a larger decoding error that was marked as completely incorrect by the annotator. For example, in the last decoded rule, the decoder generated an incorrect `cause` argument, which does not exist in the data, as well as an incorrect syntactic pattern for the `theme` argument, i.e., the protein being phosphorylated.

That is, we performed this analysis on the subset of the development partition, where each data point is accompanied by a matching hand-written rule. This reduced this dataset to approximately 60% of the total BioNLP development set. In particular, we analyzed 108, 82, and 296 event instances with matching rules for P, L, and GE events, respectively. The table shows that our rules have high BLEU overlap with hand-written rules, e.g., 93% for P, and, by and large, they exactly match them. We believe this is an exciting result, as it shows that our approach is able to decode directly from the raw text the declarative semantics necessary for the task, as well as the syntactic patterns that match the event arguments.

Lastly, Table 3 shows examples of typical decoding errors, ranging from partial mistakes that do not affect the interpretability of rules to complete decoding mistakes. As we mentioned above, we cannot ensure the validation of the generated rules with our current approach. Table 3 shows that this indeed happens in our output. For example, the decoder generates a binary operator such "!=" without the left operand (first row in the table).

5 Conclusions

We introduced an interpretable approach for event extraction that jointly trains an event classifier with a component that translates the classifier's decisions into interpretable extraction rules. We implemented this approach using an encoder-decoder architecture, where the decoder jointly optimizes the decoding of extraction rules and event classification. We evaluated the proposed approach on three biomedical events and demonstrated that the decoder generates interpretable rules, and that the joint training improves the performance of the event classifier. We also showed that the performance of our approach further improves when trained on automatically-labeled data generated by a rule-based system.

In the longer term, we envision a decoder with constraints, which enforces that the generated rules follow correct Odin syntax. We plan to include constraints as part of decoding to aid in rule synthesis. For example, in the Odin language, brackets must be paired to produce syntactically valid rules. This can be enforced with different strategies in the decoder, ranging from constrained greedy decoding to globally optimal solutions that could be implemented with integer linear programming. We suspect that including such validity constraints will further improve the quality of the decoded rules.

Further, we plan to use this decoder in an iterative, semi-supervised learning scenario akin to co-training (Blum and Mitchell, 1998). That is, the newly decoded, executable rules can be applied over large, unannotated texts to generate new training examples for the event classifier.

Acknowledgments

This work was supported by the Defense Advanced Research Projects Agency (DARPA) under grant #W911NF1810014. Mihai Surdeanu and Gus Hahn-Powell declare a financial interest in lum.ai. This interest has been properly disclosed to the University of Arizona Institutional Review Committee and is managed in accordance with its conflict of interest policies.

References

Avrim Blum and Tom Mitchell. 1998. Combining labeled and unlabeled data with co-training. In *Proceedings of the eleventh annual conference on Computational learning theory*, pages 92–100. ACM.

Phil Blunsom, Oana-Maria Camburu, Thomas Lukasiewicz, and Tim Rocktäschel. 2018. e- snli: Natural language inference with natural language explanations.

Zhengping Che, Sanjay Purushotham, Robinder Khemani, and Yan Liu. 2016. Interpretable deep models for icu outcome prediction. In *AMIA Annual Symposium Proceedings*, volume 2016, page 371. American Medical Informatics Association.

Mark Craven and Jude W Shavlik. 1996. Extracting tree-structured representations of trained networks. In *Advances in neural information processing systems*, pages 24–30.

Nicholas Frosst and Geoffrey Hinton. 2017. Distilling a neural network into a soft decision tree. *arXiv preprint arXiv:1711.09784*.

Gus Hahn-Powell, Dane Bell, Marco A. Valenzuela-Escárcega, and Mihai Surdeanu. 2016. This before that: Causal precedence in the biomedical domain. In *Proceedings of the 2016 Workshop on Biomedical Natural Language Processing*, pages 146–155. Association for Computational Linguistics.

Lisa Anne Hendricks, Zeynep Akata, Marcus Rohrbach, Jeff Donahue, Bernt Schiele, and Trevor Darrell. 2016. Generating visual explanations. In *European Conference on Computer Vision*, pages 3–19. Springer.

Jin-Dong Kim, Yue Wang, and Yamamoto Yasunori. 2013. The genia event extraction shared task, 2013 edition-overview. In *Proceedings of the BioNLP Shared Task 2013 Workshop*, pages 8–15.

Zachary C Lipton. 2016. The mythos of model interpretability. *arXiv preprint arXiv:1606.03490*.

Minh-Thang Luong, Hieu Pham, and Christopher D Manning. 2015. Effective approaches to attention-based neural machine translation. *arXiv preprint arXiv:1508.04025*.

Tomas Mikolov, Kai Chen, Greg Corrado, and Jeffrey Dean. 2013. Efficient estimation of word representations in vector space. In *Proceedings of the International Conference on Learning Representations (ICLR)*.

Marco Tulio Ribeiro, Sameer Singh, and Carlos Guestrin. 2016. Why should i trust you?: Explaining the predictions of any classifier. In *Proceedings of the 22nd ACM SIGKDD international conference on knowledge discovery and data mining*, pages 1135–1144. ACM.

Marco A. Valenzuela-Escárcega, Özgün Babur, Gus Hahn-Powell, Dane Bell, Thomas Hicks, Enrique Noriega-Atala, Xia Wang, Mihai Surdeanu, Emek Demir, and Clayton T. Morrison. 2018. Large-scale automated machine reading discovers new cancer driving mechanisms. *Database: The Journal of Biological Databases and Curation*.

Marco A. Valenzuela-Escárcega, Gus Hahn-Powell, and Mihai Surdeanu. 2016. Odin's runes: A rule language for information extraction. In *Proceedings of the 10th International Conference on Language Resources and Evaluation*. LREC.

Ashish Vaswani, Noam Shazeer, Niki Parmar, Jakob Uszkoreit, Llion Jones, Aidan N Gomez, Łukasz Kaiser, and Illia Polosukhin. 2017. Attention is all you need. In *Advances in Neural Information Processing Systems*, pages 5998–6008.

Hai Ye, Xin Jiang, Zhunchen Luo, and Wenhan Chao. 2018. Interpretable charge predictions for criminal cases: Learning to generate court views from fact descriptions. *arXiv preprint arXiv:1802.08504*.

Crossing the Line: Where do Demographic Variables Fit into Humor Detection?

J. A. Meaney
School of Informatics
University of Edinburgh
Edinburgh, UK
jameaney@ed.ac.uk

Abstract

Recent shared tasks in humor classification have struggled with two issues: scope and subjectivity. Regarding scope, many task datasets either comprise a highly constrained genre of humor which does not broadly represent the genre, or the data collection is so indiscriminate that the inter-annotator agreement on its comic content is drastically low. In terms of subjectivity, these tasks typically average over all annotators' judgments, in spite of the fact that humor is highly subjective and varies both between and within cultures. We propose a dataset which maintains a broad scope but which addresses subjectivity. We will collect demographic information about the data's humor annotators in order to bin ratings more sensibly. We also suggest the addition of an 'offensive' label to reflect the fact a text may be humorous to one group, but offensive to another. This would allow for more meaningful shared tasks and could lead to better performance on downstream applications, such as content moderation.

1 Introduction

Interest in computational humor (CH) is flourishing, and since 2017, the proliferation of shared humor detection tasks in NLP has attracted new researchers to the field. However, leading researchers in CH have bemoaned the fact that NLP's contribution is not always informed by the long and interdisciplinary history of humor research (Taylor and Attardo, 2016) (Davies, 2008). This may result in the creation of humor detection systems which produce excellent evaluation results, but which may not scale to other humor datasets, improve downstream tasks like content moderation, or contribute to our understanding of humor.

A central issue is the conception of humor classification tasks as humor-or-not, similar to image classification's view of an image as dog-or-not. However, while one can be an expert in whether or not an image depicts a dog, and this is stable within and between cultures, humor is more nuanced than that. Unlike image classification:

- Humor differs *between* cultures. Even within the same language, different nationalities perceive jokes differently. This is particularly relevant to stereotyped humor, which may be perceived as funny to one culture, but offensive to another. (Rosenthal and Bindman, 2015)

- Humor differs *within* cultures. Age, gender and socio-economic status are known to impact what is perceived as humorous. (Kuipers, 2017)

- Humor differs within the same person. Mood is thought to impact what is considered to be humorous or not. (Wagner and Ruch, 2020)

Currently in NLP shared tasks, there is scant admission of these issues. Humor is treated as a stable target, and humorous texts are subjected to binary classification and humor score prediction, with little recognition that gold standard labels for these constructs simply do not exist.

1.1 Proposal

To the extent that humor is multi-faceted, and subject to multiple interpretations, incremental improvements to shared tasks can be made by:

- Acknowledging that texts may not be perceived as humorous by all readers, and allowing for a different interpretation, e.g. offensive.

- Collecting demographic information about the annotators of humor datasets to learn more about which sectors of society find a text humorous versus offensive.

Proceedings of the 58th Annual Meeting of the Association for Computational Linguistics: Student Research Workshop, pages 176–181
July 5 - July 10, 2020. ©2020 Association for Computational Linguistics

1.2 Why Offensive as an Alternative Label?

Cultural shifts in many parts of the world have seen a decline in racist and sexist jokes, and the growth of humor that acknowledges marginalized people. Lockyer and Pickering (2005) argue that this is not just a recent phenomenon, but that all pluralist societies navigate the space between humor and offensiveness, between 'free speech and cultural respect'

Despite the shift away from using racist or sexist comments as humor, offensive language is still plentiful on the internet (Davidson et al., 2017), (Nobata et al., 2016). This can reinforce racial stereotypes, or have a damaging impact on communities. In light of the fact that many shared tasks source their data online, either by scraping Twitter, Reddit, or crowdsourcing, we believe it is worth capturing the impact of these texts on users.

1.3 Why Demographic Factors?

Studies as far back as 1937 demonstrate gender and age differences in the appreciation of jokes, where young men gave higher ratings to 'shady' (e.g. sexual) jokes than their female, and older counterparts did (Omwake, 1937).

More recently, in the Netherlands, Kuipers (2017) found significant differences in humor preferences along the lines of gender, age, and in particular, social class or education level. An interesting finding was that the older generation rated their younger counterparts' humor as offensive. This contradicts the popular opinion that the millennial generation is perpetually offended (Fisher, 2019).

In terms of gender-specific offensive humor, a US study found that males tended to give higher ratings to female-hostile jokes, and females did the same with male-hostile jokes. Both genders found female-hostile jokes more offensive overall (Abel and Flick, 2012).

The body of work from CH on demographic differences in humor perception is absent in current work, but can be incorporated into shared tasks with some simple adjustments.

2 Previous Work

SemEval 2017 posed two humor detection tasks. Task 7 (Miller et al., 2017) covered puns, which we do not include here as the identification/interpretation of puns is less ambiguous than other forms of humor, except in the case that the audience does not possess the tacit linguistic knowledge required to understand them (Aarons, 2017).

2.1 Limited Scope

Task 6, Hashtag Wars (Potash et al., 2017), sourced its name and data from a segment in the Comedy Central Show @Midnight with Chris Hardwick, which solicited humorous responses to a given hashtag from its viewers, submitted on Twitter. These submissions were effectively annotated twice: the producers selected ten tweets as most humorous, and most appropriate for the show's type of humor. The show's audience then voted on their number one submission. Task 1 was to pair the tweets, and for each pair, predict which one had achieved a higher ranking, according to the audience. Task 2 was to predict the labels given by this stratified annotation: submitted but not top-10, top-10, number one in top-10.

The task's organisers highlighted the data's limited scope, and were keen to point out that this task does not aim to build an all-purpose, cross-cultural humor classifier, but rather to characterise the humor from one source - the show @Midnight. This task's dual annotation and ecologically valid task make it arguably one of the most effective humor challenges in recent years. However, it remains to be seen how well a system built on this data would generalize to another humor detection task.

Semeval 2020 featured another humor challenge with two subtasks: predicting the mean funniness rating of each humorous text, and given two humorous texts, predicting which was rated as funnier (Hossain et al., 2019). Instead of collecting previously existing humorous texts, the organisers generated them by scraping news headlines from Reddit, and then paying crowdworkers to edit the headlines to make them funny, and annotators to rate the funniness of the new headlines.

Edits were defined as 'the insertion of a single-word noun or verb to replace an existing entity or single-word noun or verb'. The annotators rated the headline as funny from 0-4. An abusive/spam option was included, but presumably to discard ineffective edits, rather than highlight a text which would cause offense. Nonetheless, inter-annotator agreement between raters was moderately high, (Krippendorff's α 0.64)

Of interest to CH research is that the authors' analysis of the generated humor finds support for established humor theories, such as incongruity, superiority and setup and punchline being central to the this task. However, the editing rules enforced such tight linguistic constraints that many common features of language were not permitted, e.g. the use of named entities with two words, phrasal verbs, even apostrophes. This scales down the humor that can be generated, not in terms of genre, as was the case with the 2017 SemEval task, but rather in terms of arbitrary linguistic constraints.

Finally we must consider that, given that the humorous texts were presented alongside the original headline, it's possible that affirmative humor ratings do not mean that the text is humorous in and of itself, only that it is funnier than the contemporary news — arguably a low bar in the current climate.

2.2 Unlimited Scope

The HAHA challenge (Humor Analysis based on Human Annotation) has run in 2018 (Castro et al., 2018) and 2019 (Chiruzzo et al., 2019) with two subtasks: binary classification of humor, and prediction of the average humor score assigned to each text.

The data were collected from fifty Spanish-speaking Twitter accounts which typically post humorous content, representing a range of different dialects of Spanish. These were then uploaded to an online platform, which was open to the public who were asked the following questions to annotate the data:

1. Does this tweet intend to be humorous? (Yes, or No)

2. [If yes] How humorous do you find it, from 1 to 5?

A strength of this annotation process is that the first question allows the user to objectively identify the genre of the text by identifying its intention, before giving their subjective opinion of it. However, the inter-annotator agreement for the second question was extremely low (Krippendorf's α of 0.1625). It's possible that sourcing the texts from fifty different accounts introduced too many genres to gain a consensus about what was funny amongst annotators. Similarly, the organizers targeted as many different Spanish dialects as possible in their data collection, which could lead to cultural and linguistic differences in humor appreciation. Finally, the annotations were sourced on an open platform, with only three test tweets to assess whether an annotator provided usable ratings or not. There were no questions as to whether the user was a Spanish speaker, and as the task was unpaid, there may have been little incentive to do it accurately.

3 Methodology

The datasets featured in both SemEval tasks had tight constraints on the genre of humor involved. This led to high inter-annotator reliability, but may not generalize well to other forms of humor. The Spanish tasks featured no such constraints, however, there was extremely low inter-annotator agreement, suggesting that the dataset is noisy, and that a system which is built on this may also fail to generalize.

This proposal aims to include a wide range of genres, and to increase the reliability of the annotations by collecting information on well-known latent variables in humor appreciation — the demographic characteristics of the humor audience/annotators. This will allow for more nuanced tasks, as an alternative to simple humor-or-not definitions.

3.1 Data Collection

We plan to follow a similar data collection protocol to (Castro et al., 2018) and collect tweets from a wide variety of humorous Twitter accounts. However, unlike Castro et al., we plan to limit the dialect of the jokes collected to US English, and use a crowdsourcing platform which allows us to select annotators who use this dialect. This will help us to avoid introducing confounds such as lack of cultural knowledge, or divergent language usage. Furthermore, we will hand select the Twitter accounts which typically post humorous content, in order to ensure that the data features a wide variety of genres of humor, e.g. observational humor, wordplay, humorous vignettes, etc.

3.2 Annotation

As mentioned above, averaging over the opinions of the audience, similar to approaches in image detection is not ecologically valid for humor detection. For this reason, we plan to collect demographic information about the annotators, in order to bin the ratings into groups that may perceive humor in a similar way. In this way, we hope to increase inter-annotator reliability. We also plan to include a second label for each text — offensive.

Following Castro et al., annotators will be asked the following questions for each text:

1. Is the intention of this text to be humorous?

2. [If so] How humorous do you perceive this text to be?

3. Is this text offensive?

4. [If so] How offensive do you perceive this text to be?

The annotator guidelines will reflect that offensiveness can encompass an insult to the audience itself, or to others who are likely to find the text distasteful.

All annotators will be paid for their work, to incentivize quality ratings. They will be selected to undertake the task by virtue of fitting into the following demographic bins:

- Age: 18-25, 26-40, 41-55, 56-70 the bins are broadly designed to capture Generation Z, Millenials, Generation X and Baby Boomers respectively (Dimock, 2019).

- Gender: Male, Female, Non-binary

- Level of Education: High School, Undergraduate, Postgraduate. This will be used as an index of socioeconomic status (Mirowsky and Ross, 2003).

Subsequent to data annotation, we will select the demographic factor that gives the highest inter-rater reliability for this dataset. Annotations will be averaged by bin, rather than averaging over all of a text's ratings, as was the case in previous shared tasks.

3.3 Pilot Study

To examine the integrity of our assumptions, we ran a short pilot task in which we used the Prolific Academic platform to crowdsource annotations from users in the youngest and oldest age groups.

We searched for texts which related to race/origin, religion, gender, sexuality and body type. We used keywords from Fortuna's (2017) subcategories of offensive speech to source texts which could be offensive jokes, such as 'black', 'woman', 'girlfriend', 'blind', 'gay', 'Muslim', 'Jew', etc. From a readily available dataset (The Short Jokes dataset from Kaggle), we sourced 40 jokes, 20 in which the keyword also referred to the butt of the joke (average number of tokens per text = 18.4), and 20 in which it did not (average number of tokens = 19.1). Twenty neutral texts were selected from Twitter, ensuring that the semantic meaning of the keyword stayed they same, e.g. 'black' referred to race, and not to Black Friday, and that the texts were not intended to be humorous. The average number of tokens per text in this group was 20.2.

- **Keyword is not target of joke:** 'What is the Terminators Muslim name? Al Bi Baq'

- **Keyword is target of joke:** 'Mattel released a Muslim Barbie... It's a blow-up doll.'

- **Random tweet with keyword:** 'The Mosque will close this weekend due to the pandemic'.

We asked 2 groups of annotators, aged 18-25 (n=10) or aged 55-70 (n=10) to imagine they were social media moderators. Their task was to identify the genre of the texts as label them as 'humorous', 'offensive', 'humorous and offensive' and 'other'. We highlighted that they did not need to find the text humorous, or personally offensive to label them as such. If they identified the intent as humorous, or the text as possibly offensive to others, they should use the corresponding label. We omitted the numerical rating task for reasons of brevity.

In terms of results, the clearest trends emerge when the groups were split by age. Both age groups of users made use of the 'humorous and offensive' label, suggesting that annotators could identify the genre of the text as humorous, but found it in bad taste. However, there was a trend for the younger group using this label more frequently than the older group.

Examining where differences in annotation occurred, Table 1 demonstrates the disparity in labelling on the following gender-related text:

> We should really use the blackjack scale to rate women. For example: "Every girl here is ugly" "Well, what about her?" "Eh, she's like a 15 or 16. Not sure if I'd hit it"

Table 1: Variation in labelling between age groups

Age	Humorous	Offensive	Humorous & Offensive	Other
18-25	3	3	3	1
56-70	2	7	0	1

As we did not have balanced groups based on level of education, or a critical mass of non-binary users so we omit analysis for these. Similarly, regarding gender differences, there were no clear trends in terms of labelling between females and males, and there were no statistically significant differences between groups.

The results of our pilot study suggest that pursuing demographic differentiation in humor annotation/classification is worthwhile. Specifically, we can see that age group may be relevant as the demographic factor which most distinguishes annotators' response to humor.

3.4 Tasks

We will ask systems to predict, given a group with a specific set of user demographics:

- Is this text humorous to the group, and if so, how humorous?

- Is this text offensive to the group, and if so, how offensive?

Our data will comprise texts which are either humorous and not offensive, humorous and offensive, not humorous and offensive, and not humorous and not-offensive.

In the case that there are no clear distinctions between the groups in terms of labels and ratings, we will average over these annotations, as typical tasks have done and proceed with classification and regression, as above.

The evaluation metrics for the classification task will be precision, recall and F1. The metric for predicting the humor and offensiveness scores will be root mean squared error.

4   Contribution to Computational Humor

In line with CH research, we affirm that humor is a moving target in terms of differing interpretations between demographic groups and across the lifetime. Our dataset will be the first to model the reception of a wide variety of humor genres from Twitter, presented to users of different demographics. It will also be, to the best of our knowledge, the first CH dataset to take into account the ratings of non-binary annotators.

In line with Hossain (2019), we aim to use clustering methods on the humor and/or offensive texts to determine themes that evoke these classes for different groups. We also aim to explore whether theories of humor, such as surprisal, superiority and incongruity are equally appreciated among different groups.

5   Conclusion

Humor detection and rating is a multi-faceted problem. We hope that the inclusion of demographic information will shift the state of the art away from objective classification, towards a more subjective approach. Future qualitative work could also suggest further variables whose inclusion would enhance our knowledge of humor perception. This could set a new standard for shared tasks which aim to model humor in future, and could outline a methodology that can be replicated with other cultures and languages.

6   Acknowledgements

This work was supported in part by the EPSRC Centre for Doctoral Training in Data Science, funded by the UK Engineering and Physical Sciences Research Council (grant EP/L016427/1) and the University of Edinburgh.

References

Debra Aarons. 2017. Puns and tacit linguistic knowledge. In *The Routledge handbook of language and humor*, pages 80–94. Routledge.

Millicent H Abel and Jason Flick. 2012. Mediation and moderation in ratings of hostile jokes by men and women.

Santiago Castro, Luis Chiruzzo, Aiala Rosá, Diego Garat, and Guillermo Moncecchi. 2018. A crowd-annotated spanish corpus for humor analysis. In *Proceedings of the Sixth International Workshop on Natural Language Processing for Social Media*, pages 7–11.

Luis Chiruzzo, S Castro, Mathias Etcheverry, Diego Garat, Juan José Prada, and Aiala Rosá. 2019. Overview of haha at iberlef 2019: Humor analysis based on human annotation. In *Proceedings of the Iberian Languages Evaluation Forum (IberLEF 2019). CEUR Workshop Proceedings, CEUR-WS, Bilbao, Spain (9 2019)*.

Thomas Davidson, Dana Warmsley, Michael Macy, and Ingmar Weber. 2017. Automated hate speech detection and the problem of offensive language. In *Eleventh international aaai conference on web and social media*.

Christie Davies. 2008. Undertaking the comparative study of humor. *The primer of humor research, Berlin: Mouton de Gruyter*, pages 157–182.

Michael Dimock. 2019. Defining generations: Where millennials end and generation z begins. *Pew Research Center*, 17:1–7.

Caitlin Fisher. 2019. *The Gaslighting of the Millennial Generation: How to Succeed in a Society that Blames You for Everything Gone Wrong.* Mango Media Inc.

Paula Cristina Teixeira Fortuna. 2017. Automatic detection of hate speech in text: an overview of the topic and dataset annotation with hierarchical classes.

Nabil Hossain, John Krumm, and Michael Gamon. 2019. " president vows to cut¡ taxes¿ hair": Dataset and analysis of creative text editing for humorous headlines. *arXiv preprint arXiv:1906.00274.*

Giselinde Kuipers. 2017. Humour styles and class cultures: Highbrow humour and lowbrow humour in the netherlands. In *The Anatomy of Laughter*, pages 58–69. Routledge.

Sharon Lockyer and Michael Pickering. 2005. Introduction: The ethics and aesthetics of humour and comedy. In *Beyond a Joke*, pages 1–24. Springer.

Tristan Miller, Christian Hempelmann, and Iryna Gurevych. 2017. SemEval-2017 task 7: Detection and interpretation of english puns. In *Proceedings of the 11th International Workshop on Semantic Evaluation (SemEval-2017)*, pages 58–68, Stroudsburg, PA, USA. Association for Computational Linguistics.

John Mirowsky and Catherine E Ross. 2003. *Education, social status, and health.* Transaction Publishers.

Chikashi Nobata, Joel Tetreault, Achint Thomas, Yashar Mehdad, and Yi Chang. 2016. Abusive language detection in online user content. In *Proceedings of the 25th international conference on world wide web*, pages 145–153.

Louise Omwake. 1937. A study of sense of humor: its relation to sex, age, and personal characteristics. *Journal of Applied Psychology*, 21(6):688.

Peter Potash, Alexey Romanov, and Anna Rumshisky. 2017. Semeval-2017 task 6:# hashtagwars: Learning a sense of humor. In *Proceedings of the 11th International Workshop on Semantic Evaluation (SemEval-2017)*, pages 49–57.

Angela Rosenthal and David Bindman. 2015. *No laughing matter: Visual humor in ideas of race, nationality, and ethnicity.* Dartmouth College Press.

Julia M Taylor and S Attardo. 2016. Computational treatments of humor. In *Routledge Handbook of Language and Humor*.

Lisa Wagner and Willibald Ruch. 2020. Trait cheerfulness, seriousness, and bad mood outperform personality traits of the five-factor model in explaining variance in humor behaviors and well-being among adolescents. *Current Psychology*, pages 1–12.

Effectively Aligning and Filtering Parallel Corpora under Sparse Data Conditions

Steinþór Steingrímsson
Department of
Computer Science
Reykjavik University
Iceland
steinthor18@ru.is

Hrafn Loftsson
Department of
Computer Science
Reykjavik University
Iceland
hrafn@ru.is

Andy Way
School of Computing
ADAPT Centre
Dublin City University
Ireland
andy.way
@adaptcentre.ie

Abstract

Parallel corpora are key to developing good machine translation systems. However, abundant parallel data are hard to come by, especially for languages with a low number of speakers. When rich morphology exacerbates the data sparsity problem, it is imperative to have accurate alignment and filtering methods that can help make the most of what is available by maximising the number of correctly translated segments in a corpus and minimising noise by removing incorrect translations and segments containing extraneous data. This paper sets out a research plan for improving alignment and filtering methods for parallel texts in low-resource settings. We propose an effective unsupervised alignment method to tackle the alignment problem. Moreover, we propose a strategy to supplement state-of-the-art models with automatically extracted information using basic NLP tools to effectively handle rich morphology.

1 Introduction

Machine translation (MT) quality has improved substantially with the advent of neural machine translation systems (NMT). However, while the quality gains over statistical machine translation (SMT) systems can be large, in low-resource and domain mismatch settings they are significantly reduced (Koehn and Knowles, 2017). In recent years, unsupervised NMT trained only on monolingual corpora has attracted considerable attention, and has been proposed for scenarios where there is a lack of bilingual data (Artetxe et al., 2018b; Lample et al., 2018). These methods have been shown to perform well for related language pairs (e.g. Wu et al. (2019)), but as the languages differ more the unsupervised methods become less effective (Leng et al., 2019). Kim et al. (2020) show that supervised and semi-supervised baselines with only a small parallel corpus of 50K bilingual sentences

consistently outperform the best unsupervised systems for a range of languages, similar and distant. They also show that unsupervised NMT is very sensitive to domain mismatch, which poses a problem to low-resource language pairs where it can be difficult to match the data domain on both sides. Thus, it is evident that to achieve high quality MT, sentence aligned-texts in two or more languages are required.

NMT systems have been shown to be sensitive to noise in the training data (Khayrallah and Koehn, 2018), where noise is defined as segments that decrease output quality of systems trained on the data. It is, therefore, important to be able to accurately align multilingual texts and precisely filter out misalignments and bad translations that adversely affect performance. In the study, conducted on the impact of various types of noise on MT quality, untranslated and misaligned segments had the most detrimental effect. Misaligned segments were by far the most prevalent type of noise in the ParaCrawl[1] parallel corpus they used, twice as common as accepted segments. However, misalignments vary; a segment can have one extraneous word, it can have twice the content its counterpart has, or anything in between. It can be very useful to understand the intricacies of the effects different types and levels of noise have, why it is important not to have noise and whether some kinds of noise are more acceptable than others. This leads us to our first research question:

RQ1: How do different kinds of misalignments in a parallel corpus affect translation quality of an MT (SMT or NMT) system trained on that corpus?

If we can measure the effects of various misalignments, it could help us construct more effective methods to filter parallel corpora for MT.

---

[1] https://paracrawl.eu/

Proceedings of the 58th Annual Meeting of the Association for Computational Linguistics: Student Research Workshop, pages 182–190
July 5 - July 10, 2020. ©2020 Association for Computational Linguistics

As the usefulness of parallel corpora for MT was first becoming apparent, Harris (1988) pointed out that aligning such texts was a serious problem. Moreover, collecting multilingual texts is expensive and time-consuming, and for some languages it can be hard to obtain access to even small amount of texts. Thus, we need to be able to make the most out of what is available.

We describe a method using Bleualign (Sennrich and Volk, 2011) and Monoses (Artetxe et al., 2018b), an unsupervised SMT system, to align parallel corpora using only monolingual texts for training. The proposed method is language pair-independent and only assumes unaligned bitexts and monolingual corpora for both languages. It is the first step towards answering our second research question:

RQ2: How can we best build useful parallel corpora from bilingual texts, having no other resources but monolingual corpora?

In morphological typology, languages can be classified as analytic or synthetic (see e.g. Haspelmath and Sims (2013), Steinbergs (1996)). Analytic languages primarily rely on word order and auxiliary words to convey meaning, while synthetic languages use inflection. "Morphologically rich" languages are synthetic languages which commonly have a large number of different surface forms for any given lexeme. This can lead to a high rate of out-of-vocabulary (OOV) words, a data sparsity problem that machine learning algorithms struggle with.

Icelandic is a synthetic language with relatively few native speakers (approx. 350,000) where data sparsity problems are prevalent in most NLP tasks. In our work, we will focus on building a parallel corpus for the English-Icelandic language pair and confronting the issues that arise when working with a less-resourced and morphologically rich language.

When doing sentence alignment and filtering noise from parallel corpora, the sparsity problem caused by rich morphology leads to lower confidence scores for segment pairs resulting in lower classification accuracy, and thus smaller or less accurate parallel corpora. When ParIce (Barkarson and Steingrímsson, 2019), an English-Icelandic parallel corpus was compiled, the filtering process resulted in an estimated 20% reduction in corpus size. Out of what remained, about 5% was faulty (see Section 3). We will work with the same data

with the goal of minimising these numbers. This leads us to the third and last research question this research proposal centres around:

RQ3: How can we filter parallel corpora to minimize noise, and still lose little or no useful data from the original texts?

Our approach to try to answer these questions is to experiment with common and recent methods from the alignment and filtering literature. We will build a toolset that can employ various known methods and compare and contrast them. We will investigate how word embeddings, a lemmatizer, a part-of-speech (PoS) tagger or a parser can help tackle the data sparsity problem, and which known methods benefit most from them. Evaluation data sets will be created for the purposes of the project and the methods evaluated according to a set of evaluation metrics. Finally, we will train and evaluate our system on a different language pair with comparable issues.

2 Related Work

Filtering parallel data is the task of removing incorrect translations, noise and otherwise faulty data from a set of two (or more) aligned texts. Alignment is the task of finding target segments with a corresponding meaning to that of source segments in multilingual texts. While these may seem to be different tasks, the same methods may apply partly to both problems. Filtering is often done by scoring sentences and removing the lowest-scoring ones, whereas in alignment the highest-scoring sentences can be used as anchors: elements in the data that can reliably be aligned and thus direct further processing. In the next subsections, we describe alignment and filtering methods used in prior work.

2.1 Alignment

The first approaches to automatic sentence alignment were length-based. Gale and Church (1991) found that "the correlation between the length of a paragraph in characters and the length of its translation was extremely high". Motivated by that, they describe a method for aligning sentences based on a simple statistical model of character lengths. Brown et al. (1991) also describe a length-based method, but use tokens instead of characters. In addition, they use signals in the markup as anchor points to segment the corpus into smaller chunks.

Kay and Röscheisen (1993) used bilingual lexicons induced from the corpus being aligned.

Haruno and Yamazaki (1996) show that combining an induced lexicon with an external dictionary yields better results. Papageorgiou et al. (1994) use part-of-speech, commonly preserved in translation, by computing the optimum alignment based on the PoS-tags. Tschorn and Lüdeling (2003) use a morphological analyzer to improve a dictionary-based distance measure, and Ma (2006) increases the robustness of a lexicon-based aligner by assigning greater weights to less frequent translated words.

Sennrich and Volk (2010) use machine translations and BLEU (Papineni et al., 2002) as a similarity score to find reliable alignments to use as anchor points. The gaps between the anchor points are filled using BLEU-based and length-based heuristics.

Thompson and Koehn (2019) describe a method based on bilingual sentence embeddings, using the similarity between the embeddings as the scoring function for alignment.

2.2 Filtering

Recently, neural networks have been used to find anchor points and detect misalignments. Many of these methods have been devised to extract parallel sentences from comparable corpora, by training classifiers to determine if source and target sentences are parallel.

Earlier work includes employing the IBM models (Brown et al., 1993) for word alignment. Khadivi and Ney (2005) filter out the noisy part of a corpus based on IBM models 1 and 4 and length-based models, and score the alignments on a linear combination of these. Taghipour et al. (2011) do outlier detection and show that their filtered corpus results in improved translation quality, even though sentences have been removed. Sarikaya et al. (2009) use context extrapolation to boost the sentence pair coverage, checking whether the distance of the sentences from an anchor point is the same, and whether the sentences have the highest similarity score compared to other pairs within a window, despite being below a defined threshold.

Crosslingual word embeddings have been used to calculate distance between equivalences in different languages (Luong et al., 2015; Artetxe et al., 2016). Defauw et al. (2019) treat filtering as a supervised regression problem and show that Levenshtein distance (Levenshtein, 1966) between the target and MT-translated source, as well as cosine distance between sentence embeddings of the source and target, are important features. While they use InferSent (Conneau et al., 2017), BERT (Devlin et al., 2019) has recently been employed for calculating crosslingual semantic textual similarity to detect misalignment with good results (Lo and Simard, 2019).

Zipporah (Xu and Koehn, 2017) uses a logistic regression model trained to classify sentence pairs. Noisy data is synthesized and used as negative samples in training. BiCleaner (Sánchez-Cartagena et al., 2018) uses a set of handcrafted hard rules to detect flawed sentences and then proceeds to use a random forest classifier based on lexical translations and several shallow features such as respective length, matching numbers and punctuation. Finally, it scores sentences based on fluency using 5-gram language models.

In 2019, at the fourth Conference on Machine Translation, WMT, the shared task on parallel corpora filtering focused on low-resource conditions. The method central to the best-performing submission was the use of crosslingual sentence embeddings, trained from parallel sentence pairs (Chaudhary et al., 2019). Artetxe and Schwenk (2019a) devised a similar method. Both papers tackle the inconsistencies of cosine similarity by investigating the neighbourhood of a given sentence pair, outperforming systems using only cosine similarity.

3 Experimental Framework

The continuum of morphologically rich languages is quite diverse with the one end of the continuum being agglutinative languages, that primarily rely on discrete particles for inflection, and the other being fusional languages, which tend to use a single inflectional morpheme to denote multiple features. While it may be worthwhile to investigate if the same unsupervised methods work across different language categories, it can be expected that if further processing is needed, different approaches have to be taken. Decompounding (Alfonseca et al., 2008) may be more useful for agglutinative languages to tackle the OOV problem, and for many fusional languages internal change and suppletion call for different approaches. In our study we focus on fusional languages. English is primarily an analytic language and Icelandic a fusional language with moderately rich morphology. We will be using the English-Icelandic language pair as a test case.

3.1 Data

ParIce, an English-Icelandic parallel corpus, was compiled from data consisting of 4.3 million translation segments. It was aligned with LF Aligner, which uses Hunalign (Varga et al., 2005), and then filtered using a sentence-scoring algorithm based on a bilingual lexicon bag-of-words method and a comparison between the original segment and an MT-generated translation. The filtering process resulted in 3.5 million translated segments. Manual evaluation of approximately 2000 sample pairs from the corpus indicate that approximately 5% are faulty, while over 50% of the deleted segments are estimated to be faulty using automatic methods.

From these numbers we can deduce that in the raw 4.3 million segment ParIce corpus, there are approx. 3.7 million good segments and around 600K faulty ones. Many of the faulty segments in the corpus are due to misalignment. We will be working with the raw data that made up the 4.3 million segment ParIce corpus. In order to compile a better corpus, we need improved alignment methods to reduce the number of faulty alignments, and we need a classifier that is able to identify the quality of the segments with high precision and recall in order to build as big a corpus as possible with as few faulty segments as possible.

3.2 Evaluation

We are building three evaluation sets, for alignment, filtering, and MT, all sub-sampled and extracted from the ParIce corpus. The MT evaluation set will contain 3000 manually aligned and error-free segments. The alignment evaluation set will have 2000 manually aligned sentences and the filtering set 2000 automatically aligned segments, each assigned one of four classes: correct, partially misaligned, partially incorrect translation, incorrect.

To evaluate the usefulness of our methods for MT, we will use our aligned and filtered corpora to train SMT and NMT systems and compare the results to a baseline where the raw ParIce corpus is used for training.

3.3 Tools and Models

In Section 4, we will discuss some of the methods we will be experimenting with. These include applying a variety of available tools and models as well as developing our own. ABLTagger (Steingrímsson et al., 2019) will be used for PoS-tagging Icelandic texts. The tagger employs biLSTMs and an external morphological lexicon (Bjarnadóttir et al., 2019). Lemmatising will be carried out using Nefnir (Ingólfsdóttir et al., 2019). For all English processing we will use tools available in the NLTK toolkit (Bird et al., 2009) or SpaCy.[2]

We will focus on the most common word embedding models: word2vec (Mikolov et al., 2013), GloVe (Pennington et al., 2014), FastText (Bojanowski et al., 2017) and ELMo (Peters et al., 2018). As using bilingual sentence embeddings with BERT has been shown to be effective for filtering (Lo and Simard, 2019), we want to experiment with different contextualized embedding models. The main hindrance with these models is the massive computational resources needed to train, which may limit our possibilites.

For alignment and filtering we experiment with Bleualign, Hunalign and vecalign for sentence alignment, Giza++ (Och and Ney, 2003) for word alignments, and Zipporah, BiCleaner and LASER (Artetxe and Schwenk, 2019b) for filtering, and possibly to help with anchoring the parallel texts for more effective alignment.

Moses (Koehn et al., 2007) will be employed for phrase-based SMT and our NMT system uses the reference implementation of Vaswani et al. (2017) of the transformer-base architecture that is part of the Tensor2Tensor package (Vaswani et al., 2018).

4 Research Plan

Our first goal is to set up an unsupervised pipeline for aligning parallel texts. While this is the first step in tackling RQ2, it is also necessary to devise a method to answer RQ1. We will outline how we seek to answer these questions, as well as RQ3. A secondary goal is to investigate methods to improve upon the unsupervised pipeline by exploring how basic NLP tools can help us deal with the data sparsity problem inherent to many morphologically rich languages. In the following subsections we describe how we intend to research these questions.

4.1 Unsupervised Alignment

Our initial pipeline for aligning parallel texts is trained only on monolingual corpora. While this is a starting point for language pairs lacking pre-existing parallel corpora or glossaries to use with alignment, it also serves as a baseline to compare to when additional processing modules are added, such as a lemmatizer or other NLP tools.

	LF Aligner			Bleualign + Monoses		
	Regulatory texts	Literary texts	Total	Regulatory texts	Literary texts	Total
Aligned pairs	184	69	253	166	61	227
- of which correct	143	57	79.1%	154	54	91.6%
- of which faulty	41	12	20.9%	12	7	8.4%
Aligned words	2470/2485	1652/1652	4122/4137	2427/2485	1539/1652	3966/4137
- of which correct	1980	1337	80.5%	2110	1539	92.0%

Table 1: Alignment results for both systems and number of source language words in the alignments. When no alignment was found the segments were discarded.

As stated in Section 1, we initially employ Bleualign for unsupervised alignment, but instead of bootstrapping an initial training set with length-based methods like Sennrich and Volk (2011), we train Monoses and use that to provide Bleualign with machine translations of the sentences being aligned. Monoses is trained by building cross-lingual word embeddings from monolingual corpora using word2vec and Vecmap (Artetxe et al., 2018a), inducing a phrase table. An SMT system is then trained on this data and used to translate the monolingual corpus in one of the two languages. The translated data is then used to train a standard SMT system in the opposite direction. A new phrase table is built and the process iterated three times for a final model.

To investigate the feasibility of our method we aligned two parallel texts, selected randomly from the ParIce data. We compared the results to LF Aligner, which employs Hunalign. To be able to evaluate the alignment methods accurately, evaluation sets are being compiled (see Section 3.2). Here, we present preliminary results acquired by manually evaluating the alignments. Results, given in Table 1, show that the Bleualign + Monoses method gives better results as measured by accuracy of the aligned pairs, with a total of 91.6% of the resulting pairs correctly aligned, vs. only 79.1% of the alignments by LF Aligner. Although our method yields 10% fewer aligned pairs, it results in a parallel corpus which has substantially more correct alignments both in terms of absolute numbers and percentage of alignments, regardless of whether we are looking at aligned pairs or aligned words.

There are a variety of ways to improve upon the unsupervised method. By training larger word embedding models we can increase the vocabulary. By investigating common n-grams within word embedding models we may be able to better pinpoint phrases or multi-word expressions. By extending the iteration process to the bitexts by selecting the highest-scoring sentence pairs after training and alignment, and add them to the training set of the SMT system, we would have more accurate training data, and probably derive better translations after each iteration. That in turn would likely raise the confidence for selecting the best alignments.

4.2 Investigating Misalignments

After setting up alignment pipelines and creating evaluation sets, we will initiate the filtering process using methods and strategies that have previously given good results for other language pairs.

One aspect of the filtering process is to decide which noise is most important to filter out. While Khayrallah and Koehn (2018) highlight the importance of filtering out certain types of noise in parallel corpora, we want more fine-grained results. We will conduct a similar study but investigate different classes of misalignments especially. This will help us decide whether to treat all misalignments the same or if some are worse than others.

We will do this by using available tools (see Section 3.3) to aggressively filter out possible faulty alignments to have as clean a corpus as possible. We will then systematically change the alignments to introduce different types of misalignments in the corpus. The effects of these variations will be investigated by training both SMT and NMT systems, and comparing the effect on changes in resulting translations. This method is intended to give us insight into the problem we pose in RQ1. We will use the results to help us make decisions on how to best set up a filtering system.

4.3 Filtering

We then start the filtering process again, with information about which type of faulty sentences are likely to have the worst effect on MT systems trained by the data. To try to answer RQ3 we will investigate the practicality of applying different mechanisms to scoring sentences. We will look at features such as sentence length; word similarity based on dictionary lookup, both using an external dictionary and an induced one from raw parallel data; word similarity from word embeddings; distance between a machine-translated source sentence and the target sentence; and sentence similarity scores based on bilingual sentence embeddings.

4.4 Language Independence

After studying the effects of misalignments on MT systems and finding a good balance between the different mechanisms used for scoring the aligned segments, we will investigate the extent of this balance being language pair-dependent by running the same process for other language pairs. These could be English-Irish, Danish-Faroese or others that have some of the same characteristics the English-Icelandic pair has, e.g, at least one morphologically rich language and data sparsity. This will give us further insight to answer the three research questions posed in Section 1.

4.5 Aligning Morphologically Rich Languages

While the first goal is to create a completely unsupervised pipeline for building parallel corpora, applicable to any language pair, we also want to investigate the case of morphologically rich languages specifically by extracting latent information in the data that can help us tackle the data sparsity problem. This includes lemmas derived from the word forms, PoS-tags or constituent structures as additional features for sentence-pair scoring, and by training embedding models, both to help with the morphology and with semantics for unknown words. For this we use available tools such as a PoS-tagger and lemmatizer to try to outperform the unsupervised method alone. For many languages these tools are not available, as they usually rely on training data which may not exist for low-resource languages. Pursuing our second goal we will thus consider the case of a low- to medium-resource language which is morphologically rich and for which basic NLP tools are available. For the language pair selected as our test case, English-Icelandic, all necessary NLP tools are available, so successful methods can subsequently be tested on other language pairs. Furthermore, the only parallel corpus available for Icelandic is rather small and quite noisy and there is a pressing need to improve on it. For proof-of-concept we want our methods to achieve that goal.

No machine-readable English-Icelandic dictionary is available, and if we want to try to use semi-supervised methods for the language pair we will thus need to induce a lexicon from the parallel data, monolingual data or both. Other methods for building a glossary may include using external data such as Wiktionary or Wikipedia, and using available dictionaries in different languages for pivoting.

One of the products of this research will be a toolset to produce parallel corpora from multilingual texts. The software should: align bilingual parallel texts; filter bilingual parallel corpora; be modular; be language-pair independent – although optional language-specific features can be used; use external tools for linguistic annotation: PoS-tagging, parsing, lemmatising, machine translation or other methods that may be beneficial; offer a variety of strategies for aligning and filtering, depending on available resources; and it should aim at accuracy at the cost of speed.

5 Summary

We have given an overview of the literature on sentence alignment and parallel corpus filtering. We outlined challenges associated with implementing these methods for low-resource and morphologically rich languages and proposed initial experiments to tackle these challenges. The motivation for this research is to improve the quality of machine translations by making better use of and increasing the quality of parallel training data, especially in regard to sparse data scenarios. An unsupervised method that effectively aligns bilingual texts will lower the barrier for building high-quality MT systems for low-resource languages and our first results suggest that it may also play a role in improving MT for morphologically rich languages.

Acknowledgements

This work is supported by the Language Technology Programme for Icelandic 2019-2023, funded by the Icelandic government, and by the ADAPT Centre for Digital Content Technology which is funded under the Science Foundation Ireland (SFI) Research Centres Programme (Grant No. 13/RC/2106) and is co-funded under the European Regional Development Fund.

References

Enrique Alfonseca, Slaven Bilac, and Stefan Pharies. 2008. Decompounding query keywords from compounding languages. In *Proceedings of ACL-08: HLT, Short Papers*, Columbus, Ohio.

Mikel Artetxe, Gorka Labaka, and Eneko Agirre. 2016. Learning principled bilingual mappings of word embeddings while preserving monolingual invariance. In *Proceedings of the 2016 Conference on Empirical Methods in Natural Language Processing*, Austin, Texas.

Mikel Artetxe, Gorka Labaka, and Eneko Agirre. 2018a. A robust self-learning method for fully unsupervised cross-lingual mappings of word embeddings. In *Proceedings of the 56th Annual Meeting of the Association for Computational Linguistics (Volume 1: Long Papers)*, Melbourne, Australia.

Mikel Artetxe, Gorka Labaka, and Eneko Agirre. 2018b. Unsupervised Statistical Machine Translation. In *Proceedings of the 2018 Conference on Empirical Methods in Natural Language Processing*, Brussels, Belgium.

Mikel Artetxe and Holger Schwenk. 2019a. Margin-based parallel corpus mining with multilingual sentence embeddings. In *Proceedings of the 57th Annual Meeting of the Association for Computational Linguistics*, Florence, Italy.

Mikel Artetxe and Holger Schwenk. 2019b. Massively Multilingual Sentence Embeddings for Zero-Shot Cross-Lingual Transfer and Beyond. *Transactions of the Association for Computational Linguistics*, 7:597–610.

Starkaður Barkarson and Steinþór Steingrímsson. 2019. Compiling and Filtering ParIce: An English-Icelandic Parallel Corpus. In *Proceedings of the 22nd Nordic Conference on Computational Linguistics*, Turku, Finland.

Steven Bird, Ewan Klein, and Edward Loper. 2009. *Natural Language Processing with Python*, 1st edition. O'Reilly Media, Inc.

Kristín Bjarnadóttir, Kristín Ingibjörg Hlynsdóttir, and Steinþór Steingrímsson. 2019. DIM: The Database of Icelandic Morphology. In *Proceedings of the 22nd Nordic Conference on Computational Linguistics*, Turku, Finland.

Piotr Bojanowski, Edouard Grave, Armand Joulin, and Tomas Mikolov. 2017. Enriching Word Vectors with Subword Information. *Transactions of the Association for Computational Linguistics*, 5:135–146.

Peter F. Brown, Stephen A. Della Pietra, Vincent J. Della Pietra, and Robert L. Mercer. 1993. The Mathematics of Statistical Machine Translation: Parameter Estimation. *Computational Linguistics*, 19(2):263–311.

Peter F. Brown, Jennifer C. Lai, and Robert L. Mercer. 1991. Aligning Sentences in Parallel Corpora. In *Proceedings of the 29th Annual Meeting on Association for Computational Linguistics*, Berkeley, California.

Vishrav Chaudhary, Yuqing Tang, Francisco Guzmán, Holger Schwenk, and Philipp Koehn. 2019. Low-Resource Corpus Filtering Using Multilingual Sentence Embeddings. In *Proceedings of the Fourth Conference on Machine Translation (Volume 3: Shared Task Papers, Day 2)*, Florence, Italy.

Alexis Conneau, Douwe Kiela, Holger Schwenk, Loïc Barrault, and Antoine Bordes. 2017. Supervised Learning of Universal Sentence Representations from Natural Language Inference Data. In *Proceedings of the 2017 Conference on Empirical Methods in Natural Language Processing*, Copenhagen, Denmark.

Arne Defauw, Sara Szoc, Anna Bardadym, Joris Brabers, Frederic Everaert, Roko Mijic, Kim Scholte, Tom Vanallemeersch, Koen Van Winckel, and Joachim Van den Bogaert. 2019. Misalignment Detection for Web-Scraped Corpora: A Supervised Regression Approach. *Informatics*, 6(3):35.

Jacob Devlin, Ming-Wei Chang, Kenton Lee, and Kristina Toutanova. 2019. BERT: Pre-training of deep bidirectional transformers for language understanding. In *Proceedings of the 2019 Conference of the North American Chapter of the Association for Computational Linguistics: Human Language Technologies, Volume 1 (Long and Short Papers)*, Minneapolis, Minnesota.

William A. Gale and Kenneth W. Church. 1991. A Program for Aligning Sentences in Bilingual Corpora. In *Proceedings of the 29th Annual Meeting on Association for Computational Linguistics*, Berkeley, California.

Brannon C. Harris. 1988. Bi-text, a New Concept in Translation Theory. *Language Monthly*, 54:8–10.

Masahiko Haruno and Takefumi Yamazaki. 1996. High-Performance Bilingual Text Alignment Using Statistical and Dictionary Information. In *Proceedings of the 34th Annual Meeting on Association for Computational Linguistics*, Santa Cruz, California.

Martin Haspelmath and Andrea D. Sims. 2013. *Understanding Morphology*. Taylor & Francis, New York.

Svanhvít Lilja Ingólfsdóttir, Hrafn Loftsson, Jón Friðrik Daðason, and Kristín Bjarnadóttir. 2019. Nefnir: A high accuracy lemmatizer for Icelandic. In *Proceedings of the 22nd Nordic Conference on Computational Linguistics*, Turku, Finland.

Martin Kay and Martin Röscheisen. 1993. Text-Translation Alignment. *Computational Linguistics*, 19(1):121–142.

Shahram Khadivi and Hermann Ney. 2005. Automatic Filtering of Bilingual Corpora for Statistical Machine Translation. In *Natural Language Processing and Information Systems*, pages 263–274, Berlin. Springer Berlin Heidelberg.

Huda Khayrallah and Philipp Koehn. 2018. On the impact of various types of noise on neural machine translation. In *Proceedings of the 2nd Workshop on Neural Machine Translation and Generation*, Melbourne, Australia.

Yunsu Kim, Miguel Graça, and Hermann Ney. 2020. When and why is unsupervised neural machine translation useless? *ArXiv*, abs/2004.10581.

Philipp Koehn, Hieu Hoang, Alexandra Birch, Chris Callison-Burch, Marcello Federico, Nicola Bertoldi, Brooke Cowan, Wade Shen, Christine Moran, Richard Zens, Chris Dyer, Ondřej Bojar, Alexandra Constantin, and Evan Herbst. 2007. Moses: Open source toolkit for statistical machine translation. In *Proceedings of the 45th Annual Meeting of the Association for Computational Linguistics Companion Volume Proceedings of the Demo and Poster Sessions*, Prague, Czech Republic.

Philipp Koehn and Rebecca Knowles. 2017. Six challenges for neural machine translation. In *Proceedings of the First Workshop on Neural Machine Translation*, Vancouver, Canada.

Guillaume Lample, Myle Ott, Alexis Conneau, Ludovic Denoyer, and Marc'Aurelio Ranzato. 2018. Phrase-based & neural unsupervised machine translation. In *Proceedings of the 2018 Conference on Empirical Methods in Natural Language Processing*, Brussels, Belgium.

Yichong Leng, Xu Tan, Tao Qin, Xiang-Yang Li, and Tie-Yan Liu. 2019. Unsupervised pivot translation for distant languages. In *Proceedings of the 57th Annual Meeting of the Association for Computational Linguistics*, Florence, Italy.

Vladimir Iosifovich Levenshtein. 1966. Binary codes capable of correcting deletions, insertions and reversals. *Soviet Physics Doklady*, 10(8):707–710.

Chi-kiu Lo and Michel Simard. 2019. Fully unsupervised crosslingual semantic textual similarity metric based on BERT for identifying parallel data. In *Proceedings of the 23rd Conference on Computational Natural Language Learning (CoNLL)*, Hong Kong, China.

Minh-Thang Luong, Hieu Pham, and Christopher D. Manning. 2015. Bilingual Word Representations with Monolingual Quality in Mind. In *NAACL Workshop on Vector Space Modeling for NLP*, Denver, Colorado.

Xiaoyi Ma. 2006. Champollion: A robust parallel text sentence aligner. In *Proceedings of the Fifth International Conference on Language Resources and Evaluation (LREC'06)*, Genoa, Italy.

Tomas Mikolov, Kai Chen, Greg Corrado, and Jeffrey Dean. 2013. Efficient Estimation of Word Representations in Vector Space. In *1st International Conference on Learning Representations, ICLR 2013, Workshop Track Proceedings*, Scottsdale, Arizona.

Franz Josef Och and Hermann Ney. 2003. A systematic comparison of various statistical alignment models. *Computational Linguistics*, 29(1):19–51.

Harris Papageorgiou, Lambros Cranias, and Stelios Piperidis. 1994. Automatic Alignment in Parallel Corpora. In *32nd Annual Meeting of the Association for Computational Linguistics*, Las Cruces, New Mexico.

Kishore Papineni, Salim Roukos, Todd Ward, and Wei-Jing Zhu. 2002. BLEU: a Method for Automatic Evaluation of Machine Translation. In *Proceedings of the 40th Annual Meeting of the Association for Computational Linguistics*, Philadelphia, PA.

Jeffrey Pennington, Richard Socher, and Christopher Manning. 2014. GloVe: Global Vectors for Word Representation. In *Proceedings of the 2014 Conference on Empirical Methods in Natural Language Processing*, Doha, Qatar.

Matthew Peters, Mark Neumann, Mohit Iyyer, Matt Gardner, Christopher Clark, Kenton Lee, and Luke Zettlemoyer. 2018. Deep Contextualized Word Representations. In *Proceedings of the 2018 Conference of the North American Chapter of the Association for Computational Linguistic*, New Orleans, Louisiana.

Víctor M. Sánchez-Cartagena, Marta Bañón, Sergio Ortiz-Rojas, and Gema Ramírez. 2018. Prompsit's submission to WMT 2018 Parallel Corpus Filtering shared task. In *Proceedings of the Third Conference on Machine Translation: Shared Task Papers*, Belgium, Brussels.

Ruhi Sarikaya, Sameer Maskey, R. Zhang, Ea-Ee Jan, D. Wang, Bhuvana Ramabhadran, and Salim Roukos. 2009. Iterative sentence-pair extraction from quasi-parallel corpora for machine translation. In *Proceedings of INTERSPEECH 2009*, Brighton, United Kingdom.

Rico Sennrich and Martin Volk. 2010. MT-based Sentence Alignment for OCR-generated Parallel Texts. In *The Ninth Conference of the Association for Machine Translation in the Americas*, Denver, Colorado.

Rico Sennrich and Martin Volk. 2011. Iterative, MT-based Sentence Alignment of Parallel Texts. In *Proceedings of the 18th Nordic Conference of Computational Linguistics*, Riga, Latvia.

Aleksandra Steinbergs. 1996. The classification of languages. In William O'Grady, Michael Dobrovolsky, and Francis Katamba, editors, *Contemporary Linguistics*, 3rd edition, chapter 9, pages 372–415. Longman, Harlow, UK.

Steinþór Steingrímsson, Örvar Kárason, and Hrafn Loftsson. 2019. Augmenting a BiLSTM tagger with a morphological lexicon and a lexical category identification step. In *Proceedings of the International Conference on Recent Advances in Natural Language Processing (RANLP 2019)*, Varna, Bulgaria.

Kaveh Taghipour, Shahram Khadivi, and Jia Xu. 2011. Parallel Corpus Refinement as an Outlier Detection Algorithm. In *Proceedings of MT Summit XIII*, Xiamen, China.

Brian Thompson and Philipp Koehn. 2019. Vecalign: Improved Sentence Alignment in Linear Time and Space. In *Proceedings of the 2019 Conference on Empirical Methods in Natural Language Processing and the 9th International Joint Conference on Natural Language Processing (EMNLP-IJCNLP)*, Hong Kong, China.

Patrick Tschorn and Anke Lüdeling. 2003. Morphological knowledge and alignment of English-German parallel corpora. In *Proceedings of the Corpus Linguistics 2003 conference*, Lancaster, UK.

Dániel Varga, Péter Halácsy, András Kornai, Nagy Viktor, Nagy László, Németh László, and Tron Viktor. 2005. Parallel corpora for medium density languages. In *Proceedings of the International Conference on Recent Advances in Natural Language Processing (RANLP 2005)*, Borovets, Bulgaria.

Ashish Vaswani, Samy Bengio, Eugene Brevdo, Francois Chollet, Aidan N. Gomez, Stephan Gouws, Llion Jones, Łukasz Kaiser, Nal Kalchbrenner, Niki Parmar, Ryan Sepassi, Noam Shazeer, and Jakob Uszkoreit. 2018. Tensor2Tensor for Neural Machine Translation. In *Proceedings of the 13th Conference of the Association for Machine Translation in the Americas (Volume 1: Research Papers)*, Boston, Massachusetts.

Ashish Vaswani, Noam Shazeer, Niki Parmar, Jakob Uszkoreit, Llion Jones, Aidan N Gomez, Ł ukasz Kaiser, and Illia Polosukhin. 2017. Attention is All you Need. In *Advances in Neural Information Processing Systems 30*, Long Beach, California.

Jiawei Wu, Xin Wang, and William Yang Wang. 2019. Extract and Edit: An Alternative to Back-Translation for Unsupervised Neural Machine Translation. In *Proceedings of the 2019 Conference of the North American Chapter of the Association for Computational Linguistics: Human Language Technologies, Volume 1 (Long and Short Papers)*, Minneapolis, Minnesota.

Hainan Xu and Philipp Koehn. 2017. Zipporah: a fast and scalable data cleaning system for noisy web-crawled parallel corpora. In *Proceedings of the 2017 Conference on Empirical Methods in Natural Language Processing*, Copenhagen, Denmark.

Understanding Points of Correspondence between Sentences for Abstractive Summarization

Logan Lebanoff[†]   John Muchovej[†]   Franck Dernoncourt[§]
Doo Soon Kim[§]   Lidan Wang[§]   Walter Chang[§]   Fei Liu[†]

[†]University of Central Florida   [§]Adobe Research
{loganlebanoff, john.muchovej}@knights.ucf.edu   feiliu@cs.ucf.edu
{dernonco, dkim, lidwang, wachang}@adobe.com

Abstract

Fusing sentences containing disparate content is a remarkable human ability that helps create informative and succinct summaries. Such a simple task for humans has remained challenging for modern abstractive summarizers, substantially restricting their applicability in real-world scenarios. In this paper, we present an investigation into fusing sentences drawn from a document by introducing the notion of points of correspondence, which are cohesive devices that tie any two sentences together into a coherent text. The types of points of correspondence are delineated by text cohesion theory, covering pronominal and nominal referencing, repetition and beyond. We create a dataset containing the documents, source and fusion sentences, and human annotations of points of correspondence between sentences. Our dataset bridges the gap between coreference resolution and summarization. It is publicly shared to serve as a basis for future work to measure the success of sentence fusion systems.[1]

1 Introduction

Stitching portions of text together into a sentence is a crucial first step in abstractive summarization. It involves choosing which sentences to fuse, what content from each of them to retain and how best to present that information (Elsner and Santhanam, 2011). A major challenge in fusing sentences is to establish correspondence between sentences. If there exists no correspondence, it would be difficult, if not impossible, to fuse sentences. In Table 1, we present example source and fusion sentences, where the summarizer attempts to merge two sentences into a summary sentence with improper use of *points of correspondence*. In this paper, we seek to uncover hidden correspondences between sen-

---

[1] https://github.com/ucfnlp/points-of-correspondence

[Source Sentences]
Robert Downey Jr. is making headlines for walking out of an interview with a British journalist who dared to veer away from the superhero movie Downey was there to promote.
The journalist instead started asking personal questions about the actor's political beliefs **and "dark periods" of addiction and jail time.**

[Summary] Robert Downey Jr started asking personal questions about the actor's political beliefs.

[Source Sentences]
"Real Housewives of Beverly Hills" star and former child actress Kim Richards is accused of kicking a police officer after being arrested Thursday morning.
A police representative said Richards was asked to leave but refused **and then entered a restroom and wouldn't come out.**

[Summary] Kim Richards is accused of kicking a police officer who refused to leave.

[Source Sentences]
The kind of horror represented by the Blackwater case and others like it [...] may be largely absent from public memory in the West these days, but it is being used by the Islamic State in Iraq and Syria (ISIS) to support its sectarian narrative.
In its propaganda, ISIS has been using Abu Ghraib and other cases of Western abuse to legitimize its current actions [...]

[Summary] In its propaganda, ISIS is being used by the Islamic State in Iraq and Syria.

Table 1: Unfaithful summary sentences generated by neural abstractive summarizers, in-house and PG (See et al., 2017). They attempt to merge two sentences into one sentence with improper use of *points of correspondence* between sentences, yielding nonsensical output. Summaries are manually re-cased for readability.

tences, which has a great potential for improving content selection and deep sentence fusion.

Sentence fusion (or multi-sentence compression) plays a prominent role in automated summarization and its importance has long been recognized (Barzilay et al., 1999). Early attempts to fuse sentences build a dependency graph from sentences, then decode a tree from the graph using integer linear programming, finally linearize the tree to generate a summary sentence (Barzilay and McKeown, 2005; Filippova and Strube, 2008; Thadani and McKeown, 2013a). Despite valuable insights gained from

Proceedings of the 58th Annual Meeting of the Association for Computational Linguistics: Student Research Workshop, pages 191–198
July 5 - July 10, 2020. ©2020 Association for Computational Linguistics

PoC Type	Source Sentences	Summary Sentence
Pronominal Referencing	[S1] The bodies showed signs of torture. [S2] They were left on the side of a highway in Chilpancingo, about an hour north of the tourist resort of Acapulco in the state of Guerrero.	• The bodies of the men, which showed signs of torture, were left on the side of a highway in Chilpancingo.
Nominal Referencing	[S1] Bahamian R&B singer Johnny Kemp, best known for the 1988 party anthem "Just Got Paid," died this week in Jamaica. [S2] The singer is believed to have drowned at a beach in Montego Bay on Thursday, the Jamaica Constabulatory Force said in a press release.	• Johnny Kemp is "believed to have drowned at a beach in Montego Bay," police say.
Common-Noun Referencing	[S1] A nurse confessed to killing five women and one man at hospital. [S2] A former nurse in the Czech Republic murdered six of her elderly patients with massive doses of potassium in order to ease her workload.	• The nurse, who has been dubbed "nurse death" locally, has admitted killing the victims with massive doses of potassium.
Repetition	[S1] Stewart said that she and her husband, Joseph Naaman, booked Felix on their flight from the United Arab Emirates to New York on April 1. [S2] The couple said they spent $1,200 to ship Felix on the 14-hour flight.	• Couple spends $1,200 to ship their cat, Felix, on a flight from the United Arab Emirates.
Event Triggers	[S1] Four employees of the store have been arrested, but its manager was still at large, said Goa police superintendent Kartik Kashyap. [S2] If convicted, they could spend up to three years in jail, Kashyap said.	• The four store workers arrested could spend 3 years each in prison if convicted.

Table 2: Types of sentence correspondences. Text cohesion can manifest itself in different forms.

these attempts, experiments are often performed on small datasets and systems are designed to merge sentences conveying *similar* information. Nonetheless, humans do not restrict themselves to combine similar sentences, but also *disparate* sentences containing fundamentally different content but remain related to make fusion sensible (Elsner and Santhanam, 2011). We focus specifically on analyzing fusion of *disparate* sentences, which is a distinct problem from fusing a set of *similar* sentences.

While fusing disparate sentences is a seemingly simple task for humans to do, it has remained challenging for modern abstractive summarizers (See et al., 2017; Celikyilmaz et al., 2018; Chen and Bansal, 2018; Liu and Lapata, 2019). These systems learn to perform content selection and generation through end-to-end learning. However, such a strategy is not consistently effective and they struggle to reliably perform sentence fusion (Falke et al., 2019; Kryściński et al., 2019). E.g., only 6% of summary sentences generated by pointer-generator networks (See et al., 2017) are fusion sentences; the ratio for human abstracts is much higher (32%). Further, Lebanoff et al. (2019a) report that 38% of fusion sentences contain incorrect facts. There exists a pressing need for—and this paper contributes to–broadening the understanding of points of correspondence used for sentence fusion.

We present the first attempt to construct a sizable sentence fusion dataset, where an instance in the dataset consists of a pair of input sentences, a fusion sentence, and human-annotated *points of correspondence* between sentences. Distinguishing our work from previous efforts (Geva et al., 2019), our input contains *disparate* sentences and output is a fusion sentence containing important, though not equivalent information of the input sentences. Our

investigation is inspired by Halliday and Hasan's theory of *text cohesion* (1976) that covers a broad range of points of correspondence, including entity and event coreference (Ng, 2017; Lu and Ng, 2018), shared words/concepts between sentences and more. Our contributions are as follows.

- We describe the first effort at establishing points of correspondence between disparate sentences. Without a clear understanding of points of correspondence, sentence fusion remains a daunting challenge that is only sparsely and sometimes incorrectly performed by abstractive summarizers.

- We present a sizable dataset for sentence fusion containing human-annotated corresponding regions between pairs of sentences. It can be used as a testbed for evaluating the ability of summarization models to perform sentence fusion. We report on the insights gained from annotations to suggest important future directions for sentence fusion. Our dataset is released publicly.

2 Annotating Points of Correspondence

We cast sentence fusion as a constrained summarization task where portions of text are selected from each source sentence and stitched together to form a fusion sentence; rephrasing and reordering are allowed in this process. We propose guidelines for annotating *points of correspondence* (PoC) between sentences based on Halliday and Hasan's theory of cohesion (1976).

We consider points of correspondence as cohesive phrases that tie sentences together into a coherent text. Guided by text cohesion theory, we categorize PoC into five types, including pronominal referencing ("*they*"), nominal referencing ("*Johnny Kemp*"), common-noun referencing ("*five women*"),

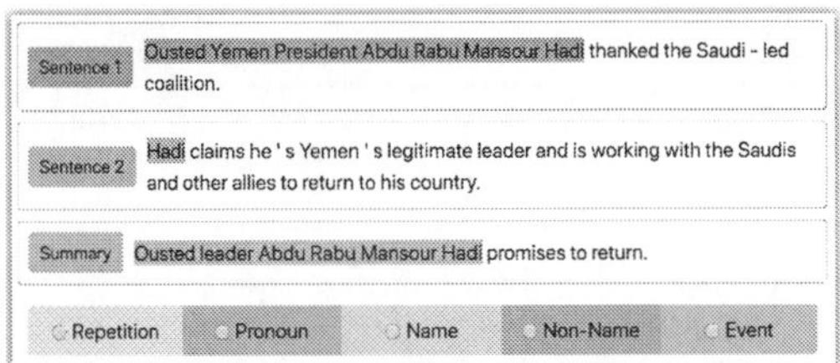

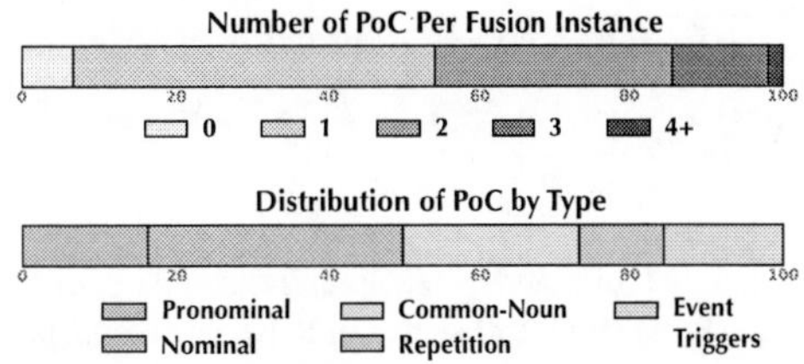

Figure 2: Statistics of PoC occurrences and types.

Figure 1: An illustration of the annotation interface. A human annotator is asked to highlight text spans referring to the same entity, then choose one from the five pre-defined PoC types.

repetition, and event trigger words that are related in meaning ("*died*" and "*drowned*"). An illustration of PoC types is provided in Table 2. Our categorization emphasizes the lexical linking that holds a text together and gives it meaning.

A human annotator is instructed to identify a text span from each of the source sentences and summary sentence, thus establishing a point of correspondence between source sentences, and between source and summary sentences. As our goal is to understand the role of PoC in sentence fusion, we do not consider the case if PoC is only found in source sentences but not summary sentence, e.g., "*Kashyap said*" and "*said Goa police superintendent Kartik Kashyap*" in Table 2. If multiple PoC co-exist in an example, an annotator is expected to label them all; a separate PoC type will be assigned to each PoC occurrence. We are particularly interested in annotating inter-sentence PoC. If entity mentions ("*John*" and "*he*") are found in the same sentence, we do not explicitly label them but assume such intra-sentence referencing can be captured by an existing coreference resolver. Instances of source sentences and summary sentences are obtained from the test and validation splits of the CNN/DailyMail corpus (See et al., 2017) following the procedure described by Lebanoff et al. (2019a). We take a human summary sentence as an anchor point to find two document sentences that are most similar to it based on ROUGE. It becomes an instance containing a pair of source sentences and their summary. The method allows us to identify a large quantity of candidate fusion instances.

Annotations are performed in two stages. Stage one removes all spurious pairs that are generated by the heuristic, i.e. a summary sentence that is not a valid fusion of the corresponding two source sentences. Human annotators are given a pair of sentences and a summary sentence and are asked

whether it represents a valid fusion. The pairs identified as valid fusions by a majority of annotators move on to stage two. Stage two identifies the corresponding regions in the sentences. As shown in Figure 1, annotators are given a pair of sentences and their summary and are tasked with highlighting the corresponding regions between each sentence. They must also choose one of the five PoC types (repetition, pronominal, nominal, common-noun referencing, and event triggers) for the set of corresponding regions.

We use Amazon mechanical turk, allowing only workers with 95% approval rate and at least 5,000 accepted tasks. To ensure high quality annotations, we first run a qualification round of 10 tasks. Workers performing sufficiently on these tasks were allowed to annotate the whole dataset. For task one, 2,200 instances were evaluated and 621 of them were filtered out. In total, we annotate points of correspondence for **1,599 instances, taken from 1,174 documents**. Similar to (Hardy et al., 2019), we report Fleiss' Kappa judged on each word (highlighted or not), yielding substantial inter-annotator agreement (κ=0.58) for annotating points of correspondence. We include a reference to the original article that each instance was taken from, thus providing context for each instance.

Figure 2 shows statistics of PoC occurrence frequencies and the distribution of different PoC types. A majority of sentence pairs have one or two points of correspondence. Only a small percentage (6.5%) do not share a PoC. A qualitatively analysis shows that these sentences often have an *implicit* discourse relationship, e.g., "*The two men speak. Scott then gets out of the car, again, and runs away.*" In this example, there is no clear portion of text that is shared between the sentences; rather, the connection lies in the fact that one event happens after the other. Most of the PoC are a flavor of coreference (pronominal, nominal, or common-noun). Few are exact repetition. Further, we find that only 38% of points of correspondence in the sentence pair share

Coref Resolver	P(%)	R(%)	F(%)	Pronominal	Nominal	Comm.-Noun	Repetition	Event Trig.
SpaCy	**59.2**	20.1	30.0	30.8	23.3	10.4	39.9	2.6
AllenNLP	49.0	24.5	32.7	36.5	28.1	14.7	47.1	3.1
Stanford CoreNLP	54.2	**26.2**	**35.3**	40.0	27.3	17.4	55.1	2.3

Table 3: Results of various coreference resolvers on successfully identifying inter-sentence points of correspondence (PoC) and recall scores of these resolvers split by PoC correspondence type.

any words (lemmatized). This makes identifying them automatically challenging, requiring a deeper understanding of what connects the two sentences.

3   Resolving Coreference

Coreference resolution (Ng, 2017) is similar to the task of identifying points of correspondence. Thus, a natural question we ask is how well state-of-the-art coreference resolvers can be adapted to this task. If coreference resolvers can perform reasonably well on PoC identification, then these resolvers can be used to extract PoC annotations to potentially enhance sentence fusion. If they perform poorly, coreference performance results can indicate areas of improvement for future work on detecting points of correspondence. In this paper, we compare three coreference resolvers on our dataset, provided by open-source libraries: Stanford CoreNLP (Manning et al., 2014), SpaCy (Honnibal and Montani, 2017), and AllenNLP (Gardner et al., 2017).

We base our evaluation on the standard metric used for coreference resolution, B-CUBED algorithm (Bagga and Baldwin, 1998), with some modifications. Each resolver is run on an input pair of sentences to obtain multiple clusters, each representing an entity (e.g., *Johnny Kemp*) containing multiple mentions (e.g., *Johnny Kemp*; *he*; *the singer*) of that entity. More than one cluster can be detected by the coreference resolver, as additional entities may exist in the given sentence pair (e.g., *Johnny Kemp* and *the police*). Similarly, in Section §2, human annotators identified multiple PoC clusters, each representing a point of correspondence containing one mention from each sentence. We evaluate how well the resolver-detected clusters compare to the human-detected clusters (i.e., PoCs). If a resolver cluster overlaps both mentions for the gold-standard PoC, then this resolver cluster is classified as a hit. Any resolver cluster that does not overlap both PoC mentions is a miss. Using this metric, we can calculate precision, recall, and F1 scores based on correctly/incorrectly identified tokens from the outputs of each resolver.

The results are presented in Table 3. The three resolvers exhibit similar performance, but the scores on identifying points of correspondence are less than satisfying. The SpaCy resolver has the highest precision (59.2%) and Stanford CoreNLP achieves the highest F1-score (35.3%). We observe that existing coreference resolvers can sometimes struggle to use the high-level reasoning that humans use to determine what connects two sentences together. Next, we go deeper into understanding what PoC types these resolvers struggle with. We present the recall scores of these resolvers split by PoC correspondence type. Event coreference poses the most difficulty by far, which is understandable as coreference resolution only focuses on entities rather than events. More work into detecting event coreference can bring significant improvements in PoC identification. Common-noun coreference also poses a challenge, in part because names and pronouns give strong clues as to the relationships between mentions, while common-noun relationships are more difficult to identify since they lack these clues.

4   Sentence Fusion

Truly effective summarization will only be achievable when systems have the ability to fully recognize points of correspondence between sentences. It remains to be seen whether such knowledge can be acquired implicitly by neural abstractive systems through joint content selection and generation. We next conduct an initial study to assess neural abstractive summarizers on their ability to perform sentence fusion to merge two sentences into a summary sentence. The task represents an important, atomic unit of abstractive summarization, because a long summary is still generated one sentence at a time (Lebanoff et al., 2019b).

We compare two best-performing abstractive summarizers: *Pointer-Generator* uses an encoder-decoder architecture with attention and copy mechanism (See et al., 2017); *Transformer* adopts a decoder-only Transformer architecture similar to that of (Radford et al., 2019), where a summary is

System	R-1	R-2	R-L	%Fuse
Concat-Baseline	36.13	18.64	27.79	99.7
Pointer-Generator	33.74	16.32	29.27	38.7
Transformer	**38.81**	**20.03**	**33.79**	50.7

Table 4: ROUGE scores of neural abstractive summarizers on the sentence fusion dataset. We also report the percentage of output sentences that are indeed fusion sentences (%Fuse)

decoded one word at a time conditioned on source sentences and the previously-generated summary words. We use the same number of heads, layers, and units per layer as BERT-base (Devlin et al., 2018). In both cases, the summarizer was trained on about 100k instances derived from the train split of CNN/DailyMail, using the same heuristic as described in (§2) without PoC annotations. The summarizer is then tested on our dataset of 1,599 fusion instances and evaluated using standard metrics (Lin, 2004). We also report how often each summarizer actually draws content from both sentences (*%Fuse*), rather than taking content from only one sentence. A generated sentence counts as a fusion if it contains at least two non-stopword tokens from each sentence not already present in the other sentence. Additionally, we include a *Concat-Baseline* creating a fusion sentence by simply concatenating the two source sentences.

The results according to the ROUGE evaluation (Lin, 2004) are presented in Table 4. Sentence fusion appears to be a challenging task even for modern abstractive summarizers. Pointer-Generator has been shown to perform strongly on abstractive summarization, but it is less so on sentence fusion and in other highly abstractive settings (Narayan et al., 2018). Transformer significantly outperforms other methods, in line with previous findings (Liu et al., 2018). We qualitatively examine system outputs. Table 1 presents fusions generated by these models and exemplifies the need for infusing models with knowledge of points of correspondence. In the first example, Pointer-Generator incorrectly conflates *Robert Downey Jr.* with the *journalist* asking questions. Similarly, in the second example, Transformer states the *police officer* refused to leave when it was actually *Richards*. Had the models explicitly recognized the points of correspondence in the sentences—that *the journalist* is a separate entity from *Robert Downey Jr.* and that *Richards* is separate from *police officer*—then a more accurate summary could have been generated.

5   Related Work

Uncovering hidden correspondences between sentences is essential for producing proper summary sentences. A number of recent efforts select important words and sentences from a given document, then let the summarizer attend to selected content to generate a summary (Gehrmann et al., 2018; Hsu et al., 2018; Chen and Bansal, 2018; Putra et al., 2018; Lebanoff et al., 2018; Liu and Lapata, 2019). These systems are largely agnostic to sentence correspondences, which can have two undesirable consequences. If only a single sentence is selected, it can be impossible for the summarizer to produce a fusion sentence from it. Moreover, if *non-fusible* textual units are selected, the summarizer is forced to fuse them into a summary sentence, yielding output summaries that often fail to keep the original meaning intact. Therefore, in this paper we had investigated the correspondences between sentences to gain an understanding of sentence fusion.

Establishing correspondence between sentences goes beyond finding common words. Humans can fuse sentences sharing *few or no* common words if they can find other types of correspondence. Fusing such disparate sentences poses a serious challenge for automated fusion systems (Marsi and Krahmer, 2005; Filippova and Strube, 2008; McKeown et al., 2010; Elsner and Santhanam, 2011; Thadani and McKeown, 2013b; Mehdad et al., 2013; Nayeem et al., 2018). These systems rely on common words to derive a connected graph from input sentences or subject-verb-object triples (Moryossef et al., 2019). When there are no common words in sentences, systems tend to break apart.

There has been a lack of annotated datasets and guidelines for sentence fusion. Few studies have investigated the types of correspondence between sentences such as entity and event coreference. Evaluating sentence fusion systems requires not only novel metrics (Zhao et al., 2019; Zhang et al., 2020; Durmus et al., 2020; Wang et al., 2020) but also high-quality ground-truth annotations. It is therefore necessary to conduct a first study to look into cues humans use to establish correspondence between disparate sentences.

We envision sentence correspondence to be related to text *cohesion* and *coherence*, which help establish correspondences between two pieces of text. Halliday and Hasan (1976) describe text **cohesion** as cohesive devices that tie two textual elements together. They identify five categories of cohesion:

(McKeown et al., 2010)
[S1] Palin actually turned against the bridge project only after it became a national symbol of wasteful spending.
[S2] Ms. Palin supported the bridge project while running for governor, and abandoned it after it became a national scandal.
[Fusion] Palin turned against the bridge project after it became a national scandal.

DiscoFuse (Geva et al., 2019)
[S1] Melvyn Douglas originally was signed to play Sam Bailey.
[S2] The role ultimately went to Walter Pidgeon.
[Fusion] Melvyn Douglas originally was signed to play Sam Bailey, but the role ultimately went to Walter Pidgeon.

Points of Correspondence Dataset (Our Work)
[S1] The bodies showed signs of torture.
[S2] They were left on the side of a highway in Chilpancingo, about an hour north of the tourist resort of Acapulco in the state of Guerrero.
[Fusion] The bodies of the men, which showed signs of torture, were left on the side of a highway in Chilpancingo.

Table 5: Comparison of sentence fusion datasets.

reference, lexical cohesion, ellipsis, substitution and *conjunction*. In contrast, **coherence** is defined in terms of discourse relations between textual elements, such as *elaboration, cause* or *explanation*. Previous work studied discourse relations (Geva et al., 2019), this paper instead focuses on *text cohesion*, which plays a crucial role in generating proper fusion sentences. Our dataset contains pairs of source and fusion sentences collected from news editors in a natural environment. The work is particularly meaningful to text-to-text and data-to-text generation (Gatt and Krahmer, 2018) that demand robust modules to merge disparate content.

We contrast our dataset with previous sentence fusion datasets. McKeown et al. (2010) compile a corpus of 300 sentence fusions as a first step toward a supervised fusion system. However, the input sentences have very similar meaning, though they often present lexical variations and different details. In contrast, our proposed dataset seeks to fuse significantly different meanings together into a single sentence. A large-scale dataset of sentence fusions has been recently collected (Geva et al., 2019), where each sentence has disparate content and are connected by various discourse connectives. This paper instead focuses on *text cohesion* and on fusing only the salient information, which are both vital for abstractive summarization. Examples are presented in Table 5.

6 Conclusion

In this paper, we describe a first effort at annotating points of correspondence between disparate sentences. We present a benchmark dataset comprised of the documents, source and fusion sentences, and human annotations of points of correspondence between sentences. The dataset fills a notable gap of coreference resolution and summarization research. Our findings shed light on the importance of modeling points of correspondence, suggesting important future directions for sentence fusion.

Acknowledgments

We are grateful to the anonymous reviewers for their helpful comments and suggestions. This research was supported in part by the National Science Foundation grant IIS-1909603.

References

Amit Bagga and Breck Baldwin. 1998. Algorithms for scoring coreference chains. In *The first international conference on language resources and evaluation workshop on linguistics coreference*, volume 1, pages 563–566. Granada.

Regina Barzilay and Kathleen R. McKeown. 2005. Sentence fusion for multidocument news summarization. *Computational Linguistics*, 31(3).

Regina Barzilay, Kathleen R. McKeown, and Michael Elhadad. 1999. Information fusion in the context of multi-document summarization. In *Proceedings of the Annual Meeting of the Association for Computational Linguistics (ACL)*.

Asli Celikyilmaz, Antoine Bosselut, Xiaodong He, and Yejin Choi. 2018. Deep communicating agents for abstractive summarization. In *Proceedings of the North American Chapter of the Association for Computational Linguistics (NAACL)*.

Yen-Chun Chen and Mohit Bansal. 2018. Fast abstractive summarization with reinforce-selected sentence rewriting. In *Proceedings of the Annual Meeting of the Association for Computational Linguistics (ACL)*.

Jacob Devlin, Ming-Wei Chang, Kenton Lee, and Kristina Toutanova. 2018. BERT: pre-training of deep bidirectional transformers for language understanding. *arXiv:1810.04805*.

Esin Durmus, He He, and Mona Diab. 2020. Feqa: A question answering evaluation framework for faithfulness assessment in abstractive summarization. In *Proceedings of the Annual Conference of the Association for Computational Linguistics (ACL)*.

Micha Elsner and Deepak Santhanam. 2011. Learning to fuse disparate sentences. In *Proceedings of ACL Workshop on Monolingual Text-To-Text Generation*.

Tobias Falke, Leonardo F. R. Ribeiro, Prasetya Ajie Utama, Ido Dagan, and Iryna Gurevych. 2019.

Ranking generated summaries by correctness: An interesting but challenging application for natural language inference. In *Proceedings of the Annual Meeting of the Association for Computational Linguistics (ACL)*.

Katja Filippova and Michael Strube. 2008. Sentence fusion via dependency graph compression. In *Proceedings of the Conference on Empirical Methods in Natural Language Processing (EMNLP)*.

Matt Gardner, Joel Grus, Mark Neumann, Oyvind Tafjord, Pradeep Dasigi, Nelson F. Liu, Matthew Peters, Michael Schmitz, and Luke S. Zettlemoyer. 2017. Allennlp: A deep semantic natural language processing platform.

Albert Gatt and Emiel Krahmer. 2018. Survey of the state of the art in natural language generation: Core tasks, applications and evaluation. *Journal of Artificial Intelligence Research*, 61:65–170.

Sebastian Gehrmann, Yuntian Deng, and Alexander M. Rush. 2018. Bottom-up abstractive summarization. In *Proceedings of the Conference on Empirical Methods in Natural Language Processing (EMNLP)*.

Mor Geva, Eric Malmi, Idan Szpektor, and Jonathan Berant. 2019. DISCOFUSE: A large-scale dataset for discourse-based sentence fusion. In *Proceedings of the North American Chapter of the Association for Computational Linguistics (NAACL)*.

Michael A. K. Halliday and Ruqaiya Hasan. 1976. *Cohesion in English*. English Language Series. Longman Group Ltd.

Hardy Hardy, Shashi Narayan, and Andreas Vlachos. 2019. HighRES: Highlight-based reference-less evaluation of summarization. In *Proceedings of the 57th Annual Meeting of the Association for Computational Linguistics*, pages 3381–3392, Florence, Italy. Association for Computational Linguistics.

Matthew Honnibal and Ines Montani. 2017. spaCy 2: Natural language understanding with Bloom embeddings, convolutional neural networks and incremental parsing. To appear.

Wan-Ting Hsu, Chieh-Kai Lin, Ming-Ying Lee, Kerui Min, Jing Tang, and Min Sun. 2018. A unified model for extractive and abstractive summarization using inconsistency loss. In *Proceedings of the Annual Meeting of the Association for Computational Linguistics (ACL)*.

Wojciech Kryściński, Nitish Shirish Keskar, Bryan McCann, Caiming Xiong, and Richard Socher. 2019. Neural text summarization: A critical evaluation. In *Proceedings of the Conference on Empirical Methods in Natural Language Processing (EMNLP)*.

Logan Lebanoff, John Muchovej, Franck Dernoncourt, Doo Soon Kim, Seokhwan Kim, Walter Chang, and Fei Liu. 2019a. Analyzing sentence fusion in abstractive summarization. In *Proceedings fo the EMNLP 2019 Workshop on New Frontiers in Summarization*.

Logan Lebanoff, Kaiqiang Song, Franck Dernoncourt, Doo Soon Kim, Seokhwan Kim, Walter Chang, and Fei Liu. 2019b. Scoring sentence singletons and pairs for abstractive summarization. In *Proceedings of the Annual Meeting of the Association for Computational Linguistics (ACL)*.

Logan Lebanoff, Kaiqiang Song, and Fei Liu. 2018. Adapting the neural encoder-decoder framework from single to multi-document summarization. In *Proceedings of the Conference on Empirical Methods in Natural Language Processing (EMNLP)*.

Chin-Yew Lin. 2004. ROUGE: a package for automatic evaluation of summaries. In *Proceedings of ACL Workshop on Text Summarization Branches Out*.

Peter J Liu, Mohammad Saleh, Etienne Pot, Ben Goodrich, Ryan Sepassi, Łukasz Kaiser, and Noam Shazeer. 2018. Generating wikipedia by summarizing long sequences. In *Sixth International Conference on Learning Representations (ICLR)*.

Yang Liu and Mirella Lapata. 2019. Hierarchical transformers for multi-document summarization. In *Proceedings of the Annual Meeting of the Association for Computational Linguistics (ACL)*.

Jing Lu and Vincent Ng. 2018. Event coreference resolution: A survey of two decades of research. In *Proceedings of the 27th International Joint Conference on Artificial Intelligence (IJCAI)*.

Christopher D. Manning, Mihai Surdeanu, John Bauer, Jenny Finkel, Steven J. Bethard, and David McClosky. 2014. The Stanford CoreNLP natural language processing toolkit. In *Association for Computational Linguistics (ACL) System Demonstrations*, pages 55–60.

Erwin Marsi and Emiel Krahmer. 2005. Explorations in sentence fusion. In *Proceedings of the ACL Workshop on Computational Approaches to Semitic Languages*.

Kathleen McKeown, Sara Rosenthal, Kapil Thadani, and Coleman Moore. 2010. Time-efficient creation of an accurate sentence fusion corpus. In *Proceedings of the North American Chapter of the Association for Computational Linguistics (NAACL)*.

Yashar Mehdad, Giuseppe Carenini, Frank W. Tompa, and Raymond T. NG. 2013. Abstractive meeting summarization with entailment and fusion. In *Proceedings of the 14th European Workshop on Natural Language Generation*.

Amit Moryossef, Yoav Goldberg, and Ido Dagan. 2019. Step-by-Step: Separating planning from realization in neural data-to-text generation. In *Proceedings of the North American Chapter of the Association for Computational Linguistics (NAACL)*.

Shashi Narayan, Shay B. Cohen, and Mirella Lapata. 2018. Don't give me the details, just the summary! topic-aware convolutional neural networks for extreme summarization. In *Proceedings of the 2018 Conference on Empirical Methods in Natural Language Processing*, pages 1797–1807, Brussels, Belgium. Association for Computational Linguistics.

Mir Tafseer Nayeem, Tanvir Ahmed Fuad, and Yllias Chali. 2018. Abstractive unsupervised multi-document summarization using paraphrastic sentence fusion. In *Proceedings of the International Conference on Computational Linguistics (COLING)*.

Vincent Ng. 2017. Machine learning for entity coreference resolution: A retrospective look at two decades of research. In *Proceedngs of the Thirty-First AAAI Conference on Artificial Intelligence (AAAI)*.

Jan Wira Gotama Putra, Hayato Kobayashi, and Nobuyuki Shimizu. 2018. Incorporating topic sentence on neural news headline generation.

Alec Radford, Jeffrey Wu, Rewon Child, David Luan, Dario Amodei, and Ilya Sutskever. 2019. Language models are unsupervised multitask learners.

Abigail See, Peter J. Liu, and Christopher D. Manning. 2017. Get to the point: Summarization with pointer-generator networks. In *Proceedings of the Annual Meeting of the Association for Computational Linguistics (ACL)*.

Kapil Thadani and Kathleen McKeown. 2013a. Sentence compression with joint structural inference. In *Proceedings of CoNLL*.

Kapil Thadani and Kathleen McKeown. 2013b. Supervised sentence fusion with single-stage inference. In *Proceedings of the International Joint Conference on Natural Language Processing (IJCNLP)*.

Alex Wang, Kyunghyun Cho, and Mike Lewis. 2020. Asking and answering questions to evaluate the factual consistency of summaries. In *Proceedings of the Annual Conference of the Association for Computational Linguistics (ACL)*.

Tianyi Zhang, Varsha Kishore, Felix Wu, Kilian Q. Weinberger, and Yoav Artzi. 2020. Bertscore: Evaluating text generation with bert. In *International Conference on Learning Representations*.

Wei Zhao, Maxime Peyrard, Fei Liu, Yang Gao, Christian M. Meyer, and Steffen Eger. 2019. MoverScore: Text generation evaluating with contextualized embeddings and earth mover distance. In *Proceedings of the 2019 Conference on Empirical Methods in Natural Language Processing and the 9th International Joint Conference on Natural Language Processing (EMNLP-IJCNLP)*, pages 563–578, Hong Kong, China. Association for Computational Linguistics.

vBLEU: Uncertainty-Aware Automatic Evaluation Method for Open-Domain Dialogue Systems

Yuma Tsuta
The University of Tokyo
`tsuta@tkl.iis.u-tokyo.ac.jp`

Naoki Yoshinaga
Institute of Industrial Science
The University of Tokyo
`ynaga@iis.u-tokyo.ac.jp`

Masashi Toyoda
Institute of Industrial Science, The University of Tokyo
`toyoda@tkl.iis.u-tokyo.ac.jp`

Abstract

Because open-domain dialogues allow diverse responses, basic reference-based metrics such as BLEU do not work well unless we prepare a massive reference set of high-quality responses for input utterances. To reduce this burden, a human-aided, uncertainty-aware metric, ΔBLEU, has been proposed; it embeds human judgment on the quality of reference outputs into the computation of multiple-reference BLEU. In this study, we instead propose a fully automatic, uncertainty-aware evaluation method for open-domain dialogue systems, vBLEU. This method first collects diverse reference responses from massive dialogue data and then annotates their quality judgments by using a neural network trained on automatically collected training data. Experimental results on massive Twitter data confirmed that vBLEU is comparable to ΔBLEU in terms of its correlation with human judgment and that the state of the art automatic evaluation method, RUBER, is improved by integrating vBLEU.

1 Introduction

There has been increasing interest in intelligent dialogue agents such as Apple Siri, Amazon Alexa, and Google Assistant. The key to achieving higher user engagement with those dialogue agents is to support open-domain non-task-oriented dialogues to return a meaningful response for any user input.

The major challenge in developing open-domain dialogue systems is that existing evaluation metrics for text generation tasks, such as BLEU (Papineni et al., 2002), correlate poorly with human judgment on evaluating responses generated by dialogue systems (Liu et al., 2016). In open-domain dialogues, even though responses with various contents and styles are acceptable (Sato et al., 2017), only a few responses, or often only one, are available as reference responses in evaluation datasets made from actual conversations. It is, therefore, hard for these reference-based metrics to consider uncertain responses without writing additional reference responses by hand (§ 2).

To remedy this problem, Galley et al. (2015) proposed ΔBLEU (§ 3), a human-aided evaluation method for text generation tasks with uncertain outputs. The key idea behind ΔBLEU is to consider human judgments on reference responses with diverse quality in BLEU computation. Although ΔBLEU correlates more strongly with human judgment than BLEU does, it still requires human intervention. Therefore it cannot effectively evaluate open-domain dialogue systems in a wide range of domains.

To remove the human intervention in ΔBLEU, we propose an automatic, uncertainty-aware evaluation metric, vBLEU. This metric exploits reference responses that are retrieved from massive dialogue logs and rated by a neural network trained with automatically collected training data (§ 4). We first retrieve diverse response candidates according to the similarity of utterances to which the responses were directed. We then train a neural network that judges the quality of the responses by using training data automatically generated from utterances with multiple responses. We also propose integrating vBLEU into the state of the art evaluation method, RUBER (Tao et al., 2018) (§ 2) to advance the state of the art by replacing its reference-based scorer.

Using our method, we experimentally evaluated responses generated by dialogue systems such as a retrieval-based method (Liu et al., 2016) and a generation-based method (Serban et al., 2017) using Twitter dialogues (§ 5). Our method is comparable to ΔBLEU in terms of its correlation with human judgment, and when it is integrated into RUBER (Tao et al., 2018), it substantially improves that correlation (§ 6).

Our contributions are the followings:

Proceedings of the 58th Annual Meeting of the Association for Computational Linguistics: Student Research Workshop, pages 199–206
July 5 - July 10, 2020. ©2020 Association for Computational Linguistics

- We developed an uncertainty-aware automatic evaluation method for dialogue systems. Our method automates the human ratings required in ΔBLEU while keeping the performance.

- We showed that integrating vBLEU into RUBER greatly improves RUBER's performance by providing the robustness to evaluate responses with uncertainty.

2 Related work

This section introduces recent studies on evaluating open-domain dialogue systems. We focus here on model-agnostic methods than can evaluate the quality of a response for a given utterance.[1]

For evaluation of dialogue systems, researchers have adopted existing evaluation metrics for other text generation tasks such as machine translation and summarization. Unfortunately, reference-based metrics such as BLEU (Papineni et al., 2002) and ROUGE (Lin, 2004) correlate poorly with human judgment on evaluating dialogue systems (Liu et al., 2016). This is because only a few responses, or often only one, can be used as reference responses when actual conversations are used as datasets, even though responses in open-domain dialogues can be diverse (Sato et al., 2017).

To consider uncertain responses in open-domain dialogues, Sordoni et al. (2015) attempted to collect multiple reference responses from dialogue logs for each test utterance-response pair. Galley et al. (2015) improved that method by manually rating the augmented reference responses and used the ratings to perform discriminative BLEU evaluation, as detailed later in § 3.2. Gupta et al. (2019) created multiple reference responses by hand for the Daily Dialogue dataset (Li et al., 2017). Although the last two studies empirically showed that the use of human-rated or -created reference responses in evaluation improves the correlation with human judgment, it is costly to create such evaluation datasets for various domains.

As for evaluation methods, ADEM (Lowe et al., 2017) learns an evaluation model that predicts human scores for given responses by using large-scale human-rated responses that are originally generated by humans or dialogue systems. The drawback of that method is the cost of annotation to train the

evaluation model. Moreover, the evaluation model has been reported to overfit the dialogue systems used for generating the training data.

RUBER (Tao et al., 2018) is an automatic evaluation method that combines two approaches: its referenced scorer evaluates the similarity between a reference and a generated response by using the cosine similarity of their vector representations, while its unreferenced scorer, trained by negative sampling, evaluates the relevance between an input utterance and a generated response. Ghazarian et al. (2019) showed that use of BERT embedding (Devlin et al., 2019) in pretrained vectors improves the unreferenced scorer but not the referenced scorer in RUBER. the referenced scorer is similar to ΔBLEU in that they both are referenced-based evaluation metrics. We later confirm that the referenced scorer in RUBER underperforms our method, and we thus propose replacing it with our method (§ 5.5).

3 Preliminaries

This section reviews ΔBLEU (Galley et al., 2015), a human-aided evaluation method for text generation tasks with uncertain outputs, after explaining the underlying metric, BLEU (Papineni et al., 2002).

3.1 BLEU

BLEU (Papineni et al., 2002) calculates an evaluation score based on the number of occurrences of n-gram tokens that appear in both reference and generated response. Specifically, the score is calculated from a modified n-gram precision p_n and a brevity penalty (BP):

$$\text{BLEU} = \text{BP} \cdot \exp\left(\sum_n \frac{1}{N} \log p_n\right), \tag{1}$$

$$\text{BP} = \begin{cases} 1 & \text{if } \eta > \rho \\ e^{(1-\rho/\eta)} & \text{otherwise} \end{cases}, \tag{2}$$

$$p_n = \frac{\sum_i \sum_{g \in n\text{-grams}(h_i)} \max_j\{\#_g(h_i, r_{i,j})\}}{\sum_i \sum_{g \in n\text{-grams}(h_i)} \#_g(h_i)}. \tag{3}$$

Here, ρ and η are the average lengths of reference and generated responses, respectively; n and N are the n-gram length and its maximum, h_i and $\{r_{i,j}\}$ are the generated response and the jth reference response for the ith utterance, respectively; $\#_g(u)$ is the number of occurrences of n-gram token g in sentence u; and $\#_g(u, v)$ is defined as $\min\{\#_g(u), \#_g(u)\}$.

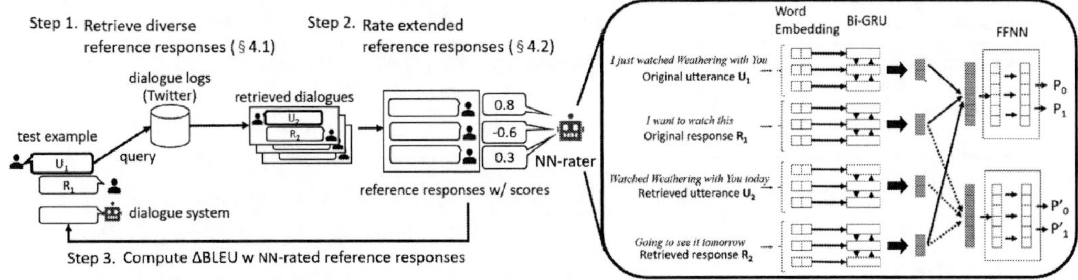

Figure 1: An overview of vBLEU: retrieving diverse reference responses from dialogue logs (§ 4.1) to augment the reference response in each test example, followed by neural network (NN)-rater that judges the their quality (§ 4.2).

3.2 ΔBLEU: Discriminative BLEU

ΔBLEU (Galley et al., 2015) is a human-aided evaluation method for text generation tasks with uncertain outputs, such as response generation in open-domain dialogues. To augment the reference responses for each test example (an utterance-response pair), following the work by Sordoni et al. (2015), ΔBLEU first retrieves, from Twitter, utterance-response pairs similar to the given pair. The similarities between utterances and between responses are next calculated by using BM25 (Robertson et al., 1994), and they are multiplied to obtain the similarity between the utterance-response pairs. Then, the responses for the top-15 similar utterance-response pairs and the utterance (as a parrot return) are combined with the original response to form an extended set of reference responses. Each of the extended references is then rated by humans in terms of its appropriateness as a response to the given utterance. Finally, ΔBLEU calculates p_n (Eq. 3) with the extended reference $r_{i,j}$ and its manual quality judgment $w_{i,j}$ for the input utterance i:

$$\frac{\sum_i \sum_{g \in n\text{-grams}(h_i)} \max_{j:g \in r_{i,j}} \{w_{i,j} \cdot \#_g(h_i, r_{i,j})\}}{\sum_i \sum_{g \in n\text{-grams}(h_i)} \max_j \{w_{i,j} \cdot \#_g(h_i)\}}.$$

In this way, ΔBLEU weights the number of occurrence of n-gram g in Eq. 3 with manual quality judgement $w_{i,j}$.

The problem with ΔBLEU is the cost of manual judgment. Although we want to evaluate open-domain dialogue systems in various domains, the annotation cost prevents effective evaluation.

4 Proposed method: vBLEU

This section describes our approach to the problems of ΔBLEU described in § 3.2. To remove the cost of human judgments of extended references, we propose using a neural network trained on automatically collected training data to rate each of the retrieved responses (Figure 1, § 4.2). In addition, to diversify the extended reference responses in terms of content and style, we propose a relaxed response retrieval approach using continuous vector representations of utterances only (§ 4.1).

4.1 Retrieving diverse reference responses

Given an utterance-response pair (test example), ΔBLEU expands the original reference response by retrieving utterance-response pairs, in which both the utterance and response are similar to the test example, from massive dialogue logs (here, Twitter). Because using the similarity between responses prevents us from retrieving diverse responses in terms of content, we propose considering only the similarity between the utterances. In addition, we use an embedding-based similarity instead of BM25 to flexibly retrieve semantically-similar responses with synonymous expressions (style variants).

We compute the similarity of utterances by using the cosine similarity between utterance vectors obtained from the average of pretrained embeddings of the words in the utterances. In addition to the retrieved responses, we add the utterance (as a parrot return) to the reference responses as in ΔBLEU.

4.2 Rating extended reference responses

ΔBLEU manually judges the appropriateness of the extended reference responses for the utterance. To remove this human intervention, we propose rating each reference response by using a neural network that outputs a probability for that response as a response to the given utterance.

Specifically, our neural network (NN)-rater takes two utterance-response pairs as inputs: a given pair of utterance U_1 and reference response R_1 (test example), and a retrieved pair of utterance U_2 and response R_2. The NN-rater is trained to output the probability that the retrieved response R_2 for

Task (method)	Unit	Training	Validation	Test
response generation	utterance-response pair	2.4M (2018)	10K (2018)	100 (2019)
NN-rater, RUBER	pair of utterance-response pairs	5.6M (2017)	10K (2017)	n/a
reference response retrieval, training for GloVe	utterance-response pair	Approximately 16M (2017)		

Table 1: Statistics of the dialogue data used to run each task. The numbers in the parentheses mean year.

U_2 can be a response to given utterance U_1 with response R_1. This probability is then used as a quality judgment after normalization to the interval $[-1, 1]$ as in ΔBLEU.

The key issue here is how to prepare the training data for the NN-rater. We use utterances with multiple responses in dialogue data (here, Twitter) as positive examples; for negative examples, we randomly sample two utterance-response pairs.

We then train the NN-rater in Figure 1 from the collected training data. Because the utterances in the two utterance-response pairs in a positive example are identical, while those in a negative example are independent, we do not feed both utterances to the NN-rater. This input design prevents overfitting.

Specifically, given a test example of utterance U_1 and response R_1 and a retrieved utterance-response pair of U_2 and R_2, we give two triplets, $\langle U_1, R_1, R_2 \rangle$ and $\langle U_2, R_2, R_1 \rangle$, as inputs to the NN-rater. Next, we make two vectors by concatenating triplet vectors returned from bi-directional gated recurrent unit (BI-GRU) (Cho et al., 2014) as the last hidden state for the utterance and the two responses. We concatenated forward and backward hidden states (h_f, h_b) in BI-GRU to represent a utterance/response vector as $v = [h_f, h_b]$. We then feed each triplet vector to feed-forward neural network (FFNN) with softmax function to obtain a pair of probabilities that R_2 can be a response to U_1 or not (similarity, another pair of probabilities that R_1 can be a response to U_2 or not). The maximum of these two probabilities is used as the qualitative judgment of the response R_2 (or R_1) and multiplied by -1 if classified as negative to normalize into $[-1, 1]$. This formulation is inspired by Tao et al. (2018) and Ghazarian et al. (2019).

5 Experimental Settings

This section describes how to evaluate our method for evaluating open-domain dialogue systems. Using utterances from Twitter (§ 5.1), responses written by humans, and responses obtained by dialogue systems (§ 5.2), we evaluated our method in terms of its correlation with human judgment (§ 5.3–5.5).

5.1 Twitter dialogue datasets

We built a large-scale Japanese dialogue dataset from Twitter posts of 2.5 million users that have been collected through the user timeline API since March 2011 (Nishi et al., 2016). Posts that are neither retweets nor mentions of other posts were regarded as utterances, and posts mentioning these posts were used as responses.

We use this dataset for training and testing dialogue systems and for training the NN-rater that judges the quality of retrieved responses. In these experiments, to simulate evaluating dialogue systems trained with dialogue data that are unseen by evaluation methods, we used dialogue data posted during 2017 for training and running the NN-rater, and dialogue data posted during 2018 for training and during 2019 for testing the dialogue systems as summarized in Table 1.

5.2 Target responses for evaluation

Following Liu et al. (2016) and Lowe et al. (2017), we adopted three methods to obtain responses for each utterance in the test set: a retrieval-based method C-TFIDF (Liu et al., 2016), with BM25 as the similarity function (C-BM25), a generation-based method VHRED (Serban et al., 2017), and HUMAN responses, which are the actual responses except for the reference response.

Following Ritter et al. (2010) and Higashinaka et al. (2011), to use a series of dialogues as training data for the above methods, we recursively follow replies from each non-reply post to obtain a dialogue between two users that consists of at least three posts. We then randomly selected pairs of the first utterances and its replies in the obtained dialogues as our dialogue data: 2.4M pairs for training VHRED and for retrieving responses in C-BM25, 10K pairs as validation data for VHRED, and 100 pairs as test data.[2] These dialogues were tokenized with SentencePiece (Kudo and Richardson, 2018) for VHRED and with MeCab 0.996 (ipadic 2.7.0)[3]

---

[2] To obtain HUMAN responses for evaluation, we only used dialogues whose first utterances had more than one responses.

[3] https://taku910.github.io/mecab/

| Metric | Reference retrieval method | | Spearman's ρ | | Pearson's r | |
	Target to compute similarity	Function to compute similarity	max	min	max	min
BLEU	(Only one reference response)		.186	.091	.276	.190
BLEU	Utterance & Response	BM25	.257	.138	.298	.173
BLEU	Utterance only	BM25	.265	.136	.296	.178
BLEU	Utterance & Response	Cosine similarity for GloVe vector	.280	.148	.322	.177
BLEU	Utterance only	Cosine similarity for GloVe vector	**.333**	.181	**.366**	**.209**

Table 2: Correlation between human judgment and BLEU with reference responses retrieved by various methods.

for C-BM25 to retrieve responses based on words that are less ambiguous than subwords.

Finally, six Japanese native speakers in our research group evaluated the 300 target responses for the 100 test examples in terms of the appropriateness as a response to a given utterance. We used a 5-point Likert-type scale with 1 meaning inappropriate or unrecognizable and 5 meaning very appropriate or seeming to be an actual response.

5.3 NN-rater to evaluate reference responses

To train the NN-rater for evaluating the extended references (§ 4.2), we randomly extracted 5.6M and 10K utterance-response pairs for training and validation data, respectively. The number of positive and negative examples were set equal in both data. Before these examples were fed to the NN-rater, they are tokenized with SentencePiece.

For the NN-rater, we used a 512-dimensional embedding layer, one Bi-GRU layer with 512-dimensional hidden units, five layers for the FFNN with 1024-dimensional hidden units, and a ReLU as the activation function. We used Adam optimizer (Kingma and Ba, 2015) with an initial learning rate of 0.001 and calculated the loss by the cross entropy. We trained the NN-rater with a batch size of 1000 and up to 15 epochs. The model with parameters that achieved the minimum loss on the validation data was used for evaluating the test data.

5.4 Response retrieval and scoring

Following Galley et al. (2015), for each test example, the 15 most similar utterance-response pairs were retrieved to augment the reference response in addition to the utterance (as a parrot return) to apply ΔBLEU and vBLEU. We retrieved utterance-response pairs from approximately 16M utterance-response pairs of our dialogue data (Table 1). These dialogue data were tokenized with MeCab for response retrieval; we then trained GloVe embeddings (Pennington et al., 2014) to compute utterance or response vectors (§ 4.1) from this data.

We then judged the quality of each retrieved reference response by humans for ΔBLEU and by NN-rater for vBLEU in terms of appropriateness as a response to a given utterance. We asked four of the six Japanese native speakers to judge the quality of each retrieved reference response.

5.5 Compared response evaluation methods

We have so far proposed two modifications to improve and automate ΔBLEU: more diverse reference retrieval (§ 4.1) and automatic reference quality judgment (§ 4.2). To see the impact of each modification, we first compare BLEU with various reference retrieval methods. We then compare BLEU with only one reference, ΔBLEU, and vBLEU. Finally, we compared vBLEU with the state of the art evaluation method, RUBER, and examined the performance of RUBER when its referenced scorer was replaced with vBLEU.

Specifically, we applied each evaluation method to the 300 responses (§ 5.2). ΔBLEU and vBLEU used the extended references in evaluation. BLEU used the original (single) references or the extended references. The reference scorer in RUBER used the original (single) references.

Following previous studies (Liu et al., 2016; Tao et al., 2018), we evaluated the performance of the evaluation methods in terms of their correlation to human judgments on the 300 responses. To calculate the correlation, we used Spearman's ρ and Pearson's r. To understand the stability of the evaluation, we computed the maximum and minimum correlation with human judgments given by each annotator. All evaluation methods using the modified n-gram precision were calculated with $n \leq 2$ (BLEU-2), following Galley et al. (2015).

6 Results

Table 2 lists the correlations between human judgment and BLEU for each reference retrieval method. In terms of Spearman's ρ, all methods using the extended reference exhibited higher maximum and

Metric	Spearman's ρ		Pearson's r	
	max	min	max	min
ΔBLEU	.366	.300	.360	.294
vBLEU	.330	.281	.394	.332
RUBER				
Unref. & Ref. Scorer	.339	.206	.325	.193
Ref. Scorer only	.188	.071	.075	.016
Unref. Scorer only	.342	.225	.336	.217
Unref. & vBLEU	**.435**	**.323**	**.450**	**.338**
human	.773	.628	.778	.607

Table 3: Correlation between each method and human judgment; human refers to the inter-rater correlations.

minimum correlation with human judgment than BLEU did with only one reference. For Pearson's r, only the proposed retrieval method, which uses an embedding-based similarity for utterances, showed higher minimum correlation than BLEU did with only one reference. This means that the proposed retrieval method was the most appropriate way to extend the reference responses. We, therefore, used reference responses extended by the proposed method for vBLEU in the following evaluation.

Next, Table 3 compares vBLEU with ΔBLEU and the state of the art evaluation method, RUBER. The comparison between vBLEU and BLEU in Table 2 revealed that the use of our NN-rater improved the minimum correlation with human judgment. Here, vBLEU was comparable to ΔBLEU, which implies that our method can successfully automate ΔBLEU, a human-aided, uncertainty-aware evaluation method. vBLEU performed better than RUBER did (unreferenced scorer + referenced scorer) for all correlations other than the maximum Spearman's ρ. We attribute the poor performance of RUBER to the poor performance of its referenced scorer, which was even worse than BLEU with only one reference in Table 2. This shows that merely adopting embedding-based similarity does not address the uncertainty of outputs. By replacing the reference scorer in RUBER with our vBLEU, however, we obtained the best overall correlations, which advances the state of the art.

Examples Table 4 shows examples of responses retrieved and evaluated by our method, along with evaluation scores for responses generated by C-BM25. The BLEU score with a single-reference response was almost zero. The vBLEU scores were the closest to human judgment, multi-reference BLEU (BLEU$_{\text{multi}}$) was the secondary closest, and single-reference BLEU was the last.

Utterance:
puma描いて一晩経ったらフォロワーが10人減っていたので時代はまだ追いついていない
(Time has not got me, because my follower reduced by 10 on the next day after I've drawn puma.)

Reference response:
おもしろすぎmiddleでしょ
(It's very funny)

Extended reference responses:	NN-rater score
此れからも素敵な作品楽しみにしてます (I'm looking forward to seeing your nice work.)	0.835
興味は持ったけどdlできないので興味を失いました (I lost an interest on it since I couldn't dl it.)	0.523

Generated response (score):
むしろ辞めたほうが良いのでは
(You'd better to stop)
(human: 0.33, BLEU: 0.01, BLEU$_{\text{multi}}$: 0.07, vBLEU: 0.25)

Table 4: Examples of responses retrieved and evaluated by our method for a given test example, along with evaluation scores for responses generated by C-BM25. BLEU refers to BLEU score with the original response, while BLEU$_{\text{multi}}$ refers to BLEU score with the extended references. For comparison, we normalized all evaluation scores to the interval for BLEU, i.e., [0, 1].

7 Conclusions

We have proposed a method to remove the need for costly human judgment in ΔBLEU (Galley et al., 2015) and obtain an automatic uncertainty-aware metric for dialogue systems. Our proposed vBLEU rates diverse reference responses retrieved from massive dialogue logs by using a neural network trained with automatically-collected training data, and it uses the responses and the scores to run ΔBLEU. Experimental results on massive Twitter dialogue data revealed that vBLEU is comparable to human-aided ΔBLEU, and that, by integrating it into RUBER, the state of the art method for evaluating open-domain dialogue systems, we can improve the correlation with human judgment.

We will release all code and datasets (tweet IDs) to promote the reproducibility of our experiments.[4] The readers are referred to our code to evaluate their dialogue systems for their native languages.

Acknowledgments

The research was supported by NII CRIS collaborative research program operated by NII CRIS and LINE Corporation.

---

[4] http://www.tkl.iis.u-tokyo.ac.jp/~tsuta/acl-srw-2020/

References

Kyunghyun Cho, Bart van Merriënboer, Dzmitry Bahdanau, and Yoshua Bengio. 2014. On the Properties of Neural Machine Translation: Encoder–Decoder Approaches. In *Proceedings of SSST-8, Eighth Workshop on Syntax, Semantics and Structure in Statistical Translation*, pages 103–111, Doha, Qatar. Association for Computational Linguistics.

Jacob Devlin, Ming-Wei Chang, Kenton Lee, and Kristina Toutanova. 2019. BERT: Pre-training of Deep Bidirectional Transformers for Language Understanding. In *Proceedings of the 2019 Conference of the North American Chapter of the Association for Computational Linguistics: Human Language Technologies, Volume 1 (Long and Short Papers)*, pages 4171–4186, Minneapolis, Minnesota. Association for Computational Linguistics.

Michel Galley, Chris Brockett, Alessandro Sordoni, Yangfeng Ji, Michael Auli, Chris Quirk, Margaret Mitchell, Jianfeng Gao, and Bill Dolan. 2015. deltaBLEU: A Discriminative Metric for Generation Tasks with Intrinsically Diverse Targets. In *Proceedings of the 53rd Annual Meeting of the Association for Computational Linguistics and the 7th International Joint Conference on Natural Language Processing (Volume 2: Short Papers)*, pages 445–450, Beijing, China. Association for Computational Linguistics.

Sarik Ghazarian, Johnny Wei, Aram Galstyan, and Nanyun Peng. 2019. Better Automatic Evaluation of Open-Domain Dialogue Systems with Contextualized Embeddings. In *Proceedings of the Workshop on Methods for Optimizing and Evaluating Neural Language Generation*, pages 82–89, Minneapolis, Minnesota. Association for Computational Linguistics.

Prakhar Gupta, Shikib Mehri, Tiancheng Zhao, Amy Pavel, Maxine Eskenazi, and Jeffrey Bigham. 2019. Investigating Evaluation of Open-Domain Dialogue Systems With Human Generated Multiple References. In *Proceedings of the 20th Annual SIGdial Meeting on Discourse and Dialogue*, pages 379–391, Stockholm, Sweden. Association for Computational Linguistics.

Tatsunori Hashimoto, Hugh Zhang, and Percy Liang. 2019. Unifying Human and Statistical Evaluation for Natural Language Generation. In *Proceedings of the 2019 Conference of the North American Chapter of the Association for Computational Linguistics: Human Language Technologies, Volume 1 (Long and Short Papers)*, pages 1689–1701, Minneapolis, Minnesota. Association for Computational Linguistics.

Ryuichiro Higashinaka, Noriaki Kawamae, Kugatsu Sadamitsu, Yasuhiro Minami, Toyomi Meguro, Kohji Dohsaka, and Hirohito Inagaki. 2011. Building a conversational model from two-tweets. In *2011 IEEE Workshop on Automatic Speech Recognition Understanding*, pages 330–335.

Diederik P. Kingma and Jimmy Ba. 2015. Adam: A Method for Stochastic Optimization. In *International Conference for Learning Representations*.

Taku Kudo and John Richardson. 2018. SentencePiece: A simple and language independent subword tokenizer and detokenizer for Neural Text Processing. In *Proceedings of the 2018 Conference on Empirical Methods in Natural Language Processing: System Demonstrations*, pages 66–71, Brussels, Belgium. Association for Computational Linguistics.

Yanran Li, Hui Su, Xiaoyu Shen, Wenjie Li, Ziqiang Cao, and Shuzi Niu. 2017. DailyDialog: A manually labelled multi-turn dialogue dataset. In *Proceedings of the Eighth International Joint Conference on Natural Language Processing (Volume 1: Long Papers)*, pages 986–995, Taipei, Taiwan. Asian Federation of Natural Language Processing.

Chin-Yew Lin. 2004. ROUGE: A Package for Automatic Evaluation of Summaries. In *Text Summarization Branches Out: Proceedings of the ACL-04 Workshop*, pages 74–81, Barcelona, Spain. Association for Computational Linguistics.

Chia-Wei Liu, Ryan Lowe, Iulian Serban, Mike Noseworthy, Laurent Charlin, and Joelle Pineau. 2016. How NOT To Evaluate Your Dialogue System: An Empirical Study of Unsupervised Evaluation Metrics for Dialogue Response Generation. In *Proceedings of the 2016 Conference on Empirical Methods in Natural Language Processing*, pages 2122–2132, Austin, Texas. Association for Computational Linguistics.

Ryan Lowe, Michael Noseworthy, Iulian Vlad Serban, Nicolas Angelard-Gontier, Yoshua Bengio, and Joelle Pineau. 2017. Towards an Automatic Turing Test: Learning to Evaluate Dialogue Responses. In *Proceedings of the 55th Annual Meeting of the Association for Computational Linguistics (Volume 1: Long Papers)*, pages 1116–1126, Vancouver, Canada. Association for Computational Linguistics.

Ryosuke Nishi, Taro Takaguchi, Keigo Oka, Takanori Maehara, Masashi Toyoda, Ken-ichi Kawarabayashi, and Naoki Masuda. 2016. Reply trees in Twitter: Data analysis and branching process models. *Social Network Analysis and Mining*, 6(1):26.

Kishore Papineni, Salim Roukos, Todd Ward, and Wei-Jing Zhu. 2002. Bleu: A Method for Automatic Evaluation of Machine Translation. In *Proceedings of 40th Annual Meeting of the Association for Computational Linguistics*, pages 311–318, Philadelphia, Pennsylvania, USA. Association for Computational Linguistics.

Jeffrey Pennington, Richard Socher, and Christopher Manning. 2014. Glove: Global Vectors for Word Representation. In *Proceedings of the 2014 Conference on Empirical Methods in Natural Language Processing (EMNLP)*, pages 1532–1543, Doha, Qatar. Association for Computational Linguistics.

Alan Ritter, Colin Cherry, and Bill Dolan. 2010. Unsupervised Modeling of Twitter Conversations. In *Human Language Technologies: The 2010 Annual Conference of the North American Chapter of the Association for Computational Linguistics*, pages 172–180, Los Angeles, California. Association for Computational Linguistics.

S. E. Robertson, S. Walker, S. Jones, M. M. Hancock-Beaulieu, and M. Gatford. 1994. Okapi at TREC-3. In *Proceedings of the 3rd Text REtrieval Conference*, pages 109–126. National Institute of Standards and Technology (NIST).

Shoetsu Sato, Naoki Yoshinaga, Masashi Toyoda, and Masaru Kitsuregawa. 2017. Modeling situations in neural chat bots. In *Proceedings of ACL 2017, Student Research Workshop*, pages 120–127, Vancouver, Canada. Association for Computational Linguistics.

Iulian Vlad Serban, Alessandro Sordoni, Ryan Lowe, Laurent Charlin, Joelle Pineau, Aaron Courville, and Yoshua Bengio. 2017. A Hierarchical Latent Variable Encoder-Decoder Model for Generating Dialogues. In *Association for the Advancement of Artificial Intelligence*, pages 3295–3301.

Alessandro Sordoni, Michel Galley, Michael Auli, Chris Brockett, Yangfeng Ji, Margaret Mitchell, Jian-Yun Nie, Jianfeng Gao, and Bill Dolan. 2015. A Neural Network Approach to Context-Sensitive Generation of Conversational Responses. In *Proceedings of the 2015 Conference of the North American Chapter of the Association for Computational Linguistics: Human Language Technologies*, pages 196–205, Denver, Colorado. Association for Computational Linguistics.

Chongyang Tao, Lili Mou, Dongyan Zhao, and Rui Yan. 2018. RUBER: An Unsupervised Method for Automatic Evaluation of Open-Domain Dialog Systems. In *AAAI Conference on Artificial Intelligence*, pages 722–729.

To Compress or not to Compress? A Finite-State Approach to Nen Verbal Morphology

Saliha Muradoğlu[1,2], Nicholas Evans[1,2], and Hanna Suominen[1,3,4]

[1]The Australian National University (ANU) / Canberra, ACT, Australia
[2]ARC Centre of Excellence for the Dynamics of Language (CoEDL) /
Canberra, ACT, Australia
[3]Data61, Commonwealth Scientific and Industrial Research Organization (CSIRO) /
Canberra, ACT, Australia
[4]University of Turku / Turku, Finland
`Firstname.Lastname@anu.edu.au`

Abstract

This paper describes the development of a verbal morphological parser for an under-resourced Papuan language, Nen. Nen verbal morphology is particularly complex, with a transitive verb taking up to $1,740$ unique features. The structural properties exhibited by Nen verbs raises interesting choices for analysis. Here we compare two possible methods of analysis: 'Chunking' and decomposition. 'Chunking' refers to the concept of collating morphological segments into one, whereas the decomposition model follows a more classical linguistic approach. Both models are built using the Finite-State Transducer toolkit foma. The resultant architecture shows differences in size and structural clarity. While the 'Chunking' model is under half the size of the full decomposed counterpart, the decomposition displays higher structural order. In this paper, we describe the challenges encountered when modelling a language exhibiting distributed exponence and present the first morphological analyser for Nen, with an overall accuracy of 80.3%.

1 Introduction

With the advance of modern technology, collecting data for the task of language documentation has become easier, but methods for coping with the influx of data have become a pressing concern. One robust solution in the realm of morphology and phonology has been Finite State methods.

This paper focuses on the development of Finite-State architecture in aid of the glossing process for building resources for Nen. Nen is a under-resourced language of the Morehead-Maro language family of Southern New Guinea (Evans, 2015). It is spoken by approximately 300–350 people in the village of Bimadbn in the Western

Province of Papua New Guinea. The resources developed here feed directly into the efforts of documentation and corpus building. This effort is globally shared amongst fieldworkers and descriptive linguistics across many languages, in response to the estimation for half of the world's languages to be extinct within the next century (Krauss, 1992). Aside from aiding the documentation process, the linguistic property of multiple exponence (ME) makes Nen an interesting case study for computational methods, as well as exasperating the already present data sparsity problem.

Though much of the recent work in Natural Language Processing (NLP) has centred around machine learning, it is still not quite feasible in low resource problem sets. Neural networks remove the need for incorporating detailed knowledge of the specific context by optimizing the mapping between input/output pairs. As a consequence a large amount of training data is required (Gorman and Sproat, 2016). In the low resource language setting, often linguistic insight can be exploited to help generate larger datasets, such as Finite-State methods being used to produce labelled data for training of neural networks (Moeller et al., 2018).

Finite-state Transducers (FSTs) are widely accepted as a standard way to computationally model the morphological structure of words in natural languages (Beesley and Karttunen, 2003; Koskenniemi, 1983). Prior works include FSTs for agglutinating languages such as Turkish, Tuvan, and Northern Haida (Çöltekin, 2014; Tyers et al., 2016; Lachler et al., 2018), and more recently so-called polysynthetic languages like Chukchi, Kunwinjku, Central Siberian Yupik, and Arapahoe (Andriyanets and Tyers, 2018; Lane and Bird, 2019; Chen and Schwartz, 2018; Kazeminejad et al., 2017).

Proceedings of the 58th Annual Meeting of the Association for Computational Linguistics: Student Research Workshop, pages 207–213
July 5 - July 10, 2020. ©2020 Association for Computational Linguistics

The novel contributions of this paper are twofold: First, we present a preliminary morphological analyser for verbs in Nen. In addition to resource building for the Nen language, this work outlines a computational approach for modelling the linguistic phenomenon of distributed exponence.

2 The Nen Language

With on-going documentation efforts, the Nen corpus is approximately $30,000$ words of natural speech, of which there are approximately $6,000$ verbs tokens (Muradoğlu, 2017). Over a third of these verb tokens ($2,379$ tokens) are varieties of the copula, which form a restricted paradigm of their own. Simply put, the amount of data is scarce. To add to this problem, Nen exhibits complex verbal morphology. In fact, verbs are morphologically the most complicated word-class in Nen (Evans, 2016, 2019). Despite this, they are often regular, allowing for generalisation of rules to analyse them. As outlined by Evans (2016), Nen verbs can be divided into two categories: prefixing and ambifixing verbs. Prefixing verbs mark the undergoer argument by prefix and ambifixing verbs employ both prefixes and suffixes to index person and number of up to two arguments. In this paper, we focus on the more complicated case of the ambifixing verb. The full prefix and suffixal paradigm can be found in Evans (2016) Table 23.3 (pg 548), Table 23.14 (pg 563) and Table 23.16 (pg 565).

The undergoer prefixes are divided into arbitrarily labelled series α, β, γ, which do not correspond to specific semantic values until they are unified with other TAM (Tense, Aspect, and Mood) markings on the verb (Evans, 2015). Following the undergoer prefixes, a directional prefix slot is available. This can be filled with {-n-} 'towards', {-ng-} 'away' or left empty to convey a directionally neutral semantic. Consider the verb *armbs* 'to climb'. When marked for direction the resultant forms are as follows: *n-armb-te* '(s)he is ascending (neutral)', *n-n-armb-te* '(s)he is coming up (towards speaker)', and *n-ng-armb-te* '(s)he is going up (away from speaker)'.

The middle prefixes simply mark the verb as a member of the middle verb type; essentially dynamic monovalent verbs. Prefix cells with more than one entry note possible allomorphy depending on the phonological environment within the verb. The suffixal system applies to both middle and transitive verb types.

Although it is convenient to segment verbs, into prefix, stem, and suffix, the Nen verbal system distributes information in a complicated way. The prefixes and suffixes are not independent values. Nen exhibits a particular kind of multiple exponence (ME), which requires prefixes and suffixes to be unified before inflectional values are known (Evans, 2016).

The possible combinatorial space for transitive and middle verbs is determined by summing the forms associated with each series (α, β, and γ) and the TAM suffixes they can co-occur with. The figure obtained is then multiplied by the possible undergoer prefixes (with only three available to the middle verbs). Lastly, this number is multiplied by three for each directional prefix available. This process yields a $1,740$ cell paradigm size for the transitive verbs.

2.1 Distributed Exponence

One of the prime motivations for choosing Nen as a case study is the phenomenon that gives rise to this combinatorial power: distributed exponence.

In linguistics, the notion of extended exponence was first introduced by Mathews (1974) and is now commonly referred to as multiple exponence (ME). Matthews defined ME as "a category if positively identified at all, would have exponents in each of two or more distinct positions" (Mathews, 1974). Distributed exponence is a kind of ME, which involves the use of more than one morphological segment to convey meaning. It requires all relevant morphs to yield a precise interpretation of the feature value in question (Carroll, 2016; Harris, 2017).

(1)   N-n-and-armb-ta-ng
      M:α-VEN-FUT.IMP-Nsg-ascend-
      Ndu:IPF-NSG.IPF.IMP

      'You|they ($>$2) climb up later! (in the future, said to a group of people)'

In the example above, no one marker marks the plural person. The information of the agent being plural is distributed across the thematic (dual/non-dual) and the desinence (single/dual/plural). If a non-dual thematic is present than the desinence cannot have dual features, and so the only options are singular or plural. Further, this is an example of the future imperative in Nen. The future imperative category is marked by an additional prefix, which also carries information about the agent. It carves up the person space in a different way to the thematic, and yet these values must be compatible. The other main feature value evident in this example is the prefix n- which serves as a dummy variable to reduce the valency of the verb, but it also yields information about the membership of the class α. Together with the desinence (and in this case the presence of the future imperative prefix), the TAM feature can be obtained.

3 Method

Several implementations of FSM compilers were available: XFST (Xerox Finite-State Transducer) (Beesley and Karttunen, 2003), foma (Hulden, 2009), and HFST (Helskini Finite-State Transducer) (Lindén et al., 2011), of which the latter two are open source. To develop a morphological analyser for Nen, we employed the foma Finite-State toolkit.

FSTs are an ideal tool for morphology, since they allow for both analysis and synthesis, meaning the user can both decompose a word and construct one, given the desired morphological features. Additionally, given the ongoing nature of language documentation, linguistic rules are constantly being added to, reviewed and revised. The incremental modularisation of FSTs allows for easy testing of set rules and addition of new rules.

FSTs are constructed in two parts: the first part deals with morphological rules and irregularities, as well as lexicon creation. The second component implements morphophonological rules.

3.1 Long Distance Dependencies (LDDs)

As with most languages, there are long-distance dependencies (LDD) that need to be resolved. This is even more true of Nen given its distributed nature. In FSTs, the transition from one state to another depends on the current state and the next input symbol. To transition to a state at time $t + 1$, the only thing considered is the state at time t (i.e., Markov assumption). In other words, there is no stack or other memory-like function that can be consulted.

One way of introducing memory is through Feature-setting and Feature-unification operations. These are practically implemented using flag diacritics (Hulden, 2011). Arcs with flag diacritics are like an epsilon transition but are conditional on the success or failure of the operation specified by the flag. In our setup, the operations used are

P (positive) and R (require). This process is often repeated through the verb, where the unification of features is required.

3.2 Future Imperative

In addition to normal imperatives, Nen has future imperatives. This type of imperative specifies that an action should be carried out at some later point, and often at a different location (Evans, ms)

As seen in example 1, the TAM category of future imperative requires another prefix. Essentially at this point the FST has three options, {-and-} for non-singular, {-ang} for singular and {-∅-}. If the verb is not a future imperative than the {-∅-} pathway is taken. The future imperative is only possible if the prefix is of the α class.

The Nen language distinguishes between SG, DU, PL persons. For the decomposition model, there needs to be restrictions for the thematic, which splits this combinatorial space in a different way: Dual (DU) or Non-Dual (ND). A non-singular future imperative prefix cannot be used with a singular actor suffix.

This licensing of information can be done in several ways. For simplicity, the LDD is recalled in the shortest way possible. If this prefix is present then the system knows the series must be α, so instead of propagating the series restrictions to the end, we require the FUT.IMP (SG/NSG) feature to be unified.

3.3 Models

In building an FST for the Nen verb, the question of whether to 'Chunk' or decompose arose. By 'Chunking', we refer to the idea of combining morphological segments rather than decomposing to the minimal units (as briefly mentioned in Lachler et al. (2018)).

There are several motivations for this distinction. First, from a technical point of view, decomposing requires more rules to govern the combinations of even more segments. By having to block the possibilities of certain combinations (i.e., negative definition), this leads to more complex rules which need to be carefully considered and tested.

Secondly, this distinction neatly parallels with psycholinguistic theories dealing with processing of agglutinative or polysynthetic languages. The basic idea is that there is a dual mechanism for processing inflected words: lexical memory and morphological decomposition/grammatical rules (Hahne et al., 2006; Ullman, 2004).

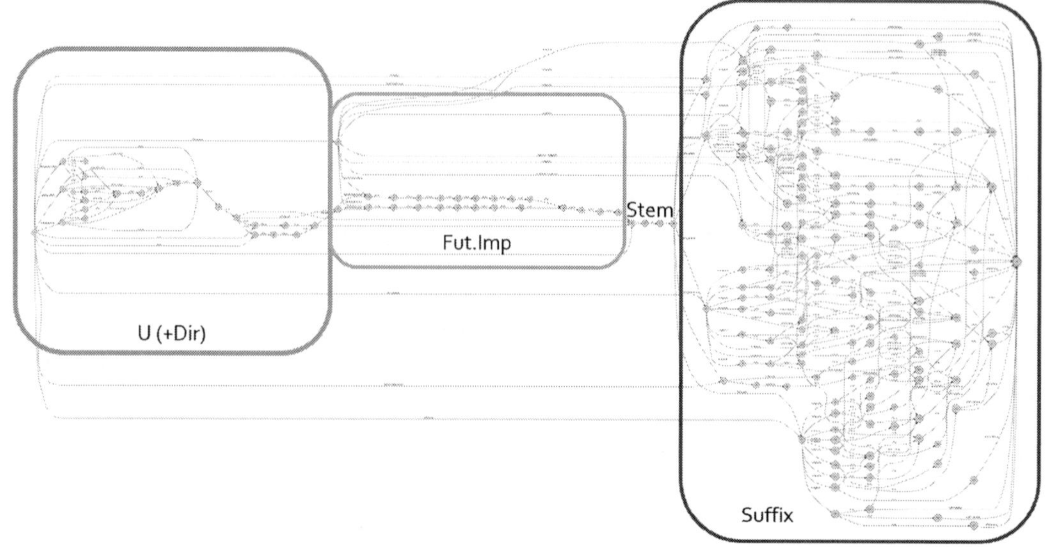

Figure 1: Overall FST architecture for 'Chunking' model. For larger view: 'Chunking'

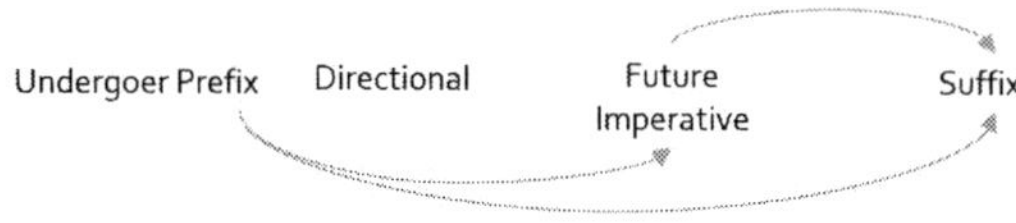

Figure 2: Information flow for the 'Chunking' model.

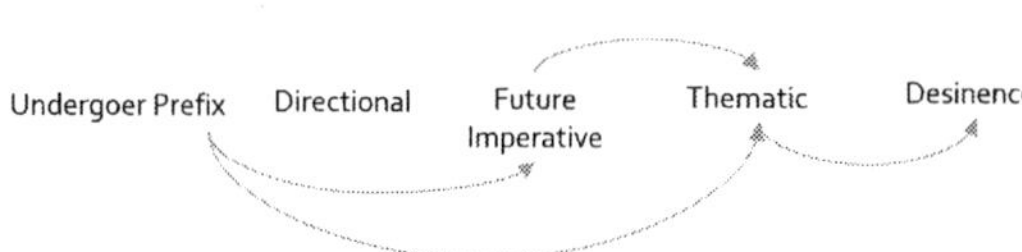

Figure 3: Information flow for decomposition model.

3.3.1 'Chunking' Model

As described above, 'Chunking' refers to the idea of combining morphological segments. In the case of Nen, this means treating the thematic and desinence as one rather than two separate segments. The thematic and desinence have the same hidden featural restrictions. That is to say, thematics of the same TAM feature can be unified with desinences of the same value. In this approach, the Undergoer prefix limits the possible allowed suffixes and forces certain TAM interpretations. Figure 2 depicts the LDD resolution for this model. We impose a prefix series restriction since the membership of the prefix (whether α, β, or γ) changes the interpretation of the suffix. It is a much more straightforward model compared with the decomposition model discussed next

3.3.2 Decomposition Model

The decomposition model follows the analysis of Evans (2016). It segments morphemes to their minimal meaningful units. This approach gives a more granular insight into the flow of information from one segment to the next. In fact, it is simply the uncompressed version of the 'Chunking' model. Decomposing into smaller units gives rise to more complex rules to constrain the FST to linguistically viable forms only. For example, Nen has {-∅-} and {-ng-} as possible thematic values, but it also has these same values in the desinence, so if no restrictions exist the system would over-assign the zero morphemes. The 'ng' suffix could be analysed as either {-∅-ng} or {-ng-∅}. Both these options are not linguistically viable because the TAM features do not match. In the decomposition model, we need to impose restrictions between all three: undergoer prefix, thematic and desinence (and the future imperative prefix). The simplest way to do this is to plan restrictions from undergoer prefix to thematic, and thematic into desinence (since they adhere to the same underlying paradigmatic structure) as seen in Figure 3. Instead of enforcing the dependency from the undergoer prefix, the range of the LDD or feature-unification is minimised. Since the future imperative and thematic already block the unsatisfactory feature-holding morphemes, the desinence only needs to be unified with the thematic morpheme.

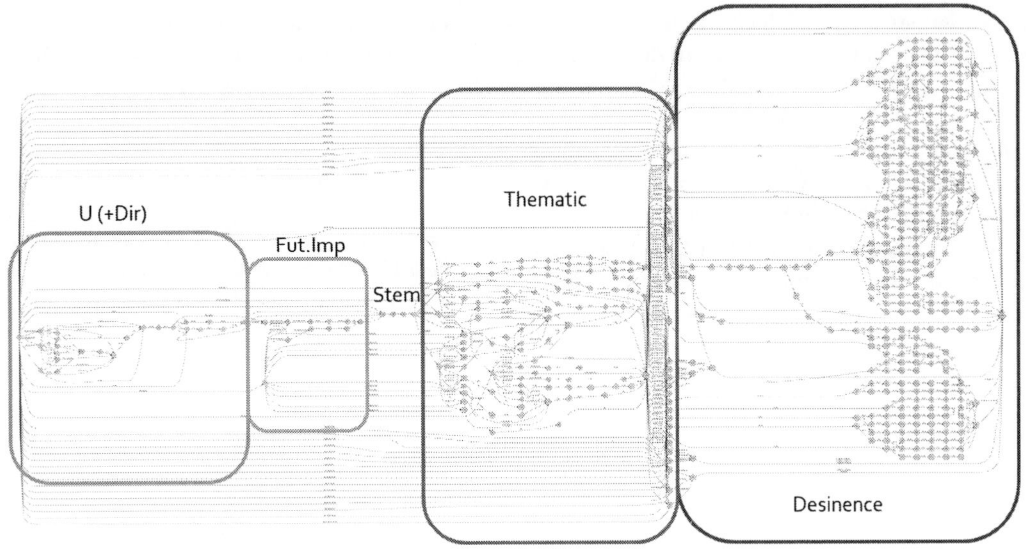

Figure 4: Overall FST architecture for decomposed model. For larger view: Decomposition model.

4   Results

The decomposition model showed a clearer level of organization than the 'Chunking' model (Figures 1 and 4, both with the flags included). Note that, one verb stem *armbs* 'to ascend' was used in both figures, for visibility of manifestation of morphological paradigm for one ambifixing verb. The particular stem was chosen because we had a full paradigm elicitation from members of the Nen community to confirm the existence of predicted forms. When comparing the specifications of both models, shown in Table 1, we could see that the decomposition was roughly double the 'Chunking' model in size, the number of states and arcs, and approximately 3.5 times more pathways.

These results questioned the benefit of decomposing further, apart from the obvious benefit of following the linguistic description. Given the added difficulty of implementing, if both yield comparable results, and the end goal is to have the highest possible accuracy of gloss than the choice of model should not matter.

4.1   Evaluation

We evaluated our FST models by comparing the glosses produced with those of a hand-annotated set (Muradoğlu, 2017). The hand-annotated corpus was derived from the Nen natural speech corpus. This included 1, 680 unique inflected forms (with the middle and transitive verbs making up approximately 58% of verbs observed) and 274 stems. Unsurprisingly, the hand-annotated corpus displays

Features	'Chunking'	Decomposition
Size	8.0kB (7.6kB)	13.7kB (15.2kB)
States	230 (197)	513 (470)
Arcs	385 (340)	709 (656)
Paths	5, 371 (26, 288)	18, 706 (811, 069)

Table 1: FST attributes for 'Chunking' and decomposition model with diacritic flags eliminated. Figures in brackets refer to the flag counterparts.

Zipfian properties, with the copula verb (and all of its inflections) being the most frequently occurring and making up 39% of the corpus. The coupla verb in Nen takes up to 40 unique forms which can be modelled perfectly.

During testing, we encountered an unexpected difference between the two proposed models. The definition of the imperfective basic non-dual thematic ({-taw-}|{-ta-}) required a morphophonological rule to drop the *a* or *aw* and attach the {-e} desinence for the 2|3sg actor. We addressed this problem in the *foma* file. This again, reiterates the notion of more rules required for further decomposition.

Both 'Chunking' and decomposition model showed an 80.3% accuracy (70.5% if only middle and transitive verbs are considered). The most common errors were attributable to spelling and/or morpholonological changes. For example, the inflected form *näramanda*, would only be recognised by the FST as *nrämnda* with the stem as *räm*. This is because, exceptionally, the verb stem *(w)ärama-* 'to give' does not appear in full in the infinitive *räms*, whereas other verbs with benefactives (e.g. *wabens* 'to feed for') do include the prefix. The verb stem for give is built by adding benefactive {wä-} 'make' (thus 'giving' is literally 'doing for') to the root *räm* (infinitive *räms*) 'to do'.

Some of the unrecognised forms can be a result of variation in transcription. With ongoing efforts of documentation, transcription decisions evolve, resulting in a distribution of forms that represent the same thing. A typical example of this variation in the corpus is *wétélés|wetls* 'to tell/say/report', with the epenthetic vowels either being written orthographically or omitted. Typically these issues would be dealt with in the pre-processing stage however, some of these cases are harder to recognise than others, as is the case of handling naturalistic data.

5   Conclusion

This paper explores options for modeling the low-resource language Nen using finite-state transducers. Nen shows distributed exponence; multiple morphs can contribute to the specification of a particular feature value. This property motivates the comparison between a 'Chunking' model, which combines the thematic and desinence segment, to a decomposition model which handles the two separately at the cost of many more parameters. Both models achieve the same accuracy of 80.3%. The choice of model depends on the primary concern of the user. Assuming that either segmentation is linguistically possible, if the size of the transducer is of concern (as a result of the size of lexicon, complexity of rules or sheer number of rules) a 'Chunking' approach can be taken with no cost to accuracy. If the user, prefers structural granularity or a one-to-one mapping between the computational implementation and the linguistic grammar then the decomposition approach can be taken. Most often, the primary use of FST grammars are to provide morphological glosses, in this case there is no computational motivation for having a high resolution description.

Future work would entail analysing and implementing more detailed underlying morphonological rules, and investigating the cross-over from FSTs to neural models. One of the prime motivations for building an FST, in the era of neural networks is to generate enough labelled data, in the appropriate format to enable testing across architectures. Additionally, the process of building an FST proves to be a great way to examine the validity of the linguistic analyses.

Acknowledgments

We are grateful for the mentoring scheme provided by the ACL student research workshop. In particular, we would like to thank Greg Durrett and Richard Sproat for their constructive feedback during the mentoring phase.

References

Vasilisa Andriyanets and Francis Tyers. 2018. A prototype finite-state morphological analyser for Chukchi. In *Proceedings of the Workshop on Computational Modeling of Polysynthetic Languages*, pages 31–40, Santa Fe, New Mexico, USA. Association for Computational Linguistics.

Kenneth R. Beesley and Lauri Karttunen. 2003. *Finite-state morphology: Xerox tools and techniques*. CSLI, Stanford.

Matthew J. Carroll. 2016. *The Ngkolmpu Language*. Ph.D. thesis, The Australian National University.

Emily Chen and Lane Schwartz. 2018. A morphological analyzer for St. Lawrence Island/Central Siberian Yupik. In *Proceedings of the Eleventh International Conference on Language Resources and Evaluation (LREC 2018)*.

Çagri Çöltekin. 2014. A set of open source tools for turkish natural language processing. In *Proceedings of the Eleventh International Conference on Language Resources and Evaluation (LREC 2014)*, pages 1079–1086.

Nicholas Evans. 2015. Valency in Nen. In Andrej Malchukov, Martin Haspelmath, Bernard Comrie and Iren Hartmann, editors, *Valency classes: A comparative handbook*, pages 1069–1116. Berlin: Mouton de Gruyter.

Nicholas Evans. 2016. Inflection in Nen. In Matthew Baerman, editor, *The Oxford Handbook of Inflection*, pages pages 543–575. Oxford University Press, USA.

Nicholas Evans. 2019. Waiting for the word: distributed deponency and the semantic interpretation of number in the Nen verb. In Andrew Hippisley Matthew Baerman, Oliver Bond, editor, *Morphological perspectives*, pages 100–123. Edinburgh: Edinburgh University Press.

Nicholas Evans. ms. Grammar of Nen.

Kyle Gorman and Richard Sproat. 2016. Minimally supervised number normalization. *Transactions of the Association for Computational Linguistics*, 4:507–519.

Anja Hahne, Jutta L. Mueller, and Harald Clahsen. 2006. Morphological processing in a second language: Behavioral and event-related brain potential evidence for storage and decomposition. *Journal of Cognitive Neuroscience*, 18(1):121–134.

Alice C Harris. 2017. *Multiple exponence*. Oxford University Press.

Mans Hulden. 2009. Foma: a finite-state compiler and library. In *Proceedings of the Demonstrations Session at EACL 2009*, pages 29–32, Athens, Greece. Association for Computational Linguistics.

Mans Hulden. 2011. Morphological analysis tutorial:a self-contained tutorial for building morphological analyzers.

Ghazaleh Kazeminejad, Andrew Cowell, and Mans Hulden. 2017. Creating lexical resources for polysynthetic languages—the case of arapaho. In *Proceedings of the 2nd Workshop on the Use of Computational Methods in the Study of Endangered Languages*, pages 10–18.

Kimmo Koskenniemi. 1983. *Two-level morphology*. Ph.D. thesis, Ph. D. thesis, University of Helsinki.

Michael Krauss. 1992. The world's languages in crisis. *Language*, 68(1):4–10.

Jordan Lachler, Lene Antonsen, Trond Trosterud, Sjur Moshagen, and Antti Arppe. 2018. Modeling northern haida verb morphology. In *Proceedings of the Eleventh International Conference on Language Resources and Evaluation (LREC 2018)*.

William Lane and Steven Bird. 2019. Towards a robust morphological analyzer for kunwinjku. In *Proceedings of the The 17th Annual Workshop of the Australasian Language Technology Association*, pages 1–9.

Krister Lindén, Erik Axelson, Sam Hardwick, Tommi A Pirinen, and Miikka Silfverberg. 2011. Hfst—framework for compiling and applying morphologies. In *International Workshop on Systems and Frameworks for Computational Morphology*, pages 67–85. Springer.

Peter H Mathews. 1974. *Morphology: an introduction to the theory of word-structure*. Cambridge, England: Cambridge University Press.

Sarah Moeller, Ghazaleh Kazeminejad, Andrew Cowell, and Mans Hulden. 2018. A Neural Morphological Analyzer for Arapaho Verbs Learned from a Finite State Transducer. pages 12–20.

Saliha Muradoğlu. 2017. *When is enough enough ? A corpus-based study of verb inflection in a morphologically rich language (Nen)*. Masters thesis, The Australian National University.

Francis Tyers, Aziyana Bayyr-ool, Aelita Salchak, and Jonathan Washington. 2016. A finite-state morphological analyser for tuvan. In *Proceedings of the Tenth International Conference on Language Resources and Evaluation (LREC 2016)*, pages 2562–2567.

Michael T. Ullman. 2004. Contributions of memory circuits to language: The declarative/procedural model. *Cognition*, 92(1-2):231–270.

AraDIC: Arabic Document Classification using Image-Based Character Embeddings and Class-Balanced Loss

Mahmoud Daif, Shunsuke Kitada, Hitoshi Iyatomi
Hosei University
Graduate School of Science and Engineering
Department of Applied Informatics
{mahmoud.daif.8h@stu., shunsuke.kitada.8y@stu., iyatomi@}
hosei.ac.jp

Abstract

Classical and some deep learning techniques for Arabic text classification often depend on complex morphological analysis, word segmentation, and hand-crafted feature engineering. These could be eliminated by using character-level features. We propose a novel end-to-end Arabic document classification framework, Arabic document image-based classifier (AraDIC), inspired by the work on image-based character embeddings. AraDIC consists of an image-based character encoder and a classifier. They are trained in an end-to-end fashion using the class balanced loss to deal with the long-tailed data distribution problem. To evaluate the effectiveness of AraDIC, we created and published two datasets, the Arabic Wikipedia title (AWT) dataset and the Arabic poetry (AraP) dataset. To the best of our knowledge, this is the first image-based character embedding framework addressing the problem of Arabic text classification. We also present the first deep learning-based text classifier widely evaluated on modern standard Arabic, colloquial Arabic and classical Arabic. AraDIC shows performance improvement over classical and deep learning baselines by 12.29% and 23.05% for the micro and macro F-score, respectively.

1 Introduction

Arabic is one of the six official languages of the United Nations and the official language of 26 states. It is spoken by as many as 420 million people making it the fifth most popular language worldwide. According to the Internet World Statistics, as of 2017, Arab users represent 4.8% of internet users[1].

Arabic can be classified into three different types each having its own purpose and morphology. The modern standard Arabic, the colloquial or dialectal Arabic and the classical or old Arabic. The modern standard Arabic is the official language used in media, government, news papers and is taught in schools. Colloquial Arabic varies between countries and regions. Old or classical Arabic survives nowadays in religious scriptures and old poetry.

Arabic has 28 basic letters all are consonants except three, which are long vowels. Arabic is written from right to left. Most Arabic letters have more than one written form depending on their position in the word. For example, " س ". " ـس ", " ـسـ ", and " سـ " are all different forms of the letter " س "(sīn). In addition, diacritical marks/short vowels that contribute to the phonology of Arabic, greatly alter the character shape. Example, " بٌ ", " بٍ ", " بِ ", " بّ ", " بْ ", " بُ ", " بَ ", and " بٌ " are combination of the letter " ب "(bā') with different diacritics. This visual nature of the Arabic letters is the main motivation for us to use image based embeddings.

The importance of text classification has increased due to the increase of textual data on the internet as a result of social networks and news sites. Common examples of text classification are sentiment analysis (Ibrahim et al., 2015), spam detection (El-Halees, 2009) and news categorization (Shehab et al., 2016). Arabic text classification is particularly challenging because of its complex morphological analysis.

Most research on Arabic text classification has used classical techniques for feature extraction (Salloum et al., 2018), which require complex morphological analysis, such as negation handling(Al-Twairesh et al., 2016), part of speech tagging (Khoja, 2001), stemming (Al-Kabi et al., 2015), and segmentation (Abdelali et al., 2016). Arabic segmentation is especially complex because Arabic words are not always separated by white spaces. It also includes some hand-crafted features

---

[1]Arabic Speaking Internet Users and Population Statistics. https://www.internet-worldstats.com/stats19.html Accessed: 16-Dec-2018,

Proceedings of the 58th Annual Meeting of the Association for Computational Linguistics: Student Research Workshop, pages 214–221
July 5 - July 10, 2020. ©2020 Association for Computational Linguistics

like document term matrix with term frequency inverse document frequency (TF-IDF) scores or word count.

Arabic text classification have been often done using classical algorithms like support vector machines (SVMs) or Naive Bayes (Salloum et al., 2018). Despite advances of text classification using deep learning techniques, little work has been done on Arabic. Soliman et al. (2017) introduced AraVec, which is a pretrained distributed word embeddings (Mikolov et al., 2013). They trained their model using the skip-gram and continuous bag of words techniques. They used data from different sources like Wikipedia and Twitter. More recently, Sagheer and Sukkar (2018) used AraVec's pretrained word embeddings with sentence convolutional neural network (CNN) originally proposed by Kim (2014) for Arabic document classification. This method still did not mitigate the problem of Arabic word segmentation.

Those combinations left two major issues unaddressed. First, performance highly depends on morphological analysis and word segmentation, which is difficult for Arabic. The same problem has been addressed for languages such as Japanese and Chinese (Peng et al., 2003). Second, obtaining appropriate embedding (i.e. building hand-crafted features) is difficult.

To solve these problems, character-based approaches utilizing deep learning methods mainly used in image processing have been proposed (Zhang et al., 2015; Shimada et al., 2016; Kitada et al., 2018).

Zhang et al. (2015) introduced a character-level CNN (CLCNN) that treats text as a raw signal at character level. The CNN then learns the language morphology and extracts appropriate features for text classification. Their method mitigated the issue of complex morphological analysis.

After that, Shimada et al. (2016) proposed image-based character embeddings for Japanese and Chinese text classification. Their model was composed of a convolutional auto-encoder (CAE) (Masci et al., 2011) and a CLCNN. They were the first to handle a character as an image and obtained character-embedding with their CAE. They also introduced wild card training as a data augmentation technique, which is dropout (Srivastava et al., 2014) on the embedding space.

Later, Liu et al. (2017) used image-based character embeddings learned through a character encoder (CE) to train a gated recurrent unit (GRU) for Japanese, Chinese, and Korean text classification.

Kitada et al. (2018) proposed CE-CLCNN that concatenated Liu et al. (2017)'s CE with CLCNN as an end-to-end system and introduced random erasing on image domain as a data augmentation method. These models using character-level features learn language morphology eliminating the need for complex morphological analysis and word segmentation.

Another problem is that large text classification datasets usually suffer from long tailed data distribution problem. This means that few classes make up majority of data. This problem often reduces the model's accuracy on the minority classes making more biased towards majority classes.

This problem can be addressed by either re-sampling (Chawla et al., 2002; Shen et al., 2016; Geifman and El-Yaniv, 2017; Buda et al., 2018; Zou et al., 2018) or re-weighting the cost function (Ting, 2000; Zhou and Liu, 2005; Huang et al., 2016; Khan et al., 2017; Cui et al., 2019).

Cui et al. (2019) noticed that re-weighting the cost function by inverse class frequency as used in vanilla schemes (Huang et al., 2016, 2019; Wang et al., 2017) could lead to poor performance on majority classes. They proposed class-balanced (CB) loss based on the effective number of classes which re-weights the loss by the inverse of the effective number of classes.

Our contributions can be summarized as follows:

- We propose AraDIC which is a framework for Arabic text classification. AraDIC is an end-to-end model of a character encoder and a classifier trained using CB loss.

- CB loss was originally intended for object detection tasks. We show that it can solve class-imbalance problems for text classification tasks.

- We introduce two datasets in the hope of becoming bench marking datasets for Arabic text classification tasks as well. The Arabic Wikipedia title (AWT) dataset and the the Arabic poetry (AraP) dataset. These two datasets contain the three types of Arabic language.

To the best of our knowledge, this is the first time an image-based character embedding model is used for Arabic text classification. Also, the first time a deep-learning based model is tested

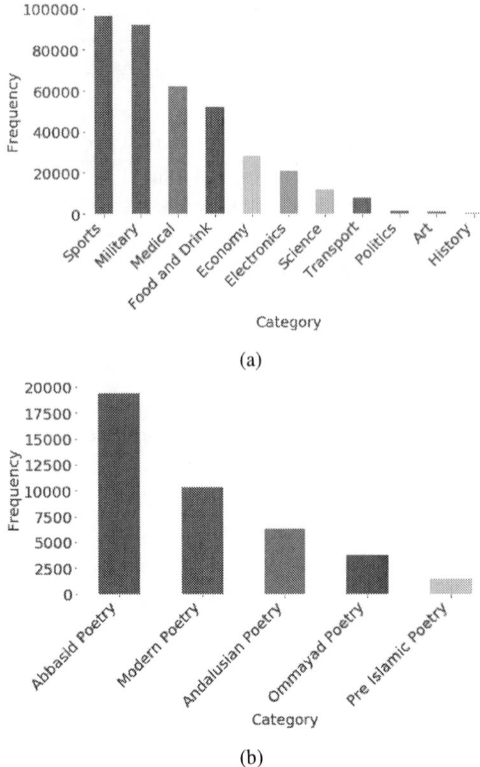

Figure 1: The category distribution for the (a) AWT and (b) AraP datasets.

on datasets containing the three types of Arabic. This shows that our method could be used to overcome Arabic's complicated morphological analysis and word segmentation for all types of Arabic. The code and datasets are released at `https://github.com/mahmouddaif/AraDIC`

2 Datasets

Arabic text classification lacks bench marking datasets. This is because it is expensive and time consuming to annotate a large dataset to be used for text classification using deep learning algorithms. We created two large datasets that do not require manual annotation and can be used as benchmarks for Arabic text classification. The AWT and the AraP datasets. Sections 2.1 and 2.2 describe how we constructed these datasets.

2.1 Arabic Wikipedia Title Dataset (AWT)

Liu et al. (2017) introduced the Wikipedia title dataset for Japanese, Chinese and Korean by making use of Wikipedia's recursive hierarchical structure to crawl 12 different Wikipedia categories and using the category as a label to all article titles under this category, and its subcategories. He assumed that an article only exists in one category. If an article existed in more that one category, it was randomly assigned to only one of them. This created some noisy annotations, however, categories were chosen as distinctive in nature as possible to reduce this problem. We crawl 11 different categories from the Arabic Wikipedia using the same method. A total of 444,911 different titles with a total of 4,196,127 different words were crawled. This dataset contains mostly modern standard Arabic. The dataset category distribution can be found in Figure 1a.

2.2 Arabic Poetry Dataset (AraP)

The AraP dataset was crawled from the Adab Website[2] It contains Arabic poetry from the 6th to 21st centuries and consists of 41,264 poems from five eras. This dataset contains mostly colloquial and old Arabic. AraP's Category distribution details can be found in Figure 1b.

3 Methodology

AraDIC is an end-to-end framework of a character encoder (CE) and a classifier. We choose two classifiers for our framework. A character CNN (CLCNN) similar to Kitada et al. (2018), but tuned to Arabic language, and a bidirectional gated recurrent unit (BiGRU) (Chung et al., 2014) based classifier. The outline of our framework is shown in Figure 2. We use wildcard training introduced by (Shimada et al., 2016) for data augmentation. Wildcard training is dropout on the embedding space so that the data changes a little every training iteration. In that sense it acts as a data augmentation technique. We use CB softmax loss to deal with class imbalance problem.

3.1 Character Encoder

The CE is a CNN where convolution is performed in a depth-wise manner. It learns to encode each input character image of size 36×36 pixels into a 128-dimension vector. The architectural configuration is shown in Table 1a.

3.2 Classifier

For classification we use two classifiers. The first one is a CLCNN, and the second is a BiGRU. Input

---

[2]Adab website for Arabic poetry from 6th to 21st centuries. `http://www.adab.com/`.

Layer	Configuration
Conv2D	(c= 1, k = 3x3, f=32) + ReLU
Max-Pool2D	(k=2x2)
Conv2D	(c=32, k = 3x3, f=32) + ReLU
Max-Pool2D	(k=2x2)
Conv2D	(c=32, k = 3x3, f=32) + ReLU
FC	(800,128) + ReLU
FC	(128,128) + ReLU

(a) Character encoder architecture.

Layer	Configuration
Conv1D	(c= 128, k = 3, f=512) + ReLU
Max-Pool1D	(k=3)
Conv1D	(c=512, k=3, f=512) + ReLU
Max-Pool1D	(k=3)
Conv1D	(c=512, k = 3, f=512) + ReLU
Conv1D	(c=512, k = 3, f=512) + ReLU
FC	(1024,1024) + ReLU
FC	(1024,nc) + ReLU

(b) CLCNN architecture.

Layer	Configuration
BiGRU	(input = 128, hidden = 128, layer = 3) + BN
FC	(256,nc)

(c) BiGRU architecture.

Table 1: AraDIC's architectural configuration, **c** is input channels, **k** is kernel size, **f** is feature maps, **nc** is number of classes and **BN** is Batch Normalization (Ioffe and Szegedy, 2015).

text is represented as an array of character images each encoded into a 128 dimension vector using the CE. Those character embeddings are the input features for both the CLCNN and the BiGRU.

The CLCNN is a character-level CNN whose architectural details can be found in Table 1b.

The BiGRU takes those characters embeddings and computes a sentence level embedding. The sentence embedding is the average of all the hidden layers outputs of the BiGRU. These sentence level features are then passed to a fully connected layer followed by a softmax for class prediction. Detailed architecture of the BiGRU can be found in Table 1c.

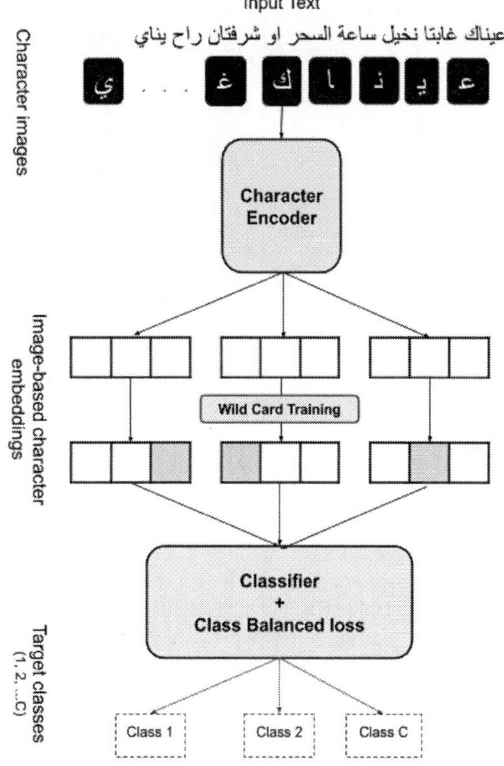

Figure 2: AraDIC's architecture outline.

3.3 Class-Balanced Loss

Both of our datasets suffer from the long tailed distribution problem as shown in Figure 1a and 1b. To deal with this problem, we use state-of-the-art method, the class balanced loss (Cui et al., 2019). The class-balanced loss could be applied by re-weighting the loss function by the inverse effective number of classes. We apply it to softmax cross entropy loss as follows:

$$-\frac{1-\beta}{1-\beta^{n_y}} \log\left(\frac{\exp(Z_y)}{\sum_{j=1}^{C} \exp(Z_j)}\right), \quad (1)$$

where $\frac{1-\beta}{1-\beta^{n_y}}$ is the inverse effective number of classes. Z_j is the model output ($j = 1, 2, ...C$), y is class label for the input sample, n_y is number of samples per class y and β is a training hyper parameter. This will assign adaptive weights to the cost function for classes with higher samples and classes with lower samples, effectively re-weighting the cost function based on effective number of classes. This method was originally intended for object detection, we show that it can be applied to text classification as well.

Model			F-score			
			Arabic Wikipedia Title		Arabic Poetry	
	Embedding	Classifier	Micro [%]	Macro [%]	Micro [%]	Macro [%]
		Majority Class	21.67	2.97	47.06	5.33
Word	Unigram	SVM	45.47	26.60	52.80	34.83
level	AraVec	CNN	45.02	25.05	69.28	41.95
Character	One-hot	CLCNN	42.76	18.71	68.24	37.72
level	**AraDIC**	CLCNN (− CB loss)	47.47	26.85	74.86	45.61
		CLCNN (+ CB loss)	49.49	30.55	74.03	48.65
		BiGRU (− CB loss)	55.71	39.04	78.93	59.88
		BiGRU (+ CB loss)	**57.76**	**44.54**	**79.53**	**65.00**

Table 2: Classification results of our model and other baselines. **Majority Class**: Due to high class-imbalance in both of our datasets, we examine the performance of majority class classifier. **CNN + AraVec**: Sentence classifier CNN (Sagheer and Sukkar, 2018; Kim, 2014) using AraVec's word embeddings (Soliman et al., 2017). **SVM**: an SVM with unigrams, stemming, and document term matrix with TF-IDF scores as features. **CLCNN**: character level CNN with one hot encoding as inputs(Zhang et al., 2015). **AraDIC**: our proposed end-to-end framework of character encoder, CLCNN and BiGRU classifiers, trained with and without class-balanced softmax loss (**CB loss**). We report two evaluation metrics, the macro and micro F-scores.

4 Experiments

To train our classifier both datasets are divided into 80% training data and 20% testing data[3].

4.1 AraDIC

The maximum character length or each document is set to 60 characters for the AWT dataset and 128 characters for the AraP dataset. That's for using the CLCNN classifiers. As for the BiGRU classifier we don't set a maximum character length, instead the whole text is used. Each character was encoded into a 128 dimension vector using the CE. Adam optimizer (Kingma and Ba, 2014) with a batch size of 64 and a learning rate of 0.001 was chosen as the optimization method. As for the CB loss we set β to 0.99 for both datasets. Wildcard training ratio is set to 10%. The training loss converged after approximately 150 epochs for AraP dataset and 500 epochs for AWT dataset.

4.2 Baselines

We use several word-based and character-based baselines to evaluate our method. They include both classical and deep learning baselines as follows:

- Due to high class imbalance in both our datasets, a majority class classifier is chosen as our first baseline.

- A classical Support Vector Machine (SVM) with a document-term matrix (DTM) of TF-IDF scores for unigrams as input was used as word-based baseline. Terms occurring only once and terms appearing in more than 90% of documents were omitted from the DTM. We performed preprocessing in the form of stop words, non-Arabic characters, diacritics removal. Then, text is stemmed using Khoja stemmer (Khoja, 2001). Farasa segmenter (Abdelali et al., 2016) was used for word segmentation.

- We also used Sagheer and Sukkar (2018)'s method of using AraVec's word embeddings as input features and sentence CNN originally introduced by Kim (2014) for classification. This is another word-based baseline.

- Another baseline is a character-level CNN (CLCNN) introduced by Zhang et al. (2015). In this baseline, input characters were one-hot encoded.

---

[3]Hyperparameters were tuned with a validation set split from the training set, and reported the predicted results of the evaluation set.

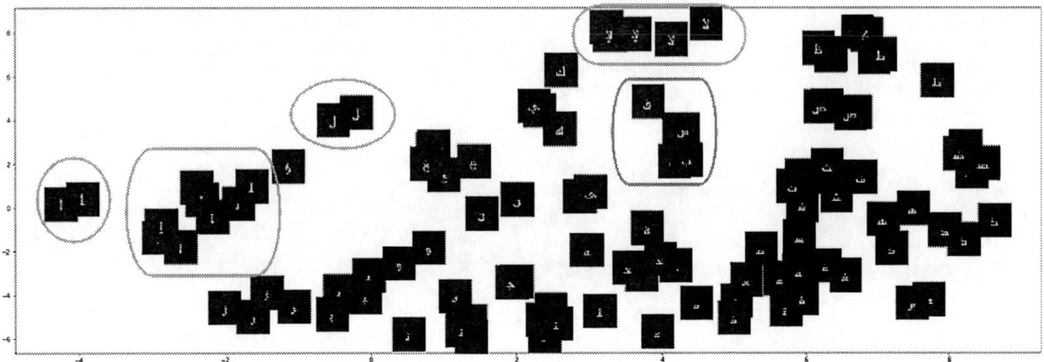

Figure 3: Character embeddings visualization using t-SNE (Maaten and Hinton, 2008). Sections circled in green show clusters of related characters with similar shapes, which was the majority of cases. Sections encircled in red show clusters of unrelated characters which was rare.

5 Results and Discussion

Classification results can be found in Table 2. It is noted that AraDIC outperforms both word based and character based deep learning and classical baselines. Performance improvement is shown over classical SVM without the need for preprocessing, word segmentation, stemming and feature engineering associated with classical methods. It was also able to beat Sagheer and Sukkar (2018) method of using sentence CNN with AraVec's word embeddings as input features without the need for word segmentation. This makes character level representations a better choice for Arabic language avoiding segmentation and feature engineering problems. It's also shown that using AraDIC's image-based character embeddings outperforms CLCNN with one-hot encoded characters as input features. Therefore, we can conclude as well that image-based character embeddings are useful for Arabic language due to the property of the language as discussed in the introduction section of this paper.

As for the classifier part of AraDIC, it can be noticed that the BiGRU significantly outperforms CLCNN for both classification tasks. This suggests that sequence-to-sequence models are more suitable for text classification using image-based character-based embeddings, especially in Arabic document classification.

Also, using CB loss improves the macro F-score of classifiers for both datasets. It can be also noted that the improvement in the macro F-score is achieved when using a CLCNN and a BiGRU. This shows that CB loss can be useful to solve class imbalance problems for text classification tasks.

Figure 3 shows character embeddings visualization using t-distributed stochastic neighbor embedding (t-SNE) method (Maaten and Hinton, 2008). As shown, embedding for related characters having similar shapes like " آ ", " ا ", " إ ", and " ﺍ " are clustered in the embedding space. This is the majority of cases. Other unrelated characters are also clustered which is rare. This however shows that using image based character embeddings gives an extra layer of visual information. Another reason why it is useful is because both the CE and the classifier are trained as an end-to-end system. This means that the CE learns the best embeddings suitable for the classifier.

6 Conclusion

In this paper, we proposed a novel end-to-end Arabic text classification framework AraDIC. We also published two large scale Arabic text classification datasets that contain the three types of Arabic language, the AWT and the AraP datasets. AraDIC's image-based character embedding strategy eliminated the need for complicated preprocessing, segmentation and morphological analysis, and achieved much better performance than conventional deep and classical text classification techniques that use word and character-based embeddings. We have shown also that class-balanced loss is useful for text classification tasks with long tailed distribution datasets.

References

Ahmed Abdelali, Kareem Darwish, Nadir Durrani, and Hamdy Mubarak. 2016. Farasa: A fast and furious segmenter for arabic. In *Proc. of NAACL*, pages 11–16.

Mohammed N Al-Kabi, Saif A Kazakzeh, Belal M Abu Ata, Saif A Al-Rababah, and Izzat M Alsmadi. 2015. A novel root based arabic stemmer. *Journal of King Saud University-Computer and Information Sciences*, 27(2):94–103.

Nora Al-Twairesh, Hend Al-Khalifa, and AbdulMalik Al-Salman. 2016. Arasenti: Large-scale twitter-specific arabic sentiment lexicons. In *Proc. of ACL*, pages 697–705.

Mateusz Buda, Atsuto Maki, and Maciej A Mazurowski. 2018. A systematic study of the class imbalance problem in convolutional neural networks. *Neural Networks*, 106:249–259.

Nitesh V Chawla, Kevin W Bowyer, Lawrence O Hall, and W Philip Kegelmeyer. 2002. Smote: synthetic minority over-sampling technique. *Journal of artificial intelligence research*, 16:321–357.

Junyoung Chung, Caglar Gulcehre, Kyunghyun Cho, and Yoshua Bengio. 2014. Empirical evaluation of gated recurrent neural networks on sequence modeling. In *Proc. of NIPS Workshop on Deep Learning*.

Yin Cui, Menglin Jia, Tsung-Yi Lin, Yang Song, and Serge Belongie. 2019. Class-balanced loss based on effective number of samples. In *Proc. of CVPR*, pages 9268–9277.

Alaa M El-Halees. 2009. Filtering spam e-mail from mixed arabic and english messages: A comparison of machine learning techniques. *Filtering Spam E-Mail from Mixed Arabic and English Messages: A Comparison of Machine Learning Techniques.*, 6(1).

Yonatan Geifman and Ran El-Yaniv. 2017. Deep active learning over the long tail. *CoRR preprint arXiv:1711.00941*.

Chen Huang, Yining Li, Chen Change Loy, and Xiaoou Tang. 2016. Learning deep representation for imbalanced classification. In *Proc. of CVPR*, pages 5375–5384.

Chen Huang, Yining Li, Change Loy Chen, and Xiaoou Tang. 2019. Deep imbalanced learning for face recognition and attribute prediction. *IEEE transactions on pattern analysis and machine intelligence*.

Hossam S Ibrahim, Sherif M Abdou, and Mervat Gheith. 2015. Sentiment analysis for modern standard arabic and colloquial. *CoRR preprint arXiv:1505.03105*.

Sergey Ioffe and Christian Szegedy. 2015. Batch normalization: Accelerating deep network training by reducing internal covariate shift. *arXiv preprint arXiv:1502.03167*.

Salman H Khan, Munawar Hayat, Mohammed Bennamoun, Ferdous A Sohel, and Roberto Togneri. 2017. Cost-sensitive learning of deep feature representations from imbalanced data. *IEEE transactions on neural networks and learning systems*, 29(8):3573–3587.

Shereen Khoja. 2001. Apt: Arabic part-of-speech tagger. In *Proc. of the Student Workshop at NAACL*, pages 20–25.

Yoon Kim. 2014. Convolutional neural networks for sentence classification. *CoRR preprint arXiv:1408.5882*.

Diederik P Kingma and Jimmy Ba. 2014. Adam: A method for stochastic optimization. *CoRR preprint arXiv:1412.6980*.

Shunsuke Kitada, Ryunosuke Kotani, and Hitoshi Iyatomi. 2018. End-to-end text classification via image-based embedding using character-level networks. In *Proc. of IEEE AIPR Workshop*, pages 1–4. IEEE.

Frederick Liu, Han Lu, Chieh Lo, and Graham Neubig. 2017. Learning character-level compositionality with visual features. In *Proc. of ACL*, pages 2059–2068.

Laurens van der Maaten and Geoffrey Hinton. 2008. Visualizing data using t-sne. *Journal of machine learning research*, 9(Nov):2579–2605.

Jonathan Masci, Ueli Meier, Dan Cireşan, and Jürgen Schmidhuber. 2011. Stacked convolutional auto-encoders for hierarchical feature extraction. In *International conference on artificial neural networks*, pages 52–59. Springer.

Tomas Mikolov, Ilya Sutskever, Kai Chen, Greg S Corrado, and Jeff Dean. 2013. Distributed representations of words and phrases and their compositionality. In *Proc. of NIPS*, pages 3111–3119.

Fuchun Peng, Xiangji Huang, Dale Schuurmans, and Shaojun Wang. 2003. Text classification in asian languages without word segmentation. In *Proc. IRAL workshop*, pages 41–48.

Dania Sagheer and Fadel Sukkar. 2018. Arabic sentences classification via deep learning. *International Journal of Computer Applications*, 182(5):40–46.

Said A Salloum, Ahmad Qasim AlHamad, Mostafa Al-Emran, and Khaled Shaalan. 2018. A survey of arabic text mining. In *Intelligent Natural Language Processing: Trends and Applications*, pages 417–431. Springer.

Mohammed A Shehab, Omar Badarneh, Mahmoud Al-Ayyoub, and Yaser Jararweh. 2016. A supervised approach for multi-label classification of arabic news articles. In *Proc. of CSIT*, pages 1–6. IEEE.

Li Shen, Zhouchen Lin, and Qingming Huang. 2016. Relay backpropagation for effective learning of deep convolutional neural networks. In *Proc. of ECCV*, pages 467–482. Springer.

Daiki Shimada, Ryunosuke Kotani, and Hitoshi Iyatomi. 2016. Document classification through image-based character embedding and wildcard training. In *Proc. of IEEE Big Data*, pages 3922–3927. IEEE.

Abu Bakr Soliman, Kareem Eissa, and Samhaa R El-Beltagy. 2017. Aravec: A set of arabic word embedding models for use in arabic nlp. *Procedia Computer Science*, 117:256–265.

Nitish Srivastava, Geoffrey Hinton, Alex Krizhevsky, Ilya Sutskever, and Ruslan Salakhutdinov. 2014. Dropout: a simple way to prevent neural networks from overfitting. *The journal of machine learning research*, 15(1):1929–1958.

Kai Ming Ting. 2000. A comparative study of cost-sensitive boosting algorithms. In *Proc. of ICML*. Citeseer.

Yu-Xiong Wang, Deva Ramanan, and Martial Hebert. 2017. Learning to model the tail. In *Advances in Neural Information Processing Systems*, pages 7029–7039.

Xiang Zhang, Junbo Zhao, and Yann LeCun. 2015. Character-level convolutional networks for text classification. In *Proc. of NIPS*, pages 649–657.

Zhi-Hua Zhou and Xu-Ying Liu. 2005. Training cost-sensitive neural networks with methods addressing the class imbalance problem. *IEEE Transactions on knowledge and data engineering*, 18(1):63–77.

Yang Zou, Zhiding Yu, BVK Kumar, and Jinsong Wang. 2018. Domain adaptation for semantic segmentation via class-balanced self-training. *arXiv preprint arXiv:1810.07911*.

Embeddings of Label Components for Sequence Labeling:
A Case Study of Fine-grained Named Entity Recognition

Takuma Kato[1]   **Kaori Abe**[1,2]   **Hiroki Ouchi**[2,1]   **Shumpei Miyawaki**[1]
Jun Suzuki[1,2]   **Kentaro Inui**[1,2]
[1] Tohoku University   [2] RIKEN

```
{takuma.kato, abe-k, miyawaki.shumpei,
   jun.suzuki, inui}@ecei.tohoku.ac.jp
        hiroki.ouchi@riken.jp
```


Abstract

In general, the labels used in sequence labeling consist of different types of elements. For example, IOB-format entity labels, such as `B-Person` and `I-Person`, can be decomposed into span (`B` and `I`) and type information (`Person`). However, while most sequence labeling models do not consider such label components, the shared components across labels, such as `Person`, can be beneficial for label prediction. In this work, we propose to integrate label component information as embeddings into models. Through experiments on English and Japanese fine-grained named entity recognition, we demonstrate that the proposed method improves performance, especially for instances with low-frequency labels.

1 Introduction

Sequence labeling is a problem in which a label is assigned to each word in an input sentence. In many label sets, each label consists of different types of elements. For example, IOB-format entity labels (Ramshaw and Marcus, 1995), such as `B-Person` and `I-Location`, can be decomposed into span (e.g., `B`, `I` and `O`) and type information (e.g., `Person` and `Location`). Also, morphological feature tags (More et al., 2018), such as `Gender=Masc|Number=Sing`, can be decomposed into gender, number and other information.

General sequence labeling models (Ma and Hovy, 2016; Lample et al., 2016; Chiu and Nichols, 2016), however, do not consider such components. Specifically, the probability that each word is assigned a label is computed on the basis of the inner product between word representation and label embedding (see Equation 2 in Section 2.1). Here, the label embedding is associated with each label and independently trained without considering its components. This means that labels are treated as mutually exclusive. In fact, labels often share some

components. Consider the labels `B-Person` and `I-Person`. They share the component `Person`, and injecting such component information into the label embeddings can improve the generalization performance.

Motivated by this, we propose a method that shares and learns the embeddings of label components (see details in Section 2.2). Specifically, we first decompose each label into its components. We then assign an embedding to each component and summarize the embeddings of all the components into one as a label embedding used in a model. This component-level operation enables the model to share information on the common components across label embeddings.

To investigate the effectiveness of our method, we take the task of fine-grained Named Entity Recognition (NER) as a case study. Typically, in this task, a large number of entity-type labels are predefined in a hierarchical structure, and intermediate type labels can be used as label components, as well as leaf type labels and B/I-labels. In this sense, the fine-grained NER can be seen as a good example of the potential applications of the proposed method. Furthermore, some entity labels occur more frequently than others. An interesting question is whether our method of label component sharing exhibits an improvement in recognizing entities of infrequent labels. In our experiments, we use the English and Japanese NER corpora with the Extended Named Entity Hierarchy (Sekine et al., 2002) including 200 entity tags. To sum up, our main contributions are as follows: (i) we propose a method that shares and learns label component embeddings, and (ii) through experiments on English and Japanese fine-grained NER, we demonstrate that the proposed method achieves better performance than a standard sequence labeling model, especially for instances with low-frequency labels.

Proceedings of the 58th Annual Meeting of the Association for Computational Linguistics: Student Research Workshop, pages 222–229
July 5 - July 10, 2020. ©2020 Association for Computational Linguistics

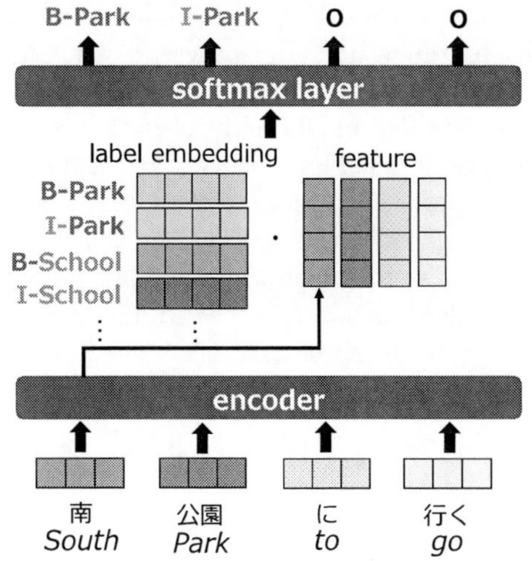

Figure 1: Overview of a standard sequence labelling model. Each label (e.g., B-Park) is annotated as a single unit, disregarding its inner structure ("B" and "Park").

2 Methods

2.1 Baseline model

We describe our baseline model in Figure 1. Given an input sentence, the encoder converts each word into its feature vector. Then, the inner product between each feature vector and label embedding is calculated for computing the label distribution. Finally, the IOB2-format label (Ramshaw and Marcus, 1995) with the highest probability is assigned to each token. The label `B-Park`, indicating the leftmost token of some entity, is assigned to 南 (*South*), and `I-Park`, indicating the token inside some entity, is assigned to 公園 (*Park*). The label `O`, indicating the token outside entities, is assigned to に (*to*) and 行く (*go*).

Formally, for each word x_i in the input sentence $X = (x_1, x_2, \ldots, x_n)$, the model outputs the label $\hat{y}_i$ with the highest probability:

$$\hat{y}_i = \arg\max_{y \in \mathcal{Y}} P(y|x_i, X), \tag{1}$$

where $\mathcal{Y}$ is a label set defined in each data set. The probability distribution is calculated as

$$P(y|x_i, X) = \frac{\exp(\mathbf{W}[y] \cdot \mathbf{f}(x_i, X))}{\sum_{y' \in \mathcal{Y}} \exp(\mathbf{W}[y'] \cdot \mathbf{f}(x_i, X))}, \tag{2}$$

where $\mathbf{W} \in \mathbb{R}^{|\mathcal{Y}| \times D}$ is a weight matrix for the label set $\mathcal{Y}$.[1] Each row of this matrix is associated with

---

[1] D is the number of dimensions of each weight vector.

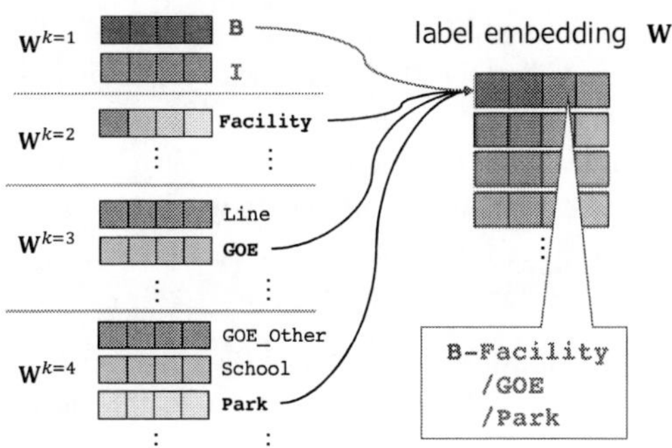

Figure 2: Label embedding calculation. Each label embedding is calculated from its component embeddings.

each label $y \in \mathcal{Y}$, and $\mathbf{W}[y]$ represents the y-th row vector. $\mathbf{f}(x, X)$ represents the vector encoded by a neural-network-based encoder.

2.2 Embeddings of label components

We propose to integrate label component information as embeddings into models. This procedure consists of two steps: (i) *label decomposition* and (ii) *label embedding calculation*.

Label decomposition   We first decompose each label into its components. Each label consists of multiple types of components. Consider the following example.

$$\texttt{B-Park} = \{\texttt{B}, \texttt{Park}\}$$

The labels defined in a general entity tag set consist of the IOB (e.g., `B`) and entity (e.g., `Park`) component types. Consider another example.

$$\texttt{B-Facility/GOE/Park} =$$
$$\{\texttt{B}, \texttt{Facility}, \texttt{GOE}, \texttt{Park}\}$$

The labels defined in the Extended Named Entity tag set (Sekine et al., 2002) consist of the four component types: IOB (e.g., `B`), top layer of the entity tag hierarchy (e.g., `Facility`), second layer (e.g., `GOE`) the third layer (e.g., `Park`). In this way, we can regard each label as a set of components (type–value pairs).

Formally, K components of each label y will be denoted by $\mathcal{C}^y = \{c_k\}_{k=1}^K$, where c_k is the index associated with the value of each component type k. The above two examples are represented as $\mathcal{C}^{y=\texttt{B-Park}} = \{c_1 = \texttt{B}, c_2 = \texttt{Park}\}$ and $\mathcal{C}^{y=\texttt{B-Facility/GOE/Park}} = \{c_1 = \texttt{B}, c_2 = \texttt{Facility}, c_3 = \texttt{GOE}, c_4 = \texttt{Park}\}$. This formalization is applicable to arbitrary label sets whose label consists of type-value components.

Label embedding calculation We then assign an embedding (i.e., trainable vector representation) to each label component and combining the embeddings of all the components within a label into one label embedding. In this study, we investigate two types of typical summarizing techniques: (a) summation and (b) concatenation.

(a) Summation The embedding of each label, $\mathbf{W}[y]$, is calculated by summing the embeddings of its components:

$$\mathbf{W}[y] = \sum_{c_k \in \mathcal{C}^y} \mathbf{W}^k[c_k]. \tag{3}$$

Here, $\mathbf{W}^k$ is an embedding matrix for each component type k, and $\mathbf{W}^k[c_k]$ denotes the c_k-th row vector. Figure 2 illustrates this calculation process. The label `B-Facility/GOE/Park` consists of four components (i.e., `B`, `Facility`, `GOE` and `Park`), each c_k value of which is associated with a row vector of each matrix $\mathbf{W}^k$.

(b) Concatenation The embedding of each label, $\mathbf{W}[y]$, is calculated by concatenating the embeddings of its components:

$$\mathbf{W}[y] = [\mathbf{W}^1[c_1], \ldots, \mathbf{W}^K[c_K]]. \tag{4}$$

Here, similarly to $\mathbf{W}^k$ is an embedding matrix for each component type k Equation 3. Unlike Equation 3, the label component embeddings are concatenated into one embedding. Compared with the summation, one disadvantage of the concatenation is memory efficiency: the number of dimensions of the label embeddings increases according to the number of label components K.

Our label embedding calculation enables models to share the embeddings of label components commonly shared across labels. For example, the embeddings of both `B-Facility/GOE/Park` and `B-Facility/GOE/School` are calculated by adding the embeddings of the shared components (i.e., `B`, `Facility` and `GOE`). Equations 3 and 4 can be regarded as a general form of the hierarchical label matrix proposed by Shimaoka et al. (2017) because our method can treat not only hierarchical structures but also any type of type–value set, such as morphological feature labels (e.g. `Gender=Masc|Number=Sing`).

3 Experiments

3.1 Settings

Dataset We use the Extended Named Entity Corpus for English[2] and Japanese.[3] fine-grained NER (Mai et al., 2018) In this dataset, each NE is assigned one of 200 entity labels defined in the Extended Named Entity Hierarchy (Sekine et al., 2002). For the English dataset, we follow the training/development/test split defined by Mai et al. (2018). For the Japanese dataset, we follow the training/development/test split of Universal Dependencies (UD) Japanese-BCCWJ. (Asahara et al., 2018)[4] Table 1 shows the statistics of the dataset.

Data statistics There is a gap between the frequencies, i.e., how many times each label appears in the training set. We categorize each label into three classes on the basis of its frequency, shown in Table 2. For example, if a label appears 0–100 times in the training set, it is categorized into the "Low" class. Moreover, we denote how many times entities with the labels belonging to each frequency class appear in the development or test set. To better understand the model behavior, we investigate the performance of each frequency class.

Model setup As the encoder $\mathbf{f}(x, X)$ in Equation 2 in Section 2.1, we use BERT[5] (Devlin et al., 2019), which is a state-of-the-art language model.[6] As the baseline model, we use the general label embedding matrix without considering label components, i.e., each label embedding $\mathbf{W}[y]$ in Equation 2 is randomly initialized and independently learned. In contrast, our proposed model calculates the label embedding matrix from label components (Equations 3 and 4). The only difference between these models is the label embedding matrix, so if a performance gap between them is observed, it stems from this point.

Hyperparameters The overall settings of hyperparameters are the same between the baseline and the proposed model. For English, we use the BERT pre-trained on BooksCorpus and English Wikipedia (Devlin et al., 2019). For Japanese, we use the BERT pre-trained on Japanese

---

[2]We e-mailed the authors of (Mai et al., 2018) and received the English dataset.

[3]`https://www.gsk.or.jp/catalog/gsk2014-a/`

[4]`https://github.com/UniversalDependencies/UD_Japanese-BCCWJ`

[5]We use the open-source NER model utilizing BERT: `https://github.com/kamalkraj/BERT-NER`.

[6]The state of the art model on the Extended Named Entity Corpus is the LSTM + CNN + CRF model that uses dictionary information (Mai et al., 2018)

Dataset	English		Japanese	
	# of Sentences	# of Entities	# of Sentences	# of Entities
train	14176	27686	34784	72318
dev	1573	3032	7009	11954
test	3942	7682	6783	11669

Table 1: Statistics of the datasets.

Frequency Classes		English		Japanese	
		Dev	Test	Dev	Test
Low	$(0\sim100)$	1125	2798	666	619
Middle	$(101\sim500)$	1224	3128	2,875	2,531
High	$(501\sim)$	683	1756	8,413	8,519

Table 2: Details of frequency classes.

Wikipedia (Shibata et al., 2019). We fine-tune them on the Extended NER corpus for solving fine-grained NER. We set the training epochs to 20 in fine-tuning. Both the baseline and the proposed models are trained to minimize cross-entropy loss during training. We set a batch size of 32 and a learning rate of 5.0×10^{-5} using Adam (Kingma and Ba, 2015) for the optimizer. We choose the dropout rate from among $\{0.1, 0.3, 0.5\}$ on the basis of the F_1 scores in each development set.[7] We set the number of dimensions of the hidden states in BERT. In the baseline model, we set the number of dimensions of the label embedding $\mathbf{W}$ in Equation 2 to 768. In the proposed models, we also use the same dimension size 768 for $\mathbf{W}$ in Equations 3 and 4.

3.2 Results

We report averaged F_1 scores across five different runs of the model training with random seeds. Table 3 shows F_1 scores for overall classes and each label frequency class on each test set.

Overall performance For the overall labels, the proposed models (PROPOSED:SUM and PROPOSED:CONCAT) outperformed the baseline model on English and Japanese datasets. These results suggest the effectiveness of our proposed method for calculating the label embeddings from label components.

Performance for each frequency class For all the label frequency classes, the proposed model with summation (PROPOSED:SUM) yielded the best results among the three models. In particular, for low-frequency labels, the proposed model with summation (PROPOSED:SUM) achieved a remarkable improvement of F_1 compared with the baseline model. Also, the proposed model with concatenation (PROPOSED:CONCAT) achieved an improvement of F_1. These results suggest that exploiting label embeddings of the components shared across labels improves the generalization performance, especially for low-frequency labels.

3.3 Analysis

Recall that the entity tag set used in the datasets has a hierarchical structure. This means that label components at higher layers appear more frequently than those at lower layers and are shared across many labels. As shown in Table 3, the proposed models achieve performance improvements for low-frequency labels. Here, we can expect that the embeddings of high-frequency shared label components help the model correctly predict the low-frequency labels. To verify this hypothesis, we compare between F_1 scores of the baseline and proposed models, shown in Table 4. Here, the targets to investigate are the three-layered, low-frequency labels[8] that have a high-frequency, second layer component.[9] As shown in Table 4, the PROPOSED:SUM model outperformed the baseline model. This indicates that for predicting low-frequency labels, it is effective for the model to use shared components. On the other hand, the PROPOSED:CONCAT model underperformed the baseline model. One possible reason is that the model obtains less information by concatenating label embeddings than by summing them.

---

[7] In our experiments, we found that the models trained with the dropout rate of 0.1 achieved the best performance on each development set.

[8] We exclude the labels that consist of only two layers, such as `Timex/Date`.

[9] In this paper, we also regard the second-layer components appearing over 100 times in the training set as high-frequency.

	Low	Middle	High	Overall
English				
BASELINE	79.83±0.27	80.29±0.46	90.82±0.32	84.99±0.27
PROPOSED:SUM	**81.15**±0.24	**80.99**±0.27	**90.87**±0.26	**85.67**±0.13
PROPOSED:CONCAT	80.40±0.38	80.31±0.28	90.75±0.23	85.20±0.16
Japanese				
BASELINE	44.39±0.29	51.73±0.50	70.82±0.32	68.06±0.27
PROPOSED:SUM	**45.34**±0.91	**51.93**±0.66	**71.04**±0.49	**68.34**±0.41
PROPOSED:CONCAT	44.76±1.12	51.45±0.40	70.52±0.29	67.77±0.23

Table 3: Comparison between the baseline and proposed models. Cells show the F_1 scores and standard deviations on each test set.

	English	Japanese
Baseline	76.58±0.26	49.66±0.68
Proposed:Sum	**77.76**±0.30	**50.05**±1.19
Proposed:Concat	76.77±0.71	49.31±1.12

Table 4: Comparison between the baseline and the proposed models in the Low frequency class.

3.4 Visualization of label embedding spaces

To better understand the label embeddings created from the label components by our proposed method, we visualize the learned label embeddings. Specifically, we hypothesize that the embeddings of the labels sharing label components are close to each other and form clusters in the embedding space if they successfully encode the shared label component information. To verify this hypothesis, we use the t-SNE algorithm (van der Maaten and Hinton, 2008) to map the label embeddings learned by the baseline and proposed models onto the two-dimensional space, shown in Figure 3. As we expected, some clusters were formed in the label embedding space learned by the proposed model, shown in Figure 3b, while there is no distinct cluster in the one learned by the baseline, shown in Figure 3a. By looking at them in detail, we obtained two findings. First, in the embedding space learned by the proposed model, we found that two distinct clusters were formed corresponding to the two span labels (i.e. B and I). Second, the labels that have the same top layer label (represented in the same color) also formed some smaller clusters within the B and I-label clusters. For example, Figure 3c shows the Product cluster whose members are the labels sharing the top layer label Product.

From these figures, we could confirm that the embeddings of the labels sharing label components (span and upper-layer type labels) form the clusters.

4 Related work

Sequence labeling has been widely studied and applied to many tasks, such as Chunking (Ramshaw and Marcus, 1995; Hashimoto et al., 2017), NER (Ma and Hovy, 2016; Chiu and Nichols, 2016) and Semantic Role Labeling (SRL) (Zhou and Xu, 2015; He et al., 2017). In English fine-grained entity recognition, Ling and Weld (2012) created a standard fine-grained entity typing dataset with multi-class, multi-label annotations. Ringland et al. (2019) developed a dataset for nested NER dataset. These datasets independently handle each label without considering label components. In Japanese NER, Misawa et al. (2017) combined word and character information to improve performance. Mai et al. (2018) reported that dictionary information improves the performance of fine-grained NER. Their methods do not consider label components and are orthogonal to our method.

Some existing studies take shared components (or information) across labels into account. In Entity Typing, Ma et al. (2016) and Shimaoka et al. (2017) proposed to calculate entity label embeddings by considering a label hierarchical structure. While their method is limited to only a hierarchical structure, our method can be applied to any set of components and can be regarded as a general form of their method. In multi-label classification, Zhong et al. (2018) assumed that the labels co-occurring in many instances are correlated with each other and share some common features, and proposed a method that learns a feature (label em-

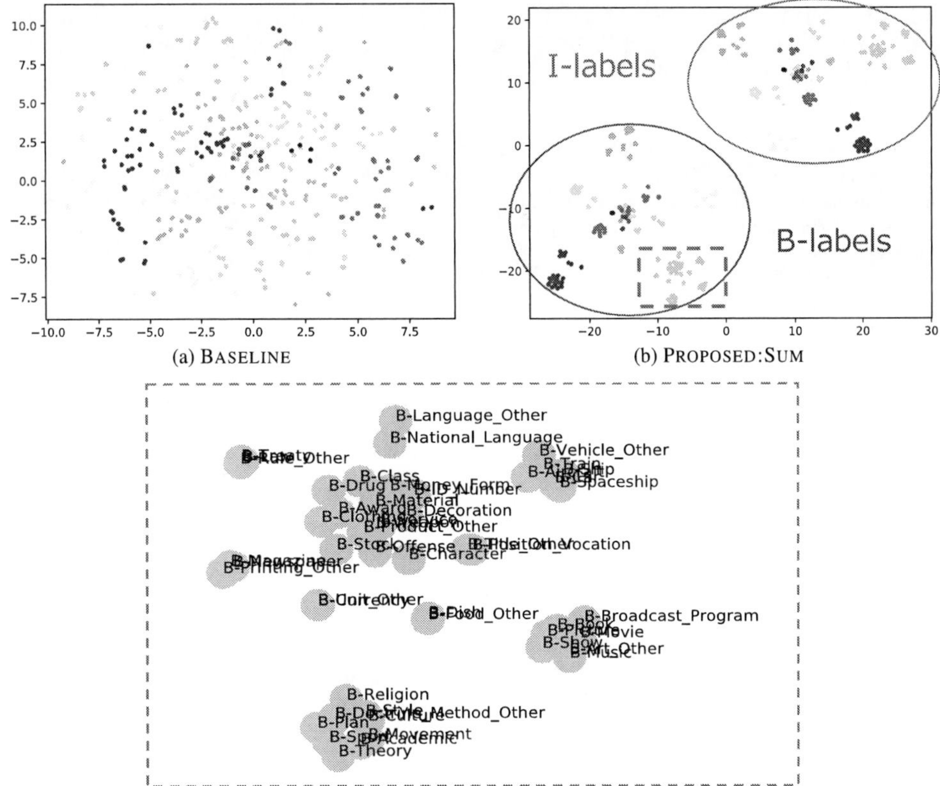

(c) Enlarged view of a cluster in (b). The embeddings of the labels sharing the top layer label `Product` form this cluster.

Figure 3: Visualization of the label embedding space. The same color represents the labels that have the same hierarchical top layer label.

bedding) space where such co-occurring labels are close to each other. The work of Matsubayashi et al. (2009) is the closest to ours in terms of decomposing the features of labels. They regard an original label comprising a mixture of components as a set of multiple labels and made models that are able to exploit the multiple components to effectively learn in the SRL task.

5 Conclusion

We proposed a method that shares and learns the embeddings of label components. Through experiments on English and Japanese fine-grained NER, we demonstrated that our proposed method improves the performance, especially for instances with low-frequency labels. For future work, we envision to apply our method to other tasks and datasets and investigate the effectiveness. Also, we plan to extend the simple label embedding calculation methods to more sophisticated ones.

Acknowledgments

This work was partially supported by JSPS KAKENHI Grant Number JP19H04162 and JP19K20351. This work was also partially supported by a Bilateral Joint Research Program between RIKEN AIP Center and Tohoku University. We would like to thank the members of Tohoku NLP Laboratory, the anonymous reviewers, and the SRW mentor Gabriel Stanovsky for their insightful comments. We also appreciate Alt inc. for providing the corpus of English extended named entity data.

References

Masayuki Asahara, Hiroshi Kanayama, Takaaki Tanaka, Yusuke Miyao, Sumire Uematsu, Shinsuke Mori, Yuji Matsumoto, Mai Omura, and Yugo Murawaki. 2018. Universal dependencies version 2 for Japanese. In *Proceedings of LREC*, pages 1824–1831.

Jason P.C. Chiu and Eric Nichols. 2016. Named entity recognition with bidirectional LSTM-CNNs. *Transactions of the Association for Computational Linguistics*, 4:357–370.

Jacob Devlin, Ming-Wei Chang, Kenton Lee, and Kristina Toutanova. 2019. BERT: pre-training of deep bidirectional transformers for language understanding. In *Proceedings of NAACL-HLT*, pages 4171–4186.

Kazuma Hashimoto, Caiming Xiong, Yoshimasa Tsuruoka, and Richard Socher. 2017. A joint many-task model: Growing a neural network for multiple NLP tasks. In *Proceedings of EMNLP*, pages 1923–1933.

Luheng He, Kenton Lee, Mike Lewis, and Luke Zettlemoyer. 2017. Deep semantic role labeling: What works and what's next. In *Proceedings of ACL*, pages 473–483.

Diederik P. Kingma and Jimmy Ba. 2015. Adam: A method for stochastic optimization. In *Proceedings of ICLR*.

Guillaume Lample, Miguel Ballesteros, Sandeep Subramanian, Kazuya Kawakami, and Chris Dyer. 2016. Neural architectures for named entity recognition. In *Proceedings of NAACL-HLT*, pages 260–270.

Xiao Ling and Daniel S. Weld. 2012. Fine-grained entity recognition. In *Proceedings of the Twenty-Sixth AAAI Conference on Artificial Intelligence, July 22-26, 2012, Toronto, Ontario, Canada.*

Xuezhe Ma and Eduard Hovy. 2016. End-to-end sequence labeling via bi-directional LSTM-CNNs-CRF. In *Proceedings of ACL*, pages 1064–1074.

Yukun Ma, Erik Cambria, and Sa Gao. 2016. Label embedding for zero-shot fine-grained named entity typing. In *Proceedings of COLING*, pages 171–180.

Laurens van der Maaten and Geoffrey Hinton. 2008. Visualizing data using t-SNE. *Journal of Machine Learning Research*, 9:2579–2605.

Khai Mai, Thai-Hoang Pham, Minh Trung Nguyen, Tuan Duc Nguyen, Danushka Bollegala, Ryohei Sasano, and Satoshi Sekine. 2018. An empirical study on fine-grained named entity recognition. In *Proceedings of COLING*, pages 711–722.

Yuichiroh Matsubayashi, Naoaki Okazaki, and Jun'ichi Tsujii. 2009. A comparative study on generalization of semantic roles in FrameNet. In *Proceedings of ACL and AFNLP*, pages 19–27.

Shotaro Misawa, Motoki Taniguchi, Yasuhide Miura, and Tomoko Ohkuma. 2017. Character-based bidirectional LSTM-CRF with words and characters for Japanese named entity recognition. In *Proceedings of the First Workshop on Subword and Character Level Models in NLP*, pages 97–102.

Amir More, Özlem Çetinoğlu, Çağrı Çöltekin, Nizar Habash, Benoît Sagot, Djamé Seddah, Dima Taji, and Reut Tsarfaty. 2018. CoNLL-UL: Universal morphological lattices for universal dependency parsing. In *Proceedings of LREC*, pages 3847–3853.

Lance Ramshaw and Mitch Marcus. 1995. Text chunking using transformation-based learning. In *Proceedings of Third Workshop on Very Large Corpora*, pages 82–94.

Nicky Ringland, Xiang Dai, Ben Hachey, Sarvnaz Karimi, Cécile Paris, and James R. Curran. 2019. NNE: A dataset for nested named entity recognition in english newswire. In *Proceedings of ACL*, pages 5176–5181.

Satoshi Sekine, Kiyoshi Sudo, and Chikashi Nobata. 2002. Extended named entity hierarchy. In *Proceedings of LREC*, pages 1818–1824.

Tomohide Shibata, Daisuke Kawahara, and Sadao Kurohashi. 2019. Improving japanese syntax parsing with bert. In *Natural Language Processing*, pages 205–208.

Sonse Shimaoka, Pontus Stenetorp, Kentaro Inui, and Sebastian Riedel. 2017. Neural architectures for fine-grained entity type classification. In *Proceedings of EACL*, pages 1271–1280.

Yongjian Zhong, Chang Xu, Bo Du, and Lefei Zhang. 2018. Independent feature and label components for multi-label classification. In *IEEE International Conference on Data Mining, ICDM 2018, Singapore, November 17-20, 2018*, pages 827–836.

Jie Zhou and Wei Xu. 2015. End-to-end learning of semantic role labeling using recurrent neural networks. In *Proceedings of ACL*, pages 1127–1137.

A Appendices

A.1 Additional results

	Top	Second	Third
English			
BASELINE	90.01±0.27	86.69±0.32	83.22±0.28
PROPOSED:SUM	**90.53**±0.06	**87.53**±0.11	**83.87**±0.20
PROPOSED:CONCAT	90.28±0.09	87.04±0.13	83.18±0.30
Japanese			
BASELINE	72.68±0.20	66.22±0.36	66.84±0.34
PROPOSED:SUM	**73.13**±0.43	**66.37**±0.42	**67.00**±0.59
PROPOSED:CONCAT	72.50±0.30	66.19±0.24	66.42±0.49

Table 5: Comparison between the baseline and proposed models for the labels at each hierarchical layer.

	English	Japanese
BASELINE	96.32±0.10	84.74±0.18
PROPOSED:SUM	96.31±0.11	85.01±0.15
PROPOSED:CONCAT	96.27±0.07	84.83±0.11

Table 6: Comparison between the baseline and the proposed models in span (only considering B, I labels).

Performance for each hierarchical category
Table 5 shows F_1 scores for each hierarchical category. The proposed model with summation (PROPOSED:SUM) outperformed the other models in all the hierarchical categories. For the labels at the top layer, in particular, PROPOSED:SUM achieved an improvement of the F_1 scores by a large margin on the Japanese dataset.

Performance for entity span boundary match
Table 6 shows F_1 scores for entity span boundary match, where we regard a predicted boundary (i.e., B and I) as correct if it matches the gold annotation regardless of its entity type label. The performance of the proposed models was comparable to the baseline model. This indicates that there is a performance difference not in identification of entity spans (entity detection) but in identification of entity types (entity typing).

A.2 Case study

We observe actual examples predicted by the proposed model with summation, shown in Table 7.

In Example (a) and (b), Both models succeeded to recognize the entity span. However, only the proposed model also correctly predicted the type label. Note that the entities `Location/Spa` and `Natural_Object/Living_Thing/Living`

Example (a)	下呂 温泉 発祥 の 地 ・・・	
	(The birthplace of Gero Spa ...)	
ENTITY	下呂 (*Gero*)	温泉 (*Spa*)
GOLD	`B-Location/Spa`	`I-Location/Spa`
BASELINE	`B-Facility/Facility_Other`	`I-Facility/Facility_Other`
PROPOSED:SUM	`B-Location/Spa`	`I-Location/Spa`
Example (b)	・・・ where clavaviridae derives from .	
ENTITY	clavaviridae	
GOLD	`B-Natural_Object/Living_Thing/Living_Thing_Other`	
BASELINE	`B-Location/Astral_Body/Constellation`	
PROPOSED:SUM	`B-Natural_Object/Living_Thing/Living_Thing_Other`	
Example (c)	・・・あお白い 日 の 光 ・・・	
	(... the pale sunlight ...)	
ENTITY	あお白い (*pale*)	
GOLD	`B-Color/Color_Other`	
BASELINE	`O`	
PROPOSED:SUM	`B-Color/Nature_Color`	

Table 7: Examples of both model outputs in fine-grained NER.

`_Thing_Other` appear rarely, but rather to the extent of the top layer components `Location` and `Natural_Object` that appear frequently in the training set. Therefore, these examples suggest that the proposed model effectively exploits shared information of label components, especially in terms of the hierarchical layer.

Although, we found that the proposed model predicts partially correct labels even though it is not totally correct in some cases. In Example (c), あお白い (*pale*) is categorized into `Color/Color_Other`, the proposed model also predicted the wrong label `Color/Nature_Color`. However, interestingly, the proposed model correctly recognized the top layer of the type label as `Color`, which is in contrast to the completely wrong prediction of the baseline model.

Building a Japanese Typo Dataset from Wikipedia's Revision History

Yu Tanaka   Yugo Murawaki   Daisuke Kawahara[*]   Sadao Kurohashi
Graduate School of Informatics, Kyoto University
Yoshida-honmachi, Sakyo-ku, Kyoto, Japan
`{ytanaka, murawaki, dk, kuro}@nlp.ist.i.kyoto-u.ac.jp`

Abstract

User generated texts contain many typos for which correction is necessary for NLP systems to work. Although a large number of typo–correction pairs are needed to develop a data-driven typo correction system, no such dataset is available for Japanese. In this paper, we extract over half a million Japanese typo–correction pairs from Wikipedia's revision history. Unlike other languages, Japanese poses unique challenges: (1) Japanese texts are unsegmented so that we cannot simply apply a spelling checker, and (2) the way people inputting kanji logographs results in typos with drastically different surface forms from correct ones. We address them by combining character-based extraction rules, morphological analyzers to guess readings, and various filtering methods. We evaluate the dataset using crowdsourcing and run a baseline seq2seq model for typo correction.

1   Introduction

For over a decade, user generated content (UGC) has been an important target of NLP technology. It is characterized by phenomena not found in standard texts, such as word lengthening (Brody and Diakopoulos, 2011), dialectal variations (Saito et al., 2017; Blodgett et al., 2016), unknown onomatopoeias (Sasano et al., 2013), grammatical errors (Mizumoto et al., 2011; Lee et al., 2018), and mother tongue interference in non-native writing (Goldin et al., 2018). Typographical errors (typos) also occur often in UGC.[1] Typos prevent machines from analyzing texts properly (Belinkov and Bisk, 2018). Typo correction systems are important because applying them before analysis would reduce analysis errors and lead to improved accuracy in various NLP tasks.

Neural networks are a promising choice for building a typo correction system because they have demonstrated their success in a closely related task, spelling correction (Sakaguchi et al., 2017). Since neural networks are known to be data-hungry, the first step to develop a neural typo correction system is to prepare a large number of typos and their corrections. However, to our best knowledge, no such dataset is available for Japanese.[2] This motivated us to build a large Japanese typo dataset.

Typos are usually collected using data mining techniques because thorough corpus annotation is inefficient for infrequently occurring typos. Previous studies on building typo datasets have exploited Wikipedia because it is large, and more importantly, keeps track of all changes made to an article (Max and Wisniewski, 2010; Zesch, 2012). In these studies, to collect typo–correction pairs, the first step is to identify words changed in revisions and the second step is to apply a spell checker to them or calculate the edit distance between them.

While these methods work well on the target languages of the previous studies, namely French and English, they cannot be applied directly to languages such as Japanese and Chinese, where words are not delimited by white space. This is because a typo may cause a word segmentation error and can be misinterpreted as a multiple-word change, making it difficult to identify the word affected. Although state-of-the-art word segmenters provide reasonable accuracy for clean texts, word segmentation on texts with typos remains a challenging problem. In addition, languages with complex writing systems such as Japanese and Chinese have typos not found in French and English. These languages use logographs, *kanji* in Japanese, and they are

---

[*]Current affiliation is Waseda University

[1]In the present study, typos may cover some grammatical errors in addition to spelling errors.

[2]Although the publicly available multilingual GitHub Typo Corpus (Hagiwara and Mita, 2020) covers Japanese, it contains only about 1,000 instances and ignores erroneous kanji-conversion, an important class of typos in Japanese.

Proceedings of the 58th Annual Meeting of the Association for Computational Linguistics: Student Research Workshop, pages 230–236
July 5 - July 10, 2020. ©2020 Association for Computational Linguistics

typically entered using input methods, with which people enter phonetic symbols, *kana* in the case of Japanese, and then select a correct logograph from a list of logographs matching the reading. Typos occurring during this process can be drastically different from the correct words.

In this paper, we build a Japanese Wikipedia typo dataset (JWTD) from Japanese Wikipedia's revision history. To address problems mentioned above, we treat adjacent changed words as one block and obtain the readings of kanji using a morphological analyzer. This dataset contains over half a million typo–correction sentence pairs. We evaluate JWTD by using crowdsourcing and use it to train a baseline seq2seq model for typo correction. JWTD is publicly available at `http://nlp.ist.i.kyoto-u.ac.jp/EN/edit.php?JWTD`. To the best of our knowledge, this is the first freely available large Japanese typo dataset.

2 Japanese Typos

We classify Japanese typos into four categories: erroneous substitution (hereafter **substitution**), erroneous deletion (hereafter **deletion**), erroneous insertion (hereafter **insertion**), and erroneous kanji-conversion (hereafter **kanji-conversion**).[3] An example and its correction for each category are shown in Table 1. Substitution is the replacement of a character with an erroneous one, deletion is the omission of a necessary character, insertion is the addition of an unnecessary character, and kanji-conversion is misconverting kanji, which needs some explanation.

To enter kanji, you first enter hiragana syllabary, either by converting roman-letter inputs or directly using a hiragana keyboard. The hiragana sequence indicates the reading, and accordingly, the input method shows a list of candidate kanji that match the reading, allowing you to choose the correct one. Errors in kanji-conversion typically occur at the last step. A typo of this category shares the reading with the correct one but in most cases, does not contain the same characters at all. For example, the typo–correction pair, "貼り付け (*harituke*) → 磔 (*harituke*)", which mean paste and crucifixion respectively, shares no character at all so that a simple edit distance-based method does not work. This is why kanji-conversion requires a special treatment.

---

[3] We do not collect erroneous transposition (Baba and Suzuki, 2012) because we observe that it occurs only infrequently in Japanese.

3 Data Construction

We construct JWTD in two steps. We first extract candidates of typo–correction sentence pairs from Wikipedia's revision history and then filter out pairs that do not seem to be typo corrections.

3.1 Mining Typos from Wikipedia

We extract candidates of typo–correction sentence pairs from Wikipedia's revision history according to the following procedure.[4]

1. For each revision of each article page, we extract a plain text from an XML dump[5] and split it into a list of sentences.[6]

2. For each article, we compare each revision with the revision immediately preceding it in a sentence-by-sentence manner using the Python3 difflib library.[7] We extract only sentence pairs that have differences. We remove pairs that have a sentence with 10 or fewer characters, or 200 or more characters. Too short sentences lack the context for us to determine whether the changes are typo corrections while too long sentences may arise from preprocessing errors. We also remove pairs with the edit distance of 6 or more because we assume that a revision having a large edit distance is not typo correction.

3. For each sentence pair, we split each sentence into a word sequence using MeCab (Kudo et al., 2004),[8] compare them using difflib, and identify *diff* blocks. Note that difflib outputs the replacement of multiple words as a single block. Therefore, typos causing a change of multiple words are also obtained.

4. We extract sentence pairs with a diff block that falls into one of the following categories:

   Substitution

   - the edit distance is 1,[9]

---

[4] Due to space limitations, we do not explain in detail additional measures to clean up the data: removing reverted revisions, removing looping revisions (for example, A→B and B→A), and replacing transitive revisions (for example, replace A→B and B→C to A→C).

[5] To strip wiki markup, we use WikiExtractor (`https://github.com/attardi/wikiextractor`)

[6] We use an in-house sentence splitter: `https://github.com/ku-nlp/textformatting`.

[7] `https://docs.python.org/3/library/difflib.html`

[8] `https://taku910.github.io/mecab/`

[9] We limit the edit distance to one because our preliminary investigation suggests that changes with the edit distance of two or more are increasingly likely to be content revisions rather than typos. The coverage problem needs to be addressed in the future.

Substitution	兄の部隊【の (*no*) → に (*ni*)】所属していた兵士でもあり、...
	(He was also a soldier belonging 〔of → to〕 his brother's unit, and ...)
Deletion	...民間レスキュー組織をもっていること【+で (*de*)】知られる。
	(... is known 〔+ for〕 having a civilian rescue organization.)
Insertion	特に免疫力の差などがそう【-う (*u*)】である。
	(In particular, differences in immunity is like that 〔- t〕 .)
Kanji-conversion	まだ、全学全てが大学院に【以降 (*ikou*) → 移行 (*ikou*)】していないため、...
	(Because all of the universities have not yet made a 〔after → transition〕 to graduate school, ...)

Table 1: Examples of Japanese typos and their corrections. +, -, and → indicate insertion, deletion, and substitution from the left hand side to the right hand side, respectively.

- the two sentences are the same in length, and
- both of the characters changed before and after the revision are hiragana, katakana, or alphabet.[10]

Deletion

- the edit distance is 1,
- the change in sentence length is $+1$, and
- the added character is hiragana, katakana, or alphabet.

Insertion

- the edit distance is 1,
- the change in sentence length is -1, and
- the deleted character is hiragana, katakana, or alphabet.

Kanji-conversion

- the two sentences have the same reading,[11] and
- both of the diff blocks before and after the revision contain kanji.

Mining typos separately for each category is a reasonable decision because each category has its own characteristics. However, this mining strategy prevents us from obtaining a balanced dataset. We leave it for future work.

3.2 Filtering

Sentence pairs obtained according to the above procedure contain pairs that do not seem to be typo corrections. We use the following three methods to remove them.

Part of speech and morphological analysis This filters out sentence pairs in which the changes concern acceptable variants, rather than typos. Based on the morphological analysis by Juman++, we remove sentence pairs that have edits related to name, number, tense, etc.

Redirect data This filters out sentence pairs that have a different spelling but the same meaning such as "ケニヤ (*keniya*)" and "ケニア (*kenia*)", both of which mean Kenya. For such close variants, Wikipedia provides special *redirect* pages that automatically send visitors to article pages. A page and its redirect can be treated as a pair of acceptable spelling variants. We obtain a list of redirects from an XML dump and remove a sentence pair if the diff block is found in the list.

Language model By using a character-level LSTM language model, we filter out sentence pairs in two ways. We trained the model by using all the latest pages of Japanese Wikipedia generated in September 2019, which contains 19.6M sentences.

The first filter measures how much the loss (negative log-likelihood) decreases by a revision. This filters out sentence pairs that seem to be spam or both sentences seem to be natural. Let $loss_{\text{pre}}$ and $loss_{\text{post}}$ be the total language model loss of the pre-revision sentence and that of the post-revision sentence, respectively. We filter out sentence pairs that satisfy the following:

$$\frac{loss_{\text{post}} - loss_{\text{pre}}}{\text{the number of characters changed in the pairs}} > \alpha,$$

where α is determined heuristically. It is set to -4 for substitution, -5 for deletion, and -6 for insertion. We do not apply this filter to kanji-conversion. We found that a change from high-frequency kanji to low-frequency kanji often yielded a large value even if the change was correct.

The second filter focused on the loss of the post-revision sentence. This filters out sentence pairs

---

[10]We use the Python3 regex library (https://pypi.org/project/regex/) to determine character types, hiragana, katakana, kanji, or alphabet.

[11]We use the morphological analyzers Juman++ (Tolmachev et al., 2018) (http://nlp.ist.i.kyoto-u.ac.jp/index.php?JUMAN++) and MeCab to get readings of kanji. If at least one of the analyses of reading matches, we regard the pairs as having the same reading.

in which the post-revision sentence seems to be unnatural. We filter out sentence pairs that satisfy the following:

$$\frac{loss_{\text{post}}}{\text{the number of characters of the post-revision sentence}} > \beta,$$

where β is set to 5 heuristically.

4 Dataset Analysis

We built JWTD by applying the method explained in Section 3 to Japanese Wikipedia's revision history generated in June 2019. The number of typo–correction pairs obtained for each category is shown in Table 2. Because the first of the two language model filters was not applied to kanji-conversion, the effect of filtering was less drastic for kanji-conversion.

The top 10 most frequent typo–correction pairs are listed in Table 3. The unit of corrections is the morpheme-level edits obtained by using Juman++ and difflib. For deletion, there were typo–correction pairs associated with colloquialism, such as "る (*ru*) → いる (*iru*)" and "た (*ta*) → いた (*ita*)" (*i*-omission), and "れる (*reru*) → られる (*rareru*)" (*ra*-omission). Both *i*- and *ra*-omissions are considered inappropriate for formal writing. For kanji-conversion, there were typo–correction pairs with similar meanings. For example, the media and entertainment industry distinguishes the homonymous pair "製作 (*seisaku*) → 制作 (*seisaku*)". The latter refers to production in a narrow sense while the former covers production management. However, people outside of the industry usually are not aware of the distinction. Perhaps for difficulty in differentiating them, we noticed that some typo–correction pairs did not seem to be genuine typo corrections but were acceptable variants. Further work is needed to remove them.

The top 5 most frequent typo–correction pairs in terms of parts-of-speech are shown in Table 4. There were many typo–correction pairs related to particles in substitution, deletion, and insertion while there were many typo–correction pairs related to nouns in kanji-conversion. The special part-of-speech "Undefined" in the substitution category were mostly related to katakana proper nouns.

5 Evaluation through Crowdsourcing

By using crowdsourcing, we evaluated the dataset. We randomly sampled 2,996 article pages and evaluated sentence pairs extracted from them. They

Typo	Before filtering	After filtering
Substitution	680,097	86,742
Deletion	490,673	89,428
Insertion	407,413	110,305
Kanji-conversion	296,757	240,219
Total	1,874,940	526,694

Table 2: Number of typo–correction pairs before and after filtering.

consisted of 1,861 substitutions, 2,147 deletions, 2,395 insertions, and 4,388 kanji-conversions. To prevent data bias, we sampled only 3 sentence pairs and discarded the others if an article page contains the same corrections more than 3 times.

5.1 Task

For each sentence pair, we presented the pre- and post-revision sentences and asked whether these are natural or unnatural in written-style texts. Note that we added the phrase "in written-style text" because, as we have seen above, Wikipedia tends to remove colloquialism. We randomly swapped pre- and post-revision sentences and presented them simply as sentences A and B so that crowdworkers were unable to figure out which is the pre-revision sentence. We asked crowdworkers to choose one from the five choices: "A is natural in written-style text, but B is unnatural", "B is natural in written-style text, but A is unnatural", "Both are natural in written-style texts", "Both are unnatural in written-style text", and "Not sure". Each sentence pair was shown to 10 crowdworkers.

5.2 Results

After aggregating crowdworkers' answers, we classified pairs with single majority votes as follows: "Correct revision" if the pre-revision sentence was unnatural and the post-revision sentence was natural, "Bad revision" if the pre-revision sentence was natural and the post-revision sentence was unnatural, "Both natural" if the choice was "Both are natural in written-style text", "Both unnatural" if the choice was "Both are unnatural in written-style text", and "Not sure" if the choice was "Not sure". We classified pairs into "Other" if no choice got more than 5 votes.

The classification results are listed in Table 5. 83.0% of substitution, 77.6% of deletion, 88.8% of insertion, and 69.8% of kanji-conversion were classified as "Correct revision". "Both natural" was more frequent in the deletion category than in the other categories, and 41% of this typo group

Substitution		Deletion		Insertion		Kanji-conversion	
の (no) → を (wo)	4.0%	る (ru) → いる (iru)	13.3%	-の (no) 14.2%		製作 → 制作 (seisaku)	2.8%
の (no) → に (ni)	3.5%	+に (ni)	10.9%	-を (wo) 11.3%		始めて → 初めて (hazimete)	1.4%
づつ (dutu) → ずつ (zutu)	3.1%	+を (wo)	10.4%	-に (ni) 10.5%		制作 → 製作 (seisaku)	1.0%
を (wo) → の (no)	2.7%	+と (to)	5.1%	-は (ha) 6.6%		運行 → 運航 (unkou)	1.0%
の (no) → が (ga)	1.9%	た (ta) → いた (ita)	4.5%	-が (ga) 6.5%		後 → 跡 (ato)	0.9%
に (ni) → の (no)	1.8%	+が (ga)	4.3%	-と (to) 4.7%		作詩 → 作詞 (sakusi)	0.9%
を (wo) → が (ga)	1.8%	+の (no)	3.8%	-で (de) 4.4%		勤めた → 務めた (tutometa)	0.8%
が (ga) → を (wo)	1.3%	れ (re) → れて (rete)	2.6%	-い (i) 1.7%		勤める → 務める (tutomeru)	0.7%
か (ka) → が (ga)	1.1%	+い (i)	2.2%	-た (ta) 1.5%		開放 → 解放 (kaihou)	0.5%
と (to) → を (wo)	1.0%	れる (reru) → られる (rareru)	1.3%	-し (si) 1.5%		付属 → 附属 (fuzoku)	0.5%

Table 3: Top 10 most frequent typo–correction pairs in JWTD. In kanji-conversion, the both hand sides are the same reading.

Substitution		Deletion		Insertion		Kanji-conversion	
Particle → Particle	28.5%	+Particle	36.8%	-Particle	57.5%	Noun → Noun	57.3%
Undefined → Noun	6.9%	Suffix → Suffix	29.6%	-Suffix	6.5%	Verb → Verb	17.0%
Noun → Noun	6.5%	Verb → Verb	5.5%	-Noun	4.4%	Noun/Noun → Noun	1.7%
Verb → Verb	5.9%	Noun → Noun	2.9%	Verb/Suffix → Verb	2.5%	Suffix → Suffix	1.6%
Noun → Suffix	3.4%	+Suffix	2.5%	-Verb	2.3%	Noun → Suffix	1.4%

Table 4: Top 5 most frequent typo–correction pairs in terms of parts-of-speech in JWTD.

Typo	Correct revision	Bad revision	Both natural	Both unnatural	Not sure	Other
Subst.	83.0	0.3	6.8	0.1	0.2	9.6
Deletion	77.6	0.1	13.1	0.0	0.0	9.3
Insertion	88.8	0.4	7.1	0.0	0.0	3.6
Kanji-conv.	69.8	7.5	3.1	0.0	0.1	19.5

Table 5: Results of crowdsourcing.

concerned *i*-omission. In our view, they should have been classified as "Correct revision" because *i*-omission is considered inappropriate in formal writing, but crowdworkers turned out to be tolerant of colloquialism. "Other" of kanji-conversion was more frequent than those of other categories. This means that the answers of crowdworkers were diverse. We conjecture that judging whether kanji is correct or not needs higher-level knowledge of kanji. Some pairs that should have been classified as "Correct revision" were classified as "Other" or "Bad revision". These imply that the quality of deletion and kanji-conversion was better than the scores indicate.

6 A Typo Correction System using JWTD

We built a baseline typo correction system using JWTD.

6.1 Settings

We used OpenNMT (Klein et al., 2017)[12], a Python toolkit of encoder-decoder-based machine translation, as a typo correction system. We trained the model separately for each category of typos. For training and validation, we used sentence pairs not used in the crowdsourced evaluation. The training set contained 79,714 substitutions, 82,227 deletions, 102,897 insertions, and 230,490 kanji-conversions and the validation set contained 5,000 sentence pairs of each category. The test set contained 1,689 substitutions[13], 1,665 deletion, 2,127 insertion, and 3,061 kanji-conversion sentence pairs classified as "Correct revision" as the result of crowdsourcing. The training and validation sets were constrained to be distinct from the test set at the level of article pages because of the sampling method used in the crowdsourced evaluation. We compared morpheme-level and character-level representations of inputs and outputs. For the OpenNMT settings, we set the train step as 200,000, and learning rate as 0.5. We used the default settings for the others: the encoder and decoder were 2-layer RNNs and the embedding size

---

[12] https://github.com/OpenNMT/OpenNMT-py

[13] In the article pages sampled for the crowdsourcing, 144 sentence pairs of substitution were almost indistinguishable to the human eye, such as revisions related to "へ (he)" (hiragana) and "ヘ (he)" (katakana). We removed these sentence pairs from crowdsourcing-based evaluation, but not from the test set for the typo correction evaluation. We manually evaluated these and confirmed that all of them are correct.

Model	Typo	P	R	$F_{0.5}$	Match	SARI
Morph	Subst.	11.9	39.8	13.8	31.6	61.2
	Deletion	23.2	69.9	26.7	60.9	80.2
	Insertion	16.8	79.7	19.9	69.3	83.8
	Kanji-conv.	30.8	57.0	33.9	48.7	71.0
Char	Subst	4.5	37.2	5.5	25.2	54.2
	Deletion	6.5	59.4	8.0	44.7	69.6
	Insertion	6.2	76.0	7.6	51.8	72.5
	Kanji-conv	10.0	43.5	11.8	33.7	60.9

Table 6: Results of the typo correction experiment.

and the hidden size were 500.

6.2 Evaluation metrics

Our evaluation metrics were precision, recall and $F_{0.5}$ score in typo correction, the percentage of exact matches between system outputs and references, and SARI (Xu et al., 2016). We defined precision and recall as follows. For each sentence, we calculate the character-level minimum edits from the input to the gold G, the character-level minimum edits from the input to the system output O, and $G \cap O$. Let N_G, N_O, and $N_{G \cap O}$ be the sums of $|G|$, $|O|$, and $|G \cap O|$ in all sentences, respectively. We calculated Precision = $N_{G \cap O}/N_O$ and Recall = $N_{G \cap O}/N_G$. We used the Python3 python-Levenshtein library[14] for calculating minimum edits. SARI is a metric for text editing. This calculates the averaged F1 scores of the added, kept, and deleted n-grams. We used character-level 4-gram.[15]

6.3 Results

The results of the experiment are presented in Table 6. The morpheme-level model outperformed the character-level model in all categories with large margins. It is interesting that for morpheme-level insertion, the precision scores were low while the exact match scores were high. In some sentences, text generation did not go well and the same token was generated repeatedly, greatly lowering precision. The SARI scores indicate improvement for all categories, given that the output identical to the input yields a score of about 30.

---

[14]https://pypi.org/project/
python-Levenshtein/

[15]We used the implementation available at https://github.com/tensorflow/tensor2tensor/blob/master/tensor2tensor/utils/sari_hook.py, setting β-deletion = 1 (Geva et al., 2019).

7 Conclusion

In this paper, we built a Japanese Wikipedia typo dataset (JWTD) which contains over half a million typo–correction sentence pairs obtained from Wikipedia's revision history. We classified Japanese typos into four categories and presented mining procedures for each of them. We evaluated JWTD using crowdsourcing and built a baseline typo correction system on top of it. To the best of our knowledge, JWTD is the first freely available large Japanese typo dataset.

While the focus of this paper was on data construction, developing a higher-quality typo correction system is the future direction to pursue. It is also interesting to apply our methods to other languages requiring word segmentation, most notably, Chinese.

References

Yukino Baba and Hisami Suzuki. 2012. How are spelling errors generated and corrected?: a study of corrected and uncorrected spelling errors using keystroke logs. In *Proceedings of the 50th Annual Meeting of the Association for Computational Linguistics: Short Papers-Volume 2*, pages 373–377. Association for Computational Linguistics.

Yonatan Belinkov and Yonatan Bisk. 2018. Synthetic and natural noise both break neural machine translation. In *International Conference on Learning Representations*.

Su Lin Blodgett, Lisa Green, and Brendan O'Connor. 2016. Demographic dialectal variation in social media: A case study of african-american english. *arXiv preprint arXiv:1608.08868*.

Samuel Brody and Nicholas Diakopoulos. 2011. Cooooooooooooooooollllllllllllll!!!!!!!!!!!!!!: using word lengthening to detect sentiment in microblogs. In *Proceedings of the conference on empirical methods in natural language processing*, pages 562–570. Association for Computational Linguistics.

Mor Geva, Eric Malmi, Idan Szpektor, and Jonathan Berant. 2019. Discofuse: A large-scale dataset for discourse-based sentence fusion. In *Proceedings of the 2019 Conference of the North American Chapter of the Association for Computational Linguistics: Human Language Technologies, Volume 1 (Long and Short Papers)*, pages 3443–3455.

Gili Goldin, Ella Rabinovich, and Shuly Wintner. 2018. Native language identification with user generated content. In *Proceedings of the 2018 Conference on Empirical Methods in Natural Language Processing*, pages 3591–3601.

Masato Hagiwara and Masato Mita. 2020. Github typo corpus: A large-scale multilingual dataset of misspellings and grammatical errors. In *Proceedings of the 12th International Conference on Language Resources and Evaluation (LREC 2020)*. To appear.

Guillaume Klein, Yoon Kim, Yuntian Deng, Jean Senellart, and Alexander M. Rush. 2017. OpenNMT: Open-source toolkit for neural machine translation. In *Proc. ACL*.

Taku Kudo, Kaoru Yamamoto, and Yuji Matsumoto. 2004. Applying conditional random fields to Japanese morphological analysis. In *Proceedings of the 2004 conference on empirical methods in natural language processing*, pages 230–237.

Lung-Hao Lee, Yuen-Hsien Tseng, and Li-Ping Chang. 2018. Building a TOCFL learner corpus for Chinese grammatical error diagnosis. In *Proceedings of the Eleventh International Conference on Language Resources and Evaluation (LREC 2018)*.

Aurélien Max and Guillaume Wisniewski. 2010. Mining naturally-occurring corrections and paraphrases from Wikipedia' s revision history. In *Proceedings of the Seventh conference on International Language Resources and Evaluation (LREC' 10)*.

Tomoya Mizumoto, Mamoru Komachi, Masaaki Nagata, and Yuji Matsumoto. 2011. Mining revision log of language learning SNS for automated Japanese error correction of second language learners. In *Proceedings of 5th International Joint Conference on Natural Language Processing*, pages 147–155, Chiang Mai, Thailand. Asian Federation of Natural Language Processing.

Itsumi Saito, Jun Suzuki, Kyosuke Nishida, Kugatsu Sadamitsu, Satoshi Kobashikawa, Ryo Masumura, Yuji Matsumoto, and Junji Tomita. 2017. Improving neural text normalization with data augmentation at character-and morphological levels. In *Proceedings of the Eighth International Joint Conference on Natural Language Processing (Volume 2: Short Papers)*, pages 257–262.

Keisuke Sakaguchi, Kevin Duh, Matt Post, and Benjamin Van Durme. 2017. Robsut wrod reocginiton via semi-character recurrent neural network. In *Thirty-First AAAI Conference on Artificial Intelligence*.

Ryohei Sasano, Sadao Kurohashi, and Manabu Okumura. 2013. A simple approach to unknown word processing in Japanese morphological analysis. In *Proceedings of the Sixth International Joint Conference on Natural Language Processing*, pages 162–170.

Arseny Tolmachev, Daisuke Kawahara, and Sadao Kurohashi. 2018. Juman++: A morphological analysis toolkit for scriptio continua. In *Proceedings of the 2018 Conference on Empirical Methods in Natural Language Processing: System Demonstrations*, pages 54–59, Brussels, Belgium. Association for Computational Linguistics.

Wei Xu, Courtney Napoles, Ellie Pavlick, Quanze Chen, and Chris Callison-Burch. 2016. Optimizing statistical machine translation for text simplification. *Transactions of the Association for Computational Linguistics*, 4:401–415.

Torsten Zesch. 2012. Measuring contextual fitness using error contexts extracted from the Wikipedia revision history. In *Proceedings of the 13th Conference of the European Chapter of the Association for Computational Linguistics*, pages 529–538. Association for Computational Linguistics.

Preventing Critical Scoring Errors in Short Answer Scoring with Confidence Estimation

Hiroaki Funayama[1,2]   **Shota Sasaki**[2,1]   **Yuichiroh Matsubayashi**[1,2]
Tomoya Mizumoto[3,2]   **Jun Suzuki**[1,2]   **Masato Mita**[2,1]   **Kentaro Inui**[1,2]
[1] Tohoku University   [2] RIKEN   [3] Future Corporation
{hiroaki, jun.suzuki, inui}@ecei.tohoku.ac.jp
{shota.sasaki.yv, tomoya.mizumoto, masato.mita}@riken.jp
{y.m}@tohoku.ac.jp

Abstract

Many recent Short Answer Scoring (SAS) systems have employed Quadratic Weighted Kappa (QWK) as the evaluation measure of their systems. However, we hypothesize that QWK is unsatisfactory for the evaluation of the SAS systems when we consider measuring their effectiveness in actual usage. We introduce a new task formulation of SAS that matches the actual usage. In our formulation, the SAS systems should extract as many scoring predictions that are not *critical scoring errors* (CSEs). We conduct the experiments in our new task formulation and demonstrate that a typical SAS system can predict scores with *zero CSE* for approximately 50% of test data at maximum by filtering out low-reliablility predictions on the basis of a certain confidence estimation. This result directly indicates the possibility of reducing half the scoring cost of human raters, which is more preferable for the evaluation of SAS systems.

1 Introduction

The automated Short Answer Scoring (SAS) is a task of estimating a score of a short-text answer written as a response to a given prompt on the basis of whether the answer satisfies the rubrics prepared by a human in advance. SAS systems have mainly been developed to markedly reduce the scoring cost of human raters. Moreover, the SAS systems play a central role in providing stable and sustainable scoring in a repeated and large-scale examination and (online) self-study learning support system (Attali and Burstein, 2006; Shermis et al., 2010; Leacock and Chodorow, 2003; Burrows et al., 2015).

The development of the SAS systems has a long history (Page, 1994; Foltz et al., 1999). Many recent previous studies, e.g., (Mizumoto et al., 2019; Taghipour and Ng, 2016; Riordan et al., 2017; Wang et al., 2019), utilize Quadratic Weighted Kappa (QWK) (Cohen, 1968) as a measure for the achievement and for the comparison of the performances of the SAS systems. QWK is indeed useful for measuring and comparing the overall performance of each system and the daily developments of their scoring models. In our experiments, however, we reveal that the SAS systems with high QWK potentially incur serious scoring errors (see experiments in Section 5.3). Such serious scoring errors are rarely incurred by trained human raters, therefore, we need to avoid containing this type of errors to ensure the sufficient scoring quality, for use in the scoring of commercial examinations, of SAS systems. When we strictly focus on measuring the effectiveness of the SAS systems in actual usage, QWK seems unsatisfactory for the evaluation of the SAS systems. Here, we assume that the following procedure is a realistic configuration for utilizing the SAS systems in actual usage: (1) apply a SAS system to score each answer, (2) treat the predicted score as the final decision if the predicted score is highly reliable, proceed to the next step otherwise, and (3) discard the unreliable predicted score and reevaluate the answer by a human rater as the final decision. Therefore, we aim to establish an appropriate evaluation scheme for accurately estimating the effectiveness of the SAS systems in actual usage instead of the current de facto standard evaluation measure, QWK.

To do so, we first introduce a key concept **critical scoring error (CSE)**, which reflects unacceptable prediction error. Specifically, CSE refers to the observation that the gap between a predicted score and the ground truth is larger than a predefined threshold, which, for example, can be determined by an average gap in human raters. Then, in our task formulation, the goal of the automated SAS is to obtain as many predictions without CSE as possible, which directly reflects the effectiveness of the SAS models in the actual usage. We also in-

Proceedings of the 58th Annual Meeting of the Association for Computational Linguistics: Student Research Workshop, pages 237–243
July 5 - July 10, 2020. ©2020 Association for Computational Linguistics

Prompt

Explain what the author means by the phrase "this tension has caused several different philosophical viewpoints in Western culture"

Student Response

Conflicts of interest in Western culture are formed on the basis of God vs. Human, ... **Score: 4 points**

Figure 1: Example of a prompt and a student's short-text response excerpted from the dataset proposed by (Mizumoto et al., 2019). The allotment score of this prompt is 16, and this response is assigned four points by a human rater. Note that the prompt and the response are translated from the original ones given in Japanese.

troduce the **critical scoring error rate (CSRate)**, which is the CSE rate in a subset of the test data selected on the basis of the confidence measure of predictions, for evaluating the performance of the SAS systems.

In our experiments, we select two methods, i.e., posterior probability and *trust score* (Jiang et al., 2018), as case studies of estimating whether or not each prediction is reliable. We use those two confidence estimation methods to obtain a set of highly reliable predictions. The experimental results show that the SAS systems can predict scores with *zero CSE* for approximately 50% of test data at maximum by filtering low-reliability predictions.

2 Short Answer Scoring

2.1 Task Description

As an example, in Figure 1, for a short answer question, a student writes a short text as a response to a given prompt. A human rater marks the response on the basis of the rubrics for the prompt. Similarly, given a student response $\mathbf{x} = \{x_1, x_2, ..., x_n\}$ for a prompt allotted N points, our short answer scoring task can be defined as predicting a score of $s \in C = \{0, ..., N\}$ for that response.

SAS models are often evaluated in terms of the agreement between the scores of a model prediction and human annotation with QWK. QWK is calculated as:

$$\kappa = 1 - \frac{\sum_{i,j} \mathbf{W}_{i,j}\mathbf{O}_{i,j}}{\sum_{i,j} \mathbf{W}_{i,j}\mathbf{E}_{i,j}}, \qquad (1)$$

where $\mathbf{O} \in \mathbb{R}^{N \times N}$ is the confusion matrix of two ratings and $\mathbf{E} \in \mathbb{R}^{N \times N}$ is the outer product of histogram vectors of the two ratings; $\mathbf{O}$ and $\mathbf{E}$ are normalized to have the same sum of their elements. $\mathbf{W}_{i,j}$ is calculated as:

$$\mathbf{W}_{i,j} = \frac{(i-j)^2}{(N-1)^2}, \qquad (2)$$

where i and j are the score rated by a human and the score predicted by a SAS system, respectively. N is allotment score defined for a prompt.

2.2 Scoring Model

Following related works (Nguyen and O'Connor, 2015; Jiang et al., 2018; Hendrycks and Gimpel, 2017) on confidence calibration, we formalize our SAS model as a classification model. Note that our focus in this paper is more on evaluating the effectiveness of the confidential scores on SAS tasks than on creating an accurate SAS model. Therefore, we employ a standard Bidirectional Long Short Term Memory (Bi-LSTM) based neural network for our scoring model as a representative model for typical SAS tasks.

Given an input student response $\mathbf{x}$, the model outputs a score $s \in \mathcal{S}$ for the response as follows. First, we convert tokens in $\mathbf{x}$ to word-embedding vectors. These embeddings are fed into a Bi-LSTM and D dimensional hidden vectors $\{\mathbf{h}_1, \mathbf{h}_2, ..., \mathbf{h}_n\}$ are obtained as the sum of the hidden vectors from forward and backward LSTMs. The response vector $\widetilde{\mathbf{h}}$ is then computed by averaging these hidden vectors.

$$\widetilde{\mathbf{h}} = \frac{1}{n}\sum_{t=1}^{n} \mathbf{h}_t \qquad (3)$$

A probability distribution of the score is calculated as:

$$p(s|\mathbf{x}) = \mathtt{softmax}(\mathbf{W}\widetilde{\mathbf{h}} + \mathbf{b}), \qquad (4)$$

where $\mathbf{W} \in \mathbb{R}^{N \times D}$ and $\mathbf{b} \in \mathbb{R}^{N}$ are learnable parameters. Finally, we select the most likely output score $\widehat{s} \in \mathcal{S}$ for given input $\mathbf{x}$ as:

$$\widehat{s} = \arg\max_{s \in \mathcal{S}}\{p(s|\mathbf{x})\}. \qquad (5)$$

3 Task Formulation

The goal in our new task formulation for applying SAS to real-world educational measurements is to obtain as many scoring predictions without CSEs as possible. This is because we can trust such predictions and markedly reduce the cost of the human scoring effort. In this section, we describe our new task formulation of the automated SAS.

	Prompt 1	Prompt 2	Prompt 3	Prompt 4	Prompt 5	Prompt 6
Length limit (char.)	70	50	60	70	70	60
Average score	7.40	4.43	5.73	5.78	4.81	5.70
Allotment score ($= N$)	16	12	12	15	15	14
Human agreement	.96 (.93)	.94 (.92)	.76 (.79)	.84 (.70)	.82 (.83)	.90 (.82)

Table 1: Statistics of the dataset used in this paper. "Length limit (char.)" is the maximum character length of the response permitted for a prompt. "Allotment score" is the maximum score for a prompt. "Human agreement" represents QWK and Cohen's Kappa (shown in brackets) between the scores annotated by two human raters.

First, to evaluate the proportion of CSEs in the predictions, we define a function on the gold dataset $\mathcal{D}$ that returns whether or not the predicted score $\widehat{s}$ of an input $\mathbf{x}$ is categorized as a CSE:

$$\mathrm{CSE}(\mathbf{x}, s) = \begin{cases} 1 & \text{if } |s - \widehat{s}| \geq \lambda \cdot N \\ 0 & \text{otherwise} \end{cases}, \quad (6)$$

where $\lambda \in [0, 1]$ is a given threshold, N is the allotment of a score for a prompt, s is the ground truth score of input $\mathbf{x}$, and $\widehat{s}$ is obtained using Equation 5. Note that we can choose the value of λ depending on the situation. For example, for an important examination such as an entrance examination, λ should be smaller than that for daily tests in schools.

Here, let $\mathcal{D}$ be a test data set. Moreover, let $\mathcal{D}'$ be a subset of $\mathcal{D}$, that is, $\mathcal{D}' \subseteq \mathcal{D}$. Then, our objective is to maximize the size of the subset $\mathcal{D}'$ on the condition that this subset does not contain CSEs. For obtaining $\mathcal{D}'$, we estimate a confidence score $C(\mathbf{x}, \widehat{s})$ for each prediction on the basis of a certain confidence measure, and then gather the predictions with high confidence scores that exceed a threshold, τ. Therefore, for the evaluation of the performance of our task formulation, we propose a *critical scoring error rate* (CSRate) defined as:

$$\mathrm{CSRate}(\mathcal{D}, \tau) = \frac{1}{|\mathcal{D}'|} \sum_{(\mathbf{x}, s) \in \mathcal{D}'} \mathrm{CSE}(\mathbf{x}, s), \quad (7)$$

$$\mathcal{D}' = \{(\mathbf{x}, s) \in \mathcal{D} | C(\mathbf{x}, \widehat{s}) \geq \tau\}, \quad (8)$$

where $\widehat{s}$ is obtained using Equation 5. In real-world tasks, the model is expected to select as large a subset D' as possible with very small or ideally zero CSRate.

4 Filtering Out Low-Reliability Estimation Using Confidence Score

As described in Equation 8, the quality of the confidence measure is important for our task configuration. In this paper, we employ two methods

for computing the confidence score: (1) *posterior probability* of the classification model and (2) *trust score* (Jiang et al., 2018) as case studies.

4.1 Posterior Probability

The most straightforward method for computing the confidence of the prediction in a classification problem is to employ a probabilistic model and use the output label probability:

$$C_{\mathrm{prob}}(\mathbf{x}, \widehat{s}) = p(\widehat{s}|\mathbf{x}). \quad (9)$$

Although a label probability is often used as a confidence score for prediction, some authors are skeptical of its utility (Guo et al., 2017; Kumar et al., 2018). In our experiments, we evaluate the effectiveness of this posterior probability in terms of a confidence estimation method for SAS models.

4.2 Trust Score

Trust score (Jiang et al., 2018) is an indicator of the reliability of prediction based on the distance between a target data point and its nearest data points in training data. The intuition behind this score is that the reliability of a prediction is higher when the target data point is closer to the nearest training data point with the same label and farther away from the nearest training data point with a different label.

In this paper, trust score is calculated as follows. Given a training data value $\{(\mathbf{x}_1, s_1), ..., (\mathbf{x}_m, s_m)\}$, a target data point $\mathbf{x}$ for prediction, and its predicted label $\widehat{s}$, we first obtain a vector representation for each data point. In our model, the representation for each data point is the sentence vector of the student response described in Section 2.2. Let $\mathcal{H} = \{\widetilde{\mathbf{h}}_1, ..., \widetilde{\mathbf{h}}_m\}$ be a set of vector representations for the training data points and let $\widetilde{\mathbf{h}}_{\mathbf{x}}$ be a vector for the target data point $\mathbf{x}$. Then we collect the representations in the training data that have the same label as the predicted label $\widehat{s}$:

$$\mathcal{H}_{\widehat{s}} = \{\widetilde{\mathbf{h}}_k \in \mathcal{H} \mid s_k = \widehat{s}\}. \quad (10)$$

The trust score C_{trust} for $\mathbf{x}$ is then calculated as the ratio of the euclidean distance $d(\cdot, \cdot)$ between the target representation $\widetilde{\mathbf{h}}_{\mathbf{x}}$ and two data-point representations $\widetilde{\mathbf{h}}_p$ and $\widetilde{\mathbf{h}}_c$ in the training data:

$$C_{\text{trust}}(\mathbf{x}, \widehat{s}, \mathcal{H}) = \frac{d(\widetilde{\mathbf{h}}_{\mathbf{x}}, \widetilde{\mathbf{h}}_c)}{d(\widetilde{\mathbf{h}}_{\mathbf{x}}, \widetilde{\mathbf{h}}_p) + d(\widetilde{\mathbf{h}}_{\mathbf{x}}, \widetilde{\mathbf{h}}_c)}, \quad (11)$$

where, $\widetilde{\mathbf{h}}_p$ is the representation of the nearest training data point having the same label as the predicted label $\widehat{s}$, and $\widetilde{\mathbf{h}}_c$ is the nearest training data point with a different label:

$$\widetilde{\mathbf{h}}_p = \underset{\widetilde{\mathbf{h}} \in \mathcal{H}_{\widehat{s}}}{\arg\min}\, d(\widetilde{\mathbf{h}}_{\mathbf{x}}, \widetilde{\mathbf{h}}), \quad (12)$$

$$\widetilde{\mathbf{h}}_c = \underset{\widetilde{\mathbf{h}} \in (\mathcal{H} \backslash \mathcal{H}_{\widehat{s}})}{\arg\min}\, d(\widetilde{\mathbf{h}}_{\mathbf{x}}, \widetilde{\mathbf{h}}). \quad (13)$$

5 Experiments

5.1 Dataset

We use the Japanese short answer scoring dataset[1] introduced by Mizumoto et al. (2019). The dataset consists of six prompts. Each prompt has its rubric, student responses, and scores. The prompts, rubrics, and student responses in the dataset were collected from the examinations conducted by a Japanese education company, Takamiya Gakuen Yoyogi Seminar. Each response was manually scored using the multiple analytic criteria for the prompt, and the subscore for each criterion was rated individually on the basis of the corresponding rubric. In the experiments, we use the sum of these analytic scores as a ground truth score of each response.[2]

Table 1 shows the statistics of the dataset. In the dataset, the randomly sampled 100 responses per prompt are annotated by two human raters. Therefore, we can calculate QWKs and their Kappa values (Cohen, 1960) between the two human raters to confirm the degree of human agreement. The Kappa values on this dataset are comparable to or higher than those on other datasets for the SAS task (Leacock and Chodorow, 2003; Mohler and Mihalcea, 2009; Mohler et al., 2011; Basu et al., 2013).

As additional statistics, we calculated the number of CSEs and CSRate in various settings of λ in

λ	#CSEs	CSRate[%]
0.05	171	28.5
0.10	93	15.5
0.15	50	8.33
0.20	38	6.33
0.25	23	3.83
0.30	7	1.17

Table 2: Changes in the number of CSEs and CSRate of two human raters with λ. 100 responses per prompt are graded by two human raters, and the number of CSEs represents the sum of the number of CSEs of each prompt.

Equation 6 over the annotated scores of two human raters. Table 2 shows the result. The number of CSEs in Table 2 represents sum of the number of CSEs for all prompts.

5.2 Settings

We split the dataset into training data $(1, 600)$, validation data (200), and test data (200). We used pretrained BERT (Devlin et al., 2019) as the embedding layer of the model.[3] We adopted the same optimization algorithm, learning rate, batch size, and output dimension of the recurrent layer as in Taghipour and Ng (2016). We trained the SAS models for 50 epochs and selected the parameters in the epoch in which the best QWK was achieved for the development set. We trained five models with different random seeds and reported the average of the results.

Choosing a reasonable λ that defines CSE is crucial for our formulation. In our experiments, we employed 0.2 as λ for CSE. There is no theoretical and statistical evidence that 0.2 is the optimal value for our formulation. However, as shown in Table 2, 0.2 is assumed to be strict considering that even for human raters make CSEs in about 6% of responses. Therefore, this selection can offer meaningful evaluations for our formulation.

5.3 Result

Can confidence scores filter out CSEs? Figure 2 shows *CSRate*s on test data when we choose a certain proportion of the predicted instances in descending order of the confidence scores. The figure illustrates that the *CSRate* in each prompt increases

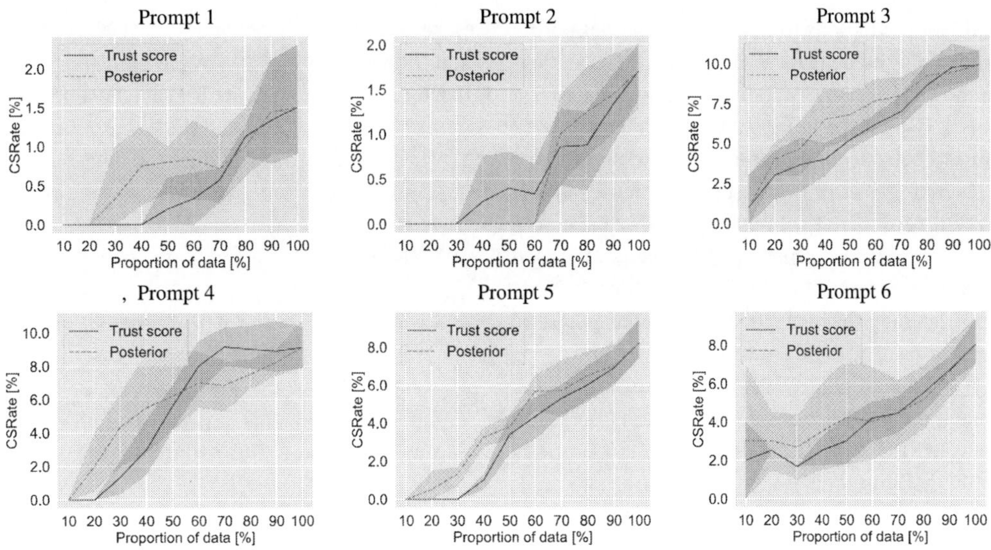

Figure 2: CSRate for test data subsets with the highest confidence scores. Proportion of data represents the ratio of $|\mathcal{D}'|$ to $|\mathcal{D}|$. The lines represent average CSRates of the trained five models and the band represents the maximum and minimum CSRates.

Prompt	Trust Score			Posteior		
	Prop[%]	#CSEs	τ	Prop[%]	#CSEs	τ
Prpt. 1	47.8	0.0	0.56	58.5	1.4	0.86
Prpt. 2	52.0	0.4	0.60	62.2	0.4	0.97
Prpt. 3	14.4	0.2	0.54	27.4	2.6	0.87
Prpt. 4	32.5	0.8	0.54	17.0	0.6	0.93
Prpt. 5	27.6	0.0	0.60	1.5	0.0	1.00
Prpt. 6	27.1	1.2	0.55	21.6	0.6	0.95

Table 3: Proportion of data (Prop[%]) and the number of CSEs (#CSEs) when using the trust score or the posterior probability to filter out unreliable predictions in test data with a certain threshold τ determined by the development set.

	10%		30%		50%		100%
	TS.	Pos.	TS.	Pos.	TS.	Pos.	(Base)
Prpt. 1	1.0	.99	.99	.98	.99	.98	.95
Prpt. 2	1.0	1.0	1.0	1.0	.99	.98	.93
Prpt. 3	.93	.84	.83	.78	.77	.74	.67
Prpt. 4	1.0	1.0	.98	.96	.93	.92	.86
Prpt. 5	1.0	1.0	1.0	.94	.91	.88	.82
Prpt. 6	.94	.92	.95	.95	.93	.92	.88

Table 4: QWK for highly confident predictions. 10%, 30%, and 50% represent the proportion of data with the highest trust score (TS.) or posterior (Pos.). The base represents our model performance on a whole test data.

almost monotonically for both confidence metrics. We can also observe that the CSRate values on four out of six prompts are suppressed to 0% with a certain amount of high confidence predictions (20% to 60% of the test data). This is an important observation for our objective; the result demonstrates that the proposed procedure using confidence scoring possibly obtains a reasonable size of highly reliable predictions. When comparing the two confidence estimation methods, the trust score is more effective for suppressing *CSE*s than the posterior probability on Prompt 1, 3, 4, 5, and 6.

Filtering CSE using the threshold In a practical situation, it is necessary to determine a certain threshold τ in the development set and use it for filtering low- reliability predictions of unknown samples. Assuming this situation, we evaluate how much CSEs in the test set can be reduced by using the threshold τ determined by the procedure described in Section 3.

Table 3 shows the proportions of the remaining test data and the number of CSEs after filtering out low-reliability predictions using the thresholds in each prompt. The results for both confidence estimation methods indicate that we can successfully filter out the unreliable predictions and achieve a sufficiently low CSRate by the proposed approach.

QWK in highly reliable predictions Additionally, we also show QWK of the top 10, 30, and 50%

confident predictions to illustrate the model performance with the de facto standard metric in Table 4. We show QWK of our model predictions on all test data as Base. The table shows that the proposed approach of selecting high-confidence predictions on the basis of confidence scores increases QWK markedly compared with using the whole test data. Moreover, we can achieve a QWK score of 1.0 in some prompts with the top 30% confident predictions, meaning that the model predictions perfectly agree with the ground truth scores.

Note that a higher QWK value does not always mean that the predictions do not contain CSEs. For example, in Table 4, the QWK values for prompts 1 and 2 are higher than 0.9. However, as shown in Figure 2, even with such high QWK values, these predictions include 1.5 to 2.0% of *CSEs*. This observation justifies the concept of CSE. QWK possibly conceals serious mispredictions, which are important to filter out in actual usage.

6 Conclusion and Future Work

In this paper, we introduced a new formulation of the SAS task to evaluate the effectiveness of the SAS systems in actual usage. We defined the concept of a critical scoring error (CSE), which represents unacceptable prediction errors. Then, we formulate the objective of the task to obtain as many predictions without CSE as possible. The experimental results show that by using our proposed procedure of selecting reliable predictions, SAS systems can predict scores with zero CSE for approximately 50% of test data at maximum. This result directly indicates the possibility of reducing half scoring cost of human raters, which, we believe, is highly preferable for the evaluation of SAS systems.

Our study revealed some potential for a better task formulation of SAS that links to actual usage. However, some issues remain, for example, how to determine the effective threshold τ that can strictly guarantee zero CSE is still unknown. This is one major challenge regarding our formulation. Moreover, we must develop a method for more accurately estimating the confidence scores, which is our primary focus in the next step.

Acknowledgments

This work was supported by JSPS KAKENHI Grant Number JP 19H04162 and 19K12112. This work was also partially supported by Bilateral Joint Research Program between RIKEN AIP Center and Tohoku University. We would like to thank the anonymous reviewers for their insightful comments. We also appreciate Takamiya Gakuen Yoyogi Seminar for providing the data.

References

Yigal Attali and Jill Burstein. 2006. Automated Essay Scoring with E-rater v.2.0. *Journal of Technology, Learning, and Assessment*, 4(3):31.

Sumit Basu, Chuck Jacobs, and Lucy Vanderwende. 2013. Powergrading: a Clustering Approach to Amplify Human Effort for Short Answer Grading. *Transactions of the Association for Computational Linguistics*, 1:391–402.

Steven Burrows, Iryna Gurevych, and Benno Stein. 2015. The eras and trends of automatic short answer grading. *International Journal of Artificial Intelligence in Education*, 25(1):60–117.

Jacob Cohen. 1960. A Coefficient of Agreement for Nominal Scales. *Educational and Psychological Measurement*, 20(1):37–46.

Jacob Cohen. 1968. Weighted Kappa: Nominal Scale Agreement with Provision for Scaled Disagreement or Partial Credit. *Psychological bulletin*, 70(4):213–220.

Jacob Devlin, Ming-Wei Chang, Kenton Lee, and Kristina Toutanova. 2019. BERT: Pre-training of Deep Bidirectional Transformers for Language Understanding. In *Proceedings of the 2019 Conference of the North American Chapter of the Association for Computational Linguistics: Human Language Technologies*, pages 4171–4186.

Peter Foltz, Darrell Laham, and T. Landauer. 1999. The Intelligent Essay Assessor: Applications to Educational Technology. *Interactive Multimedia Electronic Journal of Computer-Enhanced Learning*, 1(2):939–944.

Chuan Guo, Geoff Pleiss, Yu Sun, and Kilian Q. Weinberger. 2017. On Calibration of Modern Neural Networks. In *Proceedings of the 34th International Conference on Machine Learning*, pages 1321–1330.

Dan Hendrycks and Kevin Gimpel. 2017. A Baseline for Detecting Misclassified and Out-of-Distribution Examples in Neural Networks. In *Proceedings of 5th International Conference on Learning Representations*.

Heinrich Jiang, Been Kim, Melody Y. Guan, and Maya R. Gupta. 2018. To Trust Or Not To Trust A Classifier. In *Proceedings of Advances in Neural Information Processing Systems 31*, pages 5546–5557.

Aviral Kumar, Sunita Sarawagi, and Ujjwal Jain. 2018. Trainable calibration measures for neural networks from kernel mean embeddings. In *Proceedings of the 35th International Conference on Machine Learning*, pages 2805–2814.

Claudia Leacock and Martin Chodorow. 2003. C-rater: Automated Scoring of Short-Answer Questions. *Computers and the Humanities*, 37(4):389–405.

Tomoya Mizumoto, Hiroki Ouchi, Yoriko Isobe, Paul Reisert, Ryo Nagata, Satoshi Sekine, and Kentaro Inui. 2019. Analytic Score Prediction and Justification Identification in Automated Short Answer Scoring. In *Proceedings of the Fourteenth Workshop on Innovative Use of NLP for Building Educational Applications*, pages 316–325.

Michael Mohler, Razvan Bunescu, and Rada Mihalcea. 2011. Learning to Grade Short Answer Questions using Semantic Similarity Measures and Dependency Graph Alignments. In *Proceedings of the 49th Annual Meeting of the Association for Computational Linguistics: Human Language Technologies*, pages 752–762.

Michael Mohler and Rada Mihalcea. 2009. Text-to-text Semantic Similarity for Automatic Short Answer Grading. In *Proceedings of the 12th Conference of the European Chapter of the Association for Computational Linguistics (EACL)*, pages 567–575.

Khanh Nguyen and Brendan O'Connor. 2015. Posterior calibration and exploratory analysis for natural language processing models. In *Proceedings of the 2015 Conference on Empirical Methods in Natural Language Processing*, pages 1587–1598.

Ellis Batten Page. 1994. Computer Grading of Student Prose, Using Modern Concepts and Software. *Journal of Experimental Education*, 62(2):127–142.

Brian Riordan, Andrea Horbach, Aoife Cahill, Torsten Zesch, and Chong Min Lee. 2017. Investigating neural architectures for short answer scoring. In *Proceedings of the 12th Workshop on Innovative Use of NLP for Building Educational Applications*, pages 159–168.

M.D. Shermis, J. Burstein, D. Higgins, and Klaus Zechner. 2010. Automated essay scoring: Writing assessment and instruction. *International Encyclopedia of Education*, 4(1):20–26.

Kaveh Taghipour and Hwee Tou Ng. 2016. A Neural Approach to Automated Essay Scoring. In *Proceedings of the 2016 Conference on Empirical Methods in Natural Language Processing*, pages 1882–1891.

Tianqi Wang, Naoya Inoue, Hiroki Ouchi, Tomoya Mizumoto, and Kentaro Inui. 2019. Inject Rubrics into Short Answer Grading System. In *Proceedings of the 2nd Workshop on Deep Learning Approaches for Low-Resource NLP*, pages 175–182.

How much complexity does an RNN architecture need to learn syntax-sensitive dependencies?

Gantavya Bhatt[*1]**, Hritik Bansal**[*1]**, Rishubh Singh**[*1]**, Sumeet Agarwal**[1]
[1] Indian Institute of Technology Delhi
{gantavya.iitd, hbansal10n, rishubhsingh135}@gmail.com
sumeet@iitd.ac.in

Abstract

Long short-term memory (LSTM) networks and their variants are capable of encapsulating long-range dependencies, which is evident from their performance on a variety of linguistic tasks. On the other hand, simple recurrent networks (SRNs), which appear more biologically grounded in terms of synaptic connections, have generally been less successful at capturing long-range dependencies as well as the loci of grammatical errors in an unsupervised setting. In this paper, we seek to develop models that bridge the gap between biological plausibility and linguistic competence. We propose a new architecture, the *Decay RNN*, which incorporates the decaying nature of neuronal activations and models the excitatory and inhibitory connections in a population of neurons. Besides its biological inspiration, our model also shows competitive performance relative to LSTMs on subject-verb agreement, sentence grammaticality, and language modeling tasks. These results provide some pointers towards probing the nature of the inductive biases required for RNN architectures to model linguistic phenomena successfully.

1 Introduction

For the last couple of decades, neural networks have been approached primarily from an engineering perspective, with the key motivation being efficiency, consequently moving further away from biological plausibility. Recent developments (Song et al., 2016; Gao and Ganguli, 2015; Sussillo and Barak, 2013) have however incorporated explicit constraints in neural networks to model specific parts of the brain and have found a correlation between the learned activation maps and actual neural activity recordings. Thus, these trained networks can perhaps act as a proxy for a theoretical investigation into biological circuits.

Recurrent Neural Networks (RNNs) have been used to analyze the principles and dynamics of neural population responses by performing the same tasks as animals (Mante et al., 2013). However, these networks violate Dale's law (Dale, 1935; Strata and Harvey, 1999), which states that the neurons have either a purely excitatory or inhibitory effect on other neurons in the mammalian brain. The decaying nature of the potential in the neuron membrane after receiving signals (excitatory or inhibitory) from the surrounding neurons is also well-studied (Gluss, 1967). The goal of our work is to incorporate these biological features into the RNN structure, which gives rise to a neuro-inspired and computationally inexpensive recurrent network for language modeling, which we call a *Decay RNN* (Section 4). We perform learning using the back-propagation algorithm. Despite its differences with the way learning is believed to happen in the brain, it has been argued that the brain can implement its core principles (Hinton, 2007; Lillicrap et al., 2020). We assess our model's ability to capture syntax-sensitive dependencies via multiple linguistic tasks (Section 6): number prediction, grammaticality judgement (Linzen et al., 2016) which entails subject-verb agreement, and a more complex language modeling task (Marvin and Linzen, 2018).

Subject-verb agreement, where the *main noun* and the *associated verb* must agree in number, is considered as evidence of hierarchical structure in English. This is exemplified using a sentence taken from the dataset made available by Linzen et al. (2016):

1. *All **trips** on the <u>expressway</u> **requires** a toll.

2. All **trips** on the <u>expressway</u> **require** a toll.

The effect of agreement attractors (nouns having number opposite to the main noun; *expressway*

Proceedings of the 58th Annual Meeting of the Association for Computational Linguistics: Student Research Workshop, pages 244–254
July 5 - July 10, 2020. ©2020 Association for Computational Linguistics

in the above example[1]) between the main noun and main verb of a sentence has been well-studied (Linzen et al., 2016; Kuncoro et al., 2018). Our work also highlights the influence of non-attractor intervening nouns. For example,

- A **chair** created by a <u>hobbyist</u> as a <u>gift</u> to <u>someone</u> **is** not a commodity.[2]

In the number prediction task, if a model correctly predicts the grammatical number of the verb (singular in case of 'is'), it might be due to the (helpful) interference of non-attractor intervening nouns ('hobbyist', 'gift', 'someone') rather than necessarily capturing its dependence the main noun ('chair'). From our investigation in Section 6.2, we find that the linear recurrent models take cues present in the vicinity of the main verb to predict its number, apart from the agreement with the main noun.

In the subsequent sections, we investigate the performance of the Decay RNN and other recurrent networks, showing that no single sequential model generalizes well on all (grammatical) phenomena, which include subject-verb agreements, reflexive anaphora, and negative polarity items as described in Marvin and Linzen (2018). Our major outcomes are:

1. Designing a relatively simple and bio-inspired recurrent model: the Decay RNN, which performs on-par with LSTMs for linguistic tasks such as subject-verb agreement and grammaticality judgement.

2. Pointing to some limitations of analyzing the intervening attractor nouns alone for the subject-verb agreement task and attempting joint analysis of non-attractor intervening nouns and attractor nouns in the sentence.

3. Showing that there is no linear recurrent scheme which generalizes well on a variety of sentence types and motivating research in better understanding of the nature of biases induced by varied RNN structures.

2   Related Work

There has been prior work on using LSTMs (Hochreiter and Schmidhuber, 1997) for language modeling tasks. The work of Gers and Schmidhuber (2001) has shown that LSTMs can learn simple context-free and context-sensitive languages. However, as per the investigations carried out in Kuncoro et al. (2018), it was observed that if the model capacity is not enough, then LSTMs may not generalize the long-range dependencies. Recently many architectures have explicitly incorporated the knowledge of phrase structure trees (Kuncoro et al., 2018; Alvarez-Melis and Jaakkola, 2017; Tai et al., 2015) which have shown improvement in generalizing over long-range dependencies. At the same time, Shen et al. (2019) proposed ON-LSTMs, a modification to LSTMs that provides an inductive tree bias to the structure. However, Dyer et al. (2019) have shown that the success of ON-LSTMs was due to their proposed metric to analyze the model, not necessarily due to their architecture.

From the biological point of view, Capano et al. (2015) used a hard reset of the membrane potential in contrast to a soft decay observed in a neuronal membrane. At the same time, their learning paradigm is similar to the Hebbian learning scheme (Hebb, 1949), which does not involve error backpropagation (Rumelhart et al., 1986). Our work is closely related to the idea of modeling the population of neurons as a dynamical system (EIRNN) proposed by Song et al. (2016). However, their time constant parameter was based on the concepts described in Wang (2002) while the sampling rate was arbitrarily chosen. Given that the chosen values only considered a certain class of neurons (Yang et al., 2019), we believe that it is not necessary to have the same values of the parameters for each cognitive task. Thus, we build on their formulation by making the sampling rate and time constant learnable as manifested by our decay parameter, described in the next section.

3   Biological Preliminaries

According to Dale's principle, a neuron is either excitatory or inhibitory (Eccles, 1976). If a neuron output produces a negative (positive) change in the membrane potential of all the connected neurons via its synapse, then it is said to be an inhibitory (excitatory) neuron. In a set of N neurons, if $\mathbf{W}$ is the synaptic connection matrix, then the connection from the neuron j to neuron i is 'excitatory' if $W_{ij} > 0$, and 'inhibitory' if $W_{ij} \leq 0$. Capano et al. (2015) have argued that a balance between structural and response variability (entropy),

---

[1]Main noun and verb are highlighted in bold. Intervening nouns are underlined. Asterisks mark unacceptable sentences.

[2]Sentence taken from the dataset made available by Linzen et al. (2016).

and excitability (synaptic strength) of a network maximizes the overall learning. This balance is governed by the ratio of inhibitory and excitatory neurons. They have further shown that this balance also maximizes the overall performance in multitask learning. Catsigeras (2013) mathematically prove that Dale's principle is necessary for an optimal[3] neuronal network's dynamics.

In the postsynaptic neuron, the integration of synaptic potentials is realized by the addition of excitatory (+ve) and inhibitory (-ve) postsynaptic potentials (PSPs). PSPs are electronic voltages, that decay as a function of time due to spontaneous reclosure of the synaptic channels. The decay of the PSPs is controlled by the membrane constant τ, i.e., the time required by the PSP to decay to 37% of its peak value (Wallisch et al., 2009).

4   Decay RNN

Here we present our proposed architecture, which we call the *Decay RNN* (DRNN). Our architecture aims to model the decaying nature of the voltage in a neuron membrane after receiving impulses from the surrounding neurons. At the same time, we incorporate Dale's principle in our architecture. Thus, our model captures both the microscopic and macroscopic properties of a group of neurons. Adhering to the stated phenomena, we define our model with the following update equations for given input $\mathbf{x}^{(t)}$ at time t:

$$\mathbf{c}^{(t)} = (ReLU(\mathbf{W})\mathbf{W}_{dale})\mathbf{h}^{(t-1)} + \mathbf{U}\mathbf{x}^{(t)} + \mathbf{b}$$
$$\mathbf{h}^{(t)} = f(\alpha\mathbf{h}^{(t-1)} + (1 - \alpha)\mathbf{c}^{(t)})$$

Here f is a nonlinear activation function, $\mathbf{W}$ and $\mathbf{U}$ are weight matrices, $\mathbf{b}$ is the bias and $\mathbf{h}^{(t)}$ represents the hidden state (analogous to voltage). We define $\alpha \in (0,1)$ as a learnable parameter to incorporate a decay effect in the hidden state (analogous to the decay in the membrane potential). Here α acts as a balancing factor between the hidden state $\mathbf{h}^{(t-1)}$ and $\mathbf{c}^{(t)}$.[4] $\mathbf{W}_{dale}$ is a diagonal matrix, and based on the empirical results on the mammalian brain (Hendry and Jones, 1981), we set the last 20% of entries to -1, representing the inhibitory connections, and the rest to 1 (See Appendix A.3).[5] Unlike Song et al. (2016), we keep self-connections in the network. Besides biological inspiration, our model also has the following salient features.

First, the presence of α acts as a coupled gating mechanism to the flow of information (Figure 1), at the same time maintaining an exponential moving average of the hidden state. Thus, α values close to 1 correspond to memories of the distant past. It is worth mentioning that Oliva et al. (2017) have considered the exponential moving average in the context of RNNs. However, their approach manually selected a set of scaling parameters, whereas we have a systematic way of arriving at the values of those parameters by making them learnable for the task at hand.

Second, our model also has an intrinsic skip connection deriving out of its formulation. Yue et al. (2018) has shown that the architectures with skip connections provide an alternate path for the flow of gradients during the error backpropagation. At the same time presence of coupled gates slows down the vanishing of gradient (Bengio et al., 2013). Thus, despite of its simple un-gated structure, the features discussed above provide safeguards against vanishing gradient.

To examine the importance of Dale's principle in the learning process, we made a variant of our Decay RNN without Dale's principle, which we call the *Slacked Decay RNN* (SDRNN), with updates to $\mathbf{c}^{(t)}$ made as follows:

$$\mathbf{c}^{(t)} = \mathbf{W}\mathbf{h}^{(t-1)} + \mathbf{U}\mathbf{x}^{(t)} + \mathbf{b}$$

To understand the role of the correlation between the hidden states in the Decay RNN formulation, we devised an ablated version of our architecture, which we refer to as the *Ab-DRNN*. With the following update equation, we remove the mathematical factor $(\mathbf{W}\mathbf{h}^{(t-1)})$ that gives rise to a correlation between hidden states:

$$\mathbf{h}^{(t)} = f(\alpha\mathbf{h}^{(t-1)} + (1 - \alpha)(\mathbf{U}\mathbf{x}^{(t)} + \mathbf{b}))$$

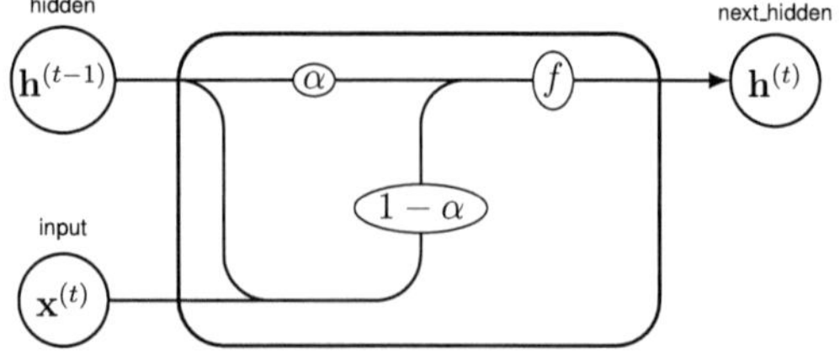

Figure 1: Decay RNN cell, comprising of a skip connection and coupled scalar gates.

5   Datasets

For the number prediction (Section 6.1) and grammaticality judgment (Section 6.3) tasks, we used a

---

[3]In the sense of showing the most diverse set of responses.

[4]It was kept bounded using a sigmoid function. Our results did not change when we used a linear function instead.

[5]Our results did not change when we chose a different set of -1 entries instead of the last 20%.

corpus of 1.57 million sentences from Wikipedia (Linzen et al., 2016), of which 10% were used for training, 0.4% for validation, and the remaining were reserved for testing. On the other hand, for the language modeling task (Section 6.4), the model was trained on a 90 million word subset of Wikipedia comprising of 3 million training and 0.3 million validation sentences (Gulordava et al., 2018).

Despite having a large number of training points, these datasets have certain drawbacks, including the lack of a sufficient number of syntactically challenging examples leading to poor generalization over the sentences out of the training data distribution. Therefore, we construct a generalization set as described in Marvin and Linzen (2018), where we generate the sentences out of templates that can be described using a non-recursive context-free grammar. The use of the generalization set allows us to test on a much broader range of linguistic phenomena. We will use this dataset for the targeted syntactic evaluation of our trained models.

6 Experiments

Here we will describe our experiments[6] to assess the models' ability to capture syntax-sensitive dependencies. Details regarding the training settings are available in Appendix A.4.

6.1 Number Prediction Task

The number prediction task was proposed by Linzen et al. (2016). In this task, the model is required to predict the grammatical number of the verb when provided a sentence up to the verb.

1. The **path** to success **is** not straight forward.

2. The path to success ______

The model will take the second sentence as input and has to predict the number of the verb (here, singular). Table 1 shows the results on the number prediction task. All the models including SRNs performed well on this task. Thus, this indicates that even vanilla RNNs can identify singular and plural words and can associate the main subject with the upcoming verb.

6.2 Joint Analysis of Intervening Nouns

So far in the literature, when looking at intervening material in agreement tasks, the research has tended

Model	No. Prediction	Grammaticality
SRN	97.70	50.12
LSTM	98.59	95.81
GRU	**98.81**	94.26
EIRNN	94.68	84.51
DRNN	98.66	95.48
SDRNN	98.65	**96.83**
Ab-DRNN	97.37	85.98

Table 1: % Accuracy of models when tested on ~ 1.4 million sentences for the number prediction and grammaticality judgement tasks.

to focus on agreement attractors, the intervening nouns with the opposite number to the main noun (Kuncoro et al., 2018). However, we posit that the role of non-attractor intervening nouns may also be important when understanding a model's decisions. For long-range dependencies in agreement tasks, a model may be influenced by the presence of non-attractor intervening nouns instead of purely capturing the verb's relationship with the main subject. Hence an analysis done solely based on the number of agreement attractors may be misleading. Table 2 shows an improvement in the verb number prediction accuracy with an increasing number of non-attractors (n), even as the subject-verb distance and the attractor count are kept fixed. This indicates that the models are also using cues present in the vicinity of the main verb to predict its number, apart from agreement with the main noun.

Model	n=0	n=1	n=2
DRNN	90.65	95.56	96.06
LSTM	90.4	95.56	95.63

Table 2: Number prediction % accuracy with an increasing number of non-attractor intervening nouns (n). The distance between the main subject and the corresponding verb is held constant at 7 and the attractor count at 1.

6.3 Grammaticality Judgement

The previous objective was predicting the grammatical number of the verb after providing the model an input sentence only up to the verb. However, this way of training may give the model a cue to the syntactic clause boundaries. In this section, we describe the grammaticality judgment task. Given an input sentence, the model has to predict whether it is grammatical or not. To perform well on this task, the model would presumably need to allocate more resources to determine the locus of ungrammaticality. For example, consider the following

---

[6]Our code is available at https://github.com/bhattg/Decay-RNN-ACL-SRW2020

pair of sentences[2] :

1. The **roses** in the vase by the door **are** red.

2. *The **roses** in the vase by the door **is** red.

The model has to decide, for input sentences such as the above, whether each one is grammatically correct or not. Table 1 shows the performance of different recurrent architectures on this task. It can be seen that SRNs, which were comparable to LSTMs and GRUs on the prediction experiment described in Section 6.1, are no better than random on the grammaticality judgment task. On the other hand, the Ab-DRNN performed better than the SRN. This highlights the importance of a balance between the uncorrelated hidden states ($\mathbf{h}^{(t)}$), and the connected hidden states ($\mathbf{Wh}^{(t)}$), which is modeled by the Decay RNN. Due to its architectural similarity with the Independent RNN (Li et al., 2018), which has independent connections among neurons in a layer, Ab-DRNN did not suffer from the vanishing gradient problem.

Importance of the generalization set

Capano et al. (2015) had argued that the inclusion of Dale's principle improved generalization abilities for multitask learning. For our models trained on a single task, we use the generalization set to determine the number prediction confidence profile over the sentences. Figure 2 describes the average number prediction confidence at each part of speech for all prepositional phrases with inanimate subjects. We note the anomalously low confidence of the SDRNN at plural inanimate subjects (like 'movies', 'books'), unlike the DRNN.

Task	DRNN	SDRNN
Across object RC (no that) anim	**0.45**	0.28
Reflexive Sentential Comp.	**0.65**	0.6
Long VP Coordination	**0.53**	0.43

Table 3: Accuracy comparison of DRNN and SDRNN when tested on the generalization set for the grammaticality judgement task; 'anim' refers to an animated noun.

In Table 3,[7] we present the result of the models trained for the grammaticality judgment task and tested on the synthetic generalization set. From the results, we can see that despite having nearly the same accuracy on the original testing data (Table

---

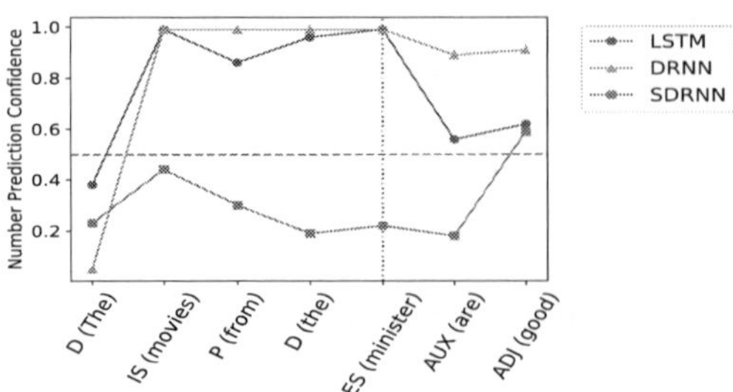

Figure 2: Number prediction confidence (for the correct verb number) averaged over the generalization set (540 sentences) for prepositional phrases with plural inanimate subjects (IS). An example word for each position is indicated in parentheses. Values at ES indicate the confidence for the following verb/auxiliary. For the example sentence, confidence < 0.5 implies singular verb number prediction, and confidence > 0.5 plural.

1), there is a substantial difference in the generalization accuracies of the DRNN and SDRNN. The DRNN shows better generalization than the SDRNN in the experiments mentioned in Table 3 and Figure 2. This might be due to regularising effects induced by Dale's constraint. This is an interesting observation that merits further investigation.

6.4 Language Modeling

Word-level language modeling is a task that helps in the evaluation of the model's capacity to capture the general properties of language beyond what is tested in specialized tasks focused on, e.g., subject-verb agreement. We use perplexity to compare our model's performance against standard sequential recurrent architectures. Table 4 shows the validation perplexity of different language models along with the number of learnable parameters for the task. From the Table 4, we observe that incorporating the components of the Ab-DRNN and the SRN in a coupled way might have led to the improved performance of the Decay RNN.

6.5 Targeted Syntactic Evaluation

Targeted syntactic evaluation (Marvin and Linzen, 2018) is a way to evaluate the language model across different classes of structure-sensitive phenomena. This includes subject-verb agreement, reflexive anaphora, and negative polarity items (NPI).[8] Table 4 shows that even with a simple architecture, the Decay RNN class of models performs

---

[7]Here, we present three tests from the targeted syntactic evaluation framework. Others test results can be found in Appendix A.2.

[8]The definitions of these linguistic terms are provided in the supplementary material of Marvin and Linzen (2018).

	SRN	GRU	LSTM	DRNN	SDRNN	Ab-DRNN	ON-LSTM
Validation Perplexity	114.74	53.78	52.73	76.67	76.88	86.42	-
Parameters	1.4M	4.2M	5.6M	1.4M	1.4M	0.55M	-
Short-Range Dependency							
SV Agreement:							
Simple	0.88	0.95	0.92	0.95	0.97	0.90	**0.99**
Sentential Complement	0.84	0.86	0.93	0.89	0.92	0.85	**0.95**
Short VP Coord	0.5	0.87	0.85	0.73	0.77	0.69	**0.89**
In an object RC	0.59	0.75	**0.87**	0.77	0.74	0.63	0.84
In an object RC (no that)	0.57	0.67	0.75	0.74	0.71	0.62	**0.78**
Reflexive Anaphora:							
Simple	0.51	0.85	0.85	0.75	0.73	0.63	**0.89**
Sentential Complement	0.56	0.78	0.83	0.68	0.65	0.62	**0.86**
Negative Polarity Items :							
Simple (grammatical vs. intrusive)	0.01	0.51	**0.56**	0.25	0.01	0.29	0.18
Simple (intrusive vs. ungrammatical)	**0.7**	0.66	0.48	0.54	0.5	0.51	0.5
Simple (grammatical vs. ungrammatical)	0.11	**0.67**	0.55	0.45	0.38	0.31	0.07
Long-Range Dependency							
SV Agreement:							
Long VP coordination	0.51	**0.8**	**0.8**	0.55	0.62	0.51	0.74
Across a PP	0.51	**0.75**	0.6	0.56	0.54	0.53	0.67
Across a subject RC	0.52	**0.67**	**0.67**	0.53	0.55	0.52	0.66
Across an object RC	0.51	0.51	0.55	**0.64**	0.58	0.57	0.57
Across an object RC (no that)	0.50	0.50	0.51	**0.65**	0.60	0.59	0.54
Reflexive Anaphora :							
Across a RC	0.51	0.58	0.57	0.62	**0.66**	0.58	0.57
Negative Polarity Items:							
Across a RC (grammatical vs. intrusive)	**0.87**	0.55	0.55	0.32	0.48	0.57	0.59
Across a RC (intrusive vs. ungrammatical)	0.02	0.29	0.22	**0.5**	0.37	0.36	0.20
Across a RC (grammatical vs. ungrammatical)	0.1	0.2	0.03	0.1	**0.3**	0.11	0.11
Mean Arithmetic Rank	5.94	3	3.31	3.52	3.68	4.73	**2.94**

Table 4: Accuracy of models on targeted syntactic evaluation. RC: Relative Clause, PP: Prepositional Phrase, VP : Verb Phrase. Closeness in the mean arithmetic rank of models (other than SRNs) across tasks suggests that within the current space of sequential recurrent models, none dominates the others.

fairly similarly to LSTMs and much better than SRNs for many tests.[9] In the case of long-range dependencies and NPI involving relative-object clauses, our models perform substantially better than LSTMs. High variability in the performance of the models in the case of NPIs might be due to non-syntactic cues as pointed out by Marvin and Linzen (2018). Based on the mean ranks observed in Table 4, we conjecture that there is no sequential recurrent structure at present which outperforms the others across the board. However, SRNs alone are not sufficient for most purposes.

7 Conclusion

In this paper, we proposed the Decay RNN, a bio-inspired recurrent network that emulates the decaying nature of neuronal activations after receiving excitatory and inhibitory impulses from upstream neurons. We have found that the balance between the free term ($\mathbf{h}^{(t)}$) and the coupled term ($\mathbf{Wh}^{(t)}$) enabled the model to capture syntax-level dependencies. As shown by McCoy et al. (2020); Kuncoro et al. (2018), explicitly modeling hierarchical structure helps to discover non-local structural dependencies. The contrast in the performance of

the language models encourages us to look at the inductive biases, which might have led to better syntactic generalization in certain cases. Recently, Maheswaranathan and Sussillo (2020) showed the existence of a line attractor in the dynamics of the hidden states for sentiment classification. Thus, similar dynamical-system-based analysis can be extended to our settings to further understand the working of the Decay RNN.

From the cognitive neuroscience perspective, it would be interesting to investigate if the proposed Decay RNN can capture some aspects of actual neuronal behaviour and language cognition. Our results here do at least indicate that the complex gating mechanisms of LSTMs (whose cognitive plausibility has not been established) may not be essential to their performance on many linguistic tasks, and that simpler and perhaps more cognitively plausible RNN architectures are worth exploring further as psycholinguistic models.

Acknowledgements

We wish to thank the anonymous reviewers, and Jakob Prange and ACL SRW for the post-acceptance mentorship program; Pankaj Malhotra for valuable comments on earlier versions of this paper; and Tal Linzen for helpful discussion.

---

[9]Results for the ON-LSTM are directly quoted from Shen et al. (2019).

References

David Alvarez-Melis and Tommi S. Jaakkola. 2017. Tree-structured decoding with doubly-recurrent neural networks. In *5th International Conference on Learning Representations, ICLR 2017, Toulon, France, April 24–26, 2017, Conference Track Proceedings*. OpenReview.net.

Yoshua Bengio, Nicolas Boulanger-Lewandowski, and Razvan Pascanu. 2013. Advances in optimizing recurrent networks. In *2013 IEEE International Conference on Acoustics, Speech and Signal Processing*, pages 8624–8628. IEEE.

Vittorio Capano, Hans J Herrmann, and Lucilla De Arcangelis. 2015. Optimal percentage of inhibitory synapses in multi-task learning. *Scientific Reports*, 5:9895.

Eleonora Catsigeras. 2013. Dale's principle is necessary for an optimal neuronal network's dynamics. *Applied Mathematics*, 4(10B):15–29.

Henry Dale. 1935. Pharmacology and nerve-endings. *Proceedings of the Royal Society of Medicine*, 28(3):319–332.

Chris Dyer, Gábor Melis, and Phil Blunsom. 2019. A critical analysis of biased parsers in unsupervised parsing. *arXiv preprint*, arXiv:1909.09428.

John Carew Eccles. 1976. From electrical to chemical transmission in the central nervous system: the closing address of the sir henry dale centennial symposium cambridge, 19 september 1975. *Notes and records of the Royal Society of London*, 30(2):219–230.

Peiran Gao and Surya Ganguli. 2015. On simplicity and complexity in the brave new world of large-scale neuroscience. *Current Opinion in Neurobiology*, 32:148–155.

Felix A Gers and E Schmidhuber. 2001. LSTM recurrent networks learn simple context-free and context-sensitive languages. *IEEE Transactions on Neural Networks*, 12(6):1333–1340.

Brian Gluss. 1967. A model for neuron firing with exponential decay of potential resulting in diffusion equations for probability density. *The Bulletin of Mathematical Biophysics*, 29(2):233–243.

Kristina Gulordava, Piotr Bojanowski, Edouard Grave, Tal Linzen, and Marco Baroni. 2018. Colorless green recurrent networks dream hierarchically. In *Proceedings of the 2018 Conference of the North American Chapter of the Association for Computational Linguistics: Human Language Technologies, Volume 1 (Long Papers)*, pages 1195–1205, New Orleans, Louisiana. Association for Computational Linguistics.

Donald O Hebb. 1949. *The organization of behavior: A neuropsychological theory*. New York: John Wiley & Sons.

Stewart H Hendry and EG Jones. 1981. Sizes and distributions of intrinsic neurons incorporating tritiated gaba in monkey sensory-motor cortex. *Journal of Neuroscience*, 1(4):390–408.

Geoffrey Hinton. 2007. How to do backpropagation in a brain. Invited talk at the NIPS'2007 Deep Learning Workshop.

Sepp Hochreiter and Jürgen Schmidhuber. 1997. Long short-term memory. *Neural Computation*, 9(8):1735–1780.

Diederik P. Kingma and Jimmy Ba. 2015. Adam: A method for stochastic optimization. In *3rd International Conference on Learning Representations, ICLR 2015, San Diego, CA, USA, May 7–9, 2015, Conference Track Proceedings*.

Adhiguna Kuncoro, Chris Dyer, John Hale, Dani Yogatama, Stephen Clark, and Phil Blunsom. 2018. LSTMs can learn syntax-sensitive dependencies well, but modeling structure makes them better. In *Proceedings of the 56th Annual Meeting of the Association for Computational Linguistics (Volume 1: Long Papers)*, pages 1426–1436, Melbourne, Australia. Association for Computational Linguistics.

Shuai Li, Wanqing Li, Chris Cook, Ce Zhu, and Yanbo Gao. 2018. Independently recurrent neural network (IndRNN): Building a longer and deeper RNN. In *Proceedings of the IEEE Conference on Computer Vision and Pattern Recognition*, pages 5457–5466.

Timothy P. Lillicrap, Adam Santoro, Luke Marris, Colin J. Akerman, and Geoffrey Hinton. 2020. Backpropagation and the brain. *Nature Reviews Neuroscience*, 21:335–346.

Tal Linzen, Emmanuel Dupoux, and Yoav Goldberg. 2016. Assessing the ability of LSTMs to learn syntax-sensitive dependencies. *Transactions of the Association for Computational Linguistics*, 4:521–535.

Niru Maheswaranathan and David Sussillo. 2020. How recurrent networks implement contextual processing in sentiment analysis. *arXiv preprint*, arXiv:2004.08013.

Valerio Mante, David Sussillo, Krishna V. Shenoy, and William T. Newsome. 2013. Context-dependent computation by recurrent dynamics in prefrontal cortex. *Nature*, 503(7474):78–84.

Rebecca Marvin and Tal Linzen. 2018. Targeted syntactic evaluation of language models. In *Proceedings of the 2018 Conference on Empirical Methods in Natural Language Processing*, pages 1192–1202, Brussels, Belgium. Association for Computational Linguistics.

R. Thomas McCoy, Robert Frank, and Tal Linzen. 2020. Does syntax need to grow on trees? Sources of hierarchical inductive bias in sequence-to-sequence networks. *Transactions of the Association for Computational Linguistics*, 8:125–140.

Junier B. Oliva, Barnabás Póczos, and Jeff Schneider. 2017. The statistical recurrent unit. In *Proceedings of the 34th International Conference on Machine Learning*, volume 70 of *Proceedings of Machine Learning Research*, pages 2671–2680, International Convention Centre, Sydney, Australia. PMLR.

David E Rumelhart, Geoffrey E Hinton, and Ronald J Williams. 1986. Learning representations by back-propagating errors. *Nature*, 323(6088):533–536.

Yikang Shen, Shawn Tan, Alessandro Sordoni, and Aaron C. Courville. 2019. Ordered neurons: Integrating tree structures into recurrent neural networks. In *7th International Conference on Learning Representations, ICLR 2019, New Orleans, LA, USA, May 6–9, 2019*. OpenReview.net.

H Francis Song, Guangyu R Yang, and Xiao-Jing Wang. 2016. Training excitatory-inhibitory recurrent neural networks for cognitive tasks: a simple and flexible framework. *PLoS Computational Biology*, 12(2):e1004792.

Piergiorgio Strata and Robin Harvey. 1999. Dale's principle. *Brain Research Bulletin*, 50(5-6):349–350.

David Sussillo and Omri Barak. 2013. Opening the black box: low-dimensional dynamics in high-dimensional recurrent neural networks. *Neural Computation*, 25(3):626–649.

Kai Sheng Tai, Richard Socher, and Christopher D. Manning. 2015. Improved semantic representations from tree-structured long short-term memory networks. In *Proceedings of the 53rd Annual Meeting of the Association for Computational Linguistics and the 7th International Joint Conference on Natural Language Processing (Volume 1: Long Papers)*, pages 1556–1566, Beijing, China. Association for Computational Linguistics.

Pascal Wallisch, Michael Lusignan, Marc Benayoun, Tanya I. Baker, Adam S. Dickey, and Nicholas G. Hatsopoulos. 2009. Synaptic transmission. In *Matlab for Neuroscientists*, pages 299–306. Elsevier.

Xiao-Jing Wang. 2002. Probabilistic decision making by slow reverberation in cortical circuits. *Neuron*, 36(5):955–968.

Guangyu Robert Yang, Madhura R Joglekar, H Francis Song, William T Newsome, and Xiao-Jing Wang. 2019. Task representations in neural networks trained to perform many cognitive tasks. *Nature Neuroscience*, 22(2):297–306.

Boxuan Yue, Junwei Fu, and Jun Liang. 2018. Residual recurrent neural networks for learning sequential representations. *Information*, 9(3):56.

A Appendix

A.1 Effect of agreement attractors

In this section, we present the trends in the testing performance of the LSTM and the Decay RNN (DRNN) for the grammaticality judgment task. Figure 3 shows the performance of the models when we fix the number of intervening nouns and vary the count of attractors between the main subject and the corresponding verb. The decreasing performance of the models with the introduction of more attractors indicates that they cause the models to get more confused about the upcoming verb number.

A.2 Comparison between DRNN and SDRNN

In Section 6.3, we saw that in terms of testing accuracy for grammaticality judgment, the Slacked Decay RNN (SDRNN) outperformed the Decay RNN (DRNN). For a robust investigation of this behaviour, we tested our models on the generalization set and mentioned a subset of our results on grammaticality judgment in Table 3. Here we present a bar graph (Figure 4) depicting the model performance when tested on the generalization set for the grammaticality judgment task. A substantial difference in the performance of the SDRNN and the DRNN reinforces the possibility of the regularizing effects of Dale's principle.

A.3 Implementation of Dale's constraint

$$\forall w_{i,j} \in ReLU(\mathbf{W}), w_{i,j} \geq 0$$

$$\mathbf{ReLU(W)W}_{dale} = \begin{bmatrix} w_{1,1} & w_{1,2} & \cdots & w_{1,n} \\ w_{2,1} & w_{2,2} & \cdots & w_{2,n} \\ \vdots & \vdots & \vdots & \vdots \\ w_{n,1} & w_{n,2} & \cdots & w_{n,n} \end{bmatrix} \begin{bmatrix} 1 & 0 & \cdots & 0 \\ 0 & 1 & \cdots & 0 \\ \vdots & \vdots & \vdots & \vdots \\ 0 & 0 & \cdots & -1 \end{bmatrix} = \begin{bmatrix} + & + & \cdots & - \\ + & + & \cdots & - \\ \vdots & \vdots & \vdots \\ + & + & \cdots & - \end{bmatrix}$$

A.4 Training settings

For the number prediction task and the grammaticality judgment task the network is trained as a binary classifier. The network is single-layered, with ReLU activation and trained with embedding and hidden layer dimension being 50, and a batch size of 1. We have reported the average accuracies after 3 separate runs in Table 1. For targeted syntactic evaluation, we have trained a language model to predict the grammaticality of a sentence. In our language model, we used a 2-layered network with $tanh$ activation, a dropout rate of 0.2 with embedding dimension 200, hidden dimension 650, and a batch size of 128. All models are trained with a learning rate of 0.001 using the Adam optimizer (Kingma and Ba, 2015).

A.5 Decay parameter (α) learning

In the main text, we describe the balancing effect of α in the Decay RNN model. We present the trend in the learned value of α throughout training for the grammaticality task for various initializations in Figure 5. We observe that for all α initializations in the range $(0,1)$, the learned value converges to around 0.8. Hence, we initialize our α to 0.8 at the start of the training process.

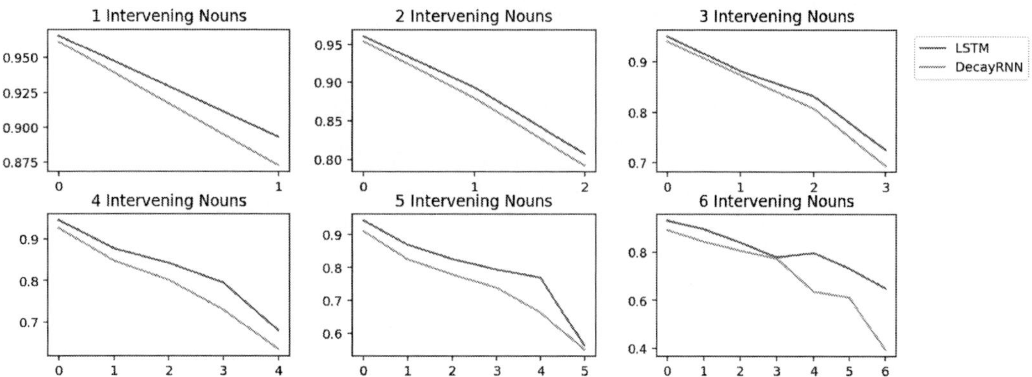

Figure 3: Trends in the performance of the LSTM (blue) and DRNN (orange) models with increasing numbers of intervening nouns. For each subplot corresponding to a fixed intervening noun number, the number of agreement attractors increases as we move from left to right on the x-axis.

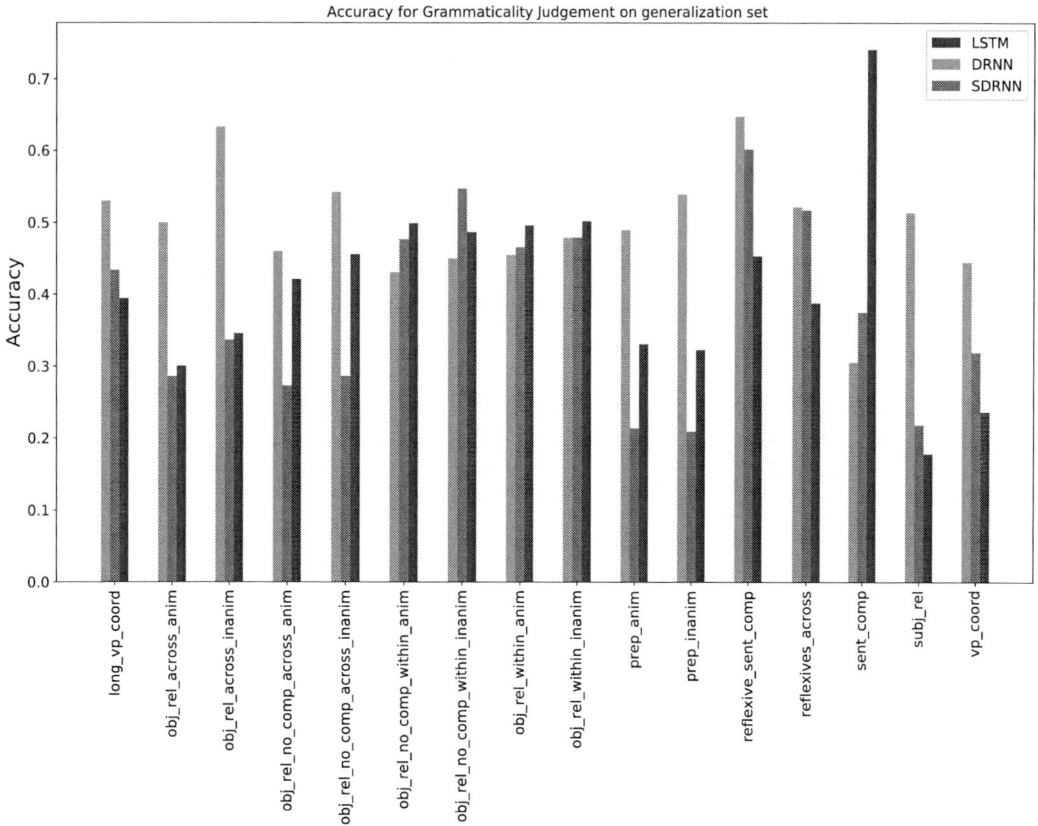

Figure 4: Performance of the LSTM (blue), DRNN (orange), and SDRNN (green) models for the different types of sentences in the generalization set, when trained for the grammaticality judgment task. There were at least 200 test sentences for each of these types.

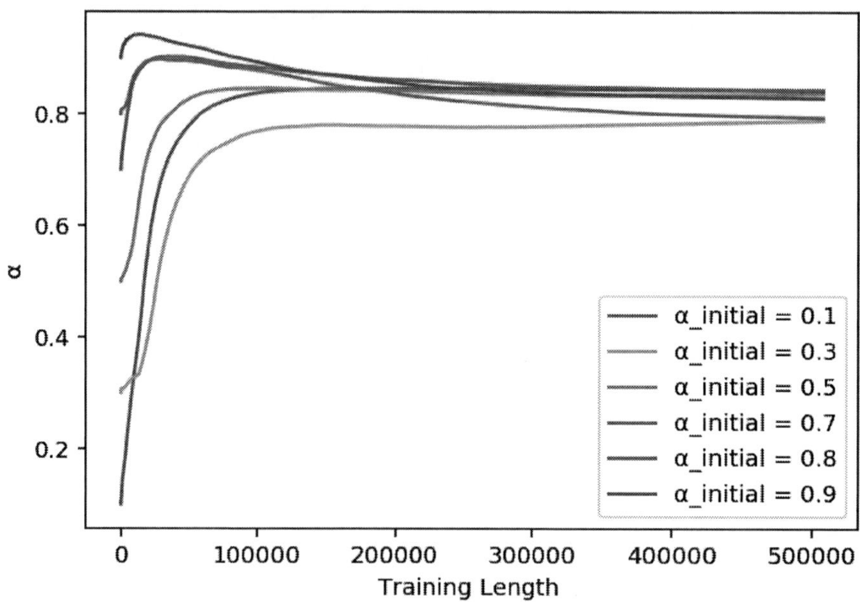

Figure 5: Moving average of α over the course of training for different initializations. 1 unit of training length is 1 forward pass.

Unsupervised Multilingual Sentence Embeddings
for Parallel Corpus Mining

Ivana Kvapilíková[‡]   Mikel Artetxe[§]   Gorka Labaka[§]
Eneko Agirre[§]   Ondřej Bojar[‡]

[‡]Institute of Formal and Applied Linguistics, Charles University (MFF UK)
`{kvapilikova,bojar}@ufal.mff.cuni.cz`
[§]Ixa NLP group, University of the Basque Country (UPV/EHU)
`{mikel.artetxe,gorka.labaka,e.agirre}@ehu.eus`

Abstract

Existing models of multilingual sentence embeddings require large parallel data resources which are not available for low-resource languages. We propose a novel unsupervised method to derive multilingual sentence embeddings relying only on monolingual data. We first produce a synthetic parallel corpus using unsupervised machine translation, and use it to fine-tune a pretrained cross-lingual masked language model (XLM) to derive the multilingual sentence representations. The quality of the representations is evaluated on two parallel corpus mining tasks with improvements of up to 22 F1 points over vanilla XLM. In addition, we observe that a single synthetic bilingual corpus is able to improve results for other language pairs.

1 Introduction

Parallel corpora constitute an essential training data resource for machine translation as well as other cross-lingual NLP tasks. However, large parallel corpora are only available for a handful of language pairs while the rest relies on semi-supervised or unsupervised methods for training. Since monolingual data are generally more abundant, parallel sentence mining from non-parallel corpora provides another opportunity for low-resource language pairs.

An effective approach to parallel data mining is based on multilingual sentence embeddings (Schwenk, 2018; Artetxe and Schwenk, 2019b). However, existing methods to generate cross-lingual representations are either heavily supervised or only apply to static word embeddings. An alternative approach to unsupervised multilingual training is that of Devlin et al. (2018) or Lample and Conneau (2019), who train a masked language model (M-BERT, XLM) on a concatenation of monolingual corpora in different languages to

learn a joint structure of these languages together. While several authors (Pires et al., 2019; Wu and Dredze, 2019; Karthikeyan et al., 2019; Libovický et al., 2019) bring evidence of cross-lingual transfer within the model, its internal representations are not entirely language agnostic.

We propose a method to further align representations from such models into the cross-lingual space and use them to derive sentence embeddings. Our approach is completely unsupervised and is applicable even for very distant language pairs. The proposed method outperforms previous unsupervised approaches on the BUCC 2018[1] shared task, and is even competitive with several supervised baselines.

The paper is organized as follows. Section 2 gives an overview of related work; Section 3 introduces the proposed method; Section 4 describes the experiments and reports the results. Section 5 concludes.

2 Related Work

Related research comprises supervised methods to model multilingual sentence embeddings and unsupervised methods to model multilingual word embeddings which can be aggregated into sentences. Furthermore, our approach is closely related to the recent research in cross-lingual language model (LM) pretraining.

Supervised multilingual sentence embeddings. The state-of-the-art performance in parallel data mining is achieved by LASER (Artetxe and Schwenk, 2019b) – a multilingual BiLSTM model sharing a single encoder for 93 languages trained on parallel corpora to produce language agnostic sentence representations. Similarly, Schwenk and Douze (2017); Schwenk (2018); Espana-Bonet

---

[1] 11th Workshop on Building and Using Comparable Corpora

Proceedings of the 58th Annual Meeting of the Association for Computational Linguistics: Student Research Workshop, pages 255–262
July 5 - July 10, 2020. ©2020 Association for Computational Linguistics

et al. (2017) derive sentence embeddings from internal representations of a neural machine translation system with a shared encoder. The universal sentence encoder (USE) (Cer et al., 2018; Yang et al., 2019) family covers sentence embedding models with a multi-task dual-encoder training framework including the tasks of question-answer prediction or natural language inference. Guo et al. (2018) directly optimize the cosine similarity between the source and target sentences using a bidirectional dual-encoder. These approaches rely on heavy supervision by parallel corpora which is not available for low-resource languages.

Unsupervised multilingual word embeddings. Cross-lingual embeddings of words can be obtained by post-hoc alignment of monolingual word embeddings (Mikolov et al., 2013) and mean-pooled with IDF weights to represent sentences (Litschko et al., 2019). Unsupervised techniques to find a linear mapping between embedding spaces were proposed by Artetxe et al. (2018) and Conneau et al. (2018), using iterative self-learning or adversarial training. Several recent studies (Patra et al., 2019; Ormazabal et al., 2019) criticize this simplified approach, showing that even the embedding spaces of closely related languages are not isometric. Vulić et al. (2019) question the robustness of unsupervised mapping methods in challenging circumstances.

Cross-lingual LM pretraining. Ma et al. (2019); Reimers and Gurevych (2019) derive monolingual sentence embeddings by mean-pooling contextualized word embeddings from BERT. Schuster et al. (2019); Wang et al. (2019b) propose mapping such contextualized embeddings into the multilingual space and report favorable results on the task of dependency parsing. Pires et al. (2019) extract contextualized embeddings directly from unsupervised multilingual LMs and use them for parallel sentence retrieval. Other authors improve the alignment of representations in a multilingual LM using a parallel corpus as an anchor (Cao et al., 2020) or using iterative self-learning (Wang et al., 2019a). None of these works apply multilingual embeddings to mine parallel sentences. Our work is the first in improving unsupervised cross-lingual models using additional unsupervised information.

3 Proposed Method

We propose a method to enhance the cross-lingual ability of a pretrained multilingual model by fine-tuning it on a small synthetic parallel corpus. The parallel corpus is obtained via unsupervised machine translation (MT) so the method remains unsupervised. In this section, we describe the pretrained model (Section 3.1), the fine-tuning objective (Section 3.2) and the extraction of sentence embeddings (Section 3.3). We provide details on the unsupervised MT system in Section 3.4.

3.1 XLM Pretraining

The starting point for our experiments is a cross-lingual language model (XLM) (Lample and Conneau, 2019) of the BERT family pretrained on concatenated monolingual texts in 100 languages using the masked language model (MLM) training objective (Devlin et al., 2018). The model processes the input in BPE subword units (Sennrich et al., 2016) with a shared vocabulary for all languages. In this work, we use the publicly available pretrained model XLM-100[2] (Lample and Conneau, 2019) with 16 transformer layers, 16 attention heads and a hidden unit size of 1280. The model was trained on monolingual corpora in 100 languages with the BPE vocabulary of 240k subwords.

3.2 XLM Fine-tuning with a Translation Objective

When parallel data is available, it can be leveraged in training of the multilingual language model using a translation language model loss (TLM) (Lample and Conneau, 2019). Pairs of sentences are concatenated, random tokens are masked from both sentences and the model is trained to fill in the blanks by attending to any of the words of the two sentences. The Transformer self-attention layers thus have the capacity to enrich word representations with the information about their monolingual context as well as their translation counterparts. This explicit cross-lingual training objective further enhances the alignment of the embeddings in the cross-lingual space.

We use this objective to fine-tune the pretrained model on a small synthetic parallel data set obtained via unsupervised MT for one language pair, aiming to improve the overall cross-lingual alignment of the internal representations of the model. In our experiments, we also compare the performance to fine-tuning on small authentic parallel corpora.

---

[2] `https://github.com/facebookresearch/XLM`

3.3 Sentence Embeddings

Pretrained language models produce contextual representations capturing the semantic and syntactic properties of word (subword) tokens in their variable context (Devlin et al., 2018). Contextualized embeddings can be derived from any of the internal layer outputs of the model. We tune the choice of the layer on the task of parallel sentence matching and conclude that the best cross-lingual performance is achieved at the 12th (5th-to-last) layer. Therefore, we use the representations from this layer in the rest of this paper. The evaluation across layers is summarized in Figure 1 in Section 4.6.

Aggregating subword embeddings to fixed-length sentence representations necessarily leads to an information loss. We compose sentence embeddings from subword representations by simple element-wise averaging. Even though mean-pooling is a naive approach to subword aggregation, it is often used for its simplicity (Reimers and Gurevych, 2019; Ruiter et al., 2019; Ma et al., 2019) and in our scenario it yields better results than max-pooling.

3.4 Unsupervised Machine Translation

Our unsupervised MT model follows the approach of Lample and Conneau (2019). It is a Transformer model with an encoder-decoder architecture. Both the encoder and the decoder are shared across languages and they are initialized with a pretrained bilingual LM to bootstrap the training. Both the encoder and the decoder have 6 layers, 8 attention heads and a hidden unit size of 768. The system is trained using the unsupervised MT training pipeline of denoising and back-translation (Lample et al., 2018).

4 Experiments & Results

In this section, we empirically evaluate the quality of our cross-lingual sentence embeddings and compare it with state-of-the-art supervised methods and unsupervised baselines. We evaluate the proposed method on the task of parallel corpus mining and parallel sentence matching. We fine-tune two different models using English-German and Czech-German synthetic parallel data.

4.1 Data

The XLM model was pretrained on the Wikipedia corpus of 100 languages (Lample and Conneau, 2019). The monolingual data for fine-tuning was sampled from NewsCrawl 2018 (10k Czech sentences, 10k German sentences, 10k English sentences).

Monolingual training data for the unsupervised MT models was obtained from NewsCrawl 2007-2008 (5M sentences per language). The text was cleaned and tokenized using standard Moses (Koehn et al., 2007) tools and segmented into BPE units based on 60k BPE splits.

4.2 Experiment Details

To generate synthetic data for fine-tuning, we train two unsupervised MT models (Czech-German, English-German) using the same method and parameters as in Lample and Conneau (2019) on 8 GPUs for 24 hours. We use these models to translate 10k sentences in each language. The translations are coupled with the originals into two parallel corpora of 20k synthetic sentence pairs.

The small synthetic parallel corpora obtained in the first step are used to fine-tune the pretrained XLM-100 model using the TLM objective. We measure the quality of induced cross-lingual embeddings from different layers on the task of parallel sentence matching described in Section 4.5 and observe the best results at the 12th layer after fine-tuning for one epoch with a batch size of 8 sentences and all other pretraining parameters intact. The development accuracy decreases with fine-tuning on a larger data set.

4.3 Baselines

We assess our method against two unsupervised baselines to separately measure the fine-tuning effect on the XLM model and to compare our results to another possible unsupervised approach based on post-hoc alignment of word embeddings.

Vanilla XLM. Contextualized token representations are extracted from the 12th layer of the original XLM-100[3] model and mean-pooled into sentence embeddings.

Word Mapping. We use Word2Vec embeddings with 300 dimensions pretrained on NewsCrawl and map them into the cross-lingual space using the unsupervised version of VecMap (Artetxe et al., 2018). As above, word embeddings are aggregated by mean-pooling to represent sentences.[4]

---

[3] Using M-BERT model yielded similar results to XLM.

[4] Weighting word embeddings by their sentence frequency (IDF) did not lead to a significant improvement over a simple average.

	en-de	en-fr	en-ru	en-zh	Supervision	
Leong et al. (2018)	-	-	-	56.00	bitext	0.5M sent.
Bouamor and Sajjad (2018)	-	76.00	-	-	bitext	2M sent.
Schwenk (2018)	76.90	75.80	73.80	71.60	9-way parallel	2M sent.
Azpeitia et al. (2018)	85.52	81.47	81.30	77.45	bitext	2-9M sent.
Artetxe and Schwenk (2019b)	**96.19**	**93.91**	**93.30**	**92.27**	2- or 3-way parallel	223M sent.
Unsup. baseline (Word Mapping)	32.04	32.94	17.68	20.65	none	n/a
Unsup. baseline (Vanilla XLM)*	62.10	64.77	61.65	44.79	none	n/a
Proposed method* (en↔de)	**80.06**	**78.77**	**77.16**	**67.04**	none	20k sent.**

Table 1: F1 score on the parallel sentence mining task (BUCC test set). The supervised (upper part) and unsupervised (lower part) winners are highlighted in bold. * The model was pretrained on Wikipedia. ** Synthetic translations produced by unsupervised MT.

	en-de	en-fr	en-ru	en-zh	en-kk	cs-zh	de-ru
Artetxe and Schwenk (2019b)	**90.30**	**87.38**	**94.34**	**83.92**	12.07	**73.41**	**88.39**
Unsup. baseline (Word Mapping)	28.45	30.79	17.81	16.04	2.28	10.86	19.55
Unsup. baseline (Vanilla XLM)	72.58	71.92	72.90	59.26	24.00	43.00	58.29
Proposed method (en↔de)	**79.32**	**77.05**	**80.98**	**65.49**	**35.41**	**48.79**	**65.91**

Table 2: F1 score on the parallel sentence mining task (News test set). The supervised and unsupervised winners are highlighted in bold. Artetxe and Schwenk (2019b) values obtained using the public implementation of the LASER toolkit.

4.4 Evaluation I: Parallel Corpus Mining

We measure the performance of our method on the BUCC shared task of parallel corpus mining where the system is expected to search two comparable non-aligned corpora and identify pairs of parallel sentences. We evaluate on two data sets – the original BUCC 2018 corpus created by inserting parallel sentences into monolingual texts extracted from Wikipedia (Zweigenbaum et al., 2017) and a new BUCC-like data set (News train and test) which we created by shuffling 10k parallel sentence from News Commentary into 400k monolingual sentences from News Crawl. The BUCC and News data sets are comparable in size and contain parallel sentences from the same source, but differ in overall domain.

In order to score all candidate sentence pairs, we use the margin-based approach of Artetxe and Schwenk (2019a) which was proved to eliminate the hubness problem of embedding spaces and yield superior results (Artetxe and Schwenk, 2019b). The score relies on cosine similarity to measure the distance between sentences but it is defined in relative terms to the average cosine similarity between the two sentences and their nearest neighbors. The optimal threshold for filtering the translation pairs is learned by tuning on the train set F1 scores. Tables 1 and 2 show the results of our proposed model on the BUCC and News test sets, resp., comparing them to related work and unsupervised baselines.

When comparing our method to related work, it must be noted that the XLM model was pretrained on Wikipedia and therefore has seen the monolingual BUCC sentences during training. This could result in an advantage over other systems, as the model could exploit the fact that it has seen the non-parallel part of the comparable corpus during training. However, since both the proposed method an the *vanilla XLM* baseline suffer from this, their results remain comparable. We also report results on the News test set which is free from such potential bias (Table 2).

The results reveal that TLM fine-tuning brings a substantial improvement over the initial pretrained model trained only using the MLM objective (*vanilla XLM*). In terms of the F1 score, the gain across four BUCC language pairs is 14.0-22.3 points. Even though the fine-tuning focused on a single language pair (English-German), the improvement is notable for all evaluated language pairs. The largest margin of 21.6 points is observed for the English-Chinese mining task. We observe that using a small parallel data set of authentic translation pairs instead of synthetic ones does not have a significant effect.

The weak results of the *word mapping* baseline can be partially attributed to the superiority of contextualized embeddings for representation of sentences over static ones. Furthermore, word mapping relies on the questionable assumption of isomorphic embedding spaces which weakens its performance especially for distant languages. In

	de-en	cs-en	cs-de	cs-fr	cs-ru	fr-es	fr-ru	es-ru
Artetxe and Schwenk (2019b)	98.78	99.08	99.23	99.37	98.77	99.42	98.60	98.77
Unsup. baseline (Word Mapping)	60.60	55.03	75.35	43.33	79.87	71.07	41.25	53.87
Unsup. baseline (Vanilla XLM)	87.15	79.83	82.87	80.55	85.15	91.07	85.28	85.73
Proposed method (en↔de)	**93.97**	**90.47**	90.48	**90.07**	92.23	**94.68**	**91.80**	**91.92**
Proposed method (cs↔de)	**94.43**	90.15	**90.50**	89.48	**92.33**	94.65	91.72	91.25

Table 3: Accuracy on a parallel sentence matching task (*newstest2012*) averaged over both matching directions.

our proposed model, it is possible that joint training of contextualized representations induces an embedding space with more convenient geometric properties which makes it more robust to language diversity.

Although the performance of our model generally lags far behind the supervised LASER benchmark, it is valuable because of its fully unsupervised nature and it works even for distant languages such as Chinese-Czech or English-Kazakh.

4.5 Evaluation II: Parallel Sentence Matching

To assess the effect of proposed fine-tuning on other language pairs not covered by BUCC, we evaluate our embeddings on the task of parallel sentence matching (PSM). The task entails searching a pool of shuffled parallel sentences to recover correct translation pairs. Cosine similarity is used for the nearest neighbor search.

We first evaluate the pairwise matching accuracy on a *newstest* multi-way parallel data set of 3k sentences in 6 languages.[5] We use *newstest2012* for development and *newstest2013* for testing. The results in Table 3 show that the fine-tuned model is able to match correct translations in 90-95% of cases, depending on the language pair, which is ∼7% more than *vanilla XLM*. It is notable that the model which was only fine-tuned on English-German synthetic parallel data has a positive effect on completely unrelated language pairs as well (e.g. Russian-Spanish, Czech-French).

Since the greatest appeal of parallel corpus mining is to enhance the resources for low-resource languages, we also measure the PSM accuracy on the Tatoeba (Artetxe and Schwenk, 2019b) data set of 0.5–1k sentences in over 100 languages aligned with English. Aside from the two completely unsupervised models, we fine-tune two more models on small authentic parallel data in English-Nepali (5k sentence pairs from the Flores development sets) and English-Kazakh (10k sentence pairs from

News Commentary). Table 4 confirms that the improvement over *vanilla XLM* is present for every language we evaluated, regardless on the language pair used for fine-tuning. Although we initially hypothesized that the performance of the English-German model on English-aligned language pairs would exceed the German-Czech model, their results are equal on average. Fine-tuning on small authentic corpora in low-resource languages exceeds both by a slight margin.

The results are clearly sensitive to the amount of monolingual sentences in the Wikipedia corpus used for XLM pretraining and the matching accuracy of very low-resource languages is significantly lower than we observed for high-resource languages. However, the benefits of fine-tuning are substantial (around 20 percentage points) and for some languages the results even reach the supervised baseline (e.g. Kazakh, Georgian, Nepali).

It seems that explicitly aligning one language pair during fine-tuning propagates through the shared parameters and improves the overall representation alignment, making the contextualized embeddings more language agnostic. The propagation effect could also positively influence the ability of cross-lingual transfer within the model in downstream tasks. A verification of this is left to future work.

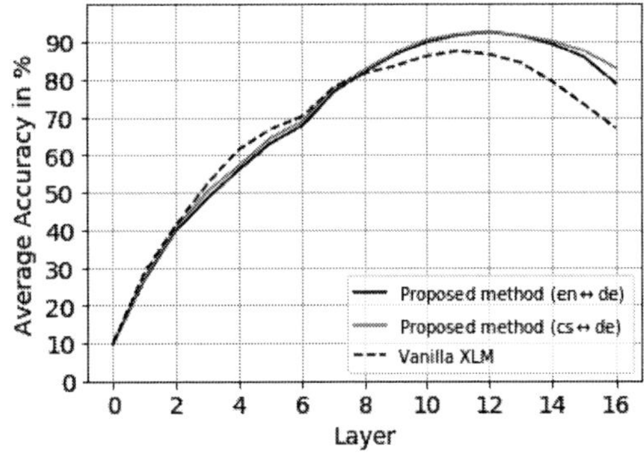

Figure 1: Average PSM accuracy on *newstest2012* before and after fine-tuning from the input embedding layer (0th) to the deepest layer (16th).

---

[5]Czech, English, French, German, Russian, Spanish

	af	ar	az	be	bg	ca	cs	de	el	eo	et	fi	fy	gl
Sup. baseline	89.5	92.0	66.0	66.2	95.0	95.9	96.5	99.0	95.0	97.2	96.7	96.3	51.7	95.5
Vanilla XLM	38.1	19.9	25.1	33.7	36.2	51.0	31.5	65.0	27.0	45.8	19.8	31.4	37.0	51.4
Proposed method:														
en↔de (synth)	57.3	41.1	46.3	58.4	56.0	66.9	53.5	83.1	51.3	68.0	39.0	47.5	48.6	66.9
cs↔de (synth)	54.2	41.2	44.2	61.8	60.7	68.9	59.9	87.3	53.1	67.4	41.4	49.5	44.8	67.3
en↔kk (auth)	58.4	45.6	51.4	60.2	59.2	72.6	53.9	87.0	54.6	72.1	43.4	51.3	51.7	72.2
en↔ne (auth)	59.9	46.6	54.2	63.1	62.9	71.0	57.6	85.0	51.0	71.2	44.6	52.7	48.6	71.0

	hi	hr	ia	is	id	ja	ka	kk	ku	la	lt	mk	ml	mn
Sup. baseline	94.7	97.2	95.2	95.6	94.5	91.8	35.9	18.6	17.2	58.5	96.2	94.7	96.9	8.2
Vanilla XLM	26.2	47.2	57.3	25.0	46.4	29.5	22.1	17.4	10.6	15.5	22.0	25.8	17.4	12.6
Proposed method:														
en↔de (synth)	53.4	68.2	71.4	43.1	64.9	54.4	41.4	33.6	16.8	24.9	43.9	48.8	51.6	29.0
cs↔de (synth)	51.7	71.8	70.5	43.7	64.1	53.3	39.8	34.7	16.2	27.7	46.2	51.1	44.3	24.5
en↔kk (auth)	60.3	71.3	79.5	45.0	66.4	59.6	44.0	46.1	20.0	28.6	46.2	54.7	54.0	32.7
en↔ne (auth)	59.3	72.1	75.7	47.1	67.8	59.6	47.8	38.4	20.9	30.0	47.7	53.8	56.0	34.9

	mr	ms	ne	nn	oc	sl	sr	sv	ta	te	tl	uk	ur	yi
Sup. baseline	91.5	96.4	20.6	88.3	61.2	95.9	95.3	96.6	69.4	79.7	50.5	94.5	81.9	5.7
Vanilla XLM	15.3	52.0	21.3	49.9	20.0	34.7	35.9	47.2	11.9	14.1	14.6	38.0	19.3	9.9
Proposed method:														
en↔de (synth)	37.3	67.0	32.8	66.8	34.3	54.9	58.6	69.7	40.9	44.7	24.0	66.1	43.7	22.1
cs↔de (synth)	34.2	65.4	31.4	67.5	35.9	59.2	64.8	71.8	31.9	37.8	20.4	70.4	43.8	22.8
en↔kk (auth)	41.9	69.8	37.3	69.2	40.3	58.0	64.3	73.3	42.8	44.0	24.4	71.6	48.2	25.8
en↔ne (auth)	43.5	72.1	42.8	69.2	36.9	58.8	65.0	72.0	41.7	53.2	26.8	71.0	49.9	26.7

Table 4: Accuracy on a parallel sentence matching task (*Tatoeba*) averaged over both matching directions (to and from English). The supervised baseline was obtained using the public implementation of the LASER model (Artetxe and Schwenk, 2019b). Our proposed models were fine-tuned on synthetic parallel data (en↔de, cs↔de) and authentic parallel data (en↔kk, en↔ne).

4.6 Analysis: Representations Across Layers

We derive sentence embeddings from all layers of the model and show PSM results on the development set averaged over all language pairs in Figure 1, both before and after fine-tuning. The accuracy differs substantially across the model depth, the best cross-lingual performance is consistently achieved around the 12th (5th-to-last) layer of the model. The TLM fine-tuning affects especially the deepest layers.

5 Conclusion

We proposed a completely unsupervised method to train multilingual sentence embeddings which can be used for building a parallel corpus with no previous translation knowledge.

We show that fine-tuning an unsupervised multilingual model with a translation objective using as little as 20k synthetic translation pairs can significantly enhance the cross-lingual alignment of its representations. Since the synthetic translations were obtained from an unsupervised MT system, the entire procedure requires no authentic parallel sentences for training.

Our sentence embeddings yield significantly better results on the tasks of parallel data mining and parallel sentence matching than our unsupervised baselines. Interestingly, targeting only one language pair during the fine-tuning phase suffices to propagate the alignment improvement to unrelated languages. It is therefore not necessary to build a working MT system for every language pair we wish to mine.

The average F1 margin across four language pairs on the BUCC task is ~17 points over the original XLM model and ~7 on the News dataset where only one of the evaluated language pairs was seen during fine-tuning. The gain in accuracy in parallel sentence matching across 8 language pairs is 7.2% absolute, lagging only 7.1% absolute behind supervised methods.

For the future we would like to apply our model on other cross-lingual NLP tasks such as XNLI or cross-lingual semantic textual similarity.

Acknowledgments

This study was supported in parts by the grants SVV 260 575, 1050119 of the Charles University Grant Agency and 19-26934X of the Czech Science Foundation, by a Facebook Fellowship, the Basque Government excellence research group (IT1343-19), the Spanish MINECO (UnsupMT TIN201791692EXP MCIU/AEI/FEDER, UE) and Project BigKnowledge (Ayudas Fundacin BBVA a equipos de investigacin cientfica 2018).

References

Mikel Artetxe, Gorka Labaka, and Eneko Agirre. 2018. A robust self-learning method for fully unsupervised cross-lingual mappings of word embeddings. In *Proceedings of the 56th Annual Meeting of the ACL*, pages 789–798, Melbourne. Association for Computational Linguistics.

Mikel Artetxe and Holger Schwenk. 2019a. Margin-based parallel corpus mining with multilingual sentence embeddings. In *Proceedings of the 57th Annual Meeting of the Association for Computational Linguistics*, Florence, Italy. Association for Computational Linguistics.

Mikel Artetxe and Holger Schwenk. 2019b. Massively multilingual sentence embeddings for zero-shot cross-lingual transfer and beyond. *Transactions of the Association for Computational Linguistics*, 7:597610.

Andoni Azpeitia, Thierry Etchegoyhen, and Eva Martnez Garcia. 2018. Extracting parallel sentences from comparable corpora with stacc variants. In *Proceedings of the Eleventh International Conference on Language Resources and Evaluation (LREC 2018)*, Paris, France. European Language Resources Association (ELRA).

Houda Bouamor and Hassan Sajjad. 2018. H2@bucc18: Parallel sentence extraction from comparable corpora using multilingual sentence embeddings. In *Proceedings of the Eleventh International Conference on Language Resources and Evaluation (LREC 2018)*, Paris, France. European Language Resources Association (ELRA).

Steven Cao, Nikita Kitaev, and Dan Klein. 2020. Multilingual alignment of contextual word representations. In *International Conference on Learning Representations (ICLR 2020)*.

Daniel Cer, Yinfei Yang, Sheng-yi Kong, Nan Hua, Nicole Limtiaco, Rhomni St. John, Noah Constant, Mario Guajardo-Cespedes, Steve Yuan, Chris Tar, Brian Strope, and Ray Kurzweil. 2018. Universal sentence encoder for English. In *Proceedings of the 2018 Conference on Empirical Methods in Natural Language Processing: System Demonstrations*, pages 169–174, Brussels, Belgium. Association for Computational Linguistics.

Alexis Conneau, Guillaume Lample, Marc'Aurelio Ranzato, Ludovic Denoyer, and Hervé Jégou. 2018. Word translation without parallel data. In *International Conference on Learning Representations (ICLR 2018)*.

Jacob Devlin, Ming-Wei Chang, Kenton Lee, and Kristina Toutanova. 2018. BERT: pre-training of deep bidirectional transformers for language understanding. *arXiv [e-Print archive]*, abs/1810.04805.

Cristina Espana-Bonet, Adam Csaba Varga, Alberto Barron-Cedeno, and Josef van Genabith. 2017. An empirical analysis of nmt-derived interlingual embeddings and their use in parallel sentence identification. *IEEE Journal of Selected Topics in Signal Processing*, 11(8):13401350.

Mandy Guo, Qinlan Shen, Yinfei Yang, Heming Ge, Daniel Cer, Gustavo Hernandez Abrego, Keith Stevens, Noah Constant, Yun-Hsuan Sung, Brian Strope, and Ray Kurzweil. 2018. Effective parallel corpus mining using bilingual sentence embeddings. In *Proceedings of the Third Conference on Machine Translation: Research Papers*, pages 165–176, Brussels, Belgium. Association for Computational Linguistics.

Kaliyaperumal Karthikeyan, Zihan Wang, Stephen Mayhew, and Dan Roth. 2019. Cross-lingual ability of multilingual BERT: An empirical study. *arXiv [e-Print archive]*, abs/1912.07840.

Philipp Koehn, Hieu Hoang, Alexandra Birch, Chris Callison-Burch, Marcello Federico, Nicola Bertoldi, Brooke Cowan, Wade Shen, Christine Moran, Richard Zens, Chris Dyer, Ondrej Bojar, Alexandra Constantin, and Evan Herbst. 2007. Moses: Open source toolkit for statistical machine translation. In *Proceedings of the 45th Annual Meeting of the ACL*, pages 177–180, Prague. Association for Computational Linguistics.

Guillaume Lample and Alexis Conneau. 2019. Cross-lingual language model pretraining. *arXiv [e-Print archive]*, abs/1901.07291.

Guillaume Lample, Ludovic Denoyer, and Marc'Aurelio Ranzato. 2018. Unsupervised machine translation using monolingual corpora only. In *International Conference on Learning Representations (ICLR 2018)*.

Chongman Leong, Derek F. Wong, and Lidia S. Chao. 2018. Um-paligner: Neural network-based parallel sentence identification model. In *Proceedings of the Eleventh International Conference on Language Resources and Evaluation (LREC 2018)*, Paris, France. European Language Resources Association (ELRA).

Jindřich Libovický, Rudolf Rosa, and Alexander M. Fraser. 2019. How language-neutral is multilingual BERT? *arXiv [e-Print archive]*, abs/1911.03310.

Robert Litschko, Goran Glavaš, Ivan Vulic, and Laura Dietz. 2019. Evaluating resource-lean cross-lingual embedding models in unsupervised retrieval. In *Proceedings of the 42nd International ACM SIGIR Conference on Research and Development in Information Retrieval*, SIGIR19, page 11091112, New York, NY, USA. Association for Computing Machinery.

Xiaofei Ma, Zhiguo Wang, Patrick Ng, Ramesh Nallapati, and Bing Xiang. 2019. Universal text representation from bert: An empirical study. *arXiv [e-Print archive]*, abs/1910.07973.

Tomas Mikolov, Quoc V. Le, and Ilya Sutskever. 2013. Exploiting similarities among languages for machine translation. *arXiv [e-Print archive]*, abs/1309.4168.

Aitor Ormazabal, Mikel Artetxe, Gorka Labaka, Aitor Soroa, and Eneko Agirre. 2019. Analyzing the limitations of cross-lingual word embedding mappings. In *Proceedings of the 57th Annual Meeting of the ACL*, pages 4990–4995, Florence. Association for Computational Linguistics.

Barun Patra, Joel Ruben Antony Moniz, Sarthak Garg, Matthew R. Gormley, and Graham Neubig. 2019. Bilingual lexicon induction with semi-supervision in non-isometric embedding spaces. In *Proceedings of the 57th Annual Meeting of the Association for Computational Linguistics*, pages 184–193, Florence, Italy. Association for Computational Linguistics.

Telmo Pires, Eva Schlinger, and Dan Garrette. 2019. How multilingual is multilingual BERT? In *Proceedings of the 57th Annual Meeting of the ACL*, pages 4996–5001, Florence. Association for Computational Linguistics.

Nils Reimers and Iryna Gurevych. 2019. Sentence-bert: Sentence embeddings using siamese bert-networks. *Proceedings of the 2019 Conference on Empirical Methods in Natural Language Processing and the 9th International Joint Conference on Natural Language Processing (EMNLP-IJCNLP)*.

Dana Ruiter, Cristina España-Bonet, and Josef van Genabith. 2019. Self-supervised neural machine translation. In *Proceedings of the 57th Annual Meeting of the Association for Computational Linguistics*, pages 1828–1834, Florence, Italy. Association for Computational Linguistics.

Tal Schuster, Ori Ram, Regina Barzilay, and Amir Globerson. 2019. Cross-lingual alignment of contextual word embeddings, with applications to zero-shot dependency parsing. *Proceedings of the 2019 Conference of the North American Chapter of the ACL*.

Holger Schwenk. 2018. Filtering and mining parallel data in a joint multilingual space. In *Proceedings of the 56th Annual Meeting of the Association for Computational Linguistics (Volume 2: Short Papers)*, pages 228–234, Melbourne, Australia. Association for Computational Linguistics.

Holger Schwenk and Matthijs Douze. 2017. Learning joint multilingual sentence representations with neural machine translation. In *Proceedings of the 2nd Workshop on Representation Learning for NLP*, pages 157–167, Vancouver, Canada. Association for Computational Linguistics.

Rico Sennrich, Barry Haddow, and Alexandra Birch. 2016. Neural machine translation of rare words with subword units. In *Proceedings of the 54th Annual Meeting of the Association for Computational Linguistics*, pages 1715–1725, Berlin. Association for Computational Linguistics.

Ivan Vulić, Goran Glavaš, Roi Reichart, and Anna Korhonen. 2019. Do we really need fully unsupervised cross-lingual embeddings? In *Proceedings of the 2019 Conference on Empirical Methods in Natural Language Processing and the 9th International Joint Conference on Natural Language Processing (EMNLP-IJCNLP)*, pages 4407–4418, Hong Kong, China. Association for Computational Linguistics.

Shuai Wang, Lei Hou, Juanzi Li, Meihan Tong, and Jiabo Jiang. 2019a. Learning multilingual sentence embeddings from monolingual corpus. In *Chinese Computational Linguistics*, pages 346–357.

Yuxuan Wang, Wanxiang Che, Jiang Guo, Yijia Liu, and Ting Liu. 2019b. Cross-lingual BERT transformation for zero-shot dependency parsing. In *Proceedings of the 2019 Conference on Empirical Methods in Natural Language Processing and the 9th International Joint Conference on Natural Language Processing (EMNLP-IJCNLP)*, pages 5720–5726, Hong Kong, China. Association for Computational Linguistics.

Shijie Wu and Mark Dredze. 2019. Beto, bentz, becas: The surprising cross-lingual effectiveness of BERT. In *Proceedings of the 2019 Conference on Empirical Methods in Natural Language Processing and the 9th International Joint Conference on Natural Language Processing (EMNLP-IJCNLP)*, pages 833–844, Hong Kong, China. Association for Computational Linguistics.

Yinfei Yang, Daniel Cer, Amin Ahmad, Mandy Guo, Jax Law, Noah Constant, Gustavo Hernandez Abrego, Steve Yuan, Chris Tar, Yun-Hsuan Sung, Brian Strope, and Ray Kurzweil. 2019. Multilingual universal sentence encoder for semantic retrieval. *arXiv [e-Print archive]*, abs/1907.04307.

Pierre Zweigenbaum, Serge Sharoff, and Reinhard Rapp. 2017. Overview of the second BUCC shared task: Spotting parallel sentences in comparable corpora. In *Proceedings of the 10th Workshop on Building and Using Comparable Corpora*, pages 60–67, Vancouver, Canada. Association for Computational Linguistics.

Logical Inferences with Comparatives and Generalized Quantifiers

Izumi Haruta[1]

`haruta.izumi@is.ocha.ac.jp`

Koji Mineshima[2]   **Daisuke Bekki**[1]

`minesima@abelard.flet.keio.ac.jp`   `bekki@is.ocha.ac.jp`

[1]Ochanomizu University, Tokyo, Japan
[2]Keio University, Tokyo, Japan

Abstract

Comparative constructions pose a challenge in Natural Language Inference (NLI), which is the task of determining whether a text entails a hypothesis. Comparatives are structurally complex in that they interact with other linguistic phenomena such as quantifiers, numerals, and lexical antonyms. In formal semantics, there is a rich body of work on comparatives and gradable expressions using the notion of degree. However, a logical inference system for comparatives has not been sufficiently developed for use in the NLI task. In this paper, we present a compositional semantics that maps various comparative constructions in English to semantic representations via Combinatory Categorial Grammar (CCG) parsers and combine it with an inference system based on automated theorem proving. We evaluate our system on three NLI datasets that contain complex logical inferences with comparatives, generalized quantifiers, and numerals. We show that the system outperforms previous logic-based systems as well as recent deep learning-based models.

1   Introduction

Natural Language Inference (NLI), or Recognizing Textual Entailment (RTE), is the task of determining whether a text entails a hypothesis and has been actively studied as one of the crucial tasks in natural language understanding. In recent years, systems based on deep learning (DL) have been developed by crowdsourcing large datasets such as Stanford Natural Language Inference (SNLI) (Bowman et al., 2015) and Multi-Genre Natural Language Inference (MultiNLI) (Williams et al., 2018) and have achieved high accuracy. NLI datasets focusing on complex linguistic phenomena, such as negation, antonyms, and numerals, have also been developed (Naik et al., 2018).

However, it has been pointed out that these datasets contain various biases that can be exploited by DL models (Dasgupta et al., 2018; McCoy et al., 2019), including easily classifying numerical expressions in inference (Liu et al., 2019) and answering by only looking at a hypothesis (Gururangan et al., 2018). This suggests that the success of NLI models to date has been overestimated and that tasks remain unresolved.

To handle inferences involving various linguistic phenomena, there are also studies to probe the effects of additional training using artificially constructed data (Dasgupta et al., 2018; Richardson et al., 2020). However, in the case of structurally complex inferences involving comparisons and numerical expressions, there is a myriad of ways to combine possible inference patterns. For example, consider the following inference.

(1) P_1:   John is taller than 6 feet.

     P_2:   Bob is shorter than 5 feet.

     H: Bob is not taller than John. (Yes)

To correctly derive H from P_1 and P_2, it is necessary to capture the predicate-argument structures of the sentences, antonyms (*tall*, *short*), numerical expressions, and negation. Note that if the hypothesis sentence H is changed to *John is not taller than Bob*, the correct answer is not an entailment (Yes) but rather a contradiction (No); even if numerical expressions are excluded, the number of combinations of sentence patterns that produces this kind of reasonable inference is enormous.

In another approach, unsupervised NLI systems based on various logics have been studied (Bos, 2008; MacCartney and Manning, 2008; Mineshima et al., 2015; Abzianidze, 2016). However, the accuracies of these systems on comparative constructions are relatively low (see Section 3). Although there have been detailed discussions in formal semantics taking into account the

Proceedings of the 58th Annual Meeting of the Association for Computational Linguistics: Student Research Workshop, pages 263–270
July 5 - July 10, 2020. ©2020 Association for Computational Linguistics

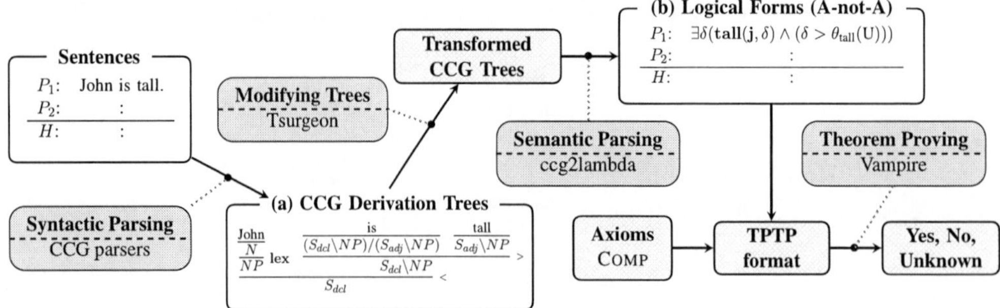

Figure 1: Overview of the proposed method. The premises and hypothesis are mapped to logical forms based on A-not-A analysis via CCG parsing and tree transformation; then a theorem prover judges *yes*, *no*, or *unknown* with the axioms for comparatives.

complexity associated with adjectives and comparative expressions (Cresswell, 1976; Kennedy, 1997; Heim, 2000; Lassiter, 2017), such theories have not yet been implemented in NLI systems. Also, some logic-based NLI systems handle comparatives (Chatzikyriakidis and Bernardy, 2019; Haruta et al., 2019), but these systems do not implement a parser and/or a prover.

The goal of this study is to fill this gap by implementing a formal compositional semantics based on the so-called A-not-A analysis (Seuren, 1973; Klein, 1980, 1982; Schwarzschild, 2008), which maps various comparative constructions in English to logical forms (LFs) via CCG (Steedman, 2000) derivation trees. Based on this, we present an inference system that computes complex logical inference over comparatives, generalized quantifiers, and numerals.[1] For evaluation, we use the FraCaS test set (Cooper et al., 1994), which contains various linguistically challenging inferences, and the Monotonicity Entailment Dataset (MED) (Yanaka et al., 2019), which contains inferences with generalized quantifiers. We also construct a new test set, the Comparative and Adjective Dataset (CAD), which extends FraCaS and collects both single-premise and multi-premise inferences with comparatives. The experiments show that our system outperforms previous logic-based systems as well as recent DL models.

2 System overview

Figure 1 shows the pipeline of the proposed system. First, the input sentences are a set of premises $P_1, \ldots, P_n$ and a hypothesis H. Next, the CCG derivation trees are obtained using CCG parsers.

Derivation trees are modified to derive appropriate LFs based on A-not-A analysis. We use the semantic parsing system ccg2lambda (Martínez-Gómez et al., 2016) based on λ-calculus to obtain LFs, which are then converted to the Typed First-order Form (TFF) of the Thousands of Problems for Theorem Provers (TPTP) format (Sutcliffe, 2017), that is, a formal expression in first-order logic with equality and arithmetic operations. Finally, together with the axiom system COMP (Haruta et al., 2019) for comparatives and numerical expressions, a theorem prover checks whether $P_1 \wedge \cdots \wedge P_n \rightarrow H$ holds or not. The system output is *yes* (entailment), *no* (contradiction), or *unknown* (neutral).

2.1 Degree semantics: A-not-A analysis

In formal semantics, comparative and other gradable expressions are usually analyzed using the notion of *degree* (Cresswell, 1976).

(2) a. Ann is *taller* than Bob.

b. John is *5 feet tall*.

c. John is *tall*.

For example, the sentence (2a), in which the comparative form *taller* of the gradable adjective *tall* is used, compares the degree of height between two persons. (2b) is an expression that includes a specific height, which is the numerical expression *5 feet*. (2c) is a sentence using the positive form of the adjective, which can be regarded as representing a comparison with some implicit standard value. In degree-based semantics, such gradable adjectives are treated as two-place predicates that have entity and degree (Cresswell, 1976). For instance, (2b) is analyzed as $\mathbf{tall}(\mathbf{john}, \mathbf{5\ feet})$,

---

Pattern	Example	Type	LF
(i)	1. John is tall.	Positive	$\exists\delta(\mathbf{tall}(\mathbf{john},\delta) \wedge (\delta > \theta_{\mathrm{tall}}(\mathrm{U})))$
	2. John is taller than Bob.	Increasing	$\exists\delta\,(\mathbf{tall}(\mathbf{john},\delta) \wedge \neg\,\mathbf{tall}(\mathbf{bob},\delta))$
	3. Ann has more children than Bob.	Numerical	$\exists\delta(\exists x(\mathbf{child}(x) \wedge \mathbf{have}(\mathbf{ann},x) \wedge \mathbf{many}(x,\delta))$
			$\wedge\neg\exists x(\mathbf{child}(x) \wedge \mathbf{have}(\mathbf{bob},x) \wedge \mathbf{many}(x,\delta)))$
(ii)	1. John is as tall as Bob.	Equatives	$\forall\delta(\mathbf{tall}(\mathbf{bob},\delta) \to \mathbf{tall}(\mathbf{john},\delta))$
	2. Mary is 2 inches taller than Harry.	Differential	$\forall\delta(\mathbf{tall}(\mathbf{harry},\delta - 2'') \to \mathbf{tall}(\mathbf{mary},\delta))$
	3. John ate 3 more cookies than Bob.	Measure	$\forall\delta(\exists x(\mathbf{cookie}(x) \wedge \mathbf{eat}(\mathbf{bob},x) \wedge \mathbf{many}(x,\delta - 3))$
			$\to \exists x(\mathbf{cookie}(x) \wedge \mathbf{eat}(\mathbf{john},x) \wedge \mathbf{many}(x,\delta)))$

Table 1: Semantic representation of comparative constructions based on A-not-A analysis

where $\mathbf{tall}(x,\delta)$ is read as "x is *at least* as tall as degree δ" (Klein, 1991).

We use A-not-A analysis of comparatives, which analyzes (3a) as (3b).

(3)   a. Ann is taller than Bob is.

     b. $\exists\delta\,(\mathbf{tall}(\mathbf{ann},\delta) \wedge \neg\,\mathbf{tall}(\mathbf{bob},\delta))$

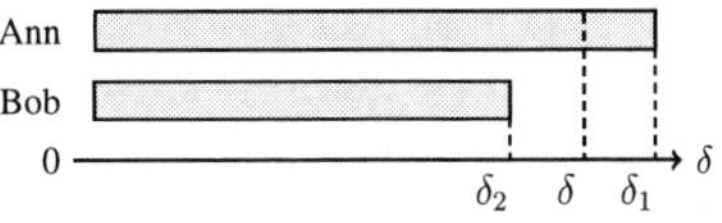

According to this analysis, (3a) is interpreted as saying that there exists a degree δ of height that Ann satisfies, but Bob does not. As shown in the figure in (3), this guarantees that Ann's height is greater than Bob's height. A-not-A analysis makes it possible to derive entailment relations between various comparative constructions in a simple way using first-order logic theorem provers.

Table 1 shows LFs for some example sentences using A-not-A analysis.[2] Here, LFs can be divided into two patterns. The examples in (i) in Figure 1 belong to the first type, where the degree of an individual **exceeds** a certain degree. For example, the sentence (i-2) means that the height of John is greater than the height of Bob. The sentence (i-3) means that the number of Ann's children exceeds the number of Bob's children. Under our analysis, this type of sentence is mapped to formulas of the form $\exists\delta(\cdots \wedge \cdots)$.

The second type includes the examples in (ii), which say that the degree of an individual is **greater than or equal to** a certain degree. For example, (ii-1) means that John's height is greater than or equal to Bob's height (Klein, 1982). The

sentence (ii-3) means that the number of cookies John ate is 3 or more greater than the number of cookies that Bob ate; in other words, if Bob ate n cookies, then John ate at least $n + 3$ cookies. Sentences of type (ii) are mapped to formulas of the form $\forall\delta(\cdots \to \cdots)$, as in Table 1.

2.2   Compositional semantics in CCG

In CCG, the mapping from syntax to semantics is defined by assigning syntactic categories to words (Steedman, 2000); the LF of a sentence is then compositionally derived using λ-calculus. However, there is a gap between the syntactic structures assumed in formal semantics and the output derivation trees of existing CCG parsers, i.e., statistical parsers trained on CCG-Bank (Hockenmaier and Steedman, 2007). For this reason, we modify the derivation trees provided by CCG parsers in post-processing. There are several types of modifications.

Syntactic features The first modification is to add syntactic features to CCG categories. For example, in the default CCG trees, a nominal adjective (*a tall boy*) has the category N/N, while a predicate adjective (*John is tall*) has the category $S_{adj}\backslash NP$. To provide a uniform degree semantics to both constructions, we rewrite N/N as N_{adj}/N for the category of nominal adjectives.

Multiword expressions Compound expressions for comparatives and quantifiers are combined as one word, such as *a few, a lot of*, and *at most*.

Empty categories We insert an empty category to systematically derive the LFs of the two patterns described in Table 1. The distinction between patterns (i) and (ii) can be controlled by an expression appearing in the adjunct position of an adjective phrase, for example, a degree modifier such as *very* or a numerical expression such as *2 cm*.

---

[2]For the positive form, the comparison class (Klein, 1982) is relevant to determining the standard of degree (e.g., tallness). We use a default comparison class such as θ_{tall} in our implementation and leave the determination of comparison classes and relevant standards (cf. Pezzelle and Fernández, 2019) to future work.

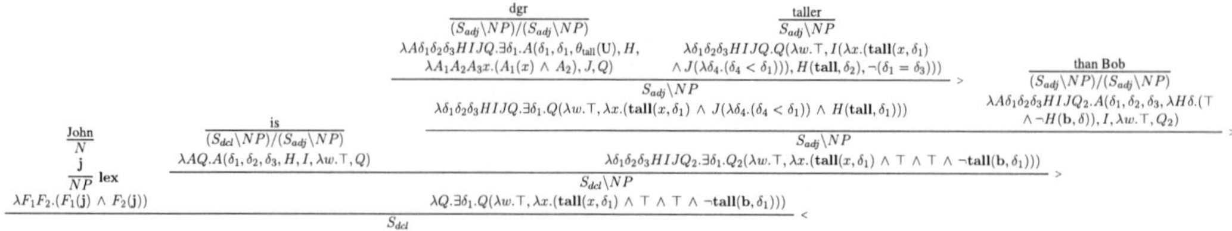

Figure 2: Derivation tree of *John is (dgr) taller than Bob*.

Example	LF
Mary has *many* dogs.	$\exists x(\mathbf{have}(\mathbf{mary}, x) \wedge \mathbf{dog}(x) \wedge \mathbf{many}(x, \theta_{\mathrm{many}}(x)))$
Ann read *two* books.	$\exists x(\mathbf{read}(\mathbf{ann}, x) \wedge \mathbf{book}(x) \wedge \mathbf{many}(x, 2))$
Most apples are red.	$\exists \delta(\exists x(\mathbf{apple}(x) \wedge \mathbf{red}(x) \wedge \mathbf{many}(x, \delta)) \wedge \neg\exists x(\mathbf{apple}(x) \wedge \neg\mathbf{red}(x) \wedge \mathbf{many}(x, \delta)))$
No more than five boys ran.	$\neg\exists x\exists\delta(\mathbf{boy}(x) \wedge \mathbf{many}(x, \delta) \wedge (5 < \delta) \wedge \mathbf{run}(x))$

Table 2: LFs of generalized quantifiers based on our degree semantics

When such an adjunct expression does not appear, we insert an empty category *dgr* into the adjunct position, which is used to derive the desired LF compositionally. Figure 2 shows an example of a modified derivation tree containing an empty element *dgr* for increasing comparatives. Similarly, we use two other types of empty categories for equatives (e.g., *as tall as*) and the positive form.

2.3 Generalized quantifiers

The analysis of comparatives by the degree-based semantics described above can naturally be extended to generalized quantifiers. In the traditional analysis (Barwise and Cooper, 1981), generalized quantifiers such as *many, few, more than*, and *most* are analyzed as denoting a relation between sets. Alternatively, an analysis based on degree semantics has been developed, which represents expressions such as *many* and *few* as adjectives (Partee, 1988; Rett, 2018) and *most* as the superlative form of *many* (Hackl, 2000; Szabolcsi, 2010). We recast this alternative analysis in our degree-based semantics. Table 2 shows the LFs for some examples. We use the binary predicate $\mathbf{many}(x, n)$, which reads "x is composed of (at least) n entities". *Most A are B* is analyzed as meaning "More than half of A is B", following the standard truth-condition (Hackl, 2000).

3 Experiments

3.1 Experimental settings

For CCG parsing, we use two CCG parsers, namely, C&C (Clark and Curran, 2007) and depccg (Yoshikawa et al., 2017), to mitigate parsing errors. If two parsers output a different answer, we choose the system answer in the following way: if one answer is *yes* (resp. *no*) and the other is *unknown*, the system answer is *yes* (resp. *no*); if one answer is *yes* and the other is *no*, then the system answer is *unknown*. For POS tagging, we use the C&C POS tagger for C&C and spaCy[3] for depccg.

To implement compositional semantics, we use ccg2lambda[4]. We extend the semantic templates proposed in Mineshima et al. (2015) to handle linguistic phenomena based on degree-based semantics. The total number of lexical entries assigned to CCG categories is 106, and the number of entries directly assigned to particular words (e.g., *than* and *as* for comparatives and items for quantifiers) is 214. For tree transformation, we use Tsurgeon (Levy and Andrew, 2006). We use 74 entries (rewriting clauses) in the Tsurgeon script. For theorem proving, we use Vampire[5], which accepts TFF forms with arithmetic operations.

For evaluation, we use three datasets. First, FraCaS (Cooper et al., 1994) is a dataset comprising nine sections, each of which contains semantically challenging inferences related to various linguistic phenomena. In this study, we use three sections: Generalized Quantifiers (GQ; 73 problems), Adjectives (ADJ; 22 problems), and Comparatives (COM; 31 problems). The distribution of gold answer labels for the three sections is (*yes/no/unknown*) = (36/5/32), (9/6/7), (19/9/3), respectively.

Second, MED[6] is a dataset that contains in-

---

[3] https://github.com/explosion/spaCy
[4] https://github.com/mynlp/ccg2lambda
[5] https://github.com/vprover/vampire
[6] https://github.com/verypluming/MED

FraCaS-235 (COMPARATIVES) Gold answer: Yes	
Premise 1	ITEL won more orders than APCOM.
Premise 2	APCOM won ten orders.
Hypothesis	ITEL won at least eleven orders.

MED-1085 Gold answer: Unknown	
Premise 1	No more than fifty campers have caught a cold.
Hypothesis	No more than fifty campers have had a sunburn or caught a cold.

CAD-011 (COMPARATIVES) Gold answer: Yes	
Premise 1	Alex is not as tall as Chris is.
Hypothesis	Chris is taller than Alex is.

CAD-034 (ADJECTIVES) Gold answer: Yes	
Premise 1	Bob is 4 feet tall.
Premise 2	John is taller than Bob.
Hypothesis	John is more than 4 feet tall.

Table 3: Examples of entailment problems from the FraCaS, MED, and CAD test sets

FraCaS				
Section		GQ	ADJ	COM
#All		73	22	31
#Single		44	15	16
Majority		.48	.39	.61
Logic	MN	.77	.68	.48
	LP	.93	.73	-
	NL	.98*	.80*	.81*
	Ours	.92	.86	.77
	+rule	**.95**	**.95**	**.84**
DL	LSTM	.64*	.47*	.56*
	DA	.59	.45	.61
	BERT	.64	.45	.58

Table 4: Accuracy on the FraCaS test suite: '#All' shows the number of all problems and '#Single' the number of single-premise problems.

ferences with quantifiers (so-called monotonicity inferences). We use a subset (498 problems) of MED that does not require world knowledge and commonsense reasoning; these problems were collected from various linguistics papers. The distribution of the gold answer is (*yes*/*unknown*) = (215/283).

Because there are only 31 problems for comparatives in FraCaS, we created the CAD test set consisting of 105 problems, which focuses on comparatives and numerical constructions not covered by FraCaS. We collected a set of inferences (9 problems) from a linguistics paper (Klein, 1982) and created more problems by adding negation, using degree modifiers (e.g., *very*), changing numerical expressions, replacing positive and negative adjectives (e.g., *large* to *small*), and swapping the premise and hypothesis of an inference. Of the 105 problems 50 are single-premise problems, and 55 are multi-premise problems. The distribution of gold answer labels is (*yes*/*no*/*unknown*) = (50/17/38). All of the gold labels were checked by an expert in linguistics. Table 3 shows some example problems.

3.2 Results and discussion

FraCaS test suite   Table 4 shows the experimental results on FraCaS. *Majority* is the accuracy of the majority baseline and *Ours* the accuracy of our system. Some errors were caused by failing to assign correct POS tags and lemmas to comparatives; for example, *cleverer* is wrongly assigned *NN* rather than *JJR* (FraCaS-217). To estimate the upper bound of the accuracy of our system by reducing error propagation, we added hand-coded rules to assign correct POS tags and lemmas (14 words). We also added two rules to join multi-word expressions to derive correct logical forms (*law lecturer* and *legal authority* for FraCaS-214, 215). In Table 4, *+rule* shows the improvement in accuracy realized by adding these rules.

We compare our system with previous logic-based NLI systems as well as three popular DL models. For logic-based systems, we use MN (Mineshima et al., 2015) and LP (Abzianidze, 2016) based on CCG parsers and theorem proving and NL (MacCartney and Manning, 2008) based on Natural Logic. NL is evaluated on single-premise problems only (indicated by *). Our system accepts both single-premise and multiple-premise problems and outperforms the previous logic-based systems on the adjectives and comparatives sections. Our system solves complex reasoning problems with multiple premises involving comparatives and numerical expressions, such as FraCaS-235 in Table 3, for which the previous systems were unable to give a correct answer.

For DL models, LSTM is the performance of a long short-term memory model trained on SNLI, which is reported in Bowman (2016) (only evaluated on single-premise problems). We also tested the Decomposable Attention (DA) model (Parikh et al., 2016), a simple attention-based model trained on SNLI. We used the implementation provided in AllenNLP (Gardner et al., 2018). Finally, BERT is the performance of a BERT model (Devlin et al., 2019). We used the `bert-base-cased` model fine-tuned with MultiNLI. We used the code available at the orig-

MED	
#All	498
Majority	.60
BERT+	.54
BERT	.56
Ours	**.84**

CAD	
#All	105
Majority	.48
DA	.51
BERT	.55
Ours	**.77**

Table 5: Accuracy on the MED and CAD datasets

inal GitHub repository.[7] Our system outperforms the three DL models by large margins.[8]

MED and CAD datasets Table 5 shows the results on MED and CAD. For MED, we compared our system with a BERT model fine-tuned with MultiNLI (**BERT**) and a BERT model with data augmentation (approximately 36K) in addition to MultiNLI (**BERT+**), both being tested in Yanaka et al. (2019). For CAD, we evaluated DA and BERT. The results show that our system achieved high accuracy on the logical inferences with adjectives, comparatives, and generalized quantifiers.

Table 6 shows examples that were solved by our system but not by DA and BERT. The DL models were particularly difficult to handle inferences related to antonyms (e.g., FraCaS-209) and numerical expressions (e.g., CAD-001). Indeed, the results on the DL models were predictable because these models were trained on datasets (SNLI and MultiNLI) that do not target the logical and numerical inferences we are concerned with in this study. However, it is fair to say that it is very challenging to generate effective training data to handle various complex inferences with comparatives, numerals, and generalized quantifiers.

There were some problems that our system could not solve. For FraCaS, the accuracy for the comparative section (COM) was relatively low (.84). This is because this section contains linguistically challenging phenomena such as clausal comparatives (FraCaS-239, 240, 241) and attributive comparatives (FraCaS-244, 245). For MED, the present system does not handle downward monotonic quantifiers (e.g., *less than*), non-monotonic quantifiers (e.g., *exactly*), and negative

---

FraCaS-209 (ADJECTIVES) Gold answer: No	
Premise 1	Mickey is a small animal.
Premise 2	Dumbo is a large animal.
Hypothesis	Mickey is larger than Dumbo.

MED-1021 Gold answer: Unknown	
Premise 1	More than five campers have had a sunburn or caught a cold.
Hypothesis	More than five campers have caught a cold.

CAD-001 Gold answer: Yes	
Premise 1	John is 5 cm taller than Bob.
Premise 2	Bob is 170 cm tall.
Hypothesis	John is 175 cm tall.

CAD-103 Gold answer: Unknown	
Premise 1	Bob is not tall.
Premise 2	John is not tall.
Hypothesis	John is taller than Bob.

Table 6: Examples of problems solved by our system but not by the DL models. The answers of the DL models are: *yes* (DA and BERT) for FraCaS-209; *yes* (**BERT** and **BERT+**) for MED-1021; *no* (DA and BERT) for CAD-001; *yes* (DA) and *no* (BERT) for CAD-103.

polarity items (e.g., *any*). Furthermore, the system needs to be extended to deal with linguistic phenomena such as comparative subdeletion and quantified comparatives that appear in CAD. To address these problems, further improvement of the CCG parsers will be needed.

4 Conclusion

In this study, we presented an end-to-end logic-based inference system for handling complex inferences with comparatives, quantifiers, and numerals. The entire system is transparently composed of several modules and can solve complex inferences for the right reason. In future work, we will extend our analysis to cover the more complex constructions mentioned in Section 3. We are also considering combining our system with an abduction mechanism that uses large knowledge bases (Yoshikawa et al., 2019) for handling commonsense reasoning with external knowledge.

Acknowledgments We are grateful to Hitomi Yanaka for sharing the detailed results on the MED dataset and Masashi Yoshikawa for continuous support. We also thank the three anonymous reviewers for their helpful comments and feedback. This work was supported by JSPS KAKENHI Grant Number JP18H03284.

---

[7]https://github.com/google-research/bert

[8]For DA and BERT, we evaluated multiple-premise problems by two methods: simply concatenating two or more premises (e.g., "S_1. S_2.") and by inserting *and* and commas between sentences (e.g., "S_1 *and* S_2."). Comparing the two methods, we used the better accuracy for each problem in MED and CAD in Table 4 and 5.

References

Lasha Abzianidze. 2016. Natural solution to FraCaS entailment problems. In *Proceedings of the Fifth Joint Conference on Lexical and Computational Semantics (*SEM)*, pages 64–74.

John Barwise and Robin Cooper. 1981. Generalized quantifiers and natural language. *Linguistics and Philosophy*, 4(2):159–219.

Johan Bos. 2008. Wide-coverage semantic analysis with Boxer. In *Proceedings of the 2008 Conference on Semantics in Text Processing (STEP)*, pages 277–286.

Samuel R. Bowman. 2016. *Modeling Natural Language Semantics in Learned Representations*. Ph.D. thesis, Stanford University.

Samuel R. Bowman, Gabor Angeli, Christopher Potts, and Christopher D. Manning. 2015. A large annotated corpus for learning natural language inference. In *Proceedings of the 2015 Conference on Empirical Methods in Natural Language Processing (EMNLP)*, pages 632–642.

Stergios Chatzikyriakidis and Jean-Philippe Bernardy. 2019. A wide-coverage symbolic natural language inference system. In *Proceedings of the 22nd Nordic Conference on Computational Linguistics (NoDaLiDa)*, pages 298–303.

Stephen Clark and James R Curran. 2007. Wide-coverage efficient statistical parsing with CCG and log-linear models. *Computational Linguistics*, 33(4):493–552.

Robin Cooper, Richard Crouch, Jan van Eijck, Chris Fox, Josef van Genabith, Jan Jaspers, Hans Kamp, Manfred Pinkal, Massimo Poesio, Stephen Pulman, et al. 1994. FraCaS–a framework for computational semantics. *Deliverable*, D6.

Max J Cresswell. 1976. The semantics of degree. In Barbara Partee, editor, *Montague Grammar*, pages 261–292. Academic Press.

Ishita Dasgupta, Demi Guo, Andreas Stuhlmüller, Samuel J. Gershman, and Noah D. Goodman. 2018. Evaluating compositionality in sentence embeddings. In *Proceedings of the 40th Annual Conference of the Cognitive Science Society*, pages 1596–1601.

Jacob Devlin, Ming-Wei Chang, Kenton Lee, and Kristina Toutanova. 2019. BERT: Pre-training of deep bidirectional transformers for language understanding. In *Proceedings of the 2019 Conference of the North American Chapter of the Association for Computational Linguistics (NAACL-HLT)*, pages 4171–4186.

Matt Gardner, Joel Grus, Mark Neumann, Oyvind Tafjord, Pradeep Dasigi, Nelson F. Liu, Matthew Peters, Michael Schmitz, and Luke Zettlemoyer. 2018. Allennlp: A deep semantic natural language processing platform. In *Proceedings of Workshop for NLP Open Source Software (NLP-OSS)*, pages 1–6.

Suchin Gururangan, Swabha Swayamdipta, Omer Levy, Roy Schwartz, Samuel Bowman, and Noah A. Smith. 2018. Annotation artifacts in natural language inference data. In *Proceedings of the 2018 Conference of the North American Chapter of the Association for Computational Linguistics: Human Language Technologies (NAACL-HLT)*, pages 107–112.

Martin Hackl. 2000. *Comparative Quantifiers*. Ph.D. thesis, Massachusetts Institute of Technology.

Izumi Haruta, Koji Mineshima, and Daisuke Bekki. 2019. A CCG-based compositional semantics and inference system for comparatives. In *Proceedings of 33rd Pacific Asia Conference on Language, Information and Computation (PACLIC 33)*, pages 67–76.

Irene Heim. 2000. Degree operators and scope. In *Proceedings of the 10th Semantics and Linguistic Theory (SALT 10)*, pages 40–64.

Julia Hockenmaier and Mark Steedman. 2007. CCGbank: A corpus of CCG derivations and dependency structures extracted from the Penn Treebank. *Computational Linguistics*, 33(3):355–396.

Christopher Kennedy. 1997. *Projecting the Adjective: The Syntax and Semantics of Gradability and Comparison*. Ph.D. thesis, University of California, Santa Cruz.

Ewan Klein. 1980. A semantics for positive and comparative adjectives. *Linguistics and Philosophy*, 4(1):1–45.

Ewan Klein. 1982. The interpretation of adjectival comparatives. *Journal of Linguistics*, 18(1):113–136.

Ewan Klein. 1991. Comparatives. In Arnim von Stechow and Dieter Wunderlich, editors, *Semantics: An International Handbook of Contemporary Research*, pages 673–691. de Gruyter, Berlin.

Daniel Lassiter. 2017. *Graded Modality: Qualitative and Quantitative Perspectives*. Oxford University Press.

Roger Levy and Galen Andrew. 2006. Tregex and Tsurgeon: tools for querying and manipulating tree data structures. In *Proceedings of the Fifth International Conference on Language Resources and Evaluation (LREC'06)*, pages 2231–2234.

Nelson F. Liu, Roy Schwartz, and Noah A. Smith. 2019. Inoculation by fine-tuning: A method for analyzing challenge datasets. In *Proceedings of the 2019 Conference of the North American Chapter of the Association for Computational Linguistics: Human Language Technologies (NAACL-HLT)*, pages 2171–2179.

Bill MacCartney and Christopher D. Manning. 2008. Modeling semantic containment and exclusion in natural language inference. In *Proceedings of the 22nd International Conference on Computational Linguistics (COLING)*, pages 521–528.

Pascual Martínez-Gómez, Koji Mineshima, Yusuke Miyao, and Daisuke Bekki. 2016. ccg2lambda: A compositional semantics system. In *Proceedings of ACL-2016 System Demonstrations*, pages 85–90.

Tom McCoy, Ellie Pavlick, and Tal Linzen. 2019. Right for the wrong reasons: Diagnosing syntactic heuristics in natural language inference. In *Proceedings of the 57th Annual Meeting of the Association for Computational Linguistics (ACL)*, pages 3428–3448.

Koji Mineshima, Pascual Martínez-Gómez, Yusuke Miyao, and Daisuke Bekki. 2015. Higher-order logical inference with compositional semantics. In *Proceedings of the 2015 Conference on Empirical Methods in Natural Language Processing (EMNLP)*, pages 2055–2061.

Aakanksha Naik, Abhilasha Ravichander, Norman Sadeh, Carolyn Rose, and Graham Neubig. 2018. Stress test evaluation for natural language inference. In *Proceedings of the 27th International Conference on Computational Linguistics (COLING)*, pages 2340–2353.

Ankur Parikh, Oscar Täckström, Dipanjan Das, and Jakob Uszkoreit. 2016. A decomposable attention model for natural language inference. In *Proceedings of the 2016 Conference on Empirical Methods in Natural Language Processing (EMNLP)*, pages 2249–2255.

Barbara H. Partee. 1988. Many quantifiers. In *Proceedings of the 5th Eastern States Conference on Linguistics (ESCOL)*, pages 383–402.

Sandro Pezzelle and Raquel Fernández. 2019. Is the red square big? MALeViC: Modeling adjectives leveraging visual contexts. In *Proceedings of the 2019 Conference on Empirical Methods in Natural Language Processing and the 9th International Joint Conference on Natural Language Processing (EMNLP-IJCNLP)*, pages 2865–2876.

Jessica Rett. 2018. The semantics of *many, much, few, and little*. *Language and Linguistics Compass*, 12(1).

Kyle Richardson, Hai Hu, Lawrence S Moss, and Ashish Sabharwal. 2020. Probing natural language inference models through semantic fragments. In *Proceedings of the AAAI Conference on Artificial Intelligence*.

Roger Schwarzschild. 2008. The semantics of comparatives and other degree constructions. *Language and Linguistics Compass*, 2(2):308–331.

Pieter A. M. Seuren. 1973. The comparative. In F. Kiefer and N. Ruwet, editors, *Generative Grammar in Europe*, pages 528–564. Riedel, Dordrecht.

Mark Steedman. 2000. *The Syntactic Process*. The MIT Press.

Geoff Sutcliffe. 2017. The TPTP Problem Library and Associated Infrastructure. *Journal of Automated Reasoning*, 59(4):483–502.

Anna Szabolcsi. 2010. *Quantification*. Cambridge University Press.

Adina Williams, Nikita Nangia, and Samuel Bowman. 2018. A broad-coverage challenge corpus for sentence understanding through inference. In *Proceedings of the 2018 Conference of the North American Chapter of the Association for Computational Linguistics: Human Language Technologies (NAACL-HLT)*, pages 1112–1122.

Hitomi Yanaka, Koji Mineshima, Daisuke Bekki, Kentaro Inui, Satoshi Sekine, Lasha Abzianidze, and Johan Bos. 2019. Can neural networks understand monotonicity reasoning? In *Proceedings of the 2019 ACL Workshop BlackboxNLP: Analyzing and Interpreting Neural Networks for NLP*, pages 31–40.

Masashi Yoshikawa, Koji Mineshima, Hiroshi Noji, and Daisuke Bekki. 2019. Combining axiom injection and knowledge base completion for efficient natural language inference. In *Proceedings of the AAAI Conference on Artificial Intelligence*, pages 7410–7417.

Masashi Yoshikawa, Hiroshi Noji, and Yuji Matsumoto. 2017. A* CCG parsing with a supertag and dependency factored model. In *Proceedings of the 55th Annual Meeting of the Association for Computational Linguistics (ACL)*, pages 277–287.

Enhancing Word Embeddings with
Knowledge Extracted from Lexical Resources

Magdalena Biesialska[*]   **Bardia Rafieian**[*]   **Marta R. Costa-jussà**
TALP Research Center, Universitat Politècnica de Catalunya, Barcelona
{magdalena.biesialska,bardia.rafieian,marta.ruiz}@upc.edu

Abstract

In this work, we present an effective method for *semantic specialization* of word vector representations. To this end, we use traditional word embeddings and apply specialization methods to better capture semantic relations between words. In our approach, we leverage external knowledge from rich lexical resources such as BabelNet. We also show that our proposed *post-specialization* method based on an adversarial neural network with the Wasserstein distance allows to gain improvements over state-of-the-art methods on two tasks: word similarity and dialog state tracking.

1 Introduction

Vector representations of words (embeddings) have become the cornerstone of modern Natural Language Processing (NLP), as learning word vectors and utilizing them as features in downstream NLP tasks is the *de facto* standard. Word embeddings (Mikolov et al., 2013; Pennington et al., 2014) are typically trained in an unsupervised way on large monolingual corpora. Whilst such word representations are able to capture some syntactic as well as semantic information, their ability to map relations (e.g. synonymy, antonymy) between words is limited. To alleviate this deficiency, a set of refinement post-processing methods–called *retrofitting* or *semantic specialization*–has been introduced. In the next section, we discuss the intricacies of these methods in more detail.

To summarize, our contributions in this work are as follows:

- We introduce a set of new linguistic constraints (i.e. synonyms and antonyms) created with BabelNet for three languages: English, German and Italian.

- We introduce an improved *post-specialization* method (dubbed *WGAN-postspec*), which demonstrates improved performance as compared to state-of-the-art *DFFN* (Vulić et al., 2018) and *AuxGAN* (Ponti et al., 2018) models.

- We show that the proposed approach achieves performance improvements on an intrinsic task (word similarity) as well as on a downstream task (dialog state tracking).

2 Related Work

Numerous methods have been introduced for incorporating structured linguistic knowledge from external resources to word embeddings. Fundamentally, there exist three categories of *semantic specialization* approaches: (a) *joint methods* which incorporate lexical information during the training of distributional word vectors; (b) *specialization* methods also referred to as *retrofitting* methods which use post-processing techniques to inject semantic information from external lexical resources into pre-trained word vector representations; and (c) *post-specialization* methods which use linguistic constraints to learn a general mapping function allowing to specialize the entire distributional vector space.

In general, *joint methods* perform worse than the other two methods, and are not model-agnostic, as they are tightly coupled to the distributional word vector models (e.g. *Word2Vec*, *GloVe*). Therefore, in this work we concentrate on the *specialization* and *post-specialization* methods. Approaches which fall in the former category can be considered local specialization methods, where the most prominent examples are: *retrofitting* (Faruqui et al., 2015) which is a post-processing method to enrich word embeddings with knowledge from semantic

---

[*]Equal contribution

Proceedings of the 58th Annual Meeting of the Association for Computational Linguistics: Student Research Workshop, pages 271–278
July 5 - July 10, 2020. ©2020 Association for Computational Linguistics

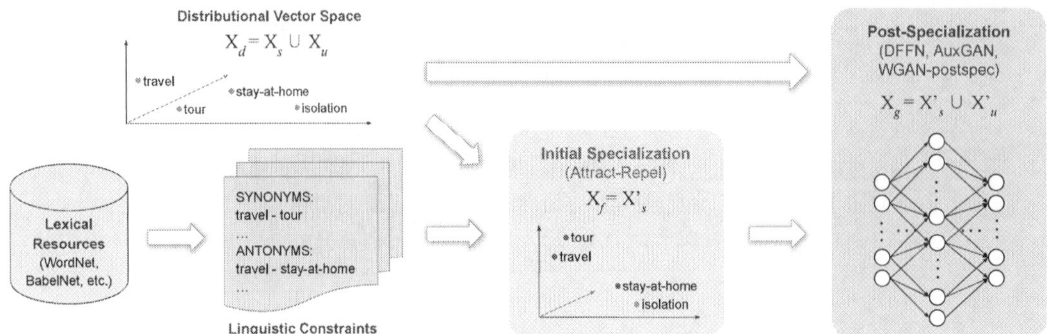

Figure 1: Illustration of the semantic specialization approach.

lexicons, in this case it brings closer semantically similar words. *Counter-fitting* (Mrkšić et al., 2016) likewise fine-tunes word representations; however, conversely to the *retrofitting* technique it counter-fits the embeddings with respect to the given similarity and antonymy constraints. *Attract-Repel* (Mrkšić et al., 2017b) uses linguistic constraints obtained from external lexical resources to semantically specialize word embeddings. Similarly to *counter-fitting* it injects synonymy and antonymy constraints into distributional word vector spaces. In contrast to *counter-fitting*, this method does not ignore how updates of the example word vector pairs affect their relations to other word vectors.

On the other hand, the latter group, *post-specialization* methods, performs global specialization of distributional spaces. We can distinguish: *explicit retrofitting* (Glavaš and Vulić , 2018) that was the first attempt to use external constraints (i.e. synonyms and antonyms) as training examples for learning an explicit mapping function for specializing the words not observed in the constraints. Later, a more robust *DFFN* (Vulić et al., 2018) method was introduced with the same goal – to specialize the full vocabulary by leveraging the already specialized subspace of seen words.

3   Methodology

In this paper, we propose an approach that builds upon previous works (Vulić et al., 2018; Ponti et al., 2018). The process of specializing distributional vectors is a two-step procedure (as shown in Figure 1). First, an *initial specialization* is performed (see §3.1). In the second step, a global specialization mapping function is learned, allowing to generalize to unseen words (see §3.2).

3.1   Initial Specialization

In this step a subspace of distributional vectors for words that occur in the external constraints is specialized. To this end, fine-tuning of seen words can be performed using any *specialization* method. In this work, we utilize *Attract-Repel* model (Mrkšić et al., 2017b) as it offers state-of-the-art performance. This method allows to make use of both synonymy (*attract*) and antonymy (*repel*) constraints. More formally, given a set $\mathcal{A}$ of *attract* word pairs and a set of $\mathcal{R}$ of *repel* word pairs, let $\mathcal{V}_S$ be the vocabulary of words seen in the constraints. Hence, each word pair (v_l, v_r) is represented by a corresponding vector pair $(\mathbf{x}_l, \mathbf{x}_r)$. The model optimization method operates over mini-batches: a mini-batch $\mathcal{B}_A$ of synonymy pairs (of size k_1) and a mini-batch $\mathcal{B}_R$ of antonymy pairs (of size k_2). The pairs of negative examples $T_A(\mathcal{B}_A) = \left[\left(\mathbf{t}_l^1, \mathbf{t}_r^1\right), \ldots, \left(\mathbf{t}_l^{k_1}, \mathbf{t}_r^{k_1}\right)\right]$ and $T_R(\mathcal{B}_R) = \left[\left(\mathbf{t}_l^1, \mathbf{t}_r^1\right), \ldots, \left(\mathbf{t}_l^{k_2}, \mathbf{t}_r^{k_2}\right)\right]$ are drawn from $2(k_1 + k_2)$ word vectors in $\mathcal{B}_A \cup \mathcal{B}_R$.

The negative examples serve the purpose of pulling synonym pairs closer and pushing antonym pairs further away with respect to their corresponding negative examples. For synonyms:

$$A(\mathcal{B}_A) = \sum_{i=1}^{k_1} \left[\tau(\delta_{att} + \mathbf{x}_l^i \mathbf{t}_l^i - \mathbf{x}_l^i \mathbf{x}_r^i) + \right.$$
$$\left. + \tau\left(\delta_{att} + \mathbf{x}_r^i \mathbf{t}_r^i - \mathbf{x}_l^i \mathbf{x}_r^i\right)\right] \quad (1)$$

where τ is the rectifier function, and δ_{att} is the similarity margin determining the distance between synonymy vectors and how much closer they should be comparing to their negative examples. Similarly,

272

the equation for antonyms is given as:

$$R\left(\mathcal{B}_R\right) = \sum_{i=1}^{k_2} \left[\tau(\delta_{rep} + \mathbf{x}_l^i \mathbf{x}_r^i - \mathbf{x}_l^i \mathbf{t}_l^i) + \right.$$
$$\left. + \tau\left(\delta_{rep} + \mathbf{x}_l^i \mathbf{x}_r^i - \mathbf{x}_r^i \mathbf{t}_r^i\right)\right] \qquad (2)$$

A distributional regularization term is used to retain the quality of the original distributional vector space using L_2-regularization.

$$Reg\left(\mathcal{B}_A, \mathcal{B}_R\right) = \sum_{\mathbf{x}_i \in V(\mathcal{B}_A \cup \mathcal{B}_R)} \lambda_{reg} \|\widehat{\mathbf{x}}_i - \mathbf{x}_i\|_2$$
$$(3)$$

where λ_{reg} is a L_2-regularization constant, and $\widehat{x}_i$ is the original vector for the word x_i.

Consequently, the final cost function is formulated as follows:

$$C(\mathcal{B}_A, \mathcal{B}_R) = A(\mathcal{B}_A) + R(\mathcal{B}_R) + Reg(\mathcal{B}_A, \mathcal{B}_R)$$
$$(4)$$

3.2 Proposed Post-Specialization Model

Once the *initial specialization* is completed, *post-specialization* methods can be employed. This step is important, because local specialization affects only words seen in the constraints, and thus just a subset of the original distributional space $\mathbf{X}_d$. While *post-specialization* methods learn a global specialization mapping function allowing them to generalize to unseen words $\mathbf{X}_u$.

Given the specialized word vectors $\mathbf{X}_s'$ from the vocabulary of seen words $\mathcal{V}_S$, our proposed method propagates this signal to the entire distributional vector space using a generative adversarial network (GAN) (Goodfellow et al., 2014). Hence, in our model, following the approach of Ponti et al. (2018), we introduce adversarial losses. More specifically, the mapping function is learned through a combination of a standard L_2-loss with adversarial losses. The motivation behind this is to make the mappings more natural and ensure that vectors specialized for the full vocabulary are more realistic. To this end, we use the Wasserstein distance incorporated in the generative adversarial network (WGAN) (Arjovsky et al., 2017) as well as its improved variant with gradient penalty (WGAN-GP) (Gulrajani et al., 2017). For brevity, we call our model *WGAN-postspec*, which is an umbrella term for the *WGAN* and *WGAN-GP* methods implemented in the proposed *post-specialization* model. One of the benefits of using WGANs over vanilla GANs is that WGANs are generally more stable, and also they do not suffer from vanishing gradients.

Our proposed *post-specialization* approach is based on the principles of GANs, as it is composed of two elements: a generator network G and a discriminator network D. The gist of this concept, is to improve the generated samples through a min-max game between the generator and the discriminator.

In our *post-specialization* model, a multi-layer feed-forward neural network, which trains a global mapping function, acts as the generator. Consequently, the generator is trained to produce predictions $G(\mathbf{x}; \theta_G)$ that are as similar as possible to the corresponding initially specialized word vectors $\mathbf{x}_s'$. Therefore, a global mapping function is trained using word vector pairs, such that $(\mathbf{x}_i, \mathbf{x}_i') = \{\mathbf{x}_i \in \mathbf{X}_s, \mathbf{x}_i' \in \mathbf{X}_s'\}$. On the other hand, the discriminator $D(\mathbf{x}; \theta_D)$, which is a multi-layer classification network, tries to distinguish the generated samples from the initially specialized vectors sampled from $\mathbf{X}_s'$. In this process, the differences between predictions and initially specialized vectors are used to improve the generator, resulting in more realistically looking outputs.

In general, for the GAN model we can define the loss $\mathcal{L}_G$ of the generator as:

$$\mathcal{L}_G = -\sum_{i=1}^{n} \log P(\text{spec} = 1 | G(\mathbf{x}_i; \theta_G); \theta_D) -$$
$$- \sum_{i=1}^{m} \log P(\text{spec} = 0 | \mathbf{x}_i'; \theta_D) \qquad (5)$$

While the loss of the discriminator $\mathcal{L}_D$ is given as:

$$\mathcal{L}_D = -\sum_{i=1}^{n} \log P(\text{spec} = 0 | G(\mathbf{x}_i; \theta_G); \theta_D) -$$
$$- \sum_{i=1}^{m} \log P(\text{spec} = 1 | \mathbf{x}_i'; \theta_D) \qquad (6)$$

In principle, the losses with Wasserstein distance can be formulated as follows:

$$\mathcal{L}_G = -\frac{1}{n} \sum_{i=1}^{n} D(G(\mathbf{x}_i; \theta_G); \theta_D) \qquad (7)$$

and

$$\mathcal{L}_D = \frac{1}{m} \sum_{i=1}^{m} D(\mathbf{x}_i'; \theta_D) -$$
$$- \frac{1}{n} \sum_{i=1}^{n} D(G(\mathbf{x}_i; \theta_G); \theta_D) \qquad (8)$$

An alternative scenario with a gradient penalty (WGAN-GP) requires adding gradient penalty λ coefficient in the Eq. (8).

4 Experiments

Pre-trained Word Embeddings. In order to evaluate our proposed approach as well as to compare our results with respect to current state-of-the-art *post-specialization* approaches, we use popular and readily available 300-dimensional pre-trained word vectors. Word2Vec (Mikolov et al., 2013) embeddings for English were trained using skip-gram with negative sampling on the cleaned and tokenized Polyglot Wikipedia (Al-Rfou' et al., 2013) by Levy and Goldberg (2014), while German and Italian embeddings were trained using CBOW with negative sampling on WacKy corpora (Dinu et al., 2015; Artetxe et al., 2017, 2018). Moreover, GloVe vectors for English were trained on Common Crawl (Pennington et al., 2014).

Linguistic Constraints. To perform *semantic specialization* of word vector spaces, we exploit linguistic constraints used in previous works (Zhang et al., 2014; Ono et al., 2015; Vulić et al., 2018) (referred to as *external*) as well as introduce a new set of constraints collected by us (referred to as *babelnet*) for three languages: English, German and Italian. We use constraints in two different settings: *disjoint* and *overlap*. In the first setting, we remove all linguistic constraints that contain any of the words available in SimLex (Hill et al., 2015), SimVerb (Gerz et al., 2016) and WordSim (Leviant and Reichart, 2015) evaluation datasets. In the *overlap* setting, we let the SimLex, SimVerb and WordSim words remain in the constraints. To summarize, we present the number of word pairs for English, German and Italian constraints in Table 1.

Let us discuss in more detail how the lists of constraints were constructed. In this work, we use two sets of linguistic constraints: *external* and *babelnet*. The first set of constraints was retrieved from WordNet (Fellbaum, 1998) and Roget's Thesaurus (Kipfer, 2009), resulting in 1,023,082 synonymy and 380,873 antonymy word pairs. The second set of constraints, which is a part of our contribution, comprises synonyms and antonyms obtained using NASARI lexical embeddings (Camacho-Collados et al., 2016) and BabelNet (Navigli and Ponzetto, 2012). As NASARI provides lexical information for BabelNet words in five languages (EN, ES, FR, DE and IT), we collected each word with its related BabelNetID (a sense database identifier) to extract the list of its synonyms and antonyms using BabelNet API.

Furthermore, to improve the list of Italian words, we also followed the approach proposed by Sucameli and Lenci (2017). The authors provided a new dataset of semantically related Italian word pairs. The dataset includes nouns, adjectives and verbs with their synonyms, antonyms and hypernyms. The information in this dataset was gathered by its authors through crowdsourcing from a pool of Italian native speakers. This way, we could concatenate Italian word pairs to provide a more complete list of synonyms and antonyms.

Similarly, we refer to the work of Scheible and Schulte im Walde (2014) that presents a new collection of semantically related word pairs in German, which was compiled through human evaluation. Relying on GermaNet and the respective JAVA API, the list of the word pairs was generated with a sampling technique. Finally, we used these word pairs in our experiments as external resources for the German language.

Initial Specialization and Post-Specialization. Although, initially specialized vector spaces show gains over the non-specialized word embeddings, linguistic constraints represent only a fraction of their total vocabulary. Therefore, *semantic specialization* is a two-step process. Firstly, we perform *initial specialization* of the pre-trained word vectors by means of *Attract-Repel* (see §2) algorithm. The values of hyperparameter are set according to the default values: $\lambda_{reg} = 10^{-9}, \delta_{sim} = 0.6, \delta_{ant} = 0.0$ and $k_1 = k_2 = 50$. Afterward, to perform a specialization of the entire vocabulary, a global specialization mapping function is learned. In our *WGAN-postspec* proposed approach, the *post-specialization* model uses a GAN with improved loss functions by means of the Wasserstein distance and gradient penalty. Importantly, the optimization process differs depending on the algorithm implemented in our model. In the case of a vanilla GAN (*AuxGAN*), standard stochastic gradient descent is used. While in the *WGAN* model we employ RMSProp (Tieleman and Hinton, 2012). Finally, in the case of the *WGAN-GP*, Adam (Kingma and Ba, 2015) optimizer is applied.

		English			German			Italian		
		overlap	*disjoint simlex/verb*	*disjoint wordsim*	*overlap*	*disjoint simlex/verb*	*disjoint wordsim*	*overlap*	*disjoint simlex/verb*	*disjoint wordsim*
Synonyms	*babelnet*	3,522,434	3,521,366	3,515,111	1,358,358	1,087,814	1,348,006	975,483	807,399	806,890
	external + babelnet	4,545,045	4,396,350	3,515,111	1,360,040	1,089,338	1,349,612	976,877	808,605	808,225
Antonyms	*babelnet*	1,024	843	1,011	139	136	136	99	99	98
	external + babelnet	381,777	352,099	378,365	1,823	1,662	1,744	883	769	851

Table 1: Number of synonym and antonym word pairs for English, German and Italian in two settings: *babelnet*, *external + babelnet*.

		English											
		GLOVE						WORD2VEC					
		overlap			*disjoint*			*overlap*			*disjoint*		
		SL	SV	WS	SL	SV	WS	SL	SV	WS	SL	SV	WS
ORIGINAL		0.407	0.280	0.655	0.407	0.280	0.655	0.414	0.272	0.593	0.414	0.272	0.593
ATTRACT-REPEL	*a*	0.781	0.761	0.597	0.407	0.280	0.655	0.778	0.761	0.574	0.414	0.272	0.593
	b	0.407	0.282	0.655	0.407	0.282	0.655	0.414	0.275	0.594	0.414	0.275	0.593
	c	0.784	0.763	0.595	0.407	0.282	0.655	0.776	0.763	0.560	0.414	0.275	0.593
DFFN	*a*	0.785	0.764	0.600	0.645	0.531	0.678	0.781	0.763	0.571	0.553	0.430	0.593
	b	0.699	0.562	0.703	0.458	0.324	0.679	0.351	0.237	0.506	0.387	0.245	0.578
	c	0.783	0.764	0.597	0.646	0.535	0.684	0.777	0.763	0.560	0.538	0.381	0.594
AUXGAN	*a*	0.789	0.764	0.659	0.652	0.552	0.642	0.782	0.762	0.550	0.581	0.434	0.602
	b	0.734	0.647	0.627	0.417	0.284	0.658	0.405	0.269	0.587	0.395	0.260	0.581
	c	0.796	0.767	0.639	0.659	0.560	0.669	0.782	0.755	0.588	0.583	0.438	0.603
WGAN	*a*	0.809	0.767	0.652	0.661	0.553	0.642	0.780	0.749	0.602	0.580	0.446	0.608
	b	0.722	0.635	0.654	0.452	0.279	0.671	0.392	0.262	0.590	0.397	0.269	0.580
	c	0.808	0.765	0.653	0.663	0.549	0.665	0.771	0.737	0.614	0.586	0.440	0.611
WGAN-GP	*a*	0.810	0.751	0.669	0.660	0.548	0.669	0.776	0.742	0.600	0.586	0.462	0.605
	b	0.722	0.622	0.646	0.461	0.282	0.676	0.396	0.254	0.567	0.398	0.267	0.581
	c	0.798	0.732	0.715	0.660	0.551	0.672	0.775	0.614	0.590	0.585	0.463	0.609

Table 2: Spearman's ρ correlation scores on SimLex-999 (SL), SimVerb-3500 (SV) and WordSim-353 (WS). Evaluation was performed using constraints in three settings: *(a) external, (b) babelnet, (c) external + babelnet*.

5 Results

5.1 Word Similarity

We report our experimental results with respect to a common intrinsic word similarity task, using standard benchmarks: SimLex-999 and WordSim-353 for English, German and Italian, as well as SimVerb-3500 for English. Each dataset contains human similarity ratings, and we evaluate the similarity measure using the Spearman's ρ rank correlation coefficient. In Table 2, we present results for English benchmarks, whereas results for German and Italian are reported in Table 3.

Word embeddings are evaluated in two scenarios: *disjoint* where words observed in the benchmark datasets are removed from the linguistic constraints; and *overlap* where all words provided in the linguistic constraints are utilized. We use the *overlap* setting in a downstream task (see §5.2).

In the tasks we report scores for *Original* (non-specialized) word vectors, *initial specialization* method *Attract-Repel* (Mrkšić et al., 2017b), and three post-specialization methods: *DFFN* (Vulić et al., 2018), *AuxGAN* (Ponti et al., 2018) and our proposed model *WGAN-postspec* (in two scenarios: *WGAN* and *WGAN-GP*).

The results suggest that the *post-specialization* methods bring improvements in the specialization of the distributional word vector space. Overall, the highest correlation scores are reported for the models with adversarial losses. We also observe that the proposed *WGAN-postspec* achieves fairly consistent correlation gains with GLOVE vectors on the SimLex dataset. Interestingly, while exploiting additional constraints (i.e. *external + babelnet*) generally boosts correlation scores for German and Italian, the results are not conclusive in the case of English, and thus they require further investigation.

| | German WORD2VEC | | | | Italian WORD2VEC | | | |
| | overlap | | disjoint | | overlap | | disjoint | |
	SL	WS	SL	WS	SL	WS	SL	WS
ORIGINAL	0.358	0.538	0.358	0.538	0.356	0.563	0.356	0.563
ATTRACT-REPEL *a*	0.360	0.537	0.358	0.538	0.376	0.568	0.364	0.565
ATTRACT-REPEL *b*	0.358	0.538	0.358	0.538	0.366	0.568	0.366	0.559
ATTRACT-REPEL *c*	0.360	0.538	0.358	0.538	0.378	0.566	0.367	0.564
DFFN *a*	0.366	0.422	0.370	0.452	0.381	0.512	0.365	0.519
DFFN *b*	0.354	0.538	0.348	0.538	0.364	0.559	0.361	0.560
DFFN *c*	0.359	0.541	0.358	0.533	0.376	0.561	0.369	0.559
AUXGAN *a*	0.331	0.532	0.325	0.535	0.362	0.561	0.348	0.560
AUXGAN *b*	0.369	0.552	0.373	0.561	0.361	0.559	0.364	0.563
AUXGAN *c*	0.369	0.564	0.365	0.556	0.365	0.566	0.368	0.563
WGAN *a*	0.331	0.528	0.327	0.531	0.361	0.558	0.344	0.558
WGAN *b*	0.364	0.558	0.367	0.559	0.359	0.553	0.367	0.559
WGAN *c*	0.371	0.559	0.364	0.560	0.367	0.567	0.370	0.562

Table 3: Spearman's ρ correlation scores on SimLex-999 (SL) and WordSim-353 (WS). Evaluation was performed using constraints in three settings: *(a) external, (b) babelnet, (c) external + babelnet.*

	GLOVE
ORIGINAL	0.797
ATTRACT-REPEL	0.817
DFFN	0.829
AUXGAN	0.836
WGAN-POSTSPEC	0.838

Table 4: DST results for English.

5.2 Dialog State Tracking

We also evaluate our proposed approach on a dialog state tracking (DST) downstream task. This task is a standard language understanding task, which allows to differentiate between word similarity and relatedness. To perform the evaluation we follow previous works (Henderson et al., 2014; Williams et al., 2016; Mrkšić et al., 2017b). Concretely, a DST model computes probability based only on pre-trained word embeddings. We use Wizard-of-Oz (WOZ) v.2.0 dataset (Wen et al., 2017; Mrkšić et al., 2017a) composed of 600 training dialogues as well as 200 development and 400 test dialogues.

In our experiments, we report results with a standard *joint goal accuracy* (JGA) score. The results in Table 4 confirm our findings from the previous word similarity task, as initial semantic *specialization* and *post-specialization* (in particular *WGAN-postspec*) yield improvements over original distributional word vectors. We expect this conclusion to hold in all settings; however, additional experiments for different languages and word embeddings would be beneficial.

6 Conclusion and Future Work

In this work, we presented a method to perform *semantic specialization* of word vectors. Specifically, we compiled a new set of constraints obtained from BabelNet. Moreover, we improved a state-of-the-art *post-specialization* method by incorporating adversarial losses with the Wasserstein distance. Our results obtained in an intrinsic and an extrinsic task, suggest that our method yields performance gains over current methods.

In the future, we plan to introduce constraints for asymmetric relations as well as extend our proposed method to leverage them. Moreover, we plan to experiment with adapting our model to a multilingual scenario, to be able to use it in a neural machine translation task. We make the code and resources available at: `https://github.com/mbiesialska/wgan-postspec`

Acknowledgments

We thank the anonymous reviewers for their insightful comments. This work is supported in part by the Spanish Ministerio de Economía y Competitividad, the European Regional Development Fund through the postdoctoral senior grant Ramón y Cajal and by the Agencia Estatal de Investigación through the projects EUR2019-103819 and PCIN-2017-079.

References

Rami Al-Rfou', Bryan Perozzi, and Steven Skiena. 2013. Polyglot: Distributed word representations for multilingual NLP. In *Proceedings of the Seventeenth Conference on Computational Natural Language Learning*, pages 183–192, Sofia, Bulgaria. Association for Computational Linguistics.

Martin Arjovsky, Soumith Chintala, and Léon Bottou. 2017. Wasserstein generative adversarial networks. In *Proceedings of the 34th International Conference on Machine Learning - Volume 70*, ICML'17, page 214–223. JMLR.org.

Mikel Artetxe, Gorka Labaka, and Eneko Agirre. 2017. Learning bilingual word embeddings with (almost) no bilingual data. In *Proceedings of the 55th Annual Meeting of the Association for Computational Linguistics (Volume 1: Long Papers)*, pages 451–462.

Mikel Artetxe, Gorka Labaka, and Eneko Agirre. 2018. Generalizing and improving bilingual word embedding mappings with a multi-step framework of linear transformations. In *Proceedings of the Thirty-Second AAAI Conference on Artificial Intelligence*, pages 5012–5019.

José Camacho-Collados, Mohammad Taher Pilehvar, and Roberto Navigli. 2016. Nasari: Integrating explicit knowledge and corpus statistics for a multilingual representation of concepts and entities. *Artificial Intelligence*, 240:36–64.

Georgiana Dinu, Angeliki Lazaridou, and Marco Baroni. 2015. Improving zero-shot learning by mitigating the hubness problem. *Proceedings of ICLR*.

Manaal Faruqui, Jesse Dodge, Sujay Kumar Jauhar, Chris Dyer, Eduard Hovy, and Noah A. Smith. 2015. Retrofitting word vectors to semantic lexicons. In *Proceedings of the 2015 Conference of the North American Chapter of the Association for Computational Linguistics: Human Language Technologies*, pages 1606–1615, Denver, Colorado. Association for Computational Linguistics.

Christiane Fellbaum. 1998. Wordnet: An electronic lexical database mit press.

Daniela Gerz, Ivan Vulić, Felix Hill, Roi Reichart, and Anna Korhonen. 2016. SimVerb-3500: A large-scale evaluation set of verb similarity. In *Proceedings of the 2016 Conference on Empirical Methods in Natural Language Processing*, pages 2173–2182, Austin, Texas. Association for Computational Linguistics.

Goran Glavaš and I. Vulić . 2018. Explicit retrofitting of distributional word vectors. In *Proceedings of the 56th Annual Meeting of the Association for Computational Linguistics (Volume 1: Long Papers)*, pages 34–45, Melbourne, Australia. Association for Computational Linguistics.

Ian J. Goodfellow, Jean Pouget-Abadie, Mehdi Mirza, Bing Xu, David Warde-Farley, Sherjil Ozair, Aaron Courville, and Yoshua Bengio. 2014. Generative adversarial nets. In *Proceedings of the 27th International Conference on Neural Information Processing Systems - Volume 2*, NIPS'14, page 2672–2680, Cambridge, MA, USA. MIT Press.

Ishaan Gulrajani, Faruk Ahmed, Martin Arjovsky, Vincent Dumoulin, and Aaron C Courville. 2017. Improved training of wasserstein gans. In I. Guyon, U. V. Luxburg, S. Bengio, H. Wallach, R. Fergus, S. Vishwanathan, and R. Garnett, editors, *Advances in Neural Information Processing Systems 30*, pages 5767–5777. Curran Associates, Inc.

Matthew Henderson, Blaise Thomson, and Jason D. Williams. 2014. The second dialog state tracking challenge. In *Proceedings of the 15th Annual Meeting of the Special Interest Group on Discourse and Dialogue (SIGDIAL)*, pages 263–272, Philadelphia, PA, U.S.A. Association for Computational Linguistics.

Felix Hill, Roi Reichart, and Anna Korhonen. 2015. SimLex-999: Evaluating semantic models with (genuine) similarity estimation. *Computational Linguistics*, 41(4):665–695.

Diederik P. Kingma and Jimmy Ba. 2015. Adam: A method for stochastic optimization. In *3rd International Conference on Learning Representations, ICLR 2015, San Diego, CA, USA, May 7-9, 2015, Conference Track Proceedings*.

B.A. Kipfer. 2009. *Roget's 21st Century Thesaurus (3rd Edition)*. Philip Lief Group.

Ira Leviant and Roi Reichart. 2015. Separated by an un-common language: Towards judgment language informed vector space modeling.

Omer Levy and Yoav Goldberg. 2014. Dependency-based word embeddings. In *Proceedings of the 52nd Annual Meeting of the Association for Computational Linguistics (Volume 2: Short Papers)*, pages 302–308, Baltimore, Maryland. Association for Computational Linguistics.

Tomas Mikolov, Ilya Sutskever, Kai Chen, Gregory S. Corrado, and Jeffrey Dean. 2013. Distributed representations of words and phrases and their compositionality. In *NIPS*.

Nikola Mrkšić, Diarmuid Ó Séaghdha, Blaise Thomson, Milica Gašić, Lina M. Rojas-Barahona, Pei-Hao Su, David Vandyke, Tsung-Hsien Wen, and Steve Young. 2016. Counter-fitting word vectors to linguistic constraints. In *Proceedings of the 2016 Conference of the North American Chapter of the Association for Computational Linguistics: Human Language Technologies*, pages 142–148, San Diego, California. Association for Computational Linguistics.

Nikola Mrkšić, Diarmuid Ó Séaghdha, Tsung-Hsien Wen, Blaise Thomson, and Steve Young. 2017a. Neural belief tracker: Data-driven dialogue state tracking. In *Proceedings of the 55th Annual Meeting of the Association for Computational Linguistics (Volume 1: Long Papers)*, pages 1777–1788, Vancouver, Canada. Association for Computational Linguistics.

Nikola Mrkšić, Ivan Vulić, Diarmuid Ó Séaghdha, Ira Leviant, Roi Reichart, Milica Gašić, Anna Korhonen, and Steve Young. 2017b. Semantic specialization of distributional word vector spaces using monolingual and cross-lingual constraints. *Transactions of the Association for Computational Linguistics*, 5:309–324.

Roberto Navigli and Simone Paolo Ponzetto. 2012. BabelNet: The automatic construction, evaluation and application of a wide-coverage multilingual semantic network. *Artificial Intelligence*, 193:217–250.

Masataka Ono, Makoto Miwa, and Yutaka Sasaki. 2015. Word embedding-based antonym detection using thesauri and distributional information. In *Proceedings of the 2015 Conference of the North American Chapter of the Association for Computational Linguistics: Human Language Technologies*, pages 984–989, Denver, Colorado. Association for Computational Linguistics.

Jeffrey Pennington, Richard Socher, and Christopher Manning. 2014. Glove: Global vectors for word representation. In *Proceedings of the 2014 Conference on Empirical Methods in Natural Language Processing (EMNLP)*, pages 1532–1543, Doha, Qatar. Association for Computational Linguistics.

Edoardo Maria Ponti, Ivan Vulić, Goran Glavaš, Nikola Mrkšić, and Anna Korhonen. 2018. Adversarial propagation and zero-shot cross-lingual transfer of word vector specialization. In *Proceedings of the 2018 Conference on Empirical Methods in Natural Language Processing*, pages 282–293, Brussels, Belgium. Association for Computational Linguistics.

Silke Scheible and Sabine Schulte im Walde. 2014. A database of paradigmatic semantic relation pairs for German nouns, verbs, and adjectives. In *Proceedings of Workshop on Lexical and Grammatical Resources for Language Processing*, pages 111–119, Dublin, Ireland. Association for Computational Linguistics and Dublin City University.

Irene Sucameli and Alessandro Lenci. 2017. Parad-it: Eliciting italian paradigmatic relations with crowdsourcing. In *Proceedings of the Fourth Italian Conference on Computational Linguistics (CLiC-it 2017), Rome, Italy, December 11-13, 2017*.

Tijmen Tieleman and Geoffrey Hinton. 2012. Lecture 6.5-rmsprop: Divide the gradient by a running average of its recent magnitude. *COURSERA: Neural networks for machine learning*, 4(2):26–31.

Ivan Vulić, Goran Glavaš, Nikola Mrkšić, and Anna Korhonen. 2018. Post-specialisation: Retrofitting vectors of words unseen in lexical resources. In *Proceedings of the 2018 Conference of the North American Chapter of the Association for Computational Linguistics: Human Language Technologies, Volume 1 (Long Papers)*, pages 516–527, New Orleans, Louisiana. Association for Computational Linguistics.

Tsung-Hsien Wen, David Vandyke, Nikola Mrkšić, Milica Gašić, Lina M. Rojas-Barahona, Pei-Hao Su, Stefan Ultes, and Steve Young. 2017. A network-based end-to-end trainable task-oriented dialogue system. In *Proceedings of the 15th Conference of the European Chapter of the Association for Computational Linguistics: Volume 1, Long Papers*, pages 438–449, Valencia, Spain. Association for Computational Linguistics.

Jason D. Williams, Antoine Raux, and Matthew Henderson. 2016. The dialog state tracking challenge series: A review. *Dialogue & Discourse*, 7:4–33.

Jingwei Zhang, Jeremy Salwen, Michael Glass, and Alfio Gliozzo. 2014. Word semantic representations using Bayesian probabilistic tensor factorization. In *Proceedings of the 2014 Conference on Empirical Methods in Natural Language Processing (EMNLP)*, pages 1522–1531, Doha, Qatar. Association for Computational Linguistics.

Pre-training via Leveraging Assisting Languages
for Neural Machine Translation

Haiyue Song[1]   Raj Dabre[2]   Zhuoyuan Mao[1]
Fei Cheng[1]   Sadao Kurohashi[1]   Eiichiro Sumita[2]

[1]Kyoto University, Kyoto, Japan
[2]National Institute of Information and Communications Technology, Kyoto, Japan

{song, feicheng, zhuoyuanmao, kuro}@nlp.ist.i.kyoto-u.ac.jp,
{raj.dabre, eiichiro.sumita}@nict.go.jp

Abstract

Sequence-to-sequence (S2S) pre-training using large monolingual data is known to improve performance for various S2S NLP tasks. However, large monolingual corpora might not always be available for the languages of interest (LOI). Thus, we propose to exploit monolingual corpora of other languages to complement the scarcity of monolingual corpora for the LOI. We utilize script mapping (Chinese to Japanese) to increase the similarity (number of cognates) between the monolingual corpora of helping languages and LOI. An empirical case study of low-resource Japanese–English neural machine translation (NMT) reveals that leveraging large Chinese and French monolingual corpora can help overcome the shortage of Japanese and English monolingual corpora, respectively, for S2S pre-training. Using only Chinese and French monolingual corpora, we were able to improve Japanese–English translation quality by up to 8.5 BLEU in low-resource scenarios.

1 Introduction

Neural Machine Translation (NMT) (Sutskever et al., 2014; Bahdanau et al., 2015) is known to give state-of-the-art (SOTA) translations for language pairs with an abundance of parallel corpora. However, most language pairs are resource poor (Russian–Japanese, Marathi–English) as they lack large parallel corpora and the lack of bilingual training data can be compensated by by monolingual corpora. Although it is possible to utilise the popular back-translation method (Sennrich et al., 2016a), it is time-consuming to backtranslate a large amount of monolingual data. Furthermore, poor quality backtranslated data tends to be of little help. Recently, another approach has gained popularity where the NMT model is pre-trained through tasks that only require monolingual data (Song et al., 2019; Qi et al., 2018).

Pre-training using models like BERT (Devlin et al., 2018) have led to new state-of-the-art results in text understanding. However, BERT-like sequence models were not designed to be used for NMT which is sequence to sequence (S2S). Song et al. (2019) recently proposed MASS, a S2S specific pre-training task for NMT and obtained new state-of-the-art results in low-resource settings. MASS assumes that a large amount of monolingual data is available for the languages involved but some language pairs may lack both parallel and monolingual corpora and are "truly low-resource" and challenging.

Fortunately, languages are not isolated and often belong to "language families" where they have similar orthography (written script; shared cognates) or similar grammar or both. Motivated by this, in this paper we hypothesize that we should be able to leverage large monolingual corpora of other assisting languages to help the monolingual pre-training of NMT models for the languages of interest (LOI) that may lack monolingual corpora. Wherever possible, we subject the pre-training corpora to script mapping which should help minimize the vocabulary and distribution differences, respectively, between the pre-training, main training (fine-tuning) and testing time datasets. This should help the already consistent pre-training and fine-tuning objectives leverage the data much better and thereby, possibly, boost translation quality.

To this end, we experiment with ASPEC Japanese–English translation in a variety of low-resource settings for the Japanese–English parallel corpora. Our experiments reveal that while it's possible to leverage *unrelated languages* for pre-training, using *related languages* is extremely important. We utilized Chinese to Japanese script mapping to maximize the similarities between the assisting languages (Chinese and French) and the languages of interest (Japanese and English).

Proceedings of the 58th Annual Meeting of the Association for Computational Linguistics: Student Research Workshop, pages 279–285
July 5 - July 10, 2020. ©2020 Association for Computational Linguistics

We show that only using monolingual corpora of Chinese and French for pre-training can improve Japanese–English translation quality by up to 8.5 BLEU.

The contributions of our work are as follows:

1. Leveraging assisting languages: We give a novel study of leveraging monolingual corpora of related and unrelated languages for NMT pre-training.

2. Empirical evaluation: We make a comparison of existing and proposed techniques in a variety of corpora settings to verify our hypotheses.

2 Related work

Our research is at the intersection of works on monolingual pre-training for NMT and leveraging multilingualism for low-resource language translation.

Pre-training has enjoyed great success in other NLP tasks with the development of methods like BERT (Devlin et al., 2018). Song et al. (2019) recently proposed MASS, a new state-of-the-art NMT pre-training task that jointly trains the encoder and the decoder. Our approach builds on the initial idea of MASS, but focuses on complementing the potential scarcity of monolingual corpora for the languages of interest using relatively larger monolingual corpora of other (assisting) languages.

On the other hand, leveraging multilingualism involves cross-lingual transfer (Zoph et al., 2016) which solves the low-resource issue by using data from different language pairs. Dabre et al. (2017) showed the importance of transfer learning between languages belonging to the same language family but corpora might not always be available in a related language. A mapping between Chinese and Japanese characters (Chu et al., 2012) was shown to be useful for Chinese–Japanese dictionary construction (Dabre et al., 2015). Mappings between scripts or unification of scripts (Hermjakob et al., 2018) can artificially increase the similarity between languages which motivates most of our work.

3 Proposed Method: Using Assisting Languages

We propose a novel monolingual pre-training method for NMT which leverages monolingual corpora of assisting languages to overcome the scarcity of monolingual and parallel corpora of

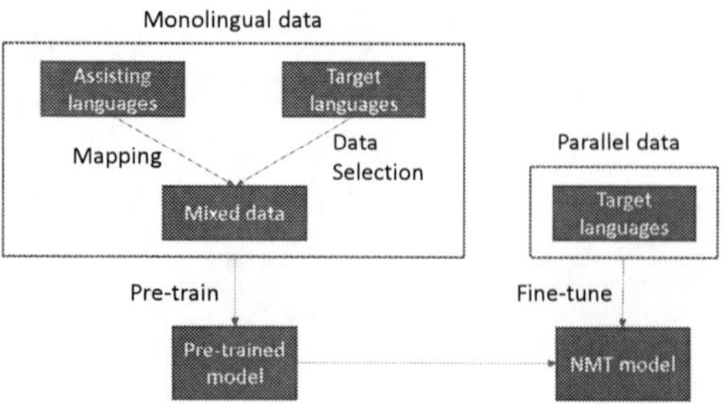

Figure 1: An overview of our proposed method consisting of script mapping, data selection, pre-training and fine-tuning

the languages of interest (LOI). The framework of our approach is shown in Figure 1 which consists of script mapping, data selection, pre-training and fine-tuning.

3.1 Data Pre-processing

Blindly pre-training a NMT model on vast amounts of monolingual data belonging to the assisting languages and LOI might improve translation quality slightly. However, divergences between the languages, especially their scripts (Hermjakob et al., 2018) and also the distributions of data between different training phases is known to impact the final result. Motivated by past works on using related languages (Dabre et al., 2017), orthography mapping/unification (Hermjakob et al., 2018; Chu et al., 2012) and data selection for MT (Axelrod et al., 2011), we propose to improve the efficacy of pre-training by reducing data and language divergence.

3.1.1 Script Mapping

Previous research has shown that enforcing shared orthography (Sennrich et al., 2016b; Dabre et al., 2015) has a strong positive impact on translation. Following this, we propose to leverage existing script mapping rules[1] or script unification mechanisms to, at the very least, maximize the possibility of cognate sharing and thereby bringing the assisting language closer to the LOI. This should strongly impact languages such as Hindi, Punjabi and Bengali belonging to the same family but written using different scripts.

For languages such as Korean, Chinese and Japanese there may exist a many to many mapping between their scripts. Thus, incorrect mapping of

---

[1]Transliteration is another option but transliteration systems are relatively unreliable compared to handcrafted rule tables.

characters (basic unit of a script) might produce wrong words and reduce cognate sharing. We propose two solutions to address this.

1. One-to-one mapping: Here we do not care about word level information and map each character in one language to its corresponding character in another language. Here, we just select the first mapping in the mapping list.

2. Many-to-many mapping with LM scoring: A more sophisticated solution is where for each tokenized word-level segment in one language we enumerate all possible combinations of mapped characters and use a language model in the other language to select the character combination with the highest score as the result.

3.1.2 Note on Chinese–Japanese Scripts

Japanese is written in Kanji which was borrowed from China. Over time the written scripts have diverged and the pronunciations are naturally different but there are a significant number of cognates written in both languages. As such pre-training on Chinese should benefit translation involving Japanese. Chu et al. (2012) created a mapping table between them which can be leveraged to further increase the number of cognates.

3.1.3 Data Selection

Often, the pre-training monolingual data and the fine-tuning parallel data belong to different domains. (Axelrod et al., 2011; Wang and Neubig, 2019) have shown that proper data selection can reduce the differences between the natures of data between different training domains and phases. In this paper we experiment with **(a)** Scoring monolingual sentences using a language model (LM) and selecting the highest scoring ones and **(b)** Selecting monolingual sentences to match the sentence length distribution of the development set sentences in the parallel corpus.

1. LM based data selection: We use a language model trained on corpora belonging to the domain that the fine-tuning data belongs to. We use this sort monolingual sentences according to LM score and use the top N sentences that are expected to be the most similar to the domain of the fine-tuning data.

2. Length based data selection: Algorithm 1 describes how to use the in-domain dataset ($TargetFile$; typically the sentences from the fine-tuning parallel corpus) to select $SelectNum$ lines from the out-of-domain dataset ($InputFile$; typ-

---

Algorithm 1: Length Distribution Data Selection

$$
\begin{aligned}
&\textbf{Input} \quad : TargetFile,\ InputFile, \\
&\qquad\qquad SelectNum \\
&\textbf{Output}: SelectedLines
\end{aligned}
$$

1   $TargetDistribution \leftarrow \{\};$
2   $CurrentDistribution \leftarrow \{\};$
3   $SelectedLines \leftarrow \{\};$
4   $TargetNum = \#\ of\ Lines\ in\ TargetFile;$
5   **foreach** $Line \in TargetFile$ **do**
6     $TargetD[len(Line)]{+}={1};$
7   **foreach** $Line \in InputFile$ **do**
8   **if** $CurrentD[len(Line)]/SelectNum < TargetD[len(Line)]/TargetNum$ **then**
9       $CurrentD[len(Line)]{+}={1};$
10      $SelectedLines \leftarrow SelectedLines \cup \{Line\};$

---

ically the monolingual corpus). When selecting monolingual data of languages of interest, we can first calculate the length distribution of parallel data as target distribution (the ratio of all lengths in $TargetFile$) and we fill the length distribution by selecting sentences from monolingual data of same language. As a result, the monolingual data and parallel data have similar length distribution.

3.2 NMT Modeling

In order to train a NMT model we first use the pre-processed monolingual data for pre-training and then resume training this model on parallel data to fine-tune for the languages of interest.

We use MASS, which is a pre-training method for NMT proposed by Song et al. (2019). In MASS, the input is a sequence of tokens where a part of the sequence is masked and the pre-training objective is to predict the masked fragments using a denoised auto-encoder model. The NMT model is pre-trained with the MASS task, until convergence, jointly for both the source and target languages. Thereafter training is resumed on the parallel corpus, a step known as fine-tuning (Zoph et al., 2016).

4 Experimental Settings

We conducted experiments on Japanese–English (Ja–En) translation in a variety of simulated low-resource settings using the "similar" assisting language pairs Chinese (Zh) and French (Fr) and the "distant" assisting language pairs Russian (Ru) and Arabic (Ar).

4.1 Datasets

We used the official ASPEC Ja–En parallel corpus (Nakazawa et al., 2016) provided by WAT 2019[2]. The official split consists of 3M, 1790 and 1872 train, dev and test sentences respectively. We sampled parallel corpora from the top 1M sentences for fine-tuning. Out of the remaining 2M sentences, we used the En side of the first 1M and the Ja side of the next 1M sentences as monolingual data for language modeling for data selection. We used Common Crawl[3] monolingual corpora for pre-training. To train LMs for data-selection of the assisting languages corpora, we used news commentary datasets [4]. While this data selection step for the assisting languages won't minimize the domain difference from the parallel corpus, it can help in filtering noisy sentences. In this paper we consider the ASPEC and news commentary data as in-domain and the rest of the pre-training data as out-of-domain.

4.2 Data Pre-processing

1. Normalization and Initial Filtering: We applied NFKC normalization to data of all languages. Juman++ (Tolmachev et al., 2018) for Ja tokenization, jieba[5] for Zh tokenization and NLTK[6] tokenization for other languages. We filtered out all sentences from the pre-training data that contain fewer than 3 and equal or more than 80 tokens. For Chinese data, we filtered out sentences containing fewer than 30 percent Chinese words or more than 30 percent English words.

2. Script Mapping: Chinese is the only assisting language that can be mapped to Japanese reliably. We converted Chinese to Japanese script to make them more similar by using the mapping table from (Chu et al., 2012) and the mapping approaches mentioned in the previous section. French and English are written using the Roman alphabet and do not need any script mapping. We did not perform script mapping for Arabic and Russian to show the impact of using distant languages (script-wise as well as linguistically).

3. Data selection: We used KenLM (Heafield, 2011) to train 5-gram LMs on in-domain data for LM scoring based data selection and use ASPEC dev set for length distribution based data selection.

5 Results and Analysis

5.1 Training and Evaluation Settings

We used the tensor2tensor framework (Vaswani et al., 2018) [7], version 1.14.0., with its default "*transformer_big*" setting.

We created a shared sub-word vocabulary using Japanese and English data from ASPEC mixing with Japanese, English, Chinese and French data from Common Crawl. We used SentencePiece (Kudo and Richardson, 2018) and obtained a vocabulary with the size of roughly 64k . We used this vocabulary in all experiments except unrelated language experiment where Arabic and Russian were used instead of Chinese and French data.

We combined monolingual data of assisting languages and languages of interest (LOI; Japanese and English) for pre-training. When mixing datasets of different sizes, we always oversampled the smaller datasets to match the size of the largest.

For all pre-training models, we saved checkpoints every 1000 steps and for all fine-tuning models, we saved checkpoints every 200 steps. We used early-stopping using approximate-BLEU as target and stops when no gain after 10,000 steps for pre-training and 2,000 steps for fine-tuning. We fine-tuned different fine-tune settings from the last checkpoint of each pre-trained model.

For decoding we averaged 10 checkpoints of the fine-tuning stage with $\alpha = 0.6$ and $beamsize = 4$. We used sacreBLEU[8] to evaluate BLEU score for all translation evaluation.

5.2 Models Trained and Evaluated

5.2.1 Pre-trained Models

We separated pre-training settings into different blocks as shown in Table 1. Baseline model without fine-tuning is shown as A1. Zero (0M), low (1M) and rich (20M) monolingual-corpus scenarios are shown in parts B, C and D, respectively. Part E explores the impact of the two script mapping techniques on pre-training. Part F shows the impact of using related versus unrelated assisting languages.

---

[2]http://lotus.kuee.kyoto-u.ac.jp/WAT/WAT2019/index.html#task.html

[3]http://data.statmt.org/ngrams/

[4]http://data.statmt.org/news-commentary/v14/

[5]https://github.com/fxsjy/jieba

[6]https://www.nltk.org

[7]https://github.com/tensorflow/tensor2tensor

[8]https://github.com/mjpost/sacreBLEU

#	Pre-training					Fine-tuning							
	Data pre-processing	Zh	Ja	En	Fr	En→Ja				Ja→En			
						3K	10K	20K	50K	3K	10K	20K	50K
A1	-	-	-	-	-	2.5	6.0	14.4	22.9	1.8	4.6	10.9	19.4
B1	1-to-1 Zh→Ja mapping + LM	20M	-	-	-	**5.3**	**14.5**	**20.0**	**26.1**	**3.7**	**11.2**	**15.6**	**20.5**
B2	LM	-	-	-	20M	3.4	9.1	14.9	23.4	2.1	6.3	11.3	17.7
B3	1-to-1 Zh→Ja mapping + LM	20M	-	-	20M	2.1	6.7	12.6	21.9	2.2	6.3	10.7	16.8
C1	LD	-	1M	1M	-	7.7	15.8	**20.7**	26.3	7.2	**12.7**	15.7	19.6
C2	1-to-1 Zh→Ja mapping + LD	20M	1M	1M	-	**8.3**	**16.4**	20.2	**26.9**	**7.5**	12.5	**16.3**	**20.7**
C3	LD	-	1M	1M	20M	**8.3**	15.3	19.3	26.7	6.8	12.3	15.4	20.4
C4	1-to-1 Zh→Ja mapping + LD	20M	1M	1M	20M	7.1	15.2	19.4	26.5	6.6	12.0	15.4	19.9
D1	LD	-	15M	15M	-	9.6	**17.2**	21.5	**28.0**	**8.6**	**13.5**	**16.8**	**20.9**
D2	1-to-1 Zh→Ja mapping + LD	20M	15M	15M	-	**9.7**	17.1	**21.6**	27.2	8.3	13.3	16.7	20.6
D3	LD	-	15M	15M	20M	7.7	15.0	19.8	26.3	6.3	11.7	15.1	20.2
D4	1-to-1 Zh→Ja mapping + LD	20M	15M	15M	20M	7.7	14.9	19.7	26.1	6.5	11.4	15.4	19.8
E1	1-to-1 Zh→Ja mapping	20M	20M	20M	20M	**7.0**	**13.4**	**19.3**	**25.7**	**5.9**	**11.1**	**15.0**	**19.8**
E2	LM-scoring Zh→Ja mapping	20M	20M	20M	20M	6.3	12.7	18.1	24.7	5.7	10.3	13.5	18.9
F1	LM-scoring	-	20M	20M	-	4.7	11.7	16.6	23.9	4.5	9.1	12.9	18.3
F2	1-to-1 Zh→Ja mapping + LM-scoring	20M	20M	20M	20M	**7.0**	**13.4**	**19.3**	**25.7**	**5.9**	**11.1**	**15.0**	**19.8**
F3	LM-scoring + Ar20M + Ru20M	-	20M	20M	-	4.8	12.1	18.1	25.1	4.4	10.2	13.5	18.9

Table 1: Low-resource pre-training experiments. Part A shows the baseline results. Part B, C, and D show results on monolingual zero, low and rich-resource scenarios. Part E shows results of two different mapping methods. And part F shows results of using related and unrelated languages. LD is with the meaning of "length distribution". Best results of each part are in bold.

5.2.2 Fine-tuned Models

We evaluated both Ja→En and En→Ja models with four parallel dataset size settings, 3K, 10K, 20K and 50K, selected from the previously selected 1M ASPEC parallel sentences.

In Table 1, we show results of several experimental settings to analyse the effect of: pre-training data size, Zh→Ja mapping methods and choices of unrelated languages versus related languages.

In our preliminary experiments we found out that 1-to-1 script mapping was not only faster but better than LM-scoring based script mapping. Furthermore, using length distribution was better than LM based data selection for the languages of interest (Japanese and English). Due to lack of space we only report core results using 1-to-1 script mapping (for assisting languages) and length distribution based data selection (for languages of interest).

5.3 Monolingual Zero and Low-resource scenario

The results of zero-resource and low-resource scenario are shown in parts B and C of Table 1. In these settings we used either no monolingual data or very little (1M) monolingual data for Japanese and English.

In part B, for a zero-monolingual data scenario, we observed large improvements, a maximum of 8.5 BLEU score over the baseline setting (A1), on all fine-tuning settings over model without fine-tuning when using only Chinese monolingual data (B1). Using only French data also gives better results on almost all fine-tuning settings, but not as large as that of using only Chinese data. Combining Chinese and French data, led to reduction in scores indicating some incompatibility between them.

In part C of the table, when there are 1M Japanese and English monolingual sentences, combining them with 20M Chinese data also gives improvements up to 1.1 BLEU points over A1. Combining with French data only gives occasional improvements. In this setting too, combining Chinese and French data led to reduction in performance.

Although French and English share cognates and have similar grammar, we have not performed explicit script mapping like we did for Chinese to make it more similar to Japanese. In the future we will investigate whether using a simple dictionary to map French to English can alleviate this issue.

We can draw the following conclusions,

1. Utilizing monolingual corpora of other languages **IS** beneficial.
2. Using similar languages (French and English) will **sometimes** give better results.
3. There may be **conflicts** between data of different assisting languages.

5.4 Monolingual resource-rich scenario

In part D, we found that there is less need to combine related language data when we use a large monolingual data of target languages. Only combining with Chinese data (D2) is comparable with pure Japanese-English monolingual pre-training (D1). Using French data degrades the translation quality in most settings. Thus, assisting languages become interfering languages in scenarios where large amounts of monolingual data are available for languages to be translated.

5.5 Chinese to Japanese mapping

In part E, we compared our two proposed script mapping methods. Results showed that the one-to-one mapping (character-level mapping) gives better BLEU score than word-level mapping consistently on most fine-tuning settings, about 0.7 to 1.0 in most cases. The word-level mapping gives lower score than baseline in Ja→En 50K case. One possible reason is that the Chinese and Japanese tokenizers cut the words in different granularity. So that applying Japanese LM to Chinese data may not work well. Therefore, we focus on 1-to-1 mapping experiments.

5.6 Unrelated language VS related language

In part F of the table, we compare pre-training on related languages versus unrelated languages. We saw that using Arabic and Russian as unrelated assisting languages in addition to Japanese and English, gives about 0.1 to 1.5 BLEU improvement over the baseline (G1) which uses only Japanese and English monolingual data. This is surprising and it shows that leveraging any additional language is better than not leveraging them. However, using (mapped) Chinese and French instead of Arabic and Russian yields about 2 to 2.7 BLEU score improvements. This clearly indicates that language relatedness is definitely important. In the future, we will consider more rigorous ways of increasing relatedness between pre-training corpora by using existing dictionaries and advanced script unification/mapping techniques instead of simple script mapping techniques.

6 Conclusion

In this paper we showed that it is possible to leverage monolingual corpora of other languages to pre-train NMT models for language pairs that lack parallel as well as monolingual data. Even if monolingual corpora for the languages of interest are unavailable, we can successfully improve translation quality by up to 8.5 BLEU, in low-resource settings, using monolingual corpora of assisting languages. We showed that the similarity between the other (assisting) languages and the languages to be translated is crucial and leveraged script mapping wherever possible. In the future, we plan to experiment with even more challenging language pairs such as Japanese–Russian and attempt to leverage monolingual corpora belonging to diverse language families.We might be able to identify subtle relationships among languages and approaches to better leverage assisting languages for several NLP tasks.

References

Amittai Axelrod, Xiaodong He, and Jianfeng Gao. 2011. Domain Adaptation via Pseudo In-Domain Data Selection. In *Proceedings of the 2011 Conference on Empirical Methods in Natural Language Processing*, pages 355–362, Edinburgh, Scotland, UK. Association for Computational Linguistics.

Dzmitry Bahdanau, Kyunghyun Cho, and Yoshua Bengio. 2015. Neural Machine Translation by Jointly Learning to Align and Translate. In *Proceedings of the 3rd International Conference on Learning Representations (ICLR)*, San Diego, USA.

Chenhui Chu, Toshiaki Nakazawa, and Sadao Kurohashi. 2012. Chinese Characters Mapping Table of Japanese, Traditional Chinese and Simplified Chinese. In *Proceedings of the Eighth International Conference on Language Resources and Evaluation (LREC'12)*, pages 2149–2152, Istanbul, Turkey. European Language Resources Association (ELRA).

Raj Dabre, Chenhui Chu, Fabien Cromieres, Toshiaki Nakazawa, and Sadao Kurohashi. 2015. Large-scale Dictionary Construction via Pivot-based Statistical Machine Translation with Significance Pruning and Neural Network Features. In *Proceedings of the 29th Pacific Asia Conference on Language, Information and Computation*, pages 289–297, Shanghai, China.

Raj Dabre, Tetsuji Nakagawa, and Hideto Kazawa. 2017. An Empirical Study of Language Relatedness for Transfer Learning in Neural Machine Translation. In *Proceedings of the 31st Pacific Asia Conference on Language, Information and Computation*, pages 282–286. The National University (Phillippines).

Jacob Devlin, Ming-Wei Chang, Kenton Lee, and Kristina Toutanova. 2018. BERT: Pre-training of Deep Bidirectional Transformers for Language Understanding. *CoRR*, abs/1810.04805.

Kenneth Heafield. 2011. KenLM: Faster and Smaller Language Model Queries. In *Proceedings of the Sixth Workshop on Statistical Machine Translation*, pages 187–197, Edinburgh, Scotland. Association for Computational Linguistics.

Ulf Hermjakob, Jonathan May, and Kevin Knight. 2018. Out-of-the-box Universal Romanization Tool uroman. In *Proceedings of ACL 2018, System Demonstrations*, pages 13–18, Melbourne, Australia. Association for Computational Linguistics.

Taku Kudo and John Richardson. 2018. SentencePiece: A simple and language independent subword tokenizer and detokenizer for Neural Text Processing. In *Proceedings of the 2018 Conference on Empirical Methods in Natural Language Processing: System Demonstrations*, pages 66–71, Brussels, Belgium. Association for Computational Linguistics.

Toshiaki Nakazawa, Manabu Yaguchi, Kiyotaka Uchimoto, Masao Utiyama, Eiichiro Sumita, Sadao Kurohashi, and Hitoshi Isahara. 2016. ASPEC: Asian Scientific Paper Excerpt Corpus. In *Proceedings of the Tenth International Conference on Language Resources and Evaluation (LREC)*, pages 2204–2208, Portorož, Slovenia. European Language Resources Association.

Ye Qi, Devendra Sachan, Matthieu Felix, Sarguna Padmanabhan, and Graham Neubig. 2018. When and Why Are Pre-Trained Word Embeddings Useful for Neural Machine Translation? In *Proceedings of the 2018 Conference of the North American Chapter of the Association for Computational Linguistics: Human Language Technologies, Volume 2 (Short Papers)*, pages 529–535, New Orleans, Louisiana. Association for Computational Linguistics.

Rico Sennrich, Barry Haddow, and Alexandra Birch. 2016a. Improving Neural Machine Translation Models with Monolingual Data. In *Proceedings of the 54th Annual Meeting of the Association for Computational Linguistics (Volume 1: Long Papers)*, pages 86–96, Berlin, Germany. Association for Computational Linguistics.

Rico Sennrich, Barry Haddow, and Alexandra Birch. 2016b. Neural Machine Translation of Rare Words with Subword Units. In *Proceedings of the 54th Annual Meeting of the Association for Computational Linguistics (Volume 1: Long Papers)*, pages 1715–1725, Berlin, Germany. Association for Computational Linguistics.

Kaitao Song, Xu Tan, Tao Qin, Jianfeng Lu, and Tie-Yan Liu. 2019. MASS: Masked Sequence to Sequence Pre-training for Language Generation. In *Proceedings of the 36th International Conference on Machine Learning, ICML 2019, 9-15 June 2019, Long Beach, California, USA*, pages 5926–5936.

Ilya Sutskever, Oriol Vinyals, and Quoc V. Le. 2014. Sequence to Sequence Learning with Neural Networks. In *Proceedings of the 27th Neural Information Processing Systems Conference (NIPS)*, pages 3104–3112, Montréal, Canada.

Arseny Tolmachev, Daisuke Kawahara, and Sadao Kurohashi. 2018. Juman++: A Morphological Analysis Toolkit for Scriptio Continua. In *Proceedings of the 2018 Conference on Empirical Methods in Natural Language Processing: System Demonstrations*, pages 54–59, Brussels, Belgium. Association for Computational Linguistics.

Ashish Vaswani, Samy Bengio, Eugene Brevdo, Francois Chollet, Aidan Gomez, Stephan Gouws, Llion Jones, Łukasz Kaiser, Nal Kalchbrenner, Niki Parmar, Ryan Sepassi, Noam Shazeer, and Jakob Uszkoreit. 2018. Tensor2Tensor for Neural Machine Translation. In *Proceedings of the 13th Conference of the Association for Machine Translation in the Americas (Volume 1: Research Papers)*, pages 193–199, Boston, USA. Association for Machine Translation in the Americas.

Xinyi Wang and Graham Neubig. 2019. Target Conditioned Sampling: Optimizing Data Selection for Multilingual Neural Machine Translation. In *Proceedings of the 57th Annual Meeting of the Association for Computational Linguistics*, pages 5823–5828, Florence, Italy. Association for Computational Linguistics.

Barret Zoph, Deniz Yuret, Jonathan May, and Kevin Knight. 2016. Transfer Learning for Low-Resource Neural Machine Translation. In *Proceedings of the 2016 Conference on Empirical Methods in Natural Language Processing (EMNLP)*, pages 1568–1575, Austin, USA.

Checkpoint Reranking: An Approach To Select Better Hypothesis For Neural Machine Translation Systems

Vinay Pandramish
International Institute of
Information Technology,
Hyderabad
`pandramish.vinay@research.`
`iiit.ac.in`

Dipti Misra Sharma
International Institute of
Information Technology,
Hyderabad
`dipti@iiit.ac.in`

Abstract

In this paper, we propose a method of reranking the outputs of Neural Machine Translation (NMT) systems. After the decoding process, we select a few last iteration outputs in the training process as the N-best list. After training a Neural Machine Translation (NMT) baseline system, it has been observed that these iteration outputs have an oracle score higher than baseline up to 1.01 BLEU points compared to the last iteration of the trained system. We come up with a ranking mechanism by solely focusing on the decoder's ability to generate distinct tokens and without the usage of any language model or data. With this method, we achieved a translation improvement up to +0.16 BLEU points over baseline. We also evaluate our approach by applying the coverage penalty to the training process. In cases of moderate coverage penalty, the oracle scores are higher than the final iteration up to +0.99 BLEU points, and our algorithm gives an improvement up to +0.17 BLEU points. With excessive penalty, there is a decrease in translation quality compared to the baseline system. Still, an increase in oracle scores up to +1.30 is observed with the re-ranking algorithm giving an improvement up to +0.15 BLEU points is found in case of excessive penalty. The proposed re-ranking method is a generic one and can be extended to other language pairs as well.

1   Introduction

Neural Machine Translation(NMT) has brought excellent results in the field of Machine TranslationSutskever et al. (2014); Bahdanau et al. (2014); Cho et al. (2014) due to generation of high-quality translations for different language pairs. Yet even higher quality can be achieved by combining multiple models by techniques like ensembles Hansen and Salamon (1990) and reranking Shen et al. (2004). Our work deals with how Neural Machine Translation (NMT) can achieve better results explicitly with reranking methods.

Neural Machine Translation has an encoder-decoder architecture that is jointly trained to maximize the probability of target given source sentences. It first encodes the source sentence into a single vector, and the decoder predicts it. With the Attention Mechanism, it tries to apply weights to the input sentence at each time step. Recent approaches like the transformer model Vaswani et al. (2017) have achieved the state-of-the-art results for Machine Translation.

Neural Machine Translation (NMT) however, leads to over-translation and under-translation as it tends to ignore the past alignment information, and it is effectively tackled by introducing a coverage vector Tu et al. (2016). Other approaches such as Mi et al. (2016a) and Mi et al. (2016b) too solve the coverage problem in NMT. Without the coverage vector, it could result in a decrease in translation quality.

We propose a method that selects a better hypothesis giving high importance to distinct words generated from decoder without the usage of any language model or data. After applying the proposed reranking method, an overall improvement in translation quality is observed as compared to the baseline system.

The rest of the paper is organized as follows; Section 2 discusses the work related to re-utilizing existing models for Machine Translation. Section 3 describes our approach for Checkpoint based Reranking. In Section 4, we present our Reranking Algorithm. In Section 5, we demonstrate all of our Experiments along with the results obtained, and finally, the paper is concluded in Section 6 with future directions.

Proceedings of the 58th Annual Meeting of the Association for Computational Linguistics: Student Research Workshop, pages 286–291
July 5 - July 10, 2020. ©2020 Association for Computational Linguistics

2 Related Work

The work of Imamura and Sumita (2017) explains the concepts of reranking and ensembling in detail. It introduces a method of bidirectional reranking in which it combines the hypothesis from l2r and r2l decoding following the works of Liu et al. (2016), which proposes an agreement model to solve unbalanced outputs of recurrent neural networks. Marie and Fujita (2018) has introduced a reranking system that uses a smorgasbord of informative features in tasks where PBSMT and NMT produce translations of different quality.

The work by Shen et al. (2004) shows how to apply perceptron-like reranking algorithms to improve the overall translation quality, and Olteanu et al. (2006) shows the usage of Language Models (LMs) for reranking on hypotheses generated by phrase-based Statistical Machine Translation systems. Wang et al. (2007) has shown linguistically motivated and computationally efficient structured language models for reranking in SMT systems.

The concept of Checkpoint ensembles is introduced by Sennrich et al. (2016) and was later on improvised to independent ensembling Sennrich et al. (2017). Vaswani et al. (2017) included a checkpoint averaging method for their model. Liu et al. (2018) has focused on decoding techniques that utilize existing models at parameter, word, and sentence level corresponding to checkpoint averaging, model ensembling, and candidate reranking and found that all of these improve the translation quality without retraining the model.

3 Checkpoint Based Reranking

In our approach, the iteration outputs are selected as the N-best list. It implies for the last K iterations; we have the corresponding K-best list for a sentence. We take our Oracle scores as the one that is having the largest BLEU Score Papineni et al. (2002) on the test reference hypothesis from this K-best list. After obtaining the oracle scores from this K-best list, we observe that this score is larger than the baseline system, and it indicates that there is scope for further improvement of translation quality. So we propose a reranking method that improves the translation quality over the baseline system without any language model or data.

We try to focus on the nature of translations that the decoder generates with and without coverage penalty. In the initial step, we keep track of the number of distinct words in the generated hypothe-sis, and the later ones we keep track of words that have repeated more than once.A higher score is given for sentences having a higher number of Distinct Tokens (D) and lower scores for those having more number of repetitive words (F).

For each sentence in the N-best list, these scores are sorted, and the sentence having the highest score is selected. This process is repeated for the entire test set, and the ones that are having the top most scores are chosen as the reranked output, as shown in Section 4.

4 Reranking Procedure

Algorithm 1 Method

  Input: Translated Target Language Sentences $H = (\, h(n-k)...,h(n)\,)$ at last k epochs for given sentence

  Output: Sentence having highest number of distinct words and lowest repetitive words

  for each sentence h_j in H **do**

    if $h_j \leftarrow (\mathrm{w}_1, w_2, w_3 ... w_l)$ **then**

      $D \rightarrow DISTINCT((\mathrm{w}_1, w_2, w_3 ... w_l))$

      $F \rightarrow FREQ(\mathrm{w}_1) \times FREQ(\mathrm{w}_2)...$

    $score_j \rightarrow D/F$

    end if

    return sentence with highest $score_j$

  end for=0

For a sentence, FREQ is the count of each word; DISTINCT is the total count of unique words. For each hypothesis in the K-best list we divide DISTINCT with FREQ and select the highest scorer.

5 Experiments and Results

5.1 DataSet

We used ILCI Jha (2010) corpus, which has eleven language pairs from which we chose Telugu and Hindi as our parallel data during the training process. The entire corpus is manually cleaned to remove the misalignments. Table 1 shows the split ratio of sentences followed in the process.

Data	Size
Training	45000
Validation	4000
Test	990

Table 1: Corpus Division

5.2 Experiments

We adopt the Keras implementation Álvaro Peris and Casacuberta (2018) for our experiments.We use a two-layer encoder-decoder model with 500-dimensional source and target embeddings and 500 units in each of the layers. The encoder layers are LSTM Hochreiter and Schmidhuber (1997) and decoder are ConditionalLSTM with Bahdanu's attention Bahdanau et al. (2014) and the optimizer used is Adam Kingma and Ba (2014) and the model is trained for 15 iterations with a batch size of 512 sentences. The rest of the parameters in the configuration file were set to their default values. We evaluate with coverage penalty and the absence of it for our experiments.

The hypotheses are collected for the last k=3, 5, 7 during decoding. We evaluate the generated hypotheses with BLEU Papineni et al. (2002) for our experiments.

5.3 Results

Hypothesis	BLEU
Checkpoint-1	0.62
Checkpoint-2	3.55
Checkpoint-3	8.83
Checkpoint-4	13.53
Checkpoint-5	17.01
Checkpoint-6	19.20
Checkpoint-7	20.72
Checkpoint-8	21.09
Checkpoint-9	21.38
Checkpoint-10	21.87
Checkpoint-11	22.39
Checkpoint-12	22.37
Checkpoint-13	22.57
Checkpoint-14	22.71
Checkpoint-15	22.92

Table 2: BLEU Scores with Baseline System

The scores obtained after each iteration are shown in Table 2. After this, we apply our proposed reranking method to the last few iteration outputs, which are selected as the N-best list. The proposed reranking method leads to an overall improvement of translation quality by +0.07, +0.15, +0.16 BLEU score compared to the baseline with oracle improvements up to +0.55, +0.90, +1.01 on the three systems. The scores obtained for each of them are shown in Tables 3, 4, 5.

System	BLEU
Baseline	22.92
Reranking	22.99 (**+0.07**)
Oracle	23.47 (**+0.55**)

Table 3: Last 3 Iterations

System	BLEU
Baseline	22.92
Reranking	23.07 (**+0.15**)
Oracle	23.82 (**+0.90**)

Table 4: Last 5 Iterations

System	BLEU
Baseline	22.92
Reranking	23.08 (**+0.16**)
Oracle	23.93 (**+1.01**)

Table 5: Last 7 Iterations

5.4 With Coverage Penalty

We also evaluate our work by adding coverage penalty Wu et al. (2016) in the training process to ensure that this algorithm works when both the under translations and over translations are addressed adequately. All the hyperparameters are kept the same as the baseline system except for the coverage penalty.

Hypothesis	0.1 penalty
Checkpoint-1	1.22
Checkpoint-2	5.59
Checkpoint-3	11.92
Checkpoint-4	16.59
Checkpoint-5	19.18
Checkpoint-6	20.51
Checkpoint-7	21.26
Checkpoint-8	21.40
Checkpoint-9	21.80
Checkpoint-10	21.72
Checkpoint-11	22.27
Checkpoint-12	22.57
Checkpoint-13	23.11
Checkpoint-14	22.93
Checkpoint-15	23.35

Table 6: BLEU Scores With 0.1 Coverage Penalty

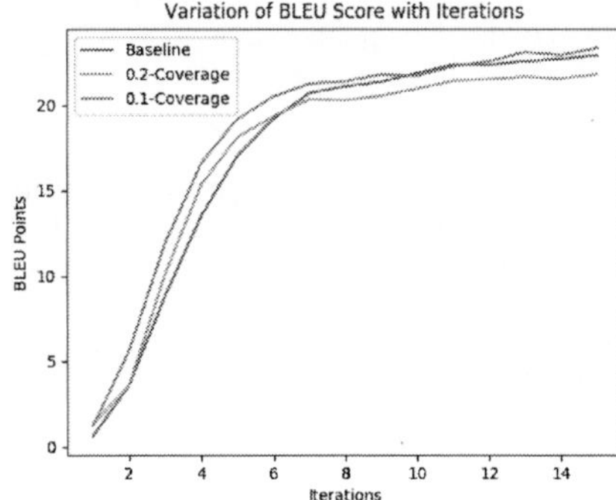

Figure 1: Comparison with Baseline System

System	0.1 penalty
Baseline	23.35
Reranking	23.40 (**+0.05**)
Oracle	23.86 (**+0.51**)

Table 7: Last 3 Iterations with 0.1 coverage penalty

System	0.1 penalty
Baseline	23.35
Reranking	23.50 (**+0.15**)
Oracle	24.17 (**+0.82**)

Table 8: Last 5 Iterations with 0.1 coverage penalty

System	0.1 penalty
Baseline	23.35
Reranking	23.52 (**+0.17**)
Oracle	24.34 (**+0.99**)

Table 9: Last 7 Iterations with 0.1 coverage penalty

From Tables 7, 8, 9 it can be inferred that there is an improvement of +0.05, +0.15, +0.17 and oracle improvements up to +0.51, +0.82, +0.99 for 0.1 coverage penalty.

With excess coverage penalty, there is a decline in translation quality compared to the baseline system without coverage penalty, as shown in Tables 2 and 10. Still, the proposed method gives an increase of +0.12, +0.15, +0.15 over baseline with oracle improvements up to +0.91, +1.30, +1.30 for the last 3, 5 and 7 checkpoints respectively as shown in Tables 11, 12, 13.

One can also observe that the improvements and the oracle scores increase correspondingly with the size of the N-best list.The variation with the baseline can be obtained as shown in Figure 1.

Hypothesis	0.2 penalty
Checkpoint-1	1.33
Checkpoint-2	3.54
Checkpoint-3	10.10
Checkpoint-4	15.36
Checkpoint-5	18.08
Checkpoint-6	19.36
Checkpoint-7	20.35
Checkpoint-8	20.29
Checkpoint-9	20.56
Checkpoint-10	20.96
Checkpoint-11	21.43
Checkpoint-12	21.52
Checkpoint-13	21.66
Checkpoint-14	21.56
Checkpoint-15	21.81

Table 10: BLEU Scores With 0.2 Coverage Penalty

System	0.2 penalty
Baseline	21.81
Reranking	21.93 (**+0.12**)
Oracle	22.72 (**+0.91**)

Table 11: Last 3 Iterations with 0.2 coverage penalty

System	0.2 penalty
Baseline	21.81
Reranking	21.96 (**+0.15**)
Oracle	23.11 (**+1.30**)

Table 12: Last 5 Iterations with 0.2 coverage penalty

System	0.2 penalty
Baseline	21.81
Reranking	21.96 (**+0.15**)
Oracle	23.11 (**+1.30**)

Table 13: Last 7 Iterations with 0.2 coverage penalty

6 Conclusions and Future Work

In this paper, we introduce a method of selecting an N-best list for NMT systems and propose a way of reranking to the generated hypotheses from the system. We observe that our approach is giving better results over the baseline model by following the proposed reranking method and is also evaluated with the coverage penalty.

One can investigate our approach with varying beam sizes and analyzing the effect of length penalty Wu et al. (2016) and comparing it with methods such as Yang et al. (2018). We also look forward to coming up with better reranking ways that are closer to the oracle scores and investigate the efficacy of the approach in low-resourced data conditions.

Language models are used for getting the likelihood of sentences and is a widely used concept for reranking hypotheses. Introducing Language Models during reranking could establish a tradeoff between perplexity and the scores to the hypotheses generated. We also plan to explore the work by Çaglar Gülçehre et al. (2017) and Çaglar Gülçehre et al. (2015) that introduces language models into the existing neural architecture with methods such as Shallow Fusion and Deep Fusion. It is another promising area to be looked upon for reranking.

Acknowledgments

The authors would like to thank some of the Anonymous reviewers for providing critical suggestions. We acknowledge Kenton Murray for the post-acceptance mentoring, Manish Shrivastava for the guidance, Vandan Mujadia for reviewing the drafts and Grammarly for their generous donation towards drafting the final manuscript.

References

Dzmitry Bahdanau, Kyunghyun Cho, and Yoshua Bengio. 2014. Neural machine translation by jointly learning to align and translate. *CoRR*, abs/1409.0473.

Kyunghyun Cho, Bart van Merrienboer, Çaglar Gülçehre, Dzmitry Bahdanau, Fethi Bougares, Holger Schwenk, and Yoshua Bengio. 2014. Learning phrase representations using rnn encoder-decoder for statistical machine translation. In *EMNLP*.

Çaglar Gülçehre, Orhan Firat, Kelvin Xu, Kyunghyun Cho, Loïc Barrault, Huei-Chi Lin, Fethi Bougares, Holger Schwenk, and Yoshua Bengio. 2015. On using monolingual corpora in neural machine translation. *ArXiv*, abs/1503.03535.

Çaglar Gülçehre, Orhan Firat, Kelvin Xu, Kyunghyun Cho, and Yoshua Bengio. 2017. On integrating a language model into neural machine translation. *Computer Speech Language*, 45:137–148.

Lars Kai Hansen and Peter Salamon. 1990. Neural network ensembles. *IEEE Trans. Pattern Anal. Mach. Intell.*, 12:993–1001.

Sepp Hochreiter and Jürgen Schmidhuber. 1997. Long short-term memory. *Neural Computation*, 9:1735–1780.

Kenji Imamura and Eiichiro Sumita. 2017. Ensemble and reranking: Using multiple models in the nict-2 neural machine translation system at wat2017. In *WAT@IJCNLP*.

Girish Nath Jha. 2010. The tdil program and the indian langauge corpora intitiative (ilci). In *Proceedings of the Seventh International Conference on Language Resources and Evaluation (LREC'10)*, Valletta, Malta. European Language Resources Association (ELRA).

Diederik P. Kingma and Jimmy Ba. 2014. Adam: A method for stochastic optimization. *CoRR*, abs/1412.6980.

Lemao Liu, Masao Utiyama, Andrew M. Finch, and Eiichiro Sumita. 2016. Agreement on target-bidirectional neural machine translation. In *HLT-NAACL*.

Yuchen Liu, Long Zhou, Yining Wang, Yang Zhao, Jiajun Zhang, and Chengqing Zong. 2018. A comparable study on model averaging, ensembling and reranking in nmt. In *NLPCC*.

Benjamin Marie and Atsushi Fujita. 2018. A smorgasbord of features to combine phrase-based and neural machine translation. In *AMTA*.

Haitao Mi, Baskaran Sankaran, Zhiguo Wang, and Abe Ittycheriah. 2016a. A coverage embedding model for neural machine translation. *ArXiv*, abs/1605.03148.

Haitao Mi, Zhiguo Wang, and Abe Ittycheriah. 2016b. Supervised attentions for neural machine translation. In *EMNLP*.

Marian Olteanu, Pasin Suriyentrakorn, and Dan I. Moldovan. 2006. Language models and reranking for machine translation. In *WMT@HLT-NAACL*.

Kishore Papineni, Salim Roukos, Todd Ward, and Wei-Jing Zhu. 2002. Bleu: a method for automatic evaluation of machine translation. In *Proceedings of the 40th Annual Meeting of the Association for Computational Linguistics*, pages 311–318, Philadelphia, Pennsylvania, USA. Association for Computational Linguistics.

Álvaro Peris and Francisco Casacuberta. 2018. NMT-Keras: a Very Flexible Toolkit with a Focus on Interactive NMT and Online Learning. *The Prague Bulletin of Mathematical Linguistics*, 111:113–124.

Rico Sennrich, Alexandra Birch, Anna Currey, Ulrich Germann, Barry Haddow, Kenneth Heafield, Antonio Valerio Miceli Barone, and Philip Williams. 2017. The university of edinburgh's neural mt systems for wmt17. In *WMT*.

Rico Sennrich, Barry Haddow, and Alexandra Birch. 2016. Edinburgh neural machine translation systems for wmt 16. In *WMT*.

Libin Shen, Anoop Sarkar, and Franz Josef Och. 2004. Discriminative reranking for machine translation. In *HLT-NAACL*.

Ilya Sutskever, Oriol Vinyals, and Quoc V. Le. 2014. Sequence to sequence learning with neural networks. In *NIPS*.

Zhaopeng Tu, Zhengdong Lu, Yang P. Liu, Xiaohua Liu, and Hang Li. 2016. Modeling coverage for neural machine translation. In *ACL*.

Ashish Vaswani, Noam Shazeer, Niki Parmar, Jakob Uszkoreit, Llion Jones, Aidan N. Gomez, Lukasz Kaiser, and Illia Polosukhin. 2017. Attention is all you need. In *NIPS*.

Weiqi Wang, Andreas Stolcke, and Jing Zheng. 2007. Reranking machine translation hypotheses with structured and web-based language models. *2007 IEEE Workshop on Automatic Speech Recognition Understanding (ASRU)*, pages 159–164.

Yonghui Wu, Mike Schuster, Zhifeng Chen, Quoc V. Le, Mohammad Norouzi, Wolfgang Macherey, Maxim Krikun, Yuan Cao, Qin Gao, Klaus Macherey, Jeff Klingner, Apurva Shah, Melvin Johnson, Xiaobing Liu, Lukasz Kaiser, Stephan Gouws, Yoshikiyo Kato, Taku Kudo, Hideto Kazawa, Keith Stevens, George Kurian, Nishant Patil, Wei Wang, Cliff Young, Jason Smith, Jason Riesa, Alex Rudnick, Oriol Vinyals, Gregory S. Corrado, Macduff Hughes, and Jeffrey Dean. 2016. Google's neural machine translation system: Bridging the gap between human and machine translation. *ArXiv*, abs/1609.08144.

Yilin Yang, Liang Huang, and Mingbo Ma. 2018. Breaking the beam search curse: A study of (re-)scoring methods and stopping criteria for neural machine translation. In *EMNLP*.

Cross-Lingual Disaster-related Multi-label Tweet Classification
with Manifold Mixup

Jishnu Ray Chowdhury[1], Cornelia Caragea[1], and Doina Caragea[2]
[1]Computer Science, University of Illinois at Chicago
[2]Computer Science, Kansas State University
jraych2@uic.edu, cornelia@uic.edu, dcaragea@ksu.edu

Abstract

Distinguishing informative and actionable messages from a social media platform like Twitter is critical for facilitating disaster management. For this purpose, we compile a multilingual dataset of over 130K samples for multi-label classification of disaster-related tweets. We present a masking-based loss function for partially labeled samples and demonstrate the effectiveness of Manifold Mixup in the text domain. Our main model is based on Multilingual BERT, which we further improve with Manifold Mixup. We show that our model generalizes to unseen disasters in the test set. Furthermore, we analyze the capability of our model for zero-shot generalization to new languages. Our code, dataset, and other resources are available on Github.[1]

1 Introduction

In times of disaster, affected individuals often turn to social media platforms, such as Twitter or Facebook, to express their feelings generated by a disaster, update friends and relatives on their status, request help or supplies, or report useful information to the disaster response teams. Response organizations can use social media to increase situational awareness by providing information about disaster status, ongoing rescue operations, and disaster warnings (Palen and Hughes, 2018). However, the low entry-barrier of social media platforms, where everybody can post their own "news" in real-time, leads to information overload, making it hard for users to find relevant and useful information (Reuter et al., 2018). Thus, it is crucial to filter out the non-informative messages, and to distinguish among different categories of informative messages to ensure that a message reaches its target users. In

turn, this can help facilitate disaster response and increase situational awareness.

Towards this goal, in recent years, many works have focused on disaster-related tweet classification (Alam et al., 2018b; Mazloom et al., 2018; Nguyen et al., 2017; Li et al., 2017; Neppalli et al., 2018; Caragea et al., 2016, 2011). However, most of these works have focused on the classification of English tweets only, with a few notable exceptions (Musaev and Pu, 2017; Khare et al., 2018; Lorini et al., 2019; Torres et al., 2019). We stress that there are a lot of disaster-prone non-English-speaking countries, which could benefit from a multilingual classifier that can be used in real-time to identify useful information on social media. Furthermore, there is a lack of a large scale standard multilingual disaster-related dataset for multi-label classification with diverse disaster types. Against this background and needs, we make the following contributions:

1. We aggregate existing datasets into a large disaster dataset using a new annotation scheme. Furthermore, by utilizing a class-mask (elaborated in Section 4.1), we make use of both binary-classification data and multi-class classification data in the same training phase.

2. We explore Manifold Mixup (Verma et al., 2019) in the natural language-based disaster domain. Manifold Mixup is a regularization technique originally introduced in computer vision tasks.

3. We employ Multilingual BERT (Devlin et al., 2019) to train multilingual classifiers. We demonstrate its generalization on unseen disasters and its zero-shot transfer-ability to languages not present in the training data.

---

[1]https://github.com/JRC1995/
Multilingual-BERT-Disaster

Proceedings of the 58th Annual Meeting of the Association for Computational Linguistics: Student Research Workshop, pages 292–298
July 5 - July 10, 2020. ©2020 Association for Computational Linguistics

2   Related Work

There are numerous prior works on disaster-related tweet classification. For example, Imran et al. (2013; 2015) focus on classifying and extracting actionable information from disaster-related tweets, assuming that sufficient labeled tweets from the ongoing disaster are available for model training. Later, Imran et al. (2016b) explore real-time classification of tweets from a target disaster using models trained on past disasters. Nguyen et al. (2017) introduce a Convolutional Neural Network that performs robustly even on out-of-event data during inference. Other works explore domain-adaptation that uses labeled tweets from past disasters and unlabeled tweets from an ongoing disaster (Li et al., 2018; Alam et al., 2018a). Kruspe (2019) take a few-shot learning approach, in which a disaster-specific model is trained using only a few (around 10) examples for disaster-related tweet detection. In contrast, we train a universal model on diverse disaster types for fine-grained classification and show that it performs remarkably well on unseen disaster types without further training (specifically, it achieves zero-shot generalization to unseen events). Wang and Lillis (2019) classify actionable tweets using ELMo contextual word embeddings, whereas Ma (2019) uses a monolingual BERT-based model for disaster-related tweet classification. In contrast, we work with a multilingual model, which we compare with multiple baselines, and augment with Manifold Mixup.

Regarding cross-lingual approaches, Dittrich and Lucas (2014) present a real-time application tool for multilingual tweet classification and disaster detection. However, this tool requires a long training phase with tweets from specific areas for robust detection, and its multilingual classifier filters messages based on shallow matching of pre-selected keywords (and their translations). Musaev and Pu (2017) construct a multilingual model for tweet classification using multilingual Wikipedia articles as knowledge repository. Khare et al. (2018) also take into account cross-lingual capabilities, however, this is limited to the fixed few number of languages that are present in their annotated training data and do not generalize to new languages without further training. M-BERT overcomes these shortcomings. Similar to us, Lorini et al. (2019) use multi-lingual word embeddings for cross-lingual classification, but they use non-contextual embeddings. Torres et al. (2019) use

contextualized word embeddings for cross-lingual analysis, but only on limited samples ($8K$) and only for two languages (English and Spanish).

A few recent works (Pires et al., 2019; K et al., 2020) also demonstrate the strong cross-lingual and zero-shot transfer capabilities of M-BERT, but not in the disaster domain.

3   Aggregated Dataset

To prepare our large multilingual dataset, we aggregated several resources from CrisisNLP,[2] together with two resources from CrisisLex.[3] Specifically, we used Resource #1 (Imran et al., 2016a), Resource #4 (Nguyen et al., 2017), Resource #5 (Alam et al., 2018c), and Resource #7 (Alam et al., 2018a) from CrisisNLP, and CrisisLexT6 (Olteanu et al., 2014) and CrisisLexT26 (Olteanu et al., 2015) from CrisisLex. The *original classes* in each resource, together with the mapping to the *new classes* included in our data set, can be seen in Table 1. Some examples from the dataset are shown in Table 2. For the dataset construction, the following classes were included:

1. **Casualties and Damage (C & D):** This class consists of tweets related to affected individuals, displaced people, building collapse, rescue operations, infrastructure and utilities damage, needs of affected people, missing or trapped people, and other topics related to situational awareness and disaster response.

2. **Donation and Volunteering (D & V):** This class consists of tweets related to donations, volunteering requests, and other needs and requests targeted to individuals following the disaster and/or supporting the victims.

3. **Caution and Advice (C & A):** This class consists of tweets recommending caution, expressing warnings, or providing advice regarding the crisis situation. Such tweets are useful for the affected individuals.

4. **Informative (I):** This is a general class, which includes: tweets belonging to any of the above three classes; tweets with niche categories that do not fit into the above classes; tweets with more vague classes (e.g., "*other useful information*"); and tweets originally labeled with only binary classes such as *relevant* or *informative*.

---

[2] https://crisisnlp.qcri.org/
[3] https://crisislex.org/data-collections.html

Original Class	New Class	Original Class	New Class	Original Class	New Class
CrisisNLP Resource #1				**CrisisNLP Resource #5**	
Other relevant info.	I	Disease signs, symptoms	C & D, I	Other relevant info.	I
Displaced people	C & D, I	Affected People	C & D, I	Affected individuals	C & D, I
Needs of those affected	C & D, I	Prevention	C & A, I	Injured or dead	C & D, I
Donations of money	D & V, I	Death Reports	C & D, I	Vehicle damage	C & D, I
Not related to crisis	N	Disease Transmission	I	Infrastructure & util.	C & D, I
Infrastructure	C & D, I	Treatment	I	Volun. & Donation	D & V, I
Shelter and supplies	D & V, I	Displaced people & evac.	C & D, I	Missing or found	C & D, I
Other relevant	I	Other Useful Info.	I	**CrisisNLP Resource #7**	
Injured and dead	C & D, I	Money	D & V, I	Relevant	I
Volunteer or Prof. services	D & V, I	Caution & Advice	C & A, I	Not relevant	N
Sympathy & emotional	N	Humanitarian Aid	D & V, I	**CrisisLexT6**	
Infrastructure & util.	C & D, I	People missing or found	C & D, I	on-topic	I
Donations supp. & volun.	D & V, I	Response Efforts	C & D, I	off-topic	N
Not related or irrelevant	N	Urgent Needs	D & V, I	**CrisisLexT26**	
Requests for Help/Needs	D & V, I	Not Informative	N	Affected individuals	C & D, I
Praying	N	**CrisisNLP Resource #4**		Not applicable	N
Missing, trapped, found	C & D, I	Other Useful Info.	I	Donations & volun.	D & V, I
Not Relevant	N	Not related or irrelevant	N	Sympathy & support	N
Informative	I	Affected Individuals	C & D, I	Caution and advice	C & A, I
Injured or dead people	C & D, I	Sympathy and support	N	Infrastructure & util.	C & D, I
Infrastructure damage	C & D, I	Donations and volunteering	D & V, I	Other Useful Info.	I
Personal, sympathy, support	N				

Table 1: Overview of mappings between the original classes and the new classes.

Examples	Original label	New label
Another typhoon named internationally as #BOPHA will hit #Southern #Mindanao. It will be named #Pablo in RP. Oh noooooes!!	Other Useful Info.	Informative
#RescuePH Rescue pls family trapped at Blk64 Lot2 Phase2 Dela Costa Homes V Burgos Montalban Rizal.Family of 4w/2 children. ..."	Affected individuals	Casualties & Damage
Methods of prevention of Coronavirus: Use a tissue when coughing or sneezing, cover your mouth and nose with it, and then get rid of it	Prevention	Caution & Advice

Table 2: Examples from the aggregated dataset with the original and new label.

5. **Non-Informative (N):** This class consists of all the tweets that are not included in the Informative class.

Some of the above classes (for example, Casualties and Damage) are very broad and could be broken down into more specific classes. However, keeping them broad simplifies the aggregation of different annotation schemes and prevents the formation of multiple fine-grained but sparse classes.

During aggregation, we treat the first four classes as mutually exclusive (they are also mutually exclusive with the Non-Informative class). We filter out duplicate tweets. For duplicates from different resources that were originally associated with more than one mutually exclusive classes, we keep only the first class, based on the order in which classes are listed above.

Statistics about the final dataset with respect to the number of tweets per class and per language are shown in Table 3.

Number of Tweets per Class				
C & D	D & V	C & A	I	N
16, 235	9, 125	3, 634	79, 473	54, 947

Number of Tweets per Language				
English	Spanish	Italian	French	Others
123, 406	4, 724	1, 581	666	4043

Table 3: Samples per class and per language.

4 Methods

4.1 Classification Approach

In general, all of our models use a sentence encoder to map a tweet to a single vector sentence representation. The vector is then fed to multiple binary classifiers. Specifically, we train four classifiers. One classifier distinguishes between *Informative* and *Non-Informative* classes, while the other three classifiers correspond to the remaining three classes: *Casualties and Damage*, *Caution and Advise*, and *Donations and Volunteers*, respectively (each classifier predicts whether a tweet belongs to a particular class or not).

We should note that there are many tweets belonging to the *Informative* class, which originally only had binary classes (informative/non-informative or relevant/non-relevant). While those tweets may also belong to one of the more fine-grained classes, their class could not be determined, if it was not available in the original resources. In other words, many of the samples in the dataset are **partially labeled** (where the binary "informative" or "Non-Informative" class is present but the other fine-grained class information is absent). However, ignoring all partially labeled tweets would result in removing nearly half of the data. In order to get the benefit from the binary-classification-only data while also enabling the same model to work on multi-label classification we devise a label masking strategy. Precisely, the mask is used to ensure that the loss signal is only propagated from classes which are annotated. The strategy is discussed in further details below.

By default, we use the negative class for the three fine-grained categories as dummy ground-truth for such cases. We then mask out (i.e., zero out) the loss from the dummy ground truth cases during training. For masking the loss from dummy ground truth, we use a class mask m_{ij} (i.e., a mask for the jth class and the ith sample), where m_{ij} is 0 if the actual j^{th} class ground truth is not present for the ith sample, otherwise it is 1. Overall, we use binary cross entropy for each of the classifiers with the class masks and class weights. The loss function can be formalized as:

$$\mathcal{L} = -\frac{1}{N}\sum_{i=1}^{N}\frac{1}{K}\sum_{j=1}^{K} m_{ij} \cdot (c_j y_{ij} \cdot \log P_\theta(y_{ij}|x_i)$$
$$+ (1 - y_{ij}) \cdot \log(1 - P_\theta(y_{ij}|x_i))) \quad (1)$$

where K is the number of classes, N is the number of samples, c_j is the class weight for the jth class, x_i is the ith tweet string, θ represents the model parameters, and $P_\theta(y_{ij}|x_i)$ is the model prediction for the ith tweet string and the jth class. We use class weights to handle class imbalance. We consider the cost of filtering out an important and urgent tweet to be higher than the cost of including a non-informative tweet. This is why we bias our model towards recall by using class-weights of value ≥ 1 for the positive classes. We use a class weight of 1 for the *Informative* versus *Non-Informative*

classes (as they are fairly balanced, with already a small bias towards the positive class). For the fine-grained classes, we use the following formula to find the class weights:

$$c_i = \frac{\max_j(\{count(class_j)|class_j \in C\})}{count(class_i)} \quad (2)$$

where $C = \{$*'Non-Informative'*, *'Casualties & Damage'*, *'Donation & Volunteering'*, *'Caution & Advice'*$\}$. We should note here that the loss function does not take the positive classes as mutually exclusive since, in principle, a single tweet could have multiple classes (for example, a tweet could have both 'Caution and Advice' and 'Casualties and Damage').[4]

4.2 Sentence Encoders

As we focus on supervised learning from large data, we use some standard text classification models, such as FastText (Joulin et al., 2017; Mikolov et al., 2018), CNN (Kim, 2014), XML-CNN (Liu et al., 2017), and BiLSTM (Adhikari et al., 2019) as baseline sentence encoders. We compare them with M-BERT (Devlin et al., 2019) encoders.

Manifold Mixup. We also adopt Manifold Mixup (Verma et al., 2019) in our main model (M-BERT). Mixup (Zhang et al., 2018) was originally introduced in the image classification domain as a data augmentation based regularization technique. The original technique augments data by linearly interpolating two different input data samples and their associated classes. In effect, this helps make a model more robust by inducing a linear behavior in-between training samples. Guo et al. (2019) show that Mixup both at the level of word embeddings and at the level of sentence embeddings (output of sentence encoder) is effective for text classification. Manifold Mixup is a more recent variant of the original input Mixup, where the hidden states of two different data samples, along with their associated classes, are linearly interpolated. To do this, a mixup ratio λ is sampled from a $Beta$ distribution, as: $\lambda \sim Beta(\alpha, \alpha)$.

Next, a hidden layer l is randomly chosen for mix up. Let h_i^l be the randomly chosen l^{th} hidden

---

[4]Even though the classifiers are not mutually exclusive, the annotated classes (excluding the more general informative class) are kept mutually exclusive because there were not many multi-label annotations in the original data and most tweets tend to belong to only one of the specific classes. One could also use mutually exclusive classifiers with the given data.

Model	F_1 (mean, std)	F_1 (mean, std)
	Meteor (802)	Cyclone (2,473)
FastText	73.79 ± 0.55	81.81 ± 0.67
FastText$_{hier}$	74.61 ± 1.19	81.59 ± 0.50
CNN	66.83 ± 2.16	82.40 ± 0.48
XML-CNN	74.34 ± 2.51	82.04 ± 1.02
BiLSTM	72.40 ± 2.47	82.65 ± 0.88
M-BERT	83.63 ± 0.78	83.99 ± 0.47
+Word Mixup	83.02 ± 0.95	**85.48 ± 0.64***
+Sentence Mixup	82.62 ± 0.55	83.78 ± 0.73
+Mixup	**84.90 ± 0.84***	85.09 ± 0.86*
	Flood (684)	Mixed (10,000)
FastText	75.53 ± 0.54	82.91 ± 0.05
FastText$_{hier}$	76.21 ± 0.81	84.09 ± 0.24
CNN	72.78 ± 3.18	83.70 ± 0.12
XML-CNN	77.03 ± 1.26	84.56 ± 0.32
BiLSTM	74.35 ± 0.25	84.33 ± 0.15
M-BERT	78.51 ± 0.93	86.77 ± 0.18
+Word Mixup	79.18 ± 0.95*	87.31 ± 0.29*
+Sentence Mixup	**79.85 ± 0.50**	87.32 ± 0.20*
+Manifold Mixup	79.36 ± 0.79	**87.39 ± 0.23***

Table 4: F_1 scores on four test datasets (English Only). * means that the difference from M-BERT is statistically significant.

layer output from the ith tweet sample, and let h_j^l be the hidden layer output from the jth sample. The two outputs can be mixed up as follows:

$$\tilde{h}^l{}_i = \lambda \cdot h_i^l + (1 - \lambda) \cdot h_j^l \qquad (3)$$

where $\tilde{h}^l{}_i$ is the augmented (mixed-up) hidden state. We use the same λ to mix the hidden states of the tweet samples i and j, and also the corresponding ground truth classes and class masks for each class k included in our dataset:

$$\tilde{y}_{ik} = \lambda \cdot y_{ik} + (1 - \lambda) \cdot y_{jk} \qquad (4)$$

$$\tilde{m}_{ik} = \lambda \cdot m_{ik} + (1 - \lambda) \cdot m_{jk} \qquad (5)$$

where, $\tilde{y}_{ik}$ and $\tilde{m}_{ik}$ are the corresponding mixed-up class and class-mask, respectively. The augmented class-masks can be intuitively thought of as indicating to what extent the loss following the corresponding augmented ground truth class should be considered. If the major fraction of the mixed up class is a dummy class, then the corresponding augmented class-mask should have a low value. We also compare Word Mixup and Sentence Mixup. Word Mixup and Sentence Mixup can be considered as special cases of Manifold Mixup where the mixup is applied on only a specific layer. In case of word mixup, it is the first embedding layer, and in case of Sentence Mixup it is the final layer output of the sentence encoder.

Model	F_1 (mean, std)	F_1 (mean, std)
	Meteor (930)	Cyclone (2,558)
M-BERT	81.39 ± 1.42	84.60 ± 1.06
+Word Mixup	80.16 ± 3.09	84.47 ± 0.81
+Sentence Mixup	80.97 ± 1.65	84.87 ± 0.71
+Manifold Mixup	**81.73 ± 0.78**	**85.15 ± 0.79***
	Flood (768)	Mixed (10,000)
M-BERT	79.24 ± 1.28	86.63 ± 0.22
+Word Mixup	78.32 ± 0.81*	87.10 ± 0.19
+Sentence Mixup	78.77 ± 0.69	86.98 ± 0.18
+Manifold Mixup	**79.84 ± 0.68***	**87.44 ± 0.11***

Table 5: F_1 scores on four test datasets (Full Dataset). * means that the difference from M-BERT is statistically significant.

5 Experiments and Results

5.1 Experimental Setup

We use four datasets for testing: Russia Meteor, Cyclone Pam, Philippines Flood, and Mixed disasters. To demonstrate the generalization capabilities of our models, we ensured that the first three datasets are from disasters that are absent in the training set. For M-BERT-based models, we use a mini batch size of 32, a learning rate of 10^{-3} for non-BERT parameters, and a fine-tuning rate of 2×10^{-5} for M-BERT parameters. We set the parameter α of the *Beta* distribution for the Mixup equation to 2. We run each model five times and report the mean and standard deviation of the results obtained in the 5 runs. For the other models, we import the parameter settings from their corresponding paper and then perform light manual tuning. The exact hyperparameters are available on Github.[5] For significance testing, we used the paired t-test ($p \leq 0.05$) (Dror et al., 2018) Note that the CNN baseline is also similar to the model used by Nguyen et al. (2017) which was demonstrated to be a strong performer in disaster-related classification.

5.2 Results

In Table 4, we show the results on English only samples, and in Table 5, we show the results on the full multilingual test sets. As can be seen in Table 4, the M-BERT outperforms all the non-BERT baseline models. Using Manifold Mixup consistently increases the performance of base M-BERT in all cases, often also working better than Word Mixup and Sentence Mixup, especially for the multilingual setting (see Table 5). Manifold Mixup

---

[5]https://github.com/JRC1995/
Multilingual-BERT-Disaster

Language	Samples	F_1 (mean, std)
French (zero shot)	666	81.33 ± 0.77
Italian (zero shot)	1,581	75.44 ± 0.67
Spanish (zero shot)	4,724	85.26 ± 0.37

Table 6: F_1 scores of M-BERT + Manifold Mixup.

C & D	D & V	C & A	I
79.8 ± 0.5	77.5 ± 1	70.3 ± 1	90.9 ± 0.2

Table 7: Per-class F_1 of M-BERT+Manifold Mixup on Multilingual Mixed Disasters.

either outperforms or is very close to the other Mixup techniques. Table 6 shows the results of the cross-lingual experiments with M-BERT and Manifold Mixup for French, Italian, and Spanish languages, respectively, in a zero shot setting (Pires et al., 2019), where no tweets in the test language are included in the training set.

As can be seen from the table, the zero shot F1-score on Spanish is 85.25% (which is comparable to the best results in the previous experiments), despite the fact that no Spanish tweets were included in the training. The zero shot F1-scores on French and Italian are 81.33% and 75.44%, respectively. These results show that the M-BERT+Manifold Mixup model has good generalization capability in the new language (zero shot) setting. Thus, we can conclude that our M-BERT+Manifold Mixup model has great capability to generalize to a disaster in a new language (unseen in the training set) as long as the language is one of the 104 languages on which M-BERT was pre-trained. This is a strong result given that disasters can happen in countries with limited resources for automated classification of social media information.

In Table 7, we check the binary classification performance of M-BERT+Manifold Mixup for each class. As we can see, our model achieves an F_1 above 90% for the binary classification task of distinguishing whether a tweet is informative or not. Interestingly, it does not perform too poorly on Caution & Advice either despite having very limited samples for this class in the training set.

6 Conclusion

We present a way to aggregate prior disaster-related resources to compile a large scale tweet dataset for multi-label classification utilizing both multi-class classes and binary classes. We motivate the use of M-BERT for disaster-related tweet classification and we demonstrate its strong performance on unseen disasters and languages. We also motivate the use of Manifold Mixup for further improvement. In the future, it would be interesting to explore weak suervision and other data augmentation techniques to improve models' robustness further.

Acknowledgments

We thank NSF and Amazon Web Services for support from grants IIS-1741345 and IIS-1912887, which supported the research and the computation in this study. We also thank NSF for support from the grants IIS-1903963, and CMMI-1541155. We are grateful to our anonymous reviewers and the ACL student mentor Valerio Basile for their constructive feedback.

References

Ashutosh Adhikari, Achyudh Ram, Raphael Tang, and Jimmy Lin. 2019. Rethinking complex neural network architectures for document classification. In *ACL*.

Firoj Alam, Shafiq Joty, and Muhammad Imran. 2018a. Domain adaptation with adversarial training and graph embeddings. In *ACL*.

Firoj Alam, Shafiq Joty, and Muhammad Imran. 2018b. Graph based semi-supervised learning with convolution neural networks to classify crisis related tweets. In *AAAI Conference on Web and Social Media*.

Firoj Alam, Ferda Ofli, and Muhammad Imran. 2018c. Crisismmd: Multimodal twitter datasets from natural disasters. In *ICWSM*.

Cornelia Caragea, Nathan J. McNeese, Anuj R. Jaiswal, Greg Traylor, Hyun-Woo Kim, Prasenjit Mitra, Dinghao Wu, Andrea H. Tapia, C. Lee Giles, Bernard J. Jansen, and John Yen. 2011. Classifying text messages for the haiti earthquake. In *8th Proceedings of ISCRAM*.

Cornelia Caragea, Adrian Silvescu, and Andrea H. Tapia. 2016. Identifying informative messages in disaster events using convolutional neural networks. In *Proceedings of ISCRAM*.

Jacob Devlin, Ming-Wei Chang, Kenton Lee, and Kristina Toutanova. 2019. BERT: Pre-training of deep bidirectional transformers for language understanding. In *ACL*.

André Dittrich and Christian Lucas. 2014. Is this twitter event a disaster?

Rotem Dror, Gili Baumer, Segev Shlomov, and Roi Reichart. 2018. The hitchhiker's guide to testing statistical significance in natural language processing. In

Proceedings of the 56th Annual Meeting of the Association for Computational Linguistics (Volume 1: Long Papers), pages 1383–1392, Melbourne, Australia. Association for Computational Linguistics.

Hongyu Guo, Yongyi Mao, and Richong Zhang. 2019. Augmenting data with mixup for sentence classification: An empirical study. *arXiv preprint arXiv:1905.08941*.

Muhammad Imran, Carlos Castillo, Fernando Diaz, and Sarah Vieweg. 2015. Processing social media messages in mass emergency: A survey. *ACM Comp. Surveys (CSUR)*.

Muhammad Imran, Shady Elbassuoni, Carlos Castillo, Fernando Diaz, and Patrick Meier. 2013. Practical extraction of disaster-relevant information from social media. In *WWW*.

Muhammad Imran, Prasenjit Mitra, and Carlos Castillo. 2016a. Twitter as a lifeline: Human-annotated twitter corpora for nlp of crisis-related messages. In *LREC*.

Muhammad Imran, Prasenjit Mitra, and Jaideep Srivastava. 2016b. Enabling rapid classification of social media communications during crises. *IJISCRAM*.

Armand Joulin, Edouard Grave, Piotr Bojanowski, and Tomas Mikolov. 2017. Bag of tricks for efficient text classification. In *ACL*.

Karthikeyan K, Zihan Wang, Stephen Mayhew, and Dan Roth. 2020. Cross-lingual ability of multilingual {bert}: An empirical study. In *ICLR*.

Prashant Khare, Grégoire Burel, Diana Maynard, and Harith Alani. 2018. Cross-lingual classification of crisis data. In *ISWC*.

Yoon Kim. 2014. Convolutional neural networks for sentence classification. In *EMNLP*.

Anna Kruspe. 2019. Few-shot tweet detection in emerging disaster events. *arXiv preprint arXiv:1910.02290*.

Hongmin Li, Doina Caragea, and Cornelia Caragea. 2017. Towards practical usage of a domain adaptation algorithm in the early hours of a disaster. In *ISCRAM*.

Hongmin Li, Doina Caragea, Cornelia Caragea, and Nic Herndon. 2018. Disaster response aided by tweet classification with a domain adaptation approach. *JCCM*.

Jingzhou Liu, Wei-Cheng Chang, Yuexin Wu, and Yiming Yang. 2017. Deep learning for extreme multi-label text classification. In *ACM SIGIR*.

Valerio Lorini, Carlos Castillo, Francesco Dottori, Milan Kalas, Domenico Nappo, and Peter Salamon. 2019. Integrating social media into a pan-european flood awareness system: A multilingual approach. In *ISCRAM*.

Guoqin Ma. 2019. Tweets classification with bert in the field of disaster management.

Reza Mazloom, HongMin Li, Doina Caragea, Muhammad Imran, and Cornelia Caragea. 2018. Classification of twitter disaster data using a hybrid feature-instance adaptation approach. In *ISCRAM*.

Tomas Mikolov, Edouard Grave, Piotr Bojanowski, Christian Puhrsch, and Armand Joulin. 2018. Advances in pre-training distributed word representations. In *LREC*.

A. Musaev and C. Pu. 2017. Towards multilingual automated classification systems. In *ICDCS*.

Venkata Kishore Neppalli, Cornelia Caragea, and Doina Caragea. 2018. Deep neural networks versus naive bayes classifiers for identifying informative tweets during disasters. In *ISCRAM*.

Dat Tien Nguyen, Kamela Ali Al Mannai, Shafiq Joty, Hassan Sajjad, Muhammad Imran, and Prasenjit Mitra. 2017. Robust classification of crisis-related data on social networks using convolutional neural networks. In *ICWSM*.

Alexandra Olteanu, Carlos Castillo, Fernando Diaz, and Sarah Vieweg. 2014. Crisislex: A lexicon for collecting and filtering microblogged communications in crises. In *AAAI Conference on Weblogs and Social Media*.

Alexandra Olteanu, Sarah Vieweg, and Carlos Castillo. 2015. What to expect when the unexpected happens: Social media communications across crises. In *CSCW*.

Leysia Palen and Amanda L. Hughes. 2018. *Social Media in Disaster Communication*, pages 497–518. Springer International Publishing, Cham.

Telmo Pires, Eva Schlinger, and Dan Garrette. 2019. How multilingual is multilingual bert? *arXiv preprint arXiv:1906.01502*.

Christian Reuter, Amanda Lee Hughes, and Marc-André Kaufhold. 2018. Social media in crisis management: An evaluation and analysis of crisis informatics research. *Int. J. of HCI*, 34(4):280–294.

Torres, Carmen Vaca, and Johnny. 2019. Cross-lingual perspectives about crisis-related conversations on twitter. In *WWW*.

Vikas Verma, Alex Lamb, Christopher Beckham, Amir Najafi, Ioannis Mitliagkas, David Lopez-Paz, and Yoshua Bengio. 2019. Manifold mixup: Better representations by interpolating hidden states. In *ICML*.

Congcong Wang and David Lillis. 2019. Classification for crisis-related tweets leveraging word embeddings and data augmentation.

Hongyi Zhang, Moustapha Cisse, Yann N. Dauphin, and David Lopez-Paz. 2018. mixup: Beyond empirical risk minimization. In *ICLR*.

Inducing Grammar from Long Short-Term Memory Networks
by Shapley Decomposition

Yuhui Zhang   Allen Nie
Stanford University
Stanford, CA 94305
{yuhuiz, anie}@stanford.edu

Abstract

The principle of compositionality has deep roots in linguistics: the meaning of an expression is determined by its structure and the meanings of its constituents. However, modern neural network models such as long short-term memory network process expressions in a linear fashion and do not seem to incorporate more complex compositional patterns. In this work, we show that we can explicitly induce grammar by tracing the computational process of a long short-term memory network. We show: (i) the multiplicative nature of long short-term memory network allows complex interaction beyond sequential linear combination; (ii) we can generate compositional trees from the network without external linguistic knowledge; (iii) we evaluate the syntactic difference between the generated trees, randomly generated trees and gold reference trees produced by constituency parsers; (iv) we evaluate whether the generated trees contain the rich semantic information. [1]

1   Introduction

Recurrent neural networks have demonstrated surprising performance on processing natural language data, surpassing traditional n-gram or hand-engineered features on a variety of tasks. Naturally, curiosity about whether these models capture aspects of linguistic knowledge increases. Recent works proposed different probing tests on whether a model learns a set of linguistic properties (Conneau et al., 2018) such as subject-verb agreement (Linzen et al., 2016), syntax-sensitive dependencies (Kuncoro et al., 2018), whether a neuron learns to recognize a group of words with special properties (such as date) (Dalvi et al., 2019), or by dropping the word in the context far away vs nearby and trace perplexity to see how neural networks leverage context (Khandelwal et al., 2018).

However, there are two major limitations of the probing tests: i) probing tests are limited in the scope of their claim; ii) probing tests often treat model as a blackbox, reaching conclusions by directly altering the testing stimuli and observing the change in the outcome. This type of research often does not yield satisfactory conclusion about the underlying complex mechanism of the blackbox model (Jonas and Kording, 2017).

More holistic approach has been explored to study whether modern neural networks understand sentences by implicitly inducing recursive structures that match the semantics and syntactic theories in linguistics (Williams et al., 2018). However, Williams et al. (2018) studied a specific type of models that explicitly build tree representations of each sentence, which are far from common text processing models such as long short-term memory (LSTM) networks (Hochreiter and Schmidhuber, 1997). In the end, the question of whether common text processing model assumes implicit linguistic structures is left unanswered.

In this work, we draw inspirations from the field of deep learning model interpretations to provide a glimpse into how LSTM networks process a sentence, and extract a tree structure that LSTM networks implicitly create. Using the techniques from contextual decomposition (Murdoch et al., 2018), we propose a tree building algorithm that mimics construction grammar in that the grammar we induce is conditionally dependent on the task and the sentence. We extend Williams et al. (2018)'s analysis on the trees generated from the LSTM networks. We evaluate whether the induced tree structures syntactically resemble constituency grammar, and we evaluate whether training a recursive neural network on the induced structure will provide performance gain over recursive neural network on the

---

[1] Codes are available at https://github.com/windweller/LSTMTree/.

Proceedings of the 58th Annual Meeting of the Association for Computational Linguistics: Student Research Workshop, pages 299–305
July 5 - July 10, 2020. ©2020 Association for Computational Linguistics

constituency grammar.

Similar to Williams et al. (2018)'s conclusion on models that explicitly build tree representation, we conclude that induced trees from LSTM networks also do not resemble semantic or syntactic formalism created by human. We hope our work can encourage future work about interpretation-based methods and their connections with semantic and syntactic theory in linguistics.

2 Method

2.1 Long Short-Term Memory Networks

Long Short-Term Memory Network is a recurrent neural network composed of a cell, an input gate, an output gate and a forget gate (Hochreiter and Schmidhuber, 1997). The cell remembers values over arbitrary time intervals and the three gates regulate the flow of information into and out of the cell. This type of network processes input from left to right, with the same cell weights.

$$
\begin{aligned}
o_t &= \sigma(W_o x_t + V_o h_{t-1} + b_o) \\
f_t &= \sigma(W_f x_t + V_f h_{t-1} + b_f) \\
i_t &= \sigma(W_i x_t + V_i h_{t-1} + b_i) \\
g_t &= \tanh(W_g x_t + V_g h_{t-1} + b_g) \\
c_t &= f_t \odot c_{t-1} + i_t \odot g_t \\
h_t &= o_t \odot \tanh(c_t)
\end{aligned}
\tag{1}
$$

2.2 Shapley Value

Given a function f and variables $F = \{z_1, ..., z_n\}$, and a subset $S \subseteq F \setminus \{z_i\}$, we can define the Shapley value ϕ_i of a given variable z_i as:

$$
\phi_i(f) = \sum_{S \subseteq F \setminus \{z_i\}} \frac{1}{Z}(f(S \cup z_i) - f(S))
\tag{2}
$$

Intuitively, Shapley value computes the contribution of a term for the final outcome by executing the function with the term z_i and without the term z_i in all possible permutations (enumerating over the presence and absence of all other variables), and then takes the average over the number of such permutations Z. Shapley value has been shown as the unifying framework that subsumes many other deep learning interpretation methods (Lundberg and Lee, 2017).

Shapley value has some desirable properties. For example, Shapley values are locally accurate, which means $f(z_1, ..., z_n) = \sum_{i=1}^{n} \phi_i(f)$. We obtain an additive linear combination of Shapley values ϕ_i that will produce the same output as the original model f. Murdoch et al. (2018) proposed to use Shapley decomposition to linearize the nonlinear activation functions in the LSTM networks.

Let $f(a, b) = \tanh(a + b)$, we can linearize tanh activation by calculating the Shapley values of variable a and b (Eq 3).

$$
\begin{aligned}
\phi_a(f) &= \frac{1}{2}(\tanh(a) + (\tanh(a + b) - \tanh(b))) \\
\phi_b(f) &= \frac{1}{2}(\tanh(b) + (\tanh(b + a) - \tanh(a)))
\end{aligned}
\tag{3}
$$

Analogously, we can linearize σ activation as well. We use $L_{\tanh}$ and L_σ to denote this linearization process, and let $L_{\tanh}(a) = \phi_a(\tanh(a + b + ...))$ and $L_\sigma(a) = \phi_a(\sigma(a + b + ...))$. It is worth noting that $L_{\tanh}$ and L_σ are functions of a, as Shapley value will change with respect to input. Also, by decomposing LSTM into a summation of Shapley values, we still retain the original output value.

2.3 The Linearly Decomposed LSTM

Murdoch et al. (2018) proposed a method to linearize the LSTM computation by computing the Shaley value of each term. We can use this linearized LSTM to understand how LSTM processes through all time steps, and why it is very powerful in terms of representing a sequence of input. By linearizing the activation functions, we can rewrite the LSTM computation in Eq 4.

$$
\begin{aligned}
o_t &= L_\sigma(W_o x_t) + L_\sigma(V_o h_{t-1}) + L_\sigma(b_o) \\
f_t &= L_\sigma(W_f x_t) + L_\sigma(V_f h_{t-1}) + L_\sigma(b_f) \\
i_t &= L_\sigma(W_i x_t) + L_\sigma(V_i h_{t-1}) + L_\sigma(b_i) \\
g_t &= L_{\tanh}(W_g x_t) + L_{\tanh}(V_g h_{t-1}) + L_{\tanh}(b_g) \\
c_t &= f_t \odot c_{t-1} + i_t \odot g_t \\
h_t &= o_t \odot \tanh(c_t)
\end{aligned}
\tag{4}
$$

Since all nonlinear computations are now linearized, we can apply the distributive law of multiplication for these additive terms and trace the computation. We note that the Hadamard product enables an efficient mixing of all additive terms.

If we trace the computation, assuming that h_0 and c_0 are initialized with $\mathbf{0}$ vector, and input

(x_1, x_2, x_3), we can collect the number of terms that are associated with input by symbolic computation. We verify that each of these terms is in fact different and can be understood as the output of a function that can take a subset of $\{x_1, x_2, x_3\}$ as input. These are interaction terms among different time steps, creating features that are mixings of these steps. We remove the bias term so that the symbolic tracing is still tractable. We provide a few examples of such mixing terms in Figure 1.

$$L_\sigma(W_o x_2) * L_{\tanh}((L_\sigma(W_f x_2) * (L_\sigma(W_i x_1) * L_{\tanh}(W_g x_1))))$$
$$L_\sigma(W_o x_2) * L_{\tanh}((L_\sigma(W_i x_2) * L_{\tanh}(W_g x_2)))$$

Figure 1: We show a few terms from the symbolic tracer's output when the LSTM has processed both x_1 and x_2.

We count the statistics of terms that are associated with each input at the first three time steps. Each term is a unique feature computation of the input from the sequence (guaranteed by the uniqueness of Shapley value). We present the result of tracing in Table 1. This shows that LSTM is implicitly mixing inputs to allow interactions, and the final hidden state h_n, assuming the sequence is of length n, can be decomposed to many terms that contain combinations of $x_1, ..., x_n$.

Terms	x_1 Step	x_2 Step	x_3 Step
x_1	1	2	16
x_2	—	1	2
$x_1 x_2$	—	9	2,574
x_3	—	—	1
$x_2 x_3$	—	—	9
$x_1 x_3$	—	—	28
$x_1 x_2 x_3$	—	—	581
Total	1	12	3,211

Table 1: Number of unique terms that are associated with inputs when the LSTM progresses. We observe an exponential increase of terms as LSTM progresses.

We show that the Hadamard product provides the much needed mixing of time steps, and each time step's feature is processed using existing weight matrices but through different ways — enabled by nonlinearity. Previous work hypothesized that the advantage of the LSTM comes from the addition in the cell state computation: $f_t \odot c_{t-1} + i_t \odot g_t$, which resembles skip-connections between time steps, or improves the effectiveness on the gradient flows (Chung et al., 2014). Our result shows an alternative explanation on why LSTM is so effective at creating representations of an entire sequence — by creating interaction terms of time steps implicitly. Our analysis shows that the high expressivity brought by the Hadamard product $\odot$ might contribute to the overall effectiveness of the LSTM network as well.

2.4 Contextual Decomposition

Murdoch et al. (2018) proposed the contextual decomposition algorithm to interpret which part of the text sequence contributes most to the LSTM prediction. Given a subsequence $x_i, ..., x_j, 1 \leq i < j \leq T$, contextual decomposition re-arranges the terms at every time step t, such that each hidden and cell state can be decomposed into a relevant part associated with $x_i, ..., x_j$, denoted by β, and an irrelevant part, denoted by γ (Eq 5).

$$c^t = c_\beta^t + c_\gamma^t$$
$$h^t = h_\beta^t + h_\gamma^t \qquad (5)$$

Since the recurrent computation is fully linear and additive, the rearrangements of Shapley values will produce the same hidden and cell state as the original computation. At the final step of LSTM recurrence, h^T is used as the feature representation of the entire sentence. In a binary classification setting, the probability for label y can be computed by the dot product between the hidden state h^T and the output layer weight W. We can easily calculate the contextual decomposition score (contribution score) s for a given subsequence $x_i, ..., x_j$ by calculating dot product between the relevant hidden state h_β^T and the output layer weight W.

$$\hat{y} = W h^T = W h_\beta^T + W h_\gamma^T$$
$$s = W h_\beta^T \qquad (6)$$

2.5 Agglomerative Contextual Decomposition

As we discussed in Section 2.3, tracing all interactive terms of all time steps is intractable. The problem of how to find out which combinations of input in a given sequence contributed the most to the final label prediction remains. Singh et al. (2019) proposed a hierarchical clustering method to discover sub-sequences that contribute the most

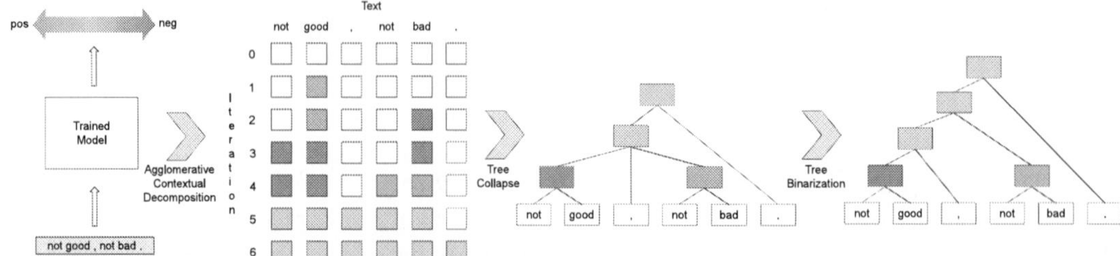

Figure 2: Overview of the tree generation algorithm. We train our model on SST-2 sentiment classification dataset. We use the Agglomerative Contextual Decomposition algorithm (ACD) for hierarchical sentiment interpretation. For each iteration, ACD selects one of the unselected words with the highest contextual score, and update scores of other unselected words. Blocks with sentiment scores (blue for negative, orange for positive, and grey for neutral) are formed through iterations. We build the tree with sentiment labels based on these blocks and binarize the tree for further evaluation and analysis.

to the final prediction, where the contribution score calculated by contextual decomposition algorithm is used as the metric to determine which clusters to join at each step.

We explain the procedure in Figure 2. We describe a simplified version of their algorithm:

- **Initialize**: Compute a contribution score for each word using the contextual decomposition algorithm and add these words to a priority queue with their scores.

- **Select**: Dequeue and obtain the word with the highest absolute contribution score.

- **Update**: Update contribution scores of other unselected words by adjusting the range of contextual decomposition algorithm to include the adjacent words.

- **Finalize**: Repeat Select and Update until the queue is empty.

2.6 Tree Generation

As the agglomerative contextual decomposition algorithm progresses, text blocks will be formed during iterations. By tracing how the merge happens at every step, we can create a tree-like structure that is the phrase-structure grammar of the sentence. We explain the procedure in Figure 2. The merging will stop when all regions are merged together. We binarize the trees by using left Chomsky normal form for further evaluation and analysis.

Connection to Construction Grammar We note that by selecting and merging text spans that have the highest contribution scores, we are letting the classifier that maps a sentence to a semantic attribute (such as sentiment) to define the structure of

the sentence. We leave to future work to examine possible connection between the structure induction through machine interpretation algorithm and construction grammar (Goldberg, 1995).

3 Experiments

3.1 Generation

3.1.1 Model Training

We trained a simple 1-layer unidirectional LSTM sentence classification model on Stanford Sentiment Treebank (SST) (Socher et al., 2013). SST contains 8544 training sentences, 1101 validation sentences and 2210 test sentences. We use pre-trained 300d GloVe embedding (Pennington et al., 2014). We use Adam optimizer (Kingma and Ba, 2014) with learning rate 0.001 to optimize the algorithm. We obtain 82.2% and 85.3% accuracy with hidden state dimension 50 and 500 on the binary classification task of positive and negative sentiment on the test dataset.

3.1.2 Tree Generation

We generate tree structures by tracing the selections made by the agglomerative contextual decomposition (ACD) algorithm, and binarize the final tree. The algorithm has $O(n^3)$ runtime, where n is the length of sequence. We find that this algorithm becomes very inefficient for any sequence longer than 20 words, so we focus on generating structures from SST sequences that are shorter than 20 words. This leads to 4980 / 633 / 1280 generated trees from training / validation / test set, respectively. An example of generated trees and the gold tree can be found in Figure 4.

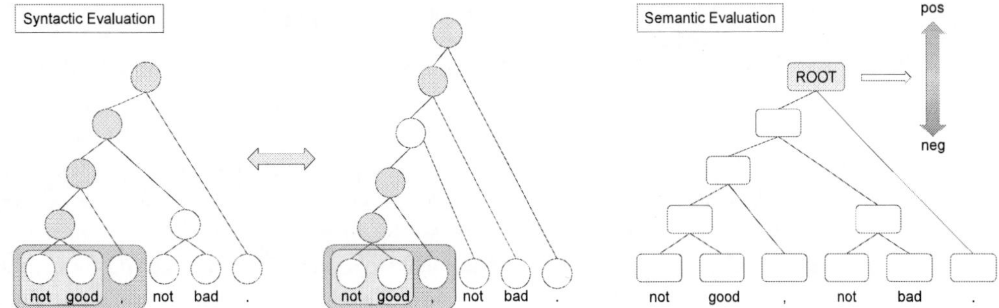

Figure 3: Syntactic and semantic evaluation of our results. For syntactic evaluation, we compare our trees with left-leaning trees, right-leaning trees and gold reference trees. An example of syntactic similarity evaluation is shown in the left part. The similarity (Jaccard index) of the two trees is 0.8. For semantic evaluation, we train a tree recursive neural network on our generated trees with sentiment labels. Each node is embedded and can represent the sentiment. We report the sentiment classification accuracy on all nodes or only the root node.

3.2 Evaluation

We are interested in two aspects: i) Syntactic: how do our generated trees compare with gold trees constructed by Stanford CoreNLP parser (Manning et al., 2014)? ii) Semantic: do our generated trees contain rich semantic information? We show an overview of the syntactic and semantic evaluation in Figure 3.

3.2.1 Syntactic Evaluation

We compare the generated tree structures with three types of trees: always left-leaning trees (**LS**), always right-leaning trees (**RS**), and gold reference trees (**GS**) produced by Stanford CoreNLP parser. We also compute the result of randomly generated trees to compare with trees generated from the ACD algorithm. Results are reported in Table 2. We use the same script from Williams et al. (2018) that computes the Jaccard similarity between set representation of two trees.

Compared with randomly generated trees, here we see that LSTM does capture structures that more closely resembles the gold reference, but there are still remarkable differences. LSTM with 500 dimension hidden states performed better on the original sentiment classification task (85.3% vs 82.2% accuracy), and generated trees are more balanced than LSTM with 50 dimension hidden states. This is also a phenomenon discovered by Williams et al. (2018) that balanced trees are often implicitly produced by the machine learning algorithms.

3.2.2 Semantic Evaluation

We also train a recursive neural network on these generated structures. We use the contribution score

Trees	LS	RS	GS	AD
Random	29.3	29.2	27.6	4.19
LSTM-50d	36.9	25.7	29.7	5.53
LSTM-500d	33.7	32.5	30.2	5.91

Table 2: The Jaccard similarity between generated trees and gold trees. **LS** means left-leaning trees. **RS** means right-leaning trees. **GS** means gold parse trees. **AD** means average tree depth.

s for each phrase as the intermediate labels and we allow the recursive computation step to be either a normal RNN or an LSTM. We evaluate the label accuracy on all nodes (All) or only on the root node (Root). The generated structure under-performed gold reference trees by a large margin, and is also below the original LSTM's performance, indicating that structures recovered by ACD are not equivalent to the true LSTM sequence computing process.

Trees	RNN		LSTM	
	All	Root	All	Root
LSTM-50d	72.7	60.4	74.8	63.3
LSTM-500d	75.1	53.6	75.9	58.0
Gold Trees	75.9	74.5	78.2	78.1

Table 3: The sentiment classification accuracy of recursive neural networks on the generated trees and gold trees. The gold tree set is also composed of trees that correspond to sequences shorter than 20 words.

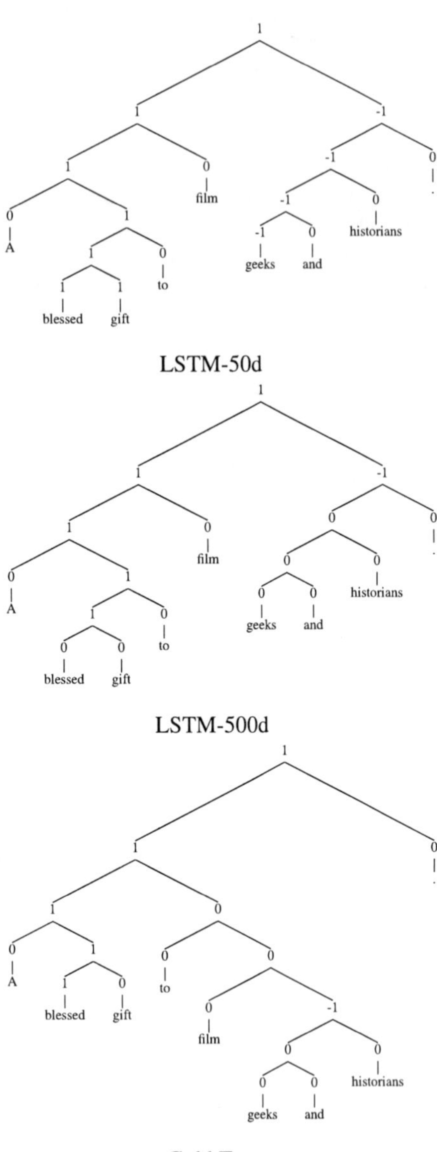

LSTM-50d

LSTM-500d

Gold Tree

Figure 4: Example of generated trees and the gold tree with sentiment labels. Labels are discretized (-1 for negative, 1 for positive, and 0 for neutral).

4 Discussion and Conclusion

In this work, we extract trees from LSTM by an interpretation algorithm — agglomerative contextual decomposition (ACD). We show empirically that the generated trees are not similar to the trees produced from formal syntactic theory. The generated trees also do not seem to provide more computational improvement when we train a recursive neural network leveraging the structure to predict the final label.

These negative observations can result from several possible reasons. Firstly, as discussed in Sec 2.6, the connection between the structure induction through machine interpretation algorithm and construction grammar remains a question — whether what is semantically important for sentiment analysis is necessarily reflected in the syntax and the way the syntactic constituents are formed in the language? Besides, while sentiment analysis requires the understandings of compositionality, models trained on linguistic tasks may better capture syntactic information. For future work, we consider conducting the same experiments on CoLA, a dataset for judging the grammatical acceptability of a sentence (Warstadt et al., 2019). Moreover, it is unclear whether models truly learned compositionality or just overfit to some spurious patterns of the dataset, as recent works have demonstrated that a well-performing natural language inference model completely fails on challenging cases generated by syntactic transformations (McCoy et al., 2019).

Nonetheless, we conclude with encouragement for the community to look deeper into interpretation-based methods and their connections with semantic and syntactic theory in linguistics.

Acknowledgments

The authors would like to thank the anonymous reviewers and our post-acceptance mentor Prof. Parisa Kordjamshidi for their careful reading of our manuscript and their many insightful comments and suggestions.

References

Junyoung Chung, Caglar Gulcehre, KyungHyun Cho, and Yoshua Bengio. 2014. Empirical evaluation of gated recurrent neural networks on sequence modeling. *arXiv preprint arXiv:1412.3555*.

Alexis Conneau, German Kruszewski, Guillaume Lample, Loïc Barrault, and Marco Baroni. 2018. What you can cram into a single $&!#* vector: Probing sentence embeddings for linguistic properties. In *Proceedings of the 56th Annual Meeting of the Association for Computational Linguistics (Volume 1: Long Papers)*, pages 2126–2136. Association for Computational Linguistics.

Fahim Dalvi, Nadir Durrani, Hassan Sajjad, Yonatan Belinkov, D Anthony Bau, and James Glass. 2019. What is one grain of sand in the desert? analyzing individual neurons in deep nlp models. In *Proceedings of the AAAI Conference on Artificial Intelligence (AAAI)*, volume 7.

Adele E Goldberg. 1995. *Constructions: A construction grammar approach to argument structure*. University of Chicago Press.

Sepp Hochreiter and Jürgen Schmidhuber. 1997. Long short-term memory. *Neural computation*, 9(8):1735–1780.

Eric Jonas and Konrad Paul Kording. 2017. Could a neuroscientist understand a microprocessor? *PLoS computational biology*, 13(1):e1005268.

Urvashi Khandelwal, He He, Peng Qi, and Dan Jurafsky. 2018. Sharp nearby, fuzzy far away: How neural language models use context. In *Proceedings of the 56th Annual Meeting of the Association for Computational Linguistics (Volume 1: Long Papers)*, pages 284–294.

Diederik P Kingma and Jimmy Ba. 2014. Adam: A method for stochastic optimization. *arXiv preprint arXiv:1412.6980*.

Adhiguna Kuncoro, Chris Dyer, John Hale, Dani Yogatama, Stephen Clark, and Phil Blunsom. 2018. Lstms can learn syntax-sensitive dependencies well, but modeling structure makes them better. In *Proceedings of the 56th Annual Meeting of the Association for Computational Linguistics (Volume 1: Long Papers)*, pages 1426–1436.

Tal Linzen, Emmanuel Dupoux, and Yoav Goldberg. 2016. Assessing the ability of lstms to learn syntax-sensitive dependencies. *Transactions of the Association for Computational Linguistics*, 4:521–535.

Scott M Lundberg and Su-In Lee. 2017. A unified approach to interpreting model predictions. In *Advances in Neural Information Processing Systems*, pages 4765–4774.

Christopher D. Manning, Mihai Surdeanu, John Bauer, Jenny Finkel, Steven J. Bethard, and David McClosky. 2014. The Stanford CoreNLP Natural Language Processing Toolkit. In *Association for Computational Linguistics (ACL) System Demonstrations*, pages 55–60.

Tom McCoy, Ellie Pavlick, and Tal Linzen. 2019. Right for the wrong reasons: Diagnosing syntactic heuristics in natural language inference. In *Proceedings of the 57th Annual Meeting of the Association for Computational Linguistics*, pages 3428–3448.

W. James Murdoch, Peter J. Liu, and Bin Yu. 2018. Beyond word importance: Contextual decomposition to extract interactions from LSTMs. In *International Conference on Learning Representations*.

Jeffrey Pennington, Richard Socher, and Christopher Manning. 2014. Glove: Global vectors for word representation. In *Proceedings of the 2014 conference on empirical methods in natural language processing (EMNLP)*, pages 1532–1543.

Chandan Singh, W. James Murdoch, and Bin Yu. 2019. Hierarchical interpretations for neural network predictions. In *International Conference on Learning Representations*.

Richard Socher, Alex Perelygin, Jean Wu, Jason Chuang, Christopher D Manning, Andrew Ng, and Christopher Potts. 2013. Recursive deep models for semantic compositionality over a sentiment treebank. In *Proceedings of the 2013 conference on empirical methods in natural language processing*, pages 1631–1642.

Alex Warstadt, Amanpreet Singh, and Samuel R Bowman. 2019. Neural network acceptability judgments. *Transactions of the Association for Computational Linguistics*, 7:625–641.

Adina Williams, Andrew Drozdov*, and Samuel R Bowman. 2018. Do latent tree learning models identify meaningful structure in sentences? *Transactions of the Association of Computational Linguistics*, 6:253–267.

Exploring the Role of Context to Distinguish Rhetorical and Information-Seeking Questions

Yuan Zhuang and Ellen Riloff
School of Computing
University of Utah
{yyzhuang, riloff}@cs.utah.edu

Abstract

Social media posts often contain questions, but many of the questions are rhetorical and do not seek information. Our work studies the problem of distinguishing rhetorical and information-seeking questions on Twitter. Most work has focused on features of the question itself, but we hypothesize that the prior context plays a role too. This paper introduces a new dataset containing questions in tweets paired with their prior tweets to provide context. We create classification models to assess the difficulty of distinguishing rhetorical and information-seeking questions, and experiment with different properties of the prior context. Our results show that the prior tweet and topic features can improve performance on this task.

1 Introduction

Questions are common in social media forums, but they can serve many pragmatic functions. Questions are often information-seeking, but social media posts also frequently contain questions that do not expect any information for what the question literally asks about. We will use the term *rhetorical question (RQ)* broadly to refer to all questions that do not seek any information. For example, rhetorical questions can express criticism (e.g., *"Can't you do anything right?"*), sentiment (e.g., *"How fun is that?"*), sarcasm (e.g., *"Who knew?"*), and agreement/disagreement (e.g., *"Is the pope catholic?"*). Distinguishing rhetorical and information-seeking questions is important for dialogue processing and conversational analysis, but only recently has begun to receive attention in the NLP community.

Our research has two main contributions. First, we created a new resource for this understudied problem. We have compiled a collection of nearly 5,000 tweets that contain a question that is respond-ing to an initial tweet, and labeled the questions as *rhetorical* or *information-seeking* with crowdsourcing. We found that 53% of the questions are information-seeking (IQ) and 47% are rhetorical (RQ), confirming that both types of questions are prevalent in social media.

Second, our research examines whether the initial tweet prior to a question can help to predict whether a question is information-seeking or rhetorical. Most prior work has focused only on the question itself, but we investigate whether the topic of the discussion may be a valuable indicator too. Our intuition was that rhetorical questions are common in contexts associated with argumentation and debate, such as politics. Conversely, we expect information-seeking questions to be prevalent in contexts about products and services, where people are actively seeking information.

In this paper, we first describe our Twitter dataset and human annotations. Next, we present classification models that exploit both the question and the initial tweet prior to the question. We explore several ways of extracting topic information from tweets to capture the prior context. Our results show that the prior context does improve performance for this task.

2 Related Work

Rhetorical questions have been studied in linguistics, primarily focused on linguistic properties and pragmatic functions (Sadock, 1971; Schmidt-Radefeldt, 1977; Frank, 1990; Gutierrez-Rexach, 1998; Han, 2002; Schaffer, 2005). However there has been relatively little work on rhetorical questions in the NLP community until recently. Work by Zhao and Mei (2013) identified the information need of questions in Twitter by extracting features from the question tweets. However, their work did not explore the usefulness of prior context in dis-

Proceedings of the 58th Annual Meeting of the Association for Computational Linguistics: Student Research Workshop, pages 306–312
July 5 - July 10, 2020. ©2020 Association for Computational Linguistics

tinguishing rhetorical questions from information-seeking questions. Ranganath et al. (2016) modeled the contextual overlap between a question and the most recent status message (MRSM) of the same user in Twitter, with the hypothesis that a rhetorical question shares context with its MRSM more than a random question with its MRSM. Bhattasali et al. (2015) found that n-gram features from utterances immediately preceding and following a question could help identify rhetorical questions. Our work differs from both works in several aspects. First our evaluation dataset contains human-assigned gold labels and a rich mix of both RQ and IQ. In contrast, Ranganath et al. (2016) automatically assigned their dataset with labels according to some heuristic rules, which may be noisy, and Bhattasali et al. (2015) used the Switchboard Dialog Act Corpus (Godfrey et al., 1992), where only 5% of questions are rhetorical. Second, neither of these works took preceding context and topic information into account.

Oraby et al. (2016) studied rhetorical questions in the context of sarcasm in debate forums, but they did not study the problem of distinguishing rhetorical questions from information-seeking questions. In contrast, we focused on distinguishing the information need of general questions in Twitter. Oraby et al. (2017) further explored distinguishing rhetorical questions from information-seeking questions. But their gold standard data consists of rhetorical questions automatically extracted from debate forums using heuristic rules. In contrast, our gold standard data consists of questions that have been manually labeled as rhetorical or information-seeking. Another difference is that Oraby et al. (2017) did not consider the prior context for questions, which we focus on in this work.

3 Data

We began by collecting tweets that contain question marks from January to December 2014.[1] We then applied a few filters to remove tweets that (1) are not in English (based on Twitter's language code), (2) contain < 5 words, (3) are retweets or have quotation marks around the question, because these questions did not originate with the tweeter, (4) contain URLs or media (e.g., photos), because the question may refer to the linked content, (5)

contain multiple questions, which could be difficult to tease apart, or (6) were posted by a VIP ("verified") account. Questions posted by VIP accounts (entities in the public interest) were predominately rhetorical questions in advertisements, and we did not want these to skew our data. We will refer to the resulting tweets as **Question Tweets (QTweets)**.

We also collected the preceding tweets, which we will refer to as **Prior Tweet (PTweets)**. Our hypothesis is that the preceding context can be important because (a) the question alone can be ambiguous, and (b) knowledge about the topic of discussion can affect the likelihood that a question will be rhetorical or information-seeking. Consequently, we only kept question tweets that responded to a prior tweet. We also required that the prior tweet was the initial tweet in the conversational thread because conversational threads often have topic shifts and questions may refer back to earlier comments. Detangling discourse threads is a challenging problem in its own right.

This process produced 5,064 question tweets[2], each paired with its prior tweet as context.

3.1 Manual Annotation

We hired three annotators from Amazon's Mechanical Turk[3] to label each of the question tweets (coupled with its prior tweet) with one of the following three labels:

Information-seeking Question (IQ): The main purpose of the question is most likely to seek some information about what it literally asks.

Rhetorical Question (RQ): The main purpose of the question is most likely *not* to seek any information about what it literally asks. Instead, the speaker uses the question mainly for some other purpose, such as suggestion or criticism.

Incomprehensible (I): The annotation sample is not in English or it is hard to understand.

We emphasized in the annotation guidelines that some questions are ambiguous and could indeed have multiple purposes at the same time. One example is the question *"The sunset is great, isn't it?"*, which may convey the speaker's admiration of the sunset and also seek the hearers' agreement at the same time. We advised the annotators to choose the most likely primary purpose of a question, according to their instincts. To further assist

---

[1] We intentionally collected tweets from several years ago because their continued presence on Twitter suggests that they are likely to remain available, so other researchers can easily reacquire our data.

[2] We originally collected 5,200 tweets, but a pre-processing error allowed 136 tweets with < 5 words to slip through so they were later discarded.

[3] https://www.mturk.com/

the annotators, we provided several examples of both rhetorical and information-seeking questions in the annotation guidelines, along with explanations for why each question belongs to its corresponding category.

The pairwise inter-annotator agreement scores using Cohen's kappa were: $\kappa = .67, .67, .68$. Of the 5,064 questions, 67 (1.3%) were annotated as Incomprehensible by at least 1 annotator and discarded. The rest were assigned a gold standard label using majority vote. The final annotated dataset contains 4,997 question tweets, with 2,332 (47%) labeled as rhetorical and 2,665 (53%) labeled as information-seeking. The final gold standard dataset is available for download at the authors' website.

4 Classifying Questions as Rhetorical or Information-seeking

We designed a variety of classification models to assess the difficulty of distinguishing rhetorical and information-seeking questions, and to examine the role of prior context for this task.

First, we applied the CMU Twokenizer (Gimpel et al., 2011), removed URLs and hashtags, and replaced acronyms with their corresponding full words or phrases using a Twitter acronym list[4]. Next, we applied the Stanford CoreNLP parser (Manning et al., 2014) to obtain lemmas and part-of-speech tags. For the embedding features, we used GloVe vectors (Pennington et al., 2014) pre-trained on 2B tweets. We experimented with both 25 and 100 dimensional vectors, and show the best results in Section 5. We then extracted three sets of features: word features, question features, and topic features.

4.1 Word Features

We explored both unigrams and embedding vectors to capture the meaning of the words in a tweet.

Unigrams: Each word is a feature with a TF-IDF value. We only include unigrams that occur $\geq$ 3 times in the training set.

Embedding (Embed): We create an embedding vector for a tweet by averaging the embedding vectors for all words in the tweet.

[4]https://sproutsocial.com/insights/social-media-acronyms/

4.2 Question Features

We suspected that rhetorical questions and information-seeking questions may be phrased differently. Hence we developed 3 features to capture the question form.

Question Attributes: (1) One feature represents the leading bigram of the question (e.g., a leading "How to" may be more likely to seek a solution), (2) one feature indicates the WH-category of the leftmost question word: {*who, when, what, where, which, why, how*}. (3) one feature counts the number of negations in the question, as rhetorical questions may have more negations (e.g., *"why don't you try this ?"*).

Post-Question Attributes: We observed that rhetorical questions in Twitter are often followed by another sentence (suggesting a self-answer) or emoji. So we created three post-question features: (1) a feature indicating whether the question is followed by additional words, (2) a feature indicating whether the question is followed by emoji and (3) a feature that counts the number of emoji after the question.

Subjectivity Features: Rhetorical questions often express an opinion (e.g., criticize), agreement/disagreement, etc. So we hypothesized that recognizing subjective language may be a helpful clue for identifying rhetorical questions. We extracted 5 features associated with subjectivity: (1) the number of elongated words (e.g., *"looooove"*), (2) the number of entirely upper case words (e.g., *"YAY"*), (3) the number of exclamation marks, (4) the number of strongly subjective words found in the MPQA lexicon (Wilson et al., 2005), and (5) the number of weakly subjective words in the MPQA lexicon.

4.3 Topic Features

Our research explores whether the topic of discussion can help distinguish rhetorical and information-seeking questions, so we created four types of features to capture topic information.

Nouns Embedding (NounEmbed): The set of nouns in a tweet, in aggregate, might sufficiently reflect the topic of a tweet. So we created a composite nouns embedding vector by averaging embeddings of all the nouns.

Specificity (Specific): Information-seeking questions often focus on a specific entity or object, so we created features to capture specificity using the MRC resource (Brysbaert et al., 2013), which assigns words with familarity and concreteness scores from 100 to 700. One feature counts the number of words with familiarity score ≥ 400, and the other feature counts the number of words with concreteness score ≥ 400.

Latent Dirichlet Allocation (LDA): We created an LDA model (Blei et al., 2003) from our training data, after removing stopwords, with $k = 25$ as the number of topics. Given input text, we extracted the latent topic distribution as k features.

Google Topic Categories (GTopic): Google's Content Classifier[5] labels text with respect to **700+** topic categories in its content hierarchy. Our dataset is small, so we only used the 27 general categories in the top level of its hierarchy. Given an input text, we used 27 features to capture the topics assigned by Google's Content Classifier.

Initially we extracted topic features directly from a tweet. But topic models and classifiers perform better on longer texts, so we also tried giving a tweet to Google as a query, and extracting the summary snippet for the top-ranked web page.[6] The resulting snippet is usually longer but similar in topic. We will call the snippet retrieved by a QTweet its **QSnippet**, and the snippet retrieved by a PTweet its **PSnippet**. In our experiments, we tried extracting the topic features from the tweet alone, its snippet, and from the tweet combined with its snippet. For the sake of brevity, we only show the best-performing results.

4.4 Learning Models

We created two types of classifiers: 1) a linear SVM (Chang and Lin, 2011) with $C = 0.1$, and 2) a 4-layer BiLSTM, implemented using PyTorch[7], with a hidden size of 100 and ReLU. We set the learning rate of the BiLSTM to 0.0001 with a dropout rate of 0.1 (Srivastava et al., 2014). For both models, we use GloVe embeddings pre-trained on 2B tweets of size 25 or 100 dimensions (Pennington et al., 2014).

5 Experimental Results

We randomly split our data into 3 partitions: training (3,200), development (797), and test (1,000). All classifiers were trained on the training set and

tuned with the development set. We report results on the test set as Precision, Recall, & F1 scores, all macro-averaged over the RQ and IQ classes.

First, we evaluated models that used features derived only from the QTweet (QT). The first two rows of Table 1 show the performance of SVMs trained with word embedding vectors and unigrams, respectively. The third row shows that the BiLSTM outperforms the SVMs, achieving an F1 score of 70.8. However, the fourth row shows that adding the Question Features to the SVM performs better than the BiLSTM, yielding an F1 score of 73.5.

Classifiers for QTweet	Prec	Rec	F1
SVM Embed(QT)^{100D}	67.6	67.8	67.6
SVM Unigrams(QT)	68.8	68.9	68.9
BiLSTM(QT)^{100D}	71.0	70.9	70.8
SVM Unigrams(QT) + QFeatures(QT)	**73.5**	**73.5**	**73.5**
Adding Topic Features			
+ NounEmbed(QT)^{25D}	72.9	72.9	72.9
+ Specific(QT)	73.1	73.1	73.1
+ LDA(QT)	73.4	73.4	73.4
+ GTopic(QT)	73.5	73.6	73.5
+ ALL topic features (**QT-SVM**)	**73.9**	**74.0**	**73.9**

Table 1: Results using only QTweet (QT)

The lower portion of Table 1 shows results when adding each type of topic feature (not cumulatively) to the best SVM model. None of them improved performance on their own, but adding them all together (shown in the last row) increased the F1 score to 73.9. We observed that the topic is often unclear from the question itself, which may explain the minimal gains. We will refer to the best model in Table 1 as QT-SVM.

Classifiers for QTweet+PTweet	Prec	Rec	F1
BiLSTM(PT + QT)^{100D}	70.3	70.1	70.2
QT-SVM+Embed(PT)^{25D}+Sbj(PT)	74.4	74.5	74.5
+ Specific(PT)	74.7	74.8	74.8
+ LDA(Psnippet)	74.7	74.8	74.8
+ GTopic(Psnippet)	74.8	74.9	74.8
+ NounEmbed(PT + Psnippet)^{25D}	75.1	75.2	75.2
Best Combination: **+ Specific + LDA + GTopic**	**75.4**	**75.5**	**75.5**

Table 2: Results using QTweet (QT) & PTweet (PT)

Table 2 shows results for classifiers that used features derived from both the QTweet and PTweet. The first row shows the BiLSTM model trained with the PTweet words followed by the QTweet words. This model performs slightly worse than the BiLSTM trained on QTweets alone. The next row shows results for QT-SVM with added features representing the PTtweet as a 25D embedding vec-

---

[5]https://cloud.google.com/natural-language/

[6]We filtered snippets from Twitter.com or any website with 'dictionary' in its url or title, because the snippet from Twitter.com is usually the tweet itself, and online dictionaries just provide definitions of the words.

[7]https://pytorch.org/

	RQ		IQ	
	Prec	**Rec**	**Prec**	**Rec**
QT-SVM	71.3	72.4	76.5	75.5
QT-SVM+Embed(PT)^{25D}+Sbj(PT)	71.7	73.3	77.1	75.7
+Topic Features	72.9	74.2	77.9	76.8

Table 3: Breakdown of Precision and Recall Scores of Different Models for Each Question Class

tor[8] and Subjectivity (Sbj) Features[9] extracted from the PTweet. The additional PTweet information improved the SVM performance from 73.9 to 74.5. The following rows show results when adding each type of topic feature extracted from the PTweet (not cumulatively). Each of them slightly improved performance. We also experimented with combining them and the last row shows the best-performing combination, which achieved an F1 score of 75.5. We conjecture that each topic feature itself does not necessarily capture useful topic information across all questions, but combined they become complementary to each other and are more useful for the classifier.

Table 3 shows the breakdown of precision and recall scores for rhetorical questions and information-seeking questions separately. Overall the scores for rhetorical questions are consistently lower than for information-seeking questions, which means that it is harder to identify rhetorical questions. This is not surprising as it often requires complex commonsense knowledge to understand that a question is not seeking information, and we will show some examples in Section 6.

Between the first row and the second row, the recall for rhetorical questions increases by about 1%, while the precision for information-seeking questions goes up. This shows that the embedding and subjectivity features from the PTweet help discover rhetorical questions that were previously mislabeled as information-seeking. In the third row, recall and precision improves for both categories as the topic features are added. This implies that the topic features from the PTweet help to identify both rhetorical and information-seeking questions that were previously mislabeled.

6 Analysis

To better understand how topics interact with rhetorical and information-seeking questions, we ana-

---

[8]We also tried adding unigrams but the embedding worked better.

[9]None of the Question Features other than the Subjectivity Features are applicable to PTweets

lyzed the distribution of RQ and IQ over topics, based on the topic labels produced by the Google Content Classifier applied to the PSnippets from our training and development sets. Table 4 shows the four topics most highly correlated with each question category. The second column shows the total number of questions identified for each topic, and the third and fourth columns show the percentages of rhetorical and information-seeking questions in each topic.

Topic	Total	**RQ%**	**IQ%**
Computers & Electronics	85	20	80
Internet & Telecom	70	23	77
Games	94	24	76
Autos & Vehicles	34	29	71
Home & Garden	41	56	44
Law & Government	74	58	42
Books & Literature	42	60	40
Sensitive Subjects	41	71	29

Table 4: Topic Associations for RQs and IQs

The four topics most highly correlated with information-seeking questions are *Computers & Electronics*, *Internet & Telecom*, *Games*, and *Autos & Vehicles*. Our analysis found that this is because people tend to ask about the details of products and services in Twitter (e.g., sale price, features of computers, and release dates of games). On the other hand, the four topics most highly correlated with rhetorical questions are *Sensitive Subjects*, *Books & Literature*, *Law & Government*, and *Home & Garden*. We inspected examples from these topics and found that they are usually related to opinion expressions and debates (e.g., debates about race and politics, and assessment of books' quality), which lead to more rhetorical questions.

We also manually inspected some questions that seemed to be difficult for our system to label correctly. Table 5 shows some examples from our development dataset that were mislabeled by our best model. Example 1 requires the model to know that the question serves as a joke. In Example 2, the question, despite its simple question structure and lack of explicitly negative words, expresses a negative emotion. But without recognizing the implicit sentiment, it is hard to determine that the question is rhetorical. In Example 3, the model needs to understand the interaction between the prior context and the question to know that the question serves as a sarcastic response. Example 4 was classified as RQ probably because it is syntactically not in a complete question form (e.g., *"Are you going to prom or nah?"*). The model mislabeled Example 5 probably because the question contains only a (complex) noun phrase and thus looks like a suggestion, which is a more common phenomenon in rhetorical questions.

Rhetorical Questions		
1	**PTweet**: Welcome anytime. You know where I live.	
	Tweet: At the bottom of a sinkhole?	
2	**PTweet**: Son of a .. How many blocked FG's do we have to endure. Going out of my mind. #smh	
	Tweet: How does this keep happening?!	
3	**PTweet**: Hans is a piece of crap.	
	Tweet: Where were you like 4 months ago with that?	
Information-seeking Questions		
4	**PTweet**: Have faith just have faith.	
	Tweet: you going to prom or nah?	
5	**PTweet**: Definitely going to send me that picture are you? Haha!	
	Tweet: The one of your cheese on toast?	

Table 5: Examples of RQ and IQ Mislabeled by the Best Model

7 Conclusions

A contribution of this work is that we have created a new dataset containing nearly 5,000 question tweets labeled as rhetorical or information-seeking coupled with their prior tweets. To our knowledge, this is the first Twitter-based dataset for studying rhetorical questions that has both human-generated gold labels and includes prior context for each question. We also presented classification models to benchmark performance on this task, and showed that including the tweet prior to a question improves performance. We also showed several ways to capture topic information, and that topic information represented in the preceding context seems to be useful for this task. Our hope is that this work will lead to further research on the role of context for recognizing rhetorical and information-seeking questions in social media.

Acknowledgement

We thank Tao Li (University of Utah) who provided expertise that assisted this work. We are also very grateful to Harald Illig, Changchen Chen, Ruijia Zhu and Fan Wu for their help in the preliminary data analysis.

References

Shohini Bhattasali, Jeremy Cytryn, Elana Feldman, and Joonsuk Park. 2015. Automatic identification of rhetorical questions. In *Proceedings of the 53rd Annual Meeting of the Association for Computational Linguistics and the 7th International Joint Conference on Natural Language Processing (Volume 2: Short Papers)*, pages 743–749. Association for Computational Linguistics.

David M. Blei, Andrew Y. Ng, and Michael I. Jordan. 2003. Latent dirichlet allocation. *Journal of Machine Learning Research*, 3:993–1022.

Marc Brysbaert, Amy Beth Warriner, and Victor Kuperman. 2013. Concreteness ratings for 40 thousand generally known english word lemmas. *Behavior research methods*, 46.

Chih-Chung Chang and Chih-Jen Lin. 2011. LIBSVM: A library for support vector machines. *ACM Transactions on Intelligent Systems and Technology*, 2:27:1–27:27. Software available at http://www.csie.ntu.edu.tw/~cjlin/libsvm.

Jane Frank. 1990. You call that a rhetorical question?: Forms and functions of rhetorical questions in conversation. *Journal of Pragmatics*, 14(5):723 – 738.

Kevin Gimpel, Nathan Schneider, Brendan O'Connor, Dipanjan Das, Daniel Mills, Jacob Eisenstein, Michael Heilman, Dani Yogatama, Jeffrey Flanigan, and Noah A. Smith. 2011. Part-of-speech tagging for twitter: Annotation, features, and experiments. In *Proceedings of the Annual Meeting of the Association for Computational Linguistics, HLT '11*, volume 2, pages 42–47.

John Godfrey, E.C. Holliman, and J McDaniel. 1992. Switchboard: telephone speech corpus for research and development. In *Proceedings of the IEEE International Conference on Acoustics, Speech and Signal Processing (ICASSP)*, volume 1, pages 517–520.

Javier Gutierrez-Rexach. 1998. Rhetorical questions, relevance and scales. *Revista Alicantina de Estudios Ingleses*, 11:139–156.

Chung-hye Han. 2002. Interpreting interrogatives as rhetorical questions. *Lingua*, 11:201–229.

Christopher Manning, Mihai Surdeanu, John Bauer, Jenny Finkel, Steven Bethard, and David McClosky. 2014. The Stanford CoreNLP natural language processing toolkit. In *Proceedings of 52nd Annual Meeting of the Association for Computational Linguistics: System Demonstrations*, pages 55–60, Baltimore, Maryland. Association for Computational Linguistics.

Shereen Oraby, Vrindavan Harrison, Amita Misra, Ellen Riloff, and Marilyn Walker. 2017. Are you serious?: Rhetorical questions and sarcasm in social media dialog. In *Proceedings of the 18th Annual SIGdial Meeting on Discourse and Dialogue,* pages 310–319, Saarbrücken, Germany. Association for Computational Linguistics.

Shereen Oraby, Vrindavan Harrison, Lena Reed, Ernesto Hernandez, Ellen Riloff, and Marilyn Walker. 2016. Creating and characterizing a diverse corpus of sarcasm in dialogue. In *Proceedings of the 17th Annual Meeting of the Special Interest Group on Discourse and Dialogue*, pages 31–41, Los Angeles. Association for Computational Linguistics.

Jeffrey Pennington, Richard Socher, and Christopher Manning. 2014. Glove: Global vectors for word representation. In *Proceedings of the 2014 Conference on Empirical Methods in Natural Language Processing (EMNLP)*, pages 1532–1543, Doha, Qatar. Association for Computational Linguistics.

Suhas Ranganath, Xia Hu, Jiliang Tang, Suhang Wang, and Huan Liu. 2016. Identifying rhetorical questions in social media. In *Proceedings of the 10th International AAAI Conference on Web and Social Meidia*, pages 667–670.

Jerrold Sadock. 1971. Queclaratives. *Papers from the 7th Regional Meeting of the Chicago Linguistic Society*, pages 223–232.

Deborah Schaffer. 2005. Can rhetorical questions function as retorts?: Is the pope catholic? *Journal of Pragmatics*, 37(4):433 – 460.

Jürgen Schmidt-Radefeldt. 1977. On so-called 'rhetorical' questions. *Journal of Pragmatics*, 1:375–392.

Nitish Srivastava, Geoffrey Hinton, Alex Krizhevsky, Ilya Sutskever, and Ruslan Salakhutdinov. 2014. Dropout: A simple way to prevent neural networks from overfitting. *The Journal of Machine Learning Research*, 15(1):1929–1958.

Theresa Wilson, Janyce Wiebe, and Paul Hoffmann. 2005. Recognizing contextual polarity in phrase-level sentiment analysis. In *Proceedings of Human Language Technology Conference and Conference on Empirical Methods in Natural Language Processing*, pages 347–354, Vancouver, British Columbia, Canada. Association for Computational Linguistics.

Zhe Zhao and Qiaozhu Mei. 2013. Questions about questions: An empirical analysis of information needs on twitter. In *Proceedings of the 22nd International Conference on World Wide Web*, pages 1545–1556, New York, NY, USA. ACM.

Compositional generalization by factorizing alignment and translation

Jacob Russin
Psychology Department
UC Davis
`jlrussin@ucdavis.edu`

Jason Jo
MILA
Université de Montréal

Randall C. O'Reilly
Psychology Department
Computer Science Department
Center for Neuroscience
UC Davis

Yoshua Bengio
MILA
Université de Montréal
CIFAR Senior Fellow

Abstract

Standard methods in deep learning for natural language processing fail to capture the compositional structure of human language that allows for systematic generalization outside of the training distribution. However, human learners readily generalize in this way, e.g. by applying known grammatical rules to novel words. Inspired by work in cognitive science suggesting a functional distinction between systems for syntactic and semantic processing, we implement a modification to an existing approach in neural machine translation, imposing an analogous separation between alignment and translation. The resulting architecture substantially outperforms standard recurrent networks on the SCAN dataset, a compositional generalization task, without any additional supervision. Our work suggests that learning to align and to translate in separate modules may be a useful heuristic for capturing compositional structure.

1 Introduction

A crucial property underlying the expressive power of human language is its systematicity (Lake et al., 2017; Fodor and Pylyshyn, 1988): syntactic or grammatical rules allow arbitrary elements to be combined in novel ways, making the number of sentences possible in a language to be exponential in the number of its basic elements. Recent work has shown that standard deep learning methods in natural language processing fail to capture this important property: when tested on unseen combinations of known elements, standard models fail to generalize (Lake and Baroni, 2018; Loula et al., 2018; Bastings et al., 2018). It has been suggested that this failure represents a major deficiency of current deep learning models, especially when they

are compared to human learners (Marcus, 2018; Lake et al., 2017, 2019).

From a statistical-learning perspective, this failure is quite natural. The neural networks trained on compositional generalization tasks fail to generalize because they have memorized biases that do indeed exist in the training set. These tasks require networks to make an out-of-domain (o.o.d.) *extrapolation* (Marcus, 2018), rather than merely *interpolate* according to the assumption that training and testing data are independent and identically distributed (i.i.d.). To the extent that humans can perform well on certain kinds of o.o.d. tests, they must be utilizing inductive biases that are lacking in current deep learning models (Battaglia et al., 2018).

It has long been suggested that the human capacity for systematic generalization is linked to mechanisms for processing syntax, and their functional separation from the meanings of individual words (Chomsky, 1957; Fodor and Pylyshyn, 1988). In this work, we take inspiration from this idea and explore operationalizing it as an inductive bias in an existing neural network architecture.

First, we notice a connection between syntactic structure and the correct alignment of words in the source sequence to meanings in the target. In our model, alignment is accomplished with an attention mechanism (Bahdanau et al., 2015) that determines the relevance of each word in the source to the translation of the next word in the target. This process must take into account the syntactic structure of both sequences (e.g. if a verb was just translated, it would be important to know whether there is in the source sequence an adverb that modifies it). We reasoned that if alignment was separated from direct translation (analogous to a separation of syntax and the meanings of individual words),

Proceedings of the 58th Annual Meeting of the Association for Computational Linguistics: Student Research Workshop, pages 313–327
July 5 - July 10, 2020. ©2020 Association for Computational Linguistics

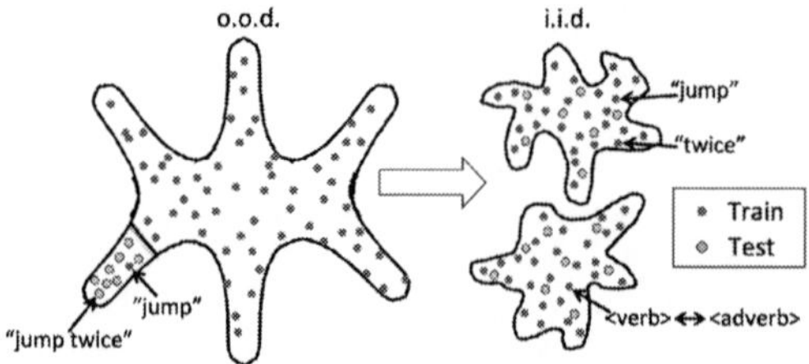

Figure 1: Illustration of the transformation of an out-of-domain (o.o.d.) generalization problem into two independent, identically distributed (i.i.d.) problems.

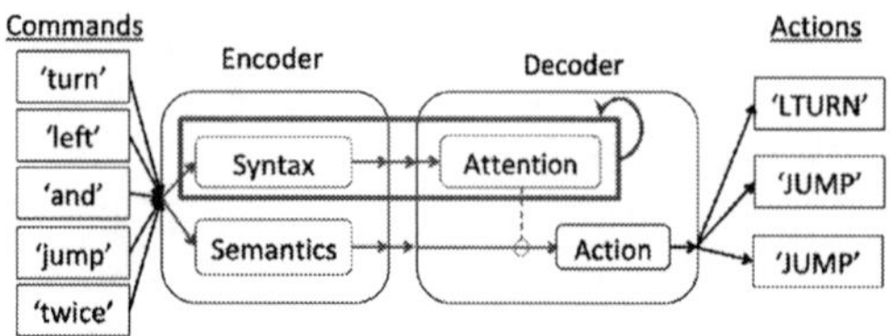

Figure 2: Syntactic Attention architecture. Information used for alignment ("syntax", shown in blue) is kept separate from information used for direct translation ("semantics", shown in red).

the difficult o.o.d. problem of composing known elements into a novel combination would be reduced to two easier i.i.d. problems, because the distributions of correct alignments and translations would be similar in training and testing data (see Figure 1).

We implemented this intuition by modifying an existing attention mechanism (Bahdanau et al., 2015), and call the resultant architecture Syntactic Attention to reflect the intuition that the attention mechanism used for alignment should operate primarily on syntactic information, which should be separated from the information relevant to translating individual words. We show that this modification achieves substantially improved compositional generalization performance over the original architecture on the SCAN dataset.

2 Syntactic Attention

The Syntactic Attention model improves the compositional generalization capability of an existing attention mechanism (Bahdanau et al., 2015) by separating two streams of information processing for alignment and translation (see Figure 2). We describe the mechanisms of this separation and the other details of the model below.

2.1 Factorizing alignment and translation

In the seq2seq problem, models must learn a mapping from arbitrary-length sequences of inputs $\mathbf{x} = \{x_1, x_2, ..., x_{T_x}\}$ to arbitrary-length sequences of outputs $\mathbf{y} = \{y_1, y_2, ..., y_{T_y}\}$: $p(\mathbf{y}|\mathbf{x})$. The underlying assumption made by the Syntactic Attention architecture is that the dependence of target words on the input sequence can be separated into two independent factors. One factor, $p(y_i|x_j)$, models the conditional distribution from individual words in the input to individual words in the target. Note that, unlike in the model of Bahdanau et al. (2015), these x_j do not contain any information about the other words in the input sequence because they are not processed with an RNN. The other factor, $p(j \rightarrow i|\mathbf{x}, y_{1:i-1})$, models the conditional probability that word j in the input is relevant to word i in the target sequence, given the entire input sequence. This alignment is accomplished from encodings of the inputs produced by an RNN. The crucial architectural assumption, then, is that any temporal dependency between individual words in the input that can be captured by an RNN should only be relevant to their alignment to words in the target sequence, and not to the translation of individual words. This assumption will be made clearer in the model description below.

2.2 Encoder

The encoder produces two separate vector representations for each word in the input sequence. Unlike the previous attention model (Bahdanau et al., 2015)), we separately extract the information that will be used for direct translation with a linear transformation: $m_j = W_m x_j$, where W_m is a learned weight matrix that multiplies the one-hot encodings $\{x_1, ..., x_{T_x}\}$. Note that these representations do not contain any information about the other words in the sentence. As in the previous attention mechanism (Bahdanau et al., 2015), we use a bidirectional RNN (biRNN) to extract the information that will be used for alignment. The biRNN produces a vector for each word on the forward pass, $(\overrightarrow{h_1}, ..., \overrightarrow{h_{T_x}})$, and a vector for each word on the backward pass, $(\overleftarrow{h_1}, ..., \overleftarrow{h_{T_x}})$. The representation of each word x_j is determined by the two vectors $\overrightarrow{h_{j-1}}, \overleftarrow{h_{j+1}}$ corresponding to the words surrounding it: $h_j = [\overrightarrow{h_{j-1}}; \overleftarrow{h_{j+1}}]$.

In all experiments, we used a bidirectional LSTM for this purpose. Note that h_j is encoding the context of the surrounding words in the sentence. Our motivation for doing this was to force the RNN in the encoder to rely on the "role" the word is playing in the sentence. Note also that because there is no sequence information in the m_j, all of the information required to align the input sequence correctly (e.g. phrase structure, modifying relationships, etc.) must be encoded by the biRNN.

2.3 Decoder

The decoder models the conditional probability of each target word given the input and the previous targets: $p(y_i|y_1, y_2, ..., y_{i-1}, \mathbf{x})$, where y_i is a target and $\mathbf{x}$ is the whole input sequence. As in the previous model, we use an RNN to determine an attention distribution over the inputs at each time step (i.e. to align words in the input to the current target). However, our decoder diverges from this model in that the mapping from inputs to outputs is performed from a weighted average of the m_j:

$$p(y_i|y_{1:i-1}, \mathbf{x}) = f(d_i) \quad d_i = \sum_{j=1}^{T_x} \alpha_{ij} m_j \quad (1)$$

where f is parameterized by a linear function with a softmax, and the α_{ij} are the weights determined by the attention model. The attention weights are computed by a function measuring how well the input representations h_j align with the current hidden state of the decoder RNN, s_i:

$$\alpha_{ij} = \frac{\exp(e_{ij})}{\sum_{k=1}^{T_x} \exp(e_{ik})} \quad e_{ij} = a(s_i, h_j) \quad (2)$$

where e_{ij} can be thought of as measuring the importance of a given input word x_j to the current target word y_i, and s_i is the current hidden state of the decoder RNN. Bahdanau et al. (2015) model the function a with a feedforward network, but we choose to use a simple dot product: $a(s_i, h_j) = s_i \cdot h_j$. Finally, the hidden state of the RNN is updated with the same weighted combination of the h_j:

$$s_i = g(s_{i-1}, c_i) \quad c_i = \sum_{j=1}^{T_x} \alpha_{ij} h_j \quad (3)$$

where g is the decoder RNN, s_i is the current hidden state, and c_i can be thought of as the information in the attended words that can be used to determine what to attend to on the next time step. Again, in all experiments an LSTM was used.

3 Experiments

3.1 SCAN dataset

The SCAN[1] dataset was specifically designed to test compositional generalization (details can be found in the appendix, or in Lake and Baroni, 2018). It is composed of 20,910 sequences of commands that must be mapped to sequences of actions, and is generated from a simple finite phrase-structure grammar that includes things like adverbs and conjunctions. The splits of the dataset include: 1) Simple split, where training and testing data are split randomly, 2) Length split, where training includes only shorter sequences, and 3) Add primitive split, where a primitive command (e.g. "turn left" or "jump") is held out of the training set, except in its most basic form (e.g. " jump" → JUMP)

Here we focus on the most difficult problem in the SCAN dataset, the add-jump split, where "jump" is held out of the training set.

3.2 Implementation details

Experimental procedure is described in detail in the appendix. Training and testing sets were kept as they were in the original dataset, but following (Bastings et al., 2018), we used early stopping by validating on a 20% held out sample of the training set. All reported results are from runs of 200,000 iterations with a batch size of 1. Unless stated otherwise, each architecture was trained 5 times with different random seeds for initialization, to measure variability in results. All experiments were implemented in PyTorch. Details of the hyperparameter search are given in the appendix. Our best model used LSTMs, with 2 layers and 200 hidden units in the encoder, and 1 layer and 400 hidden units in the decoder, and 120-dimensional vectors for the m_j. The model included a dropout rate of 0.5, and was optimized using an Adam optimizer (Kingma and Ba, 2015) with a learning rate of 0.001.

3.3 Compositional generalization results

The Syntactic Attention model achieves high compositional generalization performance on the standard seq2seq SCAN dataset (see table 1). The table shows results (mean test accuracy (%) $\pm$ standard deviation) on the test splits of the dataset. Syntactic Attention is compared to the previous models, which were a CNN (Dessì and Baroni, 2019), GRUs augmented with an attention mechanism ("+

---

[1]The SCAN dataset can be downloaded at `https://github.com/brendenlake/SCAN`

attn"), which either included or did not include a dependency ("- dep") in the decoder on the previous action (Bastings et al., 2018), and the recent model of Li et al. (2019).

Lake (2019) showed that a meta-learning architecture using an external memory achieves 99.95% accuracy on a meta-seq2seq version of the SCAN task. In this version, models are trained to learn how to generalize compositionally across a number of variants of a compositional seq2seq problem. Here, we focus on the standard seq2seq version, which limits the model to one training episode.

The best model from the hyperparameter search showed strong compositional generalization performance, attaining a mean accuracy of 91.1% (median = 98.5%) on the test set of the add-jump split. However, as in Dessì and Baroni (2019), we found that our model showed variance across initialization seeds (see appendix for details). For this reason, we ran the best model 25 times on the add-jump split to get a more accurate assessment of performance. These results were highly skewed, with a mean accuracy of 78.4% but a median of 91.0% (see appendix for detailed results). Overall, this represents an improvement in the compositional generalization performance compared to the original attention mechanism (Bahdanau et al., 2015; Bastings et al., 2018), and rivals the recent results from Li et al. (2019).

3.4 Additional SCAN experiments

We hypothesized that a key feature of our architecture was that an RNN was used to encode the information in the input sequence relevant to alignment, while one was *not* used to encode the information relevant to translation. To test this hypothesis, we conducted two more experiments:

1. *RNN for translation-encoding.* An additional biLSTM was used to process the input sequence: $m_j = [\overrightarrow{m_j}; \overleftarrow{m_j}]$, where $\overrightarrow{m_j}$ and $\overleftarrow{m_j}$ are the vectors produced for the source word x_j by a biLSTM on the forward and backward passes, respectively. These m_j replace those generated by the simple linear layer in the Syntactic Attention model.

2. *c_i used for translation.* Sequential information from the encoder RNN (i.e. the c_i) was allowed to directly influence the output at each time step in the decoder: $p(y_i|y_1, y_2, ..., y_{i-1}, \mathbf{x}) = f([d_i; c_i])$, where

again f is parameterized with a linear function and a softmax output nonlinearity.

The results of the additional experiments (mean test accuracy (%) $\pm$ standard deviations) are shown in table 2. These results partially confirmed our hypothesis: performance on the jump-split test set was worse when encodings from an RNN were directly used for translation. However, when sequential information from the biLSTM encoder was used an additional input in the final production of actions, the model maintained good compositional generalization performance. We hypothesize that this was because in this setup, it was easier for the model to learn to use the m_j to directly translate actions, so it largely ignored the sequential information. This experiment suggests that the factorization between alignment and translation does not have to be perfectly strict, as long as non-sequential representations are available for direct translation.

Additional results, including on other SCAN splits and analyses of the attention distributions, can be found in the appendix.

3.5 Machine translation experiments

Although the purpose of this work was to study the inductive biases that might encourage compositional generalization, we also validated our architecture on a small machine translation dataset to obtain a basic measure of its efficacy in a more naturalistic setting. The dataset (Lake and Baroni, 2018; Bastings et al., 2018) is composed of 10,000 English/French sentence pairs in the training set and 1,190 pairs in the test set. We trained and tested our existing model without making any changes, except for adjusting the learning rate. We also ran the same experiment with the architecture described above that used c_i for translation, as this architecture also showed strong compositional generalization performance on SCAN. BLEU scores on the test set for the best learning rate (0.00015 for both models) are shown in the table below, with comparison to previously reported results using basic recurrent architectures. Our model performs comparably in neural MT, validating it in a more naturalistic setting.

4 Related work

The principle of compositionality has recently regained the attention of deep learning researchers (Bahdanau et al., 2019b,a; Lake et al., 2017; Lake

Model	Simple	Length	Add turn left	Add jump
GRU + attn (Bastings et al., 2018)	100.0 ± 0.0	18.1 ± 1.1	59.1 ± 16.8	12.5 ± 6.6
GRU + attn - dep (Bastings et al., 2018)	100.0 ± 0.0	17.8 ± 1.7	90.8 ± 3.6	0.7 ± 0.4
CNN (Dessì and Baroni, 2019)	100.0 ± 0.0	-	-	69.2 ± 8.2
Li et al. (2019)	99.9 ± 0.0	20.3 ± 1.1	99.7 ± 0.4	98.8 ± 1.4
Syntactic Attention (ours)	100.0 ± 0.0	15.2 ± 0.7	99.9 ± 0.16	$91.0^* \pm 27.4$

Table 1: Compositional generalization results. The Syntactic Attention model achieves an improvement on the compositional generalization tasks of the SCAN dataset in the standard seq2seq setting, compared to the standard recurrent models (Bastings et al., 2018; Dessì and Baroni, 2019). Star[*] indicates median of 25 runs.

Model	Simple	Length	Add turn left	Add jump
RNN for translation-encoding	99.3 ± 0.7	13.1 ± 2.5	99.4 ± 1.1	42.3 ± 32.7
c_i *used for translation*	99.3 ± 0.85	15.2 ± 1.9	98.2 ± 2.2	88.7 ± 14.2
Syntactic Attention	100.0 ± 0.0	15.2 ± 0.7	99.9 ± 0.16	$91.0^* \pm 27.4$

Table 2: Results of additional experiments. Star[*] indicates median of 25 runs.

Model	En-Fr	Fr-En
LSTM + attn	28.6	-
GRU + attn	32.1	37.5
Syntactic Attention	36.8	35.2
c_i *used for translation*	35.1	33.8

Table 3: Results on small MT dataset (Lake and Baroni, 2018; Bastings et al., 2018).

and Baroni, 2018; Battaglia et al., 2018; Johnson et al., 2017; Keysers et al., 2020) . In particular, the issue has been explored in the visual-question answering (VQA) setting (Andreas et al., 2016; Hudson and Manning, 2018; Johnson et al., 2017; Perez et al., 2018; Hu et al., 2017). Many of the successful models in this setting learn hand-coded operations (Andreas et al., 2016; Hu et al., 2017), use highly specialized components (Hudson and Manning, 2018), or use additional supervision (Hu et al., 2017). In contrast, our model uses standard recurrent networks and simply imposes the additional constraint that mechanisms for alignment and translation are separated. In the Compositional Attention Network, built for VQA, the representations used to encode images and questions are restricted to interact only through attention distributions (Hudson and Manning, 2018). Our model utilizes a similar restriction, reinforcing the idea that compositionality is enhanced when information from different modules are only allowed to interact through discrete probability distributions.

Li et al. (2019) recently showed good performance on the SCAN tasks using a very similar approach. Our results lend additional support to the idea that separating alignment and translation can facilitate compositional generalization. The results from the meta-seq2seq version of the SCAN task (Lake, 2019) suggest that meta-learning may also be a viable approach to inducing compositionality in neural networks.

We were inspired by work in cognitive science emphasizing the relationship between systematicity and syntax (Chomsky, 1957; Fodor and Pylyshyn, 1988). Others have explored similar ideas in different natural language tasks (Bastings et al., 2017, 2019; Chen et al., 2018; Havrylov et al., 2019; Strubell et al., 2018). This work supports the suggestion that intuitions from cognitive science can aid architecture design in deep learning.

5 Conclusion

In this work we attempt to operationalize an intuition from cognitive science, implementing it as inductive bias in the form of a factorization between alignment and translation in the seq2seq setting. We showed that this can improve compositional generalization performance on the SCAN task, and that it doesn't degrade performance on a small MT task. We believe this factorization prevents the model from memorizing spurious correlations in the data, and note that similar ideas may be useful in other natural language tasks.

Acknowledgments

We would like to thank reviewers for their thorough comments and useful suggestions and references.

We would also like to thank all of the members of the Computational Cognitive Neuroscience Lab at UC Davis for helpful ongoing discussion on these topics. This work was supported by ONR N00014-19- 1-2684 / N00014-18-1-2116, ONR N00014-14-1-0670 / N00014-16-1-2128, and ONR N00014-18-C-2067.

References

Jacob Andreas, Marcus Rohrbach, Trevor Darrell, and Dan Klein. 2016. Neural Module Networks. In *2016 IEEE Conference on Computer Vision and Pattern Recognition (CVPR)*, pages 39–48, Las Vegas, NV, USA. IEEE.

Dzmitry Bahdanau, Kyunghyun Cho, and Yoshua Bengio. 2015. Neural machine translation by jointly learning to align and translate. In *3rd International Conference on Learning Representations, ICLR 2015, San Diego, CA, USA, May 7-9, 2015, Conference Track Proceedings*.

Dzmitry Bahdanau, Harm de Vries, Timothy J. O'Donnell, Shikhar Murty, Philippe Beaudoin, Yoshua Bengio, and Aaron Courville. 2019a. CLOSURE: Assessing Systematic Generalization of CLEVR Models. *arXiv:1912.05783 [cs]*.

Dzmitry Bahdanau, Shikhar Murty, Michael Noukhovitch, Thien Huu Nguyen, Harm de Vries, and Aaron C. Courville. 2019b. Systematic Generalization: What Is Required and Can It Be Learned? In *7th International Conference on Learning Representations, ICLR 2019, New Orleans, LA, USA, May 6-9, 2019*. OpenReview.net.

Joost Bastings, Wilker Aziz, Ivan Titov, and Khalil Sima'an. 2019. Modeling Latent Sentence Structure in Neural Machine Translation. *arXiv:1901.06436 [cs]*.

Joost Bastings, Marco Baroni, Jason Weston, Kyunghyun Cho, and Douwe Kiela. 2018. Jump to better conclusions: SCAN both left and right. In *Proceedings of the 2018 EMNLP Workshop BlackboxNLP: Analyzing and Interpreting Neural Networks for NLP*, pages 47–55, Brussels, Belgium. Association for Computational Linguistics.

Joost Bastings, Ivan Titov, Wilker Aziz, Diego Marcheggiani, and Khalil Sima'an. 2017. Graph Convolutional Encoders for Syntax-aware Neural Machine Translation. In *Proceedings of the 2017 Conference on Empirical Methods in Natural Language Processing*, pages 1957–1967, Copenhagen, Denmark. Association for Computational Linguistics.

Peter W. Battaglia, Jessica B. Hamrick, Victor Bapst, Alvaro Sanchez-Gonzalez, Vinicius Zambaldi, Mateusz Malinowski, Andrea Tacchetti, David Raposo, Adam Santoro, Ryan Faulkner, Caglar Gulcehre, Francis Song, Andrew Ballard, Justin Gilmer, George Dahl, Ashish Vaswani, Kelsey Allen, Charles Nash, Victoria Langston, Chris Dyer, Nicolas Heess, Daan Wierstra, Pushmeet Kohli, Matt Botvinick, Oriol Vinyals, Yujia Li, and Razvan Pascanu. 2018. Relational inductive biases, deep learning, and graph networks. *arXiv:1806.01261 [cs, stat]*.

Kehai Chen, Rui Wang, Masao Utiyama, Eiichiro Sumita, and Tiejun Zhao. 2018. Syntax-Directed Attention for Neural Machine Translation. In *Proceedings of the Thirty-Second AAAI Conference on Artificial Intelligence, (AAAI-18), the 30th Innovative Applications of Artificial Intelligence (IAAI-18), and the 8th AAAI Symposium on Educational Advances in Artificial Intelligence (EAAI-18), New Orleans, Louisiana, USA, February 2-7, 2018*, pages 4792–4799. AAAI Press.

N. Chomsky, editor. 1957. *Syntactic Structures*. Mouton & Co., The Hague.

Roberto Dessì and Marco Baroni. 2019. CNNs found to jump around more skillfully than RNNs: Compositional Generalization in Seq2seq Convolutional Networks. In *Proceedings of the 57th Annual Meeting of the Association for Computational Linguistics*, pages 3919–3923, Florence, Italy. Association for Computational Linguistics.

Jerry A. Fodor and Zenon W. Pylyshyn. 1988. Connectionism and cognitive architecture: A critical analysis. *Cognition*, 28(1-2):3–71.

Serhii Havrylov, Germán Kruszewski, and Armand Joulin. 2019. Cooperative Learning of Disjoint Syntax and Semantics. In *Proceedings of the 2019 Conference of the North American Chapter of the Association for Computational Linguistics: Human Language Technologies, Volume 1 (Long and Short Papers)*, pages 1118–1128, Minneapolis, Minnesota. Association for Computational Linguistics.

Ronghang Hu, Jacob Andreas, Marcus Rohrbach, Trevor Darrell, and Kate Saenko. 2017. Learning to Reason: End-to-End Module Networks for Visual Question Answering. In *2017 IEEE International Conference on Computer Vision (ICCV)*, pages 804–813.

Drew A. Hudson and Christopher D. Manning. 2018. Compositional Attention Networks for Machine Reasoning. In *6th International Conference on Learning Representations, ICLR 2018, Vancouver, BC, Canada, April 30 - May 3, 2018, Conference Track Proceedings*. OpenReview.net.

Justin Johnson, Bharath Hariharan, Laurens van der Maaten, Li Fei-Fei, C. Lawrence Zitnick, and Ross Girshick. 2017. CLEVR: A Diagnostic Dataset for Compositional Language and Elementary Visual Reasoning. In *2017 IEEE Conference on Computer Vision and Pattern Recognition (CVPR)*, pages 1988–1997.

Daniel Keysers, Nathanael Schärli, Nathan Scales, Hylke Buisman, Daniel Furrer, Sergii Kashubin, Nikola Momchev, Danila Sinopalnikov, Lukasz Stafiniak, Tibor Tihon, Dmitry Tsarkov, Xiao Wang, Marc van Zee, and Olivier Bousquet. 2020. Measuring compositional generalization: A comprehensive method on realistic data. page 38.

Diederik P. Kingma and Jimmy Ba. 2015. Adam: A Method for Stochastic Optimization. In *3rd International Conference on Learning Representations, ICLR 2015, San Diego, CA, USA, May 7-9, 2015, Conference Track Proceedings*.

Brenden M Lake. 2019. Compositional generalization through meta sequence-to-sequence learning. In H. Wallach, H. Larochelle, A. Beygelzimer, F. Alché-Buc, E. Fox, and R. Garnett, editors, *Advances in Neural Information Processing Systems 32*, pages 9788–9798. Curran Associates, Inc.

Brenden M. Lake and Marco Baroni. 2018. Generalization without Systematicity: On the Compositional Skills of Sequence-to-Sequence Recurrent Networks. In *Proceedings of the 35th International Conference on Machine Learning, ICML 2018, Stockholmsmässan, Stockholm, Sweden, July 10-15, 2018*, volume 80 of *Proceedings of Machine Learning Research*, pages 2879–2888. PMLR.

Brenden M. Lake, Tal Linzen, and Marco Baroni. 2019. Human few-shot learning of compositional instructions. In *Proceedings of the 41th Annual Meeting of the Cognitive Science Society, CogSci 2019: Creativity + Cognition + Computation, Montreal, Canada, July 24-27, 2019*, pages 611–617. cognitivesciencesociety.org.

Brenden M. Lake, Tomer D. Ullman, Joshua B. Tenenbaum, and Samuel J. Gershman. 2017. Building machines that learn and think like people. *The Behavioral and Brain Sciences*, 40:e253.

Yuanpeng Li, Liang Zhao, Jianyu Wang, and Joel Hestness. 2019. Compositional Generalization for Primitive Substitutions. In *Proceedings of the 2019 Conference on Empirical Methods in Natural Language Processing and the 9th International Joint Conference on Natural Language Processing (EMNLP-IJCNLP)*, pages 4293–4302, Hong Kong, China. Association for Computational Linguistics.

João Loula, Marco Baroni, and Brenden Lake. 2018. Rearranging the Familiar: Testing Compositional Generalization in Recurrent Networks. In *Proceedings of the 2018 EMNLP Workshop BlackboxNLP: Analyzing and Interpreting Neural Networks for NLP*, pages 108–114, Brussels, Belgium. Association for Computational Linguistics.

Gary Marcus. 2018. Deep learning: A critical appraisal.

Ethan Perez, Florian Strub, Harm de Vries, Vincent Dumoulin, and Aaron C. Courville. 2018. FiLM: Visual Reasoning with a General Conditioning Layer. In *Proceedings of the Thirty-Second AAAI Conference on Artificial Intelligence, (AAAI-18), the 30th Innovative Applications of Artificial Intelligence (IAAI-18), and the 8th AAAI Symposium on Educational Advances in Artificial Intelligence (EAAI-18), New Orleans, Louisiana, USA, February 2-7, 2018*, pages 3942–3951. AAAI Press.

Emma Strubell, Patrick Verga, Daniel Andor, David Weiss, and Andrew McCallum. 2018. Linguistically-Informed Self-Attention for Semantic Role Labeling. In *Proceedings of the 2018 Conference on Empirical Methods in Natural Language Processing*, pages 5027–5038, Brussels, Belgium. Association for Computational Linguistics.

A SCAN dataset details

The SCAN dataset (Lake and Baroni, 2018) is composed of sequences of instructions that must be mapped to sequences of actions (see Figure 3).

The instruction sequences are generated using the pharase-structure grammar described in Figure 4. This simple grammar is not recursive, and so can generate a finite number of command sequences (20,910 total).

These commands are interpreted according to the rules shown in Figure 5. Although the grammar used to generate and interpret the commands is simple compared to any natural language, it captures the basic properties that are important for testing compositionality (e.g. modifying relationships, discrete grammatical roles, etc.). The add-primitive splits (described in main text) are meant to be analogous to the capacity of humans to generalize the usage of a novel verb (e.g. "dax") to many constructions (Lake and Baroni, 2018).

B Experimental procedure details

The cluster used for all experiments consists of 3 nodes, with 68 cores in total (48 times Intel(R) Xeon(R) CPU E5-2650 v4 at 2.20GHz, 20 times Intel(R) Xeon(R) CPU E5-2650 v3 at 2.30GHz), with 128GB of ram each, connected through a 56Gbit infiniband network. It has 8 pascal Titan X GPUs and runs Ubuntu 16.04.

All experiments were conducted with the SCAN dataset as it was originally published (Lake and Baroni, 2018). No data were excluded, and no preprocessing was done except to encode words in the input and action sequences into one-hot vectors, and to add special tokens for start-of-sequence and end-of-sequence tokens. Train and test sets were

jump	$\Rightarrow$	JUMP
jump left	$\Rightarrow$	LTURN JUMP
jump around right	$\Rightarrow$	RTURN JUMP RTURN JUMP RTURN JUMP RTURN JUMP
turn left twice	$\Rightarrow$	LTURN LTURN
jump thrice	$\Rightarrow$	JUMP JUMP JUMP
jump opposite left and walk thrice	$\Rightarrow$	LTURN LTURN JUMP WALK WALK WALK
jump opposite left after walk around left	$\Rightarrow$	LTURN WALK LTURN WALK LTURN WALK LTURN WALK LTURN LTURN JUMP

Figure 3: Examples from the SCAN dataset. Figure reproduced from (Lake and Baroni, 2018).

C → S and S	V → D[1] opposite D[2]	D → turn left
C → S after S	V → D[1] around D[2]	D → turn right
C → S	V → D	U → walk
S → V twice	V → U	U → look
S → V thrice	D → U left	U → run
S → V	D → U right	U → jump

Figure 4: Phrase-structure grammar used to generate SCAN dataset. Figure reproduced from (Lake and Baroni, 2018).

kept as they were in the original dataset, but following (Bastings et al., 2018), we used early stopping by validating on a 20% held out sample of the training set. All reported results are from runs of 200,000 iterations with a batch size of 1. Except for the additional batch of 25 runs for the add-jump split, each architecture was trained 5 times with different random seeds for initialization, to measure variability in results. All experiments were implemented in PyTorch.

Initial experimentation included different implementations of the assumption that syntactic information be separated from semantic information. After the architecture described in the main text showed promising results, a hyperparameter search was conducted to determine optimization (stochastic gradient descent vs. Adam), RNN-type (GRU vs. LSTM), regularizers (dropout, weight decay), and number of layers (1 vs. 2 layers for encoder and decoder RNNs). We found that the Adam optimizer (Kingma and Ba, 2015) with a learning rate of 0.001, two layers in the encoder RNN and 1 layer in the decoder RNN, and dropout worked the best, so all further experiments used these specifications. Then, a grid-search was conducted to find the number of hidden units and dropout rate. We tried hidden dimensions ranging from 50 to 400, and dropout rates ranging from 0.0 to 0.5.

The best model used an LSTM with 2 layers and 200 hidden units in the encoder, and an LSTM with 1 layer and 400 hidden units in the decoder, and used 120-dimensional m_j vectors, and a dropout rate of 0.5. The results for this model are reported in the main text. All additional experiments were done with models derived from this one, with the same hyperparameter settings.

All evaluation runs are reported in the main text: for each evaluation except for the add-jump split, models were trained 5 times with different random seeds, and performance was measured with means and standard deviations of accuracy. For the add-jump split, we included 25 runs to get a more accurate assessment of performance. This revealed a strong skew in the distribution of results, so we included the median as the main measure of performance. Occasionally, the model did not train at all due to an unknown error (possibly very poor random initialization, high learning rate or numerical error). For this reason, we excluded runs in which training accuracy did not get above 10%. No other runs were excluded.

C   Skew of add-jump results

As mentioned in the results section of the main text, we found that test accuracy on the add-jump split was variable and highly skewed. Figure 6 shows a histogram of these results (proportion correct). The model performs near-perfectly most of the time, but is also prone to catastrophic failures. This may be because, at least for our model, the add-jump

$$
\begin{aligned}
&[\![\text{walk}]\!] = \text{WALK} &&[\![u \text{ opposite left}]\!] = [\![\text{turn opposite left}]\!]\ [\![u]\!] \\
&[\![\text{look}]\!] = \text{LOOK} &&[\![u \text{ opposite right}]\!] = [\![\text{turn opposite right}]\!]\ [\![u]\!] \\
&[\![\text{run}]\!] = \text{RUN} &&[\![\text{turn around left}]\!] = \text{LTURN LTURN LTURN LTURN} \\
&[\![\text{jump}]\!] = \text{JUMP} &&[\![\text{turn around right}]\!] = \text{RTURN RTURN RTURN RTURN} \\
&[\![\text{turn left}]\!] = \text{LTURN} &&[\![u \text{ around left}]\!] = \text{LTURN } [\![u]\!] \text{ LTURN } [\![u]\!] \text{ LTURN } [\![u]\!] \text{ LTURN } [\![u]\!] \\
&[\![\text{turn right}]\!] = \text{RTURN} &&[\![u \text{ around right}]\!] = \text{RTURN } [\![u]\!] \text{ RTURN } [\![u]\!] \text{ RTURN } [\![u]\!] \text{ RTURN } [\![u]\!] \\
&[\![u \text{ left}]\!] = \text{LTURN } [\![u]\!] &&[\![x \text{ twice}]\!] = [\![x]\!]\ [\![x]\!] \\
&[\![u \text{ right}]\!] = \text{RTURN } [\![u]\!] &&[\![x \text{ thrice}]\!] = [\![x]\!]\ [\![x]\!]\ [\![x]\!] \\
&[\![\text{turn opposite left}]\!] = \text{LTURN LTURN} &&[\![x_1 \text{ and } x_2]\!] = [\![x_1]\!]\ [\![x_2]\!] \\
&[\![\text{turn opposite right}]\!] = \text{RTURN RTURN} &&[\![x_1 \text{ after } x_2]\!] = [\![x_2]\!]\ [\![x_1]\!]
\end{aligned}
$$

Figure 5: Rules for interpreting command sequences to generate actions in SCAN dataset. Figure reproduced from (Lake and Baroni, 2018).

split represents a highly nonlinear problem in the sense that slight differences in the way the primitive verb "jump" is encoded during training can have huge differences for how the model performs on more complicated constructions. We recommend that future experiments with this kind of compositional generalization problem take note of this phenomenon, and conduct especially comprehensive analyses of variability in results. Future research will also be needed to better understand the factors that determine this variability, and whether it can be overcome with other priors or regularization techniques.

D Supplementary experiments

D.1 Testing nonlinear translation

Our main hypothesis is that the separation between sequential information used for alignment and information about the meanings of individual words encourages systematicity. The results reported in the main text are largely consistent with this hypothesis, as shown by the performance of the Syntactic Attention model on the compositional generalization tests of the SCAN dataset. However, it is also possible that the simplicity of the translation stream in the model is also important for improving compositional generalization. To test this, we replaced the linear layer in this stream with a nonlinear neural network. From the model description in the main text:

$$p(y_i|y_1, y_2, ..., y_{i-1}, \mathbf{x}) = f(d_i), \qquad (4)$$

In the original model, f was parameterized with a simple linear layer, but here we use a two-layer feedforward network with a ReLU nonlinearity, before a softmax is applied to generate a distribution over the possible actions. We tested this model on the add-primitive splits of the SCAN dataset. The results (mean (%) with standard deviations) are shown in Table 4, with comparison to the baseline Syntactic Attention model.

The results show that this modification did not substantially degrade compositional generalization performance, suggesting that the success of the Syntactic Attention model does not depend on the parameterization of the translation stream with a simple linear function.

D.2 Add-jump split with additional examples

The original SCAN dataset was published with compositional generalization splits that have more than one example of the held-out primitive verb (Lake and Baroni, 2018). The training sets in these splits of the dataset include 1, 2, 4, 8, 16, or 32 random samples of command sequences with the "jump" command, allowing for a more fine-grained measurement of the ability to generalize the usage of a primitive verb from few examples. For each number of "jump" commands included in the training set, five different random samples were taken to capture any variance in results due to the selection of particular commands to train on.

Lake and Baroni (2018) found that their best model (an LSTM without an attention mechansim) did not generalize well (below 39%), even when it was trained on 8 random examples that included the "jump" command, but that the addition of further examples to the training set improved performance. Subsequent work showed better performance at lower numbers of "jump" examples, with GRU's augmented with an attention mechanism ("+ attn"), and either with or without a dependence in the decoder on the previous target ("- dep") (Bastings et al., 2018). Here, we compare the Syntactic Attention model to these results.

The Syntactic Attention model shows a substantial improvement over these previous approaches

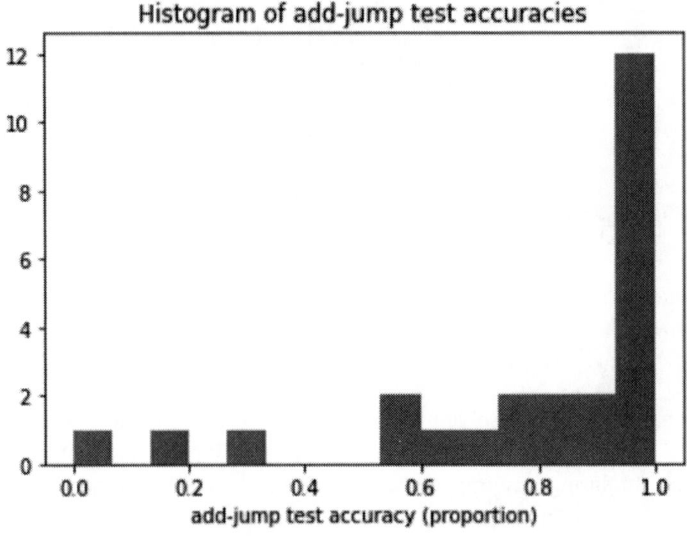

Figure 6: Histogram of test accuracies across all 25 runs of add-jump split.

Table 4: Results of nonlinear translation experiment. Star[*] indicates median of 25 runs.

Model	Add turn left	Add jump
Nonlinear translation	99.0 ± 1.7	84.4 ± 14.1
Syntactic Attention	99.9 ± 0.16	$91.0^{*} \pm 27.4$

at the lowest numbers of "jump" examples used for training (see Figure 7 and Table 5). Compositional generalization performance is already quite high at 1 example, and at 2 examples is almost perfect (99.997% correct).

D.3 Template splits

The compositional generalization splits of the SCAN dataset were originally designed to test for the ability to generalize known primitive verbs to valid unseen constructions (Lake and Baroni, 2018). Further work with SCAN augmented this set of tests to include compositional generalization based not on known verbs but on known *templates* (Loula et al., 2018). These template splits included the following (see Figure 8 for examples):

- *Jump around right*: All command sequences with the phrase "jump around right" are held out of the training set and subsequently tested.

- Primitive *right*: All command sequences containing primitive verbs modified by "right" are held out of the training set and subsequently tested.

- Primitive *opposite right*: All command se-

quences containing primitive verbs modified by "opposite right" are held out of the training set and subsequently tested.

- Primitive *around right*: All command sequences containing primitive verbs modified by "around right" are held out of the training set and subsequently tested.

Results of the Syntactic Attention model on these template splits are compared to those originally published (Loula et al., 2018) in Table 6. The model, like the one reported in (Loula et al., 2018), performs well on the *jump around right* split, consistent with the idea that this task does not present a problem for neural networks. The rest of the results are mixed: Syntactic Attention shows good compositional generalization performance on the Primitive *right* split, but fails on the Primitive *opposite right* and Primitive *around right* splits. All of the template tasks require models to generalize based on the symmetry between "left" and "right" in the dataset. However, in the *opposite right* and *around right* splits, this symmetry is substantially violated, as one of the two prepositional phrases in which they can occur is never seen with "right."

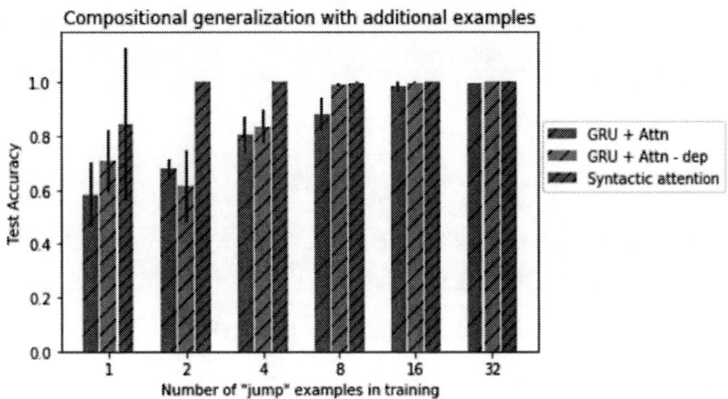

Figure 7: Compositional generalization performance on add-jump split with additional examples. Syntactic Attention model is compared to previously reported models (Bastings et al., 2018) on test accuracy as command sequences with "jump" are added to the training set. Mean accuracy (proportion correct) was computed with 5 different random samples of "jump" commands. Error bars represent standard deviations.

Table 5: Results of Syntactic Attention compared to models of Bastings et al. (2018) on jump-split with additional examples. Mean accuracy (% - rounded to tenths) is shown with standard deviations. Same data as depicted in Figure 7.

Model	Number of jump commands in training set					
	1	2	4	8	16	32
GRU + attn	$58.2_{\pm 12.0}$	$67.8_{\pm 3.4}$	$80.3_{\pm 7.0}$	$88.0_{\pm 6.0}$	$98.3_{\pm 1.8}$	$99.6_{\pm 0.2}$
GRU + attn - dep	$70.9_{\pm 11.5}$	$61.3_{\pm 13.5}$	$83.5_{\pm 6.1}$	$99.0_{\pm 0.4}$	$99.7_{\pm 0.2}$	$100.0_{\pm 0.0}$
Syntactic Attention	$84.4_{\pm 28.5}$	$100.0_{\pm 0.01}$	$100.0_{\pm 0.02}$	$99.9_{\pm 0.2}$	$100.0_{\pm 0.01}$	$99.9_{\pm 0.2}$

E   Visualizing attention

Here, we visualize the attention distributions over the words in the command sequence at each step during the decoding process. In the following figures (Figures 9 to 14), the attention weights on each command (in the columns of the image) is shown for each of the model's outputs (in the rows of the image) for some illustrative examples. Darker blue indicates a higher weight. The examples are shown in pairs for a model trained and tested on the add-jump split, with one example drawn from the training set and a corresponding example drawn from the test set. Examples are shown in increasing complexity, with a failure mode depicted in Figure 14.

In general, it can be seen that although the attention distributions on the test examples are not exactly the same as those from the corresponding training examples, they are usually good enough for the model to produce the correct action sequence. This shows the model's ability to apply the same syntactic rules it learned on the other verbs to the novel verb "jump." In the example shown in Figure 14, the model fails to attend to the correct sequence of commands, resulting in an error.

Condition	Example train commands	Example test commands
jump around right	"*jump left*", "*jump around left*", "*walk around right*"	"*jump around right*", "*jump around right and walk*"
Primitive *right*	"*jump left*", "*walk around right*"	"*jump right*", "*walk right*"
Primitive *opposite right*	"*jump left*", "*jump opposite left*", "*walk right*"	"*jump opposite right*", "*walk opposite right*"
Primitive *around right*	"*jump left*", "*jump around left*", "*walk right*"	"*jump around right*", "*walk around right*"

Figure 8: Table of example command sequences for each template split. Reproduced from (Loula et al., 2018)

Table 6: Results of Syntactic Attention compared to models of Loula et al. (2018) on template splits of SCAN dataset. Mean accuracy (%) is shown with standard deviations. **P** = Primitive

	Template split			
Model	*jump around right*	**P** *right*	**P** *opposite right*	**P** *around right*
LSTM (Loula et al. (2018))	98.43±0.54	23.49±8.09	47.62±17.72	2.46±2.68
Syntactic Attention	98.9±2.3	99.1±1.8	10.5±8.8	28.9±34.8

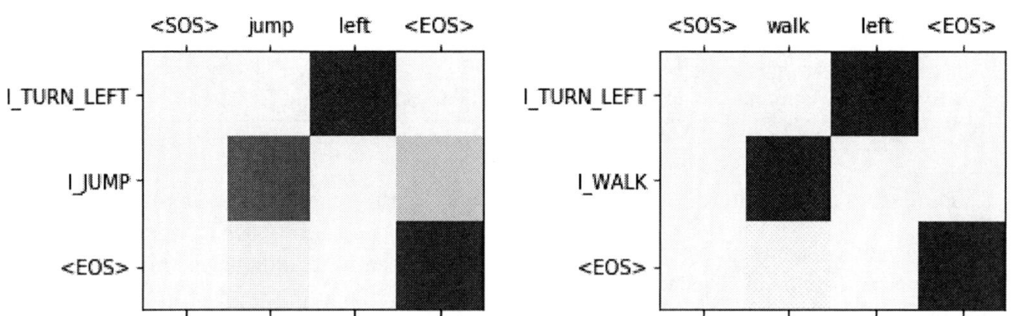

Figure 9: Attention distributions: correct example

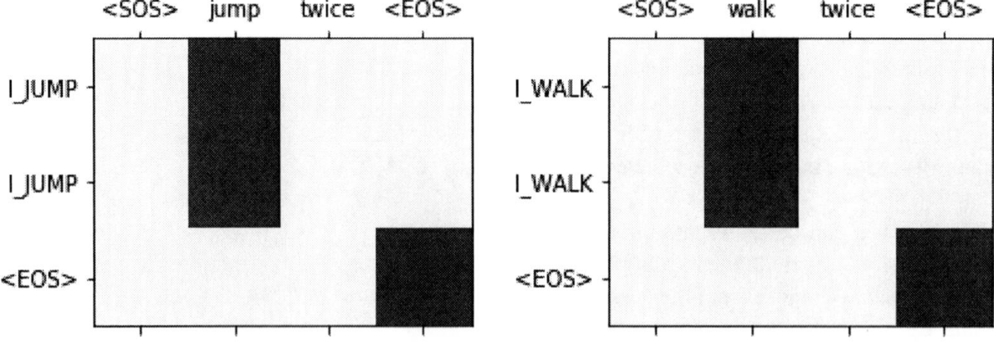

Figure 10: Attention distributions: correct example

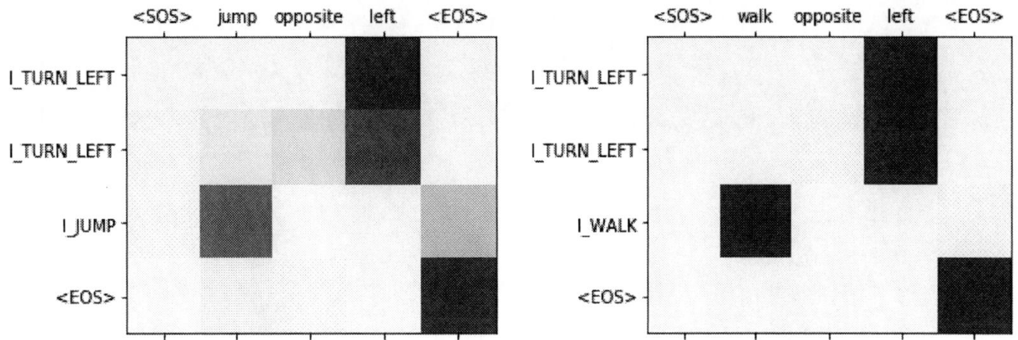

Figure 11: Attention distributions: correct example

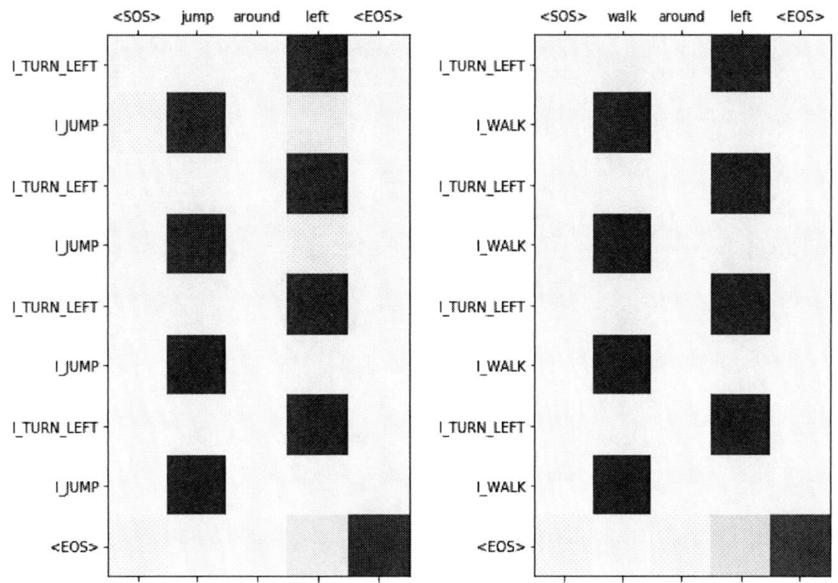

Figure 12: Attention distributions: correct example

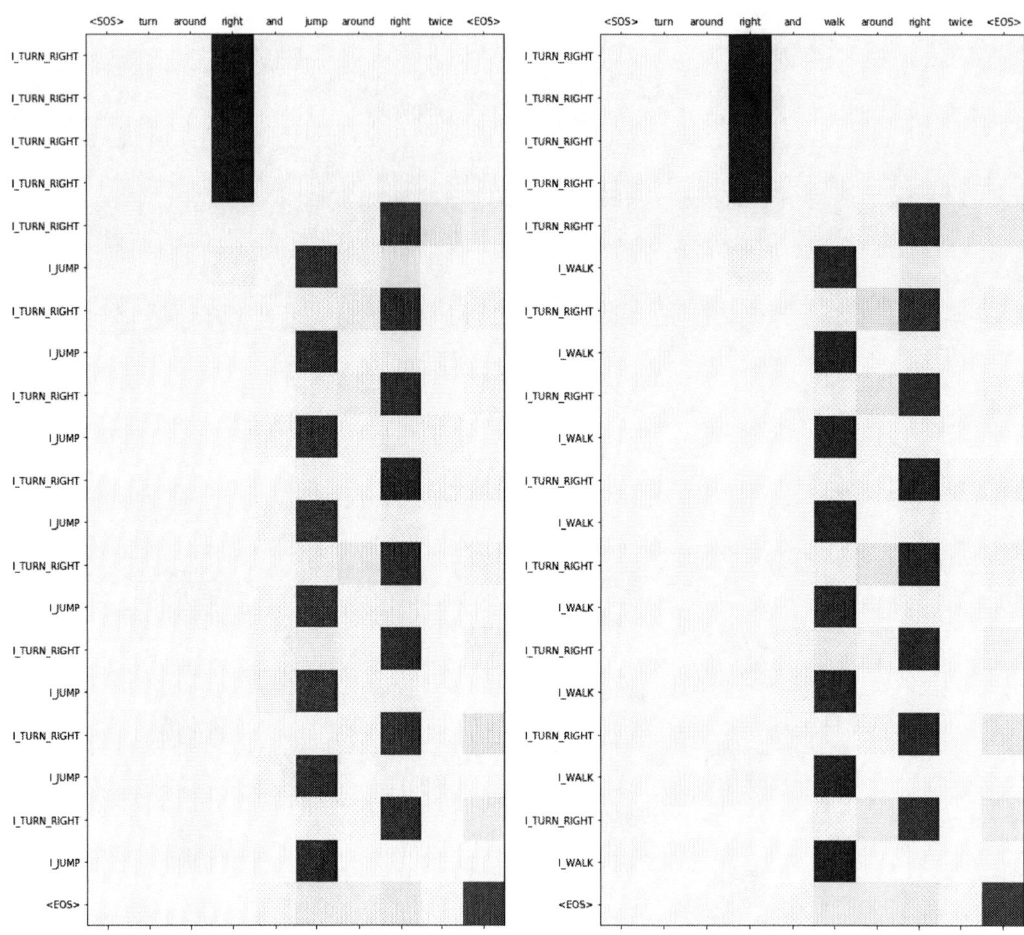

Figure 13: Attention distributions: correct example

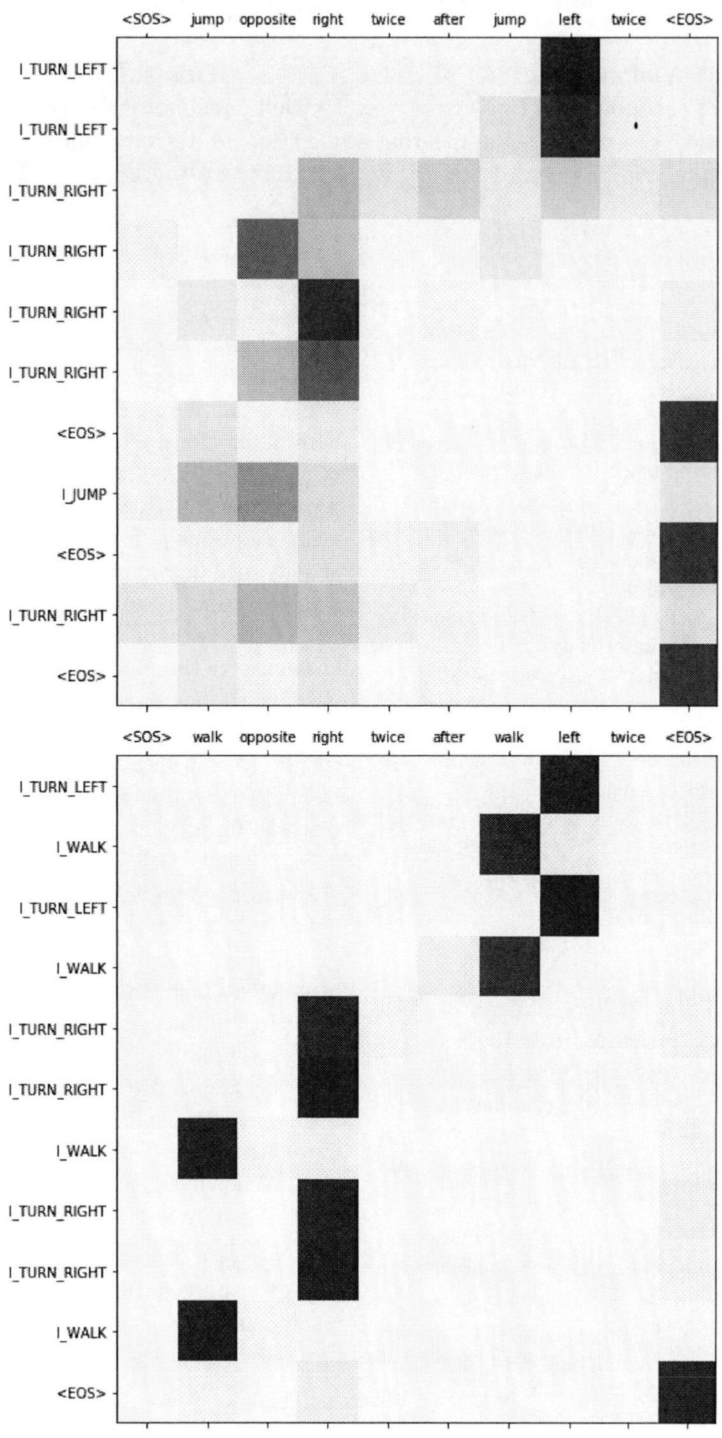

Figure 14: Attention distributions: incorrect example

#NotAWhore! A Computational Linguistic Perspective of Rape Culture and Victimization on Social Media

Ashima Suvarna[*]
Delhi Technological University
Department of Computer Engineering
asuvarna31@gmail.com

Grusha Bhalla[*]
Delhi Technological University
Department of Computer Engineering
grushabhalla@gmail.com

Abstract

The recent surge in online forums and movements supporting sexual assault survivors has led to the emergence of a 'virtual bubble' where survivors can recount their stories. However, this also makes the survivors vulnerable to bullying, trolling and victim blaming. Specifically, victim blaming has been shown to have acute psychological effects on the survivors and further discourage formal reporting of such crimes. Therefore, it is important to devise computationally relevant methods to identify and prevent victim blaming to protect the victims. In our work, we discuss the drastic effects of victim blaming through a short case study and then propose a single step transfer-learning based classification method to identify victim blaming language on Twitter. Finally, we compare the performance of our proposed model against various deep learning and machine learning models on a manually annotated domain-specific dataset.

1 Introduction

Global statistics indicate that 35% of women worldwide have experienced sexual violence at some point in their lives[1]. Popular hashtags like '#metoo', '#sexualharassment' on Twitter have encouraged victims to share their stories of sexual assault and formally report them. However, the backlash faced by the victims has been staggering. Victims of sexual assault are often held culpable for the assault, and are attacked on social forums by extremists. With the rise of such crimes, it is important to devise a computational framework that can identify and prevent online victimization of sexual assault survivors who choose to report the crime. Ambiguous interpretations of rape culture and victim blaming makes manually sorting and identifying such information an arduous task.

Hence, in our work we have attempted to identify an objectively grounded definition of victim blaming for further research in this domain.

Victim blaming occurs when the victim of a crime or any wrongful act is held entirely or partially at fault for the harm that befell them (Coates et al., 2006). Additionally, "slut shaming" is a popular form of victim blaming which refers to attacking a person's character on the basis of sexual activity, real or perceived (Ringrose and Renold, 2012). Victims of sexual assault are initially hesitant to make a sexual assault complaint and often encounter victim blaming and slut shaming attitudes when they finally do (Ahrens, 2006). This blame can appear in the form of toxic social responses from medical professionals, the media, the judiciary or a growing majority of online activists on social media platforms (Campbell et al., 2009).

Social platforms like Twitter and Facebook provide victims with a 'virtual bubble' to recollect the assault stories and seek emotional help. The victim blaming faced by these victims, however, discourages them from disclosing their personal stories and further seeking medical help (Verdun-Jones and Rossiter, 2010). Therefore, in this work, we propose a method to identify such language on Twitter and protect the victims who choose to disclose their plight. We propose a Twitter-specific classification model which can exclusively identify victim blaming tweets. The key contributions of this work are:

- Our work is the first attempt in devising a computational framework for identifying victim blaming language.

- We provide a manually annotated dataset that contains 5,070 tweets for further research in this domain.

- We propose a single step transfer learning based classification method that identifies victim blaming language and labels it. It obtained

---

[*] Authors contributed equally

[1] http://worldpopulationreview.com/countries/rape-statistics-by-country

Proceedings of the 58th Annual Meeting of the Association for Computational Linguistics: Student Research Workshop, pages 328–335
July 5 - July 10, 2020. ©2020 Association for Computational Linguistics

superior results to many deep learning and machine learning based approaches.

2 Related Work

Prior research has shown sexual assault is a crime that women are most afraid of (Koss, 1993). Oftentimes, victims of sexual assault are subjected to humiliation, blaming because of which, reasonable doubt is created about their credibility (Ullman, 2000). Popular theories such as the "just world" (Lerner, 1980) theory and the "invulnerability" (Andrew et al., 2003) theory explain the psychological motivation behind victim blaming. The "just world" theory states that people get what they deserve and deserve what they get, thereby shifting the blame of the crime to the victim while the "invulnerability" theory states that people blame the victim to project their own sense of invulnerability.

Victim Blaming, therefore, stems from an individual's personal sense of insecurity and acts as a silencing function for most victims who are discouraged to disclose their personal stories or seek any help online (Ahrens, 2006). Since victims fail to obtain the required medical assistance, they become highly susceptible to emotional difficulties that manifest as depression in the short term and acute psychological difficulties in the long run (Verdun-Jones and Rossiter, 2010). In addition to this, chronosystem factors like past instances of victimization and sexual revictimization affect the mental health outcomes of the survivor often leading to suicidal behaviour, substance use, depression etc. (Campbell et al., 2009).

With the advent of social media, a new medium has presented itself for victim blaming to occur. Social platforms like Twitter, Facebook and Reddit provide a space to publicly post comments and present an insight into community opinions for researchers and social scientists. Due to its increasing popularity, Twitter is being used for research in opinion mining (Andleeb et al., 2019), keyword extraction (Biswas, 2019), hate speech detection (Badjatiya et al., 2017) etc. It has been widely used for research on sexual violence (Wekerle et al., 2018) as well as suicidal ideation using linear and ensemble classifiers (Sawhney et al., 2018). Research has also been focused on hate speech detection for Twitter using deep learning techniques, classifying tweets as sexist, racist or neither (Badjatiya et al., 2017). Balakrishnan et al. (2020) have used Naive Bayes, Random Forest and J48 for detection of cyberbullying. Due to the similarities between victim blaming and cyberbullying, we have used Naive Bayes as one of our baseline models. Schrading (2015) analyzes discussions on domestic abuse across social media, using LSTM, Naive Bayes, Logistic Regression, and SVM which has been used as a baseline against our proposed method because of its good performance.

2.1 Motivation: Weibo Victim Scandal

Liu Jingyao, a 21 years old student at the University of Minnesota accused Liu Qiangdong the founder of Chinas largest company JD.com, of raping her. She did not report her case immediately as she was afraid that she would be blamed. After the case became popular in China, people commented things like The woman looks disgusting, She is a slut etc. on Weibo, the Chinese equivalent of Twitter. She suffered from post traumatic stress disorder and insomnia because of this.[2]

The Weibo Case study is a classic example of the drastic effects of victim blaming on the victim and it's prevalence in our society. Reporting of instances of sexual violence has shown to pre-empt blame in the talk of women reporting blame which further shows that victim blaming itself is marked by specific topics and framing of sentences that shifts the blame onto the victim. Parameters like location of incident, state of victim etc. can be used for identifying such instances (Stubbs-Richardson et al., 2018). In lieu of these specific markers of victim blaming language which can further lead to biased reporting in offline media as well, we feel it is imperative to study about it in detail. Previous works in hate speech detection classified tweets as racist or sexist only (Badjatiya et al., 2017). These works generalize all instances of sexism under one classification. However, recent research has shown important sub-classifications of sexism that may be important for online media research. (Parikh et al., 2019) classifies tweets into 14 sub categories of sexism and we identify that not all 14 categories may have as drastic effects as victim blaming and slut shaming. Victim Blaming on online media directly leads to psychological disturbances for the victim and biased responses from authorities seeking legal action for such crimes (Gruenewald et al., 2004). This does not undermine the severity of other categories but rather establishes why victim blaming

---

[2]https://www.nytimes.com/2019/12/13/business/liu-jingyao-interview-richard-liu.html

Clothing, makeup of victim (short skirt, skimpy clothes, v-neck shirts)
Victim's physiological state at time of incident (drunk, sad, depressed)
Victim's former/current job as a prostitute
Victim's sexual history or promiscuity
Victim's upbringing as explanation for behaviour (raised by lesbians, rich)
Locations that suggest victim culpability (bar, road, club)
Use of loaded terms to describe rape (alleges, accuses, she says)
self-reporting (Victim chooses to report crime on online media first)

Table 1: Coding Instrument to Identify Victim Blaming Language

should be studied separately and not as a specific instance of hate speech due to sensitivity and specific topics related to this issue. Models specific to each sub-category may not seem feasible and scalable but viewing at the issue of victim blaming from a psychological perspective we feel research in this domain is essential to devise computational frameworks to identify and prevent victim blaming on social media extensible to offline media reporting.

3 Dataset Construction

Creating our victim-blaming dataset entails a two step process: collection of data and data annotation. Due to the lack of prior work, we create a custom dataset by crawling English tweets from Twitter using the Twitter API[3] that mentioned major hashtags related to sexual harassment. A total of 4,242 tweets were scrapped from November 6, 2019 to November 19, 2019 which contained 'metoo. Also, 413 tweets were scrapped containing 'sexualharassment. We further observed that victim blaming tweets contained derogatory terms like 'whore' therefore, we used common words related to sexual harassment (rape, slut, whore) for increasing the number of positive samples. A total of 732 tweets were added after scrapping tweets from November 16, 2019 to November 29, 2019. Tweets are unstructured and noisy in nature due to the use of informal language prevalent on social media (Zappavigna, 2012). For pre-processing them, stop words are removed along with non alphanumeric text as they provide little information. URL's, emojis like ':)' and the symbol '#' are removed using regex. Usernames are also removed for anonymity. The tweets are then tokenized to run the various models. Tokenization and removal of stop words is done using NLTK. The average

number of characters in a tweet is 33 [4]. After pre-processing, we remove tweets which have less than 33 characters. The final dataset contains 5,070 tweets out of which 1562 were classified as positive samples. Under the guidance of a social scientist, a coding scheme to identify victim blaming language is devised, taking into account gender related discourse and campaigns as well as psychological analysis of rape culture and victimization from social media. Table 1 summarizes the key identifiers of victim-blaming language.

We follow a two-phase annotation process for the classification of each tweet in the final dataset. In Phase 1, two annotators, a psychology student and a social science student identify tweets which contain features listed in Table 1 and subsequently classify them by marking victim blaming tweets as '1' and other tweets as '0'. The inter annotator agreement, measured by the average of the Cohens Kappa (Cohen, 1960) is 0.712. In case of a disagreement between the annotators, a third annotator who is a social science student classifies the ambiguous tweet. Phase 2 involves checking that all the tweets have been classified and correct symbol that is, either '1' or '0' have been used for it. Table 2 shows some samples from the dataset that were labeled '1' by the annotators.

4 The Victim Blaming Language Model

NLP problems are solved using shallow machine learning models or deep learning models along with manually crafted features which fail to capture the linguistic information properly due to dimensionality problems (Khatua et al., 2018). Twitter follows a unique semantic and linguistic format (Hu et al., 2013) that makes it imperative to devise frameworks that incorporate the specific linguistic

---

[3]https://developer.twitter.com/

[4]https://techcrunch.com/2018/10/30/twitters-doubling-of-character-count-from-140-to-280-had-little-impact-on-length-of-tweets/

Tweets	Label
She went with them and got drunk. She slept with them and when they called her a whore accused them of rape	1
She is a dumb British whore who filed fake claim	1
Harvey Weinstein is a very evil man, but some of the celebrity women apart of the #Metoo movement that were "sexually assaulted" knew exactly what they were doing.	1
Another perverted Democratic! Let's see if Hollywood will say something or if #MeToo is only for Republicans.	0
They definitely raped her. Why else would they call her a whore?	0
Women don't admit they lost their power to men via rape for the fun of it. If a woman says she was raped, believe her.	0

Table 2: Examples from Annotated Dataset(Paraphrased to preserve anonymity)

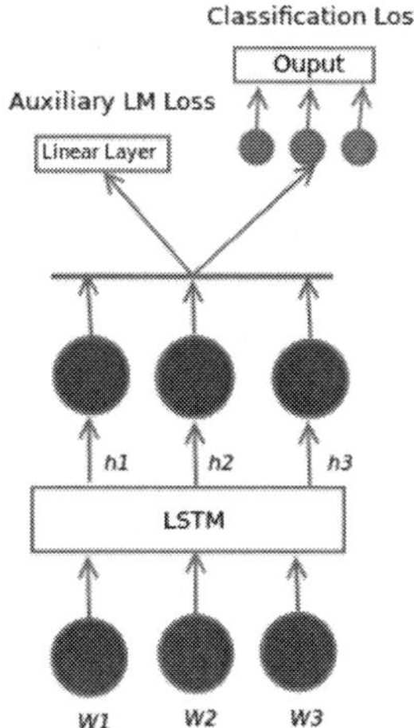

Figure 1: High Level Overview of Victim Blaming Classification Method. Blue indicates transferred layers and grey indicates randomly intialized layers

styles used on Twitter. Recent advancements in using transfer learning for tweet stance classification shows that enriching models with Twitter linguistics can improve performance (Zarrella and Marsh, 2016) Additionally, victim blaming language exhibits specific topics and syntax as shown in the coding instrument in Table 1. However, popular text classification models have failed to incorporate the subtle nuances of victim blaming language on social media specifically Twitter. Therefore, we propose a transfer learning based model that addresses this issue.

We propose a simple yet effective classification method based on single step transfer learning (Chronopoulou et al., 2019). State-of-the-art transfer learning methods employ language models (LM) trained on generic corpora with additional fine tuning of LMs for task specification. In our method, we combine the task-specification and language modelling with the help of an auxiliary loss function that is adjusted during training for task and linguistic adaptation. This prevents catastrophic forgetting and allows our model to be trained on a social media specific large corpora for e.g.: Twitter or Reddit standard datasets and then be adapted to target tasks on domain specific smaller corpora. (Chronopoulou et al., 2019) theorizes that the prevention of catastrophic forgetting for machine translation tasks is because the language model objective acts as the regularizer that limits the loss of generalizable features and evidence for the same is presented in their work. We intuitively inferred that a similar approach would be effective in capturing the subtle topics of victim blaming on Twitter due to the additional language modelling step that guides the training across the text classification task.

LM Pretraining: We train a word-level LM which consists of an embedding LSTM layer, 2 hidden LSTM layers and a linear layer.

Transfer learning and Auxiliary Loss: We transfer the weights of the pre-trained model and add an additional LSTM layer.

We introduce an auxiliary LM loss during training to incorporate the contribution of the pre-trained language model in the classification method. The joint loss is the sum of classification loss, L_{CLF} and auxiliary LM loss, L_{LM}.

$$L = L_{CLF} + L_{LM}$$

We consider equal contribution of both the loss values to effectively capture language modelling information and classification information specific

Parameter	Value
Activation function	ReLU
Dropout	0.4
Batch size	64
Epochs	20
Optimizer	Adam
Learning rate	0.0005

Table 3: Parameters for CNN Architectures

to the nature of our dataset. A High level overview of our method is shown in Figure 1.

5 Experiments

5.1 Baselines

Traditional Machine Learning (ML) Approaches
We have used two machine learning models, Support Vector Machine (**SVM**) and Naive Bayes (**NB**).

SVM: For feature extraction, TF-IDF has been used on word unigrams that is fed to the SVM

NB: Similar to SVM, TF-IDF has been used for feature extraction for classification
LSTM-Based Architectures

LSTM: The word embeddings for all the words in a post are fed to a vanilla LSTM

TextbiRNN: This is an improvement on a vanilla RNN. The word embeddings for all the words in a post are fed to a bi-directional LSTM.

CNN-Based Architectures

TextCNN: Convolutional filters we applied to the word vectors of a post followed by max-pooling layers as described by (Kim, 2014)

CharCNN: A sequence of encoded characters are fed into a CNN as described by (Zhang et al., 2015)

fasttext: fasttext classifier is used for text classification which takes into account n-grams of words to incorporate local word order (Grave et al., 2016)

5.2 Implementation of Victim-Blaming Classification Method

To pretrain the language model we create a dataset[5] of 1 million English tweets scraped from Twitter, including approximately 1M unique tokens. We use 50K most frequent tokens as our vocabulary. We then use our Victim-Blaming dataset for classification. To pre-process the tweets we use regex

<hr>

[5]https://www.kaggle.com/paoloripamonti/twitter-sentiment-analysis

to remove usernames, urls and emojis. In addition to this, we use NLTK for stop word removal and tokenization of the tweets. For neural models, we use an LM with embedding size of 300, 2 hidden layers, dropout of 0.3 and batch size of 64. We add an LSTM of size 100 with a softmax classification layer on top of the transferred LM. In pretraining, and pretrained layers (of transferred model), Adam was used with a learning rate of 0.0001. For the newly added LSTM and classification layers, Adam with learning rate of 0.0005 was used. For developing our models, we use Pytorch and Sci-kit learn.

5.3 Results

Table 4 describes the performance of the baseline models in comparison to our proposed approach across the accuracy metric. The models were trained over 60% of the dataset while 20% was held out for test and 20% was used as dev split to optimize the parameters across all the models tested. The proposed approach outperforms all baselines including RNNs, CNNs, LSTMs and traditional ML approaches SVM and NB. Fasttext model is able to generate domain specific embeddings due to the nature of embedding construction that benefits the unpredictable and unstructured Twitter semantics. CharCNNs usually have a high perplexity due to the character-by-character prediction, however, they presented similar results to the fasttext model which are better than the other baseline models. Our method shows better results when compared with the baseline models. Since we do not have a lot of data, the baseline models fail to identify linguistic features of twitter language which are significantly different from normal conversational language. Our method takes care of this using the auxiliary loss function. The language model trained on generic corpora is successfully able to capture these features and can therefore perform better when retrained for classification. In comparison to our baselines, our model architecture is simpler and computationally inexpensive.

5.4 Error Analysis

It has been observed that sometimes incidents of victim blaming are either self reported or reported by a third person. Some tweets may cite previous instances of victim blaming to speak against victim blaming. Since, these tweets consist of the marked topics and linguistic framing encoded in the coding instrument in Table 1, the proposed model classifies

Approach	Accuracy
NB	0.60
SVM	0.73
LSTM	0.74
TextbiRNN	0.74
TextCNN	0.75
CharCNN	0.77
fasttext	0.78
Proposed Method	**0.82**

Table 4: Performance Comparisons on Victim Blaming Dataset

such tweets as positive examples. This is a typical form of error encountered in even hate speech detection tasks (MacAvaney et al., 2019) where keywords marked for positive examples leads to classification errors. It should further be discussed whether such examples should be classifies as positive or negative during the annotation process and requires extensive social and psychological research. Some systemic errors we explored during our experiments:

- *She may tweet against you in #MeToo if you are not careful* : This tweet was annotated as 1, that is, victim blaming tweet since it contains implicit victim blaming. The proposed model wrongly classifies it as 0 as it lacks specific topics and keywords that the model has learned during training. This error arises due to the model failing to effectively capture sarcasm.

- *All the desi feminists....using woman card for personal gains and abusing #Metoo.*: This tweet is not classified as victim blaming by the model, however, it is annotated as victim blaming due to implicit gaslighting of victims who choose to report it. It was mis-classified since it is not directly threatening or accusing a victim. The researchers also feel this might be an oversight between the annotators while data annotation as this may be a case of general sexism and not victim blaming. To address this type of error we plan to extend our work into a multi-label categorization task which considers sub-categories of victimization, that is, secondary, primary and gender based victimization in rape cases.

- *Even if I agree, most of what it would take for that to be a valid viewpoint, you still mean that "you cant́ rape a whore." Justice should be principle based not tribe based.*: This tweet is not victim blaming but citing an instance of victim blaming directly which leads the model to classify it as victim. This is an instance which is very common in hate speech tasks as well where citing or using such phrase and words to talk against the hate or victim blaming language leads to false positives during classification.

- *I'll be a good boy and take it silently if you rape my cunt*: This tweet contains vulgar language that is identified by the model as victim blaming erroneously. This tweet is annotated as 0, not victim blaming but the specific words like 'cunt' or 'take it' has clearly confused the model as it is failing to capture long sequences here and decipher the meaning of the tweet wholly.

6 Conclusion and Future Work

In this work, we established the need to devise a computationally effective method to identify victim blaming language on Twitter. To achieve this, we proposed a single step transfer learning based classification method that effectively captures the unique linguistic structures of twitter data and victim blaming language. On a manually annotated dataset, our proposed approach could achieve significant improvement over existing methods that rely on custom textual features and popular deep learning based methods. The prevalence of rape culture and the subsequent victim blaming on unsolicited social media forums like Twitter has not been studied from a computational linguistic perspective before. Our work, therefore presents an extensive study of popular text classification methods on a niche' dataset with victim blaming semantics and further presents the significance of using a simple transfer learning approach to capture Twitter semantics on a limited dataset. We anticipate that this study encourages further research on how victims of sexual assault are portrayed on social media. Our future agenda includes further bifurcating and exploring the specific types of victim blaming and the efficacy of the proposed approach on such a multi label classification task. We plan to explore the different weighting factors for the language modelling loss and classification loss described in section 4 to determine if weighting factors can help customize the auxiliary loss for different tasks.

References

Courtney E. Ahrens. 2006. Being silenced: The impact of negative social reactions on the disclosure of rape. In *American Journal of Community Psychology*, pages 23(2), 31–34.

Aslam Andleeb, Qamar Usman, Ayesha Khan Reda, Pakizah Saqib, Aleema Aleena Ahmad, and Aiman Qadeer. 2019. Opinion mining using live twitter data. In *IEEE International Conference on Computational Science and Engineering (CSE) and IEEE International Conference on Embedded and Ubiquitous Computing (EUC)*.

Bernice Andrew, Chris R. Brewin, and Suzanna Rose. 2003. Gender, social support, and ptsd in victims of violent crime. In *Journal of Traumatic Stress*, pages (4), 16, 421–427.

Pinkesh Badjatiya, Shashank Gupta, Manish Gupta, and Vasudeva Varma. 2017. Deep learning for hate speech detection in tweets. In *Proceedings of the 26th International Conference on World Wide Web Companion*, page 759760.

Vimala Balakrishnan, Shahzaib Khan, and Hamid R. Arabnia. 2020. Improving cyberbullying detection using twitter users psychological features and machine learning. In *Computers Security*, page Volume 90.

Saroj Kumar Biswas. 2019. Keyword extraction from tweets using weighted graph. In *Advances in Intelligent Systems and Computing*.

Rebecca Campbell, Emily Dworkin, and Giannina Cabral. 2009. An ecological model of the impact of sexual assault on women's mental health. In *Trauma Violence Abuse*, pages 10(3), 225–46.

Alexandra Chronopoulou, Christos Baziotis, and Alexandros Potamianos. 2019. An embarrassingly simple approach for transfer learning from pretrained language models. In *Proceedings of the 2019 Conference of the North American Chapter of the Association for Computational Linguistics: Human Language Technologies, Volume 1 (Long and Short Papers)*, pages 2089–2095, Minneapolis, Minnesota. Association for Computational Linguistics.

Linda Coates, Cathy Richardson, and Allan Wade. 2006. Reshaping responses to victims of violent crime. In *Cowichan Bay, B.C., Canada*.

Jacob Cohen. 1960. A coefficient of agreement for nominal scales. *Educational and psychological measurement*, 20(1):37–46.

Edouard Grave, Tomas Mikolov, Armand Joulin, and Piotr Bojanowski. 2016. Bag of tricks for efficient text classification. In *EACL*.

Tara L Gruenewald, Margaret E Kemeny, Najib Aziz, and John L Fahey. 2004. Acute threat to the social self: Shame, social self-esteem, and cortisol activity. *Psychosomatic medicine*, 66(6):915–924.

Y. Hu, K. Talamadupula, and S. Kambhampati. 2013. Dude, srsly?: The surprisingly formal nature of twitter's language. *Proceedings of the 7th International Conference on Weblogs and Social Media, ICWSM 2013*, pages 244–253.

Aparup Khatua, Erik Cambria, and Apalak Khatua. 2018. Sounds of silence breakers: Exploring sexual violence on twitter. In *2018 IEEE/ACM International Conference on Advances in Social Networks Analysis and Mining (ASONAM)*, pages 397–400.

Yoon Kim. 2014. Convolutional neural networks for sentence classification. In *Proceedings of the 2014 Conference on Empirical Methods in Natural Language Processing (EMNLP)*, pages 1746–1751, Doha, Qatar. Association for Computational Linguistics.

M. P Koss. 1993. Rape: Scope, impact, interventions, and public policy responses. In *American Psychologist*, pages 48(10), 10621069. American Psychological Association.

Melvin J. Lerner. 1980. The belief in a just world: A fundamental delusion.

Sean MacAvaney, Hao-Ren Yao, Eugene Yang, Katina Russell, Nazli Goharian, and Ophir Frieder. 2019. Hate speech detection: Challenges and solutions. *PloS one*, 14(8).

Pulkit Parikh, Harika Abburi, Pinkesh Badjatiya, Radhika Krishnan, Niyati Chhaya, Manish Gupta, and Vasudeva Varma. 2019. Multi-label categorization of accounts of sexism using a neural framework. *arXiv preprint arXiv:1910.04602*.

Jessica Ringrose and Emma Renold. 2012. Slutshaming, girl power and sexualisation: Thinking through the politics of the international slutwalks with teen girls. In *Gender and Education*.

Ramit Sawhney, Prachi Manchanda, Raj Singh, and Swati Aggarwal. 2018. A computational approach to feature extraction for identification of suicidal ideation in tweets. In *Proceedings of ACL 2018, Student Research Workshop*, pages 91–98, Melbourne, Australia. Association for Computational Linguistics.

Nicolas J. Schrading. 2015. Analyzing domestic abuse using natural language processing on social media data.

Megan Stubbs-Richardson, Nicole E Rader, and Arthur G Cosby. 2018. Tweeting rape culture: Examining portrayals of victim blaming in discussions of sexual assault cases on twitter. *Feminism & Psychology*, 28(1):90–108.

S.E Ullman. 2000. Psychometric characteristics of the social reactions questionnaire. In *Psychology of Women Quarterly*.

Simon N. Verdun-Jones and Katherine Rossiter. 2010. The psychological impact of victimization: Mental health outcomes and psychological, legal, and restorative interventions.

Christine Wekerle, Negar Vakili, Sherry Stewart, and Tara Black. 2018. The utility of twitter as a toolfor increasing reach of research on sexual violence. In *Child abuse neglect*, page 85.

Michele Zappavigna. 2012. *Discourse of Twitter and social media: How we use language to create affiliation on the web*, volume 6. A&C Black.

Guido Zarrella and Amy Marsh. 2016. Mitre at semeval-2016 task 6: Transfer learning for stance detection. *arXiv preprint arXiv:1606.03784*.

Xiang Zhang, Junbo Zhao, and Yann LeCun. 2015. Character-level convolutional networks for text classification. In C. Cortes, N. D. Lawrence, D. D. Lee, M. Sugiyama, and R. Garnett, editors, *Advances in Neural Information Processing Systems 28*, pages 649–657. Curran Associates, Inc.

Author Index